THE RETURN OF STEPHEN GOLD'S

BREAKING LAW

A Judge's Guide to Legal Rights, Winning in Court or Losing Well

Better, Bigger & Bang Up To Date

Future free updates at breakinglaw.co.uk

LAW YOU CAN UNDERSTAND

First published July 2016

Second edition published June 2021

ISBN 978-1-8384390-0-2

Text © Stephen Gold

Typography © Bath Publishing

All rights reserved. No part of this publication may be reproduced in any material form (including photocopying or storing it in any medium by electronic means and whether or not transiently or incidentally to some other use of this publication) without the written permission of the copyright holder except in accordance with the provisions of the Copyright, Designs and Patents Act 1988 or under the terms of a licence issued by the Copyright Licensing Agency (www.cla.co.uk). Applications for the copyright owner's written permission to reproduce any part of this publication should be addressed to the publisher.

Stephen Gold asserts his right as set out in ss77 and 78 of the Copyright Designs and Patents Act 1988 to be identified as the author of this work wherever it is published commercially and whenever any adaptation of this work is published or produced including any sound recordings or films made of or based upon this work.

The information presented in this work is accurate and current as at 9 June 2021 to the best knowledge of the author. The author and the publisher, however, make no guarantee as to, and assume no responsibility for, the correctness or sufficiency of such information or recommendation. The contents of this book are not intended as legal advice and should not be treated as such.

Bath Publishing Limited

27 Charmouth Road

Bath

BA1 3LJ

Tel: 01225 577810

email: info@bathpublishing.co.uk

www.bathpublishing.co.uk

Bath Publishing is a company registered in England: 5209173

Registered Office: As above

"Legal bible for everyday life."

DAILY MIRROR

"Stephen Gold writes as he speaks, self-deprecating, funny, practical and wise. I loved it and recommend it with feeling."

NIGEL PASCOE QC, COUNSEL

"A practical and accessible guide to all aspects of the law – written with wit and expertise. If you think you might need a lawyer or find yourself in court, I'd highly recommend reading this first!"

PROFESSOR RICHARD SAMBROOK, CARDIFF UNIVERSITY AND FORMER DIRECTOR OF NEWS, BBC

"An essential reference book for every household – likely to repay its cost several times over."

AMAZON REVIEWER

"This book is a MUST for answering all those important legal queries such as landlords' and tenants' rights, slander and libel, what to expect in court hearings to name but a few... all explained with a wicked sense of humour. Highly recommended."

AMAZON REVIEWER

For Sonia, Lara and Sapphire

Contents

Foreword by Alastair Stewart OBE   xi

About the author   xii

Introduction from the author   xiii

Part 1   **SOME FUNNY THINGS HAPPENED TO ME ON THE WAY TO COURT**

Chapter 1	Look, No Maths	3
Chapter 2	Let Loose	17
Chapter 3	Ron And Reg	29
Chapter 4	Legal Print	53
Chapter 5	Let Right Be Done	59
Chapter 6	Let Right Be Done – For A Little Longer	69

Part 2   **HELP!!!**

Chapter 7	Lawyer Or Litigant In Person?	79
Chapter 8	The Litigant In Person Blame Game *"I'm not a bloody lawyer"*	105

Part 3   **IS THE REST OF THIS BOOK WORTH READING?**

Chapter 9	Alternatives To Court And Preserving My Premium Bonds	109

Part 4   **STARTING A CASE AND BEFORE**

Chapter 10	Before Starting A Case *Pre-match muscle flexing*	127
Chapter 11	Freezing Your Creditor *The 42 day plus paralysis*	139

Chapter 12	Where To Start *"This was a court. Do you want mushy peas with your fish and chips?"*	143
Chapter 13	Time Limits For Starting Court Proceedings *Disaster or windfall*	147
Chapter 14	Judgment Without A Hearing And Setting Aside *Watch 'yer clock*	155
Chapter 15	Getting Your Opponent's Documents *The sooner the better*	159
Chapter 16	In Full And Final Settlement *Take it or leave it*	163
Chapter 17	Court Fees *Save £s £s £s*	167

Part 5 — CRIKEY, PROCEEDINGS HAVE STARTED

Chapter 18	The Malicious Claimant *Turning the tables*	175
Chapter 19	Witnesses And Their Statements *Sock it to 'em in writing*	179
Chapter 20	The Funless Bundle *How to displease the Judge*	189
Chapter 21	Daft Cases And Daft Responses *The early kill*	193
Chapter 22	Halting The Persistent Litigator *The alternatives to strangulation*	197
Chapter 23	Outside The Courtroom For A Civil Case *Waiting about*	199
Chapter 24	Inside The Courtroom For Your Civil Case *"What am I doing here?"*	209
Chapter 25	Small Claims *But still beautiful*	221

Chapter 26	The *Tomlin Order* *Kissing and making up after proceedings started*	235

Part 6   JUDGMENT HAS BEEN GIVEN

Chapter 27	The Register Of Judgments *The ugly face of proceedings*	243
Chapter 28	Challenging The Judge's Decision *After court*	247
Chapter 29	Getting Your Money Under A Judgment *Can't pay, won't pay*	257
Chapter 30	Seizure Of Goods *The bailiff strikes*	275

Part 7   RIGHTS, WRONGS AND MANAGING YOUR AFFAIRS

Chapter 31	Covid-19 Cancellations *Frustrating!*	287
Chapter 32	Interest On Debt, Compensation And Judgments *Icing on the cake*	293
Chapter 33	Compensation For Hassle And Mental Distress *Inconvenience, distress, disappointment, annoyance, frustration, anxiety, displeasure, upset, vexation, tension, aggravation*	299
Chapter 34	Package Holidays And Other Holiday Travel Gone Wrong *Come back to sue*	301
Chapter 35	The Litigant In Person's Bill *And why not?!*	309
Chapter 36	Court Error Compensation *HMCTS blunder money*	313
Chapter 37	Money Wrongly Received *Estoppel does you good*	317

Chapter 38	Company Down Drain Owing You Money And Laughing *Getting the directors to pay*	321
Chapter 39	Protection From Your Creditors *Thou shalt not harass me*	327
Chapter 40	PPI *Mission for commission*	337
Chapter 41	Claiming On Your Credit Or Debit Card *The joy of equal responsibility or a chargeback*	343
Chapter 42	The Longest Will In The World *And some inheritance tax saving thrown in*	349
Chapter 43	Removing Executors *"We want our money!"*	361
Chapter 44	No Inheritance Claims *Gone but not forgotten*	363
Chapter 45	Joint Tenancies *Severing without pain*	371
Chapter 46	Squatters' Rights *How to become a landowner without really trying*	373
Chapter 47	Libel, Slander And Malicious Falsehood *Troublesore v Whitecock – Statement in open court*	377
Chapter 48	Bankruptcy *The ecstasy and the agony*	389
Chapter 49	Property Buying And Selling *Traps and how to avoid them*	401
Chapter 50	Residential Service Charges *Cutting 'em down*	409
Chapter 51	Eating Out Is Off *Aggro at the bistro*	419
Chapter 52	Change Of Name *From Smith to Brown*	423

Chapter 53	Drink Drive *Excess defences*	427
Chapter 54	On The Road *And off a charge or disqualification?*	435
Chapter 55	Parking On Private Land *The great escapes*	441
Chapter 56	Tax Penalties *How to beat the taxman (if you want to)*	447
Chapter 57	Knotweed *A knotty problem of the Japanese variety*	455
Chapter 58	Rights To Light *And there was insufficient light. And there was an injunction and damages*	459
Chapter 59	Ragbag	463
Chapter 60	Privacy, Dignity And Confidentiality *Keep your nose out*	481

Part 8 **GONE SHOPPING: SEE YOU IN COURT?**

Chapter 61	Supermarket Struggles *Lousy plastic bags, parking machine clocks, suspected shoplifting and expired vouchers*	489
Chapter 62	Receipts And Sale Goods And Cheques *And planes and boats and trains*	499
Chapter 63	The Newish Consumer Laws *Buyers' kit to be carried at all times when away from home*	513
Chapter 64	Unfair Trading *The price (and possibly any one of a dozen other things) is not right*	535
Chapter 65	Small Print *And bigger print*	567

Part 9   HOME UNDER ATTACK

Chapter 66	Behind With The Mortgage	583
Chapter 67	At War With Your Home Landlord *Armaments store*	599
Chapter 68	Unfit Premises *Damp dumps*	631
Chapter 69	At War With Your Business Landlord *Tenants rule, OK*	635

Part 10   RELATIONSHIPS: BEFORE AND AFTER

Chapter 70	Domestic Abuse Damages Claims *Bill for battery*	641
Chapter 71	Cohabitation *Kit for claims against swines*	649
Chapter 72	Pre-Nuptial Agreements With What Should Happen To Fifi Thrown In *"I loves you but..."*	661
Chapter 73	The No Sex Agreement *A customised marriage or civil partnership*	669
Chapter 74	Divorce, Judicial Separation, Nullity And Dissolution *That's 'yer lot!*	673
Chapter 75	After The Breakdown *The anti-stitch up guide*	699
Chapter 76	Money For The Kids *Paying for the smart phone*	735
Chapter 77	Missing Persons *Gone fishing?*	747

Index   749

Foreword by Alastair Stewart OBE

Television journalist and writer

The cry goes up, "I know my rights!", but do you?

"The law is an ass!", but is it?

In this second edition of *Breaking Law*, Stephen Gold offers an informed, accessible, insider's guide to what those rights really are and how you can saddle the tricky ass that the law sometimes can be.

The Victoria Tower, in the Palace of Westminster, groans under the weight of centuries' worth of statutes and MPs continue to pass new laws, amend the old and even strike from the statute book the redundant.

Breaking Law brings us right up to date with sections on the new divorce laws, on whiplash damages and on the legal side of Covid-19. It even ventures a cautious toe in the turbulent waters of the post-Brexit era. I suspect that may warrant a third edition at some time in the unclear but near future.

I have known Stephen Gold for decades, first as a local solicitor who proved to be a brilliant TV pundit, and through to his years as a judge, writer and commentator.

He has a gift for communication – in print as much as in the spoken word – and he has the qualifications and experience to command a hearing.

The law is a complex field and, if you need to defend your rights or seek redress, cost is added to that complexity.

This book is a great help to understanding but is replete with the wisdom of caution.

It is seldom wise to go to court but, if needs must, the book helps you understand your chances of success and the potential costs of failure; and, because it is Stephen Gold, it is funny, refreshing and rich in anecdotes from the frontline.

I began with two clichés from the law and I'll end with a third: "We are all equal under the law".

In practice, that is seldom the case: the other side may have more knowledge and more money than you. Stephen Gold won't lend you a fiver but he'll help you with the knowledge and so even up your chances.

Alastair Stewart

About the author

Stephen Gold has many years' experience as both a civil and family judge and, before that, as a practising solicitor. In numerous national and regional broadcasts and in articles, he has brought the law to the general public and lawyers alike with a unique mixture of practicality, straight language and humour.

Among the programmes Stephen has contributed to on radio and television have been *The One Show, Panorama, Top Gear, The Home Service, The Jimmy Young Programme* as a legal eagle, *Pebble Mill at One*, the Breakfast Programmes on BBC1 and Channel 4 and Radio 5 Live's *Drivetime* and he constantly appeared in a raft of commercial television programmes in Southern England.

One of the pioneers of live legal advice phone-ins, he has helped many hundreds over the airwaves on LBC, BBC Radio Solent and variously on Radio 5 as well as an early television phone-in for ITV's *Richard and Judy*.

He was an accredited media spokesman for the Law Society and subsequently for the judiciary and is a long-standing columnist for the leading legal weekly *New Law Journal*.

His columns have also appeared in *House Beautiful* and *The Independent*. He is particularly proud of his offerings on the law on pets for BBC Radio 3 – without music!

Stephen Gold

Introduction from the author

This second edition of *Breaking Law* is for everyone. Litigants in person and trainee lawyers and advisers, of course, and there's no reason why qualified barristers, solicitors and legal executives should feel ashamed to hide it under their desks. I want you to have a good read and, hopefully, a laugh at the same time as discovering how you can try and ensure that you avoid getting into a court case in the first place or achieve coming out of it as the victor or as best you can. The law can be complex. I have tried to make it understandable and digestible.

There has been a formidable quantity of new legislation and legal developments since the first edition nearly five years ago and there's more to come. You can discover how the major divorce reforms, expected to be in force in Spring 2022, will work; where and how free legal help and sometimes free representation at a court or tribunal hearing can be sourced from a multitude of organisations; how to cope with the push into remote court hearings forced on us by Covid-19 and how that wretched virus has changed court procedures and the way judges will approach their decisions. Where Brexit has made a difference, you will see in what ways. And you will find an abundance of template letters and agreements which you can use if, for example, you fancy making a will, changing your name, entering into a pre-nuptial agreement, abstaining from sex with your partner or making sure that, as a cohabitee, you will be protected if the relationship finishes. Template court documents too for claims in a multitude of areas such as cases against battering domestic abusers, malicious litigants, harassing creditors, landlords of unfit lettings, false arresting store detectives, knotweed encroachers and misleading shops.

I have included my autobiographical adventures again and brought them up to the present time to include my retirement as a permanent judge but continued sitting as a deputy judge and, during the pandemic, remotely across the South-West of England from a Richmond-upon-Thames study. By popular demand, there's much more on my dealings with the Kray Twins and I have discovered what actually happened to Ron Kray's brain after his death. My fall outs with retailers and suppliers have continued unabated and I have even managed to be deliberately overcharged by a London black cab driver. Follow how I recommend you cope with a cornucopia of consumer hitches. Don't be too hard on the consumer relations folk who are only doing their job, though a bit of teasing never goes amiss.

There are loads of new chapters on areas which may come to affect you. Drink-drive defences; parking tickets; combating the taxman; holiday claims; rights to light; privacy, dignity and confidentiality; service charges; avoiding forfeiture of your business lease when unavoidably behind with the rent; the new way that claims for whiplash injuries will be dealt with; and, as property prices rise along with the number of people bidding for the same home, how to protect yourself from losing out to a rival but getting back the money spent on legal fees and a survey. Just some. And I help you through what to do at court and before and after it, be you involved in a small claim or a great whopper of a claim.

If you have the misfortune to be a party to a financial application as part of divorce or other matrimonial proceedings or civil partnership proceedings, there's bags of advice on how to cope and, if necessary, go it alone or take in a lawyer for just part of the case. Indeed, how to make use of a private court if the queue for a judge led hearing seems interminably long.

That's just a flavour of what the pages have to offer.

The law is stated as at 9 June 2021 and applies to England and Wales. I will be regularly updating the book's contents in my blog at breakinglaw.co.uk. As before, access is free and not even a court fee.

Good luck.

Stephen Gold

Part 1

SOME FUNNY THINGS HAPPENED TO ME ON THE WAY TO COURT

Chapter 1

Look, No Maths

At 16, armed with a mediocre five GCE 'O' level passes and the tops of six *Weetabix* packets but limited small change, I rang the Law Society's careers department from a button A and button B kiosk round the corner which, being long distance, required the reinsertion of a coin every couple of seconds.

"*I've got five...*" Beep beep beep

"*O's but I haven't got...*" Beep beep beep

"*maths. Sorry, can you...*" Beep beep beep

"*hear?*"

It was all very unsatisfactory but they would send me a booklet. I managed to spout out my address and left it at that. We did have a land line at home but this was my own enterprise and I was wanting to keep it from my parents. I was suffering the sixth form at Portsmouth Grammar School at which I had been slippered on the backside by a prefect for talking at the notice board and wanted out. The booklet arrived. I found I could scrape into training as a solicitor and escape school. The training would involve entering into articles of clerkship for five years with a principal who was a qualified solicitor and passing the exams. Even if it meant joining a profession which would have an innumerate as a member, I was game. All I had to do was to find the solicitor.

Taking knocks is part of growing up and I had been well rehearsed for what was to follow. Southern Television had rejected my pre-'O' level application for appointment as a scriptwriter in its presentation department (see "*Thank you but no thank you*" on page 10). Around about the same time, Associated-Rediffusion which held the commercial television franchise for London had turned down my play, the BBC my "kind offer" to take part in *Juke Box Jury* (see "*A Miss*" on page 11) and ABC Television my request for an audition for the 'Spin-a-Disc' panel of *Thank Your Lucky Stars*. And so it had gone on. You will see from the small selection of a myriad of responses to my crank applications how desperate I had been to burn my schoolcap and insinuate myself into a television studio. Another path was to be pursued.

"My word, Gold. You are small." Having pushed out around 30 letters to every firm within bus travelling distance of my home, I had arrived at the top of the staircase of Churchers, solicitors of Gosport in Hampshire (so a walk, bus and a ferry) for my first interview. The firm's senior partner, Pip Churcher no less, had written to "grant" me an interview in view of the keenness displayed in my communication although he had not contemplated having another articled clerk. "He has one already." Here was Pip towering over me and telling me how small I was. 5' 6" actually which was short enough to give me a complex. I had prepared well and had a speech which I was to recite at every one of the dozen or so interviews which followed and which involved the interjection of such words as *contentious* and *non-contentious* and *litigation* and *conveyancing* which I had borrowed from the Law Society's booklet and I was off. Pip Churcher didn't want me (see "*First interview, first rejection*" on page 12).

The severe partner at Hubert Way, Malpas and Stanley of Portsmouth told me that if he accepted me into articles he would require a premium of £250 and I would not be paid. Even then he didn't want me, not even with a firm name which closely resembled that of a local shoe shop. No maths and my age were said in the rejection letter to have been against me (see "*Your application doesn't add up*" on page 12).

A Chichester firm Arnold Cooper & Tompkins (walk, bus and train) preferred me to finish my 'A' levels than join them. Large & Gibson of Southsea referred me to the secretary of the Hampshire Law Society "who sometimes knows of solicitors in the county who are looking for a suitable man to be articled." And so it went on until I was back in Gosport and performing before Richard (Dick) Elliott who was one of two partners in a medium sized firm of family solicitors with a litigation bias. It was called Donnelly and Elliott. I didn't buy the firm but I did become the senior partner from which you will deduce that he took me on and things went relatively well.

By deed of articles of clerkship (see "*Thou shalt obey*" ending on page 15), I of my own free will, and with the consent of my father, bound myself to Dick (I called him '*Sir*' then and later, with his permission, '*Mr Elliott*' and once I had passed my exams I was entreated to call him '*Dick*') to "truly, honestly and diligently" serve him for five years as a faithful clerk ought to do. By virtue of my tender years, there was not much enforceable covenanting I could do so it was my hapless father who had to promise I would not at any time during those five years "cancel obliterate spoil destroy waste embezzle spend or make away with any of the books papers writings money stamps or other property" of Dick or any of his clients and I would cheerfully obey and execute Dick's lawful commands. In those days, punctuation in legal documents was anathema lest it should change the sense – or nonsense – of what was being stated or enable any lay person to understand the document. I see that Dick stuck in a further promise by my father that for five years after I qualified as a solicitor (if ever) I would not practise in the law in the Borough of Gosport or down the road in the Urban District of Fareham. This was known then, and is still known now, as a covenant in restraint of trade and stops you walking off with the hard won clients of your employer for the benefit of yourself or your new employer. To be enforceable it has to be reasonable in radius and time. This covenant was neither. Dick is no longer with us but he would forgive me for saying it was very cheeky. He would also forgive me for telling you that I was not paid a penny for the first two years of my articles. This was overshadowed by the fact that in this instance no premium was required. It would have enhanced my self-worth if I had been allowed just sufficient to buy a couple of tubes of *Rolos* each week. When Dick announced after two years that I was to be paid a fiver a week, I almost prostrated myself before him and thought I had won the pools. Not that any of this came to matter as I stayed on for another 27 years once I qualified.

I loved my training. Dick specialised in crime and litigation. Before admission as a solicitor he had assisted in the investigation of war crimes and in the preparation of cases for the Nuremburg trials He was one of the most eloquent and persuasive advocates in the south of England and attracted not only a mass of criminal defence work but prosecution work for the police (this was way before the creation of the Crown Prosecution Service) and for the NSPCC (he was honorary secretary of its local branch) and the RSPCA. Of the many celebrated cases in which he had been, or was to be, involved was the 1971 court martial following the sinking of the submarine HMS Artemis at which he advocated. His one weakness was an inability to bill his clients. And so it was that, seated in the corner of his room, following him around to court and prison like a lap dog and given my own workload very soon after I started, I learnt the trade. As I attended many criminal trials, I was able to study the styles of some of the finest jury advocates on the Western Circuit and observe the idiosyncrasies of some of the most eminent judges including the Chairman of Hampshire Quarter Sessions Sir Eustace Roskill QC (later to become a Law Lord) who had the unfortunate habit of picking his nose whilst up there on the bench. I borrowed not this habit but his name, occasionally signing in as him at the 'Pomme D'or' club in Southsea but without the title.

It could have been so different if I had been articled to a conveyancing specialist with all their dry pieces and parcels of land and easements and quasi-easements. That would probably have driven me back to the sixth form. But I was not permitted to shun the conveyancing as I would be tested on the law of property in the exams which were to come my way and ultimately as a solicitor I would combine my contentious work with a large volume of conveyancing. I came to realise that for lies and deceit those involved in property sales and purchases strongly rival convicted criminals which makes litigation and conveyancing suitable bedfellows.

Barely out of short trousers and with the sexual experience of a monk, I was dazzled by the frequency with which sex manifested itself in one form or another in so many cases. Dick's secretary soon drew my attention to one file in the cabinets for which no bill had been rendered concerning a case which had gone to the Court of Appeal in which Dick had successfully represented the husband being sued by his wife for divorce on the ground (as it then was) of sodomy. It was there held that the wife's consent to the act was a good defence. And within weeks of starting my articles, Dick asked me if I knew what incest was. By coincidence my parents had recently, and in complete advance ignorance of the subject matter, taken me to the theatre to see a new play starring Robert Beatty and Diane Cilento. Beatty made a short curtain call speech at the end and told the audience to urge their friends to go and see the play. "Tell them," he said, "it is about incest – something the whole family can enjoy." I was able to give Dick a short definition and referred amongst others to a relationship between brother and sister. "And step-brother and step-sister," he corrected me for he was just about to call in a soldier charged with incest with his step-sister and who was soon to appear at the Hampshire Assizes. The couple had fallen deeply in love, completely unaware that their active sexual relationship was criminal. I attended the client's trial when having pleaded guilty and undertaken never to revive the relationship he was granted a conditional discharge.

I relished the opportunities to question clients about their sexual lives. Accident plaintiffs (as they used to be called) were asked whether their trauma had prevented them from engaging in intercourse and, if so, over what period, how frequently intercourse had occurred before the accident and whether abstinence had been a strain (for this was factor which could quite properly be reflected in an award of damages as my researches had established). It was in the field of matrimonial law, however, that I was able to excel. Divorce on the basis of two years' separation with consent or five years' separation without consent was not to arrive for another seven years and most divorce petitions were then founded on adultery or cruelty. In Gosport there was a large community of servicemen and a disproportionate number of them allegedly treated their wives with cruelty which ordinarily involved excessive sexual demands, foul and abusive language and intoxication. There was heavy concentration in the divorce petitions I drafted on the sexual demands. One particular lady had been required to submit to what seemed to me to be the most remarkable practices which she claimed she had abhorred. I spent most of that evening preparing a most comprehensive account of them in terms which would be suitable for a court of law and was bereft when the next day the lady telephoned me to say that she had decided on reconciliation. Such an outcome is something for which matrimonial practitioners now pray. As to the language and intoxication allegations, these rarely varied from one case to another and before long I was able to jog the client's memory by putting the list of the usual swearwords to her and invite her to confirm or deny what was in her spouse's vocabulary. The only variation in the allegation of intoxication related to where the spouse would urinate. It was almost invariably in the wardrobe of the matrimonial bedroom (and would often be accompanied by vomiting under the influence) and, in one case, out of the front window of the matrimonial bedroom down on to the footpath.

A very refined lady had made an appointment to see Dick on a matrimonial matter. Dick, alas, had gone missing and it was left to me to stand in for him. By now I was 17 and an expert on sexual practices, so was well qualified for the task. The lady tentatively made her way up the staircase. I extended my arm to greet her whereupon she exclaimed with horror "I'm not seeing you am I?!" turned and ran down the stairs never to reappear at Donnelly and Elliott. This was the second Gosport top of the stairs rebuff for me and it took a little time for my confidence to be restored.

Sex or No sex was the issue in a defended divorce case, the conduct of which was entrusted to me in the first year of my articles because the firm's managing clerk Gerry Combes (he became a close friend with me regularly leaving the empty shells of a packet of monkey nuts to which I was addicted on his office at lunchtime) was terrified of the client respondent. It was alleged by her husband that she had committed adultery with the naval rating who was half her age and lodged with her. She admitted habitually sleeping with the man but denied that she had been penetrated and, hence, that intercourse and thereby adultery, had occurred. Her GP compiled a report which explained the physical conditions with which she was afflicted and which he confirmed would have prevented intercourse. The cards on the table approach to litigation did not then exist and so the killer report remained secreted in the file – until the morning of the hearing of the case in the High Court. Barristers change for court in their robing rooms. It is there that outcomes are negotiated, bluff is met with counter-bluff, each side ridicules their adversary's case and – in those days at least – crushing pieces of unexpected evidence were produced and flourished, as if by magic. In our case it was the medical report. The husband's barrister turned pale, conferred with the husband and then announced that the husband had decided he must abandon his petition. Today, all would not be lost for the divorce petitioner who is unable to prove that their spouse has gone as far as having sexual intercourse with another person. Instead of alleging adultery the petitioner could rely on the alternative ground of unreasonable behaviour. No court should strain to find that having an improper relationship with someone other than your spouse (whether it is confined to sexting or fumbling in the office broom cupboard) amounted to unreasonable behaviour. Before long, as you will read, even adultery and unreasonable behaviour will be out of the window.

During my articles Dick undertook the defence case for a man charged with the murder of an elderly woman. The man was a part time fireman and had allegedly killed the woman, set fire to her home and later gone out on one of the appliances which attended the scene to extinguish the fire. His trial was held at the assizes at Devizes where the difficult defence to be run for him was that he had not committed the murder but, if he had, he was suffering from diminished responsibility at the time. The prosecution were seeking to rely on evidence of a previous arson at which the accused had attended in the course of his part-time work with the fire brigade. This is known as *similar fact* evidence and the trial judge was to be asked by the defence to exclude the evidence on the ground that the facts of the two incidents were not sufficiently similar and that, in any event, the prejudice to the accused of allowing in the evidence would outweigh its probative value. There was a leading case on the subject which had been decided by an appeal court and represented a legal precedent. Norman Brodrick QC who Dick had instructed as the leading barrister for the accused should have come to court with an authoritative report of the case to which the trial judge could be referred. This is how it is done – or should be done. He had forgotten it.

I had attended the trial with Dick. The trial was memorable for me for its drama and two other reasons. The first was that Muggins was sent out into Devizes in heavyish snow to locate and borrow an authoritative report of that leading case – on foot. I eventually found a local solicitors' firm with a decent library and a volume of law reports which included the case in question. I talked them into lending it to me. The trial judge decided – naturally, in the absence of the jury – that the prosecution could not rely on evidence of this previous incident and the law book was returned. The second ground of fascination was that Dick had instructed as junior barrister for the defence David Webster who was to become my BBC referee. So? Well, before going to the bar he had worked as an actor and appeared in *Dixon of Dock Green* on BBC television as the young police cadet Jamie. Having a celebrity in the defence team was a really big deal – for me.

The accused was convicted and sentenced to life imprisonment. Dick went down to the cells to see him afterwards and reported back that the accused had thanked him for all he had done. Dick did not speak on the journey back.

That duty of consulting with the client after a guilty verdict or custodial sentence has its inherent difficulties although the judge tends to be the target of the client's grievance. The client is entitled to advice on their rights and especially on the prospects of a successful appeal against conviction or sentence although a considered opinion a day or so after the event is probably the best time for its delivery. In the case of Robert Malcolm Weeks, this articled clerk copped out of an instant post-sentence encounter with his firm's client.

Mr Weeks at the age of 17 entered a pet shop in Gosport with a starting pistol loaded with blank cartridges, pointed it at the owner and told her to hand over the till. He stole 35p which was later found on the shop floor. Later that day, he telephoned the police to say that he would give himself up. He was apprehended locally by two police officers. He took the pistol from his pocket and it went off. In the ensuing struggle, two more blanks were fired, one of which caused a powder burn to the wrist of one of the police officers. It emerged that Mr Weeks had committed the robbery because he wanted to pay back £3 which he owed his mother who had told him that morning to find lodgings elsewhere.

Just 18 days after all this, Mr Weeks appeared before Hampshire Assizes. Dick had never expected the case to be listed so fast. We were told the day before that the case would be on. My frantic telephone calls to the prosecutor's office and the court to get the case put off were of no avail. A brief was hurriedly prepared by Dick and a barrister instructed to appear at the Assizes the next day. I was sent to represent the firm. Me and my sandwich box. Mr Weeks pleaded guilty to armed robbery, assaulting a police office and being in the unlawful possession of a firearm. The trial judge was the terrifying Mr Justice Thesiger. A prison medical officer testified that he could find no evidence that Mr Weeks was suffering from mental instability which would justify sending him to a mental institution. But a probation officer who was present characterised him in his report before the judge as being susceptible to fluctuation in mood and emotionally immature and as showing a morbid interest in the literature of violence and a fascination for guns. The officer had also written that he had taken to drinking heavily from time to time and had a high potential for aggression.

The judge passed sentence. I can hear him now. I can see his reddened face now.

> *"The facts of the offence and the evidence of the character and disposition of the accused ...satisfy me that...he is a very dangerous young man...I think that an indeterminate sentence is the right sentence for somebody of this age, of this character and disposition, who is attracted to this form of conduct. That leaves the matter with the Secretary of State who can release him if and when those who have been watching him and examining him believe that with the passage of years he has become responsible. It may not take long. Or the change may not occur for a long time – I do not know how it will work out...So far as the first count of the indictment is concerned [robbery], I think the right conclusion, terrible though it may seem, is that I pass the sentence that the law authorises me to pass for robbery and for assault with intent to rob with arms, that is life imprisonment. The Secretary of State can act if and when he thinks it is safe to act."*

Our barrister was stunned. The probation officer whose report had been instrumental in the judge's sentence was stunned. I was stunned. Perhaps everyone apart from the judge had been thinking about borstal or a fixed term of a few years. But life had not crossed minds.

It was getting late. The barrister left court without seeing Mr Weeks. I left court without seeing Mr Weeks. The next morning, back in the office, I reported to Dick. He was stunned. "What did Weeks say?" he enquired. I confessed he had not said anything to me as I had not seen him afterwards in the cells. Dick ordered me back to Winchester immediately (which was a bit rich as it was his case) and I duly saw the client there in prison. I explained the rationale of the sentence almost selling it to myself as I did so. He expressed gratitude that I had turned up because he had convinced himself that he would die in prison. Never again did I flinch away from the post conviction and post custodial sentence conference.

And what happened to Mr Weeks? He made his own attempt at getting his sentence reduced on appeal to the Court of Appeal but failed. Nine and a half years after the robbery he was released from prison on licence. Nine months later he turned up at my firm's offices asking to see me. I was then a qualified solicitor. He had broken into a beach hut and stolen a pullover. I represented him at Portsmouth Magistrates' Court where he pleaded guilty to a couple of charges and was conditionally discharged and fined. I never saw him again. After recalls to prison and further offences he was paroled and re-paroled but when some 20 years after the robbery he was required to return to prison he was at large having gone to France. Whilst in prison he had taken his case to the European Court of Human Rights which held, whilst he was still at large, that his human rights had not been violated by the recalls. A tragic story of a troubled young man who was charming and courteous in the dealings I had with him.

Before I leave this section of my life, I feel obliged to explain the maths. I had no trouble with my tables and could mentally aggregate the prices of a packet of gobstoppers and a sherbet fountain. I started to be thrown by the equations and things took a sharp turn for the worse when I stumbled upon a set of answer books at W H Smith & Son.

SOUTHERN TELEVISION
LIMITED

THE SOUTHERN TELEVISION CENTRE · NORTHAM · SOUTHAMPTON
Telephone: SOUTHAMPTON 28582/9

London Office
BRETTENHAM HOUSE
LANCASTER PLACE, W.C.2.
Telephone: Covent Garden 0941/7

Dover Studios
RUSSELL STREET
DOVER
Telephone: Dover 2200/1

AJH/SA

9th August, 1961.

Mr. S.G. Gold,
16, Burbidge Grove,
Southsea,
Hants.

Dear Mr. Gold,

    Thank you for your letter of the 27th July addressed to the Controller.

    I regret to inform you that we have no vacancies in our Presentation Department at the present time for a Script writer, but suggest that you contact us again when you have taken and passed your G.C.E. O' Levels.

                     Yours sincerely,

                       A. J. HENDERSON
                     <u>Assistant General Manager</u>

DIRECTORS:
JOHN H. DAVIS, Chairman · R. A. REDHEAD, Vice-Chairman · The Rt. Hon. LORD CORNWALLIS OF LINTON KBE, MC
G. R. COWSON · DONALD GEDDES · The Hon. V. H. E. HARMSWORTH · SIR ROBERT PERKINS · R. RICH
B. H. THOMSON TD · D. B. THOMSON · W. H. THOMSON · SIR DAVID WEBSTER · C. D. WILSON MC · K. WINCKLES MBE

"Thank you but no thank you"

THE BRITISH BROADCASTING CORPORATION
BROADCASTING HOUSE, LONDON, W.1

TELEGRAMS: BROADCASTS LONDON TELEX ★ CABLES: BROADCASTS LONDON-W1 ★ TELEX: 22182
TELEPHONE: LANGHAM 4468

Reference 28/KH   25th January 1962

Dear Mr. Gold,

Thank you for your letter of 21st January and for your kind offer to take part in "Juke Box Jury". I am afraid there is not very much likelihood of us being able to follow this up but I am bringing this letter to the producer's notice and he will get into touch with you if there is ever a possibility.

Yours sincerely,

Kathleen Haacke

(Kathleen Haacke)
Secretariat

J.A. Gold, Esq.,
16 Burbridge Grove,
Southsea,
Hants.

JMG

"A Miss"

CHURCHER & CHURCHER,
SOLICITORS.
COMMISSIONERS FOR OATHS.
R. E. CHURCHER.

TELEPHONE GOSPORT 82255 (4 LINES)
        "   COSHAM 76422 (2 LINES)

PLEASE QUOTE: RC/CRC

PLEASE REPLY TO GOSPORT.

28, High Street,
Gosport.

AND AT 62, NORTHERN ROAD, COSHAM.

21st February, 1963.

Dear Mr. Gold,

    We thank you for your letter of the 19th instant.

    At the moment Mr. Churcher was not contemplating having another articled clerk - he has one already.

    However, in view of the keeness displayed by your letter, Mr. Churcher personally would be pleased to grant you an interview.

    Perhaps you will either telephone Mr. Churcher or write saying which times of the day are convenient to yourself.

                    Yours sincerely,

Mr. Stephen G. Gold

"First interview, first rejection"

OFFICE HOURS: 10-1, 2.30-6 SAT 10-12

HUBERT WAY, MALPAS & STANLEY,
SOLICITORS.
COMMISSIONERS FOR OATHS.
B. J. STANLEY,
N. W. A. LANG, LL.B

TELEPHONE NOS.
PORTSMOUTH 21411/2
HAVANT 932.

OUR REF.   YOUR REF.
BJS/MB

22, Landport Terrace,
Southsea,
Portsmouth.

AND AT 42 NORTH STREET, HAVANT.

15th March 1963

Dear Mr. Gold,

    Further to your call, our partners have now had an opportunity of discussing your application and we feel that having regard to your age and to the fact that you have not passed your G.C.E. in the subject of mathematics, we cannot feel that you are yet ready to undertake articles of clerkship. We are accordingly not prepared to entertain your application. We must apologise for the delay in advising you of the position, due as explained to Mr. Stanley's illness.

              Yours truly,

Mr. Gold, junior,
16, Burbidge Grove,
SOUTHSEA.

"Your application doesn't add up"

ARTICLES OF CLERKSHIP made the 31st day of July 1963 BETWEEN RICHARD WILLIAM ELLIOTT of 38 Stoke Road Gosport in Hampshire, a Solicitor of the Supreme Court of Judicature (hereinafter called "the Solicitor") of the first part DAVID GOLD of 16 Burbidge Grove Southsea in the City of Portsmouth Company Director (hereinafter called "the Father") of the second part and STEPHEN GERALD GOLD son of the said David Gold (hereinafter called "the Clerk") of the third part.

WITNESS as follows that is to say :

1. In consideration of the covenants by the Father hereinafter contained the Solicitor agrees to take the Clerk as his clerk for the term of five years from the date of this deed.

2. The Clerk of his own free will and with the consent of the Father binds himself clerk to the Solicitor for the said term truly honestly and diligently to serve the Solicitor at all times during the said term as a faithful clerk ought to do.

3. The Father covenants with the Solicitor as follows :

    (a) That the clerk will well faithfully and diligently serve the Solicitor as his clerk in the profession of a solicitor for the said term.

    (b) That the Clerk will not at any time during the said term cancel obliterate spoil destroy waste embezzle spend or make away with any of the books papers writings money stamps or other property of the Solicitor or any of his clients or employers which shall be deposited in the hands of the Clerk or entrusted to his custody or possession or to the care custody or possession of the Solicitor.

    (c) That in case the Clerk shall act contrary to the last-mentioned covenant or if the Solicitor shall sustain or suffer any loss damage or prejudice by the misbehaviour neglect or improper conduct of the Clerk the Father will make good and reimburse the Solicitor the amount and value thereof.

    (d) That the Clerk will at all times during the said term keep the secrets of the Solicitor and of his partners and clients.

    (e) That the Clerk will readily and cheerfully obey and execute the lawful and reasonable commands of the Solicitor and will not depart or absent himself from the service or employ of the Solicitor during the said term without the consent of the Solicitor first obtained but will at all times during the said term conduct himself with all due diligence honesty sobriety and temperance.

(f) That the Father will at all times during the said term find and provide the Clerk with board and lodging and all necessary apparel and washing and also medicine surgery and medical advice and nursing in case of sickness and will further provide the Clerk with all necessary books of instruction and pay the fees for the instruction of and attendance by the Clerk at such courses of instruction as shall be requisite for the proper instruction of the Clerk so as to enable him to pass the required examinations for the time being prescribed by the Law Society.

(g) That the Clerk during such period as the Solicitor shall continue in practice after the expiration of the said term will not either solely or jointly with or as agent for or clerk to any other person or persons practise carry on or be engaged in the business or profession of a solicitor for the term of five years within the areas of the Borough of Gosport or the Urban District of Fareham and will not knowingly directly or indirectly act as solicitor for any person or persons who shall have been a client or clients of the Solicitor or of any partner or partners of the Solicitor during the said term either within or without those areas.

4. The Solicitor covenants with the Father and with the Clerk and each of them severally as follows :

(a) That he will accept and take the Clerk as his clerk during the said term and will by the best means he can and to the utmost of his skill and knowledge teach and instruct the Clerk or cause him to be taught and instructed in the practice and profession of a solicitor of the Supreme Court in such manner as he the Solicitor now practises and professes or shall at any time practise and profess the same.

(b) That he will at the expiration of the said term use his best endeavours at the request costs and charges of the Father and the Clerk or either of them to procure the Clerk to be admitted a solicitor of the Supreme Court provided the Clerk shall have well faithfully and diligently served his said clerkship and shall have passed the required examinations and in all respects properly qualified himself to be admitted to practise as such Solicitor.

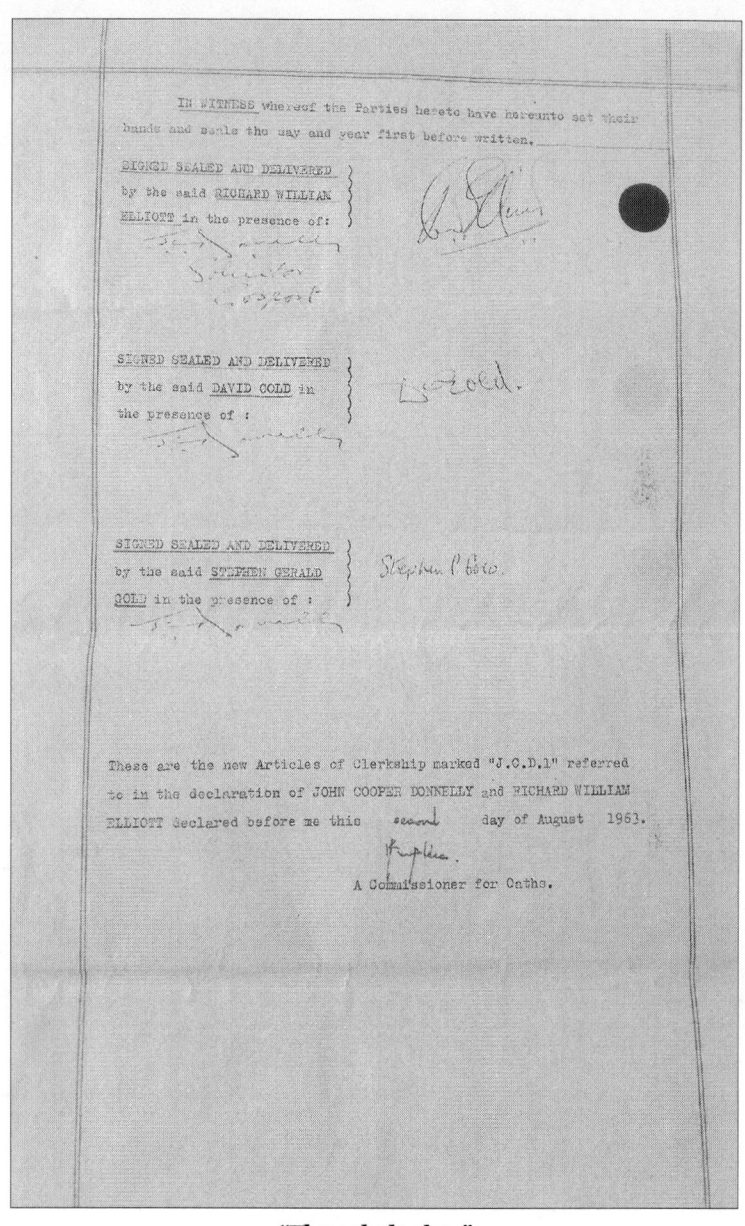

IN WITNESS whereof the Parties hereto have hereunto set their hands and seals the day and year first before written.

SIGNED SEALED AND DELIVERED)
by the said RICHARD WILLIAM)
ELLIOTT in the presence of:)

SIGNED SEALED AND DELIVERED)
by the said DAVID COLD in)
the presence of :)

SIGNED SEALED AND DELIVERED)
by the said STEPHEN GERALD)
COLD in the presence of :)

These are the new Articles of Clerkship marked "J.C.D.1" referred to in the declaration of JOHN COOPER DONNELLY and RICHARD WILLIAM ELLIOTT declared before me this second day of August 1963.

A Commissioner for Oaths.

"Thou shalt obey"

Chapter 2
Let Loose

At 22, I was deemed fit and competent to practise as a solicitor. Frightening, eh? I stayed on with Donnelly & Elliott in Gosport where I had trained. My qualification meant I was no longer commanded to run errands for my former principal Dick Elliott. The last completed fag had been executed after I had returned to the office from law school to await the results of my final exams and involved the purchase of a loaf of sliced white bread for his wife. There was no doubt that I would specialise in a wide spectrum of contentious work including crime with some conveyancing thrown in and a sprinkling of probate. And that's how it turned out with, in due course, a heavy concentration on media law. At Donnelly & Elliott I was to remain initially as assistant solicitor, then as partner and then as senior partner.

My first case was the defence of a young man charged with taking an E-type Jaguar without the owner's consent. It had been 'prepared' by Dick. The file consisted of the charge sheet and Dick's note to the effect that the car taken was red and, because of the poor street lighting when the client had driven off at night in the unlocked vehicle, he had thought it was the maroon coloured E-type that he did in fact have permission to drive. The owner of the maroon car was not to be produced by the defence. I was to meet the client for the first time at court. Mindful of Dick's mantra that it did not matter too much if you lost a case so long as you lost well, I proceeded to court with severe nervousness and the skeleton of a closing speech in my head during which I would suggest to the magistrates that driving an E-type through the streets of Portsmouth late at night was the equivalent of a naked Lady Godiva riding a horse through Coventry and was inconsistent with a guilty mind and not wanting to be noticed. As I paced the foyer of the court awaiting the client's arrival, another defendant approached me and asked: "What's up, mate? Is this your first case?" I used the Lady Godiva analogy to the magistrates. The client was convicted.

An early diversion from the staple diet of the litigation biased solicitor arrived in 1969, a few days after the end of the Isle of Wight Pop Festival which I did not attend. I was instructed to render post-festival advice to the organisers. This had been the second music festival on the island but in terms of buzz and legend it was in a different class to the first or anything since. Brothers Ron and Ray Foulk had run the event through their company Fiery Creations Limited and associated companies and Rikki Farr, the exuberant son of boxer Tommy Farr, managed it. He was also a booker. My brother Clive knew him well and swears that his booking activities involved him running up a phone bill of £29,000. Clive was given a concession at the site to sell leatherwear and accessories. He talks of a massive volume of drug consumption (not you, dear reader), a disproportionate volume of arrests and a crude toilet system involving a pit with planks over and much falling into the pit as revellers attempted to position themselves on the planks whilst they went about their business. Around 150,000 people had attended over three days. The festival turned out to be a commercial failure for the organisers and they along with two associated companies also involved could not pay their debts. There I was just as soon afterwards standing in eerie silence on flat and unremarkable land, pondering what had been. Bob Dylan, The Who, Joe Cocker, the Moody Blues and others had performed on stage and (so they say) three of the Beatles, two of the Stones, Yoko Ono and Taylor and Burton had been among those to dip into and out of the long weekend. The organising companies had to go into voluntary liquidation. Creditors of two of the companies were summoned to meetings at which it was announced that there was no alternative to a winding up. Some of them were local businesses which would be hit badly by the losses the liquidations would bring and were enraged. There was shouting and there was waving of fists. The third company to publicly collapse was Solent Graphics Limited and it was my unenviable task to turn up to a meeting of the assembled thirteen creditors and a vocal solicitor at the Clarence Pier Pavilion in Southsea (see the newspaper clippings on page 25) as sole representative of this company, walk unaccompanied along what seemed an eternal plank (with no pit thereunder) from the entrance door to a platform and announce: "It is now apparent that the company is not in a position to put forward any proposals for a moratorium and it has been advised by its accountants and lawyers that there is no alternative to placing the company into liquidation with the least possible delay. The present situation results from circumstances beyond the control of the directors." And then, as reporters of the *News of the World* were accustomed to do in other situations, I made my excuses and left.

For a short period I knuckled down to the law as a qualified solicitor. The work was stimulating and satisfying but then I saw an ad for a legal assistant – at the BBC. Yes, the station of the nation, the BB Corporation, wanted a lawyer. I could tear round the studios shouting "Broadcast and be damned" and eventually become legal correspondent on air. Or maybe I would be stuck at a desk in a pokey office approving wayleave agreements between my employer and the water authority. I got in my references and sent off the application. I was given an interview for 21 March 1969 at 11.55 am before "an Appointment Board" (see "*It's 11.55 and there's no Gold. Here is some music*" on page 26). This worried me. Who makes an appointment for 11.55 am? A little pedantic or were they seeing 63 people and allocating just five minutes to each of them? I consulted one of my referees, the barrister David Webster we have already met and who by now I was regularly briefing in criminal cases. He went on to become a QC and then a circuit judge so the boy did well. He talked me out of going to the interview. I would be far removed from "the action" he wisely predicted. What in the event the Board did at 11.55 am on that Friday, I have never discovered. Perhaps they saw the 12 noon candidate early?

Criminal work is serious stuff, for the reputation and livelihood, if not also the liberty, of the defendant are at stake, but it can also be the most exhilarating with its heavy demands and theatre. Over the years I mainly acted for the defence but also regularly prosecuted for the Crown Prosecution Service. As it had done throughout my training, the element of sex was to figure in so many cases. Frequent prosecutions were brought against men for alleged persistent importuning at public conveniences. There were many sad cases where the defendant was entrapped by plain clothed police officers effectively posing as homosexuals. One defendant I represented claimed that on the occasion charged he had positively not been importuning but since he had in fact importuned on many previous occasions and never been detected, he thought the unfounded allegation was a "fair cop" and he was insistent on pleading guilty to the charge. And another defendant was so embarrassed by the allegation against him that he could not bring himself to enter a solicitor's office. He turned up at Portsmouth Magistrates' Court as I was prosecuting a case and planted a note in my hand asking me to ring a given number so that I could arrange to represent him.

But the defence I had to run for one man charged with importuning was so incredible that I strained to keep a straight face. The reason he was seated on a promenade bench a few yards away from the gents, he claimed, was that it was a hot day (conceded by the prosecution) and on account of this, he was avoiding dehydration by drinking large quantities of water from the bottles he was carrying. This in turn induced a need for urination and so it was that he entered the toilets several times over a relatively short period of time. On the last visit, he was standing by the urinal having urinated and bent down to tighten his shoelaces. These had become loose as the act of urination had caused the foot swelling from which he suffered (verified by medical evidence) to subside. He also suffered from vertigo (verified by medical evidence) and upon rising from a bending position, he lost his balance. This led him to stumble forwards. As he was doing so, the door of a cubicle opened and my client fell into it. This was his explanation for being found by two police officers inside the cubicle with another man whose trousers were down to his knees. My client was convicted.

The *Identical Twin* defence which I had to argue was successful. It won't be available to you unless you are one of identical twins or are prepared to undergo extensive plastic surgery to give you an identical appearance to your sibling. It is essential that you are both of the same gender. In my case, the twins were male and so identical that they had trouble from telling each other apart. Twin 1 committed a string of motoring offences, ended up at the police station and passed himself off as Twin 2 to the point of producing Twin 2's driving licence which just happened to be in his pocket. Twin 2 was accordingly charged with these offences. He protested that he was not the culprit: it was my brother wot done it! Twin 1 had signed various bits and pieces at the police station in the name of Twin 2. I had the relevant documents examined by a forensic expert who compared them with the handwriting of Twin 2 and had no hesitation in concluding that the writing was not that of Twin 2. It was unnecessary to call Twin 1 to give evidence. Anyway, he was probably some miles away at the Blackpool illuminations on the day of the trial. The magistrates could not be sure beyond reasonable doubt about the true identity of the offender and so all charges against Twin 2 were dismissed and the prosecutor's face was extremely sour.

I see that the *Identical Twin* defence was set to be run in a trial at Gloucester

Crown Court in February 2016 when a man was charged with dangerous driving and possessing an offensive weapon. The prosecution offered no evidence. The court was told that inquiries to try and verify which of the twins had been arrested had drawn a blank. The charges were dismissed.

The deceiving twin could always be charged with perverting or attempting to pervert the course of justice but even that could have its difficulties. With the innocent twin unlikely to cooperate in such a prosecution the deceiving twin could always insist that it was his brother and not him who had been arrested.

One speech in mitigation to a bench of magistrates went down flat. My butcher client was prosecuted for a series of food hygiene offences by the local authority. The thrust of the case was that what sounded like a very large number of mice droppings had been found where meat was prepared and sold. The authority's solicitor who had a rodent appearance around the mouth area produced with enormous relish several packets of the droppings which had been scrupulously collected and carried away by council inspectors, no doubt before they had taken their luncheon break. "But your worships," I said. "One single mouse can be responsible for 80 droppings a day. All we are talking about here is one and a half mice on the premises."

But I did win cases too on some interesting little points (which you would call technicalities). I successfully submitted that there was no case to answer against the defendant who was summoned for breaching a local authority abatement notice which prohibited her from causing a nuisance through *barking* dogs when the evidence of the neighbours was that they had been disturbed by *howling* dogs. Another client had a charge dismissed for allegedly carrying an offensive weapon in a public place when he had spontaneously picked up a piece of wood and immediately used it offensively so that it could not be said he had *carried* it. A diner at a Gosport Chinese restaurant had a charge of stealing a salt pot dismissed on the ground that he had no case to answer and a charge of stealing a pepper pot on the same occasion dismissed after he had given evidence. I was able to submit that only a gastronomic pervert would act in the dishonest way alleged (see "*A seasoned defence*" on page 27). My racing tipster client saw off 19 charges relating to the alleged dishonest reuse of postage stamps on the envelopes he sent out daily to his punters. My market trading client who sold foodstuffs close to or over the 'sell by' date and who had previously been convicted of attempting to bribe a health inspector with two tins of dried peas (really) was found not guilty of a series of public health offences and then proceeded to bung £50 in cash into my hand in court to show – to me and the magistrates – his gratitude. A woman client charged with aiding and abetting her husband to live on her immoral earnings as a prostitute was acquitted on the basis that she could not be guilty of aiding and abetting an offence which had been created for her own protection and the husband for whom I also acted was acquitted of living on her immoral earnings on the basis that she had spent all those earnings buying jewellery for herself and so he had not derived any benefit from them. A youth alleged to have attempted to steal sweets from a stall was found not guilty as I was able to submit that, whatever his dishonest intent, there was no evidence there had been any sweets present. This element of impossibility is no longer a defence to a charge of attempt. And two clients during my career as a solicitor were rightly acquitted of charges of manslaughter but this had nothing to do with technicalities.

There were frustrating instances. A rural bench of magistrates rejected my submission that there was no case to answer for my client summoned for speeding because the one police officer giving evidence for the prosecution had failed to identify him as the driver he had stopped. The clerk to the justices asserted that the officer had pointed to the client from the witness box when he mentioned his name but I would have been unable to see this from where I was standing! Another was the falling ill of one of the three members of an employment tribunal after the 14th day of my client's application for unfair dismissal compensation which we had been winning and the opting of the employer to require the hearing to restart before a fresh tribunal before which we lost. More frustration at the decision of magistrates before whom I was prosecuting a defendant for theft of a hat to dismiss the charge. This was notwithstanding that although he said he had selected it for himself but forgotten to pay, the hat was patently no less than four sizes too big as demonstrated when I insisted he tried it on in court. On another prosecuting outing, I opened a fairly complex case to the magistrates and then asked for the first witness to be called only to discover that there were no witnesses at court. The police had messed up.

The frustrations were eclipsed by the humour which was often lurking. There was the insistence of a particular magistrate for production of a plan of the area in which the offence charged was alleged to have been committed, however straight the road or unremarkable the features. It would come fairly early on in the case. "Is there a plan?" When the enquiry was made one afternoon on the hearing of an indecency case in which I was defending, the prosecutor offered to go out and draw the plan of the relevant section of the High Street close to the court if the hearing could be adjourned and I enthusiastically agreed. We went for a cup of tea after which the prosecutor sketched out what amounted to little more than two parallel lines and this was gratefully accepted into evidence. During the course of my questioning a strange client in a domestic case about his penchant for adult pornography, my opponent lawyer passed me a note which was calculated to make me corpse and it succeeded immediately on reading. We had to adjourn.

And then there was the 1980 case of the LBC traffic reporter who successfully claimed for unfair dismissal. LBC was under different management in those days and it was to be some time before I began participating in legal phone ins on the station. So they never held it against me! The reporter's job was to broadcast live from Scotland Yard and the dismissal came after a series of incidents in which traffic control room staff wound her up. She alleged that whilst on air one officer had stood behind her and made a lewd remark. She also alleged that the staff put a dead mouse on her chair resulting in a bit of a scream just as the main studio went over to her, whistled whilst she was broadcasting, tampered with her broadcasting equipment and failed to give her adequate traffic information so that she could do her job properly. The onus was on LBC to justify the dismissal and so it was that they had to call their evidence before we did. The first question to be put to their first witness was "Did you ever say to the applicant 'I am going to pull your knickers down and smack your bum?'" It was a bizarre opener and the single agency reporter present must have thought Christmas had come early. Within ten minutes, half of Fleet Street (they hadn't moved out yet) were in residence. The tribunal decided that LBC was 80% to blame and we subsequently agreed on compensation.

In 1989 my first book, the catchily entitled *Gold's Law or how to beat the system*, was published and in my drive to sell a couple of copies, I toured as many radio and television studios as would let me in. One of the radio phone-ins was with Johnnie Walker on BBC Radio London who asked me to comment on a news story which broke during the programme that a Capital Radio technician had been arrested for alleged criminal damage for trying to drive his car away as it was being raised by a crane following impoundment for unlawful parking outside the Capital studios. Different. I declined for legal reasons which was just as well because the man was subsequently charged and engaged me to defend him. He was convicted.

I have made two visits to the House of Lords. The second was in connection with an attempt at a career change to which I shall come. The first was for a case in 1978. My client got himself into difficulties over some cannabis leaves and was charged with their unlawful possession. But was it a criminal offence to possess cannabis leaves? It seemed to me that it was not. Cannabis was then defined by statute as meaning the flowering and fruiting tops of the cannabis plant and leaves didn't look like fruiting or flowering tops to me. I advised my client to plead not guilty and to elect to have his case tried at the crown court. This is what he did and I briefed as his barrister the late Randolph Boxall who, as it happens, was then on the select panel of barristers who prosecuted cases for HM Customs & Excise so he knew his drugs and, usefully, he had read chemistry at Cambridge. For the purposes of the trial, we needed to show the jury a cannabis plant. I was granted a special licence to hold on to one. A label distinctively marked **CANNABIS** was attached to it and I ensured it was seen by as many people as possible. The argument that leaves were not fruiting or flowering tops did not go down well with the Crown Court judge at round 1 and my client was convicted. He appealed against that conviction to the Court of Appeal on round 2 where he won but they gave permission for him to be returned to the Crown Court to be tried on an alternative charge of possession of a cannabinol derivative (which is hard to say even after just two modest glasses of white wine).

Back at the Crown Court then for round 3. The prosecution contended that the cannabinol derivative was present in cannabis leaves so that if you had the leaves, you had the derivatives they contained. This was akin to saying that if you were holding an orange you were in possession of sugar. The judge did not agree with the defence and my client was convicted of this alternative offence. He put in an appeal to the Court of Appeal.

Back to the Court of Appeal for round 4. The conviction was upheld. My client asked for permission to appeal. It was refused. My client applied to the highest court in the land the House of Lords (which has since morphed into the Supreme Court) for its permission to appeal to them. At round 5 permission was granted.

And so to the House of Lords for the substantive appeal at round 6 and my first visit there. Mr Boxall – who throughout had been assisted by another barrister Roderick Cordara who is now a QC – argued that at least ten drugs classified in the same way as the cannabinol derivative relied on by the prosecution were to be found in various plants, toadstools and toads. Three types of toad produced venom in their granular and mucus glands and that venom contained bufotenine which was a controlled drug. Was it intended that possession of a toad should be a criminal offence, he asked rhetorically? The House of Lords quashed the conviction. The law was changed. It is now an offence to possess cannabis leaves. And, quite outrageously. HM Customs & Excise never gave Mr Boxall another case to prosecute.

There are stars of the law as there are stars of every profession. I had a good grounding in idolatry. I started where we all start, as an autograph hunter. I was in my early teens. The stage door at The King's Theatre, Southsea became my habitat for a season. I gazed at Margaret Lockwood and Zachary Scott as they rushed through. I had no idea who they were but they looked glamorous. I arrested Mr Scott for a photograph and he said that he would send one if I left my details with his dresser. It arrived a month or so later. I was very impressed. Nigel Stock dropped a bogey on page three of the autograph book after it had been left with him. I was not impressed. On Sunday steamer trips with my parents in the Solent between South Parade Pier and Ryde one would often encounter a star due to perform at a concert on the Isle of Wight. Eric Robinson and Dickie Henderson Junior signed my book. So did the orange haired Wee Willie Harris but he found the task arduous and applied so much pressure with my biro that it made an impression on several pages underneath. I almost passed out as I encountered Bob Monkhouse on South Parade Pier. He seemed to be in an enormous hurry. I stopped him and asked for his autograph. He pleaded for time. "I'm dying for a wee." This indulgence I extended to him and when he emerged from the gents, he duly obliged.

As an articled clerk and later a solicitor, I was not averse to sitting in the awe inspiring Lord Chief Justice's Court in the Strand Law Courts, soaking up the atmosphere and fixated at the intellect of the appeal judges. For even the most experienced criminal barrister, an appearance before the Lord Chief Justice and his two judicial colleagues to each side was an occasion for trepidation. Only once did I encounter a joke cracked there. A barrister had turned up to argue that his client's conviction had been wrong but he had received late instruction to abandon the appeal. "My Lords, I came to curse but now I bless." Not ribcage fracturing stuff but it got a laugh. At the lower end of the scale, a visit to Marlborough Street magistrates' court to listen to a stipendiary in action was always good entertainment. A street vendor convicted of obstruction of the highway asked for time to pay his fine. "Get in a moneylender," he was instructed.

These judicial heroes do not have fan clubs or sign autograph books. I suppose at the request of a law student they might be persuaded to sign a legal tome written or edited by them and even Lord Neuberger, the former president of the Supreme Court, who once balked at the idea of television cameras in the Court of Appeal, took to posing for selfies on conducted tours around his Westminster base when not being broadcast with his co-Justices. The proper way to worship a judge is read their judgments and listen to their reply to the toast to the guests at an occasional pain inducing legal dinner. In respect of the great Master of the Rolls Lord Denning, however, I did get a bit silly.

By 1982 I had notched up quite a few television and radio broadcasts as a legal talking head initially as a Law Society spokesman and then in my own right and then, quite extraordinarily, I was engaged to present a weekly current affairs programme *7 Days* on now defunct Television South. There was some pre-series editorial disagreement about its ethos. Whilst this was going on I had the hare-brained idea of a slot in which Lord Denning who had by then retired and lived on the station's patch would arbitrate on disputes between parties who were willing to bring them to the programme. This was before Judges Judy and Rinder had learnt anything about the burden of proof. I couldn't see how such a slot would comfortably meet the criteria of a current affairs programme but no matter, this would get the punters watching. I wrote off to Lord Denning who was media friendly and got a charming refusal (see "*Lord Denning regrets*" on page 28).

Then there were Ron and Reg with a smattering of Charlie.

Let Loose

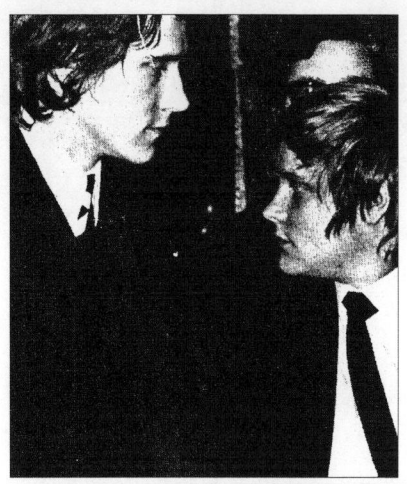

Mr. Ray Foulk (left), principal director of Fiery Creations, Ltd., addressing creditors, stands up to leave the Clarence Parade Pavilion, Southsea, with his brother Ron (right), just before the abrupt ending to the meeting.

Pop festival caterers to be wound up

Exhibition Caterers, Ltd., which handled food and drink sales for the Isle of Wight Pop Festival, is to be placed in a creditors voluntary winding-up order "with the least possible delay," creditors were told yesterday.

Mr. M. Baxter, and Mr. R. Condon, the company's two directors and shareholders, said this in a short statement issued to the 20 people present at the meeting in Portsmouth Chamber of Commerce hall.

In their statement, they told creditors: "It is now transparent that we are not in a position with regard to a moratorium and we have been advised by our accountants with our legal advisers that there is no alternative to placing the company in a creditors voluntary winding-up with the least possibly delay."

After the statement had been read, some of those present tried to pose questions, but both Mr. Baxter and Mr. Condon said they could not say anymore about the position.

Exhibition Caterers, Ltd., is an associate company of Fiery Creations, Ltd., organizers of the Festival. Ron and Ray Foulk, principal directors of Fiery Creations, Ltd., were not present at the afternoon meeting.

SOLENT GRAPHICS

A further meeting was held in Clarence Pier Pavilion, Southsea, today relating to Solent Graphics, Ltd., another company associated with the Festival.

As reported in late editions of THE NEWS yesterday, a meeting of creditors in the Pier Pavilion resulted in angry scenes when Fiery Creations, Ltd., surprised those present by issuing a short statement and refusing to answer questions.

"That's my forehead"

Third 'pop' company liquidates

THIRTEEN businessmen listened in silence at Southsea today as a solicitor read a statement announcing the liquidation of a third company associated with the Isle of Wight pop festival.

A Portsmouth solicitor, Mr. tSephen Gold, told a meeting of creditors of Solent Graphics Limited, a printing firm, that there was no alternative to voluntary liquidation.

"The present difficulties result from circumstances beyond the control of the directors," he said in a statement similarly worded to statements from two other pop festival companies read to creditors yesterday.

NOT NAMED

Mr. Gold declined to name the directors on whose behalf his firm was working and the creditors were reluctant to give the amounts owed to them.

Directors of Fiery Creations Limited yesterday appealed for time before final decision about the future of the company and directors of an associated company, Exhibition Caterers Limited, announced that they had no alternative to voluntary creditors liquidation.

"Mr Gold declines"

25

BBC

BRITISH BROADCASTING CORPORATION
PO BOX 1AA BROADCASTING HOUSE LONDON W1
TELEPHONE 01-580 4468 TELEGRAMS BROADCASTS LONDON TELEX
CABLES BROADCASTS LONDON-W1 TELEX 22182

Reference: 01/APP/   19th March 1969

. . Gold Esq.,
7 Maddison Road,
Waterlooville,
Portsmouth.

Dear Sir,

                                 65.3.21 LATIN ASSISTANT

      Referring to your application for this vacancy, will you please come for an interview with an Appointment Board at 5 Portland Place (opposite Broadcasting House), London, W.1 at 11.55 a.m. on Friday, 21st March 1969.

      Please confirm by return of post (or a telephone call) that you will be coming.

                Yours faithfully,

                Ian (M.S. Black)
                Appointments Department

"It's 11.55 and there's no Gold. Here is some music"

SALTY STORY FOR THE MAGISTRATES

A rating told Gosport Magistrates yesterday he hid a salt and pepper pot from a Chinese restaurant in his sock so he could take them to the toilet, eat the salt and pepper and return the pots afterwards.

He was alleged to have told Gosport police: "I like eating salt. I eat it all the time."

David Henry Staines (22), of Sunderland, serving in H.M.S. Resolution, denied stealing a salt pot and pepper pot, the property of Mr. Tao Ying Wan.

After a submission by Mr. S. G. Gould (defending), Mr. L. S. Vail (presiding) said the magistrates found no case to answer with regard to the salt pot but did find a case to answer for the pepper pot.

Later, the magistrates dismissed the case concerning the pepper pot but decided it had been properly brought.

Mr. Hin Tat Tang, of Avenue Road, Gosport, said he was a waiter at the Silver Capital Chinese restaurant in South Street, Gosport.

BULGE IN SOCK

While serving Staines and another man, he saw a bulge in Staines's sock and took a salt pot from it which he put on the table.

Mr. Tang alleged that when he refused to call a taxi for Staines, he was chased round the restaurant and went out to call the police. When he returned with a police officer, he found that the salt and pepper pot had disappeared again and could not be found.

P.C. R. A. Macey told the court he went to the restaurant where he saw Staines and another man in the dorway. He searched both men but found nothing.

When he asked Staines why he had put the salt pot in his sock Staines was alleged to have replied: "I like eating salt. I eat it all the time."

Staines told the magistrates he had two injections during the morning of the day the incident occurred and later drank three pints of beer. When he arrived at the restaurant he felt "dizzy and sluggish."

A JOKE

He put the salt and pepper pots in his sock as a joke.

The waiter only found the salt pot and Staines later threw the peper pot away from him. He said his friend's bill was overcharged by 10s. as payment for the salt pot.

Cross-examined by Inspector C. D. Ford (prosecuting) Staines said he put the salt and pepper pots in his sock as he intended to go to the toilet and eat the salt and pepper there.

He would then have returned the pots.

He denied chasing the waiter round the restaurant.

"A seasoned defence"

From: The Rt. Hon. Lord Denning,
Master of the Rolls.

ROYAL COURTS OF JUSTICE
STRAND, LONDON, WC2A 2LL

The Lawn,
Whitchurch, Hants.

24th August 1982.

Dear Mr. Gold,

Thank you for your letter of 29th July. I can see that your programme will be quite an interesting one for TVS, and it would be interesting for me to take some part in it as an arbitrator, but I hardly think it is my line of country. I feel it would be better for me not to take part in it.

I do hope you will not be too disappointed, but I have to limit my activities quite a lot.

Yours sincerely,

Denning

S. G. Gold, Esq.,
C/o Donnelly and Elliott,
38 Stoke Road,
GOSPORT. PO12 1JG.

"Lord Denning regrets"

Chapter 3

Ron And Reg

The place: Old Bailey, London EC4

The date: 5 March 1969

The occasion: Day 40 of the trial of Ronald Kray, Reginald Kray and others

Mr Justice Melford Stevenson sentences Ronald having been convicted of the murder of George Cornell and Reginald having been convicted of the murder of Jack McVitie.

> *"Ronald Kray, I am not going to waste words on you. The sentence upon you is that you will go to life imprisonment. In my view society has earned a rest from your activities and I recommend that you be detained for 30 years. Put him down."*

To Reginald Kray:

> *"Now, on the third count of this indictment, on which you have been convicted of murder, you will go to imprisonment for life. For reasons I have already indicated in the case of your brother, Ronald – I don't propose to repeat them – I recommend that you be detained for 30 years; and on the second count of this indictment, there will be a sentence of 10 years to run concurrently."*

They were then 34. 26 years on Ron Kray was dead from a heart attack having spent that time in prison and later as an inmate in Broadmoor, the maximum security psychiatric hospital in Crowthorne. 41 years on Reg Kray was dead from bladder cancer having spent the whole time in prison until eight weeks before his death when he was released to hospital on compassionate grounds.

I acted for both the Kray twins, not in connection with any criminal defences but in a host of civil matters over some six years until Ron's death and then for a little longer for Reg until I ceased to practise as a solicitor. Whatever their past misdeeds, they were entitled to legal advice and representation on their personal affairs and they got it from me. All my dealings with them were in person and by post and 'phone. So far as Ron was concerned, I would see him at Broadmoor where for the greater part of the period of our association he shared a ward with, amongst others, the now deceased *Yorkshire Ripper* Peter Sutcliffe (he told me he refused to have anything to do with him). Reg I would see at one of the various prisons in which he was incarcerated and at which he held considerable sway but mainly at Gartree Prison near Market Harborough in Leicestershire. When Reg was subsequently transferred to Nottingham Prison, I drove there at his request to discuss what I expected to be serious business to find him under the influence of alcohol and insistent that the interview be conducted in the presence of a young man who had become his cell mate and was in the same condition. Reg explained they had both been drinking 'hooch' which was an alcopop. It was necessary to summarily terminate the interview but not before Reg had handed me a ten-page document setting out his plans and instructions to one and all for generating an income by the exploitation of the twins' fame. This had been dictated by him to his cell mate and signed by him. It was enterprising and unrealistic in equal measure. Here's a flavour (with corrected spelling).

"We should try to get my record sold in all the cinema foyers across the country when the sequel film comes out. Our friend ... should be able to put this idea into practice. We should also be able to earn a lot of money in selling merchandise that will stem from the sequel film. It is possible that we will bring out a new book called 'Letters to the Krays'. Robert ... the publisher has shown interest in such a book. I will have to contact him re this .... Some time ago it was my idea to produce a photograph album which would stem from all our photographs. Laurie ... has come up with a similar idea so we should let him proceed with this and divide the proceeds amicably..."

The authorities would make a private room available for legal consultation at all the venues. Reg was accustomed to direct an adjournment when parched and ask me to get him a cuppa and possibly a biscuit from the prison canteen. Letters from each of them were regular and would end with a *'God Bless'* unless I had displeased so that one would check the sign-off first. The handwriting was sometimes hard to decipher, especially Ron's. They both seemed to have ready access to phones. I amused myself by pondering how the conveyancing and probate clients waiting in the reception of my Gosport office a few yards away from the trilly telephonist, reacted to hearing "Reg/Ron Kray for you, Mr Gold" as they raised their eyes from antique editions of *Horse & Hounds*. One Sunday afternoon I received a call from Ron at home instructing me to take out an injunction against Broadmoor for keeping him locked up in his room for unacceptable hours because of industrial action by staff. It was not an instruction to be relished and happily the problem was soon resolved. You may rest assured that I was not asked to do anything illegal or professionally improper but occasionally my instructions were unusual. Reg once asked me to take out the twin's brother Charlie for lunch – on him. I thought it would be an interesting experience. I met him at Graham's fish restaurant in London's Poland Street where two of the waitresses regaled him like a long lost friend. We occupied a table at the front window. During the meal, I half expected to see a limo pull up outside and a machine gun penetrate our dover soles.

The most serious mischief perpetrated by either of the twins over this period of which I was aware was on the part of Reg in reading my regular columns in the *New Law Journal* without having taken out a subscription though he had a good defence, namely that I had sent them to him and on the part of Ron in receiving visits in Broadmoor from members of the Mafia (or so he said).

In September 1989, BBC 1's *South-East at Six* regional news programme broadcast an item about the Krays presented by Duncan Kennedy to which they took exception. They claimed that what was said on air by Mr Kennedy and an unidentified male witness amounted to allegations that the

Krays were mass-murderers who had committed countless killings which had gone undetected and unpunished and that if released they intended to re-embark on their earlier careers as mass-murderers. Reg was particularly anxious about this publicity for his dream, periodically snatched away from him with parole application knock-backs, was to get out of prison.

The twins instructed me to bring libel proceedings against the BBC, the very hand that fed me £2 a time or sometimes a little more for my own local radio broadcasts. Although libel is generally devoted to defamatory words which are written rather than spoken – slander is for the spoken stuff – what is defamatorily broadcast on television and radio is classified as libel. A claim for libel had no chance of getting off the ground unless, as the law then required, it could be proved that the words complained of had "lowered the reputation of the claimant in the minds of right-thinking members of society." Now, you might reckon it was a pretty tall order to prove that anything said to the detriment of the Krays would make right-thinking members of the public think any less of them than they already did. The Krays were under no illusions about the hurdles in their way but they wanted to have a bash at trying to extract some partial withdrawal or apology from the BBC. I had to get a defamation barrister on board to draft the court document to go with the High Court writ I was to issue. The barrister's name would appear on the document and without a name there, the BBC would have deduced that yours truly, a mere solicitor, had done the drafting and so the twins were not serious about taking the case the distance if it did not capitulate. I had a furious row with the first barrister I went to, a self-satisfied practitioner who was highly regarded by his peers and the judiciary. He refused to accept that it could be respectably argued that the Krays would be thought any less of if accused of a catalogue of murders instead of the single murder for which each of them had been convicted and clearly had no desire to dirty his hands with the likes of the Krays. The second barrister I went to readily accepted the job.

A writ was duly issued (see page 41). Asked by the media for a statement on the Krays' behalf I said this: "They do not seek to make any complaint about legitimate discussion of their crimes for which they have been severely punished. But what they do object to is that having been incarcerated for so long, they should be subjected to unfounded and unsubstantiated allegations of misdeeds which have not previously been made."

The BBC put in a spirited defence (see page 43). They contended that the words complained of were true in substance and in fact and were a fair comment on a matter of public interest which was whether or not the Krays should be released from detention before their 30 years were up. The Krays, they argued, had terrorised people by proving their readiness to carry out killings and maimings and had committed countless serious crimes for which they had managed to avoid conviction and punishment. The defence pleaded that "people have good reason to be fearful at the prospect of the Plaintiffs' release from detention." The BBC also relied heavily on what the Krays had gone on record as saying in the book *Our Story* published by Sidgwick & Jackson which with Fred Dinenage they had written in 1988.

In the BBC's assessment the twins had in that book exposed themselves as cruel and ruthless men whose sole regrets lay in the mistake they had made in themselves carrying out the murders of which they had been convicted instead of engaging others to carry out the deeds for them and by failing to silence the barmaid of the Blind Beggar who had given evidence for the prosecution at the Old Bailey trial by threatening physical violence against her or her family.

The defence did the trick for the BBC. The twins decided to extricate themselves from the proceedings as fast as possible. I spoke to the BBC's lawyer who was handling the case. I tried to persuade him to drop any claim for costs if the Krays withdrew. He wasn't having it. He joked that the BBC didn't usually win civil cases and wanted to make the most of this victory. The BBC was insistent on the Krays paying the costs they had incurred. In June 1990 the High Court ordered with the consent of both sides that the action should be dismissed and that the Krays should pay the BBC's costs (see the consent order on page 44). The prospects of those costs ever being extracted by the BBC were as great as me making it to Lord Chief Justice. Wisely, they did nothing about enforcing the costs order which meant, dear licence fee payer, they were borne by you (and me) or your forefathers. And three years after that dismissal the Home Office was giving feedback to Reg to the effect that he was unlikely to be released before his 30 years were up. It is apparent that issues over lack of insight and remorse and public notoriety stood in his way. A probation officer in her parole report some 25 years following his incarceration was saying that clear messages needed to be given to Reg about expectations he needed to meet before he would be fully considered for release and he would have to work on those areas. He needed to understand that, otherwise, release would not come about.

In a second report by another probation officer at Blundeston Prison soon afterwards in August 1993 which has recently been disclosed by National Archives it was suggested that Reg held no real remorse for his crime. "The victim was one of the lads and had taken liberties and had it coming to him." He told the officer that he had tried to start a secondhand car business being run for him by outside agencies which had failed but his plans for a business in scaffolding were still in the planning stage. The officer considered that if he was released, he would need strong supervisory support which he would find it hard to accept. Although he had tried to keep abreast of life outside, he could not possibly guess at the pace of life as it then was. If he tried to drive a vehicle, could he cope? And although Reg kept himself physically fit, he had started to age considerably and his eyesight was failing slightly. He needed some indication of when he could possibly be released so that he could shake himself up and start looking more positively to the future because, although he would not admit it, there was a danger of a rapid deterioration and vegetation.

And the officer mentioned what Reg had done in prison for a very young boy who had contracted an incurable disease. Reg had read about a fund being raised to buy the boy a mobile chair. Through an "outside agency" he had mobilised contacts in the entertainment industry which had led to sufficient money coming in not only to buy the chair but to send the boy and his mother on a holiday to America. There had been media interest on what happened which the officer suspected had set back Reg's course for release. Reg was realistic enough to acknowledge that the Home Office took very little notice of the pleas to them by members of the public for his release and had confided that he wished he could drop out of the limelight so that he could concentrate on his life and plan for his release and "retirement".

Reg seems to have come over in better physical shape to the second Blundeston probation officer who compiled a third report the following month in September 1993 (see two extracts on page 45). "It is difficult not to be struck by the vitality, energy and generally, good humour displayed by Mr Kray, unexpected in a man who is nearly 60 and has been in prison for 25 years. It is not surprising that his energies have been expended in surviving for such a period." Because the "events" in which he had been involved had had no bearing on members of the public but were aimed at "competitors", he saw no real wrong. However, it did seem that he acknowledged that to take a life could not be right "although such are his expressions that one is left with the feeling that he allows for exception".

As for Ron, he never expected to get out of Broadmoor. But did he want out? He missed Reg. Indeed, one of my jobs had been to negotiate a meeting between the twins at Broadmoor which could not be overheard by third parties. Unhappily, when the meeting eventually took place, the twins' loud voices meant they could be heard outside the building and the meeting had to be terminated early because of some Kray differences of opinion.

Ron had found himself at Broadmoor after his stay at Parkhurst Prison on the Isle of Wight worked out badly. He was already at Parkhurst when Reg joined him there in February 1971. The day before Reg's arrival, Ron attacked a fellow prisoner in the special security block and injured him. Ron was removed to the prison hospital "for treatment". Once Reg had arrived, the twins met up in the hospital twice a week. A report by the prison governor, also now made public by National Archives, highlights the dilemma he faced – and the degree of control exercised by the prisoners. He reported that inmates and staff alike – with the possible exception of the assault victim! – were disturbed by what might happen if Ron was returned to the block. "Various of the prisoners have made it clear that they believe that Reginald will join with Ronald in any future attack rather than prove a restraining influence and they have prepared a contingency plan which involves neutralising both brothers if any of their number is attacked by one. In preparing this plan there has been a surprising degree of unity between the various groups of prisoners (in the block). One prisoner has also indicated that this plan will be put in operation by them if the victim of expected attack by Ronald Kray is a member of staff." Reg, nevertheless, had been accepted by the prisoners with no difficulty. He had always been more popular with fellow prisoners than his brother and had been at pains to allay the fears of the others about Ron's return to the block which Reg was very keen to happen when "treatment" had finished. The governor had concluded that the possible advantage of Reg's presence as an influence for the better on his brother had been lost and the control problem presented by both Krays being there in the same security block had been heightened by the reaction of prisoners and staff to Ron's attack. The governor expressed the view that the decision to reunite the twins had been a mistake and concluded that Ron should remain in the prison hospital "for some time". In the event, within a matter of weeks, Ron was out of the hospital and back in the block with Reg. It was not to last.

In 1989 Ron instructed me to bring divorce proceedings against a woman who had befriended him during his time in Broadmoor to which he had been transferred from prison and whom he had married. He was inside: she was outside. That made living together very problematic. He claimed that for more than two years she had ceased to visit him or to have anything to do with him. There was no suggestion that she would consent to a divorce and so the only basis on which it was likely Ron could secure his liberty from the marriage at that point was to allege that his wife had deserted him for the minimum period required of two years. And that is precisely what we did. Proceedings were started in Portsmouth county court. His wife did not take any steps to defend them. However, a district judge had declined to grant a divorce on the papers because of the relative novelty of the desertion argument we were putting forward and a hearing was ordered at which the court would need to have Ron's live evidence. Arrangements were made for him to be taken to the Portsmouth hearing from Crowthorne and the police were anticipating the possibility of a large public turn out. In the event, the day before the hearing I was notified that Ron did not wish to be there: either that or the Home Office had refused to let him out. I was to attempt to persuade the judge to pronounce a decree of divorce without the client. Fortunately, I had a sworn written statement from him setting out all the alleged facts and would have to do my best with this.

The case came before His Honour Judge Michael Brodrick. "Your Honour, I appear for the petitioner in this case. My client had the misfortune to appear before the Central Criminal Court on 5 March 1969 when he was convicted....." The judge stopped me. With a rueful smile, he said "We all know who Ronald Kray is" so I was able to cut short my introduction. Apart from a limited number of things like the date and that there are one hundred pence in the pound, a fact has to be proved by evidence and an advocate is not entitled to assume that a judge will take anything unproved for granted. That is why I had to proceed on the premise that Judge Brodrick lived in a different world to everyone else. Ron's case was that although he and his wife had never lived together, she was in law capable of deserting him if she had ceased over at least two years to have anything more to do with him in the ways which had been available to her. We were looking at desertion from a state of affairs rather than a place and, given that she could have visited him in Broadmoor as formerly she had done and he had wished these visits to continue, she had deserted him at Broadmoor. The judge agreed and pronounced a divorce decree (see "*Ron deserted*" on page 46). Ron later married Kate Kray who subsequently divorced him.

In 1990 *The Sunday People* revealed that the twins were to profit substantially from *The Krays*, the film of their lives which was then about to be premiered, in which they were being portrayed by Martin and Gary Kemp. The Inland Revenue had a couple of inspectors who spent their time or much of it trawling through newspapers to pick up on stories of money received but tax not paid. They read the story and made contact with Reg requiring a full disclosure of income. Serving prisoners, like prostitutes, are as chargeable to tax as judges and vicars. I was instructed to negotiate with the Revenue and came to an agreement subject to an interview by inspectors with Reg in prison which I set up. I attended and two Revenue men were there. Little or nothing was asked about relevant transactions. Reg treated the men to a daytime cabaret and they lapped it up. They were totally mesmerised by the man and his notoriety. Thereafter, Reg instructed me not to proceed with the agreement. I have no reason to believe that the Revenue ever collected a penny from him. In Ron, no doubt by virtue of his mental condition, they had no interest. What did happen is that a senior Revenue investigator was subsequently convicted of corruption in the course of his duties and ended up in prison. Whether or not he ever served time under the same prison roof as Reg, I know not.

The Revenue's interest in collecting some income tax on Reg's earnings sparked his short-lived desire to be registered for VAT. This was on the basis that he had received an advance under a book publishing agreement and the same agreement and others were to generate future royalties for him which could take him over the then VAT registration threshold of £25,000 a year. It would have been a unique situation for a serving prisoner to be VAT registered in relation to income from writing activities in his prison cell. I think Reg was amused at the prospect of asking the governor for special time off to devote to making up his VAT books and accounts but as I explained to the chartered accountant in the family, my brother Leonard Gold, "my client is anxious to comply with any legal obligations to which he may be subject". Yes, I had recommended Leonard as the man to sort out the VAT registration if it was to be required. The VAT office notified on what it called "an interesting registration problem" that Reg's name should appear on the VAT form for registration, the registered address should be that of Reg's agent and that Reg's books and records should be kept at that address for inspection by its control staff. Reg then decided not to pursue the matter.

I heard of Ron's death on the radio as I was driving back from London on the M3 (see pages 48 to 51 for the Order of Service, signed by Reg Kray). I was an executor of his will and, being relatively close to Broadmoor, decided it would be prudent to divert there and take charge of his personal property or at least check what was there before the memorabilia hunters burst into action. My accelerator foot got carried away with the moment and I was stopped by a traffic police officer on a motorbike for speeding, albeit modestly. It was not unknown for the motorist's words of excuse on being cautioned for an offence to make their way on to the offence information with the summons and to be passed on to the magistrates. Say "Sorry, officer. I had just heard that my client Ron Kray has died and I needed to get to Broadmoor fast?" Hardly. I accepted with grace that I had offended and without excuse and in due course collected the summons, the fine and the endorsement with no Kray mitigation put forward.

Reg was suspicious of the circumstances in which Ron had died and wanted me to investigate. I contacted the then coroner who informed me that the inquest which he had already held into Ron's death had not been notified to Ron's family. It had taken place in his office and he had heard oral evidence from a police constable. He was satisfied that Ron could be "signed up" as a routine case of someone who dies naturally by reason of heart problems and indeed he gave a verdict of death by natural causes. There is no suggestion that the coroner had been seeking to cover up evidence but he did offer to reconvene the inquest at which I could have appeared. I also arranged to instruct a private pathologist to carry out a post-mortem on behalf of Reg. Both the fresh inquest and the post-mortem were aborted after Reg telephoned me to say that he had that day seen his twin's body at the undertakers. Because he had looked so peaceful he did not wish to see the body subjected to a second post-mortem and he would accept the cause of death as certified – a heart attack – without a fresh inquest or post-mortem. What he did not know at that stage and what I could not bring myself to disclose to him was that Ron's brain had been removed. This information had been passed on to me by the private pathologist and the likelihood, it seemed to me, was that the brain was sought for research purposes there being special interest in it having come from a twin. In the event, Reg later discovered what had happened and was none too pleased.

It is not uncommon for the brain to be removed at post-mortem where this is required for the purpose of determining the cause of death. Removal for legitimate research purposes should not take place without consultation with the relatives and their consent.

Given the cause of death, I was perplexed by what had happened but, within a couple of months, I began serving as a full-time judge and so was unable to personally pursue any investigation. On retiring as a full-time judge, I felt the coast was clear to pursue a brain chase. I found out where it was from Reg's widow Roberta who told me that, while I was sitting at Kingston-upon-Thames county court trying to save tenants being evicted from their homes, Reg had instructed solicitors to procure the release of Ron's brain. Moreover, they had succeeded.

I discovered that the brain had been handed over to the funeral directors E English & Son by Wexham Park Hospital at which the pathologist (now retired) was based, 11 months after it had been removed. It was in a casket which was then buried in Ron's grave. That's the receipt for the brain which you see on page 46. But where had it been during those 11 months? In his post-mortem report the pathologist stated that he had "retained the brain for further examination by a neuropathologist."

In the year following Ron's death, former MP Harry Cohen tabled two questions in the House of Commons for the Home Office – for what reason was Ron's brain not buried with his body and what consents were obtained? This appears to have led to a flurry of activity including the brain's release. On 1 March 1996 the Home Office wrote to the then East Berkshire coroner setting out their understanding that the brain had been removed for medical research and not to establish the cause of death. In his reply on 4 March 1996 the coroner insisted that the brain had been sent away because Ron had had a mental condition and not for research. "What would the family have said had the Deceased had a tumour on the brain which had not been spotted?" he rhetorically asked. He understood that the brain was not originally buried because it was "still being studied by a neuropathologist." He had not given the pathologist express consent for the brain removal. He regarded the pathologist as having implied consent to do this. The pathologist was a skilled man and he was always happy to leave it to him to remove organs or tissue which needed specialist examination. In short, he was asserting that there had been no legislative requirement to consult with Ron's relatives before removal as research did not come into the equation. He acknowledged that the family had not been notified of the brain removal. He understood that the brain had by then been "returned" to Wexham Park Hospital and collected by the funeral directors.

Home Office Minister Tom Sackville answered Mr Cohen on 6 March 1996 in these terms:

> "I understand that at the time of Ronald Kray's funeral the brain was not buried with the body since it was still subject to an investigation to establish the cause of death. I am informed that the necessary consents were obtained from the coroner for East Berkshire."

Mr Cohen tried again. On 12 March 1996 he asked who was responsible for the decision to remove deceased prisoners' brains and who in particular was responsible for the decision to remove Ron Kray's brain. Mr Sackville answered:

> "If organs or tissue are required to be removed for further examination to establish cause of death, the decision is taken by the pathologist under the direction of the coroner."

Finally, Mr Cohen asked for a list of each of the locations in which Ron's brain was stored before being returned to the body. That was an easy one as the Home office had been told that the brain had gone from Wexham Park Hospital to the neuropathologist who was at the John Radcliffe Hospital, Oxford and then back to Wexham Park Hospital. This was the reply:

> "Arrangements for the care of the material are a matter for the pathologists involved."

There does not appear to have been any good reason for removing the brain if not for research purposes and for that there was no consultation with relatives. And another matter. Although the pathologist maintains that the brain was sent to the John Radcliffe, the NHS Trust responsible for that hospital stated to me that "the Trust did not receive the brain at any point." It maintained that it received only brain samples including blocks and histological slides – the pathologist accepts that he took "25 block" – but not the whole organ and that it received a referral from Wexham Park to provide a post-mortem neuropathological opinion on Ron in March 1996 which was after the brain had been released and buried and after Parliamentary questions were being asked.

Why did Wexham Park make such a belated request for a post-mortem opinion? I asked the Trust responsible for it. Its reply? "The information you have requested is personal information of the deceased. The Trust can confirm that this information is not held. As per the Department of Health's Records Management Code of Practice, the Trust is required to keep medical records for 8 years after the date of last treatment or 8 years after the death of the patient."

If, as claimed, the brain did not reach the John Radcliffe, where was it between removal and return in the casket?

I would not want any organs removed from my body unless I had donated them, it was really necessary for diagnostic reasons or I had consented during lifetime for the purpose of research. Nor would you. That's why I have been at pains to find out what happened in Ron's case and why.

But I hadn't finished! What happened about the testing of Ron's brain samples at the John Radcliffe? I sought disclosure of all written reports from the Trust under the Freedom of Information Act 2000. Disclosure was refused as being exempt on the ground of confidentiality. And so I complained about that refusal to the Information Commissioner. The Commissioner ruled against me on the ground that a duty of confidentiality was owed by the John Radcliffe to Wexham Park. There was no finding that such a duty was owed to Ron. I had argued that no duty could have been owed to him in respect of information created after his death and the Commissioner acknowledged the "obvious complexities" surrounding this issue.

POST MORTEM REPORT:		RI PM
NO: 96/1081		
	NEUROPATHOLOGY DEPARTMENT	
	RADCLIFFE INFIRMARY, NHS TRUST, OXFORD	
Other PM NO: A/131/95		SURNAME: KRAY
		First name: R
Hospital No:		
Physician/Surgeon		Date of Birth
		Date of Death

FIXED BRAIN REPORT –
12 MARCH 1996

Brain weight:

Post fixation – 1180 gms

Forebrain – 1005 gms

Hindbrain – 175 gms

External Appearance:

The brain has been sliced in the coronal plane prior to formalin fixation which has produced a degree of distortion. The reconstructed brain shows a moderate degree of agonal congestion. The cerebral vasculature appears patent without significant atherosclerosis and shows a normal configuration to the circle of Willis.

The hindbrain appears unremarkable.

Coronal Slices:

The partially sectioned brain was more completely sectioned in the coronal plane revealing no significant focal changes. The pigmentation of the substance nigra was within normal limits.

Histology:

Tissue sections from the following brain areas were examined: hippocampus, temporal lobe, frontal lobe, occipital lobe, cerebellum and cingulate gyrus.

Sections from these brain areas show normal brain cytoarchitecture without any evidence of significant hypoxic change nor of other acute or chronic pathological process.

Fixed brain – DISTOLOGICAL FEATURES ARE WITHIN NORMAL MORPHOLOGICAL LIMITS

Consultant Neuropathology

I decided not to appeal against the Commissioner's decision. This was because I was satisfied that there was no testing of the brain samples before March 1996 and that the samples tested did not reveal anything abnormal: in particular, they did not reveal any pathological explanation for Ron's mental condition. I had managed to obtain a copy of the Radcliffe report from another source. You will see it is described as a post-mortem report and is dated 12 March 1996 by which time, as stated, the brain had been reunited with Ron in his grave.

Incidentally, I still have the pocket watch gifted to me by the twins which is inscribed "Mr Gold From the Kray Brothers" (see page 47). When it needs attention, I prevail on someone else to deliver it to and collect it from the repairers lest they should think I am on day release from Parkhurst. And in 1988 Ron gifted me a long-playing record set of the Five Beethoven Concerti with the Boston Symphony Orchestra conducted by Erich Leinsdorf and Artur Rubintein on piano (see page 47). In *Our Story* Ron said that listening to music, along with reading and writing poetry, relaxed his mind most of all. And Ron told a psychiatrist who was preparing a report on the twins in order to establish their fitness to stand trial in 1969 that he liked classical music and singers such as Callas and Gigli. He also said he was fond of reading biographies including those of Gordon of Khartoum, Genghis Khan and Lawrence of Arabia. Well, in relation to the music, I can produce the LPs as corroborative evidence. And, no, neither the watch nor the records are up for sale.

		COURT FEES ONLY

Writ of Summons (Unliquidated Demand) (O.8r.1)

IN THE HIGH COURT OF JUSTICE

Queen's Bench Division

[Portsmouth   District Registry]

19 9 .— K — No.

Between

RONALD KRAY and REGINALD KRAY

[Stamp: HER MAJESTY'S HIGH COURT OF JUSTICE DISTRICT REGISTRY PORTSMOUTH — 19 SEP 1989]

Plaintiff s

AND

BRITISH BROADCASTING CORPORATION

Defendant

insert name.

To the Defendant (¹) British Broadcasting Corporation

insert address.

of (²) Broadcasting House, London, W1A 1AA.

This Writ of Summons has been issued against you by the above-named Plaintiffs in respect of the claim set out on the back.

Within 14 days after the service of this Writ on you, counting the day of service, you must either satisfy the claim or return to the Court Office mentioned below the accompanying Acknowledgment of Service stating therein whether you intend to contest these proceedings.

If you fail to satisfy the claim or to return the Acknowledgment within the time stated, or if you return the Acknowledgment without stating therein an intention to contest the proceedings, the Plaintiffs may proceed with the action and judgment may be entered against you forthwith without further notice.

Issued from the (³) [Central Office] [Portsmouth   District Registry] of the High Court this   19th   day of September   19 89 .

NOTE:—This Writ may not be served later than 12 calendar months beginning with that date unless renewed by order of the Court.

IMPORTANT

Directions for Acknowledgment of Service are given with the accompanying form

"We've been defamed!"

1989 K No. 781

IN THE HIGH COURT OF JUSTICE
QUEEN'S BENCH DIVISION
PORTSMOUTH DISTRICT REGISTRY
(Writ issued the 19th day of September 1989).
BETWEEN:

(1) RONALD KRAY
(2) REGINALD KRAY   Plaintiffs

–and–

BRITISH BROADCASTING CORPORATION
                                 Defendants

STATEMENT OF CLAIM

1. The First and Second Plaintiffs were respectively convicted of the murders of George Cornell and Jack McVitie at the Central Criminal Court on 8 March 1969, and were sentenced to life imprisonment. At the date hereof, both Plaintiffs remain in custody.

2. The Defendants are a corporation established by royal charter and are licensed to provide public radio and television services throughout the United Kingdom. The Defendants are responsible for the broadcast of a television programme entitled "South-East at Six", an influential news and current affairs magazine transmitted on weekdays at peak viewing-time following the early-evening news bulletin. The said programme is broadcast throughout Greater London and the Home Counties to a viewing audience of millions.

3. In the edition of the said programme for 7th September 1989, the Defendants falsely and maliciously published of and concerning the Plaintiffs the following defamatory words accompanied by certain visual images:-

Extract from document accompanying writ

IN THE HIGH COURT OF JUSTICE
QUEEN'S BENCH DIVISION
BETWEEN:-

1989 K No. 751

(1) RONALD KRAY
(2) REGINALD KRAY

-and-

BRITISH BROADCASTING CORPORATION

Defendants

D E F E N C E

1. The Defendants admit paragraph 1 of the Statement of Claim. The trial Judge, Mr. Justice Melford Stevenson, recommended that the Plaintiffs should serve a minimum of 30 years. At the date hereof, they have only served two-thirds of that recommended sentence.

2. Save that the programme for which the Defendants are responsible is entitled "Newsroom South East" and is broadcast at 6.30 each weekday night in the South East region, after the conclusion of the main national news, paragraph 2 of the Statement of Claim is admitted.

3. The Defendants admit that on the 7th September 1989, they broadcast a programme about the Plaintiffs from which short extracts have been pleaded in paragraph 3 of the Statement of Claim. The Defendants will refer at trial to the whole of the said programme for the full context in which the passages complained of were broadcast.

"We didn't do it!"

1989 K No. 2017

IN THE HIGH COURT OF JUSTICE

QUEEN'S BENCH DIVISION

B E T W E E N :

1) RONALD KRAY
2) REGINALD KRAY   Plaintiffs

– and –

BRITISH BROADCASTING CORPORATION   Defendants

CONSENT ORDER UNDER RSC ORDER 42 RULE 5A

upon parties agreeing

IT IS ORDERED BY CONSENT that :-

1. The Plaintiffs' action herein be dismissed.
2. The Plaintiffs do pay the Defendants' costs to be taxed in default of agreement on the standard basis.

We hereby consent to an order in the above terms.

"It's over!"

2.3 Whilst it is apparent that Reginald Kray maintains an allegiance to those involved with him, particularly his twin brother Ronald Kray, there is no such feeling towards the victims. Although not discussed, it seems that Mr Kray considers that his actions were justified in that the opposing faction had behaved outside the agreed code. Whilst the notion of retaliation is unacceptable to the majority within Society, it would seem that part of their code was that it was their way of ensuring that boundaries/controls were maintained.

2.4 There is no apparent sign of remorse, although to be fair to Mr Kray, I have been unable to create a situation that would enable him to explore more fully his feelings about the events/victims.

4.4 He appears to mix with few inmates through choice but is ever aware that his name attracts attention by others who may want to bask in his notoriety. He has befriended a number of the younger inmates which I know is viewed with suspicion by some, but which he tells me is out of a desire to use his experiences to try to deflect these young men from a life of crime. I know of one instance where Mr Kray has used his knowledge and outside contacts to try to help with setting up a career. Only time will tell if Mr Kray's actions are prompted out of good intent or whether there is an ulterior motive. The shame is that the notoriety of Mr Kray's case is always likely to influence individuals' perceptions as to Mr Kray's motivation. To some extent he has a calming effect on the wing.

4.5 As far as I can elicit, Mr Kray has maintained the same approach to his sentence as that displayed at previous prisons. He is not a man who attracts many disciplinary reports, he seemingly having struck a balance between retaining his own identity whilst developing systems that ensure he achieves the best for himself. I find I cannot blame him for adopting such a course.

4.6 It is difficult not to be struck by the vitality, energy and generally, good humour displayed by Mr Kray, unexpected in a man who is nearly 60 and has been in prison 25 years. It is not surprising that his energies have been expended in surviving for such a period.

4.7 His commitment to various charities is well known. There have been examples of his extraordinary generosity in this work. In some senses he sees it as a continuation of the way he was prior to sentence and although he is aware of how these activities are viewed by some, he remains philosophical and plans to continue this work.

Extracts from probation officer's parole report dated 7 September 1993 (both extracts copyright of National Archives)

Kray away day

GANGLAND killer Ronnie Kray this week divorced his wife for desertion.

Kray (55), who is serving a 30-year sentence at Broadmoor Psychiatric Hospital, was refused Home Office permission to attend the hearing at Portsmouth County Court on Monday, after concern about the effects the trip and the 40-minute hearing would have on him.

Kray, represented by lawyer Stephen Gold, brought the action on the grounds of desertion — and it was not contested by his wife, 32-year-old Elaine Mildener.

The one-time gangland chief, who with his brother Reggie was once ring-leader of the London underworld, claimed she had not visited him at Broadmoor.

"Ron deserted"

WEXHAM PARK
HOSPITAL

WEXHAM SLOUGH BERKSHIRE SL2 4HL
TEL: 01753 633000 FAX: 01753 634848

DEPARTMENT OF HISTOPATHOLOGY AND CYTOPATHOLOGY
TEL NO'S: 01753 633456 & 633482
FAX NO: 01753 633496

Our Ref:
Your Ref: 15 February 1996

W. English & Son
464a Bethnal Green Road
London
E2 0EA

Ref: Ronald KRAY - "Human Remains - Brain"

This is to certify the above named human remains are in the container which are handed to E. English & Son Funeral Directors, on 15th February 1996.

Signature .... Date 15/Feb/1996
Receiving Signature .... Date 15/Feb/96
Witness Signature .... Date 15/2/96

"The remains"

"Doing time"

"Classical gift"

ST. MATTHEW'S CHURCH
BETHNAL GREEN

In Loving Memory
of
RONALD KRAY
BORN 24th OCTOBER 1933
DIED 17th MARCH 1995

OFFICIATING PRIEST
FR. CHRISTOPHER BEDFORD

WEDNESDAY 29th MARCH 1995
at 12 NOON

ORDER OF SERVICE

Organ Music

OPENING SENTENCES

"MY WAY"
sung by Frank Sinatra

PRAYERS

Charlie and Reg would like to include in this Service
friends who cannot be here today, friends from Broadmoor and Prisons,
they are young Charlie, Mohammed, Joe, Paul, Bradley, Anton,
Jim, Rab, Ron, Pete, Lee, Andrew
and all others too many to mention, they are with us in spirit.

HYMN

Morning has broken,
Like the first morning,
Blackbird has spoken
Like the first bird.
Praise for the singing!
Praise for the morning!
Praise for them, springing
Fresh from the Word!

Sweet the rain's new fall
Sunlit from heaven,
Like the first dewfall
On the first grass.
Praise for the sweetness
Of the wet garden,
Sprung in completeness
Where his feet pass.

Mine is the sunlight!
Mine is the morning
Born of the one light
Eden saw play!
Praise with elation,
Praise every morning,
God's re-creation
Of the new day!

MESSAGES
read by Sue McGibbon

INVICTUS

Out of the night that covers me
Black as the Pit from pole to pole,
I thank whatever Gods may be
for my unconquerable soul.

In the fell clutch of circumstance,
I have not winched nor cried aloud;
Under the bludgeonings of chance
My head is bloody, but unbowed.

Beyond this place of wrath and tears
looms but the horror of the shade;
And yet the menace of the years
finds, and shall find me, unafraid.

It matters not how strait the gate,
How charged with punishments the scroll,
I am the master of my fate.
I am the captain of my soul.

By William Ernest Henley

A MESSAGE FROM CHARLIE AND REG

We wish for only good to come from Rons passing away and what is about to follow is our tribute to Ron, it is a symbol of peace in that the four pall bearers will be Charlie, Freddie Foreman, Johnny Nash and Teddy Dennis, each one represents an area of London,
North, South, East and West.

Charlie, Reg, Freddie, John and Teddy will encircle Rons coffin in a minutes silence.

SILENCE

A MESSAGE FROM REG

My Brother Ron is now free and at peace. Ron had great humour, a vicious temper, was kind and generous. He did it all his way, but above all he was a man, thats how I will always remember my twin Brother Ron.

God Bless - Reg Kray

SCRIPTURE READINGS AND PRAYERS

HYMN

Fight the good fight with all thy might,
Christ is thy Strength, and Christ thy Right;
Lay hold on life, and it shall be
Thy joy and crown eternally.

Run the straight race through God's good grace,
Lift up thine eyes, and seek His Face;
Life with its way before us lies,
Christ is the path, and Christ the prize.

Cast care aside, lean on thy Guide
His boundless mercy will provide;
Trust, and thy trusting soul shall prove
Christ is its life, and Christ its love.

Faint not nor fear, His Arms are near,
He changeth not, and thou art dear;
Only believe, and thou shalt see
That Christ is all in all to thee.

FINAL COMMENDATION

Do not stand at my grave and weep
I am not there. I do not sleep.
I am a thousand winds that blow.
I am the diamond glints on snow.
I am the sunlight on ripened grain,
I am the gentle autumn rain.
When you awaken in the morning's hush
I am the swift uplifting rush
Of quiet birds in circled flight
I am the soft stars that shine at night.
Do not stand at my grave and cry,
I am not there; I did not die.

"I WILL ALWAYS LOVE YOU"
by Whitney Houston

Organ Music

"Ron's way"

Chapter 4
Legal Print

I've put my pen to a fair bit of use. For a couple of years in the 1980's I contributed to the law page in *The Independent*. And in the 1990s I wrote a legal question and answer column for *House Beautiful*. The occasional letter seeking advice did come in from a reader but largely I made up the questions in addition to composing the answers. This is not an uncommon practice and I regard it as unobjectionable because questions and answers tend to be a lively way of disseminating diverse and sometimes technical information but so long as the published question is not succeeded by naming or indicating a fictitious reader. "My husband will not speak to me unless I wear a tight rubber skirt which I find most uncomfortable especially when shopping. Should I leave him? Mrs R. K. Macclesfield." During the lifetime of the *House Beautiful* column I was asked to sit on a panel of a couple of the magazine's experts at the Ideal Home Exhibition to answer questions from an uninvited audience and unwisely agreed. Around a paltry 30 people plonked themselves down in a lecture hall which would have accommodated several hundred to give themselves a respite from traipsing around laden with goodie bags. No audience questions emerged and so there was nothing for it but to pose a succession of questions – "I expect you want to know whether you can cut the branches of your neighbour's tree if they overhang into your garden don't you? etc etc – and proceed to answer. Very hard going but not as bad as opening the summer fete for the 7th Gosport Group Council on 3 July 1976 where I had to deliver a short opening speech and then tour the stalls in company with the chairman and make a complete fool of myself whilst failing to hit any of the usual targets. I had agreed to subject myself to this humiliation following the entreaty of a secretary in my office. I fancy that of those present, only she had a clue who I was.

For a couple of years in more recent times, I penned an anonymous spoof agony aunt column with a strong legal bias for the *New Law Journal*. 'Ask Auntie' was the inevitable title and Auntie unashamedly made it known that she would be delighted to hear from readers but could not guarantee to reply or, if she did, to be of any real help at all. In the event, Auntie never heard from anyone except the editor Jan Miller for whom I have deep respect. She thought I had gone over the top with one of my spoof questions and we sort of mutually agreed that Auntie should put her pen away. That question? It was supposedly from a judge who sought advice on how to dispose of wax if it dropped out of his ear during the course of a hearing and landed on a notebook which could be seen by the advocates and parties who were seated opposite. The irony was that a wax incident had actually happened to me. I shall spare you the solution.

One of my odder questions was from a supposed retired High Court judge on the subject of the legal principles of equity. Judges in search of a means of doing what is fair in a case may pluck one of these discretionary principles out of the sky and rely on it. If a party expects an equitable principle to be employed in their favour then it is important that they have not been up to any monkey business themselves. And so it is said *"He who comes into equity must come with clean hands"*. My invented retired judge wrote: "As a practical joke, I weaved a spoof maxim into one of my judgments a decade ago – Equity does to a cream trifle what cheddar cheese never did to clean hands. It has since been cited with approval in a number of judgments on appeal and appears in several works on the law of equity. I have discussed the situation at dinner parties with a number of friends including the editor of *The Lancet* and received conflicting advice about what I should do. Do you advise me to own up and if so should I see the Lord Chief (Justice) or Max Clifford?" Obviously, the retired judge was unaware that the late Mr Clifford's hands had been stained.

Auntie advised: "Don't be daft. Equity is a load of nebulous you-know-what and much the better for a couple of good recipes. Incidentally add a drop of cherry brandy and ensure the sponge cakes are fresh."

In October 1994 I received a telephone call from *TV Quick*, as one does. The marriage of Prince Charles and Princess Diana had broken down, ITV was about to broadcast *Diana: Portrait of a Princess* and the magazine wanted a phantom High Court judgment on issues relating to finance and the children of the family – for the next day. I'll be frank. The money offered was so good (and as I am not before the House of Commons Public Accounts Select Committee, I'll not tell you how much but give you my assurance that I paid tax on it) that I agreed despite it meaning a late night. I wasn't being identified as the writer thank you very much and so it was that the judgment of Mr Justice Piranha was duly published. I did my best with the limited information publicly available on the parties' capital and income and taking account of the law as it then was in big money cases. I awarded the Princess a lump sum of £10m on a 'clean break' basis. I ruled that the Prince's relationship with Mrs Parker-Bowles as she then was and the Princess's relationship with Major James Hewitt did not amount to conduct which was so gross and obvious that it ought to have any bearing on what the Princess should receive. In the event, rumour has it that the ultimate settlement several years later provided for a lump sum of around £17m. In relation to Princes William and Harry, I made a residence order in favour of the Princess with reasonable contact to Prince Charles which I envisaged would be liberal but limited the Princess taking the children to America for more than one month at a time without the permission of the Prince or the court. Mr Justice Piranha has not been seen or heard of since.

Which brings me back to the *New Law Journal*. Poor Auntie apart, for 38 years I have written a regular column for this respected publication. The column has for the most part appeared fortnightly and been designed to inform lawyers of legal developments and entertain them at the same time so that the overarching theme has been one of irreverence. I am not immune to the (hopefully, very) occasional error and so a lack of reader response to what I have written has always been a relief for a response generally spells trouble. I have been acidly corrected on one occasion by a former senior law lecturer and another reader's justified stricture resulted in a *mea culpa* but my warning that if he detected two further errors in the following six months, he would be required to take the column over. A practising law lecturer wrongly complained that I had misquoted him and Boy George's then solicitor that I had libelled his client. No damages have ever been paid.

My best story was exposing the conveyancing ineptitude of former Grimsby MP Austin Mitchell. In December 1983 he moved the second reading of his private member's House Buyer's Bill which was to lead to the abolition of the solicitors' conveyancing monopoly. He told the Commons that no particular skills were required for drawing up conveyancing documents other than perhaps the ability to put right and put names on a standard form. Two months later I discovered that Mr Mitchell had just bought and sold homes on behalf of himself and his wife with some help from a *Which* guide and also a public spirited solicitor acting for their purchaser who told me that Mr Mitchell has started off better than the average DIY conveyancer and got worse. He had made a considerable mess of things as he disarmingly admitted to me when I tracked him down at his Grimsby surgery at the 200th attempt one Friday evening soon after he had got back from buying some fish and chips. He told me he would get a professional to do the conveyancing work on his next transaction and that if the fee was reasonable, he would prefer to instruct a solicitor than a licensed conveyancer. Alas, all a bit late for conveyancing solicitors. How things might have been so different had the Mitchells bought and sold a bit earlier.

And then there was the case of Christmas Bigamy in 1987 which arose out of an error in the drafting of legislation which gave county courts jurisdiction to deal with defended divorce cases. The error was the inadvertent exclusion from county court jurisdiction of cases which had previously been transferred from the county court to the High Court when they became defended and then sent back to the county court. The error was not picked up for around 20 months during which time several thousand divorces were pronounced by county courts which they had no business to pronounce. It was an error which was highlighted in a case which came before the High Court and from which I concluded that those several thousand divorce decrees were null and void and that if any of the parties to them had remarried their remarriages were null and void: worse still, any children born following the remarriages would be illegitimate. The government was forced to introduce emergency legislation which was duly passed and resulted in retrospectively validating the invalid divorce decrees and any subsequent remarriages on the strength of them. I made the BBC 1 6 o'clock news on that one.

In my *New Law Journal* column I closely followed the performance of the then controversial changes in the drink-drive laws which came into force in 1983. The Home Office had approved two machines for measuring the quantity of alcohol in a suspect motorist's body through samples of their breath. Things looked a bit dodgy for the new laws when one of the machines, the Intoximeter 3000, was demonstrated to magistrates in Cannock. Despite much huffing and puffing, at least three of them found it impossible to provide the breath specimens required and could have been facing 12 months' disqualification if it had been the real thing. Every technical defence which could be conceived was run by creative lawyers on which I regularly reported. Some failed and some succeeded (see chapter 53). Writing profusely about drink-driving will eventually persuade the media that you are an expert on the subject. So it was with me. I see that *The Sun* described me in 1987 as a leading breath-test lawyer. If you are going to write about a subject then you have got to be prepared to 'do it'. I did. Firstly, I 'did it' as an alleged suspect. After a hard day's work as a solicitor I repaired to a wine bar a couple of doors away from the office where I consumed two small glasses of house white whilst reading that week's edition of the *New Law Journal*. On my way back to the office to collect my car I passed two police officers who were unknown to me. I duly collected my car and drove off whereupon I was stopped by the officers. The lead officer asked me whether I had been drinking and I admitted to consumption of the wine. He then initiated the drink-drive procedure by requiring me to give a roadside screening sample of my breath and outside my law office. Fail that and you get arrested and have to give the substantive breath test at the police station. He was out of luck because the officers did not have the breath kit with them. This was delivered after 10 minutes by a sergeant whom I knew well. During the wait, the officer refused to allow me to take the screening test out of public view and in answer to my enquiry as to why he thought I might be over the limit, all he would say was "policeman's nose" and "gut feeling". The screening test was, of course, negative which meant I was free to go off and write up the episode for... the *New Law Journal*. The officers were aware of my displeasure at this indignity and the failure to answer my enquiry in a more satisfactory way. "That's it," said the lead officer. "I told you your nose would get you into trouble. Do you want to apologise?" "No." I later established that the lead officer was new to the locality and had filed a report claiming that I had been unsteady in the gutter as they passed me by. And so it was that I did write up the episode in the *New Law Journal* under the strapline 'Sober In Charge of NLJ.'

Secondly, I 'did it' as an advocate, winning and losing. I was irked by one particular failure because I thought I – and more particularly the client – deserved a success for initiative. The point I took was highly technical. You may yourself be irked by highly technical defences but they are legitimate and it is the advocate's duty to take a point which is reasonably arguable even though it has 'technical' pouring out of its ears. The client, a film cameraman, was charged with driving with excess alcohol in his body and I was appearing for him at Thames Magistrates' Court. I took the precaution of examining the breath machine print-out showing the result of the police station test when it was produced in evidence by the police officer who had conducted the test. My client had signed the print-out as required but where the police officer should also have signed, there was a blank. I unsuccessfully submitted that my client had no case to answer on the basis that the print-out did not satisfy statutory requirements and so was not admissible in evidence. Without the print-out there was no evidence that he had been over the limit, as alleged. My client appealed against his conviction to the High Court which dismissed the appeal on the basis that the print-out was admissible under common law rules of evidence whether or not it complied with the statutory requirements.

Chapter 5
Let Right Be Done

In July 1988 it arrived. The letter. It came from the office of the Lord Chancellor at the House of Lords and invited me to apply for appointment as a deputy district judge (then known by the inferior title of registrar). The idea of going over to the establishment on a part-time basis was intriguing. I flattered myself by wondering whether somebody, somewhere, wanted to shut me up. I applied. Just in case you've had enough of working in the chippie and fancy a judicial role, starting with appointment as a deputy district judge, you may find, as did one solicitor aspiring to such an appointment, that traffic convictions could disqualify you on the ground that you are of 'bad character'. He had two live endorsements for speeding and breaking traffic lights which had earned him seven penalty points. He challenged the decision to rule him out for appointment on the strength of that record and failed in the High Court in 2014.

Naturally, I disclosed that I had collected some speeding convictions. I must come clean with you about these. On 6 November 1970 I was about 10 miles per hour over a 40 limit on my way to Lewes Prison in a hire car on a dual carriageway, perplexed why other drivers were travelling slower than me. I, idiot, never saw the police car. I shot off a letter to the police to try and persuade them not to prosecute. The summons arrived (see *"Can't wait to get to prison"* on page 65). The inevitable followed.

Then on 25 December 1971 I was clocked at 70/72 miles per hour on a 30 mph section of a dual carriageway going out of Southampton (oh, you have been done there too). There was no other traffic on the road apart from a police car and I had overlooked that I was in the slower section. No defence but I thought it worthwhile sending off a letter to the police. You know the rest. The summons duly arrived and the inevitable followed (see *"Merry Christmas!"* on page 66).

You may wonder if prosecutors can ever be persuaded not to prosecute when an offence has been committed. I once extricated a BBC television presenter from a prosecution for failing to hold a current television licence, through representations to the prosecuting authority. They may have seen the force in my argument that the media publicity which a conviction was likely to generate would be self-defeating for some of the public might conclude that if it was good enough for a BBC presenter then it was good enough for them. My success rate on no prosecution persuasion was never high but put it this way: while there's life, there's hope.

By the end of 1989, I had been appointed a deputy district judge. Those stale convictions did not turn out to be any hindrance. I got myself a few more white shirts (tab collars, mind you), cleaned my shoes and for the next four years and a bit and at the rate of about once a week, I was highly respectable and sat as a deputy judge doing much the same work as a permanent judge would do and at a number of courts in southern England. It was fascinating to be looking at those legal situations with which I had been dealing for years in my practice as a solicitor but from a different standpoint. And it was enormously satisfying to be able, wherever possible, to apply the law so that a fair result was achieved. What I was not prepared to do was eat lunch in the judges' mess. This was asking too much and I disregarded the advice given to me by one permanent judge to the effect that I could never hope to secure a full-time judicial post if I did not socialise at lunch. Though I judged, life otherwise proceeded much as usual and I certainly carried on writing and broadcasting on the law. When I was doing phone-ins for London's LBC I relaxed a little in the belief that nobody connected with the administration down south would be listening and permitted callers to address me as 'Stevie Boy'.

I did not always feel completely comfortable as a deputy judge. At Newport, Isle of Wight the county court sat once every fortnight or so at the Guildhall for cases that had to be heard in public. What seemed like hundreds congregated in an enormous council chamber. The route from the retiring room outside and through the chamber to a bench at its head – robed! – was for this newcomer to the part-time judiciary a walk too far (a little like the one after the Isle of Wight pop festival). But not as embarrassing as the ceremony for the swearing in of the new Lord Lieutenant of Hampshire in court number 1 at the Winchester Crown Court. As I was sitting there as a deputy judge for the day, I was roped in to attend this session of excruciating pomp. I was in my civvies and, happily, they couldn't find me a wig to fit my bonce which meant I could remain unrobed (see *"For painful looking judge, go to back row, second from right"* on page 67). I was directed to enter the courtroom and take a seat on the bench but to go in first. Since I was to be followed by a line of the most worthy including Mr Justice Ian Kennedy, I assumed in my naivety that this was an irrational honour. I soon discovered the truth. First in, last out. At least I didn't have to clear up after the others. One other unfortunate experience at the Winchester Crown Court was on the steps outside. It had snowed and nothing had been done to clear any of it away. I slipped on what was by then an icy step and twisted my ankle. A & E and a stick and the rest succeeded. Claims for damages arising out of snow trips are not the easiest to succeed in though in the particular circumstances I reckoned I had a good case. Put it this way. I would have awarded myself damages had I heard the case. I concluded that my prospects of a full-time position would not be enhanced by litigation and so on this rare occasion I held off.

In due course, I applied for a permanent post as a district judge. I was selected for interview at the House of Lords. This was to be my second visit there. The first was for my cannabis leaves appeal case. I was to be grilled by an informal board: a judge to fire legal conundrums at me and two senior members of the Lord Chancellor's Department. I realised I didn't like boards. I was terrible. I was not selected but persisted. By the time of my next but differently constituted board, the administrators had moved from the House of Lords to common offices in a London street and one of the civil servants had been replaced by a lay person. I was a little disturbed as I sat in the waiting room by the appearance from the interview room of another deputy district judge whom I knew well and was also up for a post. I say disturbed because my application had been a secret from the outside world. Indeed, when the lay board member asked me what my firm's partners thought of me seeking a judicial appointment, I chose to tell them in all honesty that I hadn't breathed a word to them of what I was up to as I wanted to limit the damage if I was turned down. It seemed to amuse and I got the job. I was sworn in on 24 July 1995 at Kingston-upon-Thames county court by the resident circuit judge who wondered in his short speech why on earth I had wanted to become a district judge (see *"Licence to judge"* on page 67).

After five years as a district judge I was invited to become the public relations officer of our trade union – the Association of Her Majesty's District Judges as it is now known. I remained in post for 15 years. It brought me into contact with print and radio and television legal journalists. I organised the setting up of regular columns penned by district judges in three rival legal periodicals and arranged for district judges to contribute articles to a variety of legal and non-legal publications including some which were syndicated to local newspapers. A couple of national television packages featuring a district judge were run and my colleagues began editing or writing for some of the major legal works. I arranged for a group of the better looking district judges to be media trained. The annual inauguration of the Association's president led to full coverage in the broadsheets. One president who I rang at around 10pm one night to seek to persuade him to be interviewed on a commercial station before midnight complained that I had interrupted him in a long delayed sexual act with his wife and chose to decline the invitation. The profile of district judges was gradually enhanced. We were really punching above our weight. When I bowed out, the district judges were directed from above to cease publicising themselves by way of presidential interviews and media statements without prior authority.

May I briefly digress? One of those national television packages involved a mock matrimonial dispute resolution hearing which was being filmed by Channel 5 (as it then called itself) in Harrogate. Although I, in typical self-effacing style, was not appearing, I needed to poke my nose into the filming and so made my way up to Harrogate with thoughts of afternoon tea at *Betty's* which tragically never materialised. I was booked into a hotel in the town for the night before. That experience was pretty tragic too. They had central heating problems and my room was freezing. A temporary heater never materialised. It was October. The lighting in the room was dim. There was said to be a shortage of restaurant staff and so I had to eat dinner in the room. My hotel bill was due to be reimbursed by my Association but, in all conscience, I could not countenance them having to pay out for such agony. I did not have the stomach for a reception confrontation the next morning. I paid what was asked of me and endorsed the credit card voucher "up" intending to be short for "under protest". This was evidentially important for it obviated any later suggestion by the hotel that I had accepted the accommodation and service had been satisfactory by tendering payment. Back home and thawed out, I asked the hotel for my money back. I got it without a quibble.

Then in 2007 (with a little pressure from the Lords Select Committee on Constitution) the former Lord Chief Justice Lord Phillips set up a panel of media spokespersons to represent the judiciary, when appropriate, to which I was appointed. The panel members were given special training. It was similar to the training I had received years earlier when working as a solicitor before being appointed as a Law Society spokesman. Mock interviews were recorded on video and then played back for verbal lashings delivered by the professional trainer and, this time, fellow panellists but always in the best possible taste. I appeared on *Panorama* talking about mortgage repossessions and participated in a *One Show* package dedicated to the small claims scheme and, for some of it, attired in the modern Betty Jackson designed robe for district judges (which I rarely wore in court and that positively does not mean that I sat naked). On national radio I was interviewed on several programmes including Radio 5 Live on bankruptcy from my court car park in a radio car which was a new experience for me. And I was permitted to assist the moneysaver.com website on its small claims guide. Not much. The panel was reactive and only to a very limited degree and not proactive. No member was allowed to rear their head unless the senior judiciary on advice from the judiciary's communications unit was satisfied that it was in the interests of the judiciary that they should do so. Quite rightly, the panel would never comment on another judge's decision. My personal view is that the panel was underused. I advocated an extension of its remit to inform the public on their legal rights and obligations and to regularly seek to influence public opinion and decision makers. Not a view which found favour in the right places. Incidentally, when Lord Phillips gave an early report to the Select Committee on Constitution about how the panel was doing in 2008 he said: "I certainly have not received any expressions of dissatisfaction about these interviews." That included mine. The higher judiciary does not go in for rave reviews.

In 2012, Frances Gibb, the former legal editor of The Times, was permitted through the judiciary's communications unit, to sit in with me at court while I heard cases. She was intending to write an article on the then upcoming withdrawal of most civil legal aid and the knock on effect it would have on the administration of justice with so many more litigants in person. Frances was a lively and tenacious journalist and the communications people were terrified of her. Apart from observing my cases, she wanted to ask me some questions. And I wanted to answer them. Horror, horror. I sent the unit a list of a few reasonable questions she had put together and the gist of how I would be answering them. This put them in a state of apoplexy. First I was told to keep my answers general and ask her not to quote me by name. Then I was told not to say a word outside the confines of the cases I was hearing. She was not to interview me but I assumed it would be unobjectionable for me to greet her on arrival and talk about the weather. Legal aid and litigants in person were regarded as politically sensitive areas on which judges should not be commenting. Anything I said would be taken by the government to be a direct criticism of their policies. Frances duly sat in but the unit's stance murdered any prospect of an article being published.

District judges deal with the vast majority of cases in the County Court, certain business in the High Court and a substantial proportion of cases in the now separate Family Court and the Financial Remedies Court which is operated under its umbrella although, more often than not, they are run out of the same building. All judges from the bottom to the top rung of the judicial ladder do their utmost to give every party before them a fair hearing and to reach the right decision. They would go bonkers if they became emotionally involved in the cases they hear. At the same time, they would be inhuman if they did not sometimes agonise over the right thing to do and did not find to be very heavy the burden of deciding the more substantial cases and the cases in which their judgment is to be everlastingly impacting on the parties. Decide the facts and apply the relevant law to those facts is what has to be done. Sometimes there is discretion to be exercised. It has to be exercised in a just way.

The judicial workload was intense before the pandemic. Now grappling with remote hearings and the technical difficulties they can involve hasn't made the job easier. For district judges, at least five hours a day will usually be spent deciding cases openly or privately, depending on their nature, either at face-to-face hearings or remotely by video or telephone. Familiarisation with the papers before a case is called will usually be desirable. The papers will have to be read on the morning or when hearings have finished on the previous afternoon or evening. Frequently papers will be taken home. If a hearing has taken longer than predicted or the judge needs time to consider their decision, that will have to be put off – reserved – to another day. It is common in that situation for the judge to prepare their judgment, containing the decision with full reasons, in writing and for it to be circulated to the parties before being formally 'handed down' on another court day. Preparing reserved judgments will frequently have to be squeezed in between other duties or tackled at home. But there's the so-called boxwork to be attacked as well. Lots of decisions will be made 'on paper' involving case management, enforcement of judgments, queries from parties, complaints by parties, applications for adjournments and the rest. 85 out of every 100 pieces of paper which come into the court will land on a district judge's desk or computer screen for attention. On top of all this the district judge will be working closely with court management on administration and doing extras in training, monitoring and appraising deputy district judges and liaising with the community and various agencies on diversity matters and making life easier for litigants in person. And there are would be judges who wish to sit in with – shadow – a proper judge and there's tea to be made and departing staff to be thanked and law reports and new legislation to be read. Life is much the same for judges in the upper echelons.

Yeh, the judiciary is marvellous. But it isn't loved and it is in desperate need of some tender care. Governments have been keen to blame all manner of wrongs onto the judges when all they have been doing is interpreting the legislation, using the words Parliament has given them, and applying that law. The pension arrangements on which longer sitting judges relied when they signed up have been cut down without their agreement. The dismantling of the legal aid system and the advent of lawyers' charging rates beyond the reach of most of the population have left judges with soaring numbers of litigants in person. The result? Chaotic paperwork frequently from which it is often impossible for the judge to work out what the case is about; the litigants' failure to comply with procedural directions; litigants engaging before the judge in shouting matches with their opponent; an understandable difficulty for the litigants to appreciate what is relevant to the case and what is irrelevant; the judge having to effectively undertake the questioning and the cross-questioning of the litigants and their witnesses which should not be their function; and an inability by so many litigants to look objectively at the strengths and weaknesses of their case and so compromise where compromise is the obvious course. What ensues are lengthier hearings, an increased burden on the judge and a nightmare for the litigants themselves.

Against this background, most of the judiciary lacks the support which is essential for their job to be done efficiently and without having to pull out what little hair they have left on their heads. The root cause of the problem is that there are insufficient members of court staff and, whilst the staff in post are totally dedicated and overworked, some lack the capability to do what is required of them – they are faced with a wide, complicated and forever changing raft of procedures – and have insufficient training. Sometimes, the untrained are training the untrained. Clerical positions are habitually filled on a temporary basis by casual workers who cannot reasonably be expected to know how to do what they are told to do after five minutes in their chairs. In most courts, a single usher can be found serving four or more judges leaving it to the judge to swear in witnesses and wait for the parties and any legal representatives in an individual case to be brought into court so that the case can commence. Many district judges at least feel that they are not trusted by the administrators as they should be. In April 2011 – after 16 years of service with just a couple of days off sick – I absented myself from work for a single day due to illness. My court sent off notice of this very serious absence to someone regaling in the title of District Bench Judicial Business and Deployment Officer, Judicial Secretariat for London and the South East Region who was doing her thing on the third floor of a London office. But my court had not specified from what sickness I was suffering. The officer, Helen, courteously notified me that the Presiding Judges requested to know what had been wrong with me. I assure you that the Presiding Judges – they are High Court judges who in association with HM Courts & Tribunal Service watch over judges, pull them back if they look like straying, counsel them if they appear to be twitching too often and do a host of other good things but normally follow what HM Courts & Tribunal Service would wish them to do in the context of suspected skiving – were only constructively interested in what this little judge had been up to. I asked Helen for confirmation that the Presiding Judges wanted to know from precisely which malady I had been suffering and the symptoms. She replied that the precise malady was wanted. So I gave it to 'em in these terms:

"Virus causing chronic fatigue, nausea and migraine and approximately six other symptoms. Will that do? I returned to work after one day but if it recurs I shall take a proper period of time off and send in samples."

IN THE COUNTY OF EAST SUSSEX
Petty Sessional Division of Lewes

To STEPHEN GERALD GOLD,

Any Communication should be addressed to:-
THE CLERK TO THE JUSTICES,
THE LAW COURTS,
HIGH STREET,
LEWES, SUSSEX.

INFORMATION has this day been laid before me, the undersigned Justice of the Peace, by RICHARD CUSTANCE of the Police Station, LEWES in the said County, INSPECTOR of Police, for that you on the 6th day of November, 19 70 at LEWES in the said County, did drive a motor vehicle, namely, a motor car, on a road there leading from Brighton to Lewes, at a speed exceeding 40 miles per hour; contrary to Thr Trunk Road (40 miles per hour Speed Limit) (No. 22) Order, 1969, Section 4 of the Road Traffic Act, 1960, and Section 74 of the Road Traffic Regulation Act, 1967.

YOU ARE THEREFORE HEREBY SUMMONED to appear on Tuesday, the 22nd day of December, 19 70 at the hour of ten-fifteen in the forenoon, before the Magistrates' Court sitting at the LAW COURTS, High Street, Lewes in the said County, to answer to the said Information.

DATED the 26th day of November, 19 70

Hereward Paul
Justice of the Peace for the County aforesaid.

PRODUCTION OF DRIVING LICENCE

IMPORTANT PLEASE NOTE

L

Take Notice that you are required either to:—
(a) cause your Driving Licence to be delivered to the Clerk to the Justices not later than the day before the hearing, or,
(b) send it to the Clerk by registered post or by the recorded delivery service at such a time that in the ordinary course of post it would be delivered not later than that day, or,
(c) have it with you at the hearing.

Failure to produce your Licence as above will render you liable on summary conviction to a fine not exceeding £50 and your Licence will be suspended from the time when its production was required until it is produced to the Court and will, while suspended, be of no effect.

"Can't wait to get to prison"

TAKE NOTICE that if you hold a licence you must either have it with you at the hearing or send it by hand or by registered post or recorded delivery, so as to reach the Clerk of the Court at the address shown on the enclosed notice, before the day of the hearing. Failure to do this may result in the commission of an offence and in suspension of your licence (Road Traffic Act, 1962, Section 7(4)).

In the ~~COUNTY~~/CITY/~~BOROUGH~~ of SOUTHAMPTON

~~Petty Sessional Division of~~

To: (Stephen Gerald GOLD,) .... the Defendant
of Flat 15,
Cresta Court,
Eastern Parade,
(Southsea, Portsmouth.) being the last known or usual place of abode

THE INFORMATION of Albert Corbin : Chief Inspector of Hampshire Constabulary this day laid before me that you the Defendant, on the 25th day of December, 1971, at Millbrook Road in the said ~~County~~/City/~~Borough~~ did drive a motor vehicle on a road, being a restricted road, at a speed exceeding 30 miles per hour, contrary to section 4 of the Road Traffic Act, 1960, and section 71 of the Road Traffic Regulation Act, 1967.

YOU THE DEFENDANT ARE THEREFORE HEREBY SUMMONED to appear on THURSDAY : 27TH JANUARY, 1972, at 10.30 a.m. before the Magistrates' Court sitting at THE LAW COURTS, CIVIC CENTRE, SOUTHAMPTON

to answer the said information.

DATED this 10th day of January, 1972

....
Justice of the Peace.

To: The Defendant

CLP   **STATEMENT OF FACTS** (Magistrates' Courts Act, 1957, Section 1)   25 years
The Prosecution say: Solicitor

On Saturday, 25th December, 1971 at 7.55 p.m. the defendant was seen driving a motor car at Millbrook Road, being a restricted road, at a speed of 70/72 miles per hour.

Signed .... Chief Inspector
(Informant, on behalf of the Prosecutor)

"Merry Christmas!"

Let Right Be Done

"For painful looking judge, go to back row, second from right"

I, JAMES PETER HYMERS BARON MACKAY OF CLASHFERN, Lord High Chancellor of Great Britain, by virtue of Section 6 of the County Courts Act 1984 and Section 100 of the Supreme Court Act 1981 (as amended by Section 74 of the Courts and Legal Services Act 1990) do hereby appoint

STEPHEN GERALD GOLD ESQUIRE

to be Joint District Judge for the districts of the Ashford, Aylesbury, Barnet, Bedford, Bishops Stortford, Bow, Braintree, Brentford, Brentwood, Brighton, Bromley, Bury St Edmunds, Cambridge, Canterbury, Central London, Chelmsford, Chichester, Clerkenwell, Colchester, Croydon, Dartford, Dover, Eastbourne, Edmonton, Epsom, Folkestone, Gravesend, Grays Thurrock, Great Yarmouth, Guildford, Harlow, Hastings, Haywards Heath, Hemel Hempstead, Hertford, High Wycombe, Hitchin, Horsham, Ilford, Ipswich, Kingston Upon Thames, Kings Lynn, Lambeth, Lewes, Lowestoft, Luton, Maidstone, Mayors & City, Medway, Milton Keynes, Newbury, Norwich, Reading, Reigate, Romford, Shoreditch, Sittingbourne, Slough, Southend, Staines, St Albans, Thanet, Tunbridge Wells, Uxbridge, Wandsworth, Watford, West London, Willesden, Wisbech, Woolwich and Worthing County Courts and Joint District Judge in the District Registry of the High Court at Bedford, Brighton, Bury St Edmunds, Cambridge, Canterbury, Chelmsford, Chichester, Colchester, Croydon, Dover, Eastbourne, Great Yarmouth, Guildford, Harlow, Hastings, Ipswich, Kings Lynn, Lowestoft, Luton, Maidstone, Medway, Milton Keynes, Norwich, Reading, Romford, Southend, Thanet, Tunbridge Wells and Worthing with effect from the twenty-fourth day of July 1995.

Dated this   day of   1995

"Licence to judge"

67

Chapter 6
Let Right Be Done – For A Little Longer

14 July 2016 was my birthday and you didn't send me a card. It was also the day on which I ceased to be a full-time judge. No, I was not kicked out. I retired. After 21 years in that role, I had decided on no valedictories from the staff, advocates and other judges at which their tear ducts would be opened to maximum capacity before the opening of their mouths to accommodate the scoffing of smoked salmon sandwiches, crisps and cakes. The valedictories were easily evaded. Conspiring with the listing officer who organises which cases each judge will hear on any given day, I invented a three-day final hearing of a linked Children Act and financial remedies case to cover the last three days of my tenure which I was entitled to take off as holiday. This meant that everyone, apart from the listing officer and myself, would reckon on me being present until the bitter end. On the evening before this hearing was not due to start, I scarpered out of the back door for what I thought would be forever. I had arranged a buffet lunch for staff and colleagues for one week later from which I duly absented myself. The food included an expensive chocolate cake ordered from *Waitrose* which was to be inscribed in icing sugar with the single word 'Goodbye'. Except that *Waitrose* split it into 'Good' and 'Bye' as the listing officer subsequently reported to me.

And so in my email to *Waitrose* I said:

> When I personally placed the order approximately a fortnight earlier, the lady at the customer desk who dealt with me struggled with the

> word in question. I spelt it out for her and did so without stoppage or any form of hesitation, deviation or repetition between the 'Good' and the 'bye'. Therefore, there can be no reasonable excuse for what has happened.
>
> I am told that the cake was delicious although I am perceived to be stupid, thanks to Waitrose. I would invite your comments. If there are any spelling errors in this message then I apologise but at least they have not been iced onto the email.
>
> Cheer io
>
> Stephen Gold

And they replied:

> I'm sorry you've had a poor experience with your recent Waitrose entertaining order – I've discussed this with the branch and arranged for them to refund the amount paid for the cake onto your payment card. You'll receive an email confirmation when this has happened. I hope my response has been helpful today and if you'd like to provide feedback we have a link to a short survey. It'll only take a few minutes and as a thank you for your time you'll be entered into our prize draw where you could win £500 in gift cards.

I'm afraid we'll be meeting that *Waitrose* prize draw again. Anyway, what I negotiated instead of a refund was a second chocolate cake, this time iced with the words 'Hello. Sorry Re Good Bye' which was delivered for staff only scoffing.

On the very day of my retirement, the then Lord Chief Justice The Right Honourable The Lord Thomas of Cwmghiedd wrote to me (see his letter below). He got my address wrong and so the letter was slightly delayed in reaching me but to hell with that. I was happy to hear from the Lord Chief on any day so long as it was not to berate me for swearing at a litigant. As it happens, I had never heard from Lord Thomas before and, of course, he did

---

JUDICIARY OF
ENGLAND AND WALES

THE RIGHT HONOURABLE THE LORD THOMAS OF CWMGIEDD

District Judge Stephen Gold

14 July 2016

Dear Judge

I am writing to send you my very best wishes on the occasion of your retirement and to extend my sincere gratitude for your commitment, dedication and service to the administration of justice over so many years.

I know that the Lord Chancellor will be writing to thank you on behalf of himself and the Department but I did not want to let this occasion pass without adding my own good wishes.

I hope that you have a long and happy retirement.

The Royal Courts of Justice Strand London WC2A 2LL
Telephone 020 7947 6776 Fax 020 7947 7512 Email LCJ.office@judiciary.gsi.gov.uk
Text Phone 18001 020 7947 6776 (Helpline for the deaf and hard of hearing)
Website www.judiciary.gov.uk

not know me from Adam. But it was a kind gesture. As the Lord Chief was writing, Michael Gove was being sacked as Lord Chancellor by Prime Minister Theresa May and The Right Honourable Elizabeth Truss MP was being lined up to replace him and was sworn in just one week later. Not having received the promised 'thank you' from anyone holding the office of Lord Chancellor for two months, I thought I would drop Ms Truss a line. I confirmed my correct address, sent her a copy of the Lord Chief's letter, assured her that I had no doubts as to her gender (given the Lord Chief's reference to the male gender) and went on:

> "You will see reference is made by the Lord Chief Justice to a letter I would be receiving from you. I am sure that you currently have more demanding tasks on your hands than to waste time writing to me and you may rest assured that I am not in the business of fishing for compliments. Indeed, I was at pains to escape out of the back door of my court three days early without a valedictory remark being uttered as I know what claptrap can be conjured up on retirements. I have personally been responsible for a good deal of it myself. What intrigued me was what you might have been intending to thank me for had you, in fact, written to me. If it was to congratulate me for having survived 21 years as a permanent member of the judiciary without having ever been disciplined, then I would humbly acknowledge the same with grateful thanks. If it was to recommend me for some highly paid office for the duration of my retirement then I can say that I could well be available. If and when you manage to clear your boxwork, I would deem it an honour to hear from you. In the meantime, I wish you every success and satisfaction in your office."

Alas, I did not hear from Ms Truss and, before long, she had been replaced.

A number of judges don't entirely pack in the judging when retiring as full-timers but become part-time judges for a while. Although I had vowed never to do this for fear of being treated as a form of judicial excrement, the prospect of moving in to *Waitrose* on a permanent basis and having a shopping bag soldered to my overcoat filled me with dread. So it was that I came to be appointed as a part-time judge for civil and family courts in the south-west and dealing with the same sort of cases I had dealt with in my previous incarnation. My first sitting was at the grandly called (but less salubrious than its name) Aldershot Courts of Justice. Before the court day was due to start, I took in the Aldershot air nearby when, deep in contemplation of what was to follow, I inadvertently encroached on to the car park of the police station adjoining the courts. In the course of so doing, I encountered a police officer who was suspicious of my activity. She questioned me closely as to what I was up to but not under caution. I thought I had given a good account of myself until she asked me for my name. The moral of the story is "Don't breathe in Aldershot".

In February 2011 I had joined Twitter. When I say I had joined, I mean George had joined. I won't disclose the surname I gave him for fear you might abuse him for associating with me. Had it been Gold then I would have felt more constrained in what I tweeted. I thought it would be interesting to see how many people would be prepared to follow a non-existent person. I am aware that there are various devices that can be employed to attract followers. Buying a few thousand names is no longer among them but liking and retweeting the posts of every Tom, Dick and Harry certainly is. It is obvious that I have not liked and retweeted sufficiently as, to date, I have – I mean, George has – acquired a paltry 40 followers. I grieve at the loss of any follower (oh dear, I have just lost two): in particular, the health food store which left me after apparently realising that my post offering for sale a limited number of jars of honey containing live bees, might not be serious.

The law changes with great rapidity and judges must keep up to date with those changes. To do so is mandatory and a technique has been devised to ensure it happens. The Judicial College is the school for judges. They are required to personally attend courses at regular intervals which involve considerable preparation in connection with mind blowing case studies raising a multitude of conundrums (some say conundra). They must be discussed in small groups presided over by other judges with name badges and chuffed with their title of 'tutor'. They tend to be frustrated teachers or ambitious to earn points which will elevate them up the judicial ladder. Thrashing or detention for making stupid contributions in these groups is prohibited but self-inflicted humiliation is the punishment. Until a few years ago, the course attendees were a mixture of judges of differing levels of seniority and arrogance. Obviously, none of the senior judges spoke to me but, even so, my heart went out to them. The degree of embarrassment they would have suffered for getting it wrong would have surpassed mine. I have been in groups with various High Court judges, one of whom became a Court of Appeal Lord Justice and another a Supreme Court Justice. If follows that any normal judge detests these courses unless they lack food and social intercourse at home and relish the three meals a day dished up at the residential courses, which can span four days, and enjoy boring their dining companions with repeated case anecdotes.

I certainly detested the courses with every fibre of my body. For some inexplicable reasons, I had not succeeded in turning up for one of them for a period of four years. And so it was that in March 2020 I felt compelled to participate in a two-day non-residential course – less food, better anecdotes – in Central London or else my tenure as a deputy judge would have been brought to a summary conclusion. By this time the pandemic had started to take a serious hold. I was twitchy about attending the course with a large gathering for which social distancing and face coverings were then unknown precautions but was assured by the Judicial College that government guidelines would be followed and we look forward to seeing you or else.

I left the course on its first day by cosy and closed-windowed taxi provided by Parker Cars. The driver told me he had been abroad. "Where?" "Milan". "Not bloody Milan where the pandemic is now rife?" "Yes. But I was back a fortnight ago and have had a negative blood test". I wasn't convinced and next day made contact with Parker Cars. I was given conflicting information in a series of calls. It eventually transpired that the driver had returned nine and not 14 days previously and had lied about the blood tests although he was asymptomatic.

> Hi Stephen,
>
> When I asked the driver if he had had a blood test, he said he hadn't as when he called the helpline he was told it wasn't necessary.
>
> He says he shouldn't have told you he had, but did so because he is confident he is not infected or a carrier and wanted to reassure you. I've told him that was wrong and he should have been honest.
>
> Kind regards
>
> Ian
>
> The Booking Team
>
> Parker Car Service

I secured a commitment from Parker Cars that the driver would report to them on a daily basis for five days as to whether or not he had acquired symptoms and they would notify me accordingly. They did. No symptoms. However, before I had escaped from taxi trauma, I received this communication from the Judicial College.

> 10 March 2020
>
> Dear Judge
>
> I am writing to inform you that on Monday 9 March the College became aware that one of the tutors at the Civil and Family Combined seminar last week (5-6 March) had very recently returned from a trip to Venice. On Monday 9 March, the Public Health England advice was that any traveller returning from Northern Italy (including Venice) should self-isolate, even if asymptomatic. This advice was not in place at the time of your course.
>
> The tutor self-isolated on 9 March. **I must stress that the tutor concerned is asymptomatic and there have been no concerns raised regarding their health**. However, the College felt it important to inform you as a precautionary measure.
>
> If you become concerned about your own health, please follow the NHS guidance on coronavirus symptoms – https://www.nhs.uk/conditions/coronavirus-covid-19/.
>
> Yours sincerely,
>
> Sarah Wallace
>
> Head of Operations, Governance and Policy, Judicial College

A somewhat cagey message. Who was the tutor – was it someone in my group of judges who had sneezed in my face and when had they returned from Venice anyway? After some stone walling, I prized out of the College that the tutor had returned three days before the course started and had not tutored me. Whatever the government advice was at the time, they should have known better than to turn up and put everyone else at risk. They did not become symptomatic.

I shall not be attending another Judicial College course.

Covid-19 has changed the face of civil and family justice in England and Wales. The administrators had for years dreamt of hearings remotely from court be it by video or phone, in a village hall, in a pub, in a booth outside a pub. Anywhere, except in a court. The fewer face-to-face hearings in court the fewer courts you need, and the fewer courts you have the cheaper it is to run the show. Covid-19 has realised the dream far too soon and forced many thousands of cases which pre-pandemic would have taken place face-to-face in a court room to be dealt with remotely, through one of a series of available video platforms or otherwise by telephone through the BT MeetMe platform. And that's how I have been dealing with cases, from the study at home.

From the judge's standpoint, the positives are that there's no travel, you can ignore the postman and you can turn up for work looking wholly or partially like a vagrant. An audio hearing, of course, can be conducted in total nudity or without changing out of pyjamas. This is inadvisable for video hearings where I have attired myself respectably as to the top half and run riot underneath in newscaster desk style but positively never in swimming trucks. You see, I can't swim. Care needs to be taken to ensure there is no modern art visible which might be regarded by the losing party as highly indecent and warranting a call to the *Daily Mail* newsdesk. Judges have been guided to do what they possibly can to ensure that the backdrop is neutral and appropriate. This seems to rule out children making silly faces. And guidance that lawyers need not stand when the judge appears. Really.

There are major negatives for the judge. Usually, the case documents are sent through by the court in the form of an electronic file. Reading them off a computer screen before the hearing – yes, they must be pre-read – can be draining. The file may run into 100 or 200 pages and if there is not one single case to last the day then there could be a series of five or six cases. Referring to the documents during the hearing may be technically taxing. When live evidence is being given, as almost invariably it will be at the final hearing although rarely at preliminary hearings, my preference is to have the witness relatively close by in court instead of at the other end of a telephone or on a laptop screen and I believe that the majority of trial judges would take the same view. The theory is that the demeanour of a witness when giving evidence is not a good guide to the truthfulness of what they are saying. Some people are better at lying than others and that is no different whether they are doing so remotely or in court. Yes, it will be more obvious to the judge in court what the demeanour is but that does not mean it will be more illuminating. Although it may be thought that a witness will be more likely to tell the truth if they are in the witness box in court and felt the pressure of the courtroom, this could work the other way round. They might feel less defensive and more inclined to tell the truth in a remote hearing than when feeling somewhat intimidated in court. Me not persuaded. I like to see the whites of the eyes.

There are other negatives with a remote hearing apart from the inevitable technical hiccups including too frequent image freezing. The parties may be more difficult to control. There have been many instances of extreme rudeness to the judge and constant interruptions with parties having to be warned that they are participating in court proceedings and that they risk being considered for committal to prison for contempt of court and being excluded from the hearing if their conduct persists. And how can the judge be sure that what is intended to be a private hearing is not being attended by someone who has no right to be there? Or that a party or other witness is not being prompted by someone else through notes or other forms of communication? Because of an inadequacy of court staff, accentuated by the pandemic, documentation emailed to the court by the parties or their lawyers close to a hearing is frequently not passed on to the judge sitting remotely in time for them to see it before the hearing. Sometimes it will reach the judge's computer during the hearing and not be read until afterwards.

One tip for everyone participating in a remote hearing. Be ever so cautious about what comes out of your mouth if you are not muted. Mrs Justice Judd doesn't need reminding of this. She was at court, trying a care case during the pandemic which was partly face-to-face and partly remote. A clerk took her closed laptop from the court bench into the judge's room but, unbeknown to the judge, the remote link to the court room remained open. The phone conversation the judge then had with another clerk about the mother in the case could be heard by a number of people who still remained on the call. During that conversation the judge made pejorative remarks about the mother who was in the middle of her evidence including that she was pretending to have a cough and was trying 'every trick in the book'. The mother asked the judge to stand down – to recuse herself – but the judge refused. The Court of Appeal ruled that the judge had been wrong to refuse and that the hearing would have to be restarted before another judge. It had considerable sympathy with Mrs Justice Judd but decided that, looking in from the outside, it could not do other than think that her remarks would colour the view of the mother and demonstrate a real possibility of bias.

In March 2021 the Lord Chief Justice called for a return to hearings at court with personal attendances where possible and desirable. There will be some return to how it was. But it will never be the same.

I'll have to end this part of the book now. I've got a bloody liar giving evidence this afternoon in a damages claim and must have a sandwich first.

PART 2

HELP!!!

Chapter 7

Lawyer Or Litigant In Person?

You would probably prefer to use a lawyer to advise you on a legal dispute and represent you in court if that is where the case has to end up. That's their job and not yours. For a start, you can sue a lawyer should their advice be negligent and you suffer loss as a result. But while you may self-mutilate for getting it wrong, suing yourself is not an option though, having said that, you might be able to achieve it with *Money Claim Online*. Still, what a terrible waste of a court fee.

The internet is overloaded with information about how you can find a lawyer and how you can manage without one. A good deal of it is misleading and many of the plugs are from organisations and people whose hidden agenda is to empty your pockets of what money may be left inside them. But much of it is also well meaning and often from charities committed to helping those of you caught up in a legal dispute and not having a clue where to turn. This goes some way towards filling the chasm created by the brutal chop taken to the legal aid scheme in April 2013. What is lacking is one central national organisation which can coordinate the activities of literally all the good guys: an organisation to which you can go to advise on the best advice which may be available to you wherever you may be and to get you to it as soon as possible. There is an organisation which goes some of the distance to achieving this goal. It's called Law for Life (lawforlife.org.uk) which runs a great website (advicenow.org.uk) full of stuff for litigants in person – do go to it when you have had enough of me – and they work in partnership with a handful of other charities. And there are others. I am going to give you my take on what's about and how you can get it – if you want it!

Legal aid fade

That beautiful legal aid scheme we had for bringing and defending civil cases through a solicitor plus a barrister, if necessary, is no more. Generally, legal aid is not now available for consumer and breach of contract cases and for negligence and other accident claims for compensation (except for a child on a clinical negligence claim for a neurological injury resulting in severe disablement during pregnancy, birth or the postnatal period). It is also out for family law cases (like divorce and disputes over children) except where strict criteria are met regarding child abuse or domestic violence and cases over child protection brought by local authorities. A temptation there is often succumbed to for parents to make allegations against the other which previously would never have seen the light of day and so bring themselves within the scope of legal aid.

Even when the type of case does qualify for legal aid, it may be denied to you on financial grounds. It's the capital rules that can be the killers. In most cases, someone with more than £8,000 capital is ineligible and anyone with between £3,000 and £8,000 will have to pay a contribution towards their civil legal aid costs. But there have been two recent developments which mitigate the severity of the capital rules. Firstly, let's see what happened to a victim of domestic abuse at the hands of her former partner whose challenge to a legal aid refusal met with High Court success in November 2020. She had been after legal aid for Children Act proceedings relating to her two children and a dispute over the jointly owned home. She had £28 in a bank account which had no impact on legal aid. What messed it for her was the value of a half interest in her home which took her over the capital threshold for legal aid entitlement. A fat lot of good that interest was, though. She couldn't sell the house and she couldn't borrow any money against it. The former partner wouldn't agree to either. A common problem this. The High Court ruled that in this situation the legal aid people had a discretion to disregard the whole or part of the value of any asset – other than money – so that an application could be granted. If you have been refused legal aid on the same grounds as this lady and the case is still ongoing, have another bash.

Secondly, let's take a look at what has happened when you own your home or have an interest in it but, up to the hilt, it is mortgaged or has a charging order registered against your interest. The debt had been knocked off the value of the property but up to a maximum of £100,000. So, if the house was worth £300,000 and there was £295,000 secured against it by way of mortgage or charging order, or both, your interest (if you were the sole owner but halve if you owned 50%) would have been valued by the legal aid people at £300,000 – only £100,000 = £200,000. That was way over the £8,000 capital maximum allowed for eligibility. No legal aid. But for civil legal aid applications made after 27 January 2021, the whole of the secured debt will be knocked off the value. In the example, that would mean £300,000 – £295,000 = £5,000 which is less than £8,000 so you are within the civil legal aid scheme. Again, if you have been refused because of the £100,000 cap and it is not too late, you can reapply for legal aid.

And for civil legal aid applications made after 7 January 2021 a series of one-off compensation payments for state error or serious incidents in the UK, which are still sitting in an account or your back pocket or under the bed, will be disregarded in calculating whether you have too much capital. Most impactingly, this will include compensation paid by the Criminal Injuries Compensation Scheme. Other payments disregarded are those for infected blood support, vaccine damage, variant Creutzfeldt-Jacob disease and from the National Emergencies Trust, We Love Manchester Fund and the London Emergencies Trust Fund.

Some legal help may be available in connection with an inquest into the death of a family member but legal aid will not extend to being represented by a lawyer at the inquest itself. Additionally, it might be available in a debt or housing case where your home is at risk. There's a list of what you might still get legal aid for at gov.uk/check-legal-aid.

If you reckon that the Legal Aid Agency to which your civil legal aid application has been sent has committed an obvious howler in wrongly chucking out the application or assessing your means, there's a fast 'fix it' service recently introduced under which it can be asked to take another look. This may avoid the delay of an appeal. The service is not available to you where you have put in the application yourself.

The only way of securing legal aid in one of the myriad of excluded cases is to go for exceptional funding but provided you qualify financially. This would be on the basis that a denial of legal aid would be a breach of your human rights. It is not a route which is sufficiently well known, even among litigation lawyers, and the ability of advisers at law centres and clinics during the pandemic to help those after exceptional funding with the necessary paperwork has been seriously curtailed. Nevertheless, do try and get a centre or clinic of other professional to deal with the application if you can. Otherwise, you can complete the paperwork for an application to the Legal Aid Agency yourself, if need must. For the forms and guidance, go to gov/uk/guidance/legal-aid-apply-for-exceptional-case-funding. As its name implies, the grounds for obtaining exceptional case funding must be – exceptional! In the early years of the scheme, the chances of getting an application granted were about as high as me reaching the moon before tomorrow night's BBC1 *News at Ten*. Thanks to the sterling work of the charity the Public Law Project (it's worth taking a butchers at their website – publiclawproject.org.uk), the success rate of applications has rocketed up but achieving this funding is no doddle. The key is to argue that the absence of legal aid would prevent you from effectively presenting your case, without obvious unfairness. Emphasise the complexity of any procedural rules you are going to have to comply with and why what is at stake is so important to you. The longer the hearing is likely to take, the stronger your position.

> *"English is only my secondary language. I struggle to read English. I am being assisted with this application by a friend who is better versed in the English language than me. I can be slow on the uptake. I left school at the age of 15 without having attained any academic achievements and my work has always been of a menial kind. I have had to go to advice centres and friends who are brighter than me to help me fill out official forms. I understand that the hearing will take at least three days and that there will be expert witnesses for the other side. I would find it nearly impossible to personally cross-examine non-expert factual witnesses myself. I would find it completely impossible to understand the technical expert evidence expected, let alone personally cross-examine the experts. I would be unable to cope with court case management directions concerning the disclosure of documents and the compilation of written statements of the factual evidence of myself and three essential witnesses upon whom I intend to rely. I am not in a financial position to instruct a professional McKenzie Friend to assist me in court and with pre-hearing procedures and I know of nobody who could fulfil that role for me without payment. Anyway, the case is too complex for a McKenzie Friend whose involvement is more likely to lengthen the hearing than allow it to be concluded within the estimated time. I have been treated in the past by my GP for depression and I would find the stress and demands of the proceedings to be overwhelming if I was on my own without legal advice and representation."*

Blimey, I got carried away. I would certainly accede to that plea if I had anything to do with exceptional funding which I don't so please refrain from trying to slip me a fiver.

In relation to representation by a lawyer at an inquest, obtaining exceptional funding is as difficult as it gets. It can only be granted if having an advocate at the inquest would be likely to produce significant benefits to a group of people other than you and members of your family. We might be looking at a Grenfell Tower type tragedy here. "Inquest" is a group of lawyers who are willing to provide preparation advice and help and advocacy services at inquests. Go to inquest.org.uk.

Incidentally, the Public Law Project can no longer directly assist with exceptional funding applications but could point you in the right direction if you were struggling to find help in making one.

Using a lawyer without legal aid

No win, no fee agreements

These were formerly known as conditional fee agreements and, in theory, are available for all civil cases except family cases such as divorces, financial disputes within matrimonial proceedings and children disputes. They often figure in commercial, insolvency, debt collection and defamation cases and in claims for accident compensation (as well as employment tribunal cases which are mainly outside the ambit of this book). Effectively, you and the solicitor share the risk of you losing. The best deal you are likely to reach with the solicitor where you are bringing (instead of defending) a claim is that (a) you pay them no fees if you lose, (b) if you win, the solicitor accepts for the work they have done the amount they can collect from the loser but (c) the solicitor charges you a success fee which can be anything up to 100% of what they are entitled to collect from the loser for their work and this success fee comes out of the money you have been awarded. In claims for personal injuries (other than for diffuse mesothelioma) the success fee is capped at 25% of your compensation other than for future loss (such as for future care). The capping does not apply to an appeal against a defeat in court where the success fee can be up to 100%. The solicitor may want you to take out an insurance policy for their basic bill so that they are protected if you lose. You will pay the premium but the solicitor may agree to foot it until the case is concluded. If a barrister is brought in, you can hopefully come to a similar arrangement with them. Where use is being made of an expert who won't wait around for payment you may have to advance their charges. It is usual to insure against the winner's legal costs being ordered against you should you lose. That's an after-the-event policy and the premium on that would also be down to you though, again, the solicitor may be prepared to pay it up front and get it back from you later.

But will a solicitor – and maybe a barrister too – take you on? They are unlikely to touch you unless they reckon you have at least a 60% chance of winning and you may have to yourself advance not only experts' fees but court fees and other expenses which are incurred by the solicitor as the case progresses. The solicitor may also wish to have the right to charge you for the work they have done at a rate which is higher than your loser would have to contribute. This is all up for negotiation with the solicitor. Particularly in accident claims brought by an adult on behalf of a child, I have frequently encountered scandalous conditional fee agreements providing for a 100% success fee where the risk of failure is close to non-existent, typically whiplash claims where the child has been a passenger in a stationary car which has been hit in the rear by the defendant's vehicle and the defendant's insurers have already admitted that the defendant was to blame.

You may need to haggle over the success fee sought. The solicitor will assess the risk they would be taking on in accepting the case. The bigger they assess the risk to be, the higher the success fee which will be sought. An assessment of a 60% chance of you winning may well justify a success fee of around 67% as against around 11% for a 90% chance of winning. The solicitor might be prepared to accept a staged success fee arrangement: if the case settles within say three months you pay them a success fee of x%, if it settles within say nine months you pay them a greater success fee of y% and if it settles or you win any later you pay them a success fee of a dreaded 100%. If you manage to negotiate the ultimate of not a penny from you if you lose and a success fee if you win, the level of that success fee is going to reflect the fact that no risk is being assumed by you. Where you are convinced that you have a strong case, you may wish to shop around. Sizing up the case and drafting a proposed conditional fee agreement will absorb any solicitor's time. Check beforehand whether they would charge for that and, if so, how much.

So the key info you want from the solicitor about a conditional fee arrangement is:

- Will you charge me for looking into the possibility of it and then setting it up and, if so, how much?
- If I lose, do I have to pay anything towards the cost of your work and disbursements you incur and, if so, how much do you estimate that will be and when will I have to pay?
- If I win, do I have to pay anything towards the cost of your work and disbursements you incur and, if so, how much do you estimate that will be? And what will be the rate of your success fee and will it be reduced if the case settles before trial and, if so, by how much and, if not, why not?

OK, I know you were desperate to ask. You've been charged with driving whilst disqualified and with excess alcohol in your body, you've got this cracking defence, you need an ace lawyer to argue it in court, you haven't got a black and white television set to your name and can you hire that lawyer under a conditional fee agreement? No. These agreements cannot apply to criminal proceedings except magistrates' court cases under section 82 of the Environmental Protection Act 1990 by any person aggrieved by a statutory nuisance at premises (smoke, dust, insects, badly kept animals and Uncle Tom Cobley).

83

Damages based agreements

Here is another deal you may reach with your solicitor which only became legal in April 2013 – the damages based agreement. The solicitor agrees to act for you in return for a cut of your compensation. If you lose, they get nothing. But if you win, they may do very nicely or very badly. Depends. There is a cap on their cut depending on the type of case. In personal injury cases, it is 25% of the compensation but the solicitor cannot share in any part of compensation for future loss. In other civil cases the maximum cut is 50%. In employment tribunal cases it is 35%. Any expenses which the solicitor has had to pay out such as court fees and fees for medical reports which, for whatever reason, the loser escapes having to reimburse, will be reimbursable by you. Should you lose, you would have to reimburse disbursements except for any barristers' fees. These caps do not apply to appeals where you and the solicitor are free to negotiate the percentage cut. A damages based agreement will have the solicitor in hindsight laughing if they settle the case in five minutes but they could be weeping if it goes to trial five years later. A lousy idea is for you to agree to a damages based agreement where your case is oozing with strength and the opposition is weak or non-existent or liability has already been conceded.

These agreements had been as popular with solicitors as a glass of sherry with Judge Jeffreys on one of his bad days. The reason was the ambiguity of the legislation relating to them and, in particular, the uncertainty as to whether solicitors could effectively specify in an agreement that a client who signed up and later decamped would then have to pay the solicitor's fees and disbursements up to that point. A Court of Appeal ruling in January 2021 that they could be claimed will have solicitors' faces shining on the agreements in future although some solicitors are looking for more clarification in legislation before they accept a damages based client.

Lawyer charges but you don't pay or you borrow

Third party litigation funders, they are called. Companies who will pay your legal fees and usually in return for a cut of the damages you recover. But what funders really love is multi-million commercial litigation. Could little you (or little me) ever hope to secure third party funding? There is a handful of funders who will consider "smaller" value claims but they would normally need to be worth at least £100,000 and are most likely to be negligence claims against professional advisers such as lawyers (oh no!), accountants and surveyors and claims about contested wills and intestacies, financial mis-selling, breach of contract and employment.

The funder will usually be looking for the claim value to be at least four times that of the costs which will be involved. They will usually require you to take out an insurance policy to cover any costs which may be awarded against you if you lose and the insurer would want to be satisfied that you had a minimum of a 60% chance of winning. In the current climate, it is unlikely the funder would take you on without full legal representation. Acting in person or with a direct access barrister (see below) would be a non-runner. Matrimonial financial remedy and clinical negligence claims are often avoided although some specialist lenders may back a financial remedy claim with a loan where there is a property that can be offered as security but expect to pay high interest within the range of 1.5 to 2.5% per month (that's 18 to 30% per annum). As with lawyers, the funders are generally so so so shy about going on the record as to the likely bill for backing you. The shyness has intensified since I previously sought to engage them. But I've found a few exceptions.

Affiniti Finance (affinitifinance.co.uk) looks a good bet for the more modest claims although they are in the market for the big commercial funding jobs too where their terms are going to be customized to each individual case. As to the non-big jobs, they will make a consumer credit regulated loan for the legal fees, attracting simple interest which is likely to be no less than 18% and with an average rate of 22% per annum. They will fund the insurance policy premium. A drawdown fee of £95 is charged and repayable at the end. Early repayment of the loan is allowed without penalty if, for example, you secure an interim payment of compensation in a personal injury claim or the lottery mob comes knocking at your door. The big plus is that you don't have to pay over a cut of your damages if and when you win. Matrimonial financial remedy cases will be considered for funding but Affiniti will want to be satisfied that there will be liquid assets available to repay the loan at the end. Last year it announced a £10m fund available for clients of London and Cardiff solicitors Hugh James and predominantly available for claims against the Ministry of Defence for military related injuries including military deafness and cold related injuries.

Therium (therium.com) funds what they describe as "a broad cross-section of claims with our investment ranging from a few hundred thousand pounds up to ten of millions." Among the areas for which they have a particular expertise and appetite are claims for negligence by professionals, trust litigation, international arbitration and the enforcement of judgments and awards. They will not generally touch defamation, personal injury clinical negligence or matrimonial financial remedy cases. If the funded claim is successful, then Therium would want back the capital outlayed and then the higher of a multiple of their investment, which would usually be three times the investment, or a percentage of the net damages which would depend on the specific case but is likely to be within the range of 20 to 30%. Well, you did ask!

Novitas (novitasloans.co.uk) are leading players in the market for lending for legal fees in matrimonial financial remedy cases between opposite and same sex couples without taking a share of the spoils (and they will also similarly lend for claims for clinical negligence and 'you left me out of your will' claims). The finance can cover proceedings under the Children Act 1989 which are running in tandem with a financial remedy application but not under schedule 1 to the 1989 Act. They will lend to either side of a case and often lend to both sides of the same case. You can draw down tranches of the loan as and when you need the money but only be liable for interest on what you take from the date you take it. The interest rate works out at 18% per annum. However, there is a set up fee in family cases of the greater of

£500 or 1% of the loan agreed which along with the interest is rolled up into the loan. The period of the loan is a formal 12 months but 30 days' notice can be given calling it in after 11 months have run. Novitas' managing director Jason Reeve stresses that his company seeks to be flexible about the length of the required loan period in practice and they have some loans which have been allowed to be out for three years.

There is no prescribed maximum loan at Novitas but they will want to be satisfied that the money will be available at the end of the case to repay what has been lent along with the interest. Secondary considerations include credit and reconciliation history (after all, you could be reuniting after a few months which would bring the proceedings to a close). They will arrange to have first call on the settlement proceeds to the extent necessary to get their money back and take a charge on your interest in the family home as security where that is available. If there is no security available then Novitas may wish to insure the risk of going unpaid and you would be responsible for the 10% premium; so if you were after £10,000, you would have to draw down £11,000 of which £1,000 would be passed to the insurer. About 20% of their loans are insured in this way. Novitas will insist on you taking legal advice on the proposed arrangement with them and for that advice you will have to pay.

Back to a sharing of the spoils. Augusta Ventures (augustaventures.com) describe themselves as the leading providers of litigation finance in the UK having shelled out over £15m to date in backing suitable claims. Its no go areas primarily include matrimonial applications and claims for personal injury, defamation, breach of privacy, housing disrepair and professional negligence which has allegedly led to an insufficient financial recovery (for example, against a solicitor who has acted in your litigation) although other negligence claims against solicitors will be looked at.

Augusta have financed claims worth between £20,000 (so lower than the norm) up to £40m and as a general rule of thumb look for a budget to damages ratio of 1 to 3 (that's the client seeking at least £300,000 for every £100,000 to be spent on legal costs). The legal work will be done by a firm out of their approved panel of solicitors or, if you already have a solicitor, they will work with them provided they satisfy their due diligence process. What they will not do is fund you as a litigant in person. The assessment process – it looks rigorous though they say it is no worse than applying to a bank for a loan – will include obtaining a barrister's opinion on the merits of the claim unless the matter is "small and simple". They will extend early action finance covering initial costs and a barrister's fee on merits where required and if the claim is then fully financed by them and you win, this expense will come out of the spoils plus a 25% mark up. If they refuse finance or they finance and you lose, there is no charge for the assessment.

What's in it for Augusta if they fully finance? Nothing if you lose. If you win then out of the compensation (and in this order) they are reimbursed for their outlay plus 14% per annum on the capital they have advanced, your lawyers who would have acted under a conditional fee agreement are paid (but not their success fee – yet) and you are reimbursed any funds you have contributed. Out of the balance, Augusta collect an average fee – wait for it and they aren't shy about giving us the figure – of 20%, the lawyers are paid their success fee. And the rest is yours. A win, of course, should mean the loser having to stump up for the lions' share of your costs.

Augusta's director of strategic engagement tells me they will not finance litigation unless the claimant will end up with no less than 50% of the compensation awarded after the deductions I have mentioned have been made. Oh and Augusta will want an after the event insurance policy taken out to protect you against an adverse costs order. If you have made any cash contribution to the claim costs then the policy can extend to 90% of the contribution which means that, should you lose, you will only be down for 10% of any cash contribution made and will not be in debt for costs to Augusta or the winner. The policy will involve a 15% premium. Augusta will include the premium in their finance.

Selecting a solicitor or barrister

or

"That Ponsonby-Smythe is red hot"

Like judges and weather forecasters, there are brilliant lawyers and lousy lawyers. Choose one who specialises in the type of case for which you want to *instruct* them. Yes, you don't 'hire' a lawyer or 'buy' their services. You '*instruct*' them though with most lawyers I have encountered, it is they who do the instructing. If you are embroiled in a boundary dispute with your neighbour, steer clear of a lawyer who spends most of their days on criminal trials. A friend may recommend a "good lawyer". You might even be able to extract an off the record recommendation from someone in the know, perhaps from the CAB or other advice agency. Or if your case is about making a claim against the domestic help you dismissed who went off to a tabloid newspaper with lurid details of your private life, research on *Google* which lawyers have been involved in cases on breach of confidence and who may still be alive – and won! If you want a powerful advocate to destroy your lying opponent in the witness box and can't get a recommendation from a reliable source, pop along to your local civil court, ask the usher if there are any good advocates in action that day and listen and watch but make sure you have a note of their name and address before you hop it. Advocacy can make the difference between success and failure. Any judge who swears that they will never be swayed by a persuasive advocate ought to be taking a lie detector test.

Should the lawyer's name play any part in the selection process? A really grand name like Ponsonby-Smythe could impress the opposition but distract the judge like a twitch, very greasy hair or an old-world charming barrister who sometimes appeared before me and insisted on referring to his female clients as "my lady". The most intimidating name for a firm of solicitors that I have ever come across is Wright Hassall who are based not in the East End of London but tranquil Leamington Spa and who count debt collection as one of their specialities. Their marketing director Vikki Whittemore fears that some people are likely to question the firm's credibility because of the name. Is it a joke or is the firm some sort of commoditised legal practice rather than a full service law firm with a 170 year heritage?

Solicitor, barrister or both: the choice is yours

You now have a choice of lawyer in that you can go for a solicitor or a barrister – or both. Traditionally, a litigant's first stop was a solicitor's office. The solicitor may have had someone else in the firm with legal experience (often a legal executive who can also sometimes advocate in court) who would advise and prepare the case for battle and the solicitor, especially in a complex case, would bring in a barrister to advise and also to appear in court as the advocate. If the case was proceeding in the High Court, Court of Appeal or Supreme Court the solicitor would be compelled to use a barrister for advocacy unless they had acquired authority to advocate there themselves. The majority of solicitors do not have this authority although numbers have recently been increasing. But now the solicitor can be dispensed with and you can directly engage a barrister not only to appear in court as your advocate but to advise on the law, prepare paperwork and do other things along the way. We will look at how you can source such a barrister shortly. Some barristers will only accept work via a solicitor; some will be prepared to have the litigant directly instruct them, without a solicitor, to appear in court as the advocate (and, with that chop taken to legal aid work, an increasing number are so prepared); and some will agree to do the whole case – advice, preparation and advocacy – directly instructed and without solicitor involvement.

Dilemma

What the hell do you do? Using a solicitor plus a barrister is going to be more expensive than using just one of them as there will inevitably be some duplication of work for which you will pay. For example, if a meeting with the barrister is needed – it's called a *conference* but you are unlikely to get a plastic lunch thrown in as you do with the hotel conferences I go to – the solicitor will charge you for telling the barrister in writing all about the case and the barrister will charge you for reading what the solicitor has written. The solicitor will charge you for attending the meeting with the barrister and the barrister will charge you for advising at the meeting.

That doesn't make the decision open and shut. Some cases are so complex that they demand the application of two legal brains. Less complex cases may still justify both solicitor and barrister because the preparation will be quite extensive and there may need to be concentrated contact between you and whoever is in charge of preparation. And you could also want to call on your lawyer in an attempt to settle the case, be it before proceedings have been started or hand in hand with the proceedings. Generally, solicitors and others in the firm who are on the case are better at preparatory work and they are better placed to be available to you when you want them and to keep up the momentum of settlement negotiations with the opposition. That's because they are unlikely to be occupied advocating in court with the same intensity as a barrister and they will have the office back up which will not normally be available with a barrister. "My Lord, whilst my learned friend was cross-examining, I took the liberty of checking my messages and I see that another client for whom I am in court next week urgently wants to speak to me about a settlement offer and is desperate for help on compelling some witnesses to come to court if the case does not settle. My Lord, would you be prepared to indulge me and stop this case for a few minutes so that I can deal with these matters and I apologise to your Lordship and my learned friend but, you see, I operate on direct access along with a litigation service?" It couldn't happen except in a nightmare or occasionally when only a barrister is handling the case.

Beauty parade

If you are going to instruct a solicitor with or without a barrister, you find the solicitor first. If it is to be a double act, they will almost certainly have a barrister in mind who they think is suitable for the case although you may have decided on someone else. You call the tune. Some solicitors have pet barristers and fall into the trap of using them on all their cases when sometimes a particular case may not really be in their comfort zone. In the absence of a recommendation for a solicitor or a Ponsonby-Smythe, you can use a pin in a directory – and remember that a flashy advert on a full page with a teaser on the preceding page could spell danger – or you can use the *Find a Solicitor* facility run by the Law Society (lawsociety.org.uk or telephone 020 7320 5650) or check out the websites of local law societies which are mainly established on a county basis. If I woke up one morning with every legal principle erased from my mind and needed to instruct a solicitor then unless the case revolved around a remote area of law in which the only firm having any expertise operated out of London's West End charging £2,000 an hour plus VAT, I would pick a local medium sized firm with a member who knows their stuff, would prepare, negotiate and advocate at all stages from start to finish and would not charge me an arm and a leg.

Most solicitors will be loathe to advertise in advance what they would charge you, lest it would frighten you off, so you won't generally find a price list on their websites. But since December 2018 they have been subject to Solicitors Regulatory Authority rules obliging them to be transparent in a limited number of areas (and some naughty boys and girls are awaiting a caning for failing to comply). If they have a website (and where not, the information must be available on request in other formats), they are there to present in a clear and easy to understand way their pricing, including hourly or fixed rates. These limited areas include residential conveyancing, motoring offences which are almost invariably dealt with in a magistrates' court, employment tribunal unfair dismissal cases and debt recovery cases involving up to £100,000.

You ought to be able to locate a solicitor who will see you free of charge for at least half an hour (see more later) so that you can size them up and they can size you up and, with a bit of luck, extract a bit of legal advice at the same time. You don't want a wimp and they don't want a lunatic. Ensure it is agreed when you make an appointment that there is no charge for this initial session. You will decide when you see them whether you would be able to get on with them – pompous, prat or personable – whether they appear confident and whether you would have confidence in them. And here are the questions you want answered:

- What is your experience in this sort of case?
- From what you have heard, do you think I have a good chance of success?
- Who would be dealing with my case – you personally, from beginning to end? If not, which other members of your firm would be involved and what would their tasks be?
- Will you advocate for me in court or take in a barrister?
- Why would you take in a barrister?
- Can you and will you take my case on a no win, no fee basis (and, if so, see above for the questions to ask about a no win, no fee agreement)?

If no win, no fee is out of the question:

- What will be the amount per hour you will charge me for your time and the time of anyone in the office to whom you will delegate and what do you estimate your charges will amount to for the whole case?
- How much would I have to pay you up front? How often would you send me interim bills?

Where a no win, no fee is not to be the arrangement, you could ask whether the solicitor would be prepared to take the case on a fixed fee basis so that the actual fee is fixed in advance and neither you nor the solicitor would be justified in departing from it no matter how straightforward or problematic the case turned out to be. In the world of litigation, it is unlikely that the solicitor would agree to this should you be looking at them dealing with the case in its entirety because the course of litigation is so difficult to predict. An unbundling situation is another matter (see below under **Dipping in and out with a lawyer**).

If you are going to instruct a barrister without a solicitor and are not following up a recommendation, you can go to barcouncil.org.uk which will not help you a lot except it will tell you about the Direct Access Portal. This is the website for barristers who are prepared to be instructed directly without a solicitor – directaccessportal.co.uk. For the privilege of being included on the portal, the barristers pay £150 a year. Barristers who don't want to be instructed by you directly or to pay £150 a year, won't be on the portal. Of the 8,940 barristers who will take on direct access work, around one-half of them are on the portal. The minority of portal barristers who will conduct the whole case and not just advocate for you say so on the portal. A similar website is run by mybarrister.co.uk which has a more modest 500 barristers on board. Its barristers pay an annual subscription to be included on the site of £100 per year.

clerksroom.direct.com works on a different basis and has over 1,000 barristers on its books who are available for advocacy work and drafting documents. You can select the barrister you want or ask them to find you a suitable barrister who they are satisfied is right for the job and will take it at a fee you have named or within a budget agreed in advance of the case. They will deal with all the administration involved including getting the fee agreed in advance of the case. For their service they charge you anything up to 20% of what is to go to the barrister. You'll be aware of the split between the barrister and clerksroom before you accept or reject. Most of their barristers will be prepared to spend up to half an hour by phone with you to understand precisely what service you are after and whether you are suited to direct access.

Some barristers personally advertise their availability for direct access work. Take a look at the classified ads in *Private Eye* and go onto the web and you will find plenty of barristers chambers – groups of barristers operate out of an office which they call chambers (see old videos of *Rumpole of the Bailey*) where they are terrorised by their clerk and it is probably the clerk you will speak to if you contact a set of chambers to talk about direct access – with websites imploring you to engage a barrister directly.

The minority of barristers who will conduct the entirety of the litigation for you will be no keener than a solicitor to undertake a fixed fee arrangement: if anything, even less keen. In fact, barristers won't generally even go in for advertising a fixed fee tariff for dealing with advocacy alone. One London set of chambers, however, did brandish a rather inviting list of fixed fees on their website. Alas, this took the head barrister by surprise when I questioned him about it and he said they didn't go in for fixed fees and they had been planning to alter the website the next week!

The majority of barristers operate out of clusters in London but there are plenty of sets of barristers' chambers in large cities and towns, sometimes linked to the main chambers in London. The idea that provincial barristers are second-rate is a cruel myth. The closer the base of the barrister you choose to the court at which you want them to advocate, the lower will be their fee – hopefully. There can also be another advantage in using a barrister for a case at one of their 'home' courts. They will have appeared there regularly and, unless excruciatingly irritating, will have established a good professional relationship with the judge.

Even if you are in a deliriously happy marriage or partnership, you can go to chapter 75 where you will find information about what barristers (and solicitors) are charging for acting as mediators and arbitrators in matrimonial cases but don't let your spouse or partner see what you are up to or they may think you are preparing for war. Those who openly advertise their charges for these services also advertise their charges for taking on matrimonial and other family cases as advocates.

A barrister can act on a direct access basis under a conditional fee or damages based agreement (see above under **Using a lawyer without legal aid**). I would be surprised if the barrister queue to do so is very long. If you see a queue of posh lawyers, it will probably be outside *Harrods*.

In the battle of solicitor versus barrister, my efforts to get some representatives from each profession to come to blows at a hearing centre near me didn't come off and the bosses of *mybarrister.co.uk* wouldn't be drawn. "We would prefer not to comment." In desperation, I invited the Bar Council and the Law Society to slag off the other. A Bar Council spokesman argued that it *can* be more advantageous to instruct a barrister instead of a solicitor (though this isn't always the case) and relied on the lower overheads of barristers meaning that their rates were "often very affordable" and their expertise in disputes and, in turn, their understanding of how to avoid disputes reaching the court room. And he threw in that complaints against barristers are low in number. He did point out that a barrister might actually refer a case to a solicitor if they felt they were not best suited to take it on.

Alright, we get the drift. Over to the Law Society for a knock out. Their spokeswoman said: "Solicitors provide vital support to clients in contentious matters. While clients can still instruct barristers directly and have been able to do so for some time, solicitors provide a wider range of services, which is why many clients choose to instruct a solicitor first."

If you bought tickets for the fight, you might want your money back.

Dipping in and out with a lawyer

Barristers traditionally dip in and out of a case. So it is that a barrister will take on the advocacy at a final hearing though they have never previously met you or the case and, as we have seen, so many of them now will take it on without the involvement of a solicitor. The fee will be agreed with you in advance and if you don't have to pay it before the barrister steps into court, I'll eat another one of my hats. A solicitor may possibly be more flexible than a barrister about reaching an instalment plan for their fees which has you plunging into your pocket even after the final hearing. Be it barrister or solicitor, they need to guard against the possibility of you losing and having to pay the winner's legal costs. Who will get to you first – lawyer or successful opponent- and is there enough for both? A mortgage on your home in favour of the lawyer might well be sufficient protection for them should you be desperate for their representation but lacking ready cash and unable to negotiate a loan.

If you intend to hire a barrister for the final hearing only, you should give them an opportunity as long as practically possible ahead of that hearing to see the papers and you so that they can advise on whether they have everything they require to do the best for your case.

Will a solicitor with their office backup be prepared to dip in and out of a case rather than act from start to finish should that better suit your pocket? Could you ask them just to advise whether your case is legally strong or a stinker? Just to draw up the court papers so that you can start the proceedings yourself? Just to advise you whether or not you need a particular witness or what questions to ask in cross-examination? Just to deal with the advocacy at the final hearing instead of a barrister? Just to act as *McKenzie Friend* (see more below) at a final hearing and not as an advocate which perhaps a more junior and less expensive member of the firm could more than adequately do? To look over a document setting out proposed terms of settlement of the case to ensure you are not being ripped off or that it is watertight? They would be performing what they call an *unbundling* service dealing with a discrete aspect of the case and for most solicitors it's a novel concept. Until recently, the vast majority of solicitors were nervous about it for fear that they would be highly vulnerable to a complaint by the client – or worse still, a client claim for damages – because something went wrong after they had overlooked some feature of the case they could not have known about, as they were so limited in the case information available to them and the time only a modest fee would allow them to spend on it.

Then along came a decision of the Court of Appeal in November 2015 which should have put their minds at rest. There, a lady had reached a financial remedies agreement with her husband dealing with property and finance in the course of divorce proceedings. She consulted a solicitor to deal with the redrafting of the order which set out exactly what was to happen between the couple after the unsatisfactory paperwork which had so far been prepared was rejected by a judge. She wanted the solicitor to amend the order so that it was in a form which would meet with the judge's approval. This the solicitor duly did. Subsequently, the lady came to regret the order. She sued the solicitor for damages, claiming that the solicitor should have advised or warned her against going ahead with the order as she could have done better and that the solicitor had failed to do so. When the claim was thrown out the lady appealed. The Court of Appeal upheld the throw out. It ruled that the solicitor had not been under a duty to give the broader advice or warnings for which the lady argued. There would be very serious consequences for both the courts and litigants in person if solicitors felt unable to act on a discrete part of a cased for fear of being sued in this way. This sort of solicitor service was invaluable. It was vital though, that where a solicitor was consulted for an unbundling service, the limitations of what they would be doing were carefully set out in writing.

So I asked the Law Society what they had done about compiling and publishing a register of solicitors who are prepared to do unbundling work. Nothing. So I asked the Law Society what were their plans to compile and publish such a register. None. The solution is for you to ring round to local firms of solicitors and ask whether they will unbundle.

The receptionist may query with a "Do what?" or a "How very dare you!" so request to speak to a solicitor about the possibility of instructing them on a discrete litigation matter and hopefully the line won't go dead. The level of enthusiasm for unbundling will vary. Probably better to try a smaller or medium sized firm and steer away from West End firms who may be concerned that you will spoil their waiting room carpet with your muddy boots. Some firms may prefer to reserve their unbundling services for established clients. What I am confident about is that unless the profession as a whole does show more enthusiasm and gets its unbundling act together, it will find it has lost its litigation business to barristers doing direct access work and showing much more enterprise.

Chartered legal executives can call themselves lawyers these days. Indeed, they even qualify to be appointed as judges and can become partners in solicitors' firms. Dean Talbot was one of the first legal executives to be made a partner and that was with a firm of personal injury solicitors. He gave that up and has established a business devoted to giving legal advice and assistance behind the scenes but without turning up for you at court. You'll find him at smallclaimsassistance.co.uk where he does his stuff for bringing and defending claims for up to £10,000 which will almost invariably be dealt with as small claims (see chapter 25). Effectively, you can unbundle with him or allow him to take you through the whole case with the exception of representing you at court. He will advise you on the law and draft whatever documents the case requires. He advertises his fees on the website. He will not exceed them without prior agreement. Lots of his work is charged at an hourly rate of £70. As with all unbundling services, these fees cannot be claimed back from the loser should you win the case unless you can show they have behaved unreasonably (again, see chapter 25).

Free legal help

The giant hole left by the destruction of the civil legal scheme as we knew it has been substantially tackled by volunteers, often working through charities, and mainly comprising solicitors, barristers and others with experience in the law who are willing to give their time, for no payment, to litigants in person who are without the funds to pay for legal advice or representation or both. Here's a list of the main players in the field of free help. If one turns you down – and this may well be because they have so much on that they cannot accommodate you – then try another. It's inconceivable that any of them will slam the phone down. At the worst, they will suggest who else you might try. Some will just advise; some will advise and help with paperwork; and some will advise and help you with paperwork and go to court or a tribunal for the hearing of your case and represent you there. If a solicitor is giving you free help – working on a 'pro bono' basis they call it 'cos lawyers love to throw in a bit of Latin – then, if it is heavy and complicated, the case may need some input from a barrister as well or vice versa. In that situation, there is an organisation that puts pro bono solicitors in touch with pro bono barristers and pro bono barristers in touch with pro bono solicitors and that is **Pro Bono Connect**. In a suitable case, you can always remind your adviser of their existence (if they need reminding) but do not make direct contact with the organisation.

Citizens Advice

The good old CAB. They are brilliant and operate out of 3,500 locations. You can search for your nearest location on citizensadvice.org.uk or call 03444 111 444 for pointing in the right direction in England and 03444 77 20 20 in Wales.

RCJ Advice Bureau

This is affiliated to the CAB and dispenses free legal advice for unrepresented litigants from two venues: The Royal Court of Justice in London's Strand for those involved in a court case proceeding in the county court, High Court or Court of Appeal other than contested probate and Court of Protection cases (telephone for an appointment to 0203 475 4373 on weekdays between 2pm and 4pm to see if they can offer you an appointment and, before you do, it's useful to complete and email them their civil triage form you will find at rcjadvice.org,uk). And from the Central Family Court in London's Holborn for those wanting help with a family case – positively not an appeal! – such as divorce, financial remedies and children issues (telephone to see if they can offer you an appointment to 0203 745 8921 Monday to Friday and, before you do, it's useful to complete and email them their family triage form which you will again find at rcjadvice.org.uk). It matters not where the case is being heard: or where you live – Wigan will do – but for fact-to-face meetings, you would need to attend at the appropriate London venue. In some cases, free legal representation in court might be provided and the bureau may be able to help get you free representation by a barrister in court through **Advocate** (see below). The bureau's advice is designed for those who cannot afford to pay for it. You won't be subjected to a formal means test but the bureau will want to be satisfied that the resources are not there for you to pay out of your own pocket.

If you need help with debts – they won't pay them! – or managing your money as well as bankruptcy, the bureau has a wide range of advice services they can put your way. Contact their debt team at debt@rcjadvice.org.uk.

For victims of domestic abuse who seek protection from the perpetrator by way of a non-molestation order or order putting the perpetrator out of and keeping them away from the home – or both – you can access free loadsa-help with forms and procedure through their CourtNav scheme (go to injunction.courtnav.org.uk).

Where you qualify for legal aid, then the bureau can act for you in that case in the same way as a High Street solicitor. They are qualified to do that in family and housing cases and in relation to mediation in family cases.

This lot are very switched on. Put them in your top three organisations to plague for help.

Law Centres Network

This impressive organisation supports a national network of law centres which offers free face-to-face advice and some run a telephone advice line for those who cannot afford a lawyer. You can search for your nearest centre at lawcentres.org.uk. You will find a mapped list of them on this website. Each existing centre focuses on core areas of work which are normally firmly within social welfare law and targeting their help at the most disadvantaged. Put it this way: you are more likely to get help if you are an employee or tenant rather than an employer or landlord. However, some centres will cover other areas such as mental health, family law, education rights and young people and children's rights. Recent additions to the network are Lewisham law centre and Public Interest law centre (formerly allied to Camden Community Law Centre) specialising in public interest litigation.

Some law centres have set up subsidiaries which charge for representing those who are on low incomes but outside the legal aid scheme, to deal primarily with employment and immigration cases. Charges look to be on the modest side and the lawyers doing the legal work are likely to be highly specialised in the cases they deal with so you would be doing well to get them to take you on.

Civil legal advice

This is provided by the Legal Aid Agency (gov.uk/civil-legal-advice telephone number 0345 345 4345). It's nothing like the legal aid that used to be around. It's just legal advice and often by telephone, post or email for those who pass a means test and is limited to a mere five areas of law: debt, housing, education, discrimination and family. You can have a go at working out if you would qualify financially by going to gov.uk/check-legal-aid and, if you succeed, they may offer you a job in their accounts department. If you are telephoning to find out if you are financially eligible, you should have available recent payslips, bank statements, details of any savings and investments, details of any benefits, and mortgage statements and a current valuation of any property you own. You will be relieved to hear that you can ask them to call you back. Once it is established that you are likely to be financially eligible, you will be put through to an adviser immediately. Alternatively, you can have a face-to-face meeting with a legal adviser from a firm of solicitors or law centre who are contracted by the Legal Aid Agency to provide it in one of those five areas of law. Where do you get hold of one of these advisers? You can make a search on find-legal-advice.justice.gov.uk which I have just tested. It works. Or phone the number above.

Advocate

You've heard of the Bar Pro Bono Unit? That's what **Advocate** used to be called. We have briefly met them under **RCJ Advice Bureau** above. Free of charge, they can provide a barrister to give you legal advice, draft documents, help with mediation and represent you for a specific part of your case which could be the main hearing, at any court or tribunal. A chartered legal executive may support the assigned barrister. Where your needs would involve more than three days of the barrister's time (including the hearing) their official line is that they will have to decline help. But never say never. In deciding whether a barrister can take you on, consideration will be given to the legal merits of your case, your financial circumstances and the time the barrister would be occupied on the case. Find out more at weareadvocate.org.uk (telephone 020 7092 3960). You will make yourself very unpopular if you apply to Advocate direct. They will only allow a litigant to be referred by an advice agency such as RCJ Advice Bureau, a solicitor or your member of parliament and this should be done at least three weeks before help is needed. The busiest areas of referrals for them are family, housing and employment cases.

Advocate gets my five-star award. The maximum available, which had so far only gone to the late Lord Denning and some anti-bacterial wipes I bought on Amazon. There are some really class acts who give their time without payment through **Advocate**. I have seen many of them doing their stuff while judging cases.

LawWorks

Sponsored by the Law Society, **LawWorks** is the solicitors' answer to the barristers' **Advocate** organisation. Well, sort of. It supports but does not run a nationwide network of free legal advice clinics. Some are hosted or based at law centres and around one half at universities with a law faculty or law school where advising students will be supervised by legally qualified professionals. They offer face-to-face help (subject to Covid-19) or remotely, by drop in or by appointment (usually 20 to 60 minutes' worth) to those who do not qualify for legal aid and cannot afford to pay for a lawyer. You can search for the nearest clinic for the particular area of advice you are interested in by going to lawworks.org.uk/legal-advice-individuals/find-legal-adviceclinic-near-you. Sometimes, the clinic may be able to provide follow up help and, occasionally, some representation but for more in-depth assistance, you should usually try and go after what a law centre can offer.

LawWorks additionally involves itself with a series of projects which could lead to you obtaining free advice and representation, unobtainable elsewhere but for which you would have to be referred by one of their referral organisations. Important to ever so respectfully remind the organisation of the project you are after. The tribunal representation project, for which the referral organisations include CABs, aims to make a solicitor available to represent you, if you are very vulnerable, at benefit appeal tribunals (and they were achieving a success rate of 95% when I last checked which would beat Marshall Hall at the height of his powers). An unpaid wages project is for those, often in low paid and insecure employment, owed wages or other work-related payments and help may include tribunal representation by a solicitor. Again, the referral organisations include CABs. A project run with the charity Together for Short Lives will provide legal help to parents and carers of children with life-limiting conditions over issues such as housing, including unsuitability for the child's mobility or needs. You can reach the charity's helpline on 0808 8088 100 and through children's hospices.

Free Representation Unit

The unit provides free representation to individuals making claims in social security and employment tribunals and for criminal injuries compensation for the full hearing itself and any pre-hearing settlement negotiations where such a tribunal case has been started. It cannot offer advice about making a claim. The unit has offices in London and Nottingham and so is able to attend any tribunal which is within sensible travelling distance of those cities. It also handles cases in the upper tribunal and the employment appeal tribunal from wherever they originate provided the hearing is to take place in London. Who would be representing you? Very posh counsel in a double-breasted suit (who we shall meet a little later)? Not at all. Probably a law student looking for advocacy experience but otherwise a volunteer who has plenty of knowledge in the field concerned and overseen by qualified professionals. Do not scoff. They will know their stuff, have done their homework and be dead keen to win. If you cannot afford to pay for a fully qualified lawyer to represent you then you should be blessed to be represented by someone from the unit.

In certain cases, you can ask the unit to help you directly. That's when you are claiming in an employment tribunal case which is set to last no longer than two days and subject to the travelling restriction mentioned. Then, take a look at thefru.org.uk and contact 020 7611 9555. Otherwise, you have to be referred to the agency by one of its accredited referring agencies which include a host of CABs. There's a list of the agencies who can refer on the unit's website.

Shelter

In England, this charity offers free advice on housing rights and disputes and homelessness and without delving into your financial circumstances. It does so by an urgent helpline (0808 800 4444) weekdays and 9am to 5pm on weekends. Through that, they might, for example, negotiate with the local authority to provide temporary accommodation if your family is homeless. It has a chatline at england.shelter.org.uk/get_help/webchat and there's a plethora of written material with videos and audios on its website for anyone who doesn't have a clue what I am prattling on about in relation to housing issues. If that's not enough, it can give telephone and, subject to Covid-19, face-to-face advice and help with court cases at centres based in London (Islington, Hackney and Newham), Birmingham, Bournemouth, Blackburn, Bristol, Liverpool, Manchester, Newcastle, Norwich, Oxford, Plymouth, Sheffield and Slough. When you can obtain legal aid for more extensive work or even court representation in housing cases then Shelter can take it on. This includes appeals against homelessness reviews and certain homelessness judicial review cases. There's a similar but less expansive service offered for Wales (see sheltercymru.org.uk). These guys know what they are on about: they're real specialists. If it's housing, I would try them first.

Tax Aid/Tax Help for Older People

For free tax advice **Tax Aid** will provide it so long as you are either under 60 or self-employed, on a low income and have been unable to resolve your problem with the taxman. Go to taxaid.org.uk (0345 120 3779 Monday to Friday 10am until 4pm) and see chapter 56. If you are 60 or over and not self-employed, on a low income and, again, have been unable to resolve your problem with the taxman, **Tax Help for Older People** will be at your service, free of charge. Go to taxvol.org.uk (01308 488066 Monday to Friday 9am until 5pm if urgent).

Insurance

Perhaps you have a legal expenses policy. Then you are laughing provided you didn't take it out after the dispute for which you want help actually arose. It could be that some other policy you hold, like one for household contents, includes cover for legal advice and representation. Go through your drawers. You may be pleasantly surprised.

IP Pro Bono

IP = intellectual property which has nothing to do with hiring a brain though, on second thoughts, perhaps it does. If you have an intellectual property dispute – for example, *Marks & Spencer* are trying to stop your corner shop grocery business trading as *Marks & Spencer (Bracklesham Bay)* or you are caught up in litigation over copyright or a patent – and cannot afford to pay professional fees, IP Pro Bono, managed by the Chartered Institute of Patent Lawyers, may be able to help you. There is an important proviso. Generally, they cannot help an individual with an annual income above £45,000 or a business with an annual turnover above £100,000. If you are accepted, a case officer may be able to suggest ways forward so that you understand or better understand your situation and options. If appropriate, they will endeavour to find you a legal firm or IP professional who can assist you to run your case or some part of it but you cannot expect them to take on the entire headache from beginning to end. Since its launch in late 2017, it has had nearly 600 applications for help. Go to ipprobono.org.uk

Age UK

This charity runs a free national 'advice' line at 0800 678 1602 which is open every day of the year from 8am until 7pm and so an opportunity there to ruin someone's Christmas lunch. However, you won't get legal advice but what they describe to me as "help to identify what the potential issues are and provide signposting to legal advice and representation." That amounts to helping you classify the legal area into which your problem falls and to guide you where to go from there in terms of obtaining free legal advice and, if necessary, representation in the dispute and possibly in court. Potentially, a useful service for anyone struggling to know what legal peg on which to hang their problem and in which direction to go from there and you don't have to be an antique to use it. They'll still help you if you are 19 and go clubbing. **Age Co** is not to be confused with them and is the brand name for their commercial arm. It arranges legal advice and representation through solicitors called Irwin Mitchell for which you would have to pay. Profits made by **Age Co** are gifted to Charity Age UK to support their charitable work.

Quick(ish) advice from solicitors

Many solicitors offer a free advice session by appointment for a limited time, typically half an hour, and some do the same thing for a modest fixed fee. This is aimed at indicating whether or not you have a sound case to bring or resist and with a view to – or so they would pray – instructing them to take the case on for a fee or on legal aid, if you would qualify. A sprat to catch a mackerel but no bad thing. I suppose you could go to half a dozen firms for a free ride and if they all told you roughly the same thing you could be fairly confident of the case's likely outcome. If such a service is available then it will probably be advertised in the *Pet Fancier's Weekly*, in the afternoon on *Talking Pictures* or in the phone directory.

Quality Solicitors (qualitysolicitors.com) is a group of over 100 solicitors' firms in England and Wales which runs a 45 minute scheme, ideal for small claims, under which you can obtain 45 minutes of legal help – so talk very fast – either face-to-face or by phone. Paperwork will be pre-read or read at the session and time spent on that will come off the 45 minutes. Assistance can be given within the session on writing a letter or completing a form.

An app linking would be clients to solicitors has recently been launched by Advantage Consulting. You can download the app at lawyer365.co.uk and use it on mobiles and laptops. If you hire a solicitor for your case – plenty of litigious fields are covered – then you will have to pay their fees and they are for you to negotiate. The carrot is that you will get up to 30 minutes' free advice when first put in touch with a suitable solicitor – you can book the session if you wish – and won't have your guts ripped out if you say "thank you and goodbye".

Advice now is a new service established by **Law for Life** (Advicenow. Org/Lawforlife) in conjunction with **Resolution** whose members are family lawyers and good people. The service is aimed at providing face to face or remote legal help at the most important points of a family case for a reduced fixed fee which will usually be £120 inc vat and cover up to one hour with the lawyer and half an hour for their preparation time. You start by downloading or buying a print copy of one of their guides which are about financial or children disputes so that you understand the process (or you might read *Breaking Law* which they tell me isn't bad) and then you apply for an appointment. You will be sent a form to complete which will solicit information on what the advising solicitor needs to know about your case and the solicitor will have read it before the appointment. A useful way of dipping in and out for help along the way where you can afford it.

We've already met the solicitors' professional body, the Law Society (see **LawWorks** above). The Law Society does not run a register of pro bono advice or representation schemes run by individual firms of solicitors and local law societies. Instead it refers any enquiries about free legal help to **LawWorks** or the **Law Centres Network** (see above) so you might as well go to them direct and cut out the Law Society. But the Law Society does run a register of solicitors who may be good, bad or indifferent although they have all passed their exams and not been struck off (or, if struck off, they have been reinstated for good behaviour). For this array of talent, go to Find a Solicitor at lawsociety.org.uk.

Free legal help in possession cases

If you are being taken to court by your landlord or mortgage lender or by a property owner where you are alleged to be a trespasser because you have squatted or never had a tenancy and have outstayed your welcome, you will find independent free legal advice from a duty expert available to you at the court, whatever your financial circumstances. It matters not that you have not sought that advice from any of the above sources previously, although it would have been wise to have done so.

A trial mediation scheme for possession cases was introduced in February 2021. It's free for both landlords and tenants but each side must agree to play. The trained mediator will be independent of the court. If you are the tenant, you should raise your willingness to try this mediation with the duty adviser on the review (see chapter 67). If you are the landlord and willing, you should broach the subject with any lawyer acting for you and with the tenant on or before the review. The Society of Mediators will make contact to arrange the mediation within two days of the review. The case will not be heard while mediation takes place.

Mckenzie – and other – Friends

If you don't have the benefit of a lawyer in court, you will almost always be allowed by the judge to have help from a *McKenzie Friend*. You may be forgiven for thinking that this is what they are called so that litigants in person won't have a clue what they are. Actually, it's just the law being daft with titles. *Litigant's Assistant* (even *Litigant's Pal*) would be better – or *Court Supporter* as a consultation paper from the judiciary suggested in February 2016. *McKenzie* was the surname of a divorce petitioner in a 1970 case who had been denied proper help from a friend in court. The denial was successfully challenged and the Court of Appeal ruled that help to a litigant in person from somebody they take along to court should in the ordinary course of events always be available. So now we are stuck with the unfortunate title.

Holding your pencil

Certainly the *McKenzie Friend* can do this: even a biro or a quill pen, if you have ink at the ready. They can sit by your side in court and provide you with moral support, take notes, help with case papers (find exhibit 1278b when all your documents have crashed to the floor) and quietly give you advice on any aspect of the conduct of the case, by a discreet whisper into the lughole. What they cannot do is to speak to the judge on your behalf, suggest how you answer questions when you are giving evidence or cross-examine witnesses which means, in short, that they cannot perform the role of a lawyer. That's the theory and that's more often than not the practice. However, with lawyer help being so hard for so many to come by, many judges will now allow the *McKenzie Friend* to do more. If they appear to have a better grasp of the case and the procedure than you – especially, if they have some legal or semi-legal or other professional knowledge or background – the judge may well allow them to speak on your behalf though never, never, never, ever give evidence on your behalf. According to official guidance, examples of the type of circumstances in which the *McKenzie Friend* might be permitted to turn lawyer for the day are where the *McKenzie Friend* is a close relative of the litigant or where health problems prevent the litigant from addressing the court and they cannot afford to pay a lawyer, or the litigant is inarticulate and mere prompting by the *McKenzie Friend* could prolong the proceedings. After all, what's the point in insisting they whisper into your lughole so that you can then repeat to the judge exactly what you think you have heard although it is a complete corruption of what was actually said.

> McKenzie Friend whispering into litigant's left ear: "Tell the judge that in your submission the evidence of the witness was a tissue of untruths."

> Litigant whispering into McKenzie Friend's right ear: "Don't fudge what?"
>
> McKenzie Friend whispering a little louder into litigant's left ear: "Tell the bloody judge that in your submission the witness told a pack of porkie pies."
>
> Litigant to Judge: "Your Honour, my mission was to do up my flies."

In a July 2020 case, a High Court judge allowed a *McKenzie Friend* to go further than usual and speak for a claimant – though not give the claimant's evidence for him! – where the claimant's English was very limited and he only had a partial appreciation of what he had to say. The claimant was the *McKenzie Friend's* next door neighbour and had asked for help on a neighbourhood app. The *McKenzie Friend* was not being paid.

Your *McKenzie Friend* can be anyone you trust to give you the support and assistance you may need. You can take a family member, friend or that baker or candlestick maker so long as they are willing to accompany you. Be discriminating about who you choose. If they get up the noses of people who know them they will probably get up the nose of the judge. And be careful about using someone from a pressure group who may well have their own agenda and fail to help you in the objective way that is good for you. Research by the Legal Services Consumer Panel shows that a large proportion of *McKenzie Friends* got into the job following negative experience of courts during divorce and child contact cases.

Or you can hire a *McKenzie Friend*. There are loads and loads of paid *McKenzie Friends* out there and on the internet you will find plenty of plugs by them or agencies they work through. Some are brilliant and some are dreadful. Steer clear of former solicitors and barristers who have been thrown out by their professional body for some misdeed, not because they won't be up to the job but because the judge may well be disapproving of them. Steer clear too of those who have no background in the area covered by the case. If you are involved in a dispute about the welfare of a child, for example, an ex-senior Cafcass or social services welfare officer would be handy but not an ex-electrician. Don't engage someone simply because they sound very sympathetic to your case – if they are wildly sympathetic it could be for the reason that they are desperate for your cash. Ask for a copy of their CV.

What do the paid *McKenzie Friends* charge? You can expect to pay anything within the range of £35 to £60 an hour or £100 to £400 for a full day with travelling expenses being added on. If you win, the court cannot order the loser to reimburse these charges to you. However, you might get the charges back from the loser if the court has taken the ultimate step of allowing the *McKenzie Friend* to advocate for you in court as if they were a qualified lawyer.

But for how much longer will *McKenzie Friends* be able to charge for their services? A consultation paper in February 2016 nudged towards putting a stop to it by banning them from helping in court where they are directly or indirectly being paid. There's no sign of a ban being imposed. For the time being at least, *McKenzie Friends* can certainly carry on charging.

Pros and cons

An unpaid, sane, respectful and grudgeless *McKenzie Friend*? Go for it every time if you can't get a lawyer. An unpaid, sane, respectful and grudge bearing *McKenzie Friend*? May be better than nothing. A paid *McKenzie Friend*? They are more likely to be allowed by the judge to do more for you in court than an unpaid one. But they are not answerable to a regulatory body like a qualified lawyer and they may not be covered by insurance for any claim you wanted to make against them for negligent advice. Generally, you are better off in court with a qualified lawyer than a *McKenzie Friend*. Compare what you are quoted by a solicitor or barrister for representation in court with what a *McKenzie Friend* would cost you. Sometimes, there may be little or nothing in it. Alternatively, you may be able to obtain free help in court from a support agency (see below).

Permission to use

You will need to ask the court for permission to use a *McKenzie Friend*. You should do this as soon as possible. Preferably, write to the court before the case and ask for the permission with details of the person's name and connection with you, although judges will normally allow permission to be sought on the day at the beginning of the case. Permission would almost certainly be refused if the judge thought that the *McKenzie Friend* was using you as a puppet or was giving assistance for some improper purpose.

My paid for McKenzie Friend cocked it up

Oh dear. Occasionally they do. The main risk is that they imagine they are cleverer than they actually are or, more likely, lead you to believe they have experience and skills which they do not actually possess. Can you make a claim against a *McKenzie Friend* if they have not done their job properly and you have lost out financially as a result? Probably yes. But, for heaven's sake, don't bring in a *McKenzie Friend* to help you with the case! In a 2019 High Court case called *Wright v Troy Lucas (a firm) and George Rutz* the Essex defendants sought to portray themselves as legal professionals which they were not. The claimant Paul Wright hired them to help with his clinical negligence case against Basildon & Thurrock Hospital NHS Trust. That arose from an operation which left him permanently disabled after three plastic bags were left inside him. With the purported help of our Essex non-professionals, which went well beyond what a *McKenzie Friend* would normally do, the case was being struck out bit-by-bit with costs orders being made against Mr Wright. He got rid of the Essex boys and, with his claim by then damaged beyond repair, he was forced to accept the NHS Trust's offer of £20,000 which did not do him much good as he had to pay their legal costs at around £74,000. In the subsequent 2019 High Court case, Mr Rutz was ordered to pay Mr Wright £263,759 which was to reflect how he would have ended up if he had been properly advised in the first case and he got his costs as well. The rationale of the decision was that if someone represents themselves to have the skills and experience of a legal professional then the standard of care they should apply to a case should be that of a legal professional. And that, I suggest, is the yardstick by which your *McKenzie Friend* should be judged if you assert that they messed up and were in breach of their agreement with you and negligent.

No McKenzie Friend

It may not be legal advice you want or it may be you want it but cannot get hold of it when you need it. In this situation, support from someone who knows the system could be your salvation. Over then to **Support Through Court** which used to be called the Personal Support Unit (see supportthroughcourt.org). It is a charity out to aid those otherwise going it alone in the court and operates out of several court centres in England and also in Cardiff. On-site locations include the Royal Courts of Justice in London's Strand, London's Central Family Court, West London family court and court centres at Barnet, Birmingham, Bristol, Chelmsford, Exeter, Leeds, Liverpool, Manchester, Newcastle, Nottingham, Sheffield and Wandsworth. Volunteers provide practical and emotional support to those involved in civil and family cases. They do not offer legal advice and will not speak for you at the hearing but can be present there with you and, if a hearing is adjourned, support next time can be made available. Where more is required they will signpost you to other organisations. They will also help you fill in court forms and, as they put it, help you to organise your papers and thoughts and think about your next steps. Where a court hearing is to be conducted remotely by video or telephone, it should be possible for a **Support Through Court** volunteer to join the hearing and talk things through with you afterwards.

Chapter 8

The Litigant In Person Blame Game

"I'm not a bloody lawyer"

The official line is that you get no special treatment from the courts for failing to comply with procedural rules just because you were a litigant in person and had no access to legal help. That official line has been endorsed by a majority ruling of the Supreme Court. It's a hard line but still litigants in person, who didn't do what the court order told them to do or the Civil Procedure Rules 1998 commanded them to do, can be heard every second of the court day using the fact that they are going it alone as an excuse. "I've never done this before." "I didn't understand that was necessary." "I'm not good with words."

And who can blame them? But in reality and in the right circumstances, most judges will take non-legal representation into account if this factor is approached in the right way.

Where you flouted a direction in a court order rather than in the Civil Procedure Rules, you will be in difficulty. The judge is likely to give short shrift to the argument that "But I never read it" because you should have read it. However, if you were misled by the wording of the order, make that point to the court. It may well not have made sense. It may well have been typed out by a court clerk and contain serious errors: in particular, it may omit to give a deadline for compliance with the direction in question or state what would happen in the event of non-compliance. The other error that can creep into an order and which can be fatal to its enforceability is this. An order will often be made without a request by any party but of the court's own initiative or made following a request or application but on paper, without a hearing. Where that happens, a party who dislikes the order can apply to the court to halt it, set it aside or change it in some respect. The application should usually be made within seven days of the party being treated as having received the order (which, more often than not, will be two days after the court has posted it to them). In this situation, the order should have contained a statement of the right of anyone affected by it to make an application. "Judge, although I'm thick and know nuffink about the law, a bloke in a pub told me that this order doesn't comply with rules 3.3 or 23.9 of the Civil Procedure Rules 1998 and so you can't do me for it, with respect."

And there are a couple of crumbs coming out of that Supreme Court case I mentioned that might possibly help when the judge tells you that the law expects the same standard of conduct in the case from a litigant in person as it does from the lawyer. It was suggested in the Supreme Court that the fact the errant litigant had had no lawyer might add weight to some more directly relevant factor (make what you can of that). And though it was stated that it was reasonable to expect a litigant in person to familiarise themselves with the applicable procedural rules, there would be an exception where those rules and any impacting practice direction were inaccessible or obscure.

Part 3

IS THE REST OF THIS BOOK WORTH READING?

Chapter 9
Alternatives To Court And Preserving My Premium Bonds

It's far too early to sell this book on eBay. Anyway, there could be a glut of them on offer for a while. Read on and discover a myriad of legal rights – many will surprise you – which are there for your use and protection. Allow me to show you how to achieve a good result in civil and family court cases and that may sometimes mean losing well. And better still, see how you can avoid having to sue or being sued in the first place.

It's unlikely that any of us will get through life without some involvement in a legal dispute. I've had my own fair share. Hopefully, you will feel well equipped to cope with any that come your way by the time you invite any eBay bids. What I ask of you is this. Don't sue me because you reckon you followed one of my tips and lost out as a result. That's because I can't afford to pay you out and would have to argue that, in law and just like the radio racing tipster and weather forecaster who get it wrong, I don't owe you a duty of care and so am not liable for any mistake that has caused you loss. But most important of all, legal rules and principles can easily be dislodged by some peculiarity in an individual situation. For that reason, I implore you where you possibly can to check out with a lawyer or advice agency whether there is a peculiarity in your situation before embarking on a legal course of action that could go wrong and cause you both anguish and expense. That's the end of my disclaimer.

Court proceedings should be the last resort. There are other ways of settling a dispute apart from thumping the opposition or going to court and they should be explored. Constructive negotiation is the most obvious. Try it and occasionally it will succeed. How might it go with BT, for example? I generally favour a written exchange when complaining to a business so that there is a record available of what has been said and, although an online chat, if available, can be fun where you have a few hours to waste, it may not provide you with sufficient opportunity to give a considered response to what is being pushed down your throat. All of this makes an email exchange the winner. That's certainly the view I took with BT and my two complaints to them show that tenacity can pay off.

BT botched its performance of a contract to provide me with wifi when it came to delivery of the kit; sought to insist that I had to talk to them at the second stage of its complaints procedure; and then, when a complaints manager came into the picture, acted with courtesy and efficiency. The moral is keep at BT under its complaints procedure until you obtain an offer you are prepared to accept and if you prefer to follow the procedure through the medium of correspondence, insist that you have a right to do so. Incidentally, the kit is brilliant....so far.

Me 6 July 2017

Thank you for your message. I note what you say.

This transaction has been riddled with errors by BT including-

1 Activating too early and contrary to instructions.

2 Delivering kit too early and contrary to instructions.

3 Delivering kit to wrong address and contrary to instructions.

4 Informing me that I would not be charged from 16/06/17 and subsequently informing me that I would be charged – and now informing me that I will not be charged!

5 Sending me a series of emails/letters requiring me to return the first delivered kit notwithstanding that it was misdelivered and in any event left with a neighbour (where it remains as they are currently away).

All this nonsense (and more) has caused me considerable aggravation and wastage of time. I have spent over two hours trying to sort it out. This is time I can ill afford to lose and I expect you to compensate me for it. What is your offer?

In relation to the misdelivered kit, you will need to make your own arrangements to collect from that address. I am not available to sort it out and I do not expect my neighbour to be troubled.

I await hearing from you.

BT 6 July 2017

Thanks for getting back to me............I am sorry for the aggravation and time wasted. As a goodwill gesture from our end – I would like to firstly offer to refund your account £9.99 (delivery charge for hub), as a gesture of goodwill for the above. We will make arrangements to collect any surplus kit with that address. Please get back in touch when you can – to inform me if the above would be acceptable.

Regards,

Scott

Me 6 July 2017

Thank you. I note the gesture but I hardly think that £9.99 value adequately compensates me for the aggravation that BT has caused me and the two hours plus it has taken of my life, spent on online exchanges, waiting and phone calls, etc. If I was a litigant in person on a small claim against BT (and I might yet be!), I would be entitled to £19 per hour for time spend on litigation alone. Please reconsider.

BT 6 July 2017

Dear Mr. Gold,

Thanks again for your reply.

I fully took what you have said on board and consulted with my manager to find a resolution.

Our final offer for compensation on this matter would be to credit your account with £19 – in relation to what you believe you should be entitled to.

Regards

Scott

Me 6 July 2017

Thank you. What regard have you had to my time consumed on–

[a] waiting to be spoken to

[b] abortive calls

[c] reading and, where necessary, rereading written communications passing between us and

[d] conferring with my neighbour by text and email in respect of your misdelivery of kit and subsequently their non-availability to allow collection?

What regard have you had to the aggravation you have caused me by making a mistake at every conceivable step of this wretched transaction? You appear to have allowed circa £5 which any reasonable business or person would regard as insulting, as I do.

When I said I had spent two hours plus, I meant it. I have no interest in inflating my claim. I mentioned £19 ph previously (which you appear to have adopted as a basis for your second offer) to indicate what a county court judge would award for time spent by way of costs. I was not limiting my claim to £19 ph. I am a professional person and consider my time is worth more than £19 ph.

In any event, you refer to crediting my account. If you are paying me any compensation then it should be paid "in cash". Why credit my account?

You will have gathered that I reject your second offer. Your manager should email me with his reconsideration and details of the next stage thereafter in your internal complaints procedure.

BT 6 July 2017

Dear Mr. Gold,

Thank you for your reply,

To confirm – We could credit the amount I am offering to your bank account, if requested.

I am still more than happy to apply this with your confirmation that this would be acceptable – however, as you have confirmed below, you wish to start the next stage of the escalation process.

This will require a conversation by call between yourself and my manager. We will not be able to continue the process by email.

Please reply to this email with a date and time that suits you best or give me a call on my direct number below.

As above, we cannot continue the process requested by yourself by email and this will be last correspondence until you get in touch by phone.

If we do not hear from yourselves within 28 days, we will close this case down and you will receive confirmation of this.

Regards,

Scott

Me 6 July 2016

Thank you for your message. I see that you ignore most of my comments.

I note your second paragraph and also that your manager appears to have an invincible fear of expressing himself in writing. Please send me a copy of the conditions of what you describe as an escalation process (which I take to mean an internal complaints procedure) so that I can see the basis on which I am told I must speak to you.

BT 8 July 2017

Dear Mr Gold

Scott has passed your complaint to me in line with our escalation process.

Firstly please accept my sincere apologies for both the inconvenience undoubtedly caused and the time you've had to spend dealing with the errors that has been caused. I am also sorry that Scott told you that we would not deal with your complaint by email. Although it can sometimes be quicker to resolve complaints over the telephone, it should, of course be your choice.

I've reviewed your complaint and can see the problems you've encountered and the time you've had to spend on what should have been a very straightforward process. I can assure you that I have arranged any necessary feedback and coaching for advisors when things have gone wrong.

I will arrange for the hub delivery charge to be removed as it was delivered to the wrong address. We can't begin to put a price on your time but as a gesture of goodwill I would be happy to pay £25 into your bank account by way of an apology

I hope you'll accept my offer and we can draw the matter to an amicable conclusion.

Regards

JK

Team Leader Customer Connections

BT Consumer | Customer Care

Me 8 July 2017

Dear JK

Thank you for your message. I find its terms to be courteous and reasonable and will accept your improved offer. Details of my bank account to be credited are set out below.

I do not know whether Scott's last message was based on a template. If it was, I think you should review it. I found its penultimate and final paragraphs to be aggressive and totally unreasonable. I am not easily intimidated but I believe many customers would be if communicated with in this way. It may be good to talk. It's also good to email!

[account details]

BT 10 July 09:24

Dear Mr Gold

Thank you for your prompt reply.

I've arranged the refund of £25.00 to your bank account today, you'll see it within 3 – 5 working days.

I understand your comments regarding previous emails and can assure you that has been dealt with. I'm pleased we've been able to resolve the matter amicably.

Regards

JK

Team Leader Customer Connections

BT Consumer | Customer Care

Me 14 July 11:2017

To: BT

Dear JK

Thank you.

I have today received an empty blue plastic envelope from BT – no covering letter or note – which I assume was intended to accommodate the return of the misdelivered kit. It was sent to the correct address but, as you know, the misdelivered kit was left with my neighbour at the wrong address where it remains and I made it clear that I expected you to collect from the neighbour and not to put my neighbour to any inconvenience and me to further embarrassment. So will BT get its act together and strain itself to arrange to collect from the neighbour and not expect a third party to be put to trouble through BT's incompetence? Or is that expecting too much?

BT 17 July 2017

Dear Mr Gold

Thank you for your email, I'm sorry you've had to come back to me.

The only option that we have to collect the hub from your neighbours would be by courier. I am conscious that as we can only specify a day for this and not a time it may put them to further convenience. I will ask that this hub is not chased any further and suggest that either yourself or your neighbours keep the hub as a "spare" for future use.

Regards

JK

Team Leader Customer Connections

BT Consumer | Customer Care

And then there was the case of the fault on my landline. Here's a taster.

BT 27 February 2018

I have reviewed your complaint about the compensation for the fault you have had on your line, I am sincerely sorry for any inconvenience that this fault may have caused you and can understand that it is difficult to be without a working line. I can understand from your previous conversation with my colleagues that you are not happy with the compensation offered to you which was £16.40. The refund is completely based on our Customer Service Guarantee Scheme (CSGS) policy The Customer Service Guarantee Scheme is BT compensation policy for when we are late providing or repairing service.

Me 08/04/18

Having persistently informed you that I was not prepared to discuss my complaint orally but only in writing (through email), what happened yesterday? You telephoned me to discuss the complaint!!! I reiterated my requirement whereupon your representative (whose identity is unknown to me) rapidly terminated the call. Please escalate my complaint under your Customer Review System from which I hope I will get more sense than I have so far witnessed.

BT 22 April 2018

... As a resolution I will offer the credit of £16.40 plus a £20 goodwill payment for the delay in getting a written response.

Me 26 April 2018

... I will accept £20 for delay in getting a written response and as to the £16.40 offered, I will not accept this because I do not understand the basis of the calculation. ...I do not wish to discuss by telephone. I think I have made this clear more than once, have I not?

BT 26 April 2018

I will offer the below as final resolution. £16.42 for the duration of the complaint and £25 in total goodwill as an apology.

Me 26 April 2018

I consider the offer to be too low, given that you had previously proposed a goodwill payment attributable to the delay of £20. But with a view to concluding the matter, I would be prepared – without prejudice – to split the difference and settle for £32.50 plus £19.62, namely £52.12.

BT 1 May 2018

The credits have been applied to your BT account. Thanks for giving me the opportunity to resolve this complaint .

> *Me 1 May 2018*
>
> *If the account credit is for £52.12 then I can confirm that you may close my complaint. May I wish your phone line the best of health and extend to you my earnest hope that you will never have to complain to BT.*

Out of court arbitration is a major alternative to court proceedings. An arbitrator decides who is in the right and who is in the wrong and how much the winner gets. There are two points to be alive to here. Most consumer arbitration schemes provide for a decision based on paperwork so you don't get to tear the other side to pieces in the witness box. They also bind you to the arbitrator's decision even if you think it stinks so you can't follow up the dispute with proceedings unless the arbitrator has had a seriously bad day. The ombudsman schemes are different in that you can have a second bite of the cherry with court proceedings when the decision goes against you and you will sometimes achieve compensation which a strict legal interpretation of the facts by a judge in court would have to deny you. You'll find an ombudsman for almost everything if you go to ombudsmanassociation.org. This is the home of the Ombudsman Association with whom ombudsmen can share jokes though thankfully I have not had to listen to any of them. There's a Furniture Ombudsman who must have a few settee stories to tell, an Adjudicator for complaints against the taxman and the valuation office, a Housing Ombudsman for complaints against social landlords like councils and housing associations, a Parliamentary and Health Service Ombudsman for complaints against UK government departments and the NHS in England and many, many more. Alas, they don't seem to have invented a Toilet Brush Ombudsman as yet. Or any ombudsman whose title begins with a 'z'. The tragedy is that you can't complain to the Ombudsman Association against one of its ombudsman members. You would have to go to the High Court for judicial review for that – and it has been successfully done against the Financial Ombudsman Service (see below) – although you would need a lot of stamina and anger to go along that path.

You would want me to give some prominence to the Legal Ombudsman scheme (legalombudsman.org.uk). Ironically, one of its ombudsmen who in this instance was an ombudswoman – and why not? – has recently succeeded in an employment tribunal claim against the organisation for indirect discrimination arising out of flexible working arrangements for staff. But what the scheme prefers to do is resolve around 7,000 complaints a year against what it calls legal service providers and that catches not just solicitors (its most popular group for consumer bashing), barristers and legal executives but licensed conveyancers, cost lawyers, notaries and companies which may do some law work for clients such as accountants. Failure to give advice when it should be given or poor advice is the biggest ground of complaint. Before going to the scheme you must try and resolve your complaint with the provider direct. If they come back within eight weeks and tell you to get stuffed and that's final or they ignore you for eight weeks you can then ask the scheme to help you but not before. Latest figures show that the scheme is resolving over 7,000 complaints a year but taking too long to do so. If you make contact, don't mention indirect discrimination.

I gave the Financial Ombudsman Service a go a couple of years back. It makes decisions on the basis of the law and what they consider to be fair and reasonable in the circumstances. My complaint was that *Santander UK plc* failed to notify me that a bond I held with them was about to mature. If I had had any sense, I would have jotted down the maturity date and asked for withdrawal before it arrived but I was too busy judging the negligence of others. They proceeded to reinvest the money in another bond for 12 months paying puerile interest, which their terms and conditions entitled them to do when they had not received instructions to the contrary. Had I been alerted to the maturity, I would have withdrawn and reinvested elsewhere at a superior rate. The Ombudsman recommended that *Santander* should compensate me for my loss. *Santander* refused to accept the recommendation, claiming that I had been given advance notice of maturity. The Ombudsman had to make a ruling. She decided in my favour. She was not persuaded that there was sufficient evidence *Santander* had given me notice of maturity. Whatever the terms and conditions said, that notice should have been given. I was awarded my loss of interest and £100 for distress and inconvenience (see *"The Financial Ombudsman be praised"* on page 123). *Santander* proceeded to reinvest my money for a second 12 months just 13 days after the ruling and without prior notice to me. Then they failed to pay the full award on time and I secured an additional award – around £25 – to take account of the delay. In a court of law, the result on the basis of the terms and conditions could well have been quite different. The interesting postscript is that I later received a letter from *Santander* about someone else's account and that someone else just happened to be called Stephen Gold. I wonder at night whether they had sent him my notice of maturity.

With that first result, I decided to remain a customer of the Financial Ombudsman Service to whom I have more recently returned with three complaints in less than eight weeks.

Bupa

My *Bupa* policy was due for renewal. They failed to send me renewal documentation but proceeded to take the renewal premium by debiting my credit card account. The first I knew of this was when I looked at my credit card statement. Following *Bupa*'s failure to respond to three emails about the premium taken, I did give renewal instructions but at a lower premium and with one month's free cover. *Bupa* then failed to refund the £782.03 difference between the premium taken and the lower negotiated premium.

On internal complaint, *Bupa* accepted it was wrong to have taken the premium without the renewal notice. It could not find my emails. They informed the Ombudsman that the email recipient had 'now left the business' and so the messages would never be picked up as they were going to a personal email address. *Bupa* does not like email and generally insists on contact by telephone.

The investigator's recommendation was £200 compensation together with the return of the £782.03 which both *Bupa* and myself accepted.

Paragon Bank

I applied to *Paragon* for a cash ISA and they asked me for evidence of identity. Fair enough. I could have been anyone like a judge or the author of *Breaking Law* and you have to watch folk like that. I sent it promptly and they acknowledged it and then said they had not received it. I sent fresh identification which crossed with them returning the original identification they had not received! The account was subsequently opened but later than it should have been which resulted in a loss of interest to me while the intended investment money was lying idle in my current account.

On internal complaint, *Paragon* rejected it and contended that it had been incorrect in telling me that it had received the original identification. No compensation was offered.

An Ombudsman adjudicator upheld my complaint and concluded *Paragon* had not acted fairly. She recommended compensation of £100 to reflect loss of interest, distress and inconvenience. We both accepted the recommendation.

Marks & Spencer Financial Services

My dispute this time involves a widespread practice among ISA providers when the investment is approaching maturity. It is to invite completion of an options form requesting reinvestment with that institution or withdrawal of funds but not the transfer of funds to another provider which is the investor's right. One company has frankly admitted to me that this is quite deliberate so as to encourage the investor to stick with that provider.

So it was with *M&S* with whom I had a maturing ISA. And so I quite deliberately wrote on the options form that I wished to transfer to *Paragon* (that name rings a bell!) from whom they would shortly be hearing. It came as a surprise to me, therefore, to receive a letter from *M&S* telling me that the full amount of my ISA had been reinvested "as you requested" and that under the option I had "chosen" I would receive interest at £0.00. A certificate at the bottom of the letter referred to an "advantage cash ISA option". There had been a booklet with the original options form which I did not read but which I accept explained that if the options form was not completed and returned or telephone instructions given by the maturity date then this highly appealing (nil interest) account would be opened. But I maintain the booklet was not material in the circumstances. What was material was that I was being told I had requested the reinvestment and that I had chosen the nil interest investment option. These representations, I maintained, were inaccurate. I had not requested the account and I had not chosen anything. Furthermore, I had returned the form. This computer generated letter should have been modified to fit the circumstances. It should have said that as I had not exercised any of the options on the form, the default option of putting the funds in the nil interest account (pending transfer out) was being exercised. I wasted valuable time in going through correspondence and speaking to *M&S* – after waiting to speak to *M&S* – by telephone.

My internal complaint pursued as matter of principle was rejected. My complaint to the Ombudsman was rejected by an adjudicator. I asked for it to go before an Ombudsman – this is the second and final stage of a complaint to the Ombudsman Service – and she has also turned it down. She accepted I would not agree with her – she was right about that! – but found that the letter could not be read in isolation from the booklet and so did not find the letter misleading. I beg to differ.

It would be open to me to bring a county court claim but this would be highly disproportionate and I will not do so. Nevertheless, it is to be hoped that *M&S* will rephrase its letter sent out when the default option is being exercised and that pressure will be placed on providers when seeking instructions on maturity to expressly draw attention to the transfer option alongside the other options and not bury away references to a transfer in an accompanying booklet.

Previous convictions

I may be wrong but I have a sneaking suspicion that the Financial Ombudsman Service is fed up with me. Here's why. Its complaint form asks: "Have you used our service before?" It goes on to say that this information is sought so that they can link their records. I asked it what was meant by this. Its response was that the information helps it identify possible duplicate complaints so that it can ensure it does not investigate the complaint twice. Also, some complainants may have support needs and knowing that they have used the service before helps it identify whether that may be the case. But then I asked whether the people who make decisions on a complaint, including an actual Ombudsman if they come into the process, have access to the records relating to these previous complaints. The answer, I fear, is that they do unless, for example, the complainant is in vulnerable circumstances or the previous complaints are very old. That, I suggest, is extremely unfortunate. Making a records link check is something which could be administratively conducted by a staff member who has nothing to do with the decision making process, when the complaint comes in. There is a grave risk that a decision maker's view of the complaint could be coloured by the number, nature or outcome of previous complaints, however hard they may strive to block all this from their heads. Thinks. "It's that bloody Gold again."

But what about a judicial review?

Very good question. If you don't like the decision made at the so-called second and final stage of your complaint to the Financial Ombudsman Service, you could apply to the High Court for permission to have the decision judicially reviewed. This has been successfully done but it's not a step I would recommend for the sort of case the Service normally deals with. An unsuccessful attempt at getting the High Court to review the decision could cost you megabucks and end in tears. In order to win, you would have to show that the decision was irrational in that no reasonable person, acting reasonably, could have made it. But don't go away. What you can do is to tell the Service that you intend to go down the judicial review route even if you are not welded to the idea of doing so. This would lead to a legal adviser in a different section of the Service taking a look at the case and, who knows, that could conceivably result in a reversal of the decision, though don't hold your breath.

You tell the Service about your judicial review plan in a pretty formal way, by sending it a pre-action protocol letter (see chapter 10). What has to go into the letter is set out in the Civil Procedure Rules 1998 (see judicial review protocol). Where you are required to give details of the decision to be challenged, include the assertion that the decision was 'irrational'. If justified, you can throw in 'perverse', 'erroneous' and 'unreasonable' as well.

Judicial review could be sought in relation to the decisions of other public body and regulatory Ombudsmen.

For an arbitration scheme which caters for financial claims in matrimonial proceedings where it is close to certain that the court will endorse the outcome, see chapter 75.

I'll be in trouble if I don't specifically mention mediation. That's the process by which an independent person who has been trained in getting parties at war to settle their differences will apply their skills to you and your opponent. The mediator could see you separately and then together. If the animosity between you is intense they may prefer to avoid damage to the furniture by keeping you apart under the same roof running messages from one room to another. They could try and rubbish the case of each of you so as to extract a bit of compromise here and a bit of compromise there and with the moon about to appear in a few hours and a coffee and smoked salmon sandwich consumed by each side, there's a deal. They'll have their individual styles.

Mediation could take place before court proceedings have even started or hand in hand with the proceedings. Sometimes, parties alarmed at how protracted proceedings have become and how destructive the legal costs will be for them if they lose will ask the court to halt the proceedings for a month or two so that a settlement outside the proceedings might be reached through mediation. I wouldn't expect the court to refuse because judges love mediation. Even the civil division of the Court of Appeal will ask the parties to an appeal to consider mediation where this seems appropriate. Currently, none of this mediation is compulsory but the court can take into account the unreasonable refusal of a party to participate or consider participating in it when the court ultimately comes to deal with who pays the costs of a case or an appeal. Greater judicial pressure on parties to proceedings to enter into mediation could come about in the not too distant future as the newly appointed Master of the Rolls who heads the civil division of the Court of Appeal likes mediation even more than a good law book.

Here's the rub. Generally, mediators are in the game to earn a living so they will charge a fee and the parties will share it. The Civil Mediation Council has a list of professional mediators who can be used (see civilmediation.justice.gov.uk/) and will bang your heads together – sorry, I mean who will mediate – at a fixed fee but it is important that you tell them you have located their details through the online directory of mediators. That fixed fee will be based on how much is in dispute and how long the mediation session is to last. For a claim of up to £5,000, each party pays £75 for one hour and £125 for two hours by phone or video; between £5,000 and £15,000 in issue and it's £320 per party for a three-hour session by phone or video; and between £15,000 and £50,000 you are looking at £445 per party for four hours. Once you top £50,000 in issue you will have to negotiate the fee. VAT is additional. There could be an extra charge for the use of the mediation venue. If the mediation is unsuccessful then that money has gone down the drain but the coffee and smoked salmon sandwich were nice.

Brexit Alert!!! The European Online Dispute Resolution Platform for the attempted resolution, without court proceedings, of disputes over goods and services bought online across Europe, has gone down the Brexit plughole.

In the county court there is a more simplified form of mediation for the majority of small claims – no more than £10,000 being claimed – which is free (see chapter 25), but this facility is not available unless proceedings have already been started and are being defended. And in the family court, you will be prevented from starting an application relating to financial proceedings or the care of a child unless you have found out about mediation by attending a mediation information and assessment meeting – they call it a MIAM – but there are a number of exceptions to this requirement. If you are hard up, you may qualify for legal aid to cover the cost of the MIAM. If one party qualifies then the legal aid people will foot the bill for the other party to have a MIAM even though they would be financially ineligible. And since May 2016, if the financially ineligible party pays for a MIAM out of their own pocket and attends it and then the other party attends a separate MIAM through legal aid, the first party can ask the legal aid people to refund the fee they bore.

If you want to follow up the MIAM with some actual mediation for a child dispute, you may be able to obtain a voucher for up to £500 a case towards its cost but not to cover the charge for the MIAM itself. This is under a pilot scheme launched on 26 March 2021. Ask the mediator about it. They will apply for it on your behalf and whether or not you are eligible for legal aid. Here's another rub. There's only £1 million in the pot to finance these vouchers. When they've gone, they've gone! But it is always possible that more money will be added should the scheme be a success and an appreciable number of cases get settled without court proceedings. The vouchers cannot be redeemed against your grocery order and the mediator will refuse to take in your plastic bags.

Financial Conduct Authority

Just a bit on this organisation. It does not investigate individual complaints as does the Financial Ombudsman Service but it will be pleased to hear from you, thank you very much, if you are unhappy with a financial service or product. Go to fca.org.uk. It also runs a compensation scheme which will pay you out where a financial services individual or business has gone bust and you have lost money as a consequence. Most famously, it protects building society and bank investors up to £85,000 (or £170,000 of joint accounts) in the event of the failure of the financial business. Less famously, it will pay up to £85,000 where a home finance adviser or debt management business has gone in the same direction as from 1 April 2019.

It doesn't always get it right. On its website between January 2018 and July 2019 it mistakenly published confidential details of individuals who had complained to it. In some instances, the details included names, addresses, telephone numbers and the nature of the complaint ("the bastards phoned me at 7 in the morning when I was in bed with my mistress" etc). If your data has been wrongly published then you should have been informed and you may have a claim against the authority for data breach compensation. I checked out with the authority whether I had been the victim of a breach. Unfortunately, I had not.

Private courts

See chapter 75.

Communication and Internet Services Adjudication Scheme

And I realise I shouldn't but, with your permission, may I delay you just a little longer on this chapter with CISAS (approved by Ofcom) to which you can vent your spleen over the companies which supply – or often don't supply – communication and internet services. You'll find them at cedr.com. If you've got nowhere with the company, you can go to CISAS online and free and they will adjudicate. Pre-pandemic they were taking 40 to 50 days to reach their decision. They have a scale of compensation for inconvenience and distress: up to £50 if they were moderate, £50 to £100 if significant, £100 to £200 if serious and £200 or more if very serious (yes, I know, I know, that's your type of case).

final decision
of the Financial Ombudsman Service

in the complaint reference number 1062-9813/DA/BC51
brought by Mr S Gold about Santander UK plc

complaint
Mr Gold complains that, without giving any prior notification, Santander invested his matured bond proceeds in a fixed rate account.

our initial conclusions
In the absence of any material evidence to show that Santander notified Mr Gold of the reinvestment, the adjudicator recommended that the complaint should be upheld. Santander did not agree, saying that Mr Gold would be aware of the maturity date as per the terms and conditions of the account.

my final decision
To decide what is fair and reasonable in this complaint, I have considered everything that Mr Gold and Santander have said and provided.

I am not persuaded that there is sufficient evidence to conclude safely that Santander sent advance notice to Mr Gold telling him that his bond was maturing. He therefore lost the opportunity to instruct the bank and to reinvest the money into a new account with a different lender – details of which he has provided.

Whilst the terms and conditions do provide for what happens if no maturity instructions are received from a customer, and this is the process that was followed, this is only relevant if we can be certain that notice of maturity has been sent. In this case, I therefore consider the bank is liable for the interest Mr Gold has lost and it should pay Mr Gold the difference between the rate of the Reward Saver Account and the rate of the alternative savings account that he would have moved the money into. In addition, to compensate for the distress and inconvenience caused I consider a £100 payment to be fair, reasonable and in line with awards we have made for similar complaints.

My final decision is that I uphold this complaint, as set out more fully overleaf.

Under the rules of the Financial Ombudsman Service, I am required to ask Mr Gold either to accept or reject my decision, in writing, before 23 April 2012.

signed: date: **23 March 2012**
Rebecca Connelley
ombudsman at the Financial Ombudsman Service

Financial Ombudsman Service Limited | South Quay Plaza | 183 Marsh Wall | London E14 9SR
registered as a limited company in England and Wales No. 3725015 registered office as above

"The Financial Ombudsman be praised"

Part 4

STARTING A CASE AND BEFORE

Chapter 10

Before Starting A Case

Pre-match muscle flexing

How you handle a dispute before court proceedings are started may be just as important to the outcome as your conduct during proceedings – or more so. Using the right tactics may actually avoid proceedings and bring you a good result. What those tactics should be is dependent on the legal strengths or weaknesses of your position.

Supposing you owe money but less than is being demanded from you. Then it is desirable to set out your complaints, strongly and concisely, and make an offer which takes them into account. Your letter to the other side should be calculated to give them something to seriously think about. And I advisedly urge conciseness. Too much verbiage is a sign of weakness. As a solicitor, I took great joy in answering six pages of nonsense with: *"We thank you for your letter of the 12th instant, the contents of which we have noted. Yours faithfully."* The best put down ever.

One ingredient to be avoided in correspondence is aggression. Its use may be cathartic for you but, that apart, it achieves nothing. If the dispute ever reaches a court trial, the judge will be singularly unimpressed by it and, if you lose, the aggression could even earn you a more severe order for costs against you than you might otherwise have been condemned to bear. Try and achieve a balance: a sort of cross between a Russell Brand interview and a chat with the Queen.

Lawyers occasionally try and impress their clients with aggression directed to the opponent, especially where the opponent is a litigant in person. Solicitors, barristers and legal executives should keep to guidelines set by their governing bodies in June 2015. These lawyers must adopt a professional, co-operative and courteous approach at all times when communicating with a litigant in person. An initial letter from them should briefly address the issues and avoid protracted, clearly one-sided and unnecessary arguments and assertions. In both that initial contact and at other suitable stages in any dispute, they should recommend that you seek independent legal advice or point you to other advice or support agencies. They should avoid technical language and legal jargon or explain jargon where it cannot be avoided. And they should take extra care to avoid using inflammatory words or phrases that suggest or cause a dispute where there is none or inflame a dispute that already exists. Expressing any personal opinions of the behaviour of a litigant in person is also taboo. On the other hand, the lawyer need not tolerate unacceptable behaviour from you and you have no right to expect an **immediate** response to a call or other communication.

If the lawyer on the other side has overstepped the mark with you, a carefully crafted letter to them may turn out to your advantage where they shake at the prospect of it being seen by the trial judge should the claim not settle.

> "You may be pleased with your aggression and your client may be more than impressed but it does you no credit. May I respectfully draw attention to *Excalibur Ventures LLC v Texas Keystone Inc and others* [2014] EWHC 3436 (Comm) in which Mr Justice Clarke warned that parties who engage in aggressive correspondence run the risk of an order for indemnity costs against them. Further, you would do well to read – I fancy, for the first time – the guidelines jointly agreed by the legal professional bodies in June 2015 for communication with a litigant in person such as myself. A professional, co-operative and courteous approach is demanded without the use of inflammatory and technical language and unexplained legal jargon. I reserve my right to bring this correspondence to the attention of the trial judge should my dispute with your client not be resolved to my satisfaction."

Without prejudice

But you may be concerned about putting into writing an offer which could damage your defence to a later claim if it were to come to the attention of the trial judge. Fear not. You can genuinely attempt to negotiate a settlement by marking your correspondence *"without prejudice"* (or if you are talking about settlement with the other side, by telling them at the start that you are talking on a *"without prejudice"* basis.) Then, nothing written (or said) can be used in evidence if no agreement is reached.

However, the magic words *"without prejudice"* won't give you a guaranteed licence to write or say absolutely anything and get away with it if they were a cloak for perjury, blackmail or what has been described as "unambiguous impropriety". This won't work when I say to you at the start of our discussion: "We're talking *without prejudice* now. You understand that. We'll try and settle but if we don't, lips must be sealed in court about what we say. And what I say to you sunshine, and no hard feelings and that, but if you don't agree to what I am going to put to you to get rid of this ruddy litigation then I will tell a pack of lies in court and I will be believed as I've got the gift of the gab and I will probably get my heavy mob friends to pop round to yours as well. Can't be fairer than that." But this would work.

> *149 Magnolia Crescent*
>
> *Twickenham*
>
> *KT89 4XZ*
>
> *14 July 2021*
>
> *Dear Credit Controller*
>
> *WITHOUT PREJUDICE*
>
> *Re Invoice A10/88675*
>
> *I have your invoice for advertising in two consecutive editions of The Middlesex Pet Fanciers' Recorder in the sum of £2,750.69. My princi-*

> pal – but not exhaustive – complaints about your services are that:
>
> (a) in the photograph you took and published of my shop frontage, the depiction of a double tripe sandwich in the bottom left hand corner of the window was obscured.
>
> (b) I have evidence that over 300 copies of both relevant editions had been abandoned by your distributors in a receptacle outside St Margaret's Railway Station.
>
> (c) My takings since the advertisements have appeared have plunged, leading me to the conclusion that your publication does not enjoy the volume of readership your salesman represented to me when he induced me to take advertising space and/or that few of the copies of the relevant editions were actually delivered.
>
> I have been legally advised that you are in breach of contract and that I have no liability to make any payment to you at all. Notwithstanding this advice and solely with a view to avoiding the distraction of litigation, I am prepared to make a payment to you of £750.00 in full and final settlement of the invoices. If I receive a written acceptance of this offer from you within 14 days of the date of this letter, I will remit the £750.00 to you immediately. If I do not receive such acceptance within that period, this offer will stand withdrawn and I will defend any proceedings you choose to bring against me and counterclaim for damages for loss of business.
>
> Best wishes
>
> Clive Troublesore

The fact that a letter has not been endorsed with, or a meeting has not been preceded by, the use of the words "*without prejudice*" is not fatal if it is clear from the surrounding circumstances that in that letter or at that meeting you were seeking to compromise the litigation. As a general rule, as indicated, evidence of the content of the negotiations cannot be used at a later trial should those negotiations come to nothing. But both sides should realise that the communication or meeting is about compromise. Say you write to your opponent a letter which is littered with uncomfortable admissions but do not head it "*without prejudice*"? Although you send it in an effort to strike a deal in the case, it can still later be used against you in court unless your opponent knew or should have known that you were writing because you were seeking to compromise.

The Court of Appeal recognised in a case it decided in January 2016 (a case, incidentally, in which I have a special interest because, as a judge, I dealt with a good deal of preliminary hearings before it got to trial) that where litigants in person instead of lawyers are involved in discussions, it may be more difficult to establish whether they were for negotiations genuinely aimed at a settlement. In this case, one of two tenants of a restaurant had at her own initiative gone to the offices of the landlord's solicitor to discuss the landlord's proceedings against her and the other tenant. She allegedly said things at the meeting which were used in evidence against the tenants at the ultimate trial. *"Without prejudice"* had never been mentioned. The Court of Appeal ruled that the only sensible purpose for such a meeting must have been to seek some kind of solution to the litigation for the tenant who attended and that meant that the meeting could not be relied on in later evidence. There was no justification for salami slicing an interview into bits that could be used in evidence and bits that could not be used in evidence. And the consequence? The trial that had taken place would have to be rerun – without the *"without prejudice"* evidence.

Boot switch

When the boot is on the other foot and it is you who have been poisoned, whiplashed, libelled, mis-sold or falsely imprisoned (or, on a *dreadful* day, poisoned, whiplashed, libelled, poisoned, mis-sold *and* falsely imprisoned), the approach should be different. Do you start court proceedings the moment you swallow the snail in the bottle of ginger beer or are bashed in the rear? No. Thou shalt follow a protocol which is a set of rules about claiming nicely and although there is no bar against you starting proceedings as though the protocol never existed, this could lead to the proceedings being halted for a period to give the other side an opportunity to carry out investigations which would have been available under the protocol. Non-compliance might also go against you when the court comes to deal with the costs of the proceedings. Each protocol kicks off with you sending the other side what is called a letter of claim with full details of what you are alleging and wanting.

In one situation you will not be criticised for starting proceedings without following the protocol. That's where the time limit for doing so is about to expire. There are specific time limits for bringing different types of claim (which sometimes, and not easily, the court may be prepared to extend): for example, three years for a claim for personal injury compensation, six years for breach of contract and one year for libel or slander (see chapter 13). But, again, there may be a halt of the proceedings for a couple of months to enable the other side to catch up with their enquiries.

There are separate protocols for different types of case – for personal injury claims with a value of up to £25,000 which is designed for road traffic, pavement type tripping and slipping and accident at work cases; clinical negligence (surgeon falling asleep during the op); construction; defamation (libel and slander); professional negligence (cock ups by lawyers, accountants, surveyors and the rest); disease and illness; housing disrepair; and judicial review. The protocols are composed in digestible language. The time for the other side to respond to your letter of claim ranges from a fortnight to three months. Some of the protocols were revamped in April 2015 so if you are relying on a third hand law book you bought in a car boot sale in 2000, check out the up to date protocols on at justice.gov.uk/courts/procedure-rules/civil/protocol The most recent protocol is for small claims for personal injury arising out of a road traffic accident which has occurred on or after 31 May 2021 where the injury in compensation terms has a value of up to £5,000 and the overall claim is not worth more than £10,000 (see chapter 25).

Juicy debt protocol

And we now have an often overlooked debt protocol for claims by a business and a public authority against an individual (including a sole trader). It does not cover mortgage arrears which has its own protocol (see chapter 66) and tax and duties owed to your friends at HM Revenue & Customs. The protocol requires that the debt information provided in the letter of claim includes details of whether interest is continuing; how the debt can be paid (under Margate Pier at eleven minutes past midnight to a monocled debt collector carrying a copy of *How to Stab a Debtor Without Really Trying* under his left armpit); why a court claim is being considered if you are paying or offering to pay instalments; and what you should do if you want to discuss payment options. You must also be told about any administrative or other charges they are trying to land you with, like £50 for scratching their nose before turning on their computer to send you a threatener, £75 for compiling the threatener and £100 for posting it.

You may never have heard of the people claiming against you because the debt has been bought by them from the business you originally dealt with. There may have been a series of transfers of the benefit of the debt. This can happen when the original business doesn't want the hassle of chasing the debt as they have concluded you are real trouble – sorry! The current debt chasers might have paid less than the cost of an out of date *Malteser* for the opportunity of seeking to extract from you what you actually owe and they may go after you with a vengeance. Here, the debt protocol is useful. It requires the letter of claim to give you details of the original debt and the identity of the business you dealt with, when the debt was transferred (the protocol talks of an 'assignment') and by whom.

The letter of claim is to be accompanied by various bits and pieces including an information sheet and, for you to complete, a reply form and a financial statement form about your financial circumstances. If you fail to respond, your creditor can sue their heads off after 30 days from the date which should appear at the top of the letter of claim. You are to be allowed a reasonable period to obtain advice if you indicate you are seeking it and at least 30 days from sending back the completed financial information statement or, if later, being given copies of any relevant documents you have asked for. The information sheet is to inform you that free independent advice and assistance can be obtained from organisations including National Debtline, Citizens Advice and StepChange.

Of course, your creditor may look at the protocol requirements and, one day after the debt arose, make a derogatory gesture by raising a claim form and cut throat razor into the air. It has to be emphasised that mere default by the business in complying with the protocol will not provide you with a valid defence to the claim. What it could do is allow you some more time to win the National Lottery or understand the claim and challenge the alleged debt where it appears too high by putting in a defence. That, at the least, is likely to lead to the court ordering your creditor to comply with the debt protocol and prevent the claimant from obtaining a judgment against you for the amount claimed until you have had an opportunity to respond. The defence might go something like this:

> *"1. I admit I am indebted to the claimant but deny that my indebtedness is in the amount alleged in the Particulars of Claim. From the information currently available to me, I calculate that my indebtedness is no more than £x. The Particulars of Claim do not provide a breakdown of the amount claimed and no such breakdown has been provided by or on behalf of the claimant in such pre-action communications as I have received from it.*
>
> *2. The Pre-Action Protocol For Debt Claims ('the protocol') applies to the claimant's claim in that, for the purposes of the protocol, the claimant is a business and I am an individual. The claimant is in flagrant breach of the protocol in that it has failed to send me a Letter of Claim in compliance with paragraph 3.1 to 3.3 of the protocol except for stating the alleged total sum claimed and has failed to send me any of the documentation required by the protocol. [add, if appropriate: My written request to the claimant dated 14 July 2021 for further information about the claim was ignored.]*
>
> *3. In view of the above, I request that the claimant's claim be stayed for a period of 28 days from the date on which it serves me with the information and documentation specified at paragraph 3.1(a) and (b) of the protocol and that I be granted permission to file an amended defence within 42 days of such service and an order that the costs of and consequent upon the filing of the amended defence be mine in any event.*
>
> *I believe that the facts stated in this defence are true. I understand that proceedings for contempt of court may be brought against anyone who makes, or causes to be made, a false statement in a document verified by a statement of truth without an honest belief in its truth.*
>
> *(signed) Clive Troublesore*
>
> *Defendant*
>
> *31 July 2021"*

Even if it turns out that you owe the full amount that has been claimed, the claimant's non-compliance with the protocol may give you grounds for resisting a claim by the business for their costs of bringing proceedings on the grounds that, had they complied, proceedings would not have been necessary. A claim for you to pay interest on the debt may also be disallowed or reduced because of non-compliance.

Tip for creditors. The protocol imposes obligations on the debtor too. If the creditor has done what the protocol requires of it but the debtor has not (for example, by sending back a response) then the Practice Direction for Pre-Action Conduct and Protocols which you will find with the Civil Procedure Rules 1998 kicks in. Under this, should you obtain a judgment against the creditor then the court can award you interest at a higher rate than that which would normally apply but no more than 10% above base rate.

And now for everything else

Where there is no protocol to fit a particular case, (for example, a consumer claim against a trader for substandard goods), the *Practice Direction for Pre-Action Conduct and Protocols* just mentioned above is triggered. Here, the other side should respond to any letter of claim within a reasonable period of time. Eh? Some guidelines are given on how you might quantify this. A fortnight where the matter is straightforward: no more than 30 days in a very complex case.

The Part 36 offer

This is a reference to Part 36 of the Civil Procedure Rules 1998. We've seen how to use the *"without prejudice"* communication when you wish to try and reach a settlement because you owe something to the other side. And we have seen how to follow a protocol when you are the one wanting to push a claim forward. But there's something else you can do in addition to protocol compliance and it will usually be bonkers not to do it. This is because it will concentrate the mind of the opposition more potently than a high voltage electric shock and, if it doesn't lead to a fast settlement, it could earn you mega bucks down the line. Take your partners for the Part 36 frightener offer.

Part 36 chat

Lawyers talk about Part 36 all the time and not simply because non-lawyers haven't got a clue what they are talking about. "Had a fantastic day, Rodney. Made a Part 36 for £3m. Gave the b.......s 21 days to stump up. They came back with a counter Part 36 at £750,000. Said "See you in court" and just settled at £1m and the client wasn't expecting more than 500 quid. Another double, Rodney?"

You can read Part 36 if you must – it was substantially amended in April 2015 and has been tinkered with since so, again, don't rely on old law books – but I would recommend a damp cloth and a bottle of aspirin to go with it. Note it does not apply to small claims (see chapter 25). Although we talk of an offer, you won't be paying any money. You will be offering to the other side to accept a stated sum of money in settlement of the claim. You can make an offer like this not only after you have started proceedings but beforehand. Yes, I'll repeat that. You can make a Part 36 offer before you actually start court proceedings.

The consequences for the other side could be dire if the offer is not accepted and the trial judge ultimately awards you at least the amount you offered to settle for or more. Then the likelihood is that you will collect an extra 10% of the sum you are awarded. If it's a mega-award of over half a million, it will be 10% up to half a million and only 5% on the rest. There's a limit on this bonus which is £75,000. Shame. And hold on, there are other bonuses too at the expense of the other side: you get your legal costs and with probably most of those being assessed in a more advantageous way to you than is usually the case, interest on those costs of up to 10% above base rate and interest on what you are awarded of up to 10% above base rate. The extra interest will usually run from three weeks after you made your offer. These bonuses will come your way unless the court reckons it is unjust to condemn the losing party to pay them. It will consider whether the offer was a genuine attempt to settle the case and won't lightly let the loser off the hook for the whole package of the extras. In a November 2020 case, the Court of Appeal ruled that if it was right that one of the bonuses should be awarded, then they should all be awarded. All or nothing.

The other side of the coin is that if the opposition made a Part 36 offer to you which you did not accept and you failed to better the offer with the judge's award, you will be condemned to pay their legal costs with interest, usually from three weeks after the offer unless – altogether now – the court reckons this would be unjust.

Pitching an offer at the right level is an art and it could pay you dividends to obtain legal advice just on this aspect of the case. Bearing in mind the consequences for the other side should they fare no better at a court trial then they would have done if they had accepted your offer, they will start sweating the moment your offer whizzes through their letterbox. It is also conceivable that they will have convinced themselves that the value of your claim is higher than the actual value. You might consider offering to settle high and see how they respond and subsequently go lower.

There's a form you can use to make a Part 36 offer – not essential but I recommend it and so do appeal court judges – which you can adapt if it is made prior to proceedings. It's form N242A (the 2015 version is what you want) and you can access it at assets.publishing.service.gov.uk/government/uploads/system/uploads/attachment_data/file/688550/n242a-eng.pdf. Interest can constitute a major element of an offer or court judgment (see chapter 32). A change to the Civil Procedure Rules 1998 which came into force in April 2021 clarifies that your Part 36 offer can include interest on whatever principal amount of money you are putting forward. You should calculate the interest up to the date of the offer. If you do not mention interest, it will be presumed that your offer takes interest into account. Good luck.

It is open to you to withdraw a Part 36 offer which has not been accepted within the period you have set. You should do this in writing.

You can also specify when you make it that the offer will lapse if not accepted after a stated period which must generally be not earlier than 21 days.

"Hands up. I was going too fast"

You can make a Part 36 offer which is limited to the issue of liability – not how much you want but whether you are prepared to concede that your compensation should be reduced to reflect your own conduct. It can take two to tango and to bring about an accident. If say you were one-half to blame, the court would reduce your compensation by one-half. You know it makes sense. All the time, judges are having to decide whether the claimant was partly to blame and, if so, by what percentage and how much dosh they should receive. Perhaps you aren't yet ready to put a value on your claim but you want to get any argument about blame out of the way. Perhaps your prime witness on liability is about to take off for Abyssinia and is not planning to return until Aldershot Town have won the Premier League. Making a Part 36 offer to the other side to concede 25%, 50% or whatever negligence on your part would be open to you. It could entitle you to your legal costs from when the time for acceptance is up if the case goes the distance and the judge decides you were blameless or no more to blame than you had offered to concede.

An alternative approach

In some situations, it can be tactically wise to hold off making any formal claim against the other side but instead to write explaining what you are complaining about and inviting their observations. This tends to work better when dealing with service industries and the bigger businesses. Why do this? The response is more likely to come from management or customer services rather than in-house or outside lawyers and so couched in less defensive terms and to contain an apology at the least (which could be of high evidential value to you if a claim is made later). There may even be an *ex gratia* payment which will not usually reduce your compensation on any later claim. Be careful, though, not to accept any payment in full and final settlement of any claim you were intending to make – unless it's fat enough (see chapter 16).

In my 2013 complaint to Salcombe Harbour Hotel & Spa's general manager, I outlined in a three-page letter what had gone wrong with a one week's stay by me and my companion. The hotel had reopened following substantial renovation but, unbeknown to me when I booked, works were behind and this resulted in our effectively occupying a building site instead of a prestigious hotel for the period of the stay. I acknowledged that the location was idyllic and that, when fully operational, the hotel would clearly be quite excellent and a success. In this particular instance, I went further than simply asking for comment but fell short of threatening proceedings. I put it like this:

> *"In the light of the above, I have to ask you to put forward some realistic proposals to compensate us. I would ask you to return to me with the proposals within the next seven days..."*

I declined an offer of a 25% bill refund plus two complimentary nights at the hotel, followed by offers of a £1,000 refund and then a £1,500 refund and finally settled at £1,800 which meant I paid for our food and got back the accommodation charges. This was fair to both sides. It was almost a pleasure negotiating with the hotel and I still get generic emails inviting me back. Perhaps one day – with a false beard and moustache.

This alternative approach may fail because your opponent reckons you lack the spunk to carry out your threat to sue. My encounter with the Hilton, in Manchester's Deansgate, tends to prove the point. In August 2016 with my companion, I stayed at the hotel for two nights in an executive room (sounded impressive) at the special price of £262 including breakfast. Twelve things went wrong. I won't bore you with them all: fridge door jammed close, bathroom door unopenable without application of considerable force which caused loud noise to be emitted, drilling within the building in the middle of the first night, only one armchair in room... It wasn't outrageously dreadful. It just wasn't good enough.

I wrote to the general manager and ended my letter with these words:

> "I invite your proposals for remedying what collectively amounts to a substantially sub-standard service by a monetary payment. I would not consider the acceptance of a voucher or a free or reduced charge stay at a Hilton establishment in the future as being appropriate or acceptable. I shall be glad to hear from you within the next ten days."

And his reply included this:

> "In summary I'm disappointed that you didn't raise these (complaints) at the time as we pride ourselves in providing the best possible service and ensuring every guest's (sic) depart with a memorable stay. However notwithstanding, sadly, apologies after facts seldom makes amends. As a genuine gesture of my sincerity allow me to arrange Sunday lunch, excluding wine at a convenient Hilton hotel for you in response to your disappointment with us at Hilton Deansgate Manchester."

I returned:

> "Your gesture proposal falls within the type of gestures to which I alluded in the final paragraph of my original letter and so is not suitable. For the record, I assume you had intended lunch for two and that water would have been included free of charge. Therefore, I ask for your proposals for a monetary payment and would wish to hear from you within the next seven days."

And then he said:

> "While I accept and understand your frustration however, my goodwill gesture of a complimentary Sunday lunch for 2 guests excluding wine at a convenient Hilton Hotel remains and I do hope that we are able to make the necessary arrangements for you in the near future."

And then I replied:

> "When it comes to evasion in relation to a monetary claim against your company, you have no equal. Your company's Chief Executive Officer should award you a prize.... I have told you not once but twice that I do not want the sort of gesture you have offered. I know you can read so why be silly and persist in the offer. I have lost my patience. Unless, within seven days of the date of this letter, I receive a satisfactory monetary proposal from you to settle my claim, I shall institute proceedings against your company for damages, interest and costs without further

notice. If the problem is that your company needs time to pay, then just say so and we can consider what you suggest."

No monetary proposal was received. I made an online claim on 7 November 2016 for £290 plus the £25 court fee. Hilton settled in full on 24 November 2016.

The amount claimed was intended to reflect the diminution in the value of the Hilton's accommodation and service and its guests' disappointment.

Out of court

Negotiation and court proceedings are not the only ways of achieving a settlement. There are ombudsman schemes run by trade associations and others, mediation and arbitration (see chapter 9). We also have early neutral evaluation. This involves a judge reading the papers and hearing the parties or their legal representatives before proceedings go too far and then giving their opinion on the merits and demerits of each side's case. The parties can heed what the judge has said or ignore it. What they get is a pretty good idea of who will win and who will lose, and how well or how badly, if the case continues to the bitter end. If it does continue, that judge will play no further part in the proceedings. Either of the parties or both of them can request an evaluation or the judge may float the idea. An evaluation is more likely to be ordered if the parties consent to it but their consent is not essential. It is also more likely in the High Court than in the county court.

Peanut defendants

A county court judgment to pay money is as useful as the defendant's ability to stump up the cash to settle it. Anyone who likes queues will sue an impecunious defendant so that they can stand in line behind the claimants who got in first and wait until the defendant is made bankrupt with just that packet of peanuts (probably unsalted as they are cheaper) to declare as an asset.

To avoid the queue, you can discover what the Register of Judgments (see chapter 27) has to tell you. Search online for judgments recorded against your would be defendant by going to search.trustonline.org.uk/Search/Person and pay a fee of £6 to £10, depending on how much info you want. It would be wise to find out if there are both county court and High Court judgments which are recorded. You can also make a search with a credit reference agency which may show up judgments along with other useful details. And if you reckon that your would be defendant owns a property, you can check this out online at the Land Registry by asking for copies of its records for that property. Request 'office copy entries' which will cost you £19.95 but don't waste your money on a copy of the plan of the property unless you want to find out the size of the back garden or are an architect who can't turn off. The records will disclose who are the owners, when they bought and, unless this was when George VI was on the throne, how much they paid. You will also be able to glean whether the property is mortgaged and, if it is, how many mortgages there are and whether another creditor ahead of you has obtained a charging order against the property (see chapter 29).

This info will help towards you making an assessment of how much would be left over if the property was ordered to be sold to settle your hoped for judgment, after mortgage lenders and creditors ahead of you with charging orders had been paid out. You won't usually get these search fees back from the defendant as part of your legal costs.

Default notices

This is one for the lender but is also one for the borrower 'cos if the lender does not do what the law requires, the borrower may have a defence to a court claim against them. The Consumer Credit Act 1974 says that before a lender can take certain steps in relation to most consumer credit or consumer hire agreements, they must send the borrower a default notice. The steps? They are complicated but they include terminating the agreement and demanding early repayment of what is due because the agreement has been broken. If you are the borrower, you'll have a pretty good idea that a default notice is needed as you will get one! The point of the story is that the form and content of the default notice was changed on 2 December 2020 but it is only from 2 June 2021 that the lender could be up the creek for using an out of date default notice. Research has shown that the old style default notice scared the pants off a large number of borrowers who had the misfortune to receive one and that they felt intimidated by the heavy volume of text on it which was in block capitals, albeit that it had been intended to make that text more prominent. The new default notice eliminates block capitals as a prominence tool and removes technical legal language like 'enforcement' and 'judgment'. If the old form instead of the new form is sent out after 1 June 2021 the borrower may well have a defence to some or part of any subsequent claim made against them by the lender arising out of the agreement concerned. The absence of a fully compliant notice has often been of little or no help to the borrower but things could be different in the light of the major changes now made to the notice and the reasons for them. More likely, the borrower might be able to obtain an injunction against the lender to forbid it from starting proceedings without first serving a valid default notice. If the notice that reaches you is double Dutch and scary, you'll know it's the old version.

Chapter 11

Freezing Your Creditor

The 42 day plus paralysis

Are you wanting to obtain debt advice? Or are you having a mental crisis that prevents you from coping with a debt problem? Or are you a creditor not wishing to be taken for a ride by a debtor who is prepared to use any tactic to keep you at bay? Then this chapter is for you. Spanking new laws came into force on 4 May 2021 which can help debtors and hinder creditors and will catch relevant debts which have been incurred both before and after that date. The Debt Respite Scheme – for chapter and verse go to the Debt Respite Scheme (Breathing Space Moratorium and Mental Health Crisis Moratorium) (England and Wales) Regulations 2020 – prevents your creditor taking steps to get you to pay up short of starting court or tribunal proceedings and from pressing on with them if they have already been started. Relevant court procedural rules can be found in new Practice Direction 70B of the Civil Procedure Rules 1998.

The Breathing Space moratorium

This lasts for six weeks but you can reapply after one year has passed. You apply through an approved debt counselling organisation like StepChange or the local authority and they cannot charge you for dealing with the application. Someone holding a power of attorney for you can apply on your behalf. You must be unable to pay all or some of your debt and a moratorium must be appropriate because, for example, you may be able to enter into a debt plan with your creditors during the moratorium or as soon as reasonably practicable after it has ended. You must keep up certain specified payments which fall due while the moratorium is alive including taxes and mortgage instalments, rent and service charges under a lease on your main home, insurance premiums and for the supply of water, sewerage, electricity, gas and heating oil or solid fuel. Failure to do so could lead to cancellation of the moratorium at the midway review which has to be carried out by the debt counsellor.

Joint debts such as arrears of mortgage instalments and rent can be included in the moratorium and that would give protection not only to you but to your co-debtor for those debts even though they did not have their own moratorium. If repayments under a loan to you that has been guaranteed by someone else are behind, they will be covered by the moratorium so far as you are concerned but not so far as your guarantor is concerned, unless they obtain their own moratorium.

If the court is notified of a breathing space moratorium, any hearing relating to the enforcement of a debt which is covered by it, and which was due to take place during the moratorium period, must be adjourned to the next available date after the period has ended.

The Mental Health Crisis moratorium

This lasts for the period of your mental health crisis plus 30 days but, once that time is up, you could go on to apply for a breathing space moratorium. The application is again made to an approved debt counselling organisation or the local authority. You can make the application yourself. Otherwise, it can be made on your behalf by any one of a host of others including your carer, social worker or a mental health nurse. You must be receiving certain mental health treatment in hospital or the community and this must be backed up by evidence from an approved mental health professional. The other necessity is that you are unable to pay all or some of your debt and that the moratorium would be appropriate. It can be reapplied for, without limit, as and when a mental health crisis recurs.

If the court is notified of a mental health crisis moratorium, any hearing relating to the enforcement of a debt which is covered by it, which was due to take place after the notification, must be adjourned indefinitely and permission be given to you or your creditor to ask for a new hearing in due course. In any event, a judge will look at the case papers and give appropriate directions once six months are up following notification of the moratorium.

Rules for both

Neither moratorium is available if you are: under 18, domiciled or usually resident outside England and Wales (although some or all of the debt may have been incurred outside during the course of an imprudently taken holiday); subject to a debt relief order, an interim order as a preliminary to an individual voluntary arrangement or a voluntary arrangement; or an undischarged bankrupt.

You must have at least one debt that qualifies for the moratorium. Out are debts that are secured (but mortgage arrears are in), business debts if you are registered for VAT or in partnership and the debt relates to the business and debts that aren't wiped out on bankruptcy, like child maintenance and under personal injury damages judgments (see chapter 48). A charging order or attachment of earnings order is unaffected.

If the hearing of a bankruptcy petition against you is pending when the moratorium begins and it relates to a moratorium debt, then your creditor must notify the court that there is a moratorium and the petition will be halted until the moratorium has ended. But any other case in a court or a tribunal can still go ahead, though no steps to enforce a judgment or order if the case goes against you can be taken to enforce that judgment or order during the moratorium period. That, for example, would rule out sending in a bailiff. No interest, fees, penalties or charges that would otherwise have clocked up during the moratorium period will be collectable from you.

The Insolvency Service maintains a register containing details of the moratoria. The details will be deleted 15 months after they have come to an end. You can ask to see the details as can any of your creditors who have been notified of a moratorium but not anything relating to a debt owed to another creditor.

You can request that your address is withheld from your creditors on the grounds that disclosure might reasonably be expected to lead to violence against you or a family member who normally resides with you. If the debt counselling organisation handling the moratorium application disagrees, you have a right of appeal against its decision to the county court within 28 days of it being notified to you.

FOR CREDITORS' EYES ONLY

The 'having a laugh' situation

If you reckon that your debtor is 'having a laugh', you can ask the debt counsellor to review the moratorium. This would be on the ground that it unfairly prejudices your interests or there has been some material irregularity with the application – the debtor did not meet the laid down eligibility criteria for the moratorium, your debt does not qualify for the moratorium or the debtor has sufficient funds to pay you out. You must seek the review within 20 days of the start of the moratorium so time is tight. You should receive prompt notification of the moratorium but any delay will eat into those 20 days. You can apply to the county court to cancel the moratorium if the debt counsellor has refused to do so. To the county court you must go within 50 days of the start of the moratorium. Since a breathing space moratorium cannot last for longer than 42 days, you may wonder what is the point in allowing you to make a county court challenge within 50 days. It is this. If the moratorium is cancelled by the court even after it has ended, the court can require the debtor to pay any interest, fees or charges that have accrued during the moratorium period.

The 'never mind the moratorium' situation

You can apply to a court or tribunal for permission to take enforcement action in respect of a moratorium debt or instruct an agent to do so, whether or not you already have a judgment or order in your favour. Permission – conditional or unconditional – can only be given if it is considered that it is reasonable for you to take this action and this would not be detrimental to the debtor (show me a debtor who would not suffer a detriment by being subjected to enforcement and I'll show you a WAG without sunglasses) or *significantly undermine the protections of the moratorium*.

COURT PROCEDURE

A debtor's appeal against a refusal to withhold their address from the moratoria register should be made by application notice (form N244) but in this instance a special low court fee has been set at £5 which is less than a large extra hamburger and chips. Applications by a creditor to cancel a moratorium or for permission to take enforcement action notwithstanding a moratorium should be made in the same way. If there are existing proceedings relating to the debt, the appeal or application is to be made within those proceedings. Otherwise, it should normally be made to the county court hearing centre in which it is likely that any claim would be heard and that will probably be the debtor's local centre.

Chapter 12

Where To Start

"This was a court. Do you want mushy peas with your fish and chips?"

You might just happen to live round the corner from a building at which civil or family cases – or both – are heard but most of the population does not. There have been dramatic changes in the court system and more are in store. We no longer have a county court here, there and everywhere. Instead we have a single county court with hearings and offices at civil hearing centres and they just happen to be at the very same buildings which used to house the local county courts. Loads of these buildings have been closed down and loads more are to follow. This is all to finance massive investment to belatedly bring the justice system administratively up to date and hopefully make it efficient – 'cos it creaks badly. The closed buildings will be sold off where possible. If you have the money you might want to put in a bid for one of the dilapidated buildings which would make a quirky restaurant complete with bench for the maitre d' and witness box for the waiter or could be turned into a block of luxury flats to be known as *'County Court Towers'*.

In the family arena where parties are ending their marriages and civil partnerships and battling over property and maintenance and the welfare of their children, we have a single family court. It does its stuff out of family hearing centres. Sometimes they will be in the same building as the county court civil hearing centres: other times they will be on their own. The family sections of magistrates' courts have been killed off although magistrates now often hear family cases at the new family hearing centres.

High Court or County Court for civil claims?

If you are going to bring civil proceedings – or someone brings them against you – that will most probably be in the county court. The High Court generally deals with very substantial and complex cases and those in which the outcome is important not just to the claimant but to the public in general. Trying to impress and frighten your opponent by suing them in the High Court for a case which is neither substantial nor complex won't work. The High Court will transfer a case to the county court where it should have been started there. In fact, you cannot bring a claim in the High Court for personal injury compensation under the value of £50,000 unless it is for clinical negligence, or, generally, for any other claim involving money for less than £100,000. A claim for libel or slander (see chapter 47) has to be brought in the High Court unless both sides agree that the county court can deal with it. The last time there was an agreement to this effect, I was drinking gripe water in my pram. However, the £100,000 High Court threshold for libel, slander, misuse of private information and data protection breach claims – the sort of case which would be included in what is known as the 'media and communications' list – has disappeared since October 2019.

Civil claims online

Using the Money Claim Online procedure (MCOL) is not compulsory. You can claim online for the defendant to pay you money (in the early hours and with some suitable background music) provided:

- You have access to a computer (ha ha).
- The claim is for less than £100,000 and for this purpose you disregard any interest and costs you are after but if the amount is, say, £100,002 you can be a devil and abandon £2.01 of it so that you qualify.
- The claim is for a fixed amount so you cannot claim say for a sum to be assessed by the court up to a specified ceiling. But you could – though few people do – quantify a claim for damages at a specific sum. That specific sum would need to be a reasonable and properly considered one. Otherwise, the defendant would be in a strong position to subsequently have the judgment set aside.
- You are over 18.
- You are claiming against a single defendant or just two defendants but for the same amount.
- Generally, your base and the defendant's base are in the UK.

Advantages. Speedy. No risk of the court losing the paperwork. But no longer cheaper than claiming offline as a result of online court fees having been aligned with offline fees in May 2021. Disadvantages. Fee remission unavailable. The capacity for the content of the particulars of claim which must be completed online is limited with the result that neither the judge nor the defendant may have a clue as to what the claim is about and the particulars might have to be amended with you possibly being ordered to pay some costs to the defendant. The limit is 1,080 characters and that includes spaces and the situation can be made more serious if the claimant's typing skills aren't up to much. You might get tommyrot that goes something like this – *"Ct compute not staingand smahed with hammershop rude said me fort and me mumsays claim 4 losuy hlidays."* It is possible in many uncomplicated cases to include everything that needs to be stated within 1,080 characters and you will find that we have succeeded with this on some occasions in later pages with our template particulars. Otherwise, there is a way round the potential problem for a case that cannot be adequately particularised within the available limit. In the section of the online claim form headed "Particulars of Claim" give just a brief summary of claim and say detailed particulars will follow.

PARTICULARS OF CLAIM

The claimant claims specified damages for breach of contract arising out of his purchase of a computer at the defendant's Twickenham store on 14 July 2021. Detailed particulars of claim will follow.

> At the end of the detailed particulars when they do follow add this:
>
> I am the claimant. I believe that the facts stated in these detailed particular of claim are true.
>
> (signed) C Troublesore
>
> Dated 14 July 2021

The detailed particulars of claim must then be sent to the defendant within 14 days of the defendant having been treated as receiving the claim form from the court. Within 14 days of the defendant getting the detailed particulars, you have to send the County Court Business Centre a certificate to the effect that the detailed particulars of claim were sent out (in form N215). You won't be able to obtain a judgment against the defendant for failing to respond to the proceedings until time has run out for them to do so after they have had the detailed particulars.

I have tried out the online system as a claimant. I had been handling the winding up of the estate of my late uncle who held an account with *Nationwide*. It paid out the money due to the estate but drew its cheque in his favour which was of no use at all. When it neglected to issue a fresh cheque in favour of the personal representatives including me or to respond to correspondence, I claimed – online. *Nationwide* failed to put in a defence and so I obtained judgment – online. I then put in the bailiff – online. This did the trick. *Nationwide* threw itself into action and settled the claim including interest and costs. I then made a claim for inconvenience under their internal complaints procedure and they paid up £200.

There's a similar scheme to MCOL which is the Online Civil Money Claims procedure (OCMC). Let's play *Spot the Difference* between MCOL and OCMC and you can then employ it as your specialist subject next time you compete on *University Challenge*. OCMC is a trial procedure which has just been given a boost with an extension to November 2023 and more features added. It's an alternative to MCOL and is intended to be the general procedure which will eventually apply to small claims with most, if not all, procedural steps in the case being dealt with online. But, unlike MCOL, it is only available where you are not being helped by a lawyer, you believe the defendant will be going it alone too and the claim is for no more than a specified sum of £10,000 including interest. Among the other conditions for eligibility: one claimant with an address for service of documents in the UK, one defendant with an address for service in England and Wales and both claimant and defendant at least aged 18. If you are eligible, what is the main reason you should opt to use it over MCOL? Because there is no limit on the number of characters that feature in your particulars of claim.

If you have an invincible desire to talk to a member of court staff about either of these schemes, they are waiting to take your call (or perhaps not) for MCOL on 0300 123 1057 and for OCMC on 0300 123 7050.

Other civil claims

A claim which is for money only and is not started online should be sent to the County Court Money Claims Centre, PO Box 527, Salford M5 0BY or, if you are in Wales, to the County Court Money Claims Centre (Wales), PO Box 552, Salford M5 0EG. This assumes you are using claim form N1 under the so called part 7 procedure which will usually be the case. A claim for money plus something else (say damages and an injunction) or a claim which is not for money at all (say only for an injunction or a declaration) – whether you are using form NI or form N208 for the so called part 8 procedure – may be sent to any county court civil hearing centre but it will probably avoid delay if it goes to your local centre although these days that may be some miles away. The same applies to certain applications to the court before a claim – for example, for your prospective defendant to hand over documents (see chapter 15) – which are made under part 23 of the Civil Procedure Rules 1998. Go to courttribunalfinder.service.gov.uk and search for your local court hearing centre and for a really digestible summary of starting your claim and the pre-trial process go to assets.publishing.service.gov.uk/government/uploads/system/uploads/attachment_data/file/776679/ex302-largeprint-eng.pdf. There is also a worthy *Handbook for Litigants in Person* written by six circuit judges on behalf of the Council of Circuit Judges which you can access at judiciary.uk/publications/handbook-litigants-person-civil-221013. It runs through the litigation process and I would commend it to you if you haven't got a clue what I have been on about. 160 pages but no jokes. It's up to date as at 1 April 2013. On the same site you can also devour *Interim Applications in the Chancery Division: A Guide for Litigants in Person* and *The Interim Applications Court of the Queen's Bench Division of the High Court: A Guide for Litigants in Person* though, as is evident from their titles, these guides are for the heavy stuff and not your perishing hot water bottle claim in the county court. If you want to see a human being at your local hearing centre instead of posting papers there or using a dropbox there – perhaps you are after an emergency injunction or need to make an emergency application to stop the bailiff evicting you – then you should telephone or call at the centre and ask to be seen.

Matrimonial and family cases

Please see chapters 74 and 75.

Chapter 13
Time Limits For Starting Court Proceedings
Disaster or windfall

Success in your claim may be a dead cert but if you fail to start court proceedings within the stipulated time limit for that type of claim, the general rule is that you have had it. Too late for justice. Nobody will stop you from starting the proceedings because the fact that you are late is a defence which is for your defendant, and not the judge or the court staff, to raise. If it is not raised because your defendant is too idle to take steps to defend the case or is simply unaware of the time limit law and of the cracking defence that is available to them, then you could conceivably end up with a judgment in what is a stale claim. I have seen the "too late" (lawyers call it the "statute barred") defence successfully raised many times and it has usually brought the proceedings to an end at a very early stage.

The law in this area is complicated and you will find chapter and verse, if you must, in the Limitation Act 1980. Generally, the time limits you are up against, counting from when your right to claim arose, are these:

- six years for a breach of contract (for example, a duff purchase or an unpaid loan) or 12 years if the contract was made by deed which will be readily apparent from the document as it will start with the words *THIS DEED*, look all fancy, have signatures witnessed by the vicar and make you tremble when you look at it;

- three years for a claim for compensation for a personal injury, whether the claim relates to a breach of contract (for example, you bought a used car, the brakes failed and you ran into a brick wall) or negligence (pedestrian knocked down by car) but claims for personal injuries or anxiety compensation under the Protection from Harassment Act 1997 can be brought within six years;

- six years for a nuisance (for example, habitually disturbed at night by next door neighbour playing 'Delilah' on Hammond organ) but where the nuisance continues (for example, tree roots still encroach or continue to grow or that organ) as opposed to a one-off incident (for example, a tanker oil spoil even though damage may result more than six years later) the six years restart every day of continuation;

- six years for a negligence claim relating to damage to property rather than body;

- one year for claims for defamation (libel or slander) or malicious falsehood (see chapter 47);

- six years for unpaid rent running from when it became due;

- six or 12 years for an 'unfair relationship' claim under section 140 of the Consumer Credit Act 1994 (see chapters 40 and 66); and

- within six months of probate or letters of administration for claims for provision out of a deceased person's estate although the court does have the power to allow more time (see chapter 44).

Try by the various routes available to get your claim settled without court proceedings but the moral is that if you want redress and none of those other routes bring it, pull your finger out and start proceedings. The law does not allow you to wait for ever and the longer you leave it to bring actual court proceedings, the greater the risk witnesses may disappear and that memories will fade – yours and those of your witnesses – making it difficult to prove your case. *"It's nine years since the accident, Mr Troublesore. You waited five years and 364 days before suing and the case has taken some time to get to court. I put it to you that you cannot possibly now be as sure as you make out that the driver of the other car was wearing a red polka dot dress with beige shoes and had rings in her nose and left ear lobe."*

Reviewing the situation

The Civil Procedure Rules 1998 set a special time limit for applying for permission to bring judicial review proceedings (the means for challenging the crackpot decisions of public authorities – see chapter 9 in relation to judicial review of certain arbitration decisions). You must act promptly and, in any event, generally start proceedings within three months from the date on which you say the grounds for challenge arose. The time limit can be extended by the court (but don't hold your breath). In relation to government and local authority planning decisions, that time limit is tighter at just six weeks instead of three months.

On your marks

When does your right to bring a claim arise (or as the law and lawyers poshly put it, your cause of action accrue) which sets the clock ticking? Generally, in a breach of contract claim this will usually be when the contract is broken (the date on which duff goods are purchased or a payment is missed on a loan agreement). In other claims such as for negligence, the right arises when you suffer some loss – even though you are not conscious of it at the time! (see though **Messing with the clock** below). In claims for defamation and malicious falsehood, you have one year from the date on which the words complained of were published in writing or out of the defendant's mouth. In 2020 the Court of Appeal ruled that a financial remedies client's claim against her solicitors for negligence in not obtaining expert evidence of the value of certain of her assets should have been brought within six years of the hearing and not within six years of when judgment was given. That was two and a half months later and meant she was too late.

When you come to calculate the precise date on which the six years (or whatever other period applies) expires, the general rule is that you ignore the actual day on which your right to claim is treated as arising. Let's take as an example a claim for breach of contract that arises on 2 June 2021. You ignore that day in your six year count which means you have until 3 June 2027 inclusive to start a claim. If the courts are closed on the last day then you have until the very next opening day to sue away. However, the Supreme Court ruled in a case called *Matthew and others v Sedman and others* on 21 May 2021 that this general rule did not apply in a 'midnight deadline' case. There, something had to be done by midnight on 2 June 2011 and if not done by then anyone who lost out as a result might have a claim. Because the general rule did not apply, you had to start counting the six years limitation period which would have applied to such a claim, not on 3 June but on 2 June 2011.

Credit card debts

A claim against you for defaulting under a credit card or similar agreement would be a breach of contract claim which is a six year job. But from when do the six years run – from when you first defaulted in making a monthly payment or from when you failed to pay up in response to the default notice that the creditor was obliged to send out (that's section 87(1) of the Consumer Credit Act 1974 talking) before taking court action? The bad news is that the six years run from when you fail to respond to the default notice which means that the creditor has much more time to play with before going to court than had been thought before this point was settled by the Court of Appeal in 2019. The card holder had hoped to escape a debt of £26,570 in that case but it was not to be. The possible good news is that if the creditor (be it the original credit card company or one of those businesses I hate which has bought the debt) waits an eternity before sending out a default notice, that could be regarded by the court to be sufficiently prejudicial to you as to justify letting you wholly or partly off the hook under the unfair relationship stuff in sections 140A and 140B of the Consumer Credit Act 1974 (see chapters 40 and 66).

Exploding washing machines

The clock may tick for longer before you have to start proceedings for compensation claims relating to defective products which are brought under the Consumer Protection Act 1987. Here, the manufacturer and importer of unsafe items can be rendered liable to you even though you didn't have a contract with either and without you having to prove they were negligent. You are given three years to start proceedings running from when you had knowledge about certain factors such as the effect of the defect and the identity of the defendant, with a long stop of ten years. There is a similar – but not identical – set up for negligence claims which do not involve personal injuries, such as claims for defects in property (usually buildings but not necessarily so) against builders, architects, surveyors and the rest, but here you need to claim within six years or, if later, three years of acquiring the necessary knowledge, with a long stop of 15 years.

Messing with the clock

The clock won't tick while you are under 18 or of unsound mind. So, for example, if you are injured in an accident because of someone's negligence when aged four, you have until 21 (18 plus the normal three years) to start proceedings although an adult can still sue on your behalf – the adult is called your *litigation friend* – before you reach 18.

If the claim is for a debt, there may be a bit of clock interference as a result of a breathing space moratorium or a mental health crisis moratorium which came into existence in May 2021 (see chapter 11). Should the debt be covered by the moratorium and the time for starting proceedings be due to run out within eight weeks of the moratorium coming to an end, then you are given an extra eight weeks to start, running from the end of the moratorium. Example: time to claim up on 31 July 2021, moratorium ends on 14 July 2021. 31 July 2021 extended to 25 September 2021.

Where the claim is for compensation for personal injuries (whether on the basis of a breach of contract or negligence) your three years to start proceedings can run from when you have gained sufficient knowledge about things to be able to make a claim if later than when you actually suffered some loss. The knowledge the law says you need is that your injury was significant, that it was down to some legal wrong and the identity of the person responsible.

And even more time than this could be available. Although three years from the date on which your right to claim arose and you knew about it have expired, the court may still be prepared to allow a later claim which is for personal injuries compensation if it would be "equitable" to do so. The court will take into account a host of factors: the length and reason for the delay; how stale the evidence may be for both sides; and how promptly and reasonably you acted once you knew you had a case. These are some of the factors.

The judge's discretion to allow late claims is now of special significance in civil cases arising out of sexual abuse. We are on *Jimmy Savile* type territory here. The law was effectively reversed by the judicial arm of the House of Lords (before it morphed into the Supreme Court) when it decided that the court would have to look at whether there would be a reasonable prospect of a fair trial if more time were given. And this would depend as usual on a number of matters, not least when the complaint of abuse was first made and with what effect. If a complaint had been made and recorded and, in particular, if the defendant had been convicted of the abuse, that would be one thing. On the other hand, if a complaint came out of the blue with no apparent support for it (other perhaps than that the defendant had been accused or convicted of similar abuse in the past) that would be quite another matter. By no means everyone who brings a late claim in a sexual abuse case, however genuine their complaint might be, can reasonably expect the court to allow it to continue. A High Court judge applied the House of Lords ruling in 2020 where the alleged sexual abuse by a priest had taken place around 50 years ago and the priest had since died. Because of the delay, the cogency of the evidence had been substantially diminished which would have considerably prejudiced the trustees of the priest's monastery which was being sued. There was now no prospect of a fair trial and so the claimant failed.

Very tricky Troublesores

Say you have a claim based on the defendant's fraud or the defendant has deliberately concealed from you some fact which is relevant to your right to make a claim against them. Or say you have made a mistake: perhaps you have continued to pay Clive Troublesore for eight years after you sacked him for gross misconduct. And say you haven't started a claim within the usual time limit which applies to it on account of that fraud, concealment or mistake. In these instances, the clock will not begin ticking until you have discovered the fraud, concealment or mistake or, with reasonable diligence, could have done so.

The Supreme Court gave a landmark ruling about how the clock ticks when you have made a mistake, in a November 2020 case against HMRC. You might have paid over money – to the taxman or whoever – believing that, according to the law, you were bound to do so. And then, a few years later in a case to which you are not a party, it is established that the law was not what you thought it was. That would have meant you had made a mistake – of law. The majority of the Supreme Court reaffirmed that a mistake of law is covered by this no clock tick stuff so that, until you discovered the mistake, or could have done so with reasonable diligence, your six years for suing whoever you paid under that mistake for the return of your money would not begin to run. But at what point could you, or should you with reasonable diligence, have discovered the law was different from what you had thought? This will be the point at which the basis of making the payment was legally questionable rather than the date on which you could have discovered the outcome of the court case demonstrating you had made a mistake – when you would have had good grounds for supposing that you had a valid or worthwhile claim. When should you have realised that the first decision might be dodgy? These are difficult questions to answer and courts will have to grapple with them in future cases.

Acknowledgment and part payment traps

Take this scenario. A sum of money is owed under a contract and you have six years from when it should have been repaid within which to start proceedings. But during those six years, the debtor acknowledges the debt or makes a part payment towards its settlement. Then the six years restarts from the date of the acknowledgment or part payment. In fact, the six years could repeatedly restart with each acknowledgment or part payment which is made and you, your children and your children's children might still have a right to sue although they could have to go to the debtor's graveyard to serve the court papers. But before an acknowledgment will be effective to start the six years running, it must be in writing and signed by the debtor.

> *Dear Whitewash Credit Controller*
>
> *I acknowledge that I still owe your company £15,000 for goods sold and delivered. I will pay as soon as I can.*
>
> *Yours faithfully*
>
> *Clive Troublesore*
>
> *14 July 2021*

> PS I'll be in on Saturday for some paint and grouting. Just add it on to the £15K.

That would be more than sufficient. As the creditor, it could be worthwhile you procuring a written acknowledgment where you are close to the six year expiry date for starting proceedings PLUS you are pretty sure that at long last your debtor is to show you the colour of their money PLUS you prefer not to invest time and the money you have left into beginning a claim simply to preserve your legal right to do so. A belated acknowledgment after the six years are up, however, is no good. Once a right to claim is time-barred, that right cannot be revived by a later written acknowledgment or even a part payment. A crafty debtor might try and trick you into postponing the commencement of proceedings beyond the six year limit by a *verbal* acknowledgment.

> "Hello, Whitewash man, Troublesore here. You said you were about to sue me before it was too late. Don't trouble. My life assurance is maturing next month and I'll clear what I owe with 20% interest. You can write and confirm our conversation."

Useless to you. Not in writing and any writing must emanate from the debtor and not you.

There aren't any formalities that need to be observed to make a part payment effective for the purpose of restarting the six years. But it would be wise for you to send your debtor written acknowledgment of its receipt, especially if payment has been made in cash. A payment made on behalf of the debtor and at their direction will be as effective as a payment by the debtor themselves.

24 hours to go

Your time limit runs out tomorrow? Get the ruddy claim form issued SOMEWHERE. If it's a claim for money and you can't get to the County Court Money Claims Centre at Salford then you should insist on your nearest county court civil hearing centre accepting it and passing it on to Salford. If it's for a remedy other than the payment of money or a mixture of money and something else, get it to any county court civil hearing centre. And should a hearing centre refuse to let you in, insert the claim form into their drop box. And don't forget to accompany the claim form with the correct fee. No fee or an insufficient fee will make the claim form a non-event. You will be treated as having started the proceedings when the claim form in triplicate and the correct fee with it were received at the court destination and not when they were subsequently formally issued the claim.

For defendants' eyes only

If you want to defend a claim on the ground that it has been made too late, your defence should run something like this:

> 1. The limitation period for the claimant's claim as alleged under the Limitation Act 1980 expired before the commencement of the claim and the claim should accordingly be struck out.
>
> 2. The defendant makes no admissions as to the allegations of fact contained in the particulars of claim.
>
> or
>
> 2. Further and alternatively, the defendant denies the allegations of fact made in paragraphs 1 to 13 of the particulars of claim. [go on to set out your defence to the claim to be considered by the court in the event that it rules against you on the time point or the claim is one in which the court has power to extend the claimant's time for making a claim and the claimant successfully applies for it to do so].

Now, say, for whatever reason, the claim against you is not too old but you have a valid claim which arises out of the same events which is too old for you to bring your own proceedings. Perhaps you haven't paid money due up front five years ago for building works and have been sued by the builders for what they say is owed, but you maintain that the works which were completed more than six years ago were messed up by them and that they were in breach of contract. In that situation, you could defend the case relying on the old breach of contract so as to knock out the claim entirely or reduce it. What you could not do is to also counterclaim in the proceedings with a view to collecting some damages in addition to knocking out the claim against you.

Usual time limits for starting court case*	
Type of case	**Time limit**
Breach of contract including debt	6 years
Breach of contract made by deed including debt	12 years
Claim for personal injury	3 years
Claim for negligence not including personal injury	6 years
Nuisance	6 years
Libel, slander or malicious falsehood	1 year
Money claim under Protection from Harassment Act 1977	6 years
Claim for provision out of deceased's estate	6 months (from probate or letters of administration)
Judicial review application	3 months
Unfair relationship claim	6 or 12 years
*But see above for how a longer period may sometimes be gained	

Chapter 14

Judgment Without A Hearing And Setting Aside

Watch 'yer clock

Some cases need a court hearing: for example, landlord and mortgage lender claims for possession. Other cases generally only need a hearing if the other party is contesting them, such as claims for a fixed sum of money. In those fixed money cases, the court will notify you of the date by which the other party must send their defence to the court. That will usually be within 14 days of the date the court treats them as having received the claim form. They call that the 'date of service'. The 14 days will be lengthened to 28 days if they have sent the court an 'acknowledgment of service' form stating they intend to defend within the 14 days. Tip for defendants without a hope in hell of avoiding a judgment but needing as much time as possible to get some money together – put in an acknowledgment of service and earn an extra 14 days before the evil judgment against you can be obtained.

Where the other party has failed to come up with their defence within the 14 days or the 28 days, you can send the court a request for judgment against them for whatever sum you have claimed (including any interest and costs specified on the claim form). You may ask for the judgment to be paid immediately, within a fixed period (that's frequently 14 days) or by specified instalments (which might be in accordance with an offer the other side has put forward).

If you have claimed money but not fixed how much – this is called a claim for an unspecified amount – then, in the absence of a defence from the other side within the periods we have been looking at above, you can request judgment in the same way. But the difference is that the judgment will be for a sum to be assessed by the court. The assessment will require a court hearing and the court will give directions about how this should be prepared for.

As rare as it might be and as already indicated, you can fix the amount of money you are claiming even in those cases where it would usually be left to the court to decide how much, as in a claim for compensation for injuries suffered in an accident or for distress and disappointment with a holiday from hell. What's the point? Well, if the other side fails to put in a defence in time and you obtain a judgment, it will be for the fixed sum you claimed and there won't need to be a hearing for the compensation to be assessed. Where the judgment is for a bonkers amount – £220,000 for a cut to the left buttock – this is almost certain to incite the other side to apply to the court for the judgment to be set aside. The more likely that the judgment sum exceeds the figure the claim is really worth, the more likely it is that the court will set the judgment aside. So, a bit of restraint, my dears. Remember that the greater the amount claimed, the higher the court fee for starting the case (see chapter 17).

Please make it summary, not default

Your defendant may be abroad, fail to cough up the money to be paid under a judgment and leave you to have to enforce the judgment in their country. A judgment from a judge in England and Wales who has looked at the evidence may be more readily enforceable in another country than a judgment obtained by default without a hearing. That was the position in a 2021 High Court case in which the claimant had sued a state-owned iron export company in Venezuela which had ignored the proceedings. The claimant could have gone for a default judgment. Instead it went after summary judgment (see chapter 21) so as to assist with enforcement abroad. The court obliged and summary judgment was given.

Under starter's orders

The race is on once the other party has had the claim form. Set your alarm clock to go off a nanosecond after their 14- or 28-day deadline expires or ask your partner or a pet to hit you over the head with a copy of this book when that nanosecond strikes. The race is between you and the other party to get your request for a judgment to the court before the other side gets their late defence to the court. Because of an April 2020 change to the Civil Procedure Rules 1998 rule 12.3, it is now clear that you will not be entitled to a judgment if the court receives a late defence before it receives a request for judgment. Tip for defendants who are not going to be able to put in their defence on time – apply to the court for an extension of time to take this step and, if granted, this will prevent judgment being entered against you before the extended time has come to an end. The deadline may be extended by agreement between the parties but for no longer than 28 days. If there has been an agreement to extend then the defendant must notify it to the court.

Setting aside

This is the fancy name for getting a judgment or order cancelled. The most common application to the court is for a judgment obtained without a hearing – a judgment in default – to be set aside. The application, which will almost invariably be made by the defendant against whom it has been given (though, occasionally, a claimant who has obtained the judgment in error will apply and the defendant will be only too happy to consent but may want to ask the court to order the claimant to pay their costs run up due to the cock-up) should be in form N244. You may well want to oppose the application if the judgment was in your favour. Or you may be making the application if the judgment was entered against you. Where the judgment was patently wrong – the time for the acknowledgment of service or defence to go in had not yet expired or the claimant had not served the particulars of claim before judgment was entered – the court may well set it aside without a hearing or any hearing which takes place will be concerned only with who was to blame and so who pays the defendant's costs.

If the application is made on the ground that the judgment was wrongly entered as it was premature then there is no time limit for making the application. In all other cases, the application should be made 'promptly'. There is no precise number of days, weeks or years defined. Different judges will have different views about how long that should give the defendant. But if it is you making the application and you have waited longer than 14 days after finding out about the judgment, you would be well advised to explain in your application why you didn't make the application earlier. Do it as a precaution against coming up before a mean judge. It may be that you wanted to take legal advice first, you needed to obtain important information about the case from the claimant or their solicitors before deciding what to do or you were overcome by shock when you got the judgment and passed out for a week. However, the question of promptness is something the judge must take into account when deciding whether or not to set aside. You may have been too slow in making the application but could still succeed with it. All relevant circumstances would have to be factored in by the judge and the stronger your intended defence to the claim if judgment is set aside, the more forgiving the judge is likely to be over your delay in making the application.

To win the set aside application where the judgment was not wrongly entered, and subject to what I have said about promptness, you need to show that you have a real prospect of successfully defending the claim or that there is some other good reason why the judgment should be set aside. Real prospect of success? That doesn't mean you will win but that you have a reasonable chance of doing so. The judge might think that both sides have a reasonable prospect of success! It is important for you to support your application with a draft of the form of defence you want to put forward. Some other good reason? That allows a pretty broad approach. Perhaps you want to settle the claim in full but are too late to get the judgment cancelled in the Register of Judgments, Orders and Fines (see chapter 27) in which event the judge might be persuaded to set the judgment aside on condition that you settle up within a specified period or, alternatively, adjourn the set aside application for that specified period to see if you are true to your word and then set aside at the next hearing.

I'm afraid that's not quite the end of it. If and when the judge is satisfied that you have a real prospect of successfully defending or there is some other good reason for setting aside, they have to go on to decide whether to grant you 'relief from sanction'. The sanction was the entry of judgment 'cos you didn't put in a defence. This stage involves the judge considering how serious or significant was your failure to put in a defence; the reasons for it; and whether it is just in all the circumstances for you to be let off.

It sounds like the trial of a capital murder charge. It isn't and in the majority of cases, applications to set aside will be dealt with in under 30 minutes: more often 15 minutes. A judge can pretty quickly weigh up the justice of the case.

If the judgment is set aside then the court will cancel any registration of it at the Register of Judgments, Orders and Fines and no fee for that step will be payable by you.

Chapter 15

Getting Your Opponent's Documents

The sooner the better

Whether you begin court proceedings or how you frame your case in any proceedings you do bring may be dependent on what will be revealed by certain documents held by your opponent – but not you. If these are documents which the court would compel your opponent to reveal to you as part of the process of what is called *disclosure of documents* in the course of proceedings which were brought then you may well be able to get hold of them earlier rather than later. If the documents would sink you, good to see them before you launch a claim with all the preparatory work and expense that could involve. If the documents would sink your opponent and you can demonstrate that you know it (and your opponent knows it) that may force them to capitulate and settle without proceedings. If the documents would reinforce your case and your opponent is denying any liability to you, good to see them to help you assess the risks of litigation. And if the documents would discourage you from making certain allegations in the particulars of claim but encourage you to make others, good to get them in and avoid having to amend the particulars of claim later on which might slow down the case and incur unnecessary expense.

Philip Kanal of Chichester – fresh from his 1994 success in obtaining a £300 settlement from British Airways after starting county court proceedings for allowing passenger smoking in a non-smoking row close to that occupied by himself and his family travelling from Heathrow to Toronto and because of crew neglect obliging him to attend to an adjacent passenger who was vomiting – was more recently back on the litigation trail. On a dark night in March 2015 on the B2178 his car struck a pothole and split a tyre and buckled the wheel. The highway authority West Sussex County Council rejected his claim for £629.16 but thanked him for reporting the incident. He insisted on being provided with documents relating to the authority's inspection and maintenance of the road. These documents destroyed their argument that they operated a reasonable system of maintenance and repair. When further documents were requested they offered to settle at £314.58. When told that a court claim was ready, they coughed up the full amount.

Where a pre-action protocol letter has been sent (see chapter 10) and has been met with a denial of liability, it may be that the documents you are after should have been provided by your opponent but were not. It may be that you have not reached the stage of a pre-action protocol letter. Either way, the documents you want could well come to you by courtesy of a court order on an application by you under part 31 of the Civil Procedure Rules 1998 for a *pre-action disclosure order*. The application is made on form N244 and should be backed by a written statement explaining what you want and why you want it.

Before you make your application, write to your opponent. The court will expect you to have done so. Who knows, your opponent may actually agree to comply with the request.

> "Pursuant to rule 31.16 of the Civil Procedure Rules 1998, I hereby request you to supply me with copies of the documents specified in the schedule to this letter within 14 days of the date of receipt of this letter. It is my intention to bring proceedings against you in relation to the claim about which we have already been in correspondence if you will not settle with me; the documents would be disclosable by you in such proceedings as part of standard disclosure; and disclosure before proceedings is desirable in order to dispose fairly of the proceedings or, by actually assisting us to resolve the dispute without proceedings and, in any event, would save costs.
>
> I have to require you to take this letter as formal notice that if my above request is not complied with, I shall issue an application in the county court for an order compelling you to disclose the documents to me and I shall ask the court to order you to pay the costs of such application. I am a litigant in person and will ask for such costs to be assessed on that basis.
>
> I confirm that I undertake to pay your reasonable photocopying charges for providing me with the documents in question.
>
> **Schedule of Documents**
>
> *(specify the documents you want)*

And when you are met with a refusal or silence, you can issue your application and send it to a civil hearing centre. There will need to be a hearing of the application (unless your opponent capitulates in the meantime) and so choose the most geographically convenient hearing centre. If you and your opponent are miles apart, you may well choose the centre which is closest to you. When describing the order you want on the form N244 you can adopt the wording you have utilised in the letter you sent to your opponent (unless it was unmitigated nonsense). With the application, include a draft of the order you are inviting the court to make. Not only is this good practice, but it will put you in the judge's good books.

> *Case no: BY4999786*
>
> IN THE COUNTY COURT
>
> SITTING AT PEARDROP
>
> BETWEEN
>
> CLIVE TROUBLESORE Applicant
>
> - and -
>
> WHITEWASH LIMITED Respondent

> *Before District Judge Wisdom-Solomon on 14 July 2021*
>
> *Upon hearing the applicant in person and legal representative for the respondent*
>
> IT IS ORDERED that-
>
> 1.   Subject to paragraph 2 of this order, the respondent must disclose to the applicant copies of the documents specified in the schedule to this order within 28 days of the date of this order.
>
> 2.   In the event that the respondent asserts that any of the documents referred to are no longer in its control, the respondent must serve on the applicant within 28 days of the date of this order a written statement (verified by a statement of truth) specifying which of such documents this applies to and what has happened to such documents and shall further specify such documents (if any) in respect of which it claims a right or duty to withhold inspection.
>
> 3.   The respondent do pay the applicant's costs of this application summarily assessed on the litigant in person basis at £(amount to be inserted in due course) within 14 days of the date of this order.
>
> *Schedule referred to above*
>
> *(specify the documents you want)*

In your written statement in support of the application, describe what your claim is about and how your opponent comes to be involved; produce with the statement copies of the relevant correspondence you have exchanged with your opponent about the documents in question; and explain why you say that you should have the documents at this early stage. Do not go over the top with your document requests. If you have done so in your original letter of request, there is no shame in cutting down what you ask for in your later form N244. If it is important for you to see the originals of certain documents instead of just photocopies (because, for example, you have some doubt about their authenticity) then you should adapt the paperwork to require production of those particular documents at a set time and place.

If your opponent can persuade the court that your claim is dotty and does not stand a hope in hell of success then your application will fail. That's why your statement should cover the merits of your claim.

Costs are a little unusual in these cases. If you succeed, the likelihood is that the judge will make no order for costs in favour of either side and only if your opponent has behaved particularly unreasonably, an order that they pay your costs. If you lose, you will probably be ordered to pay your opponent's costs. You should send the court and your opponent a statement of your costs before the hearing (see chapter 35).

Your opponent cannot be compelled to come up with documents they do not have in their possession and do not control – before or after proceedings have been brought. Should they say following the start of proceedings that Joe Bloggs down the road has this crucial document and they are not entitled to extract it from him themselves, then you could make an application to the court against Joe Bloggs. The procedure follows a similar pattern to the application before proceedings against your opponent. You will find more about it in rule 31.17 of the Civil Procedure Rules 1998.

Chapter 16

In Full And Final Settlement

Take it or leave it

Plump and sweet fresh strawberries dipped in the finest milk chocolate, served with a glass of chilled vintage champagne on a warm summer's evening in the gardens of your employer's estate. You reckon that's tempting? In the Temptation Stakes, it doesn't come within a mile of this (even if you could get another two glasses out of it). A cheque for £5,000 from someone who has owed you £7,000 under an invoice you sent out seven months ago and who you have been chasing for settlement ever since and who has written to say that they have tendered the cheque in full and final settlement of the invoice. That's what you call temptation, eh? Gift in the hand and all that so do you present it and write off the balance or return it and say that you are owed £7,000, it's nothing less than £7,000 that you want and it's £7,000 that you are going to get, you indescribable piece of dirt and son of unmarried parents?

Take it and DON'T leave it

But how about turning the temptation into a dilemma and consider paying in the cheque and suing your debtor for the balance? Can you successfully do this? It depends! What it depends on will usually be whether or not the debt is disputed. If it is not disputed then it should be safe for you to expeditiously bank and claim the balance, provided, that is, you do not delay in letting your debtor know that you do not accept the lesser amount in full and final settlement. Otherwise the delay may be treated as evidence that you have accepted in full and final settlement. Of course, you will want the cheque to be paid out on before you break the bad news to your debtor for otherwise the likelihood is that they will cancel it. And immediately you know that the cheque has cleared, you get off a communication to your debtor.

> *"Dear Mr Tryon*
>
> *I acknowledge receipt of your letter dated 14 July 2021 enclosing cheque for £5,000 which you have tendered "in full and final settlement" of my invoice. I have presented the cheque for payment but I positively do not accept it in full and final settlement and I have never given you any reason to suppose that I would accept anything less than the full amount due to me. The invoice has never been disputed and, as you well know, there are no grounds for dispute and you have no legitimate reason for withholding a single penny of what you owe me.*
>
> *I give you notice now that unless the balance due to me is paid within seven days of the date on which you receive this letter, I shall institute proceedings against you for the recovery of the £2,000 balance together with interest and costs.*

> Yours faithfully
>
> Clive Troublesore"

Disputed debt

The tender of a lesser amount for a disputed debt is another matter. Then your debtor may be treated as providing some legal consideration for tendering the payment – that is, providing a benefit to you by paying an amount they contend is not due – so that, if you bank the cheque, you are likely to lose out in respect of the shortfall. The dispute must be a genuine one. It would not be enough, for example, for your debtor to invent some fanciful reason for short changing you. But if at the time they believe in it and intend to pursue it in court, if necessary, even if it raises a doubtful point or some legal point which has not been ruled on before, that will be sufficient. The Court of Appeal made that clear in a 2019 case called *Simanatob v Shavleyan*. So a serious dilemma does kick in when Mr Tryon, with justification, takes issue over the invoice, and writes to you – and all the Tryons in England and Wales might adopt wording along these lines in a genuinely disputed situation – like this:

> "Dear Mr Troublesore
>
> **Without Prejudice***
>
> *You have invoiced me for £7,000. I do not owe you £7,000. You are in breach of our agreement in a number of respects. In particular, you were two months late in completing the works and various of the materials you supplied were not of satisfactory quality as I have already informed you. These breaches have caused me considerable loss which I am advised I can set off against the invoice.*
>
> *I prefer to settle this matter without suffering the expense and inconvenience of court proceedings although, rest assured that if it does not settle as now offered by me, any proceedings you choose to bring will be defended with vigour.*
>
> *I enclose my cheque in your favour for £5,000 which I tender in full and final settlement of your invoice and with a denial that you are entitled to this sum. My calculations point to the value of the set off for my own losses to which I am entitled equating to a sum in excess of £3,000 and I am advised that I would be entitled to set off the entirety of those losses against your invoice. However, I am prepared in the spirit of compromise to forgo obtaining compensation for all those losses by way of set off.*
>
> *Your presentation of the enclosed cheque for payment will constitute acceptance of the £5,000 on the basis on which it is tendered and, subject to such presentation, it will not be open to you to make any further claim against me in respect of the invoice or the works and materials supplied to which the invoice relates.*

> *Yours faithfully*
>
> *Bernard Tryon"*

*The words "without prejudice" are important (see chapter 10). If Mr Troublesore banks the cheque but sues Mr Tryon for the balance, Mr Tryon has a choice. He can ask the court to throw out the case on the basis that he and Mr Troublesore concluded a compromise agreement which binds Mr Troublesore and rely on the letter as evidence of the agreement. The inclusion of the words "without prejudice" will not prevent this. Alternatively, he can decide that he does not want to be bound by the agreement and claim that he owes nothing to Mr Troublesore because of his contract breaches. In that event, the judge will not be able to see the letter before they decide the case in view of the inclusion of the words "without prejudice" and so Mr Tryon will not be prejudiced or embarrassed by the offer.

Undisputed debt but payment by third party

For your debtor, there is one possible way round the rule that you are not barred in the case of an undisputed debt from chasing the balance when you accept a cheque for a lesser sum which is tendered "in full and final settlement". It is to procure payment by a third party.

> *"Dear Mr Troublesore*
>
> *My nephew Bernard Tryon has referred me to your outstanding invoice against him for £5,000. I am assisting him in connection with it. I am prepared to pay you on his behalf a lesser payment but on the strict condition that the lesser sum is accepted in full and final settlement of the debt.*
>
> *Therefore, I now enclose my own cheque in your favour for £3,000 which I tender in full and final settlement of the invoice and the works and materials supplied to which it relates. If you present the cheque for payment then this will be an acceptance of the terms on which it is tendered and it will not be open to you to make any claim against my nephew for the £2,000 balance or any part of it or for the works and materials which are the subject of the invoice.*
>
> *Yours faithfully*
>
> *A Vuncular Tryon"*

There the payment by the uncle being someone who has no legal responsibility to Mr Troublesore constitutes the legal consideration which is likely to bind Mr Troublesore if he banks the cheque.

Undisputed debt: lump sum payment

Your debtor can put forward a settlement proposal for payment themselves on a debt which they do not dispute which, if accepted, will bind you. Suppose they owe you £5,000 which they are paying off at the rate of £5 per month when out of the blue comes this.

> "Dear Mr Troublesore
>
> **Without Prejudice**
>
> Remember me? You agreed to accept instalments from me at the rate of £5 per month when I was in dire straits and that was, let me see, more than 20 years ago. If at all possible, I would now like to get the noose of this debt removed from my neck. I could:
>
> > borrow £1,000 from my uncle;
> >
> > or
> >
> > now I am 55, take £1,000 out of a small pension fund that I own;
> >
> > or
> >
> > sell some household items for around £1,000 which are protected from being seized by a bailiff or enforcement officer,
>
> which I would then be prepared to pay to you provided you accepted that sum in full and final settlement of the debt so that I was then fully discharged from any further liability to you.
>
> Please let me know whether you are prepared to settle with me on this basis."
>
> Yours faithfully
>
> Bernard Tryon"

If you accept and you are paid out the lesser sum in one go as agreed, you could not legally chase the rest of the money. Mr Tryon would be doing more than discharging part of his legal obligation to you. He would be doing something he was not legally obligated to do: that's the legal consideration for the deal.

Chapter 17

Court Fees

Save £s £s £s

Civil and family cases would be so much more enjoyable if it wasn't for the court fees. When you start a case and when you subsequently take some formal step during the case at court, you will almost always be asked to pay a fee for the privilege unless, as does sometimes happen, the court forgets to ask. The money is used to run the courts. If you win the case, the loser will probably have to pay those fees back to you. There are ways of making savings on the fees. You might even be able to escape paying them entirely by getting them waived under the fee remission system.

My favourite tip for saving on court fees was to use the online procedure for money and possession claims where that was possible, instead of sending in paper versions of the necessary paperwork. In an effort to sabotage this chapter (mild joke alert), the Courts and Tribunal Service scrapped the cyberspace discounts in May 2021. The fees are now the same, online and offline.

Fee saving tip 1

I was in the back of a taxi – as one is – and the driver was talking – as they do – and having covered Margaret Thatcher (it's an old story), Brexit and the state of the prisons, he moved on to small claims. He had brought a succession of them in his local county court which he had meticulously timed to coincide with the regular summer break he took when he signed on. By doing so, he managed to get the court fees waived by courtesy of the fee remission system, sometimes called 'help with fees'. At the end of the journey I told him I was a judge. He made off just as my feet touched the pavement and before I had had the chance to tip him. A gratuity remission situation, in fact. This was a few years back. The system is still with us but because it was costing the state a cool £28m a year, it was tightened up in 2013. Here's how it works now.

To get a fee remitted, you must pass a financial test. The merits of the case you want to start or application you want to make don't come into it. It may be a bag of tripe. Not too much capital and not too much income. On capital, the higher the fee, the more capital you are allowed. Take a fee of up to £1,000. It would require capital of £3,000 or more to disqualify you from remission (or £6,000 or more if you or your partner are 61 or over). Your home will be disregarded.

If you aren't knocked out on capital, you then have to pass the gross income test which applies a series of thresholds to single persons or couples with an allowance for children. Below a certain threshold, you will be granted full remission. Otherwise you will be required to make a contribution towards the fee of £5 for every £10 of your monthly income which is over the relevant threshold. The government is planning to raise these thresholds to keep pace with inflation since 2016 by about 7% and the changes are likely to take effect in around September 2021. If you have been refused remission because your income was slightly too high, you may get it for future court fees even in the same case. There is automatic remission for the main state benefits.

You can apply online for remission but, whether the application is made on or offline, the EX160 is the handle of the form to be used. There are guidance notes called the EX160A and, you've got to confess, whoever came up with that title should be penning the messages on greeting cards. The EX160 was changed in April 2020. Although the Courts and Tribunals Service won't admit it, the changes were necessary because the previous form was misleading. Where your partner has a contrary interest to you – for example, you may be litigating against your partner – their capital and income will not be taken into account: otherwise, they will. The new form makes it clear that if your partner is maintaining any child who is not living with you, then details should be provided and that liability will be taken into account. This was not apparent from the old form although it was mentioned in the old guidance notes. But, like train companies' conditions of carriage, who reads them? If your application for remission on the strength of the old form was turned down but would have been granted had your partner's payments for a child been included, then you could have a go at complaining to the Courts and Tribunals Service and asking for a refund of the court fee for which you ended up paying.

Should you have struggled to pay a court fee without applying for remission and only later discovered that you could have successfully applied for remission, you are able to make a retrospective application and obtain a refund. But don't hang about as you have just three months from the date on which you paid the fee to apply for its return.

And should your day be ruined by a court notification that your application for remission has been refused, you might want to put up a fight and ask the hearing centre's so-called delivery manager to reconsider it on the grounds of *exceptional circumstances*. There is discretion to still allow remission even though you have too much capital or income but you would have to satisfy the manager that there were extenuating reasons to remit. If, for example, your claim would be stifled by not receiving remission and though you enjoyed a relatively high income on paper you had no disposable means, you could be in with a chance but don't hold your breath.

> "*Dear Delivery Manager*
>
> *I ask you to consider/reconsider my application for fee remission under the schedule to the applicable fees order at paragraph 16. I submit that there are exceptional circumstances which justify remission and without remission I will be unable to raise the money I need to pay the fee. This would be contrary to justice because it would prevent me from pursuing a meritorious claim and to obtain the relief to which I am entitled to make the application in these proceedings which is essential*

> *if justice is to be done. The exceptional circumstances on which I rely are [specify the circumstances].*
>
> *Yours faithfully*
>
> *Clive Troublesore"*

The delivery manager turns you down? You can appeal to the operations manager for the court.

It is not possible to claim remission for the fee on starting a claim when you are doing so through Money Claim Online. You would have to issue an offline claim in that situation.

Fee saving tip 2

You can pay a court fee by debit or credit card and, with the latter, earn cashback or points on it.

Fee saving tip 3

In a defended civil case a number of procedural steps have to be taken: for example, relevant documents and witness statements exchanged. If your opponent has failed to do as ordered, the court has the power to strike out their claim or defence. Or the claim or defence may be complete nonsense and the court could strike it out at an early stage of the case (see chapter 21). In this sort of situation and in a multiplicity of others, you can apply to the court to exercise one of its appropriate powers. Trouble is a formal application is usually expected (in form N244) and that will cost you serious money, unless the fee is remitted (see **Fee Saving Tip 1** above). By serious money I mean £255 (see below for increase news) – pick the readers of this book off the floor, usher, they have just passed out – or if you are contemplating that a judge will decide the application 'on paper' without a hearing at court, the fee is a trifling £100 (see below for increase news). What you do, therefore, is try and save paying a fee by refraining from the use of a formal application form and sending a letter to the court which says:

> *"I am the claimant. The defendant has failed to comply with paragraph 8 of the order made on 14 July 2021. The defendant has previously been in breach of four orders in these proceedings. I respectfully invite the court to exercise its case management powers and, of its own initiative, order that the defence be struck out and judgment be entered in my favour for the sums I have claimed and costs to be assessed by the court in default of agreement on the litigant in person basis.*
>
> *Yours faithfully*
>
> *Clive Troublesore"*

The judge could treat that as a formal application and direct that you pay a prescribed fee. Or the judge may let it go.

Fee saving tip 4

If you do make a formal application in the course of civil proceedings (see *Fee Saving Tip 3* above) the form N244 will invite you to say whether you want it dealt with at a hearing or without a hearing. By opting for no hearing you can tender the lower fee of £100 (my prediction is that this will be increased to £108 before the end of this chapter) instead of £255 (my prediction is that this will be increased to £275 at the same time). Now the court may direct a hearing even when you have not asked for one but it may well not trouble to collect the difference between the two fees.

Fee saving tip 5

Do not over exaggerate your civil claim. It looks naff to the judge. The financial reason for not doing it is that it may waste you money. The more you claims, the more you pays. Take an online claim which is worth say £250. You could allow a bit of manoeuvre for negotiation by claiming £300 which would cost you a court fee of £35. But by going the next band up and claiming over £300 and up to £500 you will incur a fee of £50. If the case is defended and in due course you win and are awarded no more than £300, the probability is that the judge will order the loser to pay you back £35 and not £50. The value you have placed on your claim will also affect the trial fee you will later have to pay where the claim is being defended (see *Fee saving tip 7* below). You could be limited in what you get back from the loser towards the hearing fee in the same way by having gone after too much money.

Fee saving tip 6

When a civil claim is going forward as defended, there will be a full hearing: let's call it a trial. You as the claimant will be charged what is called a trial fee (but sometimes the court will call it a hearing fee). It is intended to cover the expense of laying on a judge with a roof over the heads of all participants (let's forget that the roof may sometimes leak) and all the facilities that you will suffer or enjoy with a view to attaining or evading justice. We are looking at big money with this fee. For a small claim the amount of the fee depends on how much you have claimed and ranges from £25 (though I predict soon to rise to £27) on a claim for up to £300 to £335 (though I predict soon to rise to £352) on a claim for over £3,000. On a fast track claim it is £545 and on a multi-track claim (are you seated?) it is £1,090 (though I predict soon to rise to £1,174). If, having paid the trial fee, the case settles so that no trial takes place, the chance of getting the fee back has gone. It is no longer refundable, even for a small claim. Incidentally, should the predicted increases not have materialised as yet, you may wish to consider paying the trial fee early as some increase for the fee is on its way, for sure. But see below.

The trial fee is now payable much later than it used to be. The deadline for payment is usually 28 days before the trial date and the likelihood is that the court will notify this deadline to you at the same time as it notifies the trial date. There are two exceptions. Firstly, if the trial date is fixed just 35 days or less in advance, the fee will be payable within seven days of the trial notification going out. Secondly, where there is a fee remission request pending (see **Fee saving tip 1** above) and awaiting a decision when the deadline for payment arrives, the requirement for payment will be put on hold. If you are then refused remission, the fee will have to be paid within seven days of the court sending out notice of the refusal or by 28 days before the trial date, if later. Should the court get the deadline for payment wrong, as sometimes it does, and you could do with more time for payment, then tell the court of its error. If a claim has been abandoned by the claimant or killed off by the court, the case may still be going ahead on the defendant's counterclaim. In that situation, the trial fee will be payable but by the defendant instead and rules which mirror those for the claimant will come into play.

Here's a whopping opportunity for some cash back BUT only for old cases. The former scheme for having to pay the trial fee earlier and for being able to obtain a refund on settlement before trial will still apply. That's provided, before 6 March 2017, the court has either fixed the trial date or given a date for the start of the trial window. If there has been an extraordinary delay in the progress of the case, there could still be some life in this exception.

The potential for avoiding payment of the trial fee by securing a settlement of the case can be used as a bargaining tool like this:

> "Dear Whitewash Limited
>
> *I am writing to remind you that you have not responded to my offer to you for the settlement of my claim.*
>
> *The trial fee is £x. I must pay it to the court by 14 July 2021. I will not have to pay it if the claim settles before that date. The fee will be part of my costs of the case and so, in the absence of a settlement, you will be obliged to pay back that fee to me should you be required to meet the costs, as I expect to be the position. Settling with me timeously will save you money. I hope you appreciate this.*
>
> *Yours faithfully*
>
> *Clive Troublesore"*

Beware. You fail to pay the trial fee or pay it late? Oh dear. The claim will be automatically struck out. Deaded! And you will be condemned to pay the other side's costs. But you can apply to the court for the claim to be reinstated. An application should be made on form N244 and explain why you have defaulted. Provided it is made promptly after you realise what has happened and you put forward a credible excuse for your omission ('I forgot' may be enough), I reckon you will have a very good chance of achieving reinstatement. But reinstatement will be conditional on you shelling out the trial fee or getting it remitted. The time limit for payment or producing evidence of remission will be two days from the court's order when reinstatement was granted although if you were not present or represented at the hearing, the limit will be seven days from when a copy of the order is taken to have reached you.

Fee saving tip 7

The trial fee (see *Fee saving tip 6*) for a fast track claim is cheaper than for a multi-track claim and the hearing fee on a small claim is the cheapest of all. Although the small claim limit is usually £10,000 and the fast track limit is usually £25,000, the court may be persuaded to "track down" – try a claim for over £10,000 as a small claim or a claim for over £25,000 on the fast track provided in either case it won't take longer than one day to hear. There may be considerations other than the trial fee but by securing a "tracking down" the trial fee will be substantially reduced.

Fee saving tip 8

Don't ask the court to photocopy a document for you. Unless you are a female with a Manchester City Football Club season ticket and the request is directed to a lecherous looking male usher, the charge will be £10 for ten pages or less (I predict soon to rise to £11) plus 50p for each subsequent page. And fee remission (see *Fee saving tip 1*) does not apply to copying charges.

Fee saving tip 9

A claim may involve more than one head. Take a claim for compensation arising out of a road accident. You could be after £2,000 for car repair charges and £10,000 for your injuries and loss of earnings while you were off work. You may be able to agree with the defendant what compensation you should have if the defendant was to blame for the accident but be at war as to which of you was in fact to blame for the accident. As we have seen, the amount of the court fee for starting the claim (and the amount of the trial fee) will depend on the amount being claimed. There is nothing improper in reaching an agreement with the defendant that you will bring proceedings for the recovery of the repair costs only – this will require the judge to rule on blame – and to abide by the court's decision on blame in relation to the other losses. This will keep the fees down because they will be based on a lower figure. Of course, there needs to be certainty that the defendant will honour the agreement if found to have been liable and may only work where insurance companies are involved for both of you.

Some of the other fees

The prescribed court fees can be found at court form EX50 (see gov.uk/court-fees-what-they-are). The fee for starting a possession of land claim has risen to £355 (or £325 online) and for applying for divorce, nullity, or civil partnership dissolution to £550 (though I predict a further increase soon to £592). Judicial separation is cheaper at £365. No discounts for two at the same time! Further reductions came into effect on 3 August 2020 after it was revealed that for various services performed by the courts, users were being charged more than it cost to provide them. Overcharged! But no refunds for suckers who have paid out more than they should have done. Sorry. And a raft of inflationary increases is likely to hit soon of around 7%.

Part 5

CRIKEY, PROCEEDINGS HAVE STARTED

Chapter 18

The Malicious Claimant

Turning the tables

Malicious prosecution was, until recently, only regarded as the basis of a claim for damages against the police and the occasional private crank who brought criminal proceedings without the best of intentions. But the Supreme Court has now decided that it can be the basis of a civil claim too.

Making a successful malicious prosecution claim following a civil case won't be a walkover. 'Malicious' is given a special meaning for this purpose. You would have to show that whoever brought the claim against you had 'no reasonable and probable cause' and legitimate reason for doing so. They must have deliberately misused the court system. Bringing the claim in the knowledge that it was without any foundation whatsoever should be enough. And so should bringing the claim while being indifferent to whether it could be supported or solely to gain some benefit which is unconnected with the case. If I take you to the county court for compensation on the strength of a pack of lies to the effect that you drove into the rear of my car, and the reason I do so is that you once winked at my girlfriend, you would have a cast iron malicious prosecution claim. However, the circumstances may be much more subtle but you could still succeed. The bringing of a previous claim which has been thrown out by the court could well go towards proving that this latest launch of proceedings is malicious.

As always when claiming compensation, you must have suffered some loss, be it to your health (though that might not do in a breach of contract case) or pocket or both.

Should you have wind of a claim against you which you regard as malicious, you can attempt to fend it off by a more than gentle reference to this legal development. Or you can attempt to bring to an end a claim that has already started before it goes too far. This is how your threatener can go.

> *"Dear Whitewash Limited*
>
> *I refer to your notice of the claim you intend to bring against me. As you well know, the claim is spurious. There is no reasonable and probable cause for it and you would have no good faith reason for commencing proceedings against me. I require you to take this letter as my notice to you that if you are so unwise as to proceed with the institution of proceedings against me, then not only will I apply to the court for your claim to be struck out and for you to be ordered to pay my costs, but I will institute my own proceedings against you for damages for the tort of malicious prosecution.*
>
> *I draw your attention to the majority judgments of the Justices of the Supreme Court in the case of Willers v Joyce and others [2016] EWHC 1315 and urge you to obtain legal advice on your position."*

Or

"Your claim against me now proceeding in the county court at Peardrop lacks reasonable and probable cause and you have no reasonable and probable cause for making it. The claim has already caused me injury to health and financial loss and the longer the proceedings are allowed to continue, the greater that injury and that loss are likely to be. It is my position that, in bringing and persisting with the claim, you have committed the tort of malicious prosecution. In that connection, I draw your attention to the majority judgments of the Justices of the Supreme Court in the case of Willers v Joyce and others [2016] EWHC 1315.

I hereby give you notice that unless, within seven days of the date of receipt of this letter, and in accordance with rule 3.3 of the Civil Procedure Rules 1998, you discontinue the claim and serve me with notice that you have done so, I will apply for the claim to be struck out and I will institute my own proceedings against you for damages for the tort of malicious prosecution. I should alert you to the fact that, in the event of discontinuance, I will have the right to my costs against you in connection with the claim.

Yours faithfully

Clive Troublesore"

This letter can be adapted appropriately and it would be desirable for you to set out precisely why you say the claim is malicious (for example, your car has never been damaged and "I don't drive."). Where proceedings have been started and you are requiring that they be discontinued, you could add as a carrot: *"Strictly without prejudice, if you do discontinue the claim as I have requested, without argument and within the period I have specified, I will not pursue any claim for costs against you."*

If you decide to bring your own proceedings for damages for malicious prosecution of a civil claim, your particulars of claim could run along these lines.

Particulars of Claim

1. On 14 July 2021 the defendant commenced proceedings against the claimant in the County Court Business Centre under case no20P0000678 ('the defendant's claim') which proceedings were subsequently transferred to the County Court at Peardrop.

2. The defendant's claim was for damages, interest and costs on the ground of the claimant's alleged negligence on 1 June 2020 in Magnolia Crescent, Twickenham, Middlesex KT89 4XZ at its junction with Alberta Close in driving his Vauxhall Astra motor car registration number CT4 SUE ('the claimant's car') into the rear of the defendant's Ford Escort motor car 3BAN GER ('the defendant's car') whilst the defendant's car was stationary at traffic lights. The defendant alleged that, in consequence of the collision, the defendant's car was damaged beyond economical repair and by way of damages he sought its pre-accident value which he alleged to have been £9,750.00.

3. In fact, the alleged accident never occurred and, in particular, the claimant's car was not being driven by the claimant or any other person on 1 June 2020 and was parked in the claimant's garage throughout June 2020.

4. On 6 October 2021 by order of District Judge Wisdom sitting in the County Court at Peardrop, the defendant's claim was struck out on the ground that it had no real prospect of success and the defendant was ordered to pay the claimant's litigant in person costs assessed in the sum of £72.03.

5. The defendant had no reasonable and probable cause for commencing the defendant's claim. Further, he did not have a bona fide reason for its commencement or pursuit and his commencement and pursuit of it were malicious.

Particulars of malice

The alleged facts relied on by the defendant in his particulars of claim were an invention and his statement of truth verifying such particulars was false and a contempt of the court. The defendant's motivation for commencing and pursuing the claim was to avenge what he wrongly believed was the claimant's act of having winked at the defendant's girlfriend Samantha Socrates in or about 1999.

6. In consequence of the defendant's malicious prosecution, the claimant has suffered personal injury and loss.

Particulars of personal injury

The claimant suffered anxiety, distress and depression which necessitated psychiatric treatment as set out in the annexed medical report of Dr H Shrink dated 23 December 2021.

Particulars of special loss

Loss of earnings due to inability to work – £5,500 net

AND the claimant claims –

a. Damages (the damages for personal injury and loss of amenities being limited to £1,000.00);

b. Such interest as shall be deemed just; and

c. Costs.

I believe that the facts stated in these particulars of claim are true. I understand that proceedings for contempt of court may be brought against anyone who makes, or causes to be made, a false statement in a document verified by a statement of truth without an honest belief in its truth.

Dated 5 January 2022

(signed) Clive Troublesore
Claimant

Chapter 19

Witnesses And Their Statements

Sock it to 'em in writing

There was a time when neither the court nor the other side had a clue what a witness was going to say until they got into the witness box and opened their mouths. Now we have a 'cards on the table' approach to evidence. Each side will almost always (though occasionally not so in the very simplest of small claims) be required by court order to disclose their evidence in writing in the form of a witness statement to the court and the opposition before the hearing – that's the evidence of the parties as well as the others they intend to drag along to court to back up their truths, lies or mistakes.

The court will set a deadline for this to be done. If the court has ordered documents to be disclosed, this deadline will be subsequently. If it has given permission for an expert's report to be used which has not yet been prepared, it will probably be before it has been prepared so that the expert can see the statements prior to doing their job.

Failing to adhere to the deadline is dicing with death. You will be prevented, without the court's permission, from calling a witness whose statement has not been handed over in time and such permission may be hard to come by unless you were slightly late and had good reason for it. The burning down of your house and the sustaining of a double fracture to the leg the day before could be sufficient provided it was not a case of your own arson and your dirty tackle on the referee that were responsible.

The order will usually say that the statements are to be exchanged. This simply means they are swapped round so neither side has an advantage over the other by seeing the opposition statements before they release their own. Otherwise, they might be tempted to revise their statements because of what they read from the opposition camp. Occasionally, exchange of statements will be inappropriate. In a family case, for example, where one party is alleging that the other has used domestic violence towards them, the court would order that the party making the allegations should come up with their statements first so that the other party knows what they have to answer and that the other party follows on later.

Exchange without pain

How the exchange takes place is left to you. Meet up on platform 1 at St Pancras at 4.30pm on Thursday and do it or both undertake to pop the statements into a letterbox or email them at the same time and do it. Where the process gets intriguing is with a case involving twenty parties and not just two, some of whom have lawyers and some of whom are doing it themselves. Incidentally, if one party cheats by holding on to their statements until they have peeked at those of their opponent and this can be proved, then, at the least, their evidence will be treated by the judge with enormous scepticism.

"He's mine. Stay away"

No party can be forced by another party to rely on the evidence of a particular witness but say you are desperate for that witness to be heard by the court. Well, try and get them to make a statement for you. They work for the other party and so you can't approach them? Actually, you can approach them. It is a well established principle of law that there is 'no property in a witness'. In other words, you cannot be prevented from making an approach to anyone you believe may be able to assist your case whatever their allegiance may be to the opposition. Obviously, you must not make a nuisance of yourself but you do not need opposition permission before making the approach. If the witness is the opposition's employer or one of their workers, the chances of them helping you would be somewhat reduced by an approach at work. Sometimes in this situation, a statement is refused but some useful information is gathered. "Sorry, mate, the gaffer is due back in minute. I know you were stitched up and, yeh, I did hear him tell you the old banger had never been involved in a crash though you're not getting me to court. Cheerio."

"She 'aint talking"

The next step where a witness will not cooperate? You can ask the court for permission to rely on a witness summary instead of a statement. The procedure is under rule 32.9 of the Civil Procedure Rules 1998 but does not apply to small claims (see chapter 25). The summary should set out the evidence the witness would have given in the statement if they had made one or, if this is not known, the matters about which you propose to question the witness and the name and address (care of address, if that is the best you can do) of the witness. You should explain to the court why you have not obtained a written statement and what steps you have taken to secure one. The permission application should be made and the summary sent to the other side before the deadline for exchanging witness statements.

Now, it's one thing to produce a witness summary. It's another to get the body of the witness to court. You do this by applying to the court for the issue of a witness summons which compels their attendance and which must be handed to them at least seven days before the date on which they are wanted at court and at the same time the witness must be offered their travelling expenses in getting to and from court and compensation for their loss of time. The amounts should be equivalent to what they would be entitled to if attending to give evidence at a Crown Court criminal trial and the figures which are updated from time to time can be discovered at cps.gov.uk.

And here comes the warning. Seeking to rely on a witness from the enemy camp without their written statement in advance is a risky business. They might just sink your case on the day. What might be less risky, if not downright delicious, is to procure permission from the court to rely on a witness summary without necessarily following it up with a witness summons and so terrify the opposition before any hearing so that they settle your claim or drop the claim against you. This might happen if they have not relied on the witness themselves or they have produced a statement from the witness which is at odds with what you have put in the witness summary.

We're dealing here with witness statements and not *War and Peace* so, if you can restrain yourself, don't produce books. Your statement and the statement of each of your witnesses should contain a chronological account of the relevant evidence which each of you can give as if recounting it from the witness box and be in the first person. The statement may refer to documents which are copied with it. It is a statement of fact and should not contain comment or argument about the case or the relevant law. "I consider the defendant to be a liar and, in my opinion, his witness must have Mafia connections as my wife commented on our way back from the car showroom that he was wearing a double-breasted suit that was miles too big for him and had a slight Sicilian accent." No thank you. You omit relevant facts at your peril. The judge could well preclude evidence being given in the witness box which has not been incorporated into the statement although the opposition can cross-examine on any relevant events or conversations about which there has been no or only limited mention in the witness's statement.

How to lose in one easy lesson

Now for a tip on how to lose your case. Draft the witness statements of all your witnesses in your own language. Ensure that you and each and every one of your five witnesses all refer in exactly the same words to the used car salesman mentioning that the vehicle had only clocked up 25,032 miles with a single previous owner who was a glass-eyed Peruvian belly dancer and that the salesman's boss would put in a new Doublesock multi-killer blow sound system before delivery. Nobody sees the same action or hears the same words in identical manner. It would be obvious to a judicial moron in a hurry that the words of your five witnesses were your words and that the witnesses could not all possibly recall what the salesman had said word for word in precisely the same way. You lose. Let the witnesses use their own words – see below for more on this – and, if possible, write or type their own statements. And unless a written statement is agreed by the opposition, ensure that the maker of the statement attends court and is called by you to support their written statement and is available to be cross-examined by the other side and questioned by the judge.

Naughty statements

If a statement contains irrelevant or disproportionate material or something improper then an application can be made to the court for an order that the passages objected to be excised and the statement re-served without them. That's not the sort of application that should be rushed into. Objection could always be taken at the trial instead of beforehand. "Judge, I did not want to burden the pressed court previously but I must object today to paragraphs 146 to 279 of the defendant's statement on the grounds that they are unduly prolix, irrelevant and contain extracts from 'without prejudice' correspondence I sent to the defendant before proceedings began. I ask that those paragraphs be removed from the copy of the statement in the bundle of documents." The disadvantage of objection being delayed until the trial is that the judge will probably have read the offending passages before the hearing started, although judges are adept at removing from their minds that which should not have entered.

"Without prejudice"

Of course, if any of the opposition's witness statements contain something that could actually damage your case, you would not want it to be seen by the trial judge and in that situation an application before the trial day for it to be removed may be essential. Say you have claimed damages of £10,000 but before you brought your claim you wrote to the other side to say you would be prepared to accept £50.42 rather than have the hassle of litigation. It would be better if the judge did not know about the communication for they might just possibly think your claim was a try-on. The law encourages parties to a dispute to try and settle it and details of written or verbal communications (or both) which they exchange in a genuine effort to settle should not be referred to before the judge in advance of them giving their decision on who has won and who has lost or in any documents prepared for the judge. The way to ensure that such communications with their offers and counter-offers are protected from disclosure to the court is to write at the top of the written communication the magic words "without prejudice" or say at the start of the conversation that you are speaking on a "without prejudice" basis (see chapter 10).

Second bite

Only in an exceptional case will you be granted permission to rely on a further witness statement which is designed to reply to what the opposition have said in one or more of their statements. Permission might be granted if this further evidence is really important and you could not reasonably have contemplated the points in question would be covered by the other side when your own statement was prepared.

I say, hearsay

"Max informed me that the defendant had told him he had stitched me up proper." "Max informed me that Ron had told him that the defendant had mentioned to Ron that he had stitched me up proper."

That's hearsay. These days, hearsay evidence can be used so either of those pieces of hearsay could go into your witness statement. But hearsay evidence – it could be third hand and, in theory, twenty hand hearsay by which time you would want to turn it into a song – has limited and in many cases no value whatsoever unless Max and Ron are both dead or have disappeared into oblivion and your best efforts to trace them by placing a full page ad in *The Sun* have been to no avail. If possible, you want Max in the first instance or Ron in the second instance.

Formalities

There are certain formalities which generally need to be observed in the format of a witness statement. This is not so with small claims unless the formalities are directed by the court. Nevertheless, even in small claims the observance of the formalities is no bad thing. It may well impress the judge so long as the substance of the statements does not amount to tommyrot of the highest degree.

The formalities for non-small claim cases have increased since 5 April 2020 and there is a good chance that you will be able to catch out your opponent for failing to follow them. The wording at the end of each statement about its truth – unsurprisingly it's called a 'statement of truth' – of what could well be a pack of more porkies than in a pig farm, has been extended. The witness must now acknowledge in the wording, the possibility of action being taken against them for contempt of court (which could lead to a bit of porridge) should they have lied in the statement. If the correct wording is missing then you can ask the court to disallow the statement and that would have the potential to kill off the other party's claim or defence, whether the statement is by them or one of their witnesses. In the majority of cases, the judge is likely to allow reliance, on condition that the wording is amended and the statement re-signed but the judge could go on to direct that, should you lose the case, you will not be stung for the other party's costs involved in drawing up the defective statement. The other side can apply to the court for permission to rely on it, despite its dodginess.

But when to pounce? You have a better chance of persuading the judge to disallow the statement if you have drawn the other party's attention to the defect and they have performed a 'two fingers' exercise. In that event, leave the defective statement out of the trial bundle if you are preparing it or refuse to agree to its inclusion if the other party is preparing it.

> *"Dear Claimant*
>
> *The 'statement of truth' verifying the witness statement you have served of Prudence Pilchard dated 7 July 2021 fails to comply with the Civil Procedure Rules 1998 Practice Direction 32. Unless, within 14 days from the date of this letter, you re-serve the statement with a compliant 'statement of truth' and agree to bear the costs of and incidental to you doing so, I shall ask the court to disallow reliance on the defective statement."*

> *"Dear Defendant*
>
> *Drop dead – twice, if necessary."*

A different tactic may be advisable where the other party does not intend to have the statement maker at court but to seek to rely on what they have said in writing. Then, take your objection to the statement at the trial, without prior warning to the other side, as the judge may then decide that it is too late for the 'statement of truth' to be corrected and disallow reliance on it. The judge or other side might say: "*You waived any objection to the 'statement of truth' by including or agreeing to it being included in the bundle.*" Respond with: "*With respect, I cannot waive a breach of such an important provision. It is not within my legal competence to do so."*

More formalities and this time from the Civil Procedure Rules 1998 Practice Direction 22. Again, since 5 April 2020, a non-small claim witness statement must disclose the process by which it has been prepared, whether by a lawyer or someone engaged by them or by a friend giving you a helping hand. So, if, before drawing up the statement, they took you through your evidence over the phone, face-to-face, through an interpreter or dangling from a chimney pot as you danced the conga down below, the statement should include this information. It will help the judge assess how much credence they should place on the statement's contents. The consequence of this not having been done could be the same as for a defective 'statement of truth' (see above) and how you deal with the non-compliance can be the same. If you have drawn up the statement for one of your own witnesses, the preparation process should still be included.

It has been a requirement for years that a witness statement is in the maker's own words, though it's advisable to omit the profanities. It is very often quite obvious that the requirement has been flouted. Take this from a very pleasant and intelligent shelf stacker at *Tesco* who has never claimed to be an Einstein or accident reconstruction expert, describing her road traffic accident. *"So far as liability is concerned, I say Res Ipsa Loquitur and, notwithstanding this averment, the extent and nature of the body damage to the centre rear of my vehicle show that this was a high velocity impact whilst I was stationary. So far as quantum of damages is concerned, I consulted with my registered medical practitioner several days after the accident as my right arm was immobilized and he informed me his provisional diagnosis was of a rotator cuff tear and he would refer me for an MRI scan. The result of the scan, my progress of treatment and the prognosis are covered by the medical reports requisitioned by my solicitors."* Pretty obvious they are not her words but those of the lawyer who drafted the statement. The less likely that a witness has described something crucial to the case in their own words, the more likely that the truthfulness or accuracy of what they have signed up to, can be successfully attacked.

With all the formalities – you will find them at Civil Procedure Rules 1998 Practice Directions 22 and 32 – a compliant witness statement may look like this:

Case no 21P0000678

Claimant

F Smyth-Jones

14 July 2021

FS-JD1-2

IN THE COUNTY COURT
AT PEARDROP
BETWEEN

WHITEWASH LTD Claimant

- and -

CLIVE TROUBLESORE Defendant

I FEDORA SMYTH-JONES state as follows:-

1. I live at 6b Millstone Parke, Twickenham KT46 1LA.

2. I am employed by the claimant Whitewash Ltd at its retail outlet at 149a Lower High Road, Twickenham, Middlesex KT46 1LA as a salesperson specialising in miniatures of footballers playing in the English Premier League.

3. The facts referred to at paragraph 4 of this statement are of my own knowledge and the facts referred to at paragraph 5 of this statement are based on information I have received from Ms Alethia Mcmorrow in my employer's accounts department and which I believe to be true.

4. On the 2 April 2016 at approximately 2.30pm a man I now know to be the defendant Clive Troublesore attended at the Twickenham outlet. He was accompanied by a woman who was carrying an empty beer bottle and a rattle and they were both wearing red scarves. They were unsteady on their feet and their speech was slurred. The defendant asked if we stocked Wayne Rooney miniatures and old Aldershot Town Football Club programmes. I informed him that we had no memorabilia or other products relating to Aldershot but that we had had a delivery of some very fine Wayne Rooney miniatures which were in the stockroom but unpacked. He asked me to show him every one of the miniatures which were available for purchase. I proceeded to the stock room, unpacked the miniatures and returned with them on a tray. The claimant's companion was by then lying prostrate on the floor by a full-sized cardboard cut out of David Beckham in underpants. I showed the miniatures to the defendant who said he would have them all, regardless of price. I informed him that the entire 64 could be purchased at a discounted price of £15,000. He replied that he thought this more than reasonable. He said he could give me £500 in cash with the balance to be paid within one week. He had sold some

land in Spain and was awaiting a transfer to his bank account for the sale proceeds of over £1 million within a matter of days. He was a "big shot at Old Trafford" and had once been a lay preacher. His word was his bond and he would not let me down. He showed me his passport and I satisfied myself about his identity. I re-wrapped the miniatures, accepted £500 in cash for which I wrote out a receipt a copy of which I produce marked "FS-J1" and handed it to the defendant. I also handed over to the defendant the 64 miniatures and woke up the companion who was still on the floor. The defendant and the woman left with the miniatures. On 4 April 2016 my employer's accounts department issued and posted to the defendant an invoice for the £4,500 balance due. I produce a copy of the invoice marked "FS-J2".

5. The invoice was not settled within seven days and remains unsettled at the date of this statement notwithstanding twelve telephone calls I have made to the number provided to me by the defendant and none of which he has answered.

6. This statement has been composed by me and in my own words.

I believe that the facts stated in this witness statement are true. I understand that proceedings for contempt of court may be brought against anyone who makes, or causes to be made, a false statement in a document verified by a statement of truth without an honest belief in its truth.

Signed ....F Smyth-Jones

Dated 14 July 2021

Business and Property Courts Alert

If you are involved in a case proceeding in the Business and Property Courts, bad luck. I had better qualify that. Bad luck if your witness statement or the factual witness statement of anyone else you are relying on was not signed up before 6 April 2021. That's because a new Practice Direction 57AC backed up with a statement of best practice will have to be complied with when those statements come to be prepared where they relate to the final trial rather than an interim hearing. Admiralty cases are covered by these courts but, for the time being, the Practice Direction does not apply to them but is likely to do so from 1 October 2021. If it does not, I will eat a sea captain's cap on this occasion, washed down with a bottle of rum and a Ho Ho Ho. Certain other Business and Property Courts cases are excluded from the Practice Direction and they are set out at its paragraph 1.3. They include most insolvency proceedings and claims under the Inheritance (Provision for Family and Dependants) Act 1975.

It is also possible that bits of the Practice Direction will be applied to other cases running in the High Court and county court in due course. There's nothing to stop you adopting some of them in a case to which the Practice Direction does not apply because there is a lot of sense to them but you will not be judicially thrashed if you don't.

This is what the Practice Direction says should happen where you are a litigant in person when the statements are signed and this applies to your own statement and the statements of any other witnesses you will be relying on.

- Avoid so far as possible altering or influencing the recollection of a witness other than yourself.
- Statements should be as concise as possible without omitting anything of significance.
- They should only refer to documents where necessary, if at all, and, where referred to, paragraph 3.2 of the Practice Direction and the statement of best practice should be followed,
- Do not quote at any length from a document that is referred to (the document will be available for the judge to see); attempt to argue your case (because witness statements should be about facts and polite argument about what the judge should decide in relation to the facts and the law they apply should be confined to when you have an opportunity to sum up at the end of the evidence); or include commentary on other evidence in the case (for example; "My witness Rufus Truepenny says in his statement that I have good eyesight and would never crash into a brick wall and he should know and would never lie because he is very religious and a man of integrity unlike the claimant.")
- On important disputed matters of fact, the witness should state in their own words how well they recall the matters addressed. For example: "I remember very well/I am certain/I am positive that the defendant was in the driving seat" and if, say, they are 110% positive, the judge won't believe them and if they only 'think' the defendant was in the seat, I would not bother with their statement. And whether and how and when their recollection of the matters has been refreshed by looking at documents and what were those documents.
- In relation to you and your witnesses, you should all read and understand the position set out in paragraph 4.1 of the Practice Direction before any draft statement is prepared.
- You should understand that the statements must set out only what the maker says is known personally to them or say they remember about matters personally witnessed by them.
- Statements by your witnesses may be prepared by you by reference to questions you have posed to them. Where that is done, leading questions (questions that expressly or impliedly suggest a desired answer or put words into the mouth or information into the mind of the witness ("Did you see the defendant hit me in the left eye with his right fist and then say 'You had that coming to you, Gold?'")) should be avoided where possible, especially on important points and a full record should be kept by you of the questions and answers, whatever form the witness statement takes.

- In addition to the statement of truth (see above), each witness statement must include the following confirmation signed by the witness:

"I understand that the purpose of this witness statement is to set out matters of fact of which I have personal knowledge. I understand that it is not my function to argue the case, either generally or on particular points, or to take the court through the documents in the case. This witness statement sets out only my personal knowledge and recollection, in my own words. On points that I understand to be important in the case, I have stated honestly (a) how well I recall matters and (b) whether my memory has been refreshed by considering documents, if so how and when. I have not been asked or encouraged by anyone to include in this statement anything that is not my own account, to the best of my ability and recollection, of events I witnessed or matters of which I have personal knowledge."

There are additional obligations to be discharged by a party's lawyer. In a Business and Property Courts case which is covered by these rules, you may find it worthwhile checking that the lawyer has done what was required of them. Failure to comply with the obligations could lead to the judge disallowing the statement or imposing some other sanction. And if you reckon that your opponent's witness has been swayed by what they have stated in a way abhorred by the rules, this could present you with a fertile topic for your cross-examination of them.

When you have followed the rules in a case which did not require it, you might still add the confirmation set out above to any relevant statement – so long as it is true! It might go down well with the judge.

Chapter 20

The Funless Bundle

How to displease the Judge

You will hear more about the court bundle for the trial or other final hearing than any other aspect of your case. It is the collection of the documents in the case that matter. It will save the judge having to go through a thousand pages in the court file which are out of order and some of which, if read, may disqualify them from continuing to hear the case. Where the court is operating an electronic file, it will obviate the judge having to suddenly rotate their head, leading to an attack of giddiness as they try and decipher documents which have been scanned upside down and to their side, with one-third of the contents having gone for a walk. It will enable everyone involved in the hearing to look at the same page at the same time. The unjustified absence of a bundle or a bundle inadequately prepared will cause judicial apoplexy. Remnants of the guts of culpable lawyers and litigants in person who have failed in their bundle performance remain strewn across the courtrooms and computer screens of the land, thanks to a pasting from the bench.

Before some judicial discipline was instilled into litigants about the presentation of documents, Mr Justice Sedley, who later became a Court of Appeal judge, formulated his sarcastic *Laws* on the subject and based them, no doubt, on bitter experience. Documents were to be assembled in any order, provided it was not chronological, numerical or alphabetical; in no circumstances was pagination to be continuous; no two copies of any bundle were to have the same pagination; every document was to carry at least three numbers in different places; any important documents were to be omitted; at least 10% of the documents were to appear more than once in the bundle; as many photocopies as practicable were to be illegible, truncated or cropped; at least 80% of the documents were to be irrelevant; barristers were to refer in court to no more than 10% of the documents but they could include as many irrelevant ones as the advocate deemed appropriate; only one side of any double-sided document was to be reproduced; transcriptions of manuscript documents were to bear as little relation as reasonably practicable to the original; and documents were to be held together, in the absolute discretion of the solicitor assembling them, by a steel pin sharp enough to injure the reader, a staple too short to penetrate the full thickness of the bundle, tape binding so stitched that the bundle could not be fully opened or a ring or arch-binder so damaged that the two arcs did not meet. That, my friends, was how it was. No longer.

The court or tribunal order should tell you what the bundle expectations are. It may spell out precisely what has to be done and which party has to do it. In so far as it is not exhaustive in this area of terror, it will refer to a procedural practice direction. There are separate practice directions and bundle requirements for civil, family, Court of Protection, tribunal proceedings and appeals with refinements in guidance issued for proceedings in the Chancery and Queen's Bench Divisions of the High Court and for Administrative

Court proceedings for judicial review which can all be sourced on the internet. Some county court hearing centres will have their customised versions of the bundle procedure they want to be followed in which event these will be made known and probably with the notice giving the final hearing date for the case. Only in county court small claims cases (see chapter 25) will you usually find – but not always – that the vital documents do not have to be gathered together in a bundle by any of the parties. This is largely because the job would hardly ever be done. You would earn brownie points on a small claim by preparing a bundle even though no party has been directed to do so. Prepare four sets of the bundle and shove in copies of the claim form on top and followed underneath by the particulars of claim, defence, court orders and witness statements, in that order, and number each page. Send one set to the enemy and send two sets to the court (the second set to allow for one set to be lost or otherwise to be available, if necessary, for the judge to hand to the witnesses as they give their evidence). Hold on to the final set for yourself and give it a kiss for good luck.

Let's have a look at how things should go bundle-wise in non-small claim cases. Generally, on which of the parties is this bundle purgatory inflicted? In civil proceedings it will be the solicitor for the claimant and, if none, the court will usually give the job to the defendant's solicitor. Should both parties be solicitorless, it will probably be down to the claimant personally to do the necessary. Each party will normally be ordered to use their best endeavours to agree what goes into the bundle. TRAP ALERT!!! Once you agree to a particular document being included in the bundle, you will be taken to have accepted its authenticity and that it amounts to evidence of its contents. That's unless the court says otherwise. If your opponent has sent the bundle to the court which includes a document you did not intend to go in and did not agree to going in, you should write to the court (with a copy of the communication to your opponent) as soon as you discover what has happened, make it clear that you object to the document being included and ask for it to be removed and not be seen by the trial judge. Then when the trial starts, you will need to explain to the judge that there is an issue over the bundle and why, and the judge will take it from there. The bundle should be paginated throughout and indexed with a description of each document and the page number. The documents are to be copied double-sided. Where the total number of pages exceeds 100, numbered dividers should be placed at intervals between groups of documents. A ring binder or lever arch file should normally be used. Do ensure that no binder or file is over-populated. If either explodes as the judge opens it because you were saving on the expense of a second container, the judge and your prospects of winning are likely to explode with it. Whoever is preparing the bundle should make copies for the judge, witnesses (one bundle for the lot), each of the other parties – and themselves. The bundles for the court and witnesses will generally be expected to arrive there at least three days before the hearing but – wait for it – not more than seven days before the hearing. Not too late or the judge may not have the opportunity to take a peek beforehand and not too early so that the floors aren't covered with too many binders and files, causing the mice to trip up.

Over now to family cases, whether they are proceeding in the High Court, or more likely, the Family Court and, again, just a taster. The practice direction which will generally apply is intended to catch all hearings and not merely the big final job. Each binder or file this time should be of A4 size and limited to 350 sheets. Its refreshing feature is that it tells you to keep certain documents out of the bundle unless prior permission has been granted by the court to include them. Among the excluded documents are correspondence and bank and credit card statements. As a judge who has heard more financial remedy cases than I have consumed hot dinners, the prospect of no longer having to study 7,000 pages of Dodgy Bank statements, which had no bearing on anything apart from my eyesight, is very welcome. And who prepares? The party who is making the application with which the hearing is concerned or, if that person is a litigant in person, the first person to be mentioned in the case title who is a respondent to the application and has a lawyer. If nobody around has a lawyer, a bundle can be dispensed with unless the court says otherwise and commits its preparation to one of the parties.

The trend is moving towards electronic bundles. General guidance has recently been issued on PDF bundles for civil cases and family cases and that, again, will be identified in the court order if it is to apply in your case. They say it is not immutable but that, with all or most of it, litigants in person as well as solicitors should be able to comply and, if they cannot, they should explain why not to the court. Oo-er. It is suggested that litigants in person without legal aid or means, should approach an advice centre, law centre or pro bono organisation (see chapter 7) for help in complying with requirements. If you are on your own but your opponent has a lawyer, then, says the guidance, the lawyer should consider offering to prepare the bundle. It won't go down well with the judge if they refuse. No document should appear upside down. Blast. Where the character of a document permits, it must be the subject of optical character recognition so that it can be read in text as this will facilitate word-searching and highlighting. Geddit? Page numbers, where possible, should be preceded by a letter so that, for example, it will be quick to search for 'A134' whereas searching for just '134' may throw up a number or references to that number which are not the page number and which take the computer time. *"What do you mean you have decided to abandon the case and prefer to spend your time writing a treatise on Roman law?"* Grit your teeth and make it a bundle of fun.

'Give me a break'

Okay. If all this bundle business is too much for you and you cannot pass the buck to another party or an advice or similar agency, you can pay non-lawyers who eat and sleep bundles to do the job for you. One company which will oblige for a fee is Integrated Dispute Resolution (integrated-dr.com) which is associated with Fomas who we shall meet later when we look at financial remedy cases. They will prepare paper or electronic bundles for you. For a litigant in person and with a bit of nudging from me, they say they would be prepared to compile a straightforward electronic bundle with well organised papers for £200 to £300 plus VAT. If paper bundles were required, £10 per page on top would be charged plus VAT and any courier bill at cost. If you were simply after assistance in the bundle's preparation, this could be provided by a paralegal (not a qualified lawyer but with knowledge of what is required) at an hourly late of £80 plus VAT.

Chapter 21

Daft Cases And Daft Responses

The early kill

The claim or application may be bonkers or the defence or other response not stand a hope in hell of success. But because the case is defended it has to go through the usual procedures and end up with a contested hearing at which the inevitable occurs. Or are there alternatives? You bet there are.

The more bonkers the case, the more likely that the person who has started it is subject to an order of the court that, because of their track record in the civil courts, they are prevented from making a claim or application without the permission of a judge. That order could be one declaring them to be a vexatious litigant or otherwise a civil restraint order that is limited, (and we are getting more severe) extended or (and this is for the most extreme litigants) general (see chapter 22). The likelihood is that they have not obtained permission to do what they are now doing and they could well have slipped through the net without this being picked up by the court. So check 'em out! Go to gov.uk/guidance/general-civil-restraint-orders-in-force for the list of general restraint orders in force and this will take you to the lists of the other types of order made against a number of our over-persistent lovers of the court system.

The bonkers case could be stopped in its tracks before time, labour and money have been wasted. You will usually have to make an application to the court. If what the other side has come up with is patently unadulterated rubbish, it could be worthwhile writing to the court and asking that a judge kill off (don't use that phrase whatever happens) the opposition's case of the court's own volition so that you don't have to issue an application for what is called summary judgment or you can make that request when you come to complete a form called a directions questionnaire which you will be asked to do if and when a defence has been produced. Summary judgment is what Meghan Markle, Duchess of Sussex, was after in her proceedings against Associated Newspapers Ltd and she succeeded in February 2021. The High Court ruled that there was no real prospect of a successful defence against her claims of misuse of private information and copyright infringement in respect of large parts of a letter she had sent to her father which were published in articles in the *Mail on Sunday* and *Mail OnLine*. There remain what in the whole context of the case are some minor issues to be tried on the copyright infringement claim and on what remedies the Duchess is to be granted. But the summary judgment application largely succeeded which means that considerable costs and court time will be obviated and the evidence the court hears will be enormously reduced. That's the wonder of summary judgment.

Some words

The application in a civil case should be on form N244 – it will cost you a court fee of £255 although I predict soon to be increased, unless the fee is remitted (see chapter 17) – and state that what you are applying for is:

- For claimant – *"an order that the defence [and counterclaim] be struck out and judgment be given for the claimant with costs because the defence [and counterclaim] discloses [disclose] no reasonable grounds for defending the claim [and counterclaiming] in accordance with CPR rule 3.4(2) and/or for summary judgment because the defendant has no real prospect of successfully defending the claim [and counterclaiming] in accordance with CPR rule 24.2."* * **

- For defendant – *"an order that the particulars of claim be struck out and the claim be dismissed with costs because the particulars of claim disclose no reasonable grounds for claiming (in accordance with CPR rules 3.4(2)) and/or for summary judgment because the claimant has no real prospect of successfully claiming."* **

*If there is no counterclaim or you are not after killing it off, delete the words in square brackets.

**You can rely on rule 3.4(2) or rule 24.2 or both. Frequently, both are put in. Delete as necessary. Should you at least be relying on rule 24.2, ensure that you add these words to the N244 application form (or there may be tears):

"If the respondent to this application for summary judgment wishes to rely on written evidence at the hearing, they must file the written evidence and serve copies on each other party to the application at least 7 days before the summary judgment hearing."

In so far as the early kill application is based on the particulars of claim not disclosing reasonable grounds for claiming, the defence not disclosing reasonable grounds for defending or the counterclaim not disclosing reasonable grounds for counterclaiming, there is probably nothing you need to say in the written evidence you put in or with the application – the particulars of claim, the defence and the counterclaim and their weaknesses will speak for themselves.

But in so far as the application is based on your opponent not having a real prospect of success, there will need to be supporting evidence in the quest to prove that your opponent has no hope. Where you have documents which back up what you are saying then refer to them in your written statement and include copies. If you are the claimant suing for the price of goods sold and the defendant has put in a defence alleging that the goods are substandard then you will be assisted by that wad of correspondence from them promising to pay when they have won the football pools or inherited under the estate of their 40 year old wealthy father who is in excellent health and in which they make no complaint about the goods which they have continued to use. And if you are the defendant to a claim for the balance outstanding for the supply and installation of double glazing and the claimant has written to you apologising for the fact that due to their surveyor's defective eyesight the windows don't fit properly and they will be round to fix the problem and you haven't heard from them since and you have had the windows replaced and are out of pocket and you have an expert's report to verify your case – then shove all that in.

Beware

Don't go for the early kill unless you are pretty confident of success or you could suffer failure and an order for costs against you. If you are pretty confident go for it early and with a small claim (for up to £10,000 usually – see chapter 25) go for it before the claim is formally allocated to the small claims track (which will usually be *after* completed directions questionnaires have been sent in to the court). That's because, before allocation, the other side will lack the protection of the limited costs regime for small claims so that, if the case is killed off, you can expect them to be ordered to pay your costs which will be especially handy where you have taken in a lawyer. Bear in mind that a claimant can apply for summary judgment under rule 24.2 (see above) even before the defendant has put in a defence. This would happen where the defendant has notified their intention to defend in the form of an acknowledgement of service and the claimant reckons they are playing for time and that the claim is undefendable. Why wait for the defence to come in? Should this ever so early pounce be made by the claimant, the defendant need not put in a defence before the application for summary judgment is heard.

Family cases

You are not allowed to apply for an early kill in family proceedings relating to a child. However, you may do so in other family proceedings such as divorce and matrimonial finance although such applications are rare. This time the application should be made in form D11 and the court fee will be £155, although I predict soon to rise, unless it is remitted (see chapter 17). Any application needs to rely on rule 4.4(1) of the Family Procedure Rules 2010. It empowers the court to kill off where there are no reasonable grounds for bringing or defending (for example, it is impossible to fathom out what the document starting or defending the case is about; what has been said is incoherent and makes no sense; or in an answer to a divorce, nullity, judicial separation or civil partnership dissolution or separation petition, all the respondent does is to deny every allegation made against them without advancing a positive defence) or where the document starting or defending the case is frivolous, scurrilous or obviously ill-founded. It would be extraordinarily hard to convince a judge that they should kill off a matrimonial finance application. Perhaps if you divorced 30 years ago, are on benefits, are worth a £3,000 ISA and your former wife is asking for money and property for the first time, you might just have a chance.

Chapter 22

Halting The Persistent Litigator

The alternatives to strangulation

This is about the litigant who cannot take 'no' for an answer. It could be your opponent in court proceedings. Obviously, it could not be you.

There's a deft way of dealing with the litigant who keeps making the same application in the course of a case or keeps starting new proceedings alleging the same or substantially the same things as in the previous proceedings. This can be very wasteful of your time and money: in short, a nuisance of the bloody variety unless you are crazy or want to fall madly in love with a judge.

Let's take repeated applications in the same case. This is often seen in the county court with the defendant making a series of applications to set aside the same judgment which each time is based on the same ridiculous arguments and each time is chucked out by the judge. When the first application is dismissed, you should ask the judge to certify that the application was totally without merit. These magic words will then appear in the court order. The judge may not need a prompt from you to do this. On the other hand, the judge may need a reminder! When the second and effectively the same application is dismissed, you should ask the judge to certify in exactly the same way and then to go on to make a 'limited civil restraint order'. This will prevent yet another application being made without the prior permission of a specified judge and, unless the judge has had a bad day or their stomach is rumbling at 12.50pm, that permission will be refused.

If repeated cases are started on the same grounds or repeated applications are made in them or there is a combination of the two and they are all fit for the judicial dustbin, the court can make the more severe 'extended civil restraint order'. This will prevent the litigant from making any further claims or applications relating to the same matter without the prior permission of a specified judge who will be slow to grant it even after a bumper lunch. The paralysis will last for up to two years although the period can be extended. You will almost certainly need to make a written application for such an order and, in the county court, draw attention to your understanding that the application will need to be listed in front of 'a designated civil judge or their appointed deputy.'

How many claims or applications are needed before the court can make an 'extended civil restraint order'? Three will do. And to reach the three, the court can take into account claims and applications made by someone other than a named party. So, for example, if they brought one claim in their own name and two claims in the name of a company they owned, and were all fit for the dustbin, the total of three could score you that 'extended civil restraint order'.

For the ultra crazy litigant who persists in starting proceedings and making applications and cannot be tamed by an 'extended civil restraint order', there's the deluxe 'general civil restraint order' which puts a stop to further civil proceedings about anything without prior permission. Its duration and the means of applying for such an order are similar to the 'extended civil restraint order'.

Family persistence

These restraint orders are not just for civil proceedings. They are available for family proceedings too which means, for example, that if your spouse gets a kick out of persistent applications for that maintenance order against you to be increased every time you win at dominoes, you can go for a restraint order. In relation to proceedings relating to the welfare of a child, the family court has power to prevent repeated proceedings which is additional to the restraint order. This additional power is under section 91(14) of the Children Act 1989 and allows the court, once it has dealt with an application under the Act, to direct that there is not to be any further application of the kind it will specify for a period it will specify, without the court's prior permission. It isn't strictly necessary that there should have been any previous applications, with or without merit, but too many previous cases are bound to make it more likely that this power will be exercised. The power is really designed as a weapon of last resort where there have been repeated and unreasonable applications made.

Chapter 23

Outside The Courtroom For A Civil Case

Waiting about

Have you turned up at the right place? A clue will be the runners and riders. Yes, you will find, displayed in a prominent position, lists of the various cases to be heard that day in each court in the building. Looking at the lists could ease the tension. Had you been in London's Intellectual Property Court in April 2018 you would have seen this case listed.

(1)	HENRY MARTINEZ TRADING AS PRICK
(2)	HENRY HATE STUDIO & PRICK TATTOO PARLOUR LONDON LTD

Claimants

- and -

(1)	PRICK ME BABY ONE MORE TIME LTD TRADING AS PRICK
(2)	GYNELLE LEON

Defendants

I'll just get out of the way a short summary of the case so that you can concentrate on the rest of this chapter. It was a "passing off" case involving a tattoo business in Shoreditch which had been set up in 2001 under the trading name of *Prick Tattoos* (the late Amy Winehouse was a client) and a retail cactus and succulent plant business which had been set up in Dalston in 2016 under the trading name of *Prick*. The tattoo business owners alleged that the cactus business could be confused with the tattoo business. You may have thought that such an argument would be difficult to sustain and you would be right. The claim was dismissed.

> *"Would the parties in the case of Troublesore versus Whitewash Ltd report to the usher's desk immediately."*

That's it. The judge is ready to start the case. No point now in lamenting the day you got into this. Too late to change your script. Possibly too late to expel bodily waste though if you ask them nicely and display sufficient facial tension, the usher may permit you a quick visit to the loo. After all, you could be inside the hearing room for up to a continuous three hours and the judge will have made themselves comfortable before calling for the case to come on. Judicial training urges a full wee before a full court session. Judges though do have little tricks at their disposal to secure a break if unexpected lavatorial demands are made of them. When once caught short in my previous incarnation as a solicitor, I pretended to the bench of beaks I had just remembered that I had an urgent phone call to make. They sympathetically allowed me to rush out of court at 280 urisweats per second. Later, as a judicial beginner, I relied once or twice on a need to research a point of law in the court library but as confidence has grown I have followed the more common practice of announcing a 'comfort break' which, more often than not, will be welcomed by all present. This is unlikely to last longer than five minutes so you need to get on with things.

It's vital to concentrate on the case rather than your bladder or anus or both so if nature makes its call whilst the case progresses and there is no sign of the judge being in trouble, simply ask them for a loo break. It won't lose you the case.

"Please tell the judge I'm ready – if they are"

The problem in sensibly timing the last pre-hearing court loo visit, collection of the kids from school after the case or popping out to *Primark* or for a smoke while the court is in session with other cases, is that you can never be absolutely sure when your case will be called on. Of course, you will have been sent a *notice of hearing* telling you at what time the case will start and probably how long it has been estimated to last. Here's the catch. The case may be taken dead on time or some while after it was due. Certain categories of case are bulk listed. That means, for example, that 12 claims by mortgage lenders for repossession could all be listed to begin at 10am. You won't see the 40 people involved in them invading court at the same time. Each case will be heard separately and, if you are unlucky, your turn may not come until close on to 11am.

It could be even worse. The judge may not begin the 10am batch of cases until 10.45am because of urgent business that was not expected when those 12 repossession cases were arranged. Maybe a tenant is due to be evicted from their home by a court bailiff during the day because of rent arrears and is making a last minute desperate attempt to be allowed to stay put. Or a battered wife is asking for an injunction to forbid their violent husband from molesting them after a serious assault the night before.

If, for whatever reason, you are not around when the case is ready, it is likely to be dealt with in your absence. This might result in it being *struck out* if you brought it and an order that you pay expenses to the other side or, say, an order that you give possession to your building society of the home in which you had intended to die. Then you would have to make an application for the case to be reheard. If you had genuine and reasonable grounds for your absence, a rehearing is more probable than not but coupled with an order that you compensate the blameless opposition for the loss your absence caused them.

The runner

It has been known for litigators to try and drag out proceedings by 'doing a (surreptitious) runner'. This involves clocking in with the usher so that they get marked down as present and then departing. The case is called. It is dealt with in their absence with an adverse order against them. Later they return and ask the usher why they are having to wait so long.

"Your case was called one hour ago and the judge has dealt with it."

"No it wasn't. I have been sitting here all the time and I never heard my name."

"Well I called it loud and clear."

"I want to see the judge immediately."

"He won't see you now. He's busy and the other side has left."

"This is terrible. What can I do?!"

"You'll have to apply for another hearing. Go to the court office and they will give you an application form."

Judges are skilled at sussing out the 'runner' when several weeks later they attend and remain for the hearing of their application for the previous order to be set aside.

Hug an usher

That usher I mentioned. His or her job is to know who has turned up, ferry litigants and witnesses between the waiting areas and the courtrooms, act as a link between the judge and the outside world, occasionally pour out a cup of tea for the judge and do a million other things. They've drastically cut down on the number of ushers and the poor things are rushed off their feet. They – the ushers and their feet – come in all shapes and sizes. Sometimes they wear a black robe on their back. If no robe then they can usually be identified by a booming voice and a bad temper on account of poor pay, pressure of work and insulting litigants and members of the public.

Sneer at or underestimate the usher at your peril. The first usher I encountered as an advocate at Portsmouth Magistrates' Court was my former Latin master. Having failed on so many occasions to accurately translate "Greeks build walls" into the arcane language, I was thoroughly embarrassed when he held open the court door for me and called me 'Sir'.

You never know. Your usher might report back to the judge on waiting room activities involving....you! If the judge is going to have to decide whether you are a placid wallflower or a violent maniac, you won't want the usher telling them that you shouted 'slut' at your ex-wife when she sat down opposite you and have been making menacing faces ever since. So remember you could be on trial from the moment you step into the court building. Behave and strike the right balance in your dealings with the usher. A little flattery coupled with a sympathy inducing element. You could enquire while shaking nervously how they keep so calm with such a heavy workload or ask whether they once worked as a brain surgeon because they look so like the person who operated on you. Keeping in with the usher will do you no harm.

Dress code

Oh I do hope you have dressed appropriately. You wouldn't go to a place of worship or a school prize giving ceremony ready for an outdoor barbecue. Showing you have some respect for the judge and the occasion in how you are attired is recommended. I accept that a person should not be judged by appearance and that the claimant, masquerading inside a pin-stripe job with a silk handkerchief flowing from the breast pocket, may turn out to be the mastermind behind the latest Ponsi scheme. However, if it looks like you don't give a damn for where you are, the judge may just feel that you don't give a damn about anything – your behaviour towards your opponent or keeping to court orders or whatever. The best dressed people in the past have been debtors who came to court asking the judge to make them bankrupt. Not too smart and expensive if you intend pleading poverty and not as if you have just risen from bed. Preferably, not completely naked either. A gentleman who insisted on walking without a stitch on from Land's End to John O'Groats in the course of which he was subject to arrest, prosecutions, convictions and imprisonment, lost his complaint to the European Court of Human Rights about his treatment in 2014. And men: definitely not in a tank top and a pair of shorts with your belly bulging out. And women, keep it discreet. A male judge may have a good time if ample cleavage is deliberately exposed – and I've seen many a female try it on with a bust heave or two – but the exposer will not gain any advantage in the case.

Watching lawyers go by

There's no entertainment laid on for you whilst you are waiting for your case. Watching the other litigants and, better still, their lawyers can be quite absorbing. It's not so easy these days to identify the lawyers by appearance: easier by behaviour. The solicitors are likely to rush in late with sweat running down their faces and papers spewing out of an obese file under the arm. I've had two male solicitors appear before me unjacketed. This is as serious as hitting an old lady over the head with a mallet. When I enquired of one of them whether he normally came to court unjacketed, he apologised without offering any explanation. His client, who was immaculately attired, put him to shame. As to the other, I asked him whether he was going to the beach. He apologised profusely and stated that he had been late setting off for court from his office and had simply forgotten to put his jacket on. The inspiration for the enquiry was an experience many years ago on entering Portsmouth Guildhall auditorium with a friend and very casually dressed for a Julie Felix concert – late. She publicly enquired of us: "Going to the beach?" My instant retort which, like the best of them, stayed in my head and did not leave my mouth, was: "No, the zoo, zoo, zoo. How about you?"

Barristers dealing with civil cases tend to be better attired than their solicitor counterparts (though the younger ones specialising in criminal legal aid cases for which the pay is appalling sometimes have frayed shirt cuffs) and the VPC – that's Very Posh Counsel, as they are known – can be spotted by dress and demeanour. Pinstripes for the men and fine silk tops for the women, they glide rather than walk, with the hint of an aroma under the nostrils.

Water and biro

There might be a refreshments machine or, if you are very lucky, a public canteen should you be in the mood for food or drink. Safer to carry a bottle of water with you though anything larger than a half litre may look over indulgent and if you feel constrained to have a swig after your case has started, ask the judge for permission. And you may want to arm yourself with a biro and paper because you will not find a stock of stationery available in the hearing centre for your use. There are two reasons for biro. Firstly, in the longer cases you are well advised to make notes of the evidence being given by your opponent and witnesses and they will act as a memory jogger when you come to cross-question them. And, secondly, the judge may be impressed by the care you are applying by writing down what you can. It could mean you will be writing down their judgment and are in appeal mode (after all, you're *Mr Troublesore*, aren't you?).

Leave the tape recorder at home. If you record any part of the hearing without the judge's permission, which would be refused, you would be in contempt of court and that's serious because it can lead to imprisonment, a fine or confiscation of your assets. The hearing will be recorded by the court and you can obtain a transcript of it or just part of it afterwards provided you pay the transcriber's charges for which you can ask for a quote.

Music while you wait

Unlike most public buildings, there's no background music in court buildings which is a bit of a shame. Carefully selected, it could act as a relaxant to all involved. After all, soothing music is played to womb occupants who tell me it calms them down nicely. Here's a name drop. One my nephews is Murray Gold who used to compose the *Doctor Who* music and also wrote the music for the David Attenborough *Life Stories* series and for many other television programmes and stage productions: most recently for *It's A Sin* on Channel 4. I asked him what he might write for a county court waiting room. He wasn't too keen. He has obviously had bad experiences. He says music designed to calm him in public places actually puts him more on edge and he is worried about how it would affect conversation. "If people are talking over it, everything becomes louder," he says. "Conversation is at a specific range of the frequency spectrum. Musically it is pitched in a range that is only a small part of the piano keyboard. But the more the music is in the same frequency range as human voices, the more difficult it is to hear people while it is playing because it competes. In terms of music style, the human heart tends to imitate pulses so that when there is a fast base drum that resembles a heartbeat, our hearts speed up and we get excited, agitated or nervous."

Cancel the Abbey Road Studios booking and the harpist.

> "This is the second call. Would the parties in the case of Troublesore versus Whitewash Ltd report to the usher's desk immediately".

Who's that woman over there? Is she holding a notebook? Has she come to report my case? Blimey, the neighbours might turn up too. Should I get out of here fast? Generally, the media's obsession with criminal court cases is not matched in civil cases. Unless you've just indulged in sexual intercourse on a television reality programme, it is highly unlikely that your case will be reported on. There's one exception. If your opponent has tipped off the media and the case is offbeat or otherwise highly newsworthy, either nationally or, more probably, locally then some coverage there might well be. A tactic adopted by one persistent litigant is to alert his local newspaper cronies to an upcoming hearing and have them make contact with his opponent before the hearing for a comment. This is calculated to induce the opponent to settle the case before the hearing out of fear of adverse publicity. It has worked.

Public or private

Whether or not the reporter can get into the hearing depends on the type of case. For civil cases, the general rule is that the hearing is open to the public and so a reporter can sit in and report what happened. This includes the hearing of a small claim but here the judge may decide to keep out the public and media if the litigants agree or one of certain grounds exist (for example, the hearing involves confidential information including information relating to personal financial matters and publicity would damage that confidentiality, a private hearing is necessary in the interests of justice or national security is involved so double agents please note). In 2019 the court procedural rule makers went overboard with the obsession for transparency and directed that a series of cases which, previously, had usually been heard in private should, in future, usually be heard in public. Among them were mortgage possession claims, landlord possession claims on the ground of rent arrears and applications for charging, third party debt and attachment of earnings orders and questioning of debtors. Rival creditors might well be interested to listen in on the enforcement cases. The court must make an exception when one of the factors exists which would turn a small claims hearing into a private hearing. So if there is someone at the back of the court you would prefer to see suspended from a very, very tall crane stationed in a dumping ground for putrid rat flesh, ask the judge to hear the case in private and boot them out if you have the necessary grounds, explaining why.

Sorry, I digressed. The usher will take you into court unless you are at one of the rare court buildings in which they operate a doctor's surgery type system of moving you from waiting room to courtroom by electronic board message or tardis. You enter. It may be a grand courtroom just like off the telly or it may be a shoebox. The longer and more substantial cases are likely to be in the grand courtroom. The shorter cases and small claims are likely to be in a shoebox or a room akin to an office with the judge sitting at a desk and seats for litigants and others opposite the judge. The judge or usher will tell you where to sit. You can keep your mouth shut until the judge asks you to open it. The cocky, feeling resentful that they are in court and wishing to convey an air of indifference, will come out with an "Alright, mate?" class of greeting. Never attempt to shake hands with the judge or kiss them. To do so would be construed as an attempt to curry favour which would be quite improper and could backfire. Should you take the judge by surprise and succeed in either, they might feel constrained to demonstrate that they are not partisan by shaking hands with your opponent or, worse still, kissing your opponent! I'm not serious.

Addressing the judge

"Blimey, what do I call the judge?" I have had '*My Lord*', '*Your Highness*', '*Your Honour*' (all of which are wrong but none of which I have corrected because I enjoyed them too much) and '*Sir*' (which is right). District judges who deal with the vast majority of county court hearings should be addressed as '*Sir*' or '*Madam*', depending on their gender and, if you aren't sure of that, remain silent until you get some clues. Gender detection will not be hampered by a wig on the judge's head for, these days, judicial wigs are passé except for ceremonial occasions. Circuit judges, who are senior to district judges, deal with the remainder of county court cases. They should be addressed as '*Your Honour*'. That list of cases on display in the public areas of the building will show which judge is taking which cases so you will know before whom you will be appearing. More often than not, the judge will be robed if sitting in open court.

In the absence of a robe, what can you expect? Neither nudity nor gardening clothes.

In guidance given by the former Lord Justice Leveson (who as a barrister unsuccessfully prosecuted the late comedian Ken Dodd for allegedly fiddling (no, not tickling) the tax man but put that all behind him with a distinguished judicial career – and an enquiry) it was stated that the civilian clothing should be "a dark coloured business suit or similar" so if your judge is clad in pale blue or something off the shoulder, you might turn wardrobes and suggest that they refresh their memories on the guidance. Or you might not. Perhaps just save that in case there is a judicial attempt at rebuke for your own appearance.

"Where's the jury?"

The judge will decide your case on their own. You generally only get a jury in a criminal case at the Old Bailey or in a Crown Court and sometimes at an inquest into a person's death. Once in a blue moon there may be a jury in a civil case which involves a claim for damages for defamation (libel or slander), malicious prosecution or false imprisonment. And you only get magistrates at – you guessed it – magistrates' courts and for some less complicated family court cases. You will have more than one judge for your money on most appeals to higher courts.

Remote hearings

In chapter 6 which you skipped – go back immediately and don't do that again – I dealt with the new world of remote hearings by telephone or video and sometimes by a combination of both and, every so often, a jamboree involving a combination of telephone, video and face-to-face. Remote is not reserved for the shorter, often procedural, hearings which precede the final trial but can be ordered for the final trial and this is now a frequent occurrence. Remote means that, as a litigant, you avoid the inconvenience and expense of travel. And you may reduce lawyers' fees as there's no reason why an advocate barrister or solicitor should not be asked to reflect the fact that they will be saving on travelling time to and from court (and fares) in the fees they are going to charge you for doing their stuff. Also, you can have your boiler serviced at the same time. To that extent, it's a win, win win for you.

But the prevailing consideration for you should be which type of hearing would put you in the better position to achieve a successful result. No point in saving £500 and a bus fare to and from Wigan if you are going to lose the case. You will usually be given an opportunity to make any representations against the type of hearing the court has in mind. In fact, when making an application in the course of proceedings and using the application notice which is gloriously called form N244 – it is one of the most utilised forms in the whole wild world – you will be specifically asked to say whether you want the application to be dealt with at a hearing (by which they mean a face-to-face hearing) or at a telephone hearing. Although the current N244 was modified as recently as January 2021, they didn't add the option of a remote video hearing. But you can add that in at paragraph 5 of the form as the option you select. Incidentally, the N244 also gives an option of no hearing (meaning that a judge will decide on whether to grant the application on the papers and without having the pleasure of listening to anyone apart from their usher knocking at the door with that cup of tea, if they are very lucky indeed). It is only the most straightforward application that will be suitable to be dealt with in this way and if anyone affected by the order made on paper does not like it, they will be able to ask the court, probably within seven days of getting a copy, to halt the order, cancel it or change it.

If an opportunity is not given to say the type of hearing you prefer, then you can make representations anyway and even after a particular type of hearing has already been selected by the court. It can be changed. For preliminary hearings like case management and pre-trial hearings in civil cases and dispute resolution hearings in family financial remedy cases, usually go for remote. For preliminary hearings in children cases where the input of Cafcass is likely to be involved, go for court. For a trial or other final hearing in a civil or family case which will involve the judge having to decide if there's a liar in the case, usually go for court. You are more likely to achieve court rather than remote in a family case than in a civil case. Remember, though, that the court can direct a mixture – part court and part remote – so the evidence of a particular witness or a particular expert could be taken remotely and everything else covered in court.

Remote should not be seen as an opportunity to dress down. Obviously, you don't wear ballroom attire with all your medals affixed when knocking around your home but the dress code I suggested above should still be followed with an exception for any part of the body which will not come into view. Stark nakedness is okay for telephone hearings so long as you have somewhere to put your biro. Better to use a laptop if you have one rather than a smart phone and to have it resting on a table or a chair so that you can make notes, if necessary, during the hearing.

Guidance to judges on conducting remote hearings tells them to allow more time for breaks than might happen in a court building. And it points out that parties may be tempted to agree to let a case go on for too long so as to complete it, out of a sense of deference, unassertiveness or anxiety when, in reality, their ability to absorb evidence has become impaired by tiredness. That means that should you feel enough is enough – the hearing started at 10am, there was a one hour lunch break and it is now 4.45pm – take a large spoonful of courage syrup and say to the judge after addressing them properly: *"I profusely apologise for interrupting. I don't know how you feel but I'm whacked. I just cannot take any more in. I beg of you to adjourn."*

In relation to telephone hearings, the guidance points out that the participants are relying solely on the tenor of the judge's voice because they have no visual cues from the judge or the other party. The judge should seek in their voice to avoid tension: on the blower, the judge's voice might signify impatience.

Enough of this. Let's get into court.

Chapter 24

Inside The Courtroom For Your Civil Case

"What am I doing here?"

Getting rid of the judge

Thinks. "I've seen that judge before. It's that b……d Gold." You can't cherry pick your judge but you are entitled to a fair hearing and so in certain situations you are entitled to ask the judge to stand down – to 'recuse' themselves as we say – and hand over to another judge. The judge should stand down if they are actually biased against you. That's notoriously difficult to prove and few attempt to do so. It's more common for objection to be taken on the ground of the judge's apparent bias. You have to show that a fair-minded and informed observer would reckon there was a real danger or possibility of bias – it stinks a bit. I'll give you an example. In a big money divorce case in 2007 a High Court judge had made a number of remarks during preliminary hearings about the Egyptian husband's status as a sheikh, nationality, ethnicity and Muslim faith during preliminary hearings. When the husband attempted to get rid of the judge for the final hearing, he refused to stand down. The Court of Appeal overruled him. Yes, he talked too much but he was a good judge. However, his remarks had been regrettable and unacceptable and it could be thought that the scorn and contempt that his words conveyed might be carried into his decision.

But say you are confronted by a judge you have met before in another case which you lost after the judge had decided you were the most odious, contemptible, immoral piece of excrement he had had the misfortune to encounter and had failed to utter a truthful word in evidence apart from your name and there was even some doubt about that. You would stand a good chance of persuading the judge to stand down. It is a question of the extent to which the judge had previously taken against you. The mere fact that the judge had ruled against you before or had been critical of you will usually be insufficient to warrant a recusal.

No judge should be a judge in their own cause so if they have a vested interest in the outcome of a case, they should hand over to another judge. And guidelines to judges about their conduct make it clear that a judge must not decide a case in which a member of their family legally represents a litigant or is in any way associated with the case.

The recusal request should be made at the start of the case unless you know in advance that the particular judge is due to preside, in which event you should write to the court and state your objection to the judge. If the judge refuses to stand down then you may be given permission to appeal that decision.

A warning. If your request to the judge to stand down is unsuccessful then with that judge you are stuck. Judicial continuity is often the aim. Therefore, in cases where there may be a series of preliminary hearings before the final trial, you are likely to have the same judge presiding on each occasion. In fact, that same judge may even preside over the final trial. If you have attacked them for alleged bias just be ready to be embarrassed as they continue to handle the case. Wear that false beard and nose in future in the hope that the judge does not remember you? Don't bother. The judge will remember but arguably they will bend over backwards to be fair lest it should be suggested they put the boot in out of revenge.

Getting rid of the hearing

You want an adjournment, eh? Wherever possible, that should be sought as close as possible to the hearing date being notified and after you have approached the other side to invite their consent. Even with that consent, the court may decline to adjourn. There will have to be a good reason for another date and you will struggle to obtain the court's concurrence in putting off the hearing where you have been asked to tell the court of any dates which were inconvenient to you and failed to say that the date fixed was one of them. Even if your adjournment request has already been turned down via a decision made without a hearing or even if you have crazily neglected to make the request before the day of the hearing, you can ask the judge when the case is called on to have mercy on you and adjourn at that point. You will require grounds stronger than an amalgam of Tarzan muscles – better than "The gasman is due at 2 o'clock" – and, if you persuade the judge, the odds would be in favour of you being condemned to pay the other side's legal costs and any expenses arising from the wasted outing. Of course, different considerations will apply where the adjournment is sought because of a late development beyond your control but always keep the other side informed when you reasonably can about what is going on. Every judge will be at pains to satisfy themselves that an adjournment request is not a delaying tactic.

Pregnant? In March 2021 the Court of Appeal ruled that if a pregnant woman feels unable to participate in a hearing which is shortly before her due date, the court should not adopt a 'wait and see' approach or force the woman to bring medical evidence that participation may cause her difficulty. In that case, the woman, who was involved in care proceedings relating to her children which were set to last for some ten days, was eight months' pregnant and felt unable to take an active part in the hearing. A judge's refusal to adjourn was overturned.

Menopausal symptoms? If not an adjournment, they may lead to adjustments to the hearing which can include ensuring the room has working air conditioning or open windows, cold water, easy access to toilet facilities and frequent breaks. Judges were given guidance on this in February 2021 and told of recent BMA research where 90% of doctors who had experienced the menopause said the symptoms had impacted their working lives. A significant number had reduced their hours, left management roles or intended to leave medicine altogether, despite enjoying their careers, because of the difficulties they faced when going through the menopause. The desirability for special measures should be brought to the court's attention before the day of the hearing. And judges may need to take the initiative. This is what they are told: "A woman experiencing debilitating menopausal symptoms may be too embarrassed to tell the court she needs adjustments... Judges need to be alert to subtle indicators, e.g. someone looking very hot or fanning themselves, losing concentration or becoming immediately weepy. None of these signs may be anything to do with the menopause, and that does not matter. A good rule of thumb is generally to make no assumptions, but if someone looks uncomfortable for any reason, to explore what adjustments might be of assistance. Rather than identifying why you are asking, it is sufficient to say, for example, 'It is rather hot in here. Would it help to open the window?'"

What of an adjournment request which is founded on the problems of a witness rather than one of the parties? In another March 2021 Court of Appeal case, the issue was whether a five-week Business and Property Courts case should be adjourned a fortnight before it was listed to start on account of the medical condition of one of the witnesses. An adjournment would have meant that the trial would be delayed until early or mid-2022 but by that time there were excellent prospects that the witness would be able to attend. There were allegations of dishonesty against the witness. She wanted the judge to hear her. An adverse finding about her credibility was likely to have a very significant impact on her future career, if not destroy it completely. Again, the Court of Appeal reversed the trial judge's decision to refuse an adjournment. It would be artificial to draw a distinction in this context between a party and a witness. The significance to be attached to the unavailability of an important witness to attend through illness, it was ruled, would vary from case to case but it would usually be material and might be decisive. If refusal of an adjournment would make the trial unfair, an adjournment should normally be granted, regardless of inconvenience to the other party or other court users, unless this was outweighed by injustice to the other party that could not be compensated for.

Order in court

The judge is there to control the hearing. You should submit to this control. It is self defeating to shout, be rude or offensive or interrupt the judge or, indeed, in the presence of the judge, to act in such a way towards your opponent (whose guts you may detest) or their lawyer (whose face you may like to thump with the force of a tornado). You will be given an opportunity to reply to whatever is being said against you. Wait until your time comes to crush the other side's allegations. A caveat: if your blood is boiling at a temperature in excess of 35 degrees Celsius or the other side has got it so wrong that this may send the judge off on the wrong track and an instant correction is the only reasonable course, then attempt an interruption.

> "Madam, I am sorry to interrupt but I must correct what you have been told. It is said I have made no payments under my mortgage since the 20th July 2013. I paid £7,500 off the mortgage arrears last Monday and have the lender's receipt here. The lender's representative has clearly not been fully instructed by his client."

Game, set and possibly match to you and achieved with such courtesy.

It is just conceivable that you have made a cock up by failing to follow pre-hearing directions or to comply with an order made at a previous hearing: or perhaps you did your best but, through no fault of your own, you were unable to do what was expected of you. It will go down much better with the judge if you cough your default at the start.

> "Madam, I now realise I should have sent to the court and the claimant copies of the invoices for fresh fish purchased by me over the last six months and I have not done so. I sincerely apologise. I did not read the court's order as carefully as I should have done. There is no satisfactory excuse I can offer but if the case can proceed without the invoices, I would be extremely grateful."

Another warning. That cock up could have triggered some sanction against you such as an inability to rely on certain evidence. This could be fatal to your case. You should apply before the hearing to be excused for your default: it's called an application for relief from sanctions. Where you haven't done so, you can try your luck with the grovelling apology as suggested but it may not work.

Shorter hearings

A myriad of reasons could have got you to court. The nature of the hearing will determine the procedure. Shorter hearings take place for such cases as claims for repossession because of mortgage or rent arrears, return of cars and other goods on the ground of arrears under credit agreements, petitions by creditors for bankruptcy and enforcement of judgments by way of charging order or attachment of earnings and so on. And there may also be a short hearing in what will be a long case. Take a substantial claim for damages for a serious injury sustained in a road accident which is being defended. Quite early on in the case the court will probably fix what is called a case management conference at which it will give directions to the parties about how they must prepare for the ultimate trial. Then there are those longer hearings like the full trial of that road accident claim and other defended cases where the judge has to hear evidence from the litigants and their witnesses, consider possible legal points and decide who wins and who loses. Generally, the shorter hearings will be decided by the judge on the basis of written evidence and representations on the day from each side without anyone going into the witness box. Whichever side is making the claim or application will normally go first and have its say and the judge will then turn to the other side to hear whether they oppose what the court is being asked to do, and, if so, why.

Whether or not prior to a shorter hearing you have sent to the court and your opponent any written representations about what order you are inviting the court to make, be ready to verbally recite your main points to the judge. If the judge has had an opportunity to read and digest what you have written, they will ask you in felicitously couched judicial language to belt up. In fact, the greater impact may well be made by what you say, concisely, on the day rather than what you have written in the tiniest green biro scrawl. And that reminds me. If you have the ability to type any document for the court, type it instead of putting the judge through the torture of trying to decipher your handwriting.

You may have been required in advance of the hearing to send to the court and probably the other side details of your evidence or argument. If that was so, please, please, please make copies of what you have written and any documents that have accompanied it and also write covering letters or emails with what you are sending and keep copies. There is a real possibility that your documents will not have reached the judge because they have been lost, misfiled or misinputted, gone to sleep under a court staff member's in tray, or are in a queue for attention. Alternatively or in addition, your opponent may deny ever having received what you sent them, the reason being that they are a bare-faced liar. Where you are lodging a document with the court in person and there is a human being there to take it, ask for a receipt. Where, as is the more likely, you are inserting a letter into a court 'drop box', take a selfie of you putting it in, with a newspaper front page for that day visible in the pic. I have actually seen this being done. Don't drop your lunch box in the process.

Longer hearings

The longer hearings are different (and for the rather different procedure on small claims hearings, see chapter 25 exclusively devoted to them). Usually, the litigant bringing the case – the claimant or applicant – will kick off because it's their job to prove what they are alleging. The position will be reversed where the other side – the defendant or respondent – has the task of proving the central allegation. Perhaps a manufacturer is claiming for the price of goods it has sold to a retailer and the retailer is admitting the transaction but defending on the grounds that the goods fell to pieces the moment they came out of their boxes and the retailer immediately returned them. The onus here would be on the retailer to prove that the goods were substandard and so the retailer would go first and give their evidence before the manufacturer. In the more complex cases, any lawyer representing the claimant will seek to make an opening statement drawing the judge's attention to the main factual issues and points of law they will have to decide. However, the trend is for the lawyers to have put in a written summary of those matters before the hearing in what is called a skeleton argument or position statement – only in exceptional cases would that be required from a litigant in person – and for the judge to discourage any oral opening statement from them. An unrepresented litigant will get a copy of the written summary but it may only be thrust into their hands outside court by the lawyer who has prepared it and very close to the time for going into court. If that unsettles you as a litigant in person then you should explain to the judge what has happened (to generate a few fluid ounces of sympathy) and, if it is genuinely desired, ask for a little more time outside to study the document. Generally, then, straight into the evidence. The claimant or applicant will almost invariably be the first witness and the evidence they give before they are cross-examined is called their 'evidence in chief'. Having taken the oath or affirmed, and then declared their name, address and occupation, they proceed to confirm the truth of the contents of their written statement.

If legally represented, their lawyer may try and squeeze in some additional oral evidence under the guise of wanting to clarify some matters.

> "Ma'am, if I may seek your indulgence to just put one or two supplementary questions to the witness for the assistance of the court."

Very often, the real reason is that some essential matter has been left out of the statement which could damage, if not destroy, their case, unless tackled. This might be due to the incompetence of a lawyer or someone in their employ who has drafted the statement for the witness. Be quick to stop that.

> "Objection, Ma'am. We should be told precisely what questions Mr Harbottle-Fraser-de-Monfort wishes to put to this witness and may I respectfully draw the court's attention to the fact that the witness statement should have contained all the witness's evidence in chief and I should not be ambushed with fresh evidence at this juncture. It is unfair."

If it transpires that all the lawyer wants to do is get the witness to indicate on some photographs of the accident scene which have been produced whether they had been travelling from the bottom of the photographs to the top or vice versa, the objection to this innocuous supplemental evidence can be withdrawn. Perhaps even with the mildest whiff of humour.

> "Ma'am I had been wondering whether the witness had actually been present at the accident and so this clarification is to be welcomed."

Keep an eye on where the witnesses for your opponent are looking when they are testifying. If they are asked a question they appear to be finding awkward they may look towards your opponent for a nod or some other sign before they answer. This would almost certainly be picked up by the judge if they can spot it but the courtroom geography may make this difficult so be quick to score a point.

> "Ma'am, the witness needs to be true to his oath and not my opposing party. Would the witness stop looking towards him."

When the witness has completed their evidence in chief, you get the opportunity to cross-examine them. This does not mean being angry with the witness. After that, they may be asked questions by their lawyer in what is called 're-examination' but this should be restricted to dealing with matters which have been raised in cross-examination and not with fresh matters. Then the judge may ask the witness some questions of their own which are frequently the questions that the litigants or their lawyers forgot to ask, were afraid to ask or were not entitled by the rules of evidence to ask. The remaining witnesses for the claimant or applicant are then questioned in the same sequence. Thereafter, the other side and their witnesses go into bat and we have more of the same procedure.

Each side has the right to make a closing speech to sum up at the end. Generally, the defendant or respondent sums up first and the claimant or applicant goes second. The defendant or respondent may be given the opportunity to reply purely on a point of law or to correct any inaccurate statement made by the claimant or applicant in their summing up. Phew! Summing up is not compulsory but the right to do so should be seized with both hands if it can be done well. A judge could be swayed at this late stage of the case. But if all you are going to do is to repeat your evidence then keep your trap shut and certainly don't open it to try and squeeze in some new evidence or you will be jumped on. The idea is to show why the judge should make findings of fact which are favourable to your case by linking together the salient points of evidence which the judge has heard and drawing attention to any relevant support for your account and inconsistencies in the other side's evidence. It will help you to jot down on a piece of paper the bits of evidence you may wish to refer to in your summing up as the evidence is given. And if there is a difference between you and your opponent about the relevant legal principles, this is your opportunity to argue for your interpretation of the law and to draw the judge's attention to any legal precedents that assist you. You are also meant to draw the judge's attention to any legal precedents that don't assist you! When a precedent is relied on a copy of a recognised law report of the case should be shown to the judge and your opponent. You should be able to source these reports through the internet – take a look at BAILII (that's the British and Irish Legal Information Institute) at bailii.org.

Cross-examination

Back to cross-examination. There's probably not a lawyer in the world who doesn't give some thought before they sniff the aroma of the courtroom to what they are going to say to the judge and ask in cross-examination. A prominent London QC professes to spend one hour in preparation for every minute of his court speak. If it's good enough for them, it's good enough for you. It shouldn't be hard to predict which areas the other side will wish to concentrate on when cross-examining you – the weak areas of your case. If you have asserted that it was definitely the other side who was at the wheel of the Mercedes when it drove into the back of your Skoda and that you recognise them in court, be ready to be questioned about your fishbowl-lensed specs and when you last had your eyes tested, what the driver was wearing and precisely what it is about their appearance in court that you recall from those two seconds of observation three years earlier.

Get a loved one to be cruel and put you through your paces with some really tough cross-examination involving a hypothetical situation such as whether it was you or the babysitter who stole half a cream meringue out of the fridge. Don't over rehearse or your evidence may sound false. In my former incarnation as a solicitor, I cross-examined a store detective giving evidence against my client who was charged with shoplifting, I put it to her that she was plainly wrong. She insisted that her evidence was correct and she knew it was correct because she had gone over it at home when practising for court many times. I had little difficulty in securing the dismissal of the charge on the basis that this key witness had not been testifying about the facts as she recalled them but had been delivering a well-rehearsed speech.

Conversely, think about any questions you may wish to put to the other side and their witnesses in your own cross-examination. The object of this cross-examination should be to flush out points that haven't been mentioned and will help your case – though one of the cardinal rules of cross-examination is never ask a question if you do not know the answer it will get or you could risk opening up a can of worms – and to put your own version of events to them so that they can comment on it. Make notes beforehand about the questions you want to put. Try to start and end the cross-examination with a strong point. If you possibly can – and this requires a mixture of concentration and luck – begin your cross-examination with a question which bounces straight off the last statement the witness has made in their evidence in chief. It might go something like:

> Opponent answering his own lawyer: "Because of the way the claimant behaved towards me, I had to take a fortnight off work and stayed in bed the whole time."
>
> You with your first question in cross-examination: "Apart from the Saturday when I saw you at the Spurs match, that is?"

Be circumspect about alleging that the other side or any of their witnesses have told untruths. The judge may be more susceptible to persuasion that they are mistaken rather than that they have deliberately lied. But if the only reasonable conclusion to be drawn from their evidence is that they have lied and it is important to your case to establish this, then you will need to put that allegation to them in cross-examination. Do it with a flourish. "You were a liar then and you are a liar now." Or if you want something wordier: "I put it to you that your evidence is a farrago of lies. Lie upon lie, to cover up the truth."

Giving your evidence

When you give evidence yourself, turn towards the judge and look them in the face – but not in a threatening way! While answering questions which may be coming from your own lawyer or your opponent, the temptation may be to turn towards and look at them but it is better to focus on the judge. After all, it is for the judge's benefit that you are answering questions so that they can reach a decision. In a difficult case I once tried relating to the welfare of a child, the father who was a psychiatrist of some years standing and his wife gave a master class in the technique, actually moving the witness chair so that they had a direct line to my face and stuck rigidly to that line from the beginning to the end of their testimonies. Yes, the father won but on the merits of his case.

When giving evidence, will you have to take an oath to tell the truth (the whole truth and nothing but the truth)? Something along those lines except on a small claims hearing. Under the Oaths Act 1878 – still going strong despite intermittent attempts to kill it off – a witness must take a religious oath to tell the truth or may affirm, in non-religious terms, that their evidence will be true. This is arguably a pointless exercise because a sizable proportion of witnesses then proceed to lie their heads off though there are instances of witnesses pulling back from the utterance of a porkie by virtue of the fact that they have sworn to tell the truth. Some defendants at their criminal trial are prone to declaring that they must be 'not guilty' because whenever they have been 'guilty' in the past, they have admitted the offence. That rarely works before a jury. And it never works before a civil judge to suggest they should accept your evidence is true because you have sworn on a holy book to tell the truth and you went to church only the day before. I once dismissed a claim for personal injury following a road accident by a claimant who testified to his God fearing nature and produced statements by a series of acquaintances from his religious order as to his excellent character. He had been involved in around seven previous accidents over the preceding few years and I had to decide on the evidence that his latest accident was just one whiplash too many.

One of the possible consequences of a witness telling lies at a civil trial after they have taken an oath or affirmed is that they can be charged with perjury and brought before a criminal court. If convicted, the likely sentence is one of imprisonment. If every witness who the civil judge decided had lied were charged with perjury, the queue to the Old Bailey dock would stretch to Bognor Regis promenade. And so it is that only in the more flagrant and consistent cases of porkie pieing will the civil judge refer the matter to the Director of Public Prosecutions for criminal proceedings to be considered.

It's cold outside

You will stay in court for the entire hearing but what of your witnesses? The practice in civil cases is the dead opposite to criminal cases in that the witnesses being called by each litigant come into court at the start and so hear the evidence being given before their turn arrives. Bonkers? It does give them what is sometimes perceived as the advantage of being able to change what they were going to say on account of what they have heard from the witness box. If they did so, though, they would have to explain why their written statement copies of which the judge and opposition had before them differed from the verbal evidence they were now giving. The evidential u-turn would probably reduce the value of their evidence to the price of a used pilchard. The judge always has a discretion to direct that the usual practice be dis-applied and that witnesses only come into court when they are to be called into the witness box. This might follow a request by one of the litigants or their lawyer. It could be made where they believe that their witnesses are going to be strong and impressive and that even greater weight will be attached to their evidence if they all stand up to cross-examination and give substantially the same evidence on a crucial matter, even though they were absent when the others testified.

Witness familiarisation

Of course, if you are flush with money, you will have undergone a professional witness familiarisation session. Eh? You'll recall the bitter High Court case in 2012 between the late Boris Berezovsky and Chelsea Football Club boss Roman Abramovitch. The trial judge found Abramovitch who won to be a truthful and, on the whole, reliable witness. She said: "Where he had relevant knowledge, he was able to give full and detailed answers; he took care to distinguish between his own knowledge, reconstructed assumptions and speculation." The fact he had given the entirety of his evidence in Russian through the use of a translator didn't operate to his detriment, then. Abramovitch, you see, had been through witness familiarisation with Bond Solon, the UK's leading firm specialising in the area. Firms like this won't coach anyone by guiding them through the evidence they should give in their own particular case because that's taboo. But they may subject you to a mock cross-examination, similar in ferocity to the wife's when investigating the disappearance from the fridge of the one half cream meringue and will tutor on such things as the theory, practice and procedure of giving evidence. Perhaps on the lines of some of this book, only more expensive.

For a one-to-one three hour session, Bond Solon charged a fee of £850 and boss Mark Solon assures me that Abramovitch paid that amount. I didn't ask if he collected a free Chelsea season ticket for his trouble. But Bond Solon have since changed their fee structuring. They now have two types of session: witness familiarisation and follow-up cross-examination. The first type promises to demystify the process of giving evidence and explain the techniques that cross-examining lawyers use to disconcert and discredit witnesses. The three-hour session now costs £940 for one participant. The price goes up according to the number of delegates and tops, for four to six delegates, £3095. The second type of session is intended as an optional follow up and enables delegates to undergo in-depth cross-examination. A three-hour session for one will cost £940 again and for four to six, lasting the whole day, £3095. VAT is to be added. Virtual sessions can be conducted.

If you won the case after undergoing witness familiarisation and were awarded your costs, you could include the fee paid for your session in your bill. If you were allowed the fee, I would eat my entire wardrobe.

Pass the tissues, please

Worth crying at the hearing? If you are genuinely so distressed by the possibility of an adverse outcome of the case for you, at what is being said against you or what you are describing in your evidence that you lose control and shed a tear then, so be it. The judge may feel that your reaction is relevant to your credibility. Anything from wailing to snivelling which is falsely induced so as to invoke sympathy, along with contrived panic attacks, can only assist your opponent. I usually keep a box of paper tissues handy to produce at vapour time. It would obviously give the game away to readily produce your own box. I have come across a couple of lawyers who were moved to tears in their closing addresses to me which I found puerile. Highly emotive representations to a professional judge should be eschewed. Possibly, they would be productive before a bench of lay magistrates. One experienced defence magistrates' court solicitor I knew would plead with the bench in these terms: "God never gave this man a chance. Will you?" But he never cried in court.

Putting a sock in it

It is a mistake to go on too long in cross-examining a witness or addressing the judge. A timetable for each stage of a trial may have been approved by the court and, if so, it should be adhered to. Otherwise, never trespass on the judge's patience. Use their face as a barometer. If it goes bright red, their eyebrows rise to the ceiling, their cheeks expand and they exhale hot air or words are emitted from their mouths along the lines of "How much more of this are we going to have, Mr Troublesore?" or "I've got the point" or "You've asked that question five times already" then you should think very carefully about going on. It is important not to misread what is in the judge's mind. A lay magistrate – he was a professor who was chairman of the bench – before whom I regularly appeared when advocating criminal cases had what I can only assume was an affliction. He would apparently smile broadly throughout proceedings, no matter what he may have been thinking. I had not been tipped off about this when I first encountered him in court and made the mistake of believing from what I saw that I was doing very well and could be economical in the mitigation I had to offer on behalf of my convicted client. In the event, a severe sentence was passed. The mistake was never repeated.

Occasionally it may be necessary to fall out with the judge albeit you must surrender to his control of the proceedings and accept that he is entitled to impose a time limit on cross-examination and other stages of the case. If the judge's impatience is obvious but you have not got round to your killer question or point then you must stand up for yourself and attempt to press on. You will be forgiven some mild impertinence once you have demonstrated that you had good reason to keep going.

> Judge: "Mr Troublesore, surely we don't need any more of this?"
>
> "Sir, I regret just a _little_ more."

The judgment

Where the judge has to decide the result of a case because the litigants have not agreed it, one of them will be disappointed and possibly enraged. Unruly behaviour in court when the judge gives their decision is most unwise. It's worth remembering that, quite apart from the fact that it could well lead to you being locked up for contempt, after the judge has announced his decision they will go on to deal with the costs of the case – who picks up the winner's expenses which may include their lawyer's fees if they have been legally represented at the hearing and may include a lawyer's fee for advising or otherwise helping with the case before the hearing even though they have not been legally represented at the hearing. So something like this would be unfortunate:

> Judge: "Accordingly, Mr Troublesore, your claim is dismissed."
>
> Mr Troublesore: "You idiotic cow. About time you learnt some law."
>
> Representative for Whitewash Ltd: "Most Gracious Madam, I apply for an order for costs against Mr Troublesore. I have sent him and the court a statement of my company's costs which I ask you to assess now on the litigant in person basis. You will see the amount asked for is £15,689. 23 and on top of that........."

And then there's the question of when you have to pay those costs. Oh dear.

Chapter 25

Small Claims

But still beautiful

Anyone who hasn't heard of the Small Claims Court must have been away on Planet Mars. As it happens, that's not quite right. The Small Claims Court does not actually exist except in the imagination of many or possibly at Uranus Town Hall. What does exist is a regime in the normal county court which is dedicated to small claims – generally, those for up to £10,000 – and is the pride and joy of the Courts and Tribunals Service which breaks its neck in good times to get those of them which are defended, heard within 30 weeks of being started. The regime is notable for protecting a litigant who loses against a thumping great big costs order in favour of the winner and for the relative informality of the hearing. These claims are said to be on the *small claims track* where we see real life at its rawest. Contests between buyer and seller, landlord and tenant, motorist and motorist, holidaymaker and package travel company, neighbour and neighbour and that Uncle Thomas Cobley and all again. Before they get onto this track, they are started in much the same way as a massive claim and things can go horribly wrong if they are nutty. But more of that later.

County court arbitration was the forerunner of the modern small claims track and started in the 1970s for county court cases involving a bag of sweets or a grain of sand. Lawyer involvement was considerably rare in those days. It mainly occurred when the wife of the senior partner in a solicitor's office bought a pound of cheese that was off or a solicitor owed a client a favour. As a solicitor myself, I often advised on whether the law was on the side of a client or their opponent and on the tactics to be adopted but my experience as an advocate on a county court arbitration was limited to two cases. The first was a road accident claim where for no fee I represented a female friend I was trying to impress. Whilst she had been standing in the road by the partially opened offside door of her kerb-parked vehicle, an elderly driver out for the afternoon with his wife decided to make contact with the door and remove it from its hinges. Fortunately, the client's body was left intact. The arbitrator – he was a county court judge who was then called a registrar – decided that the client was 20% to blame for having left the door open while parked near a slight bend in the road and the elderly motorist was 80% to blame. The result was that the client had to bear 20% of her repair charges. A peculiar decision which was probably intended as a consolation to the likeable elderly driver.

In my second arbitration outing as an advocate I was representing a Pompey fan against Oxford Football Club in the days of the late Robert Maxwell. The teams were playing in the Milk Cup quarter final. My client had bought stand tickets at £10 a time for himself and his three children. The tickets stated that they were sold subject to conditions displayed at the ticket office but it transpired that at the time there were no conditions displayed there. It was a disastrous evening for the family. They had a poor view of the match due to barriers and pitch perimeter fencing in front of the stand and Pompey lost. My client sued Oxford United for damages. He lost too but on the facts of the case and not the relevant law. The judge decided that the family had been able to see the flow of the game, how it evolved and how the goals were scored. As poor as their view was, it was not so poor that Oxford were in breach of contract in selling the seats. Had the seats not been reasonably fit for purpose, my client would have scored. Some years later, I used this area of the law to obtain a refund for the price of two tickets for an Abba tribute band concert at Richmond Theatre which had been ruined by most of the audience ahead spending the whole concert on their feet. I tend to prefer sitting down at concerts except when purchasing the ices.

The modern small claims scheme got going in 1999 and is destined to be given a monumental facelift but not for a while so time to enjoy what we have got. The same law of England and Wales that applies to an oligarch's case before the Supreme Court applies to your small claim in the county court and that will continue to be the case under the new regime. If the law is against you, the judge will be – must be – against you. That's why I had to throw out one person's claim against another for damages on the ground that the other had stared at them in a supermarket. If you have any doubt about the legal validity of your claim, check it out with a lawyer or advice agency first (see **Unbundling** below).

I need to make a confession. I have brought small claims during my judicial career (and before). Judges bleed when they are pricked and think about suing when they are wronged. Only occasionally, having thought about it, will they actually launch a claim. It's not the done thing. All a bit embarrassing. Difficult to find a judge who doesn't know you and just think of the humiliation if you lost. That makes me something of an exception. I have always claimed using Money Claim Online (see chapter 12) and without disclosing that I am a judge. Every time it has been my intention that, should the defendant be misguided enough to defend the case, I would either abandon it or, more probably, ask that a judge or deputy judge who was unaware of my existence should hear the case in my absence. Happily, I have never lost and either obtained a judgment in default (see below) or negotiated a settlement after a defence has gone in.

Alas, there is a further confession about which I cringe and contort every sinew of my body in shame. I, me, Judge Clever Dick, was conned. In 2008 a builder induced me to pay him £3,500 on account of his charges and those of a structural engineer he said he was to engage in connection with the preparation of plans and an application for planning permission for a loft conversion at my home. He did little or nothing but pay the money I handed over towards the debts he had incurred with others. In mitigation, I plead that I agreed to do this by telephone over dinner and after a hard day's work and the builder had been highly recommended by a friend (whose assassination I have arranged) and I had seen some impressive work the builder had done for someone else. This is scant mitigation, I know, and is not deserving of a discount of more than 10% on the number of lashings I should receive for my stupidity. And if I had taken the elementary step of making a search at the Register of Judgments, Orders and Fines (see chapter 27), I would have discovered that my plausible builder already had a string of unsatisfied county court judgments registered against him. I duly sued him and then came the not uncommon scenario. He didn't put in a defence and I obtained a default judgment. He applied to set the judgment aside and failed to turn up for the hearing of the application in Oxford County Court where I had instructed a local solicitor to represent me. His application was dismissed with costs in my favour. I then put in the bailiff. The builder was never at home when the bailiff called and nobody who was at home would open the door. All the bailiff could find outside the house that he could seize was a water feature – not even a bird seed container – but the advice was that it would cost more to remove than it would sell for. Next I obtained a charging order against the builder's interest in his home (see chapter 29). That was one of the better moves I had made since meeting him.

Then he was made bankrupt by someone else. The bankruptcy did not lose me the value of my judgment because of the charging order for this generally takes priority over other creditors who have not obtained such an order. The builder's trustee in bankruptcy had the builder's property sold and, once his mortgage was paid off along with the bankruptcy costs, the surplus was available to pay me my £3,500 and costs due to me and other charges were also paid off with the balance available for unsecured creditors to share. By the way, do you know any good loft converters who do cheap plans and don't telephone during dinner?

A chocolaty story

It's as important to assess when not to make a small claim as when to make a small claim. In 2012 my brother Clive gifted me a *Marks & Spencer* bottle of champagne with chocolates which he had ordered online. On a peckish night around three months later, I ripped open the box of chocolates to find they were past their scoff by date. They had been given a life of just two and a half months from the date of delivery. I wrote Marks and Spencer a 'letter before action' – yes, I know I was not a party to the contract for the purchase of the gift but the Contracts (Rights of Third Parties) Act 1999 gave me the standing to make a complaint and claim in my own right without involving my brother and, anyway, I could hardly have troubled him – contending that it had been implied on purchase that the scoff by date would be reasonable and that two and a half months was unreasonably short. I argued that the chocolates were not an accompaniment to a short life product but to champagne. If they had accompanied some other perishable product then I conceded that a different situation would have prevailed. Not a bad argument, eh?

As I pictured no less than the chief choc buyer from *M&S*'s head office turning up with the biggest hamper known to man and sufficient *Mountain Bars* to keep me stuffed for twenty years, customer services were instead composing a letter rejecting my claim. They wanted me to enjoy food that was as natural as possible and free from any unnecessary additives and preservatives, they said, and, as a result, some of their foods might have a shorter life than some of their competitors' products. They were sorry I had been disappointed and hoped I would continue to shop at *M&S* with confidence etc etc (see *"The life expectation of a chocolate"* below). I shook the envelope after removal of the letter but nothing dropped out: not even a chocolate peanut.

MARKS & SPENCER

Retail Customer Services
Chester Business Park
Wrexham Road
Chester
CH4 9GA

Tel: 0845 302 1234
Fax: 0845 303 0170
www.marksandspencer.com

Mr S Gold

Our Ref: 1-421238117
12 November 2012

Dear Mr Gold

The quality of our food is extremely important to us. We want you to enjoy our food at its very best and we carry out extensive tests to establish the natural life of each of our products.

We also want you to enjoy food that is as natural as possible and free from any unnecessary additives or preservatives.

As a result, some of our foods may have a shorter life than our competitors' products. We believe the benefits of our approach outweigh the negatives of a shorter shelf life, and help us achieve the higher quality our customers have come to expect.

Having said this, we are always pleased to hear from our customers on any issues that are important to them, and I have passed your comments on to our buyers. They will take them into account when we come to review the recipe and guidelines for this product.

We must also advise, that is a customers responsibility to check the best before date on items they receive, in case of any errors that may have occurred during the picking.

Concerning the chocolate in question, we do feel that 2.5 months from the date of delivery to the best before date, is more than reasonable. And in this instance we would not offer anything further.

I am sorry you were disappointed with this product. I hope my letter has been helpful in explaining how and why we date our food as we do, and that you will continue to shop at M&S with confidence.

Yours sincerely

Customer Adviser
Retail Customer Services
We're keen to know what you thought of our service. If you'd like to share any feedback, please let us know by completing our short automated telephone or online survey. You can give us a call on 0333 20 20 500 or use the web link: www.mandssurvey.co.uk/500.

"The life expectation of a chocolate"

I gave judgment against myself. A softer centred judge might well have awarded me the retail price of the chocs but a hard centred judge such as the one I saw in my mirror was not persuaded that two and half months was unreasonable.

What's the big deal?

This is all about the cost of a case on the small claims track. If you are making or defending the claim and you lose, there is a ceiling on what you will have to pay to the winner for their expenses. For a start, where the winner used a lawyer (whether for advice and help in preparing for court or just for appearing at the hearing or both) you won't have to make any contribution towards that lawyer's fees. Those fees have to be borne by the winner out of their own pocket. Apart from one ruddy great big exception (see below), there are two modest exceptions to this. If the winner made a claim for an injunction (no drum practise in the flat above after 10.30pm) or for specific performance (my landlord to be compelled to eradicate dry rot in the main bedroom) he can recover from the loser up to £260 for the cost of obtaining legal advice and assistance on the case. And if the winner made the claim and had a lawyer issue the claim form for them, then there is a standard allowance which the loser will almost invariably have to pay which takes some account of what the lawyer would have charged. This allowance depends on the amount claimed and is usually between £50 and £100 (show me a lawyer who will charge no more than £100 and I'll show you a happy corpse). Should you lose but for less than the amount which had been claimed, it would be reasonable to ask the judge to keep this allowance down to the amount applicable to the award rather than the higher figure claimed. The winner can seek payment of other expenses though, mostly with maximum sums:

- Any court fees paid by the winner (for a winning claimant who has not enjoyed remission from fees, these would be the commencement fee when you kicked off the claim and a hearing fee: the so-called allocation fee has now been abolished) – see chapter 17 for details of these fees and the system for remitting (excusing) litigants from having to pay court fees.

- Travelling expenses and expenses in "staying away from home" so as to enable court attendance for the winner and any witnesses who have attended court with them (noisy overnight box room and a sandwich at *The Wig and Duck* might get through with a double bedroom at *The Dorchester* and a Full English being more problematic). No maximum but the expenses must have been reasonably incurred. Don't get too panicky here as expenses tend in the majority of cases to stay under £100. Nevertheless, there is potential in some cases for the bill to be quite substantial. The court will direct the hearing to take place at the most convenient venue and the number of witnesses to be called by each side and where they live or carry on business will be highly relevant. If you live on the Isle of Wight and the other side has three witnesses all of whom come from Cumbria it might be worth agreeing to a hearing in Carlisle unless you are as sure as eggs that you are going to win so won't be saddled with having to pay one new pence by way of travelling or accommodation expenses. It may be productive to challenge such expenses claimed on the grounds that they are unreasonable and/or that one or more of the witnesses were unnecessary and/or that you were not alerted by the other side before the hearing that a particular witness was to be relied on. Further, it is always prudent when having sight of copies of the other side's witness statements in advance of the hearing to consider agreeing one or more of those statements and letting the other side know that you do agree so that the agreed witnesses are not dragged along to court. You won't want to agree the statement of a witness where you dispute the truth or accuracy of something in their statement which is material to the issues in the case. You will want the witness at court so that you can cross-examine them and the judge can question them too. The potential for heavy travelling expenses and long travelling times to and from court can be obviated by a remote hearing by telephone or video which Covid-19 has encouraged (see chapters 6 and 24). Pre-pandemic, the idea of that happening might have been scoffed at by the court. See more on this below.

- Loss of earnings for attending at court or "staying away from home" so as to enable a court attendance for the winner and any witnesses who have attended court with them at the rate of £95 each per day (increased from £90 in April 2015). If time off in lieu of holiday has been taken so that there is no financial loss but loss of holiday, the same allowance applies. Take home pay only will be reckoned and the employed and self-employed can qualify because they both (hopefully) "earn". The comments above on challenges to travelling and accommodation expenses and how to try and avoid exposure to liability for them equally apply.

- Experts' fees with a maximum of £750 per expert. The majority of small claims do not involve an expert's report. Sometimes, though, the court will give permission for an expert's report to be obtained (see below).

The ruddy great big exception

Here it comes. It's the major exception to the rule that the loser is protected by the limits on what they have to pay in respect of the winner's expenses. Where the judge decides that the loser has behaved unreasonably they can order the loser to pay the winner expenses which fall into the categories summarised above but uncapped PLUS any other reasonable expenses on the case that the winner has incurred (for example, on postage, telephone calls and stationery used for the case) PLUS an allowance to a litigant who has conducted the whole or any part of the case without a lawyer at what might be the rate of £19 per hour for the time they have been personally occupied on the case or an hourly sum to compensate for the actual earnings they have lost if more than £19 per hour (see chapter 35). And it's getting potentially worse. If the winner has been represented by a lawyer then the unreasonable loser could have to compensate the winner for the lawyer's fees or part of them. Big Businesses may well be represented by a lawyer and defend the case not because it is financially viable to do so but because they do not wish to be regarded by the social media community as a soft touch and thereby vulnerable to those claimants who are out to make a fast buck.

What's unreasonable behaviour?

Very good question, There's no definition of it. Like that elephant, it's hard to describe but you know it when you see it – and so does the judge. The Court of Appeal summed up unreasonable behaviour in a 2017 case called *Dammermann v Lanyon Bowdler LLP*. Behaviour, they said, could not be described as unreasonable just because it led to an unsuccessful result. Nor, of itself, would following a course which a more cautious litigant (or lawyer!) or less optimistic litigant would not have followed, amount to such behaviour. It was emphasised that it would be unfortunate if litigants were too easily deterred from pursuing a small claim by the risk of being condemned to pay more than the restricted costs that normally apply.

It could be doing everything required to defend the case and then failing to turn up for the final hearing. Telling lots of small whoppers or a couple of sizeable ones could amount to unreasonable behaviour. The judge will be used to a bit of lying by one of the litigants (sometimes both!) in a high proportion of cases so it would probably take some serious stuff before they were prepared to remove costs protection on the basis of unreasonableness. Behaviour both before and after a claim has been started can be reckoned. Take a claimant who alleges he was sold substandard goods but makes no contact with the seller and simply launches a court claim without any warning. Then when the seller puts in a defence saying they need an opportunity to examine the goods so that they can decide on their stance, the claimant denies them that opportunity. Finally, the judge concludes that the goods were up to standard when sold but were damaged when the claimant threw them at his wife the next night. In my book, that's unreasonable behaviour.

Unbundling

If you want advice or help on paperwork from a lawyer, be it on the merits or your proposed claim or defence to it or on preparing particulars of claim or your defence, or whatever, then see chapter 7 on how to go about getting it. However, unless you win and can show the loser has behaved unreasonably (see above), you will have to bear the cost of doing it out of your own money box.

Staying small

There's nothing to stop you gaining the benefits of the small claims track by limiting a claim to £10,000 even though it is actually worth more. This would involve giving up the chance of recovering the excess over £10,000 in return for lower court fees, an earlier hearing, the more informal procedure and the normal shield against a swingeing bill for the other side's costs if you lose. A calculated decision has to be made.

In assessing whether the claim goes over £10,000, you disregard any interest sought, any costs you intend to seek including the court fee for starting the case – and any undisputed amount. So, for example, if the claim is for repayment of a loan made of £25,000 and in their defence the other side admits they owe you £17,000 but deny the rest, the claim should go onto the small claims track because the amount in dispute is only £8,000.

You won't normally be allowed onto the small claims track where the hearing is likely to take longer than one day – that generally means five hours of hearing time – or one side is alleging dishonesty against the other side and the allegation is disputed. Another type of claim which is sometimes excluded from the small claims track is for housing repairs involving over £1,000. Most traffic accident personal injury claims have also been outside the scope of the track on account of their value but a whole new regime for them has now been introduced which, as a special treat, I have saved to the end of this chapter.

Now to what could be your saving grace. The court has a discretion to allocate a claim involving more than £10,000 to the small claims track whether or not the parties consent. It is not something which is often done and the power to do it is not always in the forefront of judges' minds but the power is there. You might be able to persuade a judge to exercise the power where, for example, both sides are litigants in person, the case is uncomplicated, the hearing will take less than one day and the judge is in a good mood.

You will get an opportunity to make written representations about whether a case should be allocated to the small claims track when you complete a form called a *directions questionnaire*. This will be sent out for completion (to litigants in person but lawyers for the parties have to download their copies) if and when a defence is put in. It solicits information to enable the court to ensure the case is allocated to the appropriate track and that it is not listed for hearing on your silver wedding anniversary when you are due to be baking on a Mediterranean beach.

The wobbles

You've made or defended a claim and notice of the hearing arrives. The hearing is 500 miles away or you have a panic attack – or both. Is there an alternative to throwing in the towel to avoid the hassle of a long return journey or palpitations? Yes. You can approach the other side and ask whether they would agree to dispense with an oral hearing and, if they do, write to the court with a copy of their letter of agreement and a request that a judge decides the case on the papers in the absence of the parties. The other side would be daft to agree because they should realise you might capitulate if they disagree or the court might well refuse the request. But you can always try.

And without the permission of anyone you can request the court in writing to decide the case in your absence but it must receive the request at least seven days before the hearing date. Also, you must have told the other side that you will be absent and sent them copies of your statements and any other documents at least seven days before the hearing date.

> "Pursuant to rule 27.9 of the Civil Procedure Rules 1998, I hereby give notice that I will not attend the hearing of this case. I request that the Judge please decide it in my absence taking into account the statements of evidence and other documents I have already lodged with the court. I confirm that I have given the other party notice of my intended absence and sent them copies of my statements and other documents so that they will have received them at least seven days before the hearing date".

Absence is by no means the best way of dealing with the case and may put you at a disadvantage. You will not be present to answer what your opponent in attendance and their witnesses have to say and personal representations and evidence have the potential to be a million times more powerful than the written word. However, if a personal attendance is not economically viable – and commercial organisations sometimes take this view – or is just too much trouble or panic has set in, this may be the answer for you.

For the post-pandemic court tendency to itself seek to have cases heard without a hearing or through a remote telephone or video hearing, see **Preparing for the hearing** below.

Experts

An expert is someone who tells you what you already knew but in words you cannot understand. That tends to be the general view held by judges. The trend is to keep an expert out of a case if at all possible but sometimes you just can't do without one. The judge knows the law but they may not be too hot on whether the reconditioned engine caused the car to conk out on the M25 1,000 miles after it had been fitted or whether the windows fell out because of subsidence or the stupidity of the builder. In that sort of situation, the judge might be assisted by the opinion of someone who is qualified in the discipline concerned like a vehicular mechanical engineer or a building surveyor. The expert does not decide the case and the judge is quite entitled to form the view that the expert is wrong if factual evidence in the case strongly points in an opposite direction. An expert can be relied on in small claims just as in the bigger cases but the court's permission to take advantage of an expert's report must be obtained. The time to ask for that permission is usually in the directions questionnaire we have already met which you will be asked to complete once a defence has been sent to the court. It is rare for an expert to give live evidence in a small claim. What the expert has to say will usually be said in a written report. Where persuaded to allow an expert, the court frequently directs that it is a single expert who is to be used and that they are to be jointly instructed by both sides. That almost invariably means that both sides will have an input in what the expert is told about the case. One side should take the lead in drafting a letter of instructions to the expert which should be accompanied by copies of all documents including the claim form and particulars of claim and the defence (sometimes witness statements as well) and then send it to the other side to approve. If there is any dispute about what should go into or with the letter, the court would have to be asked to resolve it. Each party will usually be required to shell out for the expert's fees and expenses up front on a 50/50 basis. The court will probably order the losing party to reimburse the winning party for the share they have borne.

Experts can be expensive and, if at all possible, the fee paid to them should not exceed the £750 which the loser can be ordered to pay to the winner for an expert's report (see above) or the parties to the case or one of them will find themselves having to meet the excess. The court does have the power to impose a limit on the amount of the expert's fee, and often exercises it, when giving the necessary permission for the expert to be used. Anecdotal evidence suggests that experts' fees range from £32 to £500 an hour with an average of £177. You may have to haggle over the fee. Don't be afraid to do that. The volume of work for experts has dropped significantly in the last couple of years. You can always remind them of the fee they would be paid if they were producing a report in a legal aid case: £85 for a housing repair surveyor (£115 if London based), £64 for an accountant and £72 for a cell telephone site analyst or telecoms expert. This might lead to a reduction in what they were asking or an invitation for you to take a one-way standing room only trip to Hell.

It's risky to pay out for an expert's report before the court has given permission for an expert to be relied on. The reason is that the court might well order that a single expert jointly instructed by the parties be used even though you had already obtained your own report. Then the cost of your early report would be money down the drain.

> "But I got this builder bloke in and he told me that Whitewash had really cocked up the job and he said he'd give me a report I could take to court and he also said that he would come in and do the job for half the price Whitewash had ripped me off for."

That sort of report would be as good as a chocolate teapot. An expert's report must be independent and the expert's overriding duty is to the court and not to the person who is paying their charges. If the expert has a vested interest in the outcome of the case – for example, they will get a job from you if the case goes your way – then the expert lacks independence and relying on them could severely prejudice your case.

The formalities that have to be observed in relation to the contents of the expert's report and certain other matters which apply to the bigger cases do not apply to small claims. Nevertheless, you don't want the report typed out on the back of a bus ticket and it's useful even in a small claim for the expert to confirm that they understand their duty to the court and that they have complied with that duty and also to give details of their qualifications.

Because an expert will not normally attend the actual small claims hearing, it is crucial that if they have failed to deal with a particular point they were asked to address, there is some ambiguity in the report or a question screams out to be answered, then you put written questions to the expert and ask that they answer them by a particular date: say by 14 days from receipt. You should send a copy of the questions to the other side where the report is from an expert they have alone instructed or the expert has been jointly instructed. Beware. This may generate a fee for replying so be selective in what you ask.

Preparing for the hearing

The pandemic has resulted in an unprecedented number of small claims hearings taking place remotely – by telephone or video – at the initiative of the court but with the parties being given an opportunity to object to what the court has in mind. If you have ignored chapter 23 – how dare you! – then have a look at it now to find out how to play a court's move towards remote. In the simplest of cases, the court may want to decide a small claim on the strength of the documents put in and without an actual hearing. Again, you can object to this. But as mentioned above, you can yourself ask for this to be done even where an actual hearing has been scheduled to take place (see **The wobbles** above).

Before the hearing the court will probably have required each side send to the court and each other statements of the evidence of themselves and their other witnesses and copies of any documents they will be relying on. Ensure that is done by the deadline set. In the bigger cases, statements are exchanged: swapped. That way neither side gains an advantage over the other by seeing their statements before they have parted with their own. In small claims, exchange is unusual so there may not be any merit in getting your statements in before those of the opposition. You could legitimately hang fire in the hope that you get to see the opposition statements first so long as you beat the deadline but it's not a good idea to blatantly comment on their statements in your own. Incidentally, as a party to the case, you are your own witness so don't answer the questions in the directions questionnaire about how many witnesses you have with 'none' unless you intend to be mute at the hearing. In chapter 19 we look at how a witness statement should read.

The claim will be decided on the evidence and the evidence comes from you and your witnesses. In so far as there is a dispute between you and the other side about what was or was not said and what did or did not happen, anyone who can back up your account or can deal with some relevant event at which you were not present, is a potential witness and you should consider relying on them. Obviously you don't want a busload of witnesses or the hearing might never end. You need to be selective about this too. As indicated, the directions questionnaire will ask you to state how many witnesses you will be relying on. Whenever I see an answer in a small claims questionnaire that more than say four witnesses were to be used, I have a pretty good idea that the party was "having a laugh". Not only will each witness in addition to you need to make a written statement but they will need to come to court if any real weight is to be placed on what they say unless the other side is prepared to agree their statement in advance. That's so they can be questioned by the other side and the judge. Should you drag a witness to court who had nothing of relevance to say and win, the judge will probably refuse to order the other side to pay that witness's expenses if you win. Ouch.

If you follow the tips at chapters 23 and 24, your chances of winning should be enhanced. Be ready though for the judge to seize the case by the scruff of the neck, suspend the court niceties and weigh in at an early stage. Each judge has their own way of conducting a small claim hearing but the majority will be interventionist and will get to the root of the dispute pretty quickly. This should put you in no doubt what they think about each side's case. Concentrate on any indication the judge gives to you about any aspects of your case which concern them and attempt to persuade.

Mediation

You can take advantage of the court's own mediation scheme for most small claims which you will be told about if and when a case becomes defended. You cannot be forced into it but the number of cases which are settled through the scheme is enormously high. Trained mediators will speak to each side separately and usually by telephone to sound them out about a compromise. What is said in the course of mediation will not reach the ears of the judge and a willingness to use the scheme will not be construed as any sort of acceptance that you are legally liable to your opponent. The service is free. If you wish, you can appoint somebody else to participate in the mediation on your behalf.

Small intellect

Copyright claims ("I took those snaps of you naked on Brighton Beach and own the copyright in them and you've put them up on the internet without my permission"), trade mark claims ("My trade mark is registered and you have been illegally using it") and passing off claims ("I've been running *The Clive Troublesore Café* and you've stolen half my business by opening up *The Clive Troublesoretothesky Café* and the public reckon it's my joint") are specialised intellectual property claims. There's a court dedicated to them in which the judges have expertise in this area of the law. It's the Intellectual Property Enterprise Court at The Rolls Building, 7 Rolls Building, Fetter Lane, London EC4A 1NL. The good news is that it has its own small claims track which operates in a similar way to the general small claims regime in the county court for claims of up to £10,000. The same costs protection applies as does the free court service mediation scheme. A claim intended to be dealt with in the Enterprise Court should be started at The Rolls Building from which a guidance booklet is available. The small claims though are actually heard at The Strand's Royal Courts of Justice where the judges are treated as sitting in the Croydon District Registry of the High Court. Now should you think that sounds odd, you would be right. It is odd and it has happened to get over a legislative drafting cock up but that's another story.

That special treat

If you have suffered personal injury as a result of a road traffic accident which occurred before 31 May 2021 you can carry on whistling and lap up the *Tomlin Order* which you will find as the next chapter. Provided you are not seeking compensation for your pain and suffering and loss of amenity (that last bit takes account of the impact on your life that your injury has caused) for more than £1,000 and provided also that the total amount of the claim once other losses such as car repairs are added in does not exceed £10,000, the small claims track should be yours. The Blooming Great Change is for this type of claim where the accident occurred on or after 31 May 2021. Then, the small claims track will take in a claim for personal injury for up to £5,000 so long as the total claim does not top £10,000. This £4,000 difference may not strike you as earth shattering but it has been for a number of lawyers and that will have its effect on you. Because for the claims which were previously outside the small claims track but have now been welcomed inside it, the solicitors' costs rewards for acting for claimants in these cases has been axed down to what most will find to be uneconomic levels. This has meant many firms specialising in the cases packing up business. Although the solicitor choice has been reduced, there are still law firms out there who advertise on the internet and remain willing to take on this type of case and, with a bit of luck, you will have opted for free legal representation as an extra under your motor insurance policy. However, with a lot of solicitors now out of the picture for these more modest cases, claims management companies will be ultra-hungry for your business. My advice is to source a solicitor instead. With savings to insurers in claimants' costs and in whiplash compensation (see below) we are led to expect that premiums will be going down. Oh, yeh! We shall see. One firm of solicitors which has already come out and announced its willingness to take on these cases is NewLaw (new-law.co.uk/) which will act for you under a damages-based agreement (see chapter 7) and be looking for a cut of up to 25% of personal injury damages and between 20% and 30% of the other damages recovered for doing so.

Or you can go it alone. For a personal injury road traffic accident claim under the new regime which falls within the small claims track, you should follow a pre-action protocol which describes the behaviour expected from you and what will normally be the insurance company on the other side, before a rush to start court proceedings. Its aim is to get the claim settled fairly without proceedings and by taking various steps under a specially designed portal which is intended to be user friendly. You can contact the portal centre – it's called Official Injury Claim – at 0800 118 1631 or customer.service@officialinjuryclaim.org.uk. They will provide support on the portal's use if you are not represented. Obtaining a medical report on you will be dealt with through the portal. If liability for the accident is admitted by the other side and a settlement can be achieved, all well and good. If there is a dispute about who was to blame or how much you should get, small claims track court proceedings will be needed. There are a few instances where for an accident on or after 31 May 2021, the £5,000 small claims track limit, the protocol and the portal procedure will not apply and the claim will be dealt with as before with the small claims track only being usable if the claim for compensation for the injury, pain and suffering and loss of amenity does not go over £1,000. These are mainly where you were under 18 or lacked the mental capacity to make decisions about the claim when proceedings were started or, at the time of the accident, you were using a motor cycle, pedal cycle, wheelchair or mobility scooter; riding a horse; or were a pedestrian.

And now for whiplash claims. The vast majority are caught by the new regime. You bet they are. Without them, there would probably not be a new regime. They have a lot to answer for. The problem with whiplash claims is that one quarter of the world believes they are fraudulent. Because the proof of injury and symptoms may wholly or largely depend on how good a story the claimant tells their doctor preparing a medical report on them and because of the antics of some claims management companies in urging claimants to go to A&E before they realised they had any pain, they have acquired a bad name. All claims by *Breaking Law* readers, of course, have been genuine and pure. What the new regime does in relation to whiplash claims, is to cut right down the compensation that can be awarded by the court for the injury and, inevitably, the protocol offer that an insurer makes will be bolted on to what the court would award if it had to decide. The level of compensation that can be awarded for accidents on or after 31 May 2021 is set by the Whiplash Injury Regulations 2021 and ranges from £240 to £4,345, depending on the actual or likely duration of the injury. These amounts will not apply if the injury symptoms last or are likely to last for more than two years and, in that event, the compensation figure will not be constrained by the regulations. The amounts are considerably less than the courts have been and will continue to be awarding for whiplashes sustained before 31 May 2021. For example, a whiplash from which there has been a complete recovery within three months and has been earning between £1,290 and £2,300 will now generate a measly award of £240 or £260 if there are associated minor psychological injuries. And for a soft tissue neck injury with a complete recovery within one to two years that has been earning between £4,080 and £7,410, an award of between £4,215 or £4,345 is allowed for. There can be a 20% enhancement in the new figures if that is appropriate because of exceptional severity of the injury or because the claimant's exceptional personal circumstances have increased the pain, suffering or loss of amenity.

But what exactly is a whiplash injury? It is treated as a soft tissue injury to the neck, back or shoulder. However, if you have suffered multiple bruising to the buttocks, this will attract compensation on top of the lousy whiplash fixed compensation. The new procedure will still apply so long as the total personal injury compensation is not worth more than £5,000. But how will the courts approach valuing the unfixed compensation alongside the fixed compensation? The new legislation does not help them and most sane people involved with the new procedure see this as a massive lacuna. A group of principal players is collaborating on identifying suitable cases that can be taken to the Court of Appeal to provide the clarity that is desperately needed.

BREXIT ALERT!!! The European Small Claims Procedure for tiddly claims against defendants elsewhere in the EU and the European Order for Payment Procedure for uncontested small money claims against them have disappeared with Brexit unless you kicked off before 11pm on 31 December 2020. Good job as nobody could understand them and, if they could, the procedures normally went wrong. Protests on a postcard to this book's publishers, please. Leave me out of it.

Chapter 26

The *Tomlin Order*

Kissing and making up after proceedings started

The *Tomlin Order* is a very fine order indeed. Where litigants have reached a compromise agreement after a court case has been started, they can jointly ask the court to make this order which records the terms of the agreement and halts the case so that the agreement can be implemented. At the same time, it gives the litigants permission to return to court to enforce any of those terms should one of them fail to do what they agreed to do. Those terms sometimes go beyond what the court would have the jurisdiction to direct if it was deciding the case although the terms should not be remote from the subject matter of the case as there could then be difficulty in getting the court to enforce them should default occur.

So what's the big appeal of it? It doesn't constitute a judgment and so is not registrable in the Register of Judgments, Orders and Fines (see chapter 27) but it commits the litigants to keep to the agreement and formally sets out all its details. Not a black mark against the debtor's credit record and protection for the creditor as they can obtain a judgment based on the broken agreement should the debtor default. It's also a way of keeping what has been agreed away from prying eyes, as we shall see shortly. The *Tomlin Order* can be used to replace a judgment which has already been entered (if the judge who considers it is prepared to allow it to go through) or, and this is more common, before any judgment has been obtained.

Pick and Mix the paragraphs which might be suitable for your very own *Tomlin Order*. Here goes.

Case No 21P0000678

IN THE COUNTY COURT

SITTING AT PEARDROP

BETWEEN

WHITEWASH LTD Claimant

- and -

CLIVE TROUBLESORE Defendant

UPON the parties having reached terms of compromise

IT IS ORDERED BY CONSENT that-

1. Judgment for the claimant entered on 14th May 2021 be set aside.

2. The claim be stayed on the terms set out in the schedule to this order save and except that there be permission to the parties to apply

235

for the purpose of enforcing any of such terms.

The schedule

(1) The defendant will pay to the claimant the sum of £4,500 to the credit of the claimant's account numbered 1098667 with Comic Bank plc sort code 14-09-06 by 4 pm on 14th July 2021.

or

(1) The defendant will pay to the claimant the sum of £4,500 by instalments of £500 per calendar month payable calendar monthly on the first day of each month with the first instalment being made on 1 July 2021 (time being of the essence) to the credit of the claimant's account numbered 1098667 with Comic Bank plc sort code 14-09-06 and in the event of default in the payment of any one instalment on the due date then the full outstanding balance shall become immediately due to the claimant who shall be entitled to the entry of judgment against the defendant for such outstanding balance together with interest thereon from the date of the default until the date of judgment at the rate of 8% per annum.

(2) The defendant will deliver to the claimant at its head office 65 Wayne Rooney miniatures (being part of the goods the subject of the claim) during normal business hours in the same condition as when sold and delivered to the defendant by 4 pm on 14th July 2021.

(3) The claimant will send the defendant a VAT credit note for the sum of £750 plus VAT within 7 days of the date of the discharge by the defendant of his liability under paragraph 1 above.

(4) The defendant will carry out the works of repair to the claimant's head office without payment in accordance with the specifications contained in the letter from the claimant to the defendant dated 11th June 2021 to a satisfactory standard and using good materials by 14th September 2021.

(5) The claimant will accept the sum of £4,500 and the carrying out of the works referred to in paragraph 4 above in full and final settlement of its claim and costs.

(6) The defendant withdraws any claims he has or may have against the claimant arising out of the sale of the goods the subject of these proceedings.

We hereby consent to this order

(signed) Arthur B Clematis   (signed) C Troublesore

On behalf of the Claimant   Defendant Dated 1 July 2021

Someone other than a party to proceedings – they are called nosey-parkers in this book and that could embrace the man at the end of the road with a pair of binoculars welded to his eyeballs or a journalist who won't be let out of their newsroom until they have come up with a decent story – will generally be entitled to obtain a copy of your *Tomlin Order*. You might be personally or commercially embarrassed by what has been agreed or you might just take the simple view that the agreement is nobody's else's business and should remain confidential while everybody else takes a running jump.

You can secure confidentiality. Choose one of two ways to do this.

First route to confidentiality

Add this paragraph to the schedule of the order:

> *(7) The claimant and the defendant agree that the terms of this agreement shall be confidential and that they will not publish or otherwise disclose them to any other person and through any medium whatsoever and, for the avoidance of any doubt, including radio, television, internet and social network sites save and except as may be required by law and to professional advisers in connection with such enforcement of the terms as may be required AND in the event that either party breaches this term of the agreement the other party shall become immediately entitled to exercise the option of giving written notice to the other party to be discharged from this agreement and shall thereupon be entitled to the refund of any monies paid thereunder together with interest at the rate of 8% per annum as from the date of breach until refund and/or property delivered thereunder and to damages for such breach and further to the removal of the stay imposed by this order.*

Second route to confidentiality

Use this form of order:

> Case No: 21P0000678
>
> IN THE COUNTY COURT
>
> SITTING AT PEARDROP
>
> BETWEEN
>
> WHITEWASH LTD Claimant
>
> - and -
>
> CLIVE TROUBLESORE Defendant
>
> UPON the parties having reached terms of compromise
>
> IT IS ORDERED BY CONSENT that the claim be stayed on the terms set out in the schedule to this order save and except that there be permission to the parties to apply for the purpose of enforcing any of such terms.

> **The schedule**
>
> The terms of settlement are set out in a confidential settlement agreement in writing made between the parties dated 5 July 2021 the original of which has been retained by the claimant and a copy of which has been retained by the defendant.
>
> We hereby consent to this order
>
> (signed) Arthur B Clematis   (signed) C Troublesore.
>
> On behalf of the claimant   Defendant
>
> Dated 14 July 2021

The court does not need to concern itself with the confidential terms of settlement or see the settlement agreement referred to in the schedule. It would only poke its nose into those terms if the agreement was broken by one party and the other party applied to the court for the stay of the proceedings to be lifted and for the settlement terms to be enforced. The only exception to this is in the Commercial Court (part of the High Court) and unless you have zillions about to ooze in or out of your bank account, your case won't be proceeding there. Should the judge or some court official tell you that you cannot follow this confidential route tell them to get stuffed. Oops, I mean tell them that with the greatest of grovelling respect, they should refer to the judgment of Mr Justice Warby in *Zenith Logistics Services (UK) Limited and others v Coury and another* case decided on 3 April 2020 in the High Court, Queen's Bench Division.

Breaking a *Tomlin Order*

The party which alleges that one or more of the scheduled terms of the order has not been complied with, applies to the court for a judgment. If, for example, the defendant was meant to pay the claimant £4,500 by 14 July 2021 and failed to do so, the claimant will ask the court for a judgment that the defendant makes the payment, probably within 14 days of the date of the judgment. Almost always, the claimant will also ask for their costs of the application to be added on to what is due and possibly some interest or extra interest as well. The application will be made using form N244 and, more likely than not, if it makes sense, the judge who considers it will approve the judgment without a hearing. If the defendant still fails to pay up, the claimant can enforce the judgment in the same way as if they had obtained it in the first place without following the *Tomlin Order* route. Should the claimant be telling a pack of lies and have collected the money from the defendant on time or jumped the gun and made their application before the money was due, the defendant will have good grounds to apply for the judgment to be set aside within seven days of it being served on them. Otherwise, where a hearing has been directed, the defendant can challenge the application at court.

A very pleasant surprise for defaulting debtors

For this, defaulting debtors who are individuals should blow that kiss, which should be big, at the Court of Appeal for its decision in February 2021 in a case called *CFL Finance Ltd v Laser Trust* where it was ruled that a debtor's agreement to pay the creditor money under the schedule to a *Tomlin Order* was capable of amounting to a regulated credit agreement within the Consumer Credit Act 1974. If it did amount to a regulated agreement, the chances are that the technical hoops through which a creditor must jump before their credit agreement is enforceable if broken, were not jumped. And, if not jumped, the creditor could not enforce the *Tomlin Order* against the debtor. Those hoops can be found at sections 40, 61-64, 77A and 86B of the 1974 Act.

How does the defaulting debtor know whether the scheduled terms of their *Tomlin Order* did amount to a regulated agreement? It will usually depend on whether what was agreed constituted the granting of credit in the form of the deferment of a debt. And that, in turn, will depend on how plain it was that the money the debtor agreed to pay over was actually owed. If it was as plain as a pikestaff that the money was owed and that the debtor believed it was owed, a claimant's agreement to give the debtor more time to pay would be classified as credit. The fact that the debtor had put in a bogus defence would not change the position. But it may be that a defence was put forward which the debtor believed has some substance even though they may have been mistaken and that they subsequently reached a compromise with their creditor which was embodied in the *Tomlin Order*'s schedule. In that situation, it is highly arguable that credit was not granted, with the result that the agreement is enforceable, where broken. For the time being, that is a legally grey order.

> "Notice of opposition to claimant's application for judgment on the ground of alleged non-compliance with schedule to Tomlin Order.
>
> The defendant opposes the claimant's application. If, which is not admitted, the defendant has failed to comply with the schedule to the order as alleged, the defendant says that the agreement incorporated within the schedule constituted an agreement for credit within the meaning of the Consumer Credit Act 1974 and is unenforceable on account of the claimant's failure to comply with the provisions of one or more of sections 40, 61-64, 77A and 86B of the 1974 Act. The defendant puts the claimant to strict proof of such compliance."

Let's suppose that an agreement in the schedule to a *Tomlin Order* is unenforceable. Drinks all round – whiskies for the debtor, arsenic with soda water for the claimant – or wait for another day when the creditor can repounce? It might be possible for the creditor to jump later through some of the hoops and ask the court to grant permission to enforce in relation to the others but the court would not be bound to do so. Because proceedings had already been brought, any attempt to start a second set of proceedings ought to fail. My bet is that the creditor would give up but if the signs were that they were going to try every trick in the book to salvage the wreck, a compromise highly favourable to the debtor ought to be within reach, at the least.

The appeal of a *Tomlin Order* to creditors in the know and owed money by debtors who are individuals and not companies or limited liability partnerships, will have been materially diminished by this Court of Appeal ruling. In future, they can be expected to require any compromise agreement to be incorporated in a court judgment rather than in a schedule to a *Tomlin Order*.

Part 6

JUDGMENT HAS BEEN GIVEN

Chapter 27

The Register Of Judgments

The ugly face of proceedings

How do you avoid being sued? Stay at home, do not hang out of the window, feed the dog, speak to nobody and never use the internet. If sued, how do you avoid a judgment being recorded against you in the Register of Judgments, Orders and Fines? That's more difficult.

The register is run by Registry Trust Ltd and onto it go details of the majority of judgments that are given in the civil courts for the payment of money. Note, only money – so if the court has ordered you to take down an extension because it is partially encroaching on your neighbour's land, that won't be recorded. The register is checked out by would be creditors who are contemplating lending you money or extending you credit, and by wise would be claimants who have a good case against you but no wish to join that queue of creditors who have already obtained a civil court judgment against you but 'aint been paid (see chapter 10). Inevitably, details of registered judgments are collected by the credit reference agencies. The longer term consequences of having a judgment recorded in the register and making its way on to the agencies' files can be more catastrophic than the judgment itself. For example, a business may find itself unable to obtain credit from suppliers and thereby strangled and an individual may be refused a mortgage loan all because there is a solitary judgment of which details are stained against their name.

The job of sending details to Registry Trust of each judgment eligible for registration falls to staff at the court which gave the particular judgment. Human error leads to ineligible judgments being registered and eligible judgments not being registered. When the former occurs, the offending court should be told to cancel the registration immediately.

Registration escapees

Let's have a look at some of the judgments which should not be registered.

- A judgment in family proceedings such as an order that you pay maintenance to your former spouse or partner or make a lump sum payment to them.
- A judgment where the hearing was contested. This is the Big One. If you put in a defence to the claim which led to the judgment, you escape its registration. It matters not that the defence was spurious, farcical or the biggest load of nonsense ever to be committed to a piece of paper, or all three. It matters not that you failed to turn up at court when the case was heard. If a defence had gone in, then for these purposes, the hearing was contested. In fact, it is not unknown for a defendant to put in a defence with no intention whatsoever of appearing at any hearing but simply to escape the registration of the

judgment which they know will follow. But hold on to the champers. The court is required to register the judgment, though it was not previously registrable because of the contest, should your creditor apply for an order that the judgment be paid by instalments and such an order be made; you apply yourself for an instalment order; or your creditor takes certain steps to enforce the judgment.

- A judgment for you to pay money in a claim involving arrears of mortgage payments or rent – you may well have been ordered to give up possession at the same hearing – unless and until your mortgage lender or landlord takes a step to enforce the judgment.

Cancellation or satisfaction

If the judgment has been rightly recorded in the register then it stays put for six years from the date of the judgment (but not six years from the date of the registration which could be some time later). However, the registration will be cancelled should the judgment be set aside. Strictly speaking, judgments should only be set aside in limited situations (see chapter 14). Nevertheless, it is common for a debtor with a judgment against them to enter into an agreement with their creditor which provides for the judgment to be set aside so that hopefully its registration can be cancelled. The dialogue goes something like this.

> Debtor: "You reptile. You are killing my business. May you rot in hell."

> Creditor: " I'm not being spoken to like that. You've had the goods and sold them on and not paid me a penny. You are a despicable rogue."

> Debtor: "Come on, angel face. Be reasonable. Tell you what, if my business goes down the pan, you'll get nothing. The judgment's for six grand. I'll sell the mother-in-law and borrow a few quid. I can come up with three grand in a fortnight. Accept that. I'll pay the money to my solicitor and he'll undertake to pay it over to you the moment the court makes an order setting aside the judgment and staying the claim on terms that I'll pay you the three grand and you'll accept it in full and final settlement of the claim and costs. I think they call it a Tommy Order or something. Have we got a deal? And if you happen to be my way over the weekend, pop in for a beer. It would be good to catch up."

So the creditor collects £3,000 and the debtor gets rid of the judgment and its registration. Everyone is happy – well almost. Some judges will go along with that sort of arrangement because it makes commercial sense in that it has the blessing of the creditor and it leads to the creditor collecting a substantial part of what they were owned when there was a real risk they might have had to whistle for the lot. And some judges may refuse to set the judgment aside even though the creditor will not enforce payment of what is unpaid because the strict criteria for setting aside a judgment have not been met.

Now there is a way of guaranteeing the cancellation of the registration. That's to pay the judgment in full. Novel, eh?! Time is of the essence. No guarantee here unless you pay within one month of the date of the judgment. Once the court has evidence of settlement in time, it will have the registration cancelled. However, this is not the same as the judgment being set aside. Setting aside means the judgment never existed. Cancellation of the registration where the judgment has been paid off within one month means it existed but the world may never find out about it, though if you were to truthfully answer certain questions put to you by a lie detector operator on the subject of your financial history, you might find yourself having to cough it!

For debtors who settle a judgment after one month, there is a consolation prize. On the register, it will be noted by the entry relating to the judgment that it has been satisfied. At least anyone then searching the register will know that you are only 50% unreliable. You will need to apply to the court for a 'certificate of satisfaction' and, if you can, accompany the application with evidence that you have settled. Where you have no satisfactory evidence that you can produce in your possession, you should ask the creditor to confirm settlement. If the creditor returns your request torn into 1,006 pieces and then stapled, the court will write to the creditor and ask them to confirm within one month that you have settled and, when that meets with silence, the court will treat the judgment as having been satisfied.

"I've seen that face before"

It has occurred to some debtors who dwell within the register that a change of name could be their salvation. That does not overcome the problem that their address will still be blacklisted with credit reference agencies. Their greater problem is that even if they change their name and move, any dishonest information given to a prospective credit provider could earn them a charge of obtaining or attempting to obtain by deception. Mr Troublesore may now call himself Lord Lucan but he is still the subject of a county court judgment entered against him in Macclesfield County Court in 2013 for goods sold and delivered.

Tommy Order

Our rather dodgy debtor who we just met negotiating a deal to pay off his creditor £3,000 instead of £6,000 referred to a Tommy Order. There's no such thing though he was close. It's called a *Tomlin Order*. It's a gem (see chapter 26).

Credit repair services

Don't waste money on paying a firm to repair your credit by procuring the setting aside of a registered judgment. What they can do, you can do. They don't have a direct line to the judge. Applications to set aside judgments which have been prepared by a credit repair company can often be spotted in the dark. Some I have seen rely as grounds for setting aside that the defendant never received the claim form or, if they did, they were on holiday at the time and the dog ate it so that it was not available when they returned and that, in any event, they were too distressed to read any official documents that might have been delivered because their spouse had just left them and that they may have just moved to another address and that they do not owe the claimant any money and have never heard of the claimant and if they have heard of the claimant, they demand a copy of any agreement they allegedly signed and reserve the right to contend that the claimant's charges are unfair and should be reduced. I exaggerate but only a bit.

The double entry

If a registered judgment is set aside by a court order made by a judge, it is that order and that order alone which does away with the judgment and that order alone which should lead to cancellation of the registered entry. Despite this, some court clerks have the habit of drawing up a second order of their own stating that the judgment is set aside and automatically sending that to the Registry. This can have the potential to give the appearance on the court record of the setting aside of two separate judgments for two separate debts. Ensure this is not done.

Chapter 28

Challenging The Judge's Decision

After court

It is fashionable to complain about the judge after the hearing to the Judicial Conduct Investigations Office. No, I won't give you their address. You have three months from the date on which the judge allegedly transgressed to make the complaint although this time limit can be extended in exceptional circumstances. If you are saying that the judge has got it wrong then that's not a situation for complaint but for appeal to a more senior judge. The complaint route is often seen by the losing litigant as a means of reeking revenge or a cathartic experience after the shock of the case going against them. It is sometimes even threatened during the actual hearing in an attempt to put pressure on the judge to avoid trouble by finding in favour of the would-be complainant. Court staff are required to plaster waiting room walls with posters about how to make a complaint against the judge. One of my former colleagues was fond of ripping them down.

OK, so you think I've had a catalogue of complaints about me.

Complaints, I've had a few

But then again, too few to mention

I said what I had to say and saw it through without exemption

I judged each legal case, each stage along the byway

And more, much more than this, I did it my way

My first experience of a seriously unhappy litigant was at Guildford county court in the 1990s after I decided that a young motorist had negligently caused damage to the claimant's car in a road accident and so had to compensate him. He was the last to leave the court- always an ominous sign when the loser holds back and in due course I began to insist that everyone left together – and, as he departed, he called me a "four-eyed c..t" which deserved one month inside for contempt but with no usher or other member of court staff about – and, yes, I was and am bespectacled but, no, to the other thing – I had to let him go on his way.

At around the same time at Kingston-upon-Thames county court I heard a small claim in favour of the claimant dating agency. It had sued their female client for the cost of a dinner they had promoted and she had attended in the hope that it would lead to her betrothal. Her case was that the concert hall conductor she had expected to be at her side for the first course turned out to be an electric organist and the childless male (she had insisted on no offspring) substituted for consumption of the main course turned out to be the father of two children. She left the dessert unfinished and made her escape. Thereafter, she refused to pay on the ground of breach of contract and misrepresentation. My judgment in favour of the dating agency reduced her to a weeping state and so I exited the courtroom when she showed no sign of voluntarily removing herself. I took sanctity in a neighbouring courtroom of a free colleague along the corridor. As I was relating to him the unusual facts of the case I had just tried, the losing lady burst in and went to claw me with her very long talons. My colleague gallantly intervened and the lady was taken away with his assistance and that of some court staff who were hastily summoned. I survived intact.

In 2007 a litigant appeared before me claiming against the Courts Service certain losses he alleged he had suffered arising out of the misaddressing of communications relating to the hearing of an appeal he had launched against his conviction for a parking offence. You may have to read that again! The Courts Service was applying for the claim to be struck out. The claim was hopeless and the claimant sensed that the hearing was not going his way. As I embarked on my judgment, explaining why the claim would have to be struck out, the claimant took to repeatedly banging on the desk at which he was seated. I warned him that I would be obliged to expel him from the hearing if he did not desist. He carried on. I expelled him. Subsequently, he complained about my conduct to the Office for Judicial Complaints (the forerunner of the Judicial Conduct Investigations Office). The complaint was thrown out. The claimant's response was to open a website partially dedicated to me. In the ordinary course of events I would have been flattered but not so in this instance because the site carried a photograph of a noose and promised that further photographs would follow. This suggested to me that he might have plans to secure my decapitation.

I was advised by the Judicial Office which looks after judges' welfare that if closure of the website was procured, this could backfire and fuel the claimant to go onto bigger and better things. Instead, a police officer was despatched to visit the claimant and warn him off. He was belligerent to the officer and promptly posted an update on the site to the effect that I had taken fright and involved the police. In due course and with my head still in position and my car tyres intact, the site disappeared. The man's conduct was seriously contemptuous and, on reflection, I believe it was a mistake to let him off the hook.

Later that year, a defendant who lost his case took his grievance towards me to the Office for Judicial Complaints. He suggested, among other things, that I had "stared down at his desk as if trying to conceal his impatience"; "had the characteristic of flicking his right hand as if flicking away an irritant"; and treated the claimants more favourably than him as exemplified by leaning encouragingly towards them and thereby increasing his sense of isolation. All these complaints were rejected though I now think twice before blinking lest this be construed as a wink at one of the parties and on no account will I scratch my ear for this could be taken as a secret sign to someone at the bus stop opposite the court that I am bored stiff and could do with a coffee.

At the start of 2011 a new complainant told the Office for Judicial Complaints that his mouth had dried up when appearing before me and, when he asked for some water, I had refused point blank to give him some despite having a carafe (of the finest Thames non-drinking water) on my desk.

There was some alleged rudeness thrown in. The complaints were rejected. As to the water deprivation, it was concluded that the complaint was without substance (!) or, even if substantiated, would not require any disciplinary action to be taken. In fact, I have never denied a request for water if there were water and a free glass available. In this instance, there was just my own glass and when there was a break in the hearing almost immediately after the water request, I asked my usher to fetch some water for the dry throated litigant.

Later in 2011 the Office of Judicial Complaints opened a letter from a claimant who was a former solicitors' managing clerk and whose case I had struck out at an early stage of its life on the ground that it had no real prospect of success. "Ethel, it's another one against Gold." "What's he done this time, Ron? Stared out of the window?" Not quite. This time I had allegedly told the complainant to sit down and keep quiet or I would otherwise have him removed from the court. He had also, he maintained, made five applications to the court to be heard and been refused by other judges and so "I can only assume that as colleagues of Judge Gold they are also on the square so they cannot contradict him no matter how wrong they know him to be." I have never been "on the square" – not even Albert's. This particular complainant had also taken to writing to me at court in abusive terms wondering how I could look at myself in the mirror. I agree this can be an uncomfortable experience. In the event, the complaint about my behaviour had no merit: the man had been represented by a barrister at the hearing before me who spoke on his behalf and the occasion did not call for any oral evidence or representations from the complainant. Because the complaint had come 18 months after the hearing in question, it was too late. In relation to the suggestion that I had wrongly struck out the claim, the man's application for permission to appeal was ultimately refused by a circuit judge.

Well, those are the complaints I can remember. That's probably a below-average number for a judicial career spanning over 25 years. All judges including myself (well, most of us) strive to give a fair hearing to every litigant and to treat them with courtesy and respect but pressure of court business does mean there may be a limit imposed on how much time can be allowed to them to state their case. And it does mean that very often they have to be curtailed and to this they do not always take kindly. The most innocuous gesture or judicial attempt to lighten the mood can be taken the wrong way and become a festering wound when a decision goes against the party to whom it was directed. Enter the Judicial Conduct Investigations Office.

Appealing

So what about an appeal then? That's certainly a more constructive approach to attempting to right what you see as a miscarriage of justice. However, if for whatever reason you were absent from the hearing at which the decision about which you are aggrieved was made then the appropriate course is almost invariably to apply for the decision to be set aside and for a rehearing. This application would go to the same level of judge who made the decision.

The appeal route is for when you or your legal representative or both of you were present at the original hearing and either you reckon the judge made an error or some new evidence has come your way since the hearing which ought to result in a different outcome. The appeal would go to a superior judge.

It should be appreciated that you cannot appeal merely because you are cheesed off at the judge's decision. You will need to establish that it was wrong or was unjust because of a serious procedural or other irregularity at the hearing. In practice, you should look to demonstrate that the judge made a mistake of law: in deciding on the facts (what actually happened) or in exercising their discretion, they took into account something they should have disregarded, failed to take into account something they should have regarded or that they were plainly wrong (a decision only a crackpot would have made); or because of fresh evidence you have obtained since the original decision, it would be unjust to allow it to stand (although it's unlikely you would succeed on this last ground unless you could not have reasonably obtained this evidence earlier, it is apparently credible and it would probably change the result).

Serious procedural error or other irregularity at the hearing? This can cover all manner of sins. The judge's refusal to allow you to give evidence or to grant you a reasonable opportunity to sum up your case after all the evidence had been heard might be enough, where you are disgruntled about what happened at a full as against a directions hearing. Something rather iffy. Take the case of *Notting Hill Finance Ltd v Sheikh* which was decided by the Court of Appeal in 2019. It involved a third mortgage for six months at an interest rate of 30.04%, rising if there was default to 289.6%, which might be regarded by some as verging on the high side. The borrower fell behind with his payments and so the lender took him to the county court for possession. He turned up for the hearing which took seven minutes. He had the duty solicitor present to give him advice but they must have been preoccupied with staring at a flea dancing on the ceiling. The breakdown of the mortgage debt was contained in a statement of account towards the end of an 85 page document. The judge was told by the lender's representative that the only relevant figure in the case was the balance owed of £99,749. Nobody mentioned the interest. The judge granted the lender judgment for the figure they were after and possession of the borrower's property.

The borrower wisely appealed and succeeded. When the lender appealed against that successful outcome, the Court of Appeal affirmed it. The possession hearing, it said, had not been in any real sense a trial. If the borrowers' arguments on the appeal about the punitive rate of interest and other consumer credit points had been raised at the original hearing, the judge would almost certainly have adjourned for a longer hearing. The borrower had acted promptly after the hearing in raising these new points and, even without them, some alarm bells might have been sounded in the judge's ears. Regard should be had to the fact that the proceedings had been short lived and the hearing had been 'summary' (short but not sweet!)

Still, mistake of law by the original judge is your best bet. When it comes to trying to show that the judge was wrong on their decision on the facts (what actually happened), you will have a more difficult task. The judge would have seen and heard the parties and their witnesses and so was in a better position than the appeal judge to assess their credibility. Decisions made by a judge when exercising their discretion such as who should pay the costs of a case and how much they should pay are notoriously difficult to successfully appeal as are case management decisions made as a case is being prepared for a contested trial.

You want to know how many times I have been successfully appealed? Mind your own business!

Permission to appeal

In three instances you don't need anyone's permission to appeal. Two of them are so remote, I won't bore you with them. The third I will bore you with. That's when a civil or family judge has sent you to prison (say for contempt of court). Otherwise, there can't be an appeal in civil or family cases without permission and we aren't into parking ticket adjudicator type territory here. And from whom do you obtain permission? From the judge who made the decision you hate! Really. You wind them up when they have completed announcing their decision and say "I ask for permission to appeal" and go on to explain why (and be in no doubt, a losing advocate or party can assuage some of the anger they feel at defeat by attempting to needle the judge by criticism of their performance). The high chance is that the judge will refuse permission on the ground that an appeal would have no real prospect of success. Judges have been divided on whether that real prospect means better than a 50% chance of winning an appeal. The point was settled by the Court of Appeal in 2019 in a case called *R (a child)* which decided it meant no such thing. There had to be a realistic as opposed to a fanciful prospect of success and there was no requirement that success was probable or more likely than not. The sort of exceptional situation in which the judge might grant permission is where the case has involved a novel or difficult point of law and they believe an appeal court might well reach a contrary decision. Where you are refused permission, the judge must tell you to which superior judge you can renew your permission request and give you certain other information which may appear in their written order you will receive after the hearing.

It is conceivable you want time to reflect on whether to try to appeal or to take legal advice about it. Should that be the position, you can ask the judge to adjourn the hearing so you can do so and then apply for permission to appeal next time. Not a brilliant idea to follow this course because it could increase your liability for the winning litigant's costs on a further outing. The better course is usually to write off the prospect of getting permission from the judge you wish to appeal and seek permission subsequently from an appeal judge. The principle is that, so far as possible, an appeal is to be determined by a judge or pack of judges the next level up. Generally, then, you would usually appeal from a district judge to a circuit judge (possibly in the same court building). An appeal from a circuit judge would also usually go to a High Court judge. An appeal from a High Court judge would go to the

Court of Appeal and the final stop would be the Supreme Court. If a circuit judge has heard an appeal from a district judge and there has been a further appeal from them to a High Court judge, then only the Court of Appeal can grant permission for a third appeal from the High Court judge. Phew.

As from 24 May 2021, appeals in family financial remedies cases against orders made by a district judge in the principal registry of the family division will, generally, no longer go to a High Court judge but instead to a circuit judge

For the application for permission to the appeal judge, you have to put in a notice of appeal and generally do so within three weeks of the decision you hate. Where the judge has announced their decision and has said that their reasons or more detailed reasons for it will follow, the 21 days start to run from the date of the announcement. However, the standard practice, unless there are very unusual circumstances, should be for the judge to extend the time for appealing to run from the date that the reasons or more detailed reasons have been provided. If you are late, you can ask for an extension of time for applying for permission. Should the original judge have failed to give you the required information when refusing you permission to appeal that might be a good reason for a late permission application to the appeal judge. The permission application is incorporated within the notice of appeal. The appeal judge will often decide whether or not to grant permission on the papers and so without a hearing. If you are refused permission on the papers you can insist on an oral hearing at which your application for permission is reconsidered except in some situations where the application is considered to be totally without merit (a complete waste of time).

Judgment transcript, please

It is almost certain that a transcript of the judgment you are attacking – the judge's summary of the case and the reasons they gave for their decision – will be required by the higher court when considering whether to grant you permission to appeal or when considering the appeal after giving permission. Sometimes, the judge will have supplied a copy of the judgment. That will suffice. Otherwise, the judge's words when giving the judgment which will have been recorded in court will usually need to be transcribed and that costs money. You would have to request the transcript through the office of the hearing centre where the decision under challenge was made. This will lead to a quote. You can't afford to pay? The court can order that the transcript of the judgment – and any part of the evidence given before the judgment – should be paid for out of public funds provided you qualify for fee remission or you are in such poor financial circumstances that the cost would be an excessive burden to you, plus that it is satisfied it is necessary in the interests of justice for the transcript to be obtained. If, in a civil case, you are having an emotional discussion with a court official about whether this power really does exist, say "Civil Procedure Rules 1998 rule 52.14, mate." In a family case, refer instead to "Family Procedure Rules 2010 rule 3.1132, mate." If you have already put in your notice of appeal when you realise that the transcript is wanted then complete form EX105 which may be required of you anyway. There's another course which may be open to you in a civil case where you have no lawyer but the winning side is represented by a lawyer. You could follow it if you have decided you want to appeal but would like to avoid paying out for a transcript or you are anxious to have an accurate note of what the judge has just said in their judgment so you can have it quickly available to take to a lawyer for advice on an appeal. It is to ask the judge to give directions for the lawyer to provide you with a note of their judgment based on what the lawyer has written down as the judge was speaking or for the judge to hand over a copy of any notes they may have made of what they were going to say (but see **Judge's notes, please** below). Gently tell the judge they have power to do this under a 2019 change to the Civil Procedure Rules 1998 rule 39.9.

Anecdotal evidence suggests that permission to appeal within the county court is granted in around one case in every four and that around one half of appeals are then upheld. Appeals to the Court of Appeal succeed in around one-half of those cases in which permission has been granted.

Judge's notes, please

The judge will have made a written note of the evidence given in the case. Almost invariably, the note will include a summary of representations made by the parties or their lawyers and any important matter that has arisen during the hearing. The less there is the stronger would be any argument you wished to advance on an appeal that the judge wasn't paying attention or had made up their minds before the case started and so were deaf to what was being said at the hearing. The note could contain a doodle here and a doodle there but, more significantly, a comment that could embarrass the judge and might go down well for you on an appeal like "Troublesore back again – a liar last time so why listen to him this time?" or "Defendant is well endowed" (which might help you if the defendant won). The notes might even show that the judge was going to decide the case in your favour right up to clearing their throat after all the evidence and representations to start giving their judgment – against you!

You can ask the court for a copy of the judge's notes and it may be that a clerk on the first day of work experience will comply with your request. I did know of one case in which the judge had reserved judgment, drafted a judgment which went one way, changed their mind and redrafted it in a diametrically opposed way. A court clerk, without any reference to the judge, sent out to the parties an order based on the second judgment and a copy of the first judgment!

The chances are that your request for a copy of the judge's notes will be refused (politely, I hope). The reason is that most notes taken by judges in the course of proceedings are their private deliberations and that deliberations are not – to borrow jargon from the Data Protection Act 1998 – the personal data of a party to the proceedings. But the position is regarded by the Information Commissioner to be different if the notes have been added to the court file because they then form part of the official record. The court could possibly even then seek to avoid disclosure on the ground that it would be a danger to the judge but that would be a difficult ground to sustain.

Notes made in digital case files and stored on IT equipment – and this would have happened with particular frequency during the Covid-19 pandemic – could be argued to be akin to notes placed in a physical court file.

Grounds of appeal

The notice of appeal will have to set out the grounds of appeal.

> 1. *The Learned Judge wrongly refused my request for him to recuse himself from trying the claim which I had made on the ground that he was biased or gave the appearance of bias in that the claim was against a hotel at which, over the years, he and his wife had holidayed.*
>
> 2. *The Learned Judge closed his eyes and emitted a snoring noise during material parts of my evidence leading me to conclude that he was asleep or not paying any or sufficient attention to the evidence.*
>
> 3. *The Learned Judge wrongly refused to adjourn the trial so that I could take steps to compel the attendance of a material and necessary witness whose evidence was challenged by the defendant and who had failed to attend voluntarily notwithstanding his promise to me to be present.*

Anything to lose by appealing in a civil case? There's a court fee to be paid when you put in the notice of appeal (whether or not it incorporates an application for permission to appeal): in the county court that's £120 in a small claims case and £140 in any other, and in the High Court the fee is £240. Appeals to the Court of Appeal are costlier. If you have lost in the Court of Appeal and fancy your chances in the Supreme Court – and it doesn't get higher than up there – you would have to shell out a £1,000 court fee for applying for permission to appeal (the Court of Appeal rarely grants permission itself) and £1,600 for putting in a notice of appeal. Well, you do get no fewer than five Justices of the Supreme Court for your money. The fee remission scheme is open for appeal fees as with other fees (see chapter 17). An unsuccessful appeal is likely to increase the bill you have to face. Apart from what you pay out on appealing, you will probably have to pay the other litigant's expenses on resisting the appeal (which could be substantial if they took in a lawyer) and even an unsuccessful application for permission to appeal could add to your bill where it has led to an oral hearing. Any exception to this rule? Of course! The restriction on an order for costs against the loser of a small claim (see chapter 25) is replicated on an appeal (and application for permission to appeal). This means that unless the court finds that the loser has behaved unreasonably (and there has to be something more than just losing again) the appeal bill will effectively be limited to the other litigant's travelling expenses to and from court plus loss of earnings capped at £95 per day. In family cases, the court fee will be £125 or £215, depending on the type of case and different principles on costs orders against a party who loses on appeal will apply.

Some use the appeal route as a device to put off the evil day – the day they have to stump up what they have been ordered to pay to the winner – though they realise they have no prospect of an appeal succeeding, let alone procuring permission to appeal. If they have cash flow problems then the extra time may be invaluable though it carries the burden of an increase in their costs liability along with having to pay interest to the other litigant on the amount of the judgment, if that is at least £5,000, from the date of judgment until settlement. The device doesn't work unless enforcement of the judgment is stayed (paralysed) pending a decision on the application for permission to appeal (or the appeal itself where permission is actually given). An application for the stay can be made at the same time as the application to the original judge for permission to appeal (and, where permission to appeal is refused, the original judge can be invited to stay enforcement provided that a notice of appeal is issued within the 21 days available). The application can be repeated before the appeal judge. Where permission to appeal is obtained, it would be unusual for a stay not to be granted until the appeal is decided.

Chapter 29

Getting Your Money Under A Judgment

Can't pay, won't pay

"Two glasses of the finest champers – nicely chilled. And we'll both start with the fois gras. Is the lobster fresh?"

"Of course, Mr Troublesore. Are you by chance celebrating this evening?"

"Why yes. I have had a bit of a victory at the county court at Peardrop."

STOP!!!!! You've got the judgment. You haven't got the money. Hopefully, you checked up before you ever made a claim that the defendant was probably good for the amount you wanted out of them (see chapter 10). It doesn't follow that they are going to pay up without a bit of delay and a bit of evasion. The battle of wits may only just have started. It will be a consolation that so long as the county court judgment was for at least £5,000, interest on what is due will be attracted at the fixed rate of 8% from the date of the judgment until full payment (see chapter 32). It won't be a consolation to the defendant that the judgment will be recorded against them at the Register of Judgments, Orders and Fines in a case which was undefended, if not settled within one month and, in a case which was defended, if and when the claimant takes enforcement action (see chapter 27).

There are a variety of lawful means by which you can extract from the defendant the amount they should be paying you. None of them involves a cut throat razor or any degree of intimidation. Around one-third of judgments are settled in full and one-third are settled in part. No prizes for guessing what happens to the rest. Nothing is paid at all. The present system for judgment enforcement is highly unsatisfactory for the creditor. The court will not automatically do what is required to induce the defendant to settle. It will follow through whatever request or application you make for a particular means of enforcement but there is no point in kidding you. The process has sometimes reduced fully grown steroid ingesting body builders to a state of weeping. It could be much better. There is a brilliant system devised by section 95 of the Tribunals, Courts and Enforcement Act 2007 as an effective aid to enforcement for the court to get information about the true circumstances of the debtor from a government department and elsewhere. There's a problem. 14 years on the system has still not been brought into operation.

Let's see how we can use the lousy system we have got to advantage. The methods to be looked at are available for the enforcement of maintenance orders as well as county court and High Court civil judgments although the process of an application for the court to consider the appropriate method of enforcement (see below) is peculiar to the enforcement of maintenance orders. For maintenance orders which used to be enforced by family proceedings courts (sometimes called magistrates' courts) the job of enforcement has now been taken over by the Family Court which is just as well 'cos the family proceedings courts were killed off in April 2014.

On your marks

You cannot enforce a judgment until the defendant has defaulted. If you have requested the court to enter judgment against them because they have admitted the claim or failed to put in a defence, you will be asked whether you want settlement forthwith – immediately – or within a fixed period or by instalments. Unless the defendant has asked for time to pay which does not coincide with your request, you will get what you wanted. On the other hand, if you have obtained the judgment at a hearing, the judge will usually direct that it be settled within 14 days of the hearing date although you can always ask the judge to make it sooner. Should you be pretty sure that you will have to take enforcement action, ask for payment to be made forthwith which would enable you to start the enforcement action immediately. The judge could well be sympathetic to payment forthwith where the defendant has put in a defence but then stayed away from the hearing as this indicates they were simply playing for time.

Following a judgment in your favour, the defendant may apply to the court to vary the judgment to allow them to pay by instalments or by lower instalments than may have already been ordered (that's under rule 40.9A of the Civil Procedure Rules 1998). Or the defendant may apply for a longer period within which to pay the lot in one go (and that's under rule 40.11 of the 1998 Rules). If the defendant cannot really afford to pay anything then you can trot out a Court of Appeal ruling in a 2018 case called *Loson v Brett Stack and another party* where the defendant owed £8,000, was on the verge of bankruptcy and had offered instalments of £50 per month. In such a situation, it was held, the court should not interfere with the claimant's right to seek to enforce the judgment by any means they seek to adopt. The court's decision should respect the claimant's rights which have been vindicated by the judgment or order they have obtained. On the other hand, an instalment order may still be justified without the circumstances being exceptional and without the defendant being solvent. But the defendant must present the court with a realistic repayment schedule backed up by evidence that the claimant can expect to receive their money, including any interest due, within a reasonable period of time. To that extent, the claimant's interests will be paramount. Quite where the balance will be struck will depend on the particular facts of the case. There may be less room for allowing time where the claimant has their own cash-flow problems. Equally, there will be cases where a limited period of time will enable the debt to be paid in full without any significant prejudice to the claimant, particularly where interest is attracted on the judgment (for at least £5,000) in the meantime. The Court of Appeal decided that the defendant's £50 per month offer was just not good enough and there would be no variation to allow payment by instalments.

A few words to our debtor friends: If the court has ordered you to pay up sooner than you can afford then, whether you were present or absent when the order was made, you can do something about it. Where you admitted the claim once you received the claim form and made a proposal as to how you should pay which was opposed by the claimant, a decision – called a *determination* – on this will almost certainly have been made by a member of the court staff on paper. You have a right to ask for a *redetermination* which will result in a judge reconsidering how you are to pay at a hearing you would be well advised to participate in. There's no fee for asking for the *redetermination* which you must do within 14 days of receiving details of what the staff member has decided. Where you put forward no proposals and an order was made without a hearing or there was a hearing at which the judge set a time for payment without an enquiry into your means, you can issue an application for the order to be varied to allow you to pay by instalments (form N245 costing a court fee of £50 but you could qualify for remission which would mean no fee – see chapter 17). You would be well advised to participate in any hearing of that application if one is fixed. What is important is that you issue the application before the time for payment has arrived for once it has arrived and you have failed to come up with the cash, your creditor can start enforcement action. Where enforcement action has already started you can request the court to *stay* (halt) the enforcement action pending a decision being made on your application to vary. Should there be a change in your circumstances for the worse after a date for payment or a rate of instalments has been fixed on paper or at a hearing, you can ask the court to reconsider how you pay by making an application for variation (as above). Make at least two applications which are totally without merit and you can expect the court to put a stop to any more in the absence of a judge's prior permission. And remember that each time you make an unsuccessful application which leads to a hearing, the chances are that you will add to the bill against you by being ordered to pay any legal costs and other expenses the claimant has incurred as a result.

And a few more words to our debtor friends 'cos I can't stop: A High Court judgment along with a county court judgment which is for at least £5,000 will attract interest at the rate of 8% as from the date of the judgment until you have settled in full (see chapter 32). This is in addition to any interest ordered in favour of the claimant from when the money was due up to the date of the judgment. 8% is a swingeing rate but is automatic. Under the County Courts (Interest on Judgment Debts) Order 1991, the interest stops for a county court judgment, however, if the claimant takes enforcement action against you unless that enforcement action fails to produce a single new pence for the claimant in which event interest will continue to clock up as if the enforcement action had not been taken. Interest will not run while an attachment of earnings order or administration order are in force. An application for a charging order or for an order to obtain information from you will not rank as enforcement. It might be said that the kindest thing your creditor with a £5,000 plus judgment can do for you is to send in the bailiff who seizes your copy of this book (nominal value) and so stops the interest clock.

And, I promise you, just these further words and I'll get on with some other stuff: You can always attempt to do a deal with the claimant along the lines that "*Without Prejudice* I owe you £6,000. I am unemployed with no prospects of a job. We live on benefits. My tenanted home has only basic contents. If you want to bankrupt me then so be it but I would just about prefer to stay afloat. How about you accept £750 in full and final settlement of the judgment which I could borrow from a third party?"

Time limits and judgments on judgments

You need permission of the court to put in a bailiff or enforcement agent (see below) once the judgment is six years old. Otherwise there is generally no time limit on taking any enforcement action although you won't be entitled to interest on a judgment for any period beyond those six years. In certain circumstances, it might be useful for you to sue the defendant for non-payment of the original judgment: a judgment on a judgment. Really. You would be obtaining a second judgment based on default under the first judgment and you could include in what you claim second time around, any interest which had accrued since the first judgment to which you are entitled for up to six years from the first judgment.

What would be the purpose of this apparent madness? You would have six years to enforce the second judgment and would not have to apply for permission to put in a bailiff or enforcement agent to enforce the first judgment once it was six years old. You would also overcome the problem that any permission granted to enforce the first judgment after six years would have a life of only one year so that multiple applications to extend the one year could be necessary. The defendant might have gone missing with it likely to take a while to find him or the defendant might be down and out though with a good prospect of eventually becoming a multi-millionaire with an invention to prevent hard boiled eggs from stinking or perhaps you still lack sufficient information to decide on the most effective enforcement route to take. A warning. Going after a second judgment could lead to the defendant applying to the court for the second claim to be struck out as an abuse of the court's process. So long as what you were doing was regarded as rational and reasonable in the circumstances, such an application by the defendant should fail.

Enforcement menu

Imprisonment

Calm down. Hardly ever. As a general rule, these days a debtor cannot be sent to prison for non-payment of a debt. Except in relation to certain taxes (and, in practice the tax collectors go for the loot and not the stir), prison is out unless the debt is for spousal, civil partner or child maintenance payable under a court order and even then the court will not impose a sentence unless satisfied beyond reasonable doubt (no less) not only that the debtor has refused or neglected to pay but has had the means to do so: a high threshold. If a sentence is imposed in one of these excepted situations, it would probably be suspended so long as the debtor paid off the debt by a specified date or by specified instalments. There are a couple of indirect ways the debtor could end up being entertained by Her Majesty: failing to produce a statement of means on an attachment of earnings application, for example (see below) but only then as a last resort.

*Attachment of earnings**

Generally available provided at least £5 is owed and the defendant is employed (and not self-employed or unemployed). The employer docks the defendant's pay each week or month for a sum fixed by the court and it is transferred to you through the court. Pretty useless unless you can identify their employer. The court can compel the debtor to disclose the employer's identity during the course of the attachment of earnings application or you can ascertain it by having the defendant forced to attend at court for questioning which is a step independent of any specific means of enforcement (see below). Should it transpire that the defendant is unemployed, ask the court to "adjourn the application generally with permission to restore it." This would enable you to reactivate the application if and when the defendant did get another job without having to make a fresh application and so pay a second court fee. The employed defendant would be well advised to ask for a *suspended* attachment of earnings order and state why and will be asked on the form they must complete about their financial circumstances, whether they seek suspension. With suspension, their employer would not come to know about the unsatisfied judgment unless any of the weekly or monthly payments required by the suspended order were missed and then you could ask for the employer to go into action and make the deductions. The managers of a pension scheme can be ordered to make regular payments from any private pension the defendant draws in the same way as an employer would deduct under the scope of an attachment of earnings order. For this purpose, the pension entitlements are treated as earnings. If you have the benefit of a High Court judgment, you will have to request the transfer of the case to the county court as only the county court has the power to make an attachment of earnings order.

As from April 2016 all applications for an attachment of earnings order (other than to the family court in connection with the enforcement of a maintenance order) have to be issued in the County Court Money Claims Centre (PO Box 527, Salford M5 OBY) which will manage them until the making of an order. But should the debtor fail to complete a statement of their financial circumstances, the application will be sent to the hearing centre which covers the debtor's home or business address who will take it over. If there is an existing attachment of earnings order against your debtor, you can ask for your debt to be added on so as to produce what is called a consolidated attachment of earnings order. Whatever is deducted under the order will then be divided up among the creditors who have the benefit of the order. A consolidated order will mean that you get paid out less often. Disadvantage. But it will probably mean you escape paying an issue fee. Advantage. You can find out whether the debtor already has an attachment of earnings order against them with a free search of the index of attachment of earnings orders. Useful anyway in deciding which is likely to be the best method of enforcement to use. Complete form N336. You can do it online at gov/uk/government/collections/court-and-tribunal-forms.

***a few words to our debtor friends:** Note what I have just said about your ability to ask for any attachment of earnings order that is made to be suspended.

Third party debt order

Money which a bank or building society is holding in an account to the credit of the debtor is diverted to you up to the limit needed to settle the judgment. The same device can be used to divert money owed to the debtor by a customer or trader (for example, where the defendant has done some decorating work for Joseph Bloggs who has not yet settled the invoice the defendant has rendered to them). The court would initially make an *interim third party debt order* which effectively freezes the money and a hearing follows a month or two later at which the court decides whether or not to confirm the order and have the frozen sum thawed out and paid over to you. The magic is that the debtor does not find out about the *interim* order until after it has been made and so is deprived of the opportunity to withdraw money or ensure it is paid over to them before you engage your snatching tactic. Should the debtor who is an individual (not say a company) be suffering hardship in meeting ordinary living expenses because of the freezing of money in their bank or building society account, they can make an emergency application for a hardship payment to be made to them from the account. Where your application falls flat on its face as the defendant no longer has an account as you had believed or it is overdrawn, don't forget to ask the court to order the defendant to pay you the fee you have wasted on the application, to be added to what they already owe.

> *"I am the claimant. I refer to my application for a final third party debt order. In view of the information supplied to the court and myself by the third party, I am obliged to ask you to dismiss the application for the final order but I would respectfully request that the court should order the defendant to pay to me the court fee I have incurred on making the application, such amount to be added to the judgment debt and I would also ask to be excused attendance at the hearing in view of my work commitments."*

That an account is in debit today does not mean that it will not be in credit next week. You can make a second or subsequent application in respect of the same account – I have seen it work – but eventually the debtor will cotton on.

Warrant or writ of control*

A warrant of control used to be called a warrant of execution and meant then and means now that a county court bailiff will attempt to seize sufficient of the debtor's goods to sell and pay off the debt and fees. Sadly, using the bailiff can be a frustrating experience. Time and resources are limited and the wily debtor may play the system and give the bailiff a right run-around. For a judgment of at least £600 you can have the case transferred to the High Court for enforcement (completing form N293A) where the warrant of control becomes a writ of control: for a judgment of over £5,000 it is mandatory for you to do so (unless the judgment arises out of an agreement regulated by the Consumer Credit Act 1974 which can only be enforced in the county court). There are three advantages in a transfer. Firstly, the enforcement will be carried out not by a court bailiff but by a possibly more savvy enforcement agent who is not in the court's employ but has been appointed by the Lord Chancellor to go about seizing goods. Secondly, a county court judgment for less than £5,000, which would not otherwise attract post-judgment interest, will attract it at the rate of 8% once transferred as from the transfer date. Thirdly, a warrant of control support centre will be avoided when it is likely to be a complete waste of time (see chapter 30). But enforcement agents are much more expensive than the county court bailiff (although again see chapter 30 about them reaching controlled goods agreements remotely). Where the debtor has limited assets, there may be less over for you once the agent's charges have been satisfied and you could end up paying all or some of those charges if little or nothing is available for seizure. Various items are exempt from seizure such as those which are essential in the household like clothing and bedding and, subject to a cap of £1,350, items or equipment for use in the debtor's employment or business. If property, including a motor vehicle, is owned not by the debtor but a finance company then it will not be taken.

Two or more creditors may be chasing one debtor for their money and have applied for writs of control at around the same time. Where this happens and, whether or not the writs have gone to the same enforcement agent or different enforcement agents, they are to be prioritised in the order in which they were received. This means that if Cutthroat Ltd receives your writ on Monday and Causeaseizure plc receives a rival creditor's writ on the following Friday, your writ must take priority and Cutthroat Ltd must go after your debtor's goods first. If there are no goods left for your rival, that's tough on them. Should Causeaseizure get to the debtor first and obtain from them money or goods which are sold, while being fully aware of the existence of your writ, then Causeaseizure can be compelled to hand over to you what has been obtained in so far as it is needed to satisfy what you are owed. If Causeaseizure was unaware of the existence of your writ then it is most unlikely that the court would order them to cough up although you could go after your rival creditor for the money. All this was decided in a 2020 case called *365 Business Finance Ltd v Bellagio Hospitality WB Ltd and another* (along with the rival case). There seems no reason why similar principles on priority should not operate where county court bailiffs are involved with rival warrants of control.

*a few words to our debtor friends: You can apply to the court to suspend the warrant (form N245 – £50 fee unless you are granted remission – see chapter 17) which would have the effect of paralysing the bailiff or enforcement agent so long as you paid up by a specified extended date or by specified instalments. Fail to do so, and seizure of your goods could proceed without any further court hearing. The bailiff or enforcement agent should give you at least seven days' warning that they are coming in though the court is empowered to cut down on this time if it reckons you may otherwise make off with your goods and so frustrate seizure. They may come on any day of the week but generally only between 6am and 9pm unless the court has directed some other time. If you are trading from the premises at which the bailiff or enforcement agent seek to seize your goods outside of those hours then they can enter and do their business then. They may enter by any door or by "any usual means by which entry is gained" which rules out the chimney (unless we are talking about a grotto) and probably through the window. To use force to get in the court must give prior permission and even then the force will need to be no more than is reasonable. If the bailiff or enforcement agent has gone further than the law permits, you may be entitled to claim compensation (see chapter 30).

*Charging order**

This is mainly made in relation to freehold or leasehold property which the debtor owns, whether solely or jointly with others, but it can also be made in relation to the debtor's stocks and shares.

Let's concentrate on freehold or leasehold property. The order puts you in a similar position to a mortgage lender. In practice, the order is aimed at preventing the debtor from selling or mortgaging or remortgaging their interest in the property without paying you off. The court does have the power to follow up a charging order with an order for the property to be sold and the debt repaid out of the sale proceeds. That would involve an application by you for an order for sale and an application could well fail where the debtor was making headway with settling by instalments. Such an application is precluded where the judgment arises out of a regulated consumer credit agreement and the amount owed is less than £1,000. An order for sale is harder to obtain than a charging order.

The procedure for obtaining a charging order changed in April 2016. As with applications for attachment of earnings, charging order applications to the county court have been centralised and must now be made to the County Court Money Claims Centre (see above for address). They are dealt with in two stages. The first stage involves a consideration of the application on paper without a hearing and without notification to the debtor. If the application is granted then an interim charging order is made and it is notified to the debtor and certain others including any co-owner, other creditors and, if they are known to you, the debtor's spouse or civil partner (which I can foresee leading to more than a few relationship breakdowns). The co-owner is interested because they could be losing their home if an order for sale was made subsequently. Where the co-owner is a spouse or civil partner and there are already proceedings for divorce etc, the court can be asked to link up the application for a final charging order to be considered alongside any financial remedy application in those other proceedings. The other creditors who are unsecured will be interested because a charging order in your favour will give you security which ranks in priority to them: should the property be sold (even after a bankruptcy) your judgment would be paid off before what they are owed.

The second stage has been streamlined. If nobody objects – and they have 28 days from being notified of the interim charging order to do so – then a final charging order will now generally follow on paper without a hearing. If there is any objection then the application will be taken over by the hearing centre covering the debtor's home or place of business.

There is no minimum debt required for a charging order to be made though some judges will be reluctant to make one for less than the £200 mark. Once upon a time, an application for a charging order could not be made where the judgment was to be paid by instalments and the debtor had kept them up. This is no longer the case. The charging order can be applied for immediately the time for payment of the judgment has passed: a nanosecond later. However, the absence of default will be taken into account by the court in deciding whether to make the order.

But if having obtained a charging order, you fail to register it against the property at the Land Registry, the whole exercise may turn out to have been a complete waste of time and you will be left feeling as sick as a cage of parrots whose sherry cream trifle has been stolen by an eagle. Where the debtor is the sole owner of the property you should register what is known as a *notice* and that ought to scupper a sale, mortgage or remortgage. You cannot do this, though, where the debtor is not the sole owner. Then, you need to register a *restriction*. There is a standard restriction and a non-standard restriction. With a *standard* restriction – which, unfortunately, is the norm – notice of a transaction has to be given to you but only after it has been effected. You're right. Potentially, rubbish. More often than not, once the prospective buyer or lender gets wind of the registered standard restriction which will happen when they make a Land Registry search before completing the transaction, they will require the charging order to be paid off but there is no guarantee this will happen. So, my prudent creditor, what you do is to instead request a *non-standard restriction* using land registry form L which will ensure you are given notice of the proposed sale, mortgage or remortgage before it takes place and can engineer getting paid out from the sale, mortgage or remortgage proceeds. You should ask the court when you make your application and again when, at the second stage, you request the final charging order to add this verbiage to the order:

> "IT IS ORDERED pursuant to section 46 of the Land Registration Act 2002 that HM Land Registrar shall enter a non-standard restriction in respect of the title referred to in this order in these terms, namely:
>
> No disposition of the registered estate is to be registered without a certificate signed by the applicant for registration or their conveyancer that written notice of the disposition was given to Whitewash Limited of 231 Queen Alexandra Crescent, Richmond-upon-Thames, Surrey TW11 7FL being the person with the benefit of an interim/final charging order on the beneficial interest of Clive Troublesore made on 14 July 2021 in the County Court in proceedings under claim number BLK161679 no later than 14 days prior to the disposition or without an order of the County Court which ordered this restriction."

Some creditors register both the interim and final charging orders: others just rest on the interim order. If you secured the extra wording on the final but not the interim order, you should be registering both.

You may not be the debtor's only creditor. Apologies for shocking you. Two or more creditors with unsatisfied judgments against a debtor who owns property with some equity in it equals an unholy race to be the first to obtain a charging order and so have the prospect of being paid out from the proceeds of sale of that property in priority to their rivals who obtain their charging orders at a later date. Lord Goddard said way back in 1949 (before subsequently sentencing Derek Bentley to death in the "Let him have it" murder case): "It not infrequently happens that where there are several claims against money, the person who gets in first gets the fruits of his diligence." Do things still work the same way? In my experience, more often than not, they do. In a 2018 High Court case called *Midtown Acquisitions LP v Essar Global Fund Ltd* two creditors of the same debtor had obtained interim charging orders around six weeks apart. The creditors were owed $171m and $588m respectively. They each wanted priority over the other when it came to making the charging order final. The judge suggested that there was not an automatic first pass the post rule and the court had a discretion in deciding which of the creditors was to prevail. But first past the post was a consideration! The court could have put the creditors on an equal footing so that they shared the spoils in the proportions they were owed money although that would have been unusual. Both creditors were significant commercial parties, well able to look after their own interests. Neither had been dilatory and it was not inequitable to prefer one creditor over the other. The result was that the creditor who got the first interim order would take priority over its rival.

*a few words to our debtor friends: The charging order will not evict you from your home. Only a later order for sale would do that and different considerations apply when a court is deciding whether to order sale than when deciding whether to make a final charging order. The court might not make a final charging order if the property is in negative equity or close to it and/or the debt is small and/or you have already started to reduce the debt. Sometimes the creditor will say to the judge: "Just give me the protection of a charging order though I have no intention of trying to get the property sold so long as Mr Troublesore pays me regular instalments." If the judge looks set to go along with that, you pipe up with this: "I respectfully ask you to order that the claimant be debarred from applying for an order for sale so long as I pay instalments on account of the judgment debt at the rate of £x per month or at such other rate as the court may from time to time determine." But a charging order is an insidious form of enforcement. It gives your creditor security over your property and if you subsequently found that there was just no way you could settle the debt, you might eventually be thrown out of your home where the order was against that property with the debt then being settled out of the sale price. Better off then without a charging order. You can object to an interim charging order being followed up with a final charging order and, if you were successful, the interim order would be cancelled. Persuading the judge to throw out the application may be an uphill task but you never know. You have 28 days from being notified of the interim order to send in your objection to a final order to the court and your creditor and, if you do so, there will be a hearing at the hearing centre covering your home or place of business. The document setting out your objection should contain a statement of truth (see chapter 19).

> "Pursuant to CPR rule 73.10(2), the grounds of my objection to a final charging order are that:
>
> 1. I was ordered to pay the judgment by instalments and I have religiously kept up those instalments.
>
> OR
>
> 1. I have paid whatever my financial circumstances have permitted since the judgment was entered. Particulars of the dates and amounts of the instalments I have paid are set out on the attached schedule (complete and staple a schedule to the statement).
>
> OR
>
> 1. I put forward written proposals to the claimant on 14 June 2021 to pay the judgment by instalments of £25 per month and to set up a standing order for this amount but despite hastening letters the claimant has completely ignored me (or refused to accept any instalments at all).
>
> OR
>
> 1. On 1 June 2021 the claimant obtained a suspended attachment of earnings order against me under which I am required to pay £25 per month. I have already made the first payment and intend to comply with the order to the letter. In these circumstances, the making of a final charging order would be too severe and disproportionate.
>
> OR
>
> 1. I believe that the claimant has purchased the benefit of the judgment debt from my original creditor for a tiny fraction of the amount involved since when it has pursued me with aggression and unreasonableness and refuses or neglects to engage with me in my attempts to reach an agreement with it.
>
> 2. The amount of the judgment debt is relatively modest and the making of a final charging order would be disproportionate and would involve me in costs which it would be inequitable for me to have to bear.
>
> OR
>
> 3. The property against which the final order is sought is in negative equity. I attach copies of a market appraisal of the property from Flogarama plc and statements from my first and second mortgagees as to balances on my mortgage accounts (staple copies to the statement). There is no reasonable expectation that the property would go

into positive equity within the next 20 years, if ever, and so to make the order final would be of no value to the claimant and involve me in costs which should never have been incurred and would not have been incurred had the claimant heeded these figures which I provided to them before this misconceived application was made.

OR

2.   There is ample equity in the property against which the final order is sought. I attach copies of a market appraisal of the property from Flogarama plc and statements from my first and second mortgagees as to balances on my mortgage accounts (staple copies to the statement). I have no other debts and so the claimant does not have to compete with other creditors to gain priority over them in obtaining a charging order. There is no evidence that I would sell the property or remortgage it without paying off the claimant. I am paying the claimant by instalments. In all the circumstances, the claimant's application is disproportionate.

Statement of truth

I believe that the facts stated in this witness statement are true. I understand that proceedings for contempt of court may be brought against anyone who makes, or causes to be made, a false statement in a document verified by a statement of truth without an honest belief in its truth.

(signed) C Troublesore

Dated 14 July 2021

Appointing a receiver

This one is a bit of a secret and an application – the full blown title is an application for the appointment of a receiver by way of equitable execution – is fairly rare though, if granted, should be effective. Best for the larger judgment. What you would be asking the court to do is appoint someone to receive money which will fall due to your debtor and account to you for it after their inevitable bill for doing so has been met. You could ask for say your accountant to be appointed. The most likely straightforward situation in which an appointment might be appropriate is where your debtor is a landlord who is entitled to monthly rent for the premises they have let. The receiver could catch rent already due but unpaid as well as future rent as and when it becomes due and until the judgment debt has been satisfied. You would not be able to catch future rent with a third party debt order (see above). The procedure for applying is in part 69 of the Civil Procedure Rules 1998.

Choosing the right course

Where your debtor is employed and you are willing to suffer payment by instalments, it's probably worth going for an attachment of earnings order. No good if you want your money quickly unless the debtor is a City trader.

Swooping on a bank or building society account by way of a third party debt order makes a lot of sense if you reckon there is a reasonable chance it is in credit. And provided your debtor appears to have a reasonable lifestyle, trying the bailiff or an enforcement agent (concurrently with a third party debt order application, if you wish) could be a good bet, especially when they have a Morgan parked in the garage and it's not on HP. You can back up other action with a charging order application should your debtor own their home (even jointly with their spouse or partner). And, if you have patience, go for a charging order alone. The time could well come when your debtor wants or needs to sell or remortgage and then they will find they are obliged to pay you off. Provided the judgment was for at least £5,000, it will be earning interest at the rate of 8% and so a nice investment as you wait to be paid. Once you get tired of waiting you can apply on the back of the charging order for the property to be sold. Enforcement other than by a charging order application can stop interest running (see above).

"But how do I discover what they've got?"

You can apply for an order to obtain information about your debtor's circumstances. Use form N316 if the debtor is an individual or form N316A if the debtor is a company and you want one of its directors to answer questions (£55 fee unless you qualify for remission but I predict soon to be increased to £59). The debtor or the director will be compelled to attend at the civil hearing centre local to them and to produce such items as pay slips, bank statements, mortgage statements and any outstanding bills. In the case of a business, production of bills owed to it and two years' accounts will also be required. The debtor or director will be quizzed at court by a member of staff who will complete a questionnaire and get them to sign it. You will then be supplied with a copy. The staff member will be quite competent to do the job properly but you can't expect a Rumpole impersonation. Should you want the debtor or director to produce at court information or documents over and above what will normally be required of them then you can give details in the application form. Should the debt be big enough to make the exercise viable, you can ask for the questioning to come before a judge instead of a staff member and either conduct it yourself or send a lawyer to do it on your behalf.

> "The judgment creditor requests that the judgment debtor/officer of the company be questioned by the judgment creditor before a judge. The reasons for this request are that (1) the judgment debt is substantial and/or (2) the judgment creditor is seized of certain information which needs to be put to the judgment debtor/director for confirmation and elaboration and/or (3) the judgment creditor submits that the judgment debtor/director is likely to be unhelpful and evasive (consistent with their conduct so far in these proceedings) and expert examination of them is considered to be desirable and proportionate."

One of my favourite tricks as a former advocate on these examinations before a judge was to ask the debtor to empty out their pockets. If they decline (and it is doubtful that the judge would force them to do the emptying), you will know you are on to something (like money or property) and they might even stutter out a bit of useful information before they re-establish their equilibrium in response to a supplementary like: "Don't be embarrassed about the car keys, Mr Troublesore, where did you park?" And who knows what might come out of the pockets if the debtor is compliant?

The debtor or director is frequently struck, on the way to be being quizzed, by a speck of dust in the eye and doesn't get to court. Shock, horror. There is then a streamlined procedure which the court will adopt which is to order the absentee to be committed to prison but to suspend the prison stay so long as they extract the dust and do turn up for an adjourned quizzing. There is a grander alternative route to forcing the debtor or director to court which should be reserved for the more complex case and that is an application (under part 81 of the Civil Procedure Rules 1998) for them to be committed to prison for contempt of court. This can also be used where the debtor or director is abroad and permission to serve them with the committal paperwork, wherever they may be, is not required in this instance.

*and a few words to our debtor friends: Empty your pockets before you get to court! And one other thing. You can ask your creditor for reasonable travelling expenses to get to and from court. You must make this request with seven days of receiving the order to attend.

"But how do I discover <u>both</u> what they've got <u>and</u> what I should do about it?"

There is a special procedure which can be used for enforcement of maintenance orders (as well as orders for the payment of lump sums) made in matrimonial and other family cases. This is *an application for enforcement by such method of enforcement as the court may consider*. The application form is called a D50K and the court fee is £50 (but I predict soon to be increased to £54). The application is not well known but it could work well for some. What happens is that the debtor is ordered to attend court on the hearing of the application. They will be questioned about their means much in the same way as they would on questioning in relation to a civil court judgment (see above) but there are two distinct differences. Firstly, the questioning will always be conducted by a judge and, secondly, the judge will effectively point you in the right direction about which method or methods or enforcement (you can use more than one method at a time) is or are right. Different judges will deal with the procedure in different ways. You may find you are required to go on and make a further application for the actual enforcement order you want and pay the additional court fee which is attracted by it...or you may not! If the judge seems disinclined to make an enforcement order of some kind there and then, mention to them the case of *Kaur v Randhawa* and that it can be found at [2015] EWHC 1592 (the judge will know what you are talking about though you won't!) in which Mr Justice Mostyn made a final third party debt order for £108,000 there and then on one of these applications. The one potential disadvantage with the procedure is that it gives the debtor advance notice of what is to be happening so that if they empty their bank account or sell, mortgage or remortgage a property they own before they get to court for the hearing or before appropriate paperwork can be produced to cover the method of enforcement to be followed, you could be left whistling.

The special treat*

The *statutory demand* is a very fine demand. It just could get you your money without taking enforcement action through the court and with relative swiftness and little or no expense. But to succeed, you need:

- a debtor who does not want to be made bankrupt;
- a debt of at least £5,000; and
- a debt for a fixed sum so you cannot use the demand for say a claim for damages for restaurant poisoning.

The demand is a prelude to bankruptcy proceedings in relation to an individual or winding up proceedings in relation to a company. The form of demand tells the debtor they must pay you what is owed and that their failure to do so within 21 days of getting the document could result in them being made bankrupt or wound up. The very last thing you want is to have to bring bankruptcy or winding up proceedings because they are expensive and should the debtor (not having been induced by the demand to settle the debt) be prepared to lie down and have the court declare them bankrupt or wound up – see chapter 48), the chances are you will have paid handsomely to recover not a penny. But if you are pretty sure your debtor is solvent (or not hopelessly insolvent) and what's stopping them from settling the debt to you is bloody-mindedness, laziness, cash flow problems, meanness or insanity then bankruptcy or winding up – the ultimate method of enforcement – may be unavoidable. Bankruptcy and so the statutory demand are not available to enforce maintenance orders but there is instead the judgment summons procedure which can lead to the defaulter being potted makes up for it (see rules 33.9 to 33.17 of the Family Procedure Rules 2010).

Whilst the demand will normally come subsequently to a court judgment, that is not essential. It can be used where a debt has been run up and no court proceedings have been brought. But not a good idea to use it in the absence of a judgment if the debtor has some genuine and reasonable ground for disputing the debt or does not quarrel with the debt but maintains you owe them money and that what you owe cancels out what they owe you. In either of those situations, the law expects you to make a court claim rather than speeding down the statutory demand road. If you did, the likelihood is that the debtor would apply to the court to set the demand aside and you would be left with a red face, indigestion, a bad night's sleep (maybe seven nights' worth) and possibly a court order for costs against you. The moral is save the procedure for where you already have a court judgment or you have no judgment but the claim is cast iron or as close to that as it gets.

Unless your claim is based on a contract which entitles you to interest on the debt until it is paid, the disadvantage of a demand without a judgment is that the debt will not carry an entitlement to interest and it should not be claimed in the form of demand. You must use a prescribed form of demand (go to gov.uk/statutory-demands: form 6.1/2 or 3 for an individual or 4.1 for a company). In the case of a demand against an individual you must insert, where the form invites you to do so, the insolvency hearing centre at which they are entitled to apply for the demand to be set aside. The best way of finding this out is to contact the Insolvency Service's enquiry line on 0300 678 0015 or go to insolvency.enquiryline@insolvency.gsi.gov.uk.

*and a few words to our debtor friends: You can apply to the insolvency hearing centre identified in the demand for it to be set aside if you contend it is misconceived, unjustified or makes no sense whatsoever or you have a good defence to the claim or a counterclaim. The application should be made within 18 days of getting the demand. Should you be late, you will have to additionally apply for a time extension. Or you could actually pay up or put forward settlement proposals to your creditor which are designed to obviate bankruptcy or winding up proceedings. A company cannot apply to set aside a statutory demand which it receives. The appropriate course of challenge then would be an application to the court to restrain the institution of winding up proceedings.

Should the statutory demand be based on a default court judgment which you contest, the likelihood is that the application to set aside the statutory demand will usually be adjourned to facilitate an application by you to set aside the actual judgment but a tight timetable will be imposed

If the application to set aside the demand is unsuccessful, the court will allow a breathing space before your creditor can petition for your bankruptcy. The norm is seven days. Where you aim to pay off the debt but would require more than seven days to raise the money, ask the judge to allow longer and say why. By paying up before a bankruptcy petition can be issued, you will avoid being condemned to pay the costs that the bankruptcy case would involve and which you would most probably have to pay even though the proceedings were abandoned because you had eventually settled. Beware. It is commonplace for the dodgier creditor to insist on their costs of bringing bankruptcy proceedings being settled as a condition of dropping the case. They can insist on an order for costs against you but not on you producing the money for them before the bankruptcy petition can be dropped. Payment of these costs would be for another day and non-payment cannot stand in the way of the court dismissing the petition on the ground that there is no longer a debt. Not a good idea to refuse forever to settle those costs whether the amount of them has been agreed between you and your creditor or the court has fixed them because of non-agreement. Your creditor could come up with a new statutory demand followed on by a second bankruptcy petition for the costs of the first bankruptcy petition (so long as the costs amounted to £5,000 or more). In fact, it could go on forever. Nice where you have taken a fancy to the court clerk but not nice if you can't afford to take them out for a drink.

Something to watch should you be thinking of agreeing the amount of your costs liability with the creditor. When starting the bankruptcy case, your creditor would have paid over to the court a deposit of a cool £990 towards the expenses of the Insolvency Service which through the official receiver deals with the administration of your affairs after the bankruptcy order. That deposit will be repaid to the creditor should there be no bankruptcy as the case has been dismissed. Therefore, the £990 must not appear in the creditor's costs bill against you. Surprising how often it is.

Where the creditor has failed to follow the procedural rules in relation to the statutory demand, you may be able to successfully contest the later bankruptcy petition. The creditor must do all that is reasonable to bring the demand to your attention and, if practicable, have you personally served with it. Should the judge tell you that rule 12.4 of the Insolvency Rules 2016 allows them to overlook a defect or irregularity over service of the demand, tell them: "Balderdash. I apologise. For just a moment, I thought I was taking to my son. What I meant to say, with the greatest unctuous respect I can muster, is that the 2017 High Court case of *Canning v Irwain Mitchell LLP* decided otherwise." Since December 2017, the court has been empowered to decline to accept a bankruptcy petition if not satisfied that the creditor has complied with this service obligation.

Covid-19 ALERT!!! Temporary pandemic restrictions on the service of statutory demands against companies and the issue of winding up petitions against companies are due to expire on 30 June 2021. If you want to do either after this date, you should check whether the restrictions have been extended.

And a few more words to our debtor friends who haven't paid their taxes

The tax man – more affectionately known as HM Revenue & Customs (HMRC) – has a new and neat way of procuring settlement of your unpaid tax bill introduced by section 51 of the Finance (No 2) Act 2015 (and if you don't believe me go to section 51 and schedule 8). The process is called direct recovery of debt (DRD). It swoops on money you hold in any accounts – typically, with a bank or building society – and after a temporary holding period it settles the tax bill out of the credit and all without any prior court order. Before the swoop, you must owe at least £1,000 with the timetables for appealing having passed and HMRC must leave at least £5,000 across all your accounts after the earmarked tax money has been deducted. Then, you are given the bad news and you have 30 days to object. Grounds include that you have already paid, the action taken is causing or will cause you exceptional hardship or someone else has an interest on one of the affected accounts (for example, your mother-in-law asked you to look after £25,000 for her and you popped it into the account). There is also a right to object on the part of that someone else or a joint account holder. HMRC must consider the objection within the next 30 days and, if they remain unmoved, there is a right of appeal on the same grounds within the next 30 days to the county court.

HMRC is committed to undertake a face-to-face visit with you before considering a DRD (so that's something to look forward to) at which you will be offered a Time to Pay arrangement and they must assess whether you are vulnerable and, if you are, they will offer you support from a specialist team. In coming to a conclusion about vulnerability, account must be had not only to a disability or long-term health condition but to temporary conditions which prevent you from putting your tax affairs in order or personal issues that affect you or say an immediate family member (including a bereavement, redundancy, serious illness and domestic or financial abuse). If any account held by a non-vulnerable debtor remains in credit after one of these face-to-face visits, I will be eating a few wigs. The hats could give me indigestion.

Chapter 30

Seizure Of Goods

The bailiff strikes

Sounds chilling. It is. Your goods seized to satisfy a debt which is subject to a court judgment or which is due under some other legal process. It's a terrible thing for you but it may be the last resort (or close to it) for your creditor. The seizure is known as execution and is carried out by what, since 2014, are generally known as enforcement agents. They include the good old county court bailiffs who additionally now have the distinction of being family court bailiffs. The enforcement agents who are not county court bailiffs are licensed to execute and are in it for the money about which there is no shame so long as they obey the rules. They take on as part of their business the pleasure of seizing goods under judgments of the High Court and sometimes judgments of the county court which have been transferred to the High Court for enforcement usually because the creditors reckon that the county court bailiffs are too soft and insufficiently aggressive (see chapter 29). There are also certificated enforcement agents who are authorised by the county court to seize goods and will be the guys who go after such debts as council tax.

If you owe money then you should pay it and, if you are not in a position to pay it when required, you should put forward reasonable proposals to pay in the future – probably by instalments – and keep to them so long as that is reasonably possible. When execution is under a High Court or county court judgment, you can apply to the court to fend off the enforcement agent. Your creditor will have obtained a *writ of control* in the High Court or a *warrant of control* in the county court. That application would be for the *writ* or the *warrant* to be suspended (halted) so long as you paid up as and when required under the proposals you put forward. But the rules which the enforcement agents must obey are there for your protection. They can only go so far and if they overstep the mark, you, the defaulting debtor, have legal rights and you can do something about it.

Those rules are in the Taking Control of Goods Regulations 2013 which every self respecting debtor should have under their bed. Depending on the circumstances, your set of the regulations may be protected from seizure and almost certainly the enforcement agent won't be able to make off with the bed even if you are out of it. So let's go to the regulations and see what the enforcement agent cannot take towards the debt and what are the rules of the game.

Can't take

Only goods which you own should be taken for a debt: not, say, those belonging to your spouse or partner or a finance company which are on hire-purchase to you. Some other goods are exempt from seizure. As odious as you are and as much as you owe, the enforcement agent cannot take:

- Items or equipment which are necessary for use by you in your employment, business, trade, profession, study or education (so if you are training to be a law professor, you could say that your copy of the regulations under the bed are exempt from seizure on that basis). Included as exempt might be tools, books, telephones, computers and vehicles. The exemption in this category applies only up to goods to the total value of £1,350. Over that figure, the enforcement agent can seize away. This exemption does not apply where the debt is for taxes or non-domestic rates.

- Clothing, bedding, furniture, household equipment, items and provisions as are reasonably required to satisfy the basic domestic needs of yourself and the other members of the household (be they young or old, big or small). What we are looking at here are, for example:
  - a cooker (but probably not two cookers unless you have 200 people living in your home);
  - microwave;
  - fridge;
  - washing machine;
  - beds and bedding;
  - a landline phone or, if no landline, a mobile (but not a landline and a mobile);
  - a dining table large enough for you and the rest of the household and chairs (ten chairs and only three occupiers would put seven chairs at risk but anything short of solid oak circa 1750 and the enforcement agent is unlikely to be interested);
  - lighting and heating equipment sufficient to satisfy your basic needs and those of your household;
  - any item or equipment reasonably required for the care of someone under 18, a disabled person or an older person;
  - a guide dog (!); and
  - a vehicle on which a valid disabled person's badge is displayed because it is actually used to carry a disabled person or the enforcement agent has reasonable grounds to believe that this is so.

If you are saying that an exempt item has been seized then you must notify this to the enforcement agent as soon as practicable and certainly within seven days of it having been removed. You need to give your name and address and state that this address is where you can be sent (served with) documentation about the matter; state the goods concerned; and provide the grounds for saying they are exempt. The creditor will be given an opportunity of admitting or disputing what you say. If there is a dispute, the enforcement agent will notify you of it and you will then need to apply to the court – on form N244 – to resolve the dispute within seven days of receiving the notification. With the application should go a written statement specifying the goods you claim to be exempt and the grounds for doing so and any available documentation to back you up. Where the goods seized belonged to someone else, the owner wishing to challenge their seizure should give notice within seven days of removal.

"I'm coming"

The enforcement agent must give you at least seven clear days' written notice (with prescribed information) that they are coming. In calculating whether sufficient notice has been given, you should ignore Sunday, a bank holiday, Good Friday and Christmas Day. For obvious reasons, most creditors would say that the notice requirement is a bit loopy. That's why the enforcement agent can apply to the court for the period of notice to be reduced (to five minutes?). The court can only oblige if satisfied that your goods will otherwise be moved out or disposed of so as to evade the enforcement agent taking control of them. You haven't had at least seven days' notice? Ask the enforcement agent to show you the court order which reduced the period.

When?

The enforcement agent can do their evil deed on any day of the week and generally only between 6am and 9pm but the court may be prepared to extend that time frame. If the enforcement agent turns up at 11.30pm you should ask to see a copy of the court order which authorises them to seize after 9pm. Important exceptions coming up. If the goods are on business premises which are open outside 6am to 9pm then the enforcement agent may seize away (two crates of champers and a ton of smoked salmon from a restaurant?) during those extended hours. Generally, if they have started the deed within the permitted period but it is reasonably necessary to take a bit longer, they can finish it so long as the total time taken up is reasonable. Guidance issued to bailiffs in March 2016 tells them to have regard to religious holidays for the debtor when deciding whether to get into seizure mode.

It isn't a condition of the enforcement agent seizing that you are present. However, the agent must not act where the only person present is under 16 or vulnerable. Whether you are present or absent, should the item the enforcement agent wishes to take be in use – by anyone – then the agent should not take if it is likely that this would cause a breach of the peace.

Where?

The enforcement agent may seize goods from where you usually live or carry on a trade or business. They may also enter other premises if they have obtained authority (by a warrant) from the court to do so. That authority will be given where the court is satisfied that there are goods at these premises which can be seized and that it is reasonable in all the circumstances for the authority to be given.

Down the chimney?

No! Generally, the enforcement agent may only enter premises through a door or any other usual means of access such as via a loading bay in respect of trade premises. So apart from the chimney, a window would also be precluded. And the general rule is that the enforcement agent cannot use force to gain entry. This means, for example, that they cannot axe down your front door or push past you. In fact, you don't even need to open the door to them though, of course, it's always good to chat. Two exceptions to the 'no force' rule. If necessary, force can be used by an enforcement agent who is after goods to settle an unpaid criminal fine or income tax or stamp duty. Reasonable force can also be used if the enforcement agent has applied to the court for and been granted a warrant which authorises it. The agent must have explained to the court the likely means of entry and the type and amount of force that will be required.

The motor

Your vehicle might possibly be exempt from seizure (see above). Otherwise, it can be taken. If the enforcement agent comes across your vehicle on the road, they can immobilise it unless you voluntarily surrender the keys. On immobilisation, a warning notice must be fixed to the vehicle with prescribed information including a 24 hour telephone number for enquiries. The vehicle must stay put for at least two hours after which the enforcement agent can have it stored unless you pay the debt in the meantime or reach some arrangement with the agent.

More notices – and more time to pay up

There are strict requirements for the enforcement agent to give you written notice about property they have seized and removed for storage. And you must also be given at least seven days' notice before seized items are sold (with no particular days excluded this time). The agent must achieve the best price that can reasonably be obtained.

Be back soon

The enforcement agent is frustrated. You have nothing on the premises which they can take or what is there is insufficient to pay off the debt. They may return – more than once – if they have reason to believe that since their last visit you have brought fresh goods on to the premises which they can nab. However, you must be given prior written notice of the intention to re-enter. The scheme for this notice is the same as for notice of the initial entry (see above) except that this time only two clear days' notice is required unless the court shortens the period. The guidance issued to bailiffs in March 2016 is that in the course of attempting to get the creditor their money, they should typically conduct three visits to the debtor on different days and at different times and, if they have still not scored, they should liaise with their manager to consider the prospect of further meetings or seizing goods. Once four weeks are up, the creditor should expect either their money or an interim report.

If the enforcement agent is not frustrated but leaves your premises with nothing except a few sheets of paper, it is because you have signed a controlled goods agreement. By this, the agent will have assumed control of specified goods on the premises but left them where they are in return for you coming to an arrangement to pay off what is due. In the document you will have agreed not to remove or dispose of the goods or permit anyone else to do so until you have settled up but you can continue to use them. You break the agreement? The agent can remove the goods into storage or sell them. And if, say, you have sold them or taken them elsewhere "without a lawful excuse" (for example, you were rescuing them from destruction in a fire which you did not deliberately start yourself or a madman invited to the premises by your wayward daughter was about to massacre them) you will be guilty of a criminal offence and risk a fine or imprisonment.

The bill

You give the enforcement agent a hard time at your peril. Of course, if you don't possess a sherry glass to spit in, that may not cause you anxiety. Equally, if you intend to apply for your own bankruptcy or are content for a creditor to bankrupt you, there's not too much to worry about. Otherwise, the more the enforcement agent does, the greater their charges and so the greater your debt 'cos you pay those charges though the bill is less painful with the bailiff in the county court and family court. You will find the enforcement agent's price list in the Taking of Goods (Fees) Regulations 2014. Here's an example. With a High Court debt, there are four separate stages which each trigger a separate charge: compliance (all activities from the agent's receipt of instructions up to but excluding the commencement of enforcement) generating a mild £75; first enforcement (from the first attendance at the premises to completion or breach of a controlled goods agreement) generating a fee of £190 plus 7.5% of the sum to be recovered in excess of £1,000; second enforcement (further steps up to but excluding sale of goods taken) generating a fixed fee of £495; and sale generating a fee of £525 plus 7.5% of the sum to be recovered. On top are court fees and other disbursements such as charges for storage, a locksmith and auction.

Enforcement agents play gentle

Where your creditor has issued a county court warrant of control, there will be a lapse of around twelve days before anything nasty happens. This will be good for you but send your creditor crazy and have them vowing to keep away from the county court for seizure in the future and use the High Court enforcement agents whenever the amount of the debt allows. During this period, the warrant will be referred to one of the warrant of control support centres covering the whole of England and Wales. They will attempt to contact you to break the news that the warrant has been issued, tell you what can happen, give you the options open, endeavour to get you to pay up or agree a payment plan and signpost you to debt advice agencies where appropriate. If you are vulnerable, this will be identified and information about the vulnerability passed on to your creditor. And if, by the end of the period, the debt remains unpaid or there is no plan and the creditor wishes to bash on, a bailiff will take over.

Over in the High Court, we can expect to see a change in how many enforcement agents follow through the issue of a writ of control. This is thanks to a decision of the High Court in January 2021 that it is lawful for an enforcement agent to get you to sign up to the controlled goods agreement we just met (see **Be back soon**) without entering your property but by courtesy of an arrangement made with you remotely be video. This would mean an enforcement agent breathing fire down your laptop instead of your neck but could save you money as agents using this means of procuring an agreement do not intend to charge that fee of £190 plus 7.5% of the debt to be recovered for their first visit which would otherwise be added to your bill. I do not expect this practice to be followed in the county court, at least for the time being, although it does have those support centres.

Enforcement agent gets executed

If an enforcement agent acts illegally – breaches schedule 12 to the Tribunals, Courts and Enforcement Act 2007 or acts under a defective power – you may get back the goods that have been seized and recover damages from the enforcement agent for any loss you have suffered. It is a defence to the damages claim but not to the claim for return of the goods that the enforcement agent acted in the reasonable belief that he was not breaching the law or acting under a defective power. Proceedings relating to a High Court writ of control must be brought in the High Court and relating to a county court warrant of control in the county court. In any other case they may be brought in the High Court or county court but almost invariably only the county court will be appropriate. Where the alleged culprit is a county court bailiff then a claim should be made against the Ministry of Justice which will accept responsibility should the bailiff have erred. The proceedings may be brought by application notice in form N244 which will mean a fee of £255 (I predict an increase soon to £275) and be supported by a written statement setting out where the enforcement agent has gone wrong. Where the goods have not yet been sold, you can ask the court to halt any auction or other sale process. Alternatively, you can start proceedings by issuing a Part 7 claim form (see chapter 12). The particulars of claim (and an application notice and the supporting statement can cover the same ground) might go like this:

Case no 970000678

IN THE COUNTY COURT

SITTING AT PEARDROP

BETWEEN

CLIVE TROUBLESORE Claimant

- and -

BERTRAND GRABWELL Defendant

PARTICULARS OF CLAIM

1. This claim is made under paragraph 66 of schedule 12 ("schedule 12") to the Tribunals, Courts and Enforcement Act 2007.

2. At all material times -

a. the claimant was indebted to Peardrop Borough Council ("the council") for unpaid parking charges and penalties ("the debt") in the total sum of £13,546 and

b. the defendant was an enforcement agent instructed by the council to recover the debt and costs by taking control of the claimant's goods under a warrant of control.

3. On 14th July 2021 at about 10.30pm the defendant in the course of seeking to take control of the claimant's goods entered the claimant's premises at 149 Magnolia Crescent, Twickenham, Middlesex KT89 4XZ ("the premises") and took control of and removed cash in the sum of £14,000 and a Ford Escort van registration number CT3 belonging to the claimant ("the van") (together referred to as "the goods").

4. Wrongfully and in breach of paragraph 7 of schedule 12 and paragraph 6 of the Taking Control of Goods Regulations 2013 ("the regulations"), the defendant failed to give the claimant not less than seven clear days' notice before taking control but gave him only two clear days' notice.

5. Further and alternatively, wrongfully and in breach of paragraph 10 of the regulations, the defendant entered the premises when the only person present was the claimant's child Clive Troublesore Junior aged 1.

6. Further and alternatively, wrongfully and in breach of schedule 12, the defendant took control of goods the aggregate value of which was more than the debt and an amount in respect of future costs calculated in accordance with the regulations when there were goods of lower value on the premises.

7. Further and alternatively, wrongfully and in breach of paragraph 19 of the regulations and in the absence of exceptional circumstances, the defendant removed the goods and secured them in a place which was not within a reasonable distance from the premises, namely at the Dodgy Depository, Poole, Dorset.

8. Further and alternatively, wrongfully and in breach of paragraph 20 of the regulations, the defendant entered the premises through an unsecured ground floor rear window and by applying force to the doors of the garage within the premises.

9. Further and alternatively, wrongfully and in breach of paragraph 22 of the regulations, the defendant entered the premises at a prohibited time.

10. Further and alternatively, wrongfully and in breach of paragraph 28 of schedule 12 to and paragraph 30 of the regulations, the

defendant failed to give notice of entry to the claimant by leaving such notice in a conspicuous place on the premises or otherwise.

11. Further and alternatively, wrongfully and in breach of paragraph 34 of schedule 12 to and paragraph 33 of the regulations, the defendant failed to provide the claimant with a list of goods of which he had taken control as soon as reasonably practicable or at all.

12. Further and alternatively, wrongfully and in breach of paragraph 35 of schedule 12 to and paragraph 34 of the regulations, the defendant failed to take reasonable care of the van following its removal from the premises in that he littered the interior or caused the interior to be littered with cigarette butts and damaged the bodywork or caused it to be so damaged requiring repairs at the cost to the claimant of £921 (inc VAT).

13. As a result of the defendant's breaches the claimant has suffered loss.

Particulars of loss

- cost of repairs to garage doors – £128;
- cost of repairs to and cleaning of the interior of the van – £951 (inc VAT);
- loss of earnings due to inability to use van – £150 per day as from 14 July 2021 and continuing; and
- bank charges incurred in arranging and servicing emergency overdraft – £35 with interest continuing as from the date of this claim at the rate of £x per day.
- travelling expenses in seeking to recover the goods – £98.

AND the claimant claims-

a. Return of the cash and van removed by the defendant;

b. Damages limited to £20,000;

c. Interest for such period and at such rate as the court shall think just; and

d. Costs.

I believe that the facts stated in these particulars of claim are true. I understand that proceedings for contempt of court may be brought against anyone who makes, or causes to be made, a false statement in a document verified by a statement of truth without an honest belief in its truth.

(signed) Clive Troublesore

Claimant

Dated 14 July 2021

Nice execution

The Ministry of Justice has issued national standards which enforcement agents are expected to follow. Their failure to do so will not entitle you to legal redress (though you may well be justified in making a complaint about them which could lead to them losing their certificate to do their job). However, the failure could help you in any claim you do bring along the lines we have looked at: in particular, to rebut a defence to a claim for damages that the agent reasonably believed they were not breaking the law. Here's a taster of these standards. Enforcement agents must:

- not act in a threatening way when visiting a debtor's premises by making gestures;
- always produce relevant identification and, where appropriate, written authorisation to act for the creditor;
- carry out their duties in a professional, calm and dignified manner;
- dress and speak appropriately and act with discretion and fairness;
- as far as practical, avoid disclosing the purpose of their visit to anyone other than the debtor or someone like an advice agency representative assisting the debtor; and
- provide an itemised account of their charges if requested to do so in writing.

During Covid-19 lockdowns and restrictions, enforcement agents have been prevented from doing anything about seizure of goods for various periods. When they have been able to lawfully pounce, they should have followed additional guidance issued by the Ministry of Justice. Among that guidance, make every reasonable effort to maintain social distancing, make reasonable attempts to contact households prior to visits in order to assess risk; and avoid unduly raising their voice because of the potential for increased risk of infection.

Part 7

RIGHTS, WRONGS AND MANAGING YOUR AFFAIRS

Chapter 31

Covid-19 Cancellations

Frustrating!

Wedding cancelled. Hotel closed. Toilet paper can't be delivered until next year. Birthday bash at the local chippie off. "We can no longer extract your five molars and three incisors next week and we regret you will have to see to them yourself. It is recommended that you do one at a time. Every good wish." Groceries drop off postponed for one week due to overwhelming demand. And on and on.

What's the legal position for each side? The Competition and Markets Authority has proclaimed what it considers should happen with cancellations and refunds under consumer contracts. However, as useful and legally correct as its assessment may appear, that assessment is not binding on traders and their customers and 2021 and beyond will see loadsalitigation coming to the fore in the courts arising out of Covid-19. That will be between business and business, business and consumer, private individual and private individual and any other permutations you can think of but I can't think of any right now as I haven't had my black coffee yet. Consumer customers will chip in with what the Authority has said and that can be expected to be clocked by the judge but it is the judge who will decide and general principles may be disapplied because of the peculiar circumstances of individual cases. Here's my take.

We covered that

A written contract may set out what should happen when an event occurs that makes it impossible for the goods in question to be delivered or the service in question to be carried out, on time or at all. If it does and there was nothing that could reasonably be done to change that, the contract will prevail and, apart from stabbing themselves or getting in a very clever lawyer (or both), there's nothing an aggrieved party can do about it. They call it a *force majeure* clause, just to be difficult, and that title often appears in the contract, but it's the substance of the clause and not the title that counts. Whether or not the clause is triggered will require a detailed examination of the contract through a lexiconic microscope while wearing telescopic lenses under a 500 watt lamp. If it says the clause comes into play during a pandemic or on a law coming into force which makes it illegal for the contract to be performed then bingo, there's a trigger. However, the fact that to do whatever has been contracted to be done would cost extra or be an enormous pain in the neck won't be good enough. And the fact that performance of the contract would involve doing something which was contrary to just government guidance as opposed to any associated national or regional legislation might well not trigger a *force majeure* clause.

But the *force majeure* clause is unfair or unreasonable

Then if we are looking at a contract between a trader and consumer, the Consumer Rights Act 2015 and its unfair contract terms regime comes into play (see chapter 63). A contract that excuses a trader from delivering goods or performing a service which was made illegal by pandemic legislation would hardly be unfair. However, if the contract went on to allow the business to keep the consumer's money for doing nothing, that can be expected to be ruled as unfair and void. And if the trader seeks to rely on contract wording which purports to give them the right to change a key part of the contract without the permission of the consumer – they call that a 'variation clause' in all the best legal circles – there's a good chance that would be regarded as unfair as well and so could be ignored. Where neither party is a consumer and they have reached their agreement on the basis of standard terms – the take it or leave it situation – the Unfair Contract Terms Act 1977 may come to the rescue of the aggrieved party. Should those standard terms seek to exclude or limit liability if a party has failed to do what the contract required of them or done something substantially different from what was required, then that bit of the contract can be struck down if it was unreasonable.

Bye bye *force majeure*

If there isn't a *force majeure* clause or one that is going to apply, we are into frustration and we all know about that. But not the sort of frustration it is my pleasure to bring to you now. A contract may be effectively brought to an end and so legally treated as frustrated when, after it was made, something happened that made it physically impossible to do what was required or transformed what was required into something radically different – provided that what happened had not been foreseeable. In some cases which were decided by the courts many years before either of us were thought of, it was ruled that the hire of a music hall for performing concerts was frustrated by the music hall burning down (obvious) and the hiring of a flat in London's Pall Mall to watch the coronation procession of Edward VII was frustrated by the cancellation of the coronation (not so obvious). But a contract for the hire of a steamboat to cruise round the fleet at Spithead and witness the naval review of the coronation was not frustrated because the cruise was still possible (not so obvious).

What will be at the root of punch-ups over whether or not the contract has been frustrated will be the issue of foreseeability. Could the pandemic and the consequences of it have been foreseen? There are likely to be strong arguments, for and against. If the pandemic was well into its destructive course when the contract was made it might take some persuasion that impossibility of performance was not foreseeable. It would depend on the state of the pandemic then and when things were to be done as well as the legislative prohibitions and restrictions at those points: perhaps also what the government was recommending although that might be of less importance.

The fact that the customer did not take out an insurance policy to cover the risk of the contract having to be cancelled could count against them on the basis that this showed they were willing to run the risk of cancellation which could prevent frustration being relied on. The greater the sum of money at stake, the less likely frustration would work in this situation.

If Brexit was regarded by the courts as a frustrating event, then it might be thought that judges would take the same view of Covid-19. That's what makes a case decided by the High Court in February 2019 so interesting. It involved a 25 year lease granted in 2014 of commercial premises in London's Canary Wharf to the European Medicines Agency which wanted to extricate itself on account of the ramifications of Brexit. Trouble was that, although it has been judicially accepted that a lease is capable of being frustrated, no court has ever ruled that a lease was in fact frustrated. And this case did not make legal history. No frustration, ruled the judge, and the Agency has abandoned an appeal against the decision after an agreement was reached between the parties.

The contract is frustrated scenario

If there is frustration of the contract, the Law Reform (Frustrated Contracts) Act 1943 takes over with more than a bit of help from a judge where the parties are not agreed. Deposits and money paid over before the frustrating event are to be refunded. Any obligation to pay over more money (like a second instalment of the contract price) disappears. Some valuable benefit has been enjoyed before frustration? This may well have to be paid for if that would be just but the court will look at the value of the end product rather than the direct value of the service. Doing very little may lead to a substantial benefit. And if one party has incurred expenditure before frustration towards carrying out their contractual obligations (hired the marquee, the portaloos and the vicar), this may well have to be paid for by the other party, where that would be just. Any insurance pay out to one party to cover their loss for what happened is to be disregarded when the liability of the other party is assessed unless the contract or the law expressly mandated that insurance was to be taken out. The policy conditions, though, might provide for the insured party to refund to the insurer what it has paid out if that money has been recovered from the other side.

The 1943 Act will not apply to the frustration of insurance policies but that does not matter too much because it is a well established legal principle that an insurer cannot recover a premium where whatever has been insured against has ceased to exist during the currency of the policy. Insured house burns down to the ground under a fire insurance policy. Insurer has to whistle for any premium owed. And it will also not apply to an order for specifically identified goods which perish before legal responsibility for them has passed to the buyer. Forget the Act too if those who have made the contract have opted out of it. But when you last signed up for a wedding reception, did the hotel's conditions say: "We hereby agree that the provisions of Law Reform (Frustrated Contracts) Act 1943 shall not apply to this contract in the event that the wedding is cancelled because of thunder and lightning bla bla bla..."? The chances are that the Act has never been mentioned in any contractual document or conversation and, even if it had, the attempt to exclude it would only be effective in the case of Covid-19 if it was clear from the words used that something so dire had been contemplated by the parties and an alternative way of dealing with what should happen had been agreed on.

Obtaining redress

If it seems that the law of frustration catches your situation, it is to be hoped that the party who has had your money, and might be expecting more of it, comes up with an acceptable solution. Should you be entitled to money back and release from any future obligations under the contract, you are not legally compelled to instead accept a voucher or credit note or to agree to it all happening when Covid-19 has been beaten. Of course, you may be willing to do so and will naturally have sympathy for the other party. But it is only reasonable for you to factor into your decision, whether or not there is a risk that the other party will be forced out of business before it can come up with the service required. A certain Stephen Gold was in a quandary about what to do about his Lyme Regis hotel booking during the pandemic when the hotel had closed and would have remained closed throughout the booked stay. I won't name the hotel. I'm not suggesting they would poison me if given the opportunity but we earnestly hope it will continue to trade and we can go back there.

> *To a Hotel in Lyme Regis*
>
> *25 March 2020*
>
> *Good Morning*
>
> *You telephoned me on Monday when we discussed the deposit I had paid to you in connection with the reservation below and you invited me to agree to the deposit standing over for a period of 12 months on the basis that the booked holiday would not stand. I explained that we were long-standing hotel guests and would wish to stay with you again as soon as circumstances permitted it but that I would wish the deposit to be refunded. You were to refer to your general manager and come back to me but I have not heard from you since. Would you confirm that you have initiated a return of the deposit.*
>
> *We wish you well in the current difficult situation.*
>
> *Kind regards*
>
> *Stephen Gold*

There had been no acceptance during the telephone conversation I was referring to that the contract had been frustrated. But on 27 March 2020 the hotel stated it would refund the deposit as soon as it could. It repeated this on 10 April 2020. The deposit was refunded on 17 April 2020.

Getting tougher

> *Dear Trader*
>
> *Agreement no ABx432180*
>
> *The services you contracted to supply to me (or goods you contracted to deliver to me) under the above numbered agreement have not been*

> supplied (or delivered) in accordance with the agreement because of the outbreak of Covid-19 and consequential legislation and Government guidance which have rendered performance of the agreement to be impossible. In these circumstances, the agreement is at an end under the legal doctrine of frustration. That being so, I am entitled to the return of the deposit of £350.00 which I have paid to you. My previous requests for the return of the deposit have gone unheeded. Accordingly, I now require you make the refund to me in full within 14 days of the date of receipt of this communication.
>
> If you fail to comply with my refund requirement, I shall bring county court proceedings against you for its return, interest at the rate of 8% as from the date of frustration until the date of judgment and costs.
>
> Yours faithfully
>
> Clive Troublesore

Where the contract price was more than £100, even though the deposit was less, and you have made a payment by credit card, you would have an alternative claim against the card company or against both the trader and the card company. If you paid by debit card, whatever the contract price, or by credit card for a contract price of £100 or less, you may be able to take advantage of the charge back system (see chapter 41).

Chapter 32

Interest On Debt, Compensation And Judgments

Icing on the cake

If you are entitled to receive money through court proceedings, be it for what you were owed or for compensation, then you are probably entitled to receive interest on that money. The rate of interest and the period for which it is payable will depend on what the money is for. Except for debts payable by one business to another business and for interest payable under the terms and conditions of a contract, it will have been necessary for you to have started proceedings so as to qualify for interest. That's one of the disadvantages of seeking to extract money you are due by serving the debtor with a statutory demand instead of obtaining a judgment (see chapter 29). The statutory demand route limits you to any interest to which the contract entitled you. While there will generally be a right to interest up to the date of a judgment, that right will stop (unless any contract says otherwise) once the judgment is given unless it was for £5,000 or more or enforcement of the judgment has been transferred to the High Court (for which the claimant can apply if the debt is for at least £600). Where proceedings have been started and the defendant coughs up the principal sum claimed but not the interest, the claimant can ask the court to enter judgment for the outstanding interest and the court will normally oblige and do so without a hearing having to take place.

Debt not due from one business to another business

Interest on unpaid debts will usually be awarded at the rate of 8% from when the money was due until the date of judgment and the liability for interest will continue from the date of judgment until settlement on claims for £5,000 or more. The rate could have been adjusted by legislation but as the bank base rate has plummeted the 8% has steadfastly stuck with us since 1993. The interest is generally simple and not compound (interest on interest) except that bankers are able to collect compound interest even though they often don't go for it.

Interest can be very substantial. Despite this, claimants are frequently unaware of their right to claim it or just do not bother. Regard should be had to the possibility that the defendant will defend a claim and it could be many months before a trial takes place and during which the claimant will be out of their money.

Any claim for interest must be made in the particulars of claim when the claimant starts a court case and with online claims, the claimant will be prompted to state whether or not there is an interest claim and the appropriate calculations will have to go in. The amount of interest up to the date of the claim form will be specified and the daily rate sought after then. The interest figure up to the date of the claim should be added on to the amount of the debt and the court fee for starting the case will be based on the total figure. If no interest has been claimed but the claimant later decides they want to claim it then the claim form and particulars of claim would have to be amended, either with the defendant's consent or the permission of the court where consent is not forthcoming. It is by no means a forgone conclusion that permission would be given. The claimant would be refused permission after judgment. And if the claimant asks for permission at the final hearing (and often the claimant does so, especially on a small claim), the likelihood is that the claimant will be given the thumbs down.

The interest regime can operate harshly against a debtor who has collected a judgment and is struggling to pay it off by instalments. The amount of the instalments may be less than the amount of interest which is accruing on the judgment with the result that the judgment sum is never reduced. There is a possible loophole. The creditor's right to interest comes to an end in the county court when they take action to enforce the judgment – by applying for a bailiff to seize the debtor's goods or for the debtor to be questioned about their financial circumstances (see chapter 29) – and that action produces a payment. Interest will not come to an end if the creditor simply applies for a charging order (see chapter 29). And if the court makes an attachment of earnings (see chapter 29) or administration order against the debtor (see chapter 48), no interest will be clocked up during the lifetime of that order. So it comes down to this. By failing to pay up when they should and thereby forcing the claimant to take some enforcement action (other than applying for a charging order), the defendant can do themselves an enormous favour interestwise so long as they make some payment in response to the step taken by the claimant. Should the claimant attempt to enforce only by bringing bankruptcy proceedings, however, the liability to pay interest will continue to run.

In some cases, it may be possible to persuade the court to cut down on the claimant's interest claim. Where it's an 8% claim, the court may be persuaded to reduce it on account of an unreasonable delay by the claimant in starting or continuing the claim which has led to a whopping interest figure. Or 8% being tantamount to extortion, by comparison with the Bank of England's base rates and the much lower rate of interest the creditor would have been required to pay if they had borrowed or would have earned with a building society if they had invested over the period in question. Should the level of interest be the defendant's only argument, they should put in a defence to the claim which takes this point and the court will in all likelihood then enter judgment in the claimant's favour for everything apart from interest and fix a shortish hearing at which interest can be argued out. The defendant should not lightly embark on this course for it can lead to an increased liability for the claimant's legal costs if the argument fails. Much will depend on whether the amount of interest claimed makes a challenge worthwhile. A defence may, of course, facilitate some compromise on the claimant's part.

If the parties had come to an agreement that, in the event of default by the defendant, interest should be payable at a higher rate than 8% or on a compound basis then that agreement will prevail unless the defendant can show that what the contract says amounts to a penalty. This would require satisfying the court that the interest provided for did not represent a true estimate of the financial loss that the defendant's default would cause the claimant.

> *DEFENCE*
>
> 1. *The defendant admits his liability for the principal sum claimed.*
>
> 2. *The defendant denies the claimant's claim for interest. The defendant says that interest in the circumstances of this claim is discretionary and that the rate at which it is claimed is excessive and unreasonable. The defendant further says that the claimant should not be awarded interest (or a reasonable rate of interest would be £x per cent per annum). The claimant relies on the following matters-*
>
> a. *the claimant has delayed for an unreasonable period of time in the institution of the claim with the result that the defendant had reasonably believed that the claim had been abandoned until he was served with the instant proceedings;*
>
> b. *during the period covered by the claim for interest, the Bank of England's base rate has been radically lower that £8 per cent per annum, namely (insert particulars of the base rate for each segment of the period);*
>
> c. *during the period covered by the claim for interest, the claimant could have borrowed had it been reasonably necessary to do so at a radically lower rate that £8 per cent per annum or, had it been paid the principal sum in the instant proceedings, could have invested it but would earned interest at a radically lower such rate (as the case may be);*
>
> d. *the defendant puts the claimant to proof as to whether it did in fact borrow during the period covered by the claim for interest and, if so, on what terms as to interest or otherwise and whether it suffered any loss by virtue of the non-payment of the principal sum in the instant proceedings and, if so, the claimant should provide full particulars; and*
>
> e. *in view of the foregoing, the award of interest to the claimant as claimed would be an unreasonable windfall and would constitute a penalty which was unduly severe for the defendant.*
>
> 3. *The defendant disputes the claimant's claim for costs and relies on the matters set out in paragraph 2 of this defence.*
>
> *I believe that the facts stated in this defence are true. I understand that proceedings for contempt of court may be brought against anyone who makes, or causes to be made, a false statement in a document verified by a statement of truth without an honest belief in its truth.*
>
> *(signed) Clive Troublesore*

Defendant

Dated 14 July 2021

Losses exceeding interest

The object of interest is to compensate the claimant for being deprived of their money. But it may well be the case that the actual loss to the claimant from that deprivation is far greater than the interest which will be awarded. Mr Clive Troublesore refuses to pay Mr Sucker the £25,000 which is due for building works. As a direct result, Mr Sucker's business collapses, he falls behind with his mortgage repayments, his home is repossessed, his wife leaves him and takes the children and his hair falls out. What can he claim from Mr Troublesore? £25,000 debt plus 8% interest. That's tough on the claimant but in this situation the general rule is that they are limited to recovering interest from the defendant.

Pin back your lugholes for the exception to the rule. Take an agreement by Mr Sucker to lend his best friend Mr Troublesore the sum of £10,000 to be repaid after 12 months. Unfortunately, Mr Troublesore is blacklisted for credit and so can't borrow from a commercial lender. Mr Sucker can only make the loan by borrowing the money himself on the basis that if he doesn't repay within 12 months he will have to pay his lender compound interest as from the expiration of the 12 months until he settles and Mr Troublesore is aware of this. When Mr Troublesore defaults in making the repayment, Mr Sucker could claim the extra interest from Mr Troublesore as damages for his loss on the basis that it was in the contemplation of the parties when the agreement was made that the loss would be suffered if Mr Troublesore defaulted.

Business to business

Where money is due for goods or services from one business to another business and goes unpaid, the Late Payment of Commercial Debts (Interest) Act 1998 says it attracts interest at the rate of 8% above the Bank of England base rate which currently stands at 0.1%. For those of you like me who scored the bottom grade for maths 'O' level, they tell me that adds up to 8.1% and even I can work out that is not something to currently get too excited about. The interest starts to run on the date agreed for payment or, if no date has been agreed, from 30 days after supply of the goods or services or, if later, from the date of invoicing. This is simple and not compound interest and it applies between businesses that are small, large, huge and ugly. It would even apply to businesses run by sole proprietors. On top of the enhanced interest rate, the defaulting business is liable to pay a fixed sum for enforcement costs which is a little more exciting – £40 for debts of under £1,000, £70 for debts of £1,000 or more but less than £10,000 and £100 for debts of £10,000 and over. The moment the enhanced interest rate is triggered, the entitlement to this office biscuit barrel subsidy is also triggered and the fixed sum is payable on top of permitted legal costs incurred by a claimant who starts proceedings.

This business interest differs from the 8% regime in that the obligation to pay it arises without proceedings having to be started. The defaulting business might, for example, settle an invoice late but fail to pay the interest and fixed sum. The supplier could nevertheless then sue just for the interest and the fixed sum – and if feeling especially cheeky add to the claim interest on the interest (!) and fixed sum at the standard rate of 8% on a graduating basis which it might be left to Archimedes to calculate.

Of course, when a business gets litigious with another business with whom it has been in a contractual bed, that's likely to be the end of a beautiful relationship. This has to be borne in mind when a decision is taken about how long should be allowed for an invoice to be paid and how heavy the creditor should get. If there is no serious concern about the long term financial stability of the debtor business and the business owed money is without cash flow problems, why not tarry a while and watch the interest mount up at 8.1% which is better than it is likely to enjoy in a savings account? A court claim for debt though must be started within six years of the date on which the money should have been paid (see chapter 13). The alternative with a claim for at least £5,000 is to obtain a judgment and tarry a while with enforcement as interest on the judgment is clocked up at 8%. Unreasonable delay in instituting proceedings could lead to a challenge by the debtor to the ultimate interest claim or the rate sought. The court can say 'no interest' or 'reduced interest' if that is "in the interests of justice" because of the conduct of the creditor business.

Other cases

In most other cases, the court has a discretion to order interest to be paid on the sum awarded at what it considers to be the appropriate rate and for an appropriate period. This would include a claim for damages for breach of contract (say where duff goods have been sold) and the norm here is for the claimant to ask for 8% interest as from the date on which the loss was incurred in the transaction and take what they get. Where damages for personal injury and financial losses are claimed, for example, against a car driver who has negligently caused a road accident, the court must order interest if more than £200 is awarded unless there are special reasons not to do so. The claimant will normally be entitled to interest at the rate of 2% on the damages they collect for their pain and suffering and loss of amenities as from the date proceedings were started. In relation to compensation for specific sums such as an accident victim's ruined motor cycle helmet, the award could be anything from 0.5% to 3% and, if the loss has accumulated over a period – say, earnings lost through absence from work due to accident injuries – the rate may be halved.

Interim payments

Because personal injury interest rates are relatively low, it may make sense once building society investment rates pick up for the claimant who has a strong case which is taking anything from 79 days to an eternity to come on for trial, to apply to the court for the defendant to put hands in pocket of defendant or defendant's insurers and bring out an interim payment. That could then be invested at a superior interest rate which might be available and the interest from the investment would belong to the claimant. The claimant might otherwise find some money handy for a purchase, perhaps even for a deposit on a home purchase. Yes, the court can order a payment on account of what it is satisfied the claimant will probably be ultimately awarded and in fact can do so in any case where money is being claimed. Strict conditions have to be met. The court must have given judgment for the claimant for an amount to be decided or the defendant must have admitted liability – or the court must be satisfied that the claimant will recover a substantial amount at trial. The amount of the interim payment is likely to be anything up to between 75% and 90% of a conservative valuation of what the claimant will ultimately be awarded. And if the court gets it wrong and the claimant gets less or nothing at trial, they will be ordered to pay it back! If on a personal injury case the claimant has a lawyer acting for them (which is likely) then they should insist in an appropriate case that they advise them about an interim payment application.

Chapter 33

Compensation For Hassle And Mental Distress

Inconvenience, distress, disappointment, annoyance, frustration, anxiety, displeasure, upset, vexation, tension, aggravation

A night out with Stephen Gold? When, if ever, are you entitled to compensation for what we can loosely describe as inconvenience or mental distress, or both? There have been loads of decided cases on the subject and many contradict others. The law could even change with a decision of the Supreme Court but what I recommend is that you ensure it is not your case that goes there as that could be expensive. This is how it looks and the county court and High Court are likely to deal with any claim by or against you by applying these general principles.

Inconvenience

In a claim for breach of a contract, you should be entitled to compensation for inconvenience if it is of the physical type such as that suffered, along with discomfort, by a claimant who had to endure living in his defective home because of the unsatisfactory way the damp course system had been installed. And way back in 1875 there was compensation for a man and his family who were put out at the wrong train station on a wet night when it was too late for them to get transport or book a hotel so that they had to walk several miles home in the pouring rain. Otherwise, you may struggle to obtain compensation under this head of loss unless you can show that the inconvenience would have been contemplated by the defaulter if the contract was broken and the contract was related to your personal or family life.

When the claim is not for breach of contract but for what is known as a tort – say for the negligent driving of a car – you will normally get compensation for the inconvenience of having to travel around by public transport instead of using your vehicle because it is off the road due to damage and you have not hired an alternative. And on a claim for what the law calls nuisance – excessive and unreasonable noise from the trombone in the flat above or a disgusting pong from next door – compensation for inconvenience and probably some annoyance thrown in will normally come your way. But courts almost invariably balk at awarding compensation after a road accident for the innocent party's inconvenience in having to deal with insurers, repairers, hirers and the rest, on the basis, as one circuit judge put it, that this was all part of the rough and tumble of being involved in an accident (although this should not eclipse the fact that the innocent driver would be entitled to compensation for the cost of postage, telephone calls and other out of pockets which post-accident arrangements usually involve).

Mental distress

For breach of a contract, you won't generally score compensation for mental distress so if you suffer mentally because the computer for your work was delivered weeks too late, that's no good (although loss of income because you were computerless might be available). You may also be able to recover compensation for alarm, distress or physical inconvenience or discomfort under the Consumer Protection from Unfair Trading Regulations 2008 as amended (see chapter 64). There is a massive exception to this general rule on mental distress compensation and that is under a contract for what judges call *pleasure, relaxation, piece of mind or freedom from molestation*. Mental distress compensation is typically awarded in lousy holiday claims where it all started with the 1973 case of solicitor Mr Jarvis. He paid £63.45 for a fortnight away at a house party in Switzerland over Christmas and the new year with a special resident host and a hotel owner who supposedly spoke English. The travel company's brochure promised all manner of delights including a welcoming party on arrival, afternoon tea and cake, a yodelling evening, a bar that would be open several days a week and a great time. In the event, there were only 13 guests in the first week and none in the second. There was no welcome party; no representative for the second week; the tea was dry nut cake and there were some crisps thrown in; the yodeller evening consisted of a local man in his working clothes singing a few songs very quickly; the bar was open on only one evening; and the hotel owner did not speak English. Just a flavour. There was more. The Court of Appeal ruled that Mr Jarvis should have compensation not simply for the diminution in the value of the holiday but for disappointment, distress, upset and frustration. It has since been established that the amount of this compensation should not be linked to the cost of the holiday so, if it was justified on the facts, you could be awarded more for a couple of weeks' hell at Knobbly Knees Holiday Camp than on The Queen Victoria Luxury Floating Hotel.

This massive exception could well also apply, for example, to claims for ruined weddings, chronic wedding photographs, lack of health club facilities and wrongly dyed hair (green instead of black).

For a non-contract case, the general position is that compensation for mental distress will not be recoverable. The exception is for some cases (but not those brought by a company) that mainly protect your reputation such as libel and some slanders and breach of confidence along with harassment and assault where compensation for injury to feelings is often collected.

Chapter 34

Package Holidays And Other Holiday Travel Gone Wrong

Come back to sue

Coronavirus willing, there's nothing to beat a package holiday: sunshine, surfing, plenty of others to join you in moaning. And the potential of a successful claim against the company you booked with if the contract has been broken. The big deal is that the company will be legally liable to you not only for their own sins but the sins of others who they have arranged should perform some part of the package on which they have messed up. That could be the hotel which poisoned you (or as the Supreme Court is likely to rule in a pending case, the hotel whose employee raped and assaulted you), the tour guide who never turned up or the transport firm for which you are still waiting. For this big deal, give thanks to 1992 regulations which were inspired by the European Union, amended six times and then replaced by the Package Travel etc Regulations 2018. Those 2018 regulations still apply although they have been tweaked by Brexit regulations made in the same year which cover insolvency protection and you would find more boring than my chapter on bankruptcy. Not only conventional packages booked through one company for one price are caught but now the more modern holidays, usually booked on the internet, where you select different elements of the holiday, like flight and hotel, by way of a tailor made trip.

The regulations do not exclude the operation of the normal law about a package travel company or any other travel company breaking its contract with you. They add to that law by treating other obligations as being part of the contract. Here are some of the extras.

- If things have not gone as agreed, the company must put things right within a reasonable period unless that is impossible or would involve disproportionate costs BUT you should have informed them of the failure without undue delay. Where putting things right would be impossible or only possible at a disproportionate cost, the company must offer you an appropriate price reduction and compensation BUT not compensation as well as the price reduction if a third party unconnected with the package was to blame and this was unforeseeable or unavoidable or if things went wrong due to unavoidable and extraordinary circumstances.

- Where the company refuses to put things right, you can do so yourself and the company must reimburse the expense in doing so. This also applies where immediate action is required as, for example, where the hotel is full or has burnt down (so long as it was not you who took a match to it).

- Where, say, the company needs to fix you up at another hotel, the alternative must be of the same or higher standard than the hotel at which you were meant to have been staying. A similar principle applies to organising other substitute services. Should the standard of the package have dropped because of the lower standard of the substitute service then you must be allowed an appropriate price reduction.

- If things have gone badly wrong – we are looking here at what the regulations would regard as a 'substantial' under-performance of the contract – and the company has failed to put things right within a reasonable period, you don't have to continue to suffer purgatory but may end the holiday without paying any fee to the company for doing so. And, where appropriate, you may be entitled to a price reduction or compensation or both unless a third party or unavoidable and extraordinary circumstances were responsible for what has happened (as above).

- Should unavoidable and extraordinary circumstances mean that the company cannot get you home as agreed, it must bear the cost of necessary accommodation (of equivalent standard, if possible so, usually, not *The Fleapit Rest* for *The Ritz*) for generally up to three nights for you and your party. The three nights limit will not apply where you or a member of your party has reduced mobility, is pregnant or is in need of specific medical assistance and this was notified to the company at least 48 hours before the holiday started.

- The information which the company gives to you about the package before you sign up has been widened and extends to the kitchen sink. And you will have to be told that the agreement will amount to a package holiday protected by the regulations if that is the case – watch out for confirmation on this – and failure to disclose a package as a protected package will amount to a criminal offence.

- There's a cap on an attempt to increase the price of the package by more than 8% after you have signed up. Any increase, be it 8% or less, must be notified, with justification for it and a calculation, at least 20 days before the start of the holiday. Where the increase tops 8%, you are entitled to cancel without being charged for the privilege and to the return of any money you have paid over.

Post-holiday blues

Many holidaymakers have a go at easing the depression of a return home by litigating with the package travel company pending next year's break. If the claim is for gastric illness worth up to £25,000, you are expected to follow a pre-action protocol (see chapter 10). You will find it in the Civil Procedure Rules 1998 which you are probably sick of hearing about by now but that would not give you the right to make a bookreading vomit claim against the publishers of this book or me. Gastric illness claims have a high bar and package holiday companies took heart from comments in the Court of Appeal in 2017 by Lord Justice Leveson when he said: "I agree that it will always be difficult (indeed, very difficult) to prove that an illness is a consequence of food or drink which was not of a satisfactory quality, unless there is cogent evidence that others have been similarly affected and alternative explanations would have to be excluded." If you are unable to squeeze a claim like this into the county court small claims regime (see chapter 25), I would strongly recommend that you hire a solicitor to deal with it for you under a 'no win, no fee' agreement (see chapter 7). Where none of the firms dealing in this area will touch it on this basis then it is probably not worth pursuing.

For the more modest holiday claim, you might want to try your luck with arbitration or mediation through ABTA (abta.com) so long as the company is a member. Otherwise, get your letter off to the package travel company as you should normally do before launching court proceedings for any type of claim. And when they tell you to get lost because the holiday snaps you have provided to them at their request show the beams on the faces of yourself and your party to be wider than the Amazon River, you will be more than ready for that county court small claim. And what can you claim for? The difference in value between what was agreed you would get and what you actually got – call it 'diminution in value' damages to be smart; compensation for physical inconvenience and distress; compensation for mental distress, disappointment, upset and frustration; and compensation for financial losses you have suffered because of what went wrong, such as travelling expenses and additional cost of eating out instead of being poisoned by the hotel chef who last washed their hands in 1986. By the way, these very same heads of compensation can be sought in holiday claims across the board and so even where there was no package holiday and you signed up directly with the hotel and everyone else. You saw how it worked for Mr Jarvis in pre-package travel legislation days at chapter 33 (and, if you skipped that chapter, shame on you and I claim damages for my disappointment with you). In this category of case, there is an exception to the general rule that every person who is entitled to make a claim must sue in their own name. The person who made the booking can claim on behalf of themselves and the rest of their party. In the likely event they have fallen out – "I'm not going away with that bloody [please insert appropriate swearword/s] again" – it ought to be possible for individual claims to be started and for them to be heard together in due course.

Case no: 21P48999R

IN THE COUNTY COURT BUSINESS CENTRE

BETWEEN:

CLIVE TROUBLESORE Claimant

- and -

HOLIDAYS FROM HELL PLC Defendant

PARTICULARS OF CLAIM

1. *The claimant who is aged 76 claims on behalf of himself and his*

wife Mavis Troublesore who is aged 70.

2. At all material times the claimant and his wife were travellers and the defendant was a trader and organiser within the meaning of the Package Travel and Linked Travel Arrangements Regulations 2018 as amended ('the regulations').

3. By a contract in writing dated 1 June 2021 the claimant on behalf of himself and his wife entered into a written package travel contract ('the contract') with the defendant within the meaning of the regulations by which the defendant was to provide to the claimant the services specified therein including accommodation at the Wiggling Washtower Hotel, Cleethorpes, Lincolnshire ('the hotel') for seven nights ('the stay') with full board and coach travel to and from the hotel at a total price of £1,300.00.

4. The following were express terms of the contract and/or terms of the contract implied by what was the intention of the parties and so as to give it commercial efficacy and/or the regulations, namely that –

a. the hotel had and would continue to have throughout the performance of the contract a four-star rating;

b. the accommodation, facilities, food and beverages, cleanliness and hygiene at the hotel would be commensurate with a four-star rating;

c. the hotel was a two-minute walk from the promenade;

d. the hotel was in a quiet and peaceful location;

e. a complimentary bottle of fortified wine with a packet of dried prunes would be awaiting the claimant and his wife upon their arrival in their hotel bedroom;

f. a working lift was installed and operated at the hotel;

g. a tea-dance would be held each afternoon which would be exclusively open to guests staying under contracts with the defendant;

h. a dinner-dance with high-class cabaret was held at the hotel on Saturday nights; and

i. a massage and toenail-clipping therapist was available to visit guests by appointment.

5. Further and in the alternative, it was a term of the contract as implied by the Consumer Rights Act 2015 that the defendant would exercise reasonable care and skill in the recommendation, selection and monitoring of the services including the accommodation to be provided to the claimant and his wife.

6. Further and in the alternative, the acts and omissions relied on by the claimant in support of his claim for breach of contract, were due to the negligence of the hotel or its servant or agents for which the defendant is liable under the regulations.

7. In breach of the terms specified above and/or due to the negligence of the hotel or its servants or agents -

a. at no stage of the stay of the claimant and his wife were the accommodation, facilities, food and beverages and cleanliness and hygiene at the hotel commensurate with a four-star rating hotel;

Particulars

The common areas of the hotel and the bedroom allocated to the claimant and his wife were unclean. The reception had an unpleasant odour. The bed linen was badly stained. The bedroom curtains were torn. There was no plug in the bathroom sink. The bath was unclean and its plughole was stuffed with hairs. The guests' lounge was small and crowded and there was insufficient seating. Food was habitually served cold or lukewarm when it should have been hot. Waiting staff wore grubby outfits and frequently dropped plates of food onto the table and had their uncovered fingers in the food. The table allocated to the claimant and his wife had one short leg so that the table rocked.

b. the hotel was a 15 minute walk from the promenade;

c. the hotel was located on a busy main road and next to an iron foundry on one side and a Morris dancing practice centre on the other;

d. no complimentary wine or prunes were provided;

e. the lift was out of order throughout the stay and the promise of the hotel porter being available to carry guests up to their rooms never materialized;

f. a tea dance was held on one afternoon only during the stay at which the only music played was by an accordionist and trumpeter who were out of time with one another, the rest of the band having failed to appear and the event thereby being a shambles;

g. for the Saturday night dinner dance a harpist and drummer only performed to which it was impossible to dance and the room incorporating the dance floor was at the other end of the hotel building at which the dinner comprising a prawn cocktail and beef burger with tap water were served: the cabaret comprised a fire eater who ignited the room's curtains involving the summary termination of their act and the forced exit of guests;

h. the pre-booked therapist for one session for each of the claimant and his wife was inexperienced, having trained through an online three-hour course, and incompetent, performing a useless massage, and had no experience in toenail clipping, offering the claimant and his wife an ear syringe in lieu which offer was declined.

8. As a result of the matters set out at paragraph 7 above, the claimant and his wife have suffered injury, loss and damage.

Particulars

The value of the package was substantially diminished and the claimant and his wife derived little enjoyment from it. On the contrary, they suffered distress, disappointment, upset and frustration throughout their stay causing sleeplessness, tearfulness, loss of appetite and lethargy and these reactions and feelings continued for two months following their return home. This was their first holiday for six years which they had eagerly awaited.

And the claimant claims:

a.   damages limited to £5,000.00;

b.   interest under section 69 of the County Court Act 1984 for such period and at such rate as shall be just; and

c.   costs.

I believe that the facts stated in these particulars of claim are true. I understand that proceedings for contempt of court may be brought against anyone who makes, or causes to be made, a false statement in a document verified by a statement of truth without an honest belief in its truth.

(signed) Clive Troublesore

Claimant

Dated 14 July 2021

And whatever happened to those flight cancellation and delay compensation rules?

Calm down, readers. They are still there post-Brexit but you will now be compensated in sterling rather than euros. And they have been given a boost by a ruling of the Court of Appeal in March 2021 in a case called *Lipton v City Flyer Ltd*. The only way an airline can escape paying out compensation for a cancellation or delay claim which otherwise qualifies is to prove – it's for them to do the proving – that the cancellation or delay was due to an 'extraordinary circumstance' which they couldn't have avoided by taking all reasonable measures. The ruling establishes that the illness of the flight captain which has started before they were due to clock on for work will not amount to an 'extraordinary circumstance' capable of getting the airline out of trouble. The same principle would apply to the illness of any other airline worker which impacted on the decision to cancel or delay the flight. It would also apply, probably with even more force, if the illness started after clock in. The airline might still try and argue that the court should look at when, why and how the worker became ill but the court can usually be expected to give this argument short shrift, particularly if the airline fails to produce any medical records for the allegedly sick worker.

You may well have been refused compensation by an airline in a staff absence case and so abandoned the claim. If you never started court proceedings, you can revive the claim now on the strength of this Court of Appeal ruling. And you have up to six years from when the flight was cancelled or delayed within which to start county court proceedings against the airline.

Chapter 35

The Litigant In Person's Bill

And why not?!

Legal costs are not the exclusive preserve of the winning party who was legally represented. Yes, you Mr, Mrs, Ms or Mx Nobody who acted in person – with or without a lawyer in the background – can claim costs just like the winner with a legal entourage. You are known as a litigant in person. Some procedural practice directions may call you a self-represented party but that title is out of fashion now. You can ask for costs if you win (you could ask for them if you lose but you would almost certainly be laughed out of court) and you will get them if a legally represented party would have got them in your shoes. You won't get paid as handsomely as a lawyer. However, your potential is habitually underestimated by lawyers on the other side and it is as well to keep them informed on how that potential is clocking up. As they try and intimidate you with costs budgets and costs estimates going through the roof, offer them a taste of what it might cost their client if they actually lost. It will give them something to think about.

How much?

Steady on. First, let's look at the work you have done and the time you have spent on the case for which you can be remunerated. If a lawyer would have had to do the work and spend time on it then you can claim for it and generally at the set rate of £19 per hour. This, for example, can catch preparing the claim form and particulars of claim, reading and considering the defence, preparing your list of documents and witness statements and considering those sent to you by the other side, preparing for the final hearing and attending at court including getting there and back. We might be looking at 20 hours plus on these items alone. There is one important caveat. You cannot collect more than two-thirds of what a lawyer would have collected if they had represented the loser so if you are a particularly slow reader and claim 480 hours for perusing the other side's documents you may run into trouble. You can also claim for the expenses you incurred (we call them *disbursements* in the law) so long as they would have been allowed if a lawyer had incurred them and the two-thirds limitation does not apply to these expenses. This could cover court fees, the cost of medical and other expert reports, travelling expenses and payments you have reasonably made for legal services in the case which might include taking advice from a lawyer and even having a lawyer to advocate for you at court. And you can sling in the expense of getting a lawyer, costs lawyer or a law costs draftsman to help you with your costs claim.

Should the time you have spent on the case have actually lost you more than £19 per hour then you can claim the higher amount. You would need to send to the court and the other side any written evidence you were intending to rely on to prove the loss at least 24 hours before the relevant hearing. This could take the form of a suitable letter from an accountant or employer.

On winning at a fast track trial, in addition to these rules applying to the work you have done up to the trial date, there is a special allowance for the day of the trial. Tell the judge you are claiming it under the Civil Procedure Rules 1998 rule 45.39(5). If you can prove any financial loss for the day, you will collect two-thirds of a sum within the range of £485 and £1,650, depending on what the claim was worth: if you can't prove any financial loss, you will collect £19 per hour. Unnecessarily complicated, I know – but nice.

Statement of costs

If you intend to ask for costs at a hearing, you should complete form N260 (access at gov.uk/government/collections/court-and-tribunal-forms). It is not ideal for a litigant in person but follow it as closely as possible. Ignore the certificate close to the end. The form has changed in recent times. Ensure you use the latest version which has a "schedule of work done on documents" at the very bottom. If you want to be ultra cocky, you can instead use form N260A for any hearing which takes place before the final hearing or trial or form N260B for the final hearing or trial. These two forms are being tried out. If the printers of this book have gone on a prolonged tea break and you are reading it in or after July 2021, the use of the trial forms instead of form N260 may well have been made permanent and compulsory. The party against whom you hope to ask for your costs and the court must have a copy of whichever form you use at least 24 hours before the time fixed for the hearing or, if the hearing is a fast track trial, at least two days beforehand. If you fail to comply with these requirements then the amount of costs you are awarded may be reduced – on a bad day to nil!

Small claims

None of this directly applies when you win a small claim (see chapter 25). Nevertheless, it could have some indirect relevance on winning and being able to persuade the court that the loser has behaved unreasonably and so should be deprived of the costs protection which generally applies to small claims cases.

> "Judge, I have put a lot of sweat, toil and time into preparing my case before you today. If this was a fast track or multi-track case, I would be entitled to £19 an hour for my time without having to prove I had suffered any financial loss by sitting up to midnight every night for the past two months pouring over Breaking Law*. Would you rule that my opponent has behaved unreasonably and award me costs against him at the same rate – say £19 an hour for a minimum of ten hours?"

*On second thoughts, better keep quiet about *Breaking Law*.

Not so small claims

In fact, claims worth more than £25,000 and up to £10 million. These will generally be allocated to what is called the multi-track and the procedures applied to them will be more detailed. They may have started in the High Court, or have been transferred there by the county court, and so be tried by a High Court judge. However, the majority will have been started in the county court and be tried by a circuit judge although quite often by a district judge instead. We are looking at fine dining as against a bacon sandwich. The stakes are higher with a multi-track case because of the amount of money in issue and because of the greater amount of preparatory work which has to be put into the case as reflected in the costs of the parties. In most multi-track cases, the court will make a 'costs management order' at an earlyish stage of the proceedings which is designed to ensure the parties plan in advance what they are spending on the case – it will need to be reasonable and proportionate – and that they keep within their budget. They are required to produce a detailed budget form which may be approved by the court as it is or reduced after the other party has attacked it. There's a name for the form of budget – Precedent H (again, access at gov.uk/government/collections/court-and-tribunal-forms) – which is at least a better name than Peregrine, unless you are a falcon,

You, as a litigant in person, are not required to produce a budget but will see the other side's Precedent H and can argue that it is too high. The reason you might want to do this is that, if you lose the case, the probability is that you will be ordered to pay those costs. You will find it an uphill struggle to get the winner's bill against you reduced if they have not exceeded their budget, so attack sooner to strengthen the possible attack later.

Although I have never known it to happen (but remember, I don't go out much), the court can order a litigant in person to produce a Precedent H of their own costs. The Royal Bank of Scotland applied for such an order in a High Court case against it by litigants in person in November 2020. It failed. However, the judge accepted that he had the power to order one. The question the judge had to decide was whether there was a significant benefit to the bank in having the form when weighed against the difficulties faced by litigants in person in seeking to estimate the costs necessary to go into the budget in a way which made the figures realistic. But it may be to your advantage as a litigant in person to consent to an order that you produce a Precedent H or even ask the court to order you to do so. Indeed, it may be to your advantage to volunteer a Precedent H to the other side without an order requiring it which would not have to be agreed by them or approved by the court. Why? Because, if it is going to be for a substantial sum, it could scare the pants off the other side and make them apply their mind to the potential bill for them if they lose the case! It is not uncommon for legally represented parties to say to themselves: "It doesn't matter if I lose. Snodgrass is a litigant in person. All I'd have to pay them is their bus fare to get to and from court. That's no deterrent. Let's fight on."

Snodgrass may have a lawyer advising in the background; may lose mega earnings as they devote themselves to preparing the case and complying with court orders; and may intend to instruct a senior barrister on a direct access basis to advocate for them at trial. All this could be reflected in the budget. The only consideration against is that the budget, as explained, could put them in a straitjacket if they won and limit them to the budgeted total.

Once a budget has been approved by the court, it can be varied by the court to take account of factors that have developed since it was produced.

Pipeline alert

Legislation is likely which would fix the amount of costs that a winner can generally extract from the loser in cases involving a value of up to £100,000. This would be under a so-called 'fixed recoverable costs' regime which already applies to a limited extent to certain cases and steps in civil proceedings. This could happen in October 2021: perhaps a little later. I'll keep you posted on my blog.

Chapter 36

Court Error Compensation

HMCTS blunder money

I don't know how to say this.....pause for embarrassment.......further pause for checking nobody is watching or listening.......coast looks clear.......in very soft voice......sometimes court staff make mistakes and the court user (otherwise punter otherwise party to proceedings) suffers financial loss as a result. It happens in the best of organisations. It tends to happen a bit more in the court service for the reasons I have already identified. To be fair, some of you swines can give the staff a very hard time – "I wrote yesterday asking for an order that Boris Johnson be subpoenaed to attend my trial and for permission to bring my Rottweiler to court to speak on my behalf and for a blanket to be provided just in case he pees on the floor and for an interpreter because swearing is the only language I speak and I haven't heard back yet. What the hell is going on?" This can hold them up and make them upset.

When a member of court staff tells you to turn up to the wrong hearing centre for your case or does not notify you of a hearing date for your case or fails to send you a copy of a crucial court order or makes your divorce final when you asked for it to be cancelled because you had become reconciled or wrongly notifies your employer that it must dock your salary for a debt against you when in fact there was no such debt or you attended court for your hearing but the judge wasn't there as they had gone on holiday or loses your case file or or or... And when the result of the error is to cause you loss or just irritation, you can make a complaint and, if appropriate, claim for compensation to Her Majesty's Courts & Tribunals Service (HMCTS) which makes up for the fact that you won't be able to sue them in the court as you might a commercial organisation for poor performance. You will be relieved and possibly surprised to know that there is no court fee payable when you take the step of complaining. It's useful to use complaint form EX343QA which you can download at government/collections/court-and-tribunal-forms.

Here's the blow. You can't use this route for complaining about the judge. So there. HMCTS has a leaflet nicknamed EX343 which explains what you can do if you are unhappy with its service. It tells you about the complaints procedure. It does not mention compensation. I think it should.

The complaint and claim should go to the hearing centre at which the case is being or has been conducted or to the head of the customer service team at the county court business centre where guilt rests with the handling of an online claim. You should get a meaningful response within ten working days or an explanation within that time frame as to why the response will take longer. If you are dissatisfied with the response whenever it comes – and you could make a second complaint if the response does not come within a reasonable period – you may take your complaint to the Customer Service Team, HMCTS Post Point 10.34, 102 Petty France, London SW1H 9AJ which should come back to you within 15 working days.

And that's exactly where Clive Gold went (no relation to Clive Troublesore but a brother of that judge Stephen Gold who has been known to dispense advice to various members of his family which he is normally told is wrong and, I hasten to add, for no reward although Clive did once buy Stephen lunch after a notable success). In one of Clive's money online claims, the court committed almost every conceivable administrative blunder possible. In this instance, Clive's complaint went to the operations manager at the online centre who saw only good in what admin had perpetrated. Clive escalated his complaint to the Customer Service Team on the grounds that the operations manager had "ignored the majority of the points of complaint and such conclusions as he has reached are irrational and/or fail to reflect the evidence." That did the trick in that there was a 'hands up' to some, but not all, of the cock ups and this which now appears in a mounted frame on Clive's toilet wall: "...I believe HMCTS' handling of your complaint could have been better....If you would accept the total sum of £50 please let me know..." He did accept.

If you are still doing your nut after Post Point 10.34 has looked at the complaint, the next step should be to make contact with your MP and ask them to refer your complaint to the Parliamentary and Health Service Ombudsman who can recommend to HMCTS that it pays you compensation. You cannot go to the Ombudsman directly.

You should back up a claim for compensation with documentary proof where available although consideration is to be given to making a monetary payment to you where mistakes have had a serious or significant impact on you even though you cannot show that a financial loss has been suffered. This could mean a payment if errors have led to a sustained period of distress or anxiety which has affected your health or severe embarrassment or damage to your reputation. If you should have received some money from the court and the court has delayed paying it over, you may claim for any interest you have lost as a result. In one case, because HMCTS delayed and generally messed up where it was dealing with the enforcement of maintenance arrears due to an ex-wife from the ex-husband, arrears spanning some three and a half years accrued. Part of the loss made up by HMCTS was the interest at the prevailing rates which the ex-wife would have earned had she invested the money if it had been efficiently collected.

Between £250 and £300 has been paid where a party was extremely upset and concerned as their personal and sensitive information including bank details and pension arrangements had been sent in error to someone else. And again where another party had been turned down for a mortgage because the entry of a judgment at the Register of Judgments, Orders and Fines had not been cancelled when the judgment itself was cancelled and the party suffered a lot of inconvenience. There was delay before a mortgage could be obtained.

Claims by solicitors for work done and expenses incurred by their client because of court maladministration are sometimes made albeit not as often as might be justified. When made they can be substantial. Compensation then will be based on the solicitors' hourly charging rates according to where they are located, the qualifications of the person who was handling the case in the office and possibly the type of case.

Chapter 37
Money Wrongly Received
Estoppel does you good

"*Mavis.*"

"*Yes, Clive.*"

"*My bank statement says I'm three grand in the black. And I thought I would have to tap up Uncle Ted for a grand. Must have been that life policy that paid out. Tell you what. Let's try out that new five star place in the New Forest for a week.*"

"*What with the spa?*"

"*Yeh and full body massages, stark naked. I'll have some of that.*"

"*You're a dirty beast, Troublesore.*"

Your bank wrongly credits your account. Your former employer overpays you on your final salary. You were expecting a cheque but it's for a couple of zeros too many. It was all down to a mistake but with computers giving the orders and staff thinking about what time *I'm a Celebrity* is on tonight, mistakes like this are as common as a cup of tea. Do you have to pay the money back? Possibly not.

Enter the defence of *estoppel by representation*. By making the payment, the payer was representing that you were entitled to it and the lot of it and should now be debarred from arguing to the contrary. You relied on that representation. You have altered your position because of the payment and so acted to your detriment and it just wouldn't be 'on' for you to have to make a refund. That's how it goes. In order to escape repayment, you would need to prove that you had spent the money in question or committed yourself to do so in an exceptional and irretrievable way, believing that it was yours to do so. Buying this book wouldn't be enough, as commendable as your action has been (and if you're reading this in a library, do us a favour and order a copy, eh?) as I know you would have done that anyway. We are really looking at some expenditure which, but for the money in question, you would never have incurred.

Has this defence ever worked? Yes, it has and I'm not teasing. In an 1825 case, a bank fed a customer's account with excessive sums over some five years as a result of which he spent more than otherwise he would have done. Bank lost. In a 1950 case Lloyds Bank over-credited a customer's account. She saw what was going in from her statements, relied on them as being accurate and spent more. Bank lost. In a 1983 case, Avon County Council overpaid a sick employee by £1,007 during an absence from work which spanned nearly two years. Of the £1,007, he spent £546.61 including £53.50 on clothes from *Burtons* and £130 by way of deposit on a car taken on HP. The Court of Appeal ruled that not only was he free from an obligation to repay what he had spent and could account for but the Council had to whistle for the balance too.

And because the recipient may usually be hard put to say precisely where every penny has gone, this all or nothing approach will usually apply. But not always. In 2000 Philip Collins Ltd (*"Yeh, it was him, Mavis. Phil Collins, the singer"*) was after clawing back the royalties it had overpaid two musicians against future royalties they would become entitled to when it was thought they had performed on all 15 tracks of *"Serious Hits...Live!"* whereas they had only performed on three of them. The High Court ruled that just one-half of the royalties – so around £14,000 – and not the lot could be clawed back because the musicians had changed their position by increasing their level of outgoings after they were paid and it would be inequitable to require them to suffer a clawback of the entirety of the money. A defence here of change of position rather than the not dissimilar defence of *estoppel by representation* and being partially successful.

You will fail in your *estoppel* defence if you knew the money had been paid by mistake before you spent it and probably also if you suspected the mistake but turned a blind eye. And where you knew of the mistake and spent away, that could land you in the wrong sort of court – a criminal court and on a charge of theft. The prosecution would need to show you had been dishonest. If you were a jury member at a Crown Court trial in one of these cases, how would you cast your vote? In the 1988 case of a Bristol man who had been earning £100 per week, the jury heard that his building society had wrongly credited his deposit account with a cool £20,000. He protested that the money was not his. Staff insisted it was. So he used about half the money to refurbish his council flat, buy a new car along with a dog and some tropical fish, take a holiday and settle some outstanding bills. When the building society discovered that another investor with the same name should have had the money, the police were brought in and the man was charged with 20 offences of theft. The jury acquitted him of them all.

In the same year, a sales representative was acquitted of stealing £18,700 from her employers who had increased her wages tenfold thanks to a computer error. She spent it on meals, clothes and holidays. She testified that she believed the money had been compensation for an injury at work.

Now say you have come by money which you thought was yours to deal with but no representation has been made to that effect? Mr Troublesore's brother Cedric steals £10,000 from his boss and loses it at the tables at your casino. Being a philanthropic casino proprietor and hoping this might get you into the next Queen's Honours List you give the £10,000 to charity. Can Cedric's boss get the £10,000 back from you? In this situation you can seek to rely on the defence of *change of position* as in the Phil Collins case (see above) which is more flexible than the *estoppel* defence. You would have to persuade the court that the injustice of requiring you to repay outweighs the injustice of denying repayment.

Case no 21P0000678

IN THE COUNTY COURT MONEY CLAIMS CENTRE

BETWEEN

WHITEWASH LIMITED Claimant

- and -

CLIVE TROUBLESORE Defendant

DEFENCE

1. The defendant admits that between on or about 6 January 2021 and 14 July 2021 the claimant credited his account with Dodgy Bank plc with the total sum of £14,260.18 by the payments ("the payments") alleged in the Particulars of Claim.

2. The defendant denies that he is liable to make restitution to the claimant for the payments or any part of them or that he is liable to the claimant to pay any interest as claimed.

3. The defendant says that by making the payments the claimant was representing to him that he was entitled to them; that the defendant believed he was so entitled; and in consequence and in good faith, he acted to his detriment by changing his position. Accordingly, the defendant says that the claimant is estopped from denying such entitlement and from recovering the payments or any part of them.

4. In the alternative, in the event that the Court decides that no representation was made by the claimant that the defendant was entitled to the payments, the defendant says that at all times the defendant acted in good faith and changed his position in consequence of believing that he was entitled to the payments so that it would be an injustice for him to be ordered to make restitution of the payments which injustice would outweigh any injustice (which is denied) which the claimant would suffer if restitution was not ordered.

5. The particulars of the defendant's change of position are that:

[set out details of payments made which would not otherwise have been made and any other ways in which you assert you have acted to your detriment in believing that the money was yours]

[add, if necessary – "These are the best particulars the defendant can give. The defendant cannot now recall how the balance of the payments was applied but it his case that he generally changed his position in respect of them."]

I believe that the facts stated in this defence are true. I understand that proceedings for contempt of court may be brought against anyone who makes, or causes to be made, a false statement in a document verified by a statement of truth without an honest belief in its truth.

(signed) Clive Troublesore

Defendant
Dated 14 July 2022

Chapter 38

Company Down Drain Owing You Money And Laughing

Getting the directors to pay

Enormously gigantic companies: itsy bitsy teeny weenie companies. It makes no difference. The general rule is that the company's directors are not personally responsible for the company's debts or breaches of contract. A notable exception is a director who has been directing at a time when he was disqualified from doing so or had given an undertaking not to do so because they had previously been up to no good. Generally, then, it is pointless claiming against a director for money owed to you by their company no matter how diabolical their behaviour towards you may have been. It is equally pointless to play the common trick of bringing proceedings against a named managing director with whom you have been corresponding about the jar of pickled onions containing a set of false teeth which you bought from their company. You will lose.

Breaking down the wall of immunity

Surely, you say, there must be some situations in which the directors can be made personally liable when the company has gone bust with no hope for you of recovering from its assets what you are owed or more than one new pence of it? Of course there are but you will need tenacity. Here goes.

The phoenix company

If a company has gone bust (insolvent liquidation, should you want to be posh), another company must not re-use the bust company's name or another name which is so similar to that of the bust company as to suggest that the two companies are associated (for example, *Whitewash Ltd/Whitish Wash Ltd*; *Breaking Law Ltd/Broken Law Ltd*; *Air Equipment Co Ltd/Air Component Co Ltd*). Any name used during the 12 months before the first company went down the drain will be relevant. And for five years from the date of insolvent liquidation (alright, I've gone posh), no one may be involved without the court's permission in the management of the second company as a director or in any other direct or indirect way. If they are so involved they will be liable for the second company's debts which have been incurred during that involvement as will someone who allows themselves to be used as a 'front man'. If you are a creditor of the second company you can make a claim against them in their own name. You'll find the relevant law in sections 216 and 217 of the Insolvency Act 1986. A lovely read.

Case no 21P0000678

IN THE COUNTY COURT MONEY CLAIMS CENTRE

BETWEEN

CLIVE TROUBLESORE Claimant

- and -

BERNARD TRYON Defendant

PARTICULARS OF CLAIM

1. The claimant claims against the defendant under section 217 of the Insolvency Act 1986 ("the Act").

2. On 26 January 2020 Whitewash Ltd ("the first company") went into insolvent liquidation. During the immediately preceding 12 months, the defendant was a director of the first company.

3. From 5 January 2021 the defendant has been a director of or has otherwise been involved in the management of Whitish Wash Ltd ("the second company").

4. On 14 July 2021 the second company agreed to sell to the claimant a suite of furniture ("the suite") for the price of £5,500.00. ("the agreement"). It was a term of the agreement that the suite would be delivered by the second company to the claimant on 20 July 2021 and that time was of the essence. The claimant paid to the second company on 14 July 2021 the full purchase price of £5,500.00 by cheque which was duly presented by the second company and paid out on.

5. In breach of the agreement the second company failed to deliver the suite to the claimant on 20 July 2021 and has since failed to respond to numerous requests by the claimant to make delivery and has refused or neglected to provide the claimant with any explanation for non-delivery.

6. On 2 August 2021 the claimant notified the second company by email that he terminated the agreement for non-delivery of the suite and demanded the immediate return of £5,500. The second company has failed to repay any sum to the claimant.

7. At all material times Whitish Wash Ltd was a prohibited name within section 216(2) of the Act in that it was so similar to Whitewash Ltd as to suggest an association with Whitewash Ltd and on and since 5 January 2021 the defendant has accordingly acted in contravention of section 216(2) of the Act thereby rendering him personally liable to the claimant for the return of the said sum of £5,500.

The claimant claims:

a. return of the price of £5,500.00;

b. interest on the sum of £5,500.00 pursuant to section 69 of the County Courts Act 1984 from 20 July 2021 to 4 September 2021 at the rate of 8%, the daily rate of interest being £1.21 and thereafter interest at the daily rate until judgment or earlier payment; and

c. costs.

I believe that the facts stated in these particulars of claim are true. I understand that proceedings for contempt of court may be brought against anyone who makes, or causes to be made, a false statement in a document verified by a statement of truth without an honest belief in its truth.

(signed) Clive Troublesore

Defendant

Dated 14 September 2022

Fraudulent and wrongful trading

When a director has been up to monkey business before their company goes into insolvent liquidation, the company's liquidator may apply to the court for them to make a contribution towards its debts. The more money the liquidator can get in, the greater the chances of you and your co-creditors taking a holiday next year. The route to a court order is open only to the liquidator and not to you personally. That's why it is important that you give the liquidator as much information as you can about any company wrongdoings of which you are aware and encourage the other creditors to do likewise. This time you will have to delve into sections 213 and 214 of the Insolvency Act 1986 if you don't believe me.

What's needed is evidence that the company has carried on its business with the intention of defrauding creditors or for some other fraudulent purpose. The court can then order that anyone who was a party to this – it is not essential that they were a director – should cough up a suitable sum. Alternatively, what will be enough is evidence that a director – and this time it is only a director in the firing line – knew or ought to have concluded that there was no reasonable prospect that the company would avoid going down the drain. For example, the company might have continued to trade and notch up further debts or paid out a fat dividend to the director. The liability of the culpable director would be to pay a suitable amount. However, if the director can show that they took every step they ought to have taken to minimise the potential loss to creditors then they will escape liability and the director will not be responsible for wrongful conduct during the period 1 March 2020 to 30 June 2021 as a result of a temporary coronavirus suspension of the law that normally applies. It is not inconceivable that the period will be extended. The liquidator will know.

A liquidator's court application could be expensive. They won't do anything unless they know they are going to be paid for it and, if there is little in the kitty from the company's assets, from where are their costs going to come? From you and your co-creditors? Perhaps not an idea that appeals to you but here's another one which you can put to the liquidator. They could go to an insolvency funder who would take a transfer of a claim with legs on terms that would be negotiated. One of the prominent funding leaders in this field is Manolete Partner (manolete-partners.com) which is prepared to look at a variety of claims connected with director wrongdoing. What it was not prepared to do was to discuss with me the financial terms which might apply.

Big blow

The big blow is to directors who have been disqualified under the Company Directors Disqualification Act 1986 from being a company director or concerned in the management of a company or given an undertaking not to so act instead of a disqualification, because of their culpable behaviour as directors which makes them unfit for office. It is in the form of sections 104 to 106 and 108 to 110 (among others) of the Small Business, Enterprise and Employment Act 2015 – well they had to find somewhere to stick it all in – which catches director misconduct after 30 September 2015.

The court is given the power to order compensation in your favour where you have been caused loss due to the conduct of a person for which, following a company's insolvency (we are looking at liquidation or administration here), they have been disqualified or given an undertaking under the 1986 Act. Proceedings may be avoided or compromised if the person undertakes to pay the compensation. To be taken into account are the amount of the loss, the nature of the conduct and whether any other financial contribution has been made in recompense for the conduct. It is the Secretary of State who must take the initiative to go after the compensation and he has two years from disqualification or undertaking to bring proceedings. This liability may attack non-directors as well as directors. If the conduct of the person disqualified (or the person who has given a disqualification undertaking) came about because they followed the instruction or direction of a third party then the third party may also now be disqualified, as also may a director on the strength of an overseas conviction for an office concerning the promotion, formation or management of an overseas company.

The sort of conduct which can lead to disqualification – for between two and 15 years – is obtaining credit when the person knew that the company was in grave danger of going down the drain, acting incompetently, trading whilst insolvent and drawing money out of the company for their own benefit when insolvency was staring them in the face.

So to have any hope of getting your loss made good, what you need is misconduct by (usually) a director PLUS that director's disqualification or an undertaking in the place of disqualification PLUS the Secretary of State being persuaded to go after the director for the benefit of creditors like yourself unless, of course, the director agrees to cough up without proceedings. As with fraudulent or wrongful trading (see above), the liquidator should be informed by you and other creditors of all misconduct on a director's part you know about in the hope that disqualification proceedings are brought. The Insolvency Service set up an online tool called the Conduct Assessment Service in April 2016 to facilitate liquidators and official receivers reporting on misconduct by directors so that their disqualification can be considered.

The report has to go in within three months of the company's failure so you need to get on with passing on relevant information.

This relatively recent law is likely to be impacting. Former directors could be less inclined to put their hands up to a disqualification order or undertaking in its stead for fear that a compensation claim will be the consequence. And we may see aggrieved creditors approaching former directors for a compensation deal off their own bats to which those former directors might accede if they think that pressure will otherwise be put on the liquidator to encourage the Secretary of State to institute disqualification proceedings.

Chapter 39

Protection From Your Creditors

Thou shalt not harass me

You owe money. This is because of genuine hardship or because you are a distrustful piece of work, empty of morals and full of *Fosters*. Either way, the law protects you against the creditor who goes over the top in trying to extract from you what is rightfully due to them. They may be committing a criminal offence or gifting you a claim for damages – or both. And if they actually start civil proceedings against you which the law classes as malicious, that may give the opportunity to turn the tables on them and claim damages against them (see chapter 18).

Crime street

The Malicious Communications Act 1988 outlaws the sending of a threatening letter where the purpose is to cause distress and anxiety to the recipient or to anyone else who was intended to read it. It is a defence for the sender to show he believed the threatening letter was a proper means of reinforcing their demand. A separate offence is created by section 40 of the Administration of Justice Act 1970 which criminalises the making of demands which are likely to cause a debtor or their family alarm, distress or humiliation because of their frequency or the way they are made or any threat or publicity which goes with them. And completing this triumvirate are sections 1(1) and 2 of the Protection from Harassment Act 1997 which make it an offence to pursue a course of conduct which amounts to harassment so long as whoever was responsible knew or ought to have known that is what it did. Harassment includes alarming someone or causing them distress. Certain conduct could amount to more than one of these three offences, if not the lot.

Side roads

Your creditor's conduct may well break the rules of any professional body to whom they are answerable, like the Law Society in the case of a solicitor, the Institute of Chartered Accountants in the case of a chartered accountant or a trade association to which they belong. The Financial Conduct Authority would be interested in the malpractice of anyone involved in debt collection and could cancel the authority they need to carry on their business. Banks, building societies and credit card companies which go too far in their efforts to increase bonuses and profits may well be breaching the Lending Code which most of them will have agreed to observe and this would justify use of their internal complaints procedure and, if you are dissatisfied with the outcome, a complaint to the Financial Ombudsman Service which I have utilised (see chapter 9).

Route map

Your creditor is legally entitled to demand the payment of the debt. It would be quite in order for them to write a couple of letters, maybe make a few telephone calls or even knock on your door, always at reasonable hours, and ask you to pay up. The creditor may legitimately warn you of what can or will happen if you don't pay – a county court claim, a credit blacklisting if there is a judgment which goes unsatisfied and what means might be adopted to enforce the judgment. How far the creditor can go is a matter of degree.

If you believe the creditor just won't stop, you should write to them. This may do the trick and at the same time get rid of them for ever. The letter and any response will also be of evidential value should you find it necessary or to your likely financial advantage to make a civil claim against them.

> 149 Magnolia Crescent
>
> Twickenham
>
> KT89 4XZ
>
> 14 July 2021
>
> Dear Creditor
>
> I owe you £2,000 under invoice number 000000000000000000000698/x. Due to circumstances completely beyond my control and which I have repeatedly and fully explained both to your company and the succession of debt collectors you have sent to my home, I am in no position at the present time to settle the debt or make any proposals for payments by instalments and this is likely to be the situation for some while yet. I am advised that your conduct amounts to harassment under civil law and is also offends the criminal law. Unless you and your agents immediately desist from communicating with me otherwise than by service of properly constituted court proceedings, I shall institute proceedings against you for an injunction to restrain contact and for damages for harassment together with costs. I shall also take steps to report you for prosecution under the Malicious Communications Act 1988, section 40 of the Administration of Justice Act 1970 and the Protection from Harassment Act 1997.
>
> Yours faithfully
>
> Clive Troublesore

And now, ladies and gentlemen, we present a nice little earner

The Protection from Harassment Act 1997 not only makes harassment a crime but gives the person harassed – that could be anyone from the actual debtor to a current or former spouse, civil partner or cohabitee – the right to claim damages from the perpetrator and an injunction to forbid any repetition of their objectionable behaviour.

Ms Lisa Ferguson, a self-employed property investor, used to be a customer of British Gas Trading Ltd for the supply of her domestic gas. She left them.

Over the following five months she was subjected to letter after letter and threat after threat to cut off her supply, start legal proceedings against her and report her to credit reference agencies – all without justification. She said this caused her considerable anxiety. She wanted to bring British Gas to book so she made a county court claim for damages against them under the Protection from Harassment Act. They attempted to get the claim thrown out, arguing that it was so weak that it should be killed off before a trial (see chapter 21). The Court of Appeal would have none of it. It ruled in 2009 that the conduct complained of was capable of amounting to harassment and was oppressive and unacceptable. Then in 2013 the Court of Appeal upheld an award of £7,500 damages under the Protection from Harassment Act to a customer of Royal Bank of Scotland plc. She had exceeded her overdraft or credit limit on one or more of her accounts. Although she had made it plain that she did not want to speak to the bank, they spoke or attempted to speak to her over the phone on 547 occasions. The calls constituted intimidation and had been wholly unjustified. The existence of a debt did not give the creditor the right to bombard the debtor with calls. It was the right of the debtor to decide whether they wanted to discuss the matter with the creditor. Good stuff, eh?

Courts are likely to follow the damages guidelines set by the Court of Appeal in a case where a police officer who had been harassed and discriminated against by colleagues was entitled to compensation for injury to feelings (as distinct from compensation for psychiatric or similar personal injury). They said the most serious cases (where, for example, there had been a lengthy campaign of discriminatory harassment on the ground of sex and race) should command between £15,000 and £25,000. The middle band of between £5,000 and £15,000 should be used for serious cases which were not serious enough to fall within the top band. And awards of between £500 and £5,000 were appropriate for the less serious cases such as where the act of discrimination was an isolated or one-off occurrence. These figures would need to be updated to take account of inflation since 2002.

Let right be done

If you make a civil claim for Protection from Harassment Act damages and an injunction or either you will need to complete a part 8 claim form (see chapter 12 and the claim form is reproduced on page 335) and a written statement in support. If anyone at court tells you that this is not the right procedure then say: "May I respectfully refer you to rule 65.28 of the Civil Procedure Rules 1998" or "Look here, mate, you having a bad day? Take a gander at 65.28." Whichever you are more comfortable with, really. You will not be able to use the money claim online procedure. Unless you are urgently after an injunction – if you are, you must additionally complete an application for an injunction in form N16A in triplicate and include with the rest of your court papers – you should first send a letter to your harasser (see chapter 10). You could even back the letter up with a draft of the documents you will use if there is no settlement and you take the claim to court. That would look quite impressive and ought to convince the harasser that you mean business. Under no circumstances should you falsely suggest you have already started proceedings.

> "If my claim is not settled by you to my satisfaction then I shall institute proceedings against you and lodge with the court a claim form and supporting evidence in accordance with the draft documents, copies of which I enclose with this letter."

DETAILS OF CLAIM FOR PART 8 CLAIM FORM

1. At all material times the claimant has been indebted to the defendant in the sum of £7,500 for goods sold and delivered. Due to hardship for reasons beyond his control, the claimant has been unable to discharge the liability ("the liability").

2. Between 1 January and 30 June 2021 the defendant has pursued or caused to be pursued a course of harassing conduct towards the claimant with the intention of thereby forcing him to discharge the liability which has put the claimant in fear and caused him to suffer injury and loss.

The claimant claims:

a. an injunction to restrain the defendant from harassing the claimant and from contacting him in any way whatsoever except for the purpose of serving him with court proceedings brought against him by the defendant and for the purpose of complying with any order, rule of court or practice direction in the course of such proceedings and from instructing or encouraging any person to do so;

b. damages;

c. interest on damages at such rate and or such period as the court shall deem just; and

d. costs.

Dated 14 July 2021

(Signed) Clive Troublesore (Claimant)

Statement in support

IN THE COUNTY COURT AT PEARDROP

Case no 21P0000678

Claimant C Troublesore

1st CT1-CT3

14 July 2021

CLIVE TROUBLESORE Claimant

- and -

WHITEWASH LIMITED Defendant

I CLIVE TROUBLESORE state as follows:

1.   I live at 149 Magnolia Gardens, Twickenham, Middlesex KT89 4XZ ("the premises").

2.   I am a local authority pest control officer.

3.   I am the above-named claimant.

4.   On 16 December 2020 I purchased building materials and equipment from the defendant for £7,500.00. I was a long-standing customer of the defendant and it accepted my cheque for the full price. Several days before the purchase I had paid a cheque for £10,000.00 into my back account which I had received from a relative by way of repayment of a personal loan. I drew the £7,500.00 cheque against the £10,000.00 cheque. I had no reason to suppose that the £10,000.00 cheque would not clear. I was amazed and embarrassed to be informed by my bankers after my purchase and delivery of the goods that the £10,000.00 cheque had been returned marked "refer to drawer". I have since represented it but it has not gone through. As a result, I am not yet in a position to settle with the defendant although it is my earnest intention to do so.

5.   I accept that the defendant is entitled to take reasonable steps to recover what I owe it. However, the steps taken have been excessive and totally unreasonable.

6.   Between 1 January and 30 June 2021 the defendant:

a.   made numerous telephone calls to my home which often exceeded ten in a single day and which were frequently at unsociable hours;

b.   on six occasions made personal visits to my place of employment through its employees or other agents during the course of which they shouted various statements within the presence and earshot of my work colleagues concerning the liability such as that if I did not settle the liability within one week I would be imprisoned and that I would be debarred from following my employment as a pest controller;

c.   on twelve occasions made personal visits to my home through its employees or other agents who then threatened me, usually in the presence and earshot of my wife: for example, if I did not discharge the liability immediately my ears would be cut off, a "heavy" would parade up and down my street with a sandwich board attached to them proclaiming that "Troublesore is a Big Time Con Artist" and the amount of the liability would be quadrupled and carry interest on the increased sum calculated from 1 January 1189 at the rate of 100% compounded with monthly rests until payment; and

d.   sent 124 letters to me by post true copies of which I produce marked "CT1" containing demands for the discharge of the liability which were couched in threatening and intimidating terms and 12 of which purported to have come from the Lord Chief Justice of England and Wales.

7. Further particulars of each event or series of events relied on by me as constituting the defendant's harassing conduct are contained in the schedule to this statement.

8. As a result of the defendant's harassment of me, I have suffered injury to my feelings, depression and anxiety. I produce a true copy of the medical report of my GP* Dr Goodfor A Sicanote dated 13 July 2021 marked "CT2". I also suffered loss of earnings due to my absence from work because of my state of health attributable to the defendant's conduct in the sum of £648.19 net. I produce a true copy of the letter from my employer marked "CT3" in support of such claim.

[*It is worthwhile consulting your doctor whilst harassment persists not only because you may actually need a prescription but because the doctor's report is likely to be of evidential value in any civil claim you may bring. If the harassment is over or your symptoms have ceased, your doctor may still be able to prepare a report recounting what you have told them about the symptoms and expressing a view as to whether they find your account to be credible from a medical standpoint, having particular regard to any relevant medical history].

SCHEDULE as referred to in paragraph 7 above

[set out under numbered paragraphs and in chronological order, the date of each event or period of any series of events, a short description of what happened and, where applicable, the identity of the defendant's employee or other agent involved: where a very large number of incidents are relied on, a schedule of this kind should assist the judge to separate the various incidents and to quickly get a good appreciation of the facts you assert – you can always seek permission to expand on the schedule with a fuller statement if what you say happened is being denied by the defendant].

No	Date/Period	Event	Person involved for defendant
...	...	...	...
...	...	...	...
...	...	...	...

I believe that the facts stated in this witness statement are true. I understand that proceedings for contempt of court may be brought against anyone who makes, or causes to be made, a false statement in a document verified by a statement of truth without an honest belief in its truth.

(signed) Clive Troublesore

Claimant

Dated 14 July 2021

By the way

In response to your protocol letter of claim (see chapter 10) or in their defence, your creditor may seek to shift all blame onto their debt collectors saying, in terms, that the collectors are independent contractors who are required to act within the law and that your creditor did not know and could not reasonably have known the collectors were acting in the way alleged. In any proceedings, you would be entitled to see written communications (or records of them) passing between the creditor and the debt collectors. You could play safe by making the claim against both the creditor and the debt collectors and leave them to fight out liability between themselves. Otherwise, just claim against the creditor and, if their defence seeks to shift blame, add the debt collectors as second defendant at that stage. The claim form would then have to be amended to name the debt collectors as would the particulars of claim to show how they come into the picture. You would require the written consent for the amendments from the creditor or, if not forthcoming, you would have to apply to the court (on form N244) for its permission to amend.

In the amended particulars you would wish to add at paragraph 1 that the second defendant was instructed by the first defendant to collect the liability on its behalf. Then at paragraph 2, you would state: ".... the first defendant and/or the second defendant have pursued or caused to be pursued...." Finally, you would make consequential amendments by referring to "the first and/or the second defendant".

"It's your fault, you shouldn't have given me credit"

The argument that a debtor can blame their creditor for extending them credit and so bring about their financial downfall may sound like a crazy one but it has been tried. You would have an uphill struggle to successfully use it to resist a claim or make your own claim. In a 2008 case, a greyhound trainer who had been a pathological gambler sued William Hill Credit Ltd for nearly £2m he had lost with them on telephone betting. He had previously reached an agreement with the bookmakers that they would not accept telephone bets from him over a six month period. He wanted to be protected from himself. Because of that specific agreement, it was held that the bookmakers had been in breach of the duty they owed to him not to take the bets but the claim failed because if William Hill had turned him down he would probably have lost the money anyway with other bookmakers. The trial judge rejected the idea that a bookmaker owed a general duty of care to a customer to restrain them from gambling away their money: it was the specific agreement reached in the case that could have made the difference. But the judge did not exclude the possibility that a court might decide a bookmaker was legally responsible where the customer's behaviour had become so extreme as to demonstrate that their gambling was wholly outside their control. There could yet be a case which falls into this category although the gambler would still have to overcome any suggestion that they would have lost the money somewhere else. This "you shouldn't have given me credit" line could conceivably be adopted in a non-gambling context, say by a pathological borrower against a lender who was fully aware of the borrowers' weakness and it might even find favour with a court as part of an *unfair relationship* claim (see chapters 40 and 66).

Despite the setback of the greyhound trainer, a not dissimilar argument was put forward in 2015 by a man who had gambled away £2m on the roulette tables at London's The Ritz Hotel casino. He signed a cheque for that amount on one evening in return for gambling chips. The cheque was dishonoured and the casino sued him for the money. His defence included the argument that the casino had owed him a duty to take reasonable steps to ensure he was not harmed or exploited by their provision of gambling facilities. However, the trial judge rejected the gambler's evidence that he was suffering any gambling disorder at the relevant time and there was certainly no evidence that his gambling was outside his control.

If a gambler ever does succeed on this argument they would be highly vulnerable to a finding that they had contributed to their downfall which would lead to a reduction of any damages awarded against the gaming company.

Claim Form (CPR Part 8)

In the

Claim no.

Fee Account no.

Claimant

SEAL

Defendant(s)

Does your claim include any issues under the Human Rights Act 1998? ☐ Yes ☐ No

Details of claim *(see also overleaf)*

	£
Court fee	
Legal representative's costs	
Issue date	

Defendant's name and address

For further details of the courts www.gov.uk/find-court-tribunal.
When corresponding with the Court, please address forms or letters to the Manager and always quote the claim number.

N208 Claim form (CPR Part 8) (05.14) © Crown copyright 2014

N208 form - page 1

	Claim no.	

Details of claim *(continued)*

Statement of Truth
*(I believe)(The Claimant believes) that the facts stated in these particulars of claim are true.
* I am duly authorised by the claimant to sign this statement.

Full name

Name of claimant's legal representative's firm

signed _____ position or office held _____
　　　*(Claimant)(Litigation friend)　　(if signing on behalf of firm or company)
　　　(Legal representative's solicitor)

*delete as appropriate

Claimant's or claimant's legal representative's address to which documents should be sent if different from overleaf. If you are prepared to accept service by DX, fax or e-mail, please add details.

N208 form - page 2

Chapter 40
PPI
Mission for commission

PPI = payment protection insurance. That was the insurance you took out but did not realise you were taking out when you signed up for some credit agreement and which covered you if you fell under a bus or lost your brain through watching too much daytime television. You then spent the next ten years wondering what the direct debit payment for £30 per month which showed up on your bank statements was all about. You probably know as much about PPI as Boris Johnson knows about not cutting your hair. In fact, you probably took Martin Lewis's advice and made a successful PPI claim and blew the premium refund aeons ago.

Well, here's a different take on PPI. It relates to the commission which was probably paid to the credit company (be it a finance company or bank) by the insurance company for getting you to sign up for PPI. If the commission was excessive – and anything over one-half of a single payment premium or the total of monthly premiums could be regarded as excessive – and you were not told by the credit company that commission was being collected, how much it was or the true amount, then you may well be on strong ground for asking for some of the commission to be paid to you or the premiums you paid under the policy to be repaid to you. And if a demand to the credit company does not trigger a satisfactory payment then you could make a claim against it in the county court. The claim would be under sections 140 A–B of the Consumer Credit Act 1974 on the basis that what happened in respect of the secret commission created an unfair relationship between you and the credit company (see chapter 66 for how an 'unfair relationship' can be used against mortgage lenders). If the credit company has been actively misleading as opposed to simply staying mute about commission (for example, it falsely told you no commission was being paid or gave you an untruthful figure for it) you may additionally allege negligence or misrepresentation on its part.

If you have made a successful PPI claim and been repaid all of the premiums paid, you have reached the end of the PPI road. But if you have not been repaid the lot, it may not be too late to launch a second claim relating to commission. It will depend on whether or not the payment you accepted was in full and final settlement of all claims against the credit company arising out of the PPI. If your first claim was unsuccessful then the fact you had made it would not bar you making a county court unfair relationship claim based on excessive undisclosed commission.

Now, here's the big news. If you have bravely read what came before this chapter, you will remember that there are time limits for taking civil cases to court (see chapter 13). These limits apply to unfair relationship claims too. In the majority of situations, the PPI and the secret commission we have been looking at will go back many years. The time for making a claim for secret commission will be six years from when the agreement ended. In most cases, this would mean you were now too late – but for section 32 of the Limitation Act 1980. This says that the six years will not begin to run if some relevant fact (like secret PPI commission) has been deliberately concealed from you by the party you want to sue, where it was unlikely to be discovered for some time. Then, the six years will start when you discover the secret or could have discovered it with reasonable diligence.

And what was established in a major High Court case in March 2020 called *Canada Square Operations Ltd v Beverley Potter* was this. For the six year time limit to be postponed, it is enough that the credit company took the conscious decision to keep quiet about the commission. It was not necessary to show it had actively misled. In that particular case, the credit company, formerly known as Egg Banking plc, had collected commission of a cool 95% of an aggregate premium of just shy of £4,000 net of interest. The High Court upheld a county court decision to extend the limitation period where the claimant had only discovered that the commission had been paid eight and a half years after the credit agreement had ended and she could not with reasonable diligence have discovered the position earlier. In March 2021 the Court of Appeal upheld what the High Court had decided.

But watch for this trap. The credit company may argue that your time for making a claim should not be extended because, with reasonable diligence, you could have discovered earlier than you did that commission had been paid and all about it. In one case I dealt with as a judge, it was contended that anyone who had read the papers, or looked at social media, would have been well aware of the practice of large sums being paid over as commission and could have done something about it ages before. Your position may well be that you did not know about the commission and there was no reason for you to have been suspicious and to have made enquiries on the subject sooner than you did. It is vital that you tackle this point in your witness statement in support of any court proceedings you bring.

> To the Chief Executive
>
> Dodgy Bank
>
> Dear Chief Executive
>
> Credit agreement number BX50- 2AKJY6678910*
>
> *On 26 July 2006 I entered into the above-numbered regulated loan agreement with your company which was repaid on 26 July 2010. A payment protection insurance policy with Laughter Insurance plc was linked to the loan agreement. I was not told that the policy was optional. In fact, I was informed by your representative that your Bank would be unable to make the loan if I refused to take out the policy.*
>
> *I now have reason to believe that your Bank was paid a commission by or on behalf of Laughter Insurance plc for arranging the policy. I was never informed by your Bank or anyone else that such a commission was being paid. Had I been aware that it was payable then I am sat-*

isfied that I would have reconsidered the terms of the loan agreement which were being offered to me.

I hereby require you to disclose to me the amount of the above commission which your Bank did receive and when it was received. I no longer have a copy of the policy and so I additionally require you to disclose to me the aggregate amount of the premiums which I was required to (and did) pay under the policy. This information is required in connection with proceedings I propose to bring against the Bank under section 140A of the Consumer Credit Act 1974.

I request that you comply with my above requests within 21 days of the date of this letter. If you fail to do so, I shall be obliged to make a complaint to the Financial Ombudsman Service and/or issue a county court application for pre-action disclosure.**

Yours faithfully

Clive Troublesore

*If you no longer have a copy of the agreement or the agreement reference number then provide as much information as you can so that the agreement can be identified and records accessed.

**For a pre-action disclosure application, see chapter 15.

PARTICULARS OF CLAIM**

1. On 26 July 2006 the claimant entered into a loan agreement with the defendant which was regulated by the Consumer Credit Act 1974 ("the loan agreement") and a linked payment protection policy with Laughter Insurance plc ('the PPI agreement').

2. By the loan agreement the defendant lent the claimant the principal sum of £17,000.00 repayable over 48 months at an interest rate of 7.9%.

3. By the PPI agreement the claimant agreed with Laughter Insurance plc to pay an aggregate premium of £4,000.00.

4. Unbeknown to the claimant, the defendant received a commission from Laughter Insurance plc for the introduction of the claimant and setting up the PPI agreement of £3,800.00 representing 95% of the aggregate premium.

5. The claimant discharged her obligations under the loan agreement and the PPI agreement as and when the payments fell due and her account with the defendant was closed on 26 July 2010.

6. The claimant entered into the PPI agreement at the initiative of the defendant. At no stage prior to doing so or subsequently did the defendant inform the claimant that the PPI agreement or payment protection insurance was an option OR prior to entering into the PPI agreement the defendant informed the claimant that she was required

to enter into the PPI agreement if the defendant was to enter into the loan agreement AND/OR the defendant failed to inform the claimant prior to entering into the PPI agreement that the premium payable under it would be so payable as a lump sum and would be added to the principal sum lent under the loan agreement and attract interest AND/OR* the PPI agreement was of no benefit to the claimant whatsoever because (state reasons – for example, "the claimant at the date of the agreement and as was known to the defendant was self-employed and, further, remained self-employed and was likely to so remain throughout the duration of the PPI agreement whereas the claimant has ascertained since 26 July 2010 that the PPI agreement would only cover her for any inability to work as an employee.").

7. In view of the matters set out above, the claimant says that at all material times the relationship between the claimant and the defendant arising out of the loan agreement and/or the PPI agreement and/or the loan agreement taken with the PPI agreement was unfair for the purposes of section 140A of the Consumer Credit Act 1974.

AND the claimant claims:

a. an order for return of the premiums paid or payable by the claimant under the PPI agreement; and/or

b. an order for payment to the claimant of the commission received by the defendant from Laughter Insurance plc; and/or

c. an order for return to the claimant of such interest as was charged to the claimant on the PPI agreement premiums; and/or

d. interest on the above sums at such rate and for such periods as the court shall deem just; and/or

e. such other relief pursuant to section 140B of the Consumer Credit Act 1974 as the court shall deem just; and

f. costs.

I believe that the facts stated in these particulars of claim are true. I understand that proceedings for contempt of court may be brought against anyone who makes, or causes to be made, a false statement in a document verified by a statement of truth without an honest belief in its truth.

(signed) Clive Troublesore

Claimant

Dated 14 July 2021

*Adapt appropriately.

**These particulars of claim should accompany a claim form. There is a special procedure for these unfair relationship claims. It is set out in Practice Direction 7B of the Civil Procedure Rules 1998. The court should fix a hearing date for the claim when the claim form is issued. It is not essential for the defendant to put in a defence although it will normally do so if it intends to defend. Show me a financial business against whom an unfair relationship claim is made which does not defend (or start off defending) and I will show you a quiz show without any questions. If, as is likely, the defendant wishes to take the point that the claim is too late then it will need to do so in a defence. You do not need to deal with this point unless and until the defendant takes it. Should the point be taken then the court will almost certainly want you to respond to it in a written document called a 'reply'. Good name, eh? Where the claim is defended, it is virtually certain that the court will not fully deal with it at the first hearing but will then give directions for how the case should be prepared for a full hearing at a later date.

Chapter 41

Claiming On Your Credit Or Debit Card

The joy of equal responsibility or a chargeback

Imagine a scheme which enables you to go to your lender and saddle them with the sins of the seller of goods or supplier of services who has let you down on the ground that it was the lender's money, or some of it, which was used for the transaction. The engine of the car you have just bought conks out on the drive home. The furniture shop to whom you paid up front for a new suite goes bust. The self-catering chalet owner told you the place was a one-minute walk from the sea but it transpires it's a ten second hop from the sewer. The double glazing leaks and the installer never speaks.

There is such a scheme. It's in section 75 of the Consumer Credit Act 1974. Generally, the scheme applies when you paid for the goods and services using a credit card like Mastercard, Visa and American Express or a store card or finance was through a credit agreement for that particular transaction (even a credit sale or hire agreement though not a hire-purchase agreement).

And when the scheme applies, the credit card company or whoever else provided the finance is equally responsible with the trader for any false or fraudulent representation on which you relied in reaching an agreement with them and which has caused you loss or for any breach of contract (including selling goods which were of unsatisfactory quality or unfit for purpose or doing duff work). That doesn't let the trader off the hook. It means, though, that you can claim against – and, if necessary, sue – whoever provided the credit without bothering with the trader who may give you aggro by the loads and never satisfy a judgment. Of course, it's sniffle time for the credit provider but they were in the deal for the money, weren't they, and they have a right to reclaim from the trader whatever they are stuck with having to pay you. As it happens, they will probably try and get a judgment against the trader in the course of any proceedings you bring against the credit provider alone.

Have I ever used the system? Muggins here ordered a new desk through a newspaper ad and paid for it with his Barclaycard. Desk never arrived. Trader went down the financial drain. I claimed from Barclaycard the price of the desk plus the difference between the price I had paid (which, on the premise that the desk would be delivered, was relatively cheap) and the price I was going to have to pay to another trader for a comparable desk which was at least another £200. Barclaycard came up with the price alright but acted dumb on the rest of the claim. They knew as well as I did that they were liable not only for my direct loss but for what the law calls *consequential* loss like the extra I would have to expend on a comparable desk. For you that *consequential* loss might be distress and disappointment for a ruined holiday because of that no sea but plenty of sewer. Whatever the trader would have to pay you for the misrepresentation or breach of contract if your claim was against them alone, the finance supplier must pay you. Barclaycard eventually settled the balance of the claim for the extra I would have to pay – and did pay for the comparable desk on which I am now tapping out this story. Thank you Barclaycard.

I hate to do this but there are some exceptions to the scheme applying. Please don't be hard on me.

The scheme:

- WON'T APPLY unless the cash price for the goods or the service you are complaining about was more than £100. £99.99 or £100 won't do. Buying a selection of items which are all individually priced under £100 won't do in respect of any of those items even though the total bill came to more than £100.

- WON'T APPLY if the cash price for the goods or services was more than £30,000 but do not despair because section 75 A may apply (see below).

- WON'T often APPLY if another company comes into the picture – an intermediary – and is involved in processing payments like PayPal, Amazon Marketplace, Worldpay and Google Pay. It will depend on the precise contractual arrangement between the other parties although you may not always be aware of the intermediary's involvement. If you make a section 75 claim against the credit card company and it reckons it is off the hook because of the intermediary's involvement, it will be quick off the mark to say so and you can always test its assertion with a complaint to the Financial Ombudsman's Service (see chapter 9) which is well used to deciding this issue. Its decisions have gone both ways. They say that on such a complaint they carry out a full investigation and establish what each party in the chain was responsible for and the activity they were actually carrying out. This is done on a case by case basis. The intermediary may well have a buyer protection scheme to compensate for the loss of section 75 rights but, generally, this will be inferior to those rights. Take PayPal's scheme. It requires that the seller and buyer are to take any action it specifies in connection with a dispute and entitles PayPal to make a final decision in favour of the other party if there is a refusal to comply. In the 2020 case of *PayPal Europe Sarl Et Cie SCA v Jivoui* the buyer had invoked the scheme with a view to getting a refund of the price for a defective laser machine from a Chinese seller. PayPal directed that the machine be returned to an address it provided which was mainly in Chinese script. The buyer contacted the seller direct who provided his address in Latin script and the laser was sent there but it was returned. PayPal contended that the buyer was in breach of its direction as to the return address to be used and so he was not entitled to a refund. A High Court judge ruled that Chinese script was not within the buyer's competence and performance of PayPal's requirement was impossible and unreasonable. Although PayPal operates from Luxembourg, the law of England and Wales applied to the contract and PayPal's direction fell outside what it had been entitled to impose. It had to pay up.

- BUT WILL usually APPLY if PayPal has itself provided you with credit and there is no credit card company in the picture.
- WON'T APPLY if your card is in a company's name as the customer.
- BUT WILL APPLY although you paid by a mixture of credit card and cash/cheque. So say the price was £1,500 and you paid £5 on your credit card and £1,495 by cheque. The extent of the liability of the credit card company to you will be as great as if the whole £1,500 had gone onto your card.
- BUT WILL generally APPLY if you used your credit card for a transaction abroad or in relation to goods purchased from a trader abroad for delivery here.
- AND WILL APPLY even though the transaction takes you over your credit limit or you are behind with repayments to the credit card company.

OK. Take it away section 75A of the Consumer Credit Act 1974. This is for you flash folks. It works like section 75 and covers transactions in which the cash price was over £30,000 and the credit was for no more than £60,260. But that credit agreement must have been directly linked to the transaction so you were being lent money for a particular purchase or service. Either the trader must have dealt with the preparation or making of the credit agreement on behalf of the lender or the specific goods or service must have been explicitly specified in the credit agreement. For example, it would cover a credit loan made to you for the specific purpose of installation of a lift to take you from the ground floor to the third floor of your desirable residence where the trader dealt with the loan paperwork. Then s75A lumbers whoever provided the credit with liability for the trader's breach of contract (not misrepresentation) if the trader cannot be traced, has failed to respond to you after you have contacted them, is insolvent or has failed to satisfy your claim after you have taken reasonable steps to pursue them.

Here's something for you more modest consumers where you want justice – which means money – from your credit card company.

Particulars of Claim

1. On 14 July 2021 the claimant purchased a mattress from Horrorsleep, Hounslow for £102.99. The mattress should have been of satisfactory quality. It was not in that no less than 20 of the mattress springs tore through the upper cover within two days of delivery. The claimant rejected the mattress on 19 July 2021.

2. The claimant paid for the mattress using his credit card number 456791229 issued to him by the defendant. The defendant is equally responsible for the seller's breach of contract under s 75 of the Consumer Credit Act 1974.

Particulars of the claimant's loss

Price – £102.99

Extra paid for substitute comparable mattress – £75.00

Travelling expenses – £30.00

AND the claimant claims:

a. Damages of £207.99.

b. Interest under s69 of the County Courts Act 1984 at 8% from 19 July 2016 to date of claim of £2.82 and thereafter at the daily rate of 4p.

c. Costs.

I believe that the facts stated in these particulars of claim are true. I understand that proceedings for contempt of court may be brought against anyone who makes, or causes to be made, a false statement in a document verified by a statement of truth without an honest belief in its truth.

(signed) Clive Troublesore

Claimant

Dated 14 August 2021

For debit card kids

Section 75 will not apply where you paid with a debit card unless you also made use of a credit card for the same transaction, provided the other conditions needed are met. So, if the cash price was £200 and you paid £50 on your credit card and £150 on your debit card, that's okay.

But where section 75 does not apply, a different regime may help you. This again is inferior to the section 75 regime. The best thing you can say about it is that it may help you where the cash price for goods or services is £100 or less. The scheme is called – wait for it – CHARGEBACK and arises because of the contract between the card issuer and the card scheme such as VISA, MasterCard or Maestro. It's a transaction reversal. The card issuer, probably your bank, asks the bank or other financial business that facilitates the trader to accept card payments, to claw back from the trader's account what you paid. As you would expect, the trader can dispute the Chargeback. Most card issuers play the Chargeback game but not all, although rules may differ between them. You won't get back any consequential losses (see above) through Chargeback such as cost of repairs, as with the section 75 scheme. If you want to try it, get in touch with your card issuer – there will be a time limit which is likely to be around 120 days from the date on which the transaction has appeared on your card account as against the six years from the transaction date with section 75 – and, if you are dissatisfied with how your card issuer responds then the Financial Services Ombudsman may entertain a complaint. Typically, they will poke in their nose if your card issuer has refused to attempt a Chargeback. The Ombudsman is likely to uphold your complaint where you had challenged the transaction and, taking account of the card scheme rules, it appeared on the face of it that a Chargeback request might have succeeded. There may also be a nose poke and successful complaint where a Chargeback was refused and your card issuer neglected to appeal against the refusal. You would be onto a winner with the Ombudsman if they considered that an appeal should have been pursued and, had it been, it would likely have succeeded. The Ombudsman cannot deal with a complaint by you against the card scheme. But the trader may make a complaint to the Ombudsman where the Chargeback has worked and the trader maintains that their account should not have been debited.

But remember

The section 75 and Chargeback remedies do not preclude direct action against the trader.

Masterstroke?

If you have ever paid for something, settle down and read on. Between 1992 and 2008 millions (or trillions) of customers paid for their goods and services by using a Mastercard credit or debit card. It turns out that each time a business accepted the card, it was charged a fee by Mastercard which was unlawful. The unlawfulness was decided by the European Commission. More than half a million businesses in the UK including major supermarkets who were charged this way, passed the fees on (as you would) to us by upping prices. So we, it is said, have lost out whether or not we personally used a Mastercard or even possessed one, by having to pay more for our goods and services than would otherwise have been the case.

Walter Merricks who is a lawyer and former financial ombudsman didn't reckon this was fair and so he brought a claim against Mastercard in the Competition Appeal Tribunal on behalf of anyone who had lost out because of the higher prices. He did so by way of the first collective action ever started under the Consumer Rights Act 2015. He is after £14billion on behalf of 46 million UK customers who are likely to include you and you – and me, please.

So far, so good. The Tribunal threw out the case. Walter Merricks appealed.

The Court of Appeal ruled that the Tribunal had been wrong and recognised that its decision would have frustrated the will of Parliament that there should be an effective route for consumers to be compensated when businesses broke competition law. Mastercard appealed. The Supreme Court ruled that the Court of Appeal had been right. The action has now gone back to the Tribunal to reconsider whether the action can proceed. It held a remote hearing in March 2021. I plugged into the hearing. At the end it was announced that judgment would be reserved. I shouted out: "Can't you give a decision now? I've got a book coming out shortly and want to be able to tell the readers whether to celebrate with a crate of prosecco or drown their sorrows with a glass of water." Only the next door neighbour heard. I was muted, of course. See my blog for what happens and be prepared. There could be another....appeal.

Chapter 42

The Longest Will In The World

And some inheritance tax saving thrown in

Inheritance tax (death duties) is payable on what you are worth (your estate) when you die. No inheritance tax on your first £325,000 (after debts have been knocked off). Yippee but the allowance has been frozen until 2026 thanks to the 2021 Budget. Anything over £325,000 is taxed at 40%. Blimey. So get yourself a spouse or civil partner – unless you already have one or you will be charged with bigamy. Loveable tax-hating comedian Ken Dodd married his long-time girlfriend Anne Jones just two days before he died. Eh? What you leave your spouse or civil partner is exempt from inheritance tax which means that you can gift the lot to them and no inheritance tax will be payable on your death. Perhaps the lot to them is too indulgent. The answer is, where practicable, to effect a hive off and gift £325,000 to the gardener and children and the rest to your spouse or civil partner and there will be no inheritance tax payable on your death or just 40% of anything over £325,000 going to anyone other than your spouse or civil partner and the estate of your spouse or civil partner will be just that bit smaller when inheritance tax on their death comes to be calculated.

Say your estate is worth less than £325,000? The difference between what it is worth and £325,000 is transferred over to your spouse or civil partner so that, when they die, no inheritance tax is payable on that difference plus their first £325,000. Or say, whatever your estate is worth, you gift the lot to your spouse or civil partner? Then, the whole £325,000 is transferred over to be used when they die, with the result that there is no inheritance tax payable on the first £650,000 of what they are worth on their death.

Increasing the £325K with a gift to charity

What you leave to a charity is discounted when inheritance tax is calculated. Or should you be minded to make a gift in your will to a charity of more than 10% of what you are worth over £325,000, then you get a discount of 4% on the inheritance tax payable without even having to enter a promotion code into the probate paperwork.

Increasing the £325K with a home gift

Do you own a home or part of it? Have you lived in it at some time? Is it in the United Kingdom? Are you happy to gift the home or your interest in it to a direct descendant – that's a child (including a step, adopted or foster child or a direct descendant of theirs)? Then, congratulations. You qualify for an extra inheritance tax free amount on your death. It's called the Residence Nil-Rate Band, if you wish to impress your funeral director buddies. This extra allowance has been available for deaths since 5 April 2017 and was due to go up annually in accordance with the consumer price index but was frozen in the 2021 Budget until 2026. The amount of the allowance is the value of the home or your interest in it, subject to a cap. For the 2020/2021 tax year the allowance is £175,000. This means that if you give your son the home – or the home is included in his share of your estate to be carved up, without being specifically mentioned – and it is worth £500,000 then an additional 40% inheritance tax will be saved on £175,000.

Where part of this additional allowance might be lost because you downsized to a less valuable residence or ceased to own a home after 7 July 2015, that part will still be available provided you left that smaller residence, or assets of equivalent value, to direct descendants. Insofar as this allowance is not used then it is available to be taken advantage of on the death of your spouse or civil partner in the same way as that £325,000 allowance (see above). Just one other thing. If your estate after debts, reliefs and allowances is over £2m then this additional allowance is tapered down and – fasten your safely belts – may potentially be extinguished.

Lifetime gifts

If you make gifts during your lifetime, you can brag about them on social media, use them in support of an application for an honour, delight their recipients and, most pleasurably, reduce the inheritance tax bill on your death. Gifts during your lifetime to your spouse or civil partner domiciled in the United Kingdom are disregarded on death, no matter their value. Just think of it. Give every penny you possess to the other half during your lifetime so that they can then chuck you out of your own home and then you don't need to bother with a will and can save the two sheets of paper it would otherwise have gone onto. Also disregarded on death and without any limit on the amount are gifts to qualifying political parties, United Kingdom registered charities and regular lifetime gifts, such as at Christmas and birthdays, which you make out of your income and not out of your capital and so long as you can maintain your standard of living having done so.

Some gifts with limits on their amounts may also be made and ignored on your death, no matter how close to your death they may have been. These are gifts amounting to a total of £3,000 for any tax year and gifts of up to £250 for any tax year to as many people as you can find to take the money. Then there are gifts which can be made during your lifetime and ignored on your death on the occasion of someone's marriage or civil partnership. That's £5,000 by either parent of either party, £2,500 by a grandparent or great grandparent and £2,500 to your other half. Or guarantee a place on the top table and the Loyal Toast with a gift of up to £1,000 to anyone else who is marrying or entering into a civil partnership.

Now, so far we have been dealing with child *Monopoly* money. On to the potentially big stuff. Give away what you like, without limit to whomsoever you like and survive for at least three years and inheritance tax will be saved on your death. Die within three years and the amount you have gifted will be added on to what you were worth on death and so will have the potential to be taxed at the rate of 40%. Make it to three years and the inheritance tax rate goes down to 32%, to four years and it's 24%, to five years and it's 16%, to six years and its 8%. And survive for at least seven years and, champers and unsalted cashews (modest salt prolongs life) come out as the gift will be totally disregarded for inheritance tax purposes.

There are special rules for gifts to trusts and transfers of business and agricultural property and certain shareholdings.

The $64,000 questions

Here are some questions you may want to ask yourself, apart from how important to you it is to avoid or save on inheritance tax, before deciding what to say in your will. They may drive you crazy.

Q1 If my child does not survive me, do I want the gift intended for them to go to any of their children and, if so, in what shares?

Q2 Do my family and friends really need anything from me – indeed, would I not be overloading what they are worth when they die and upping inheritance tax for their estate – or would it be better for the bulk of my estate to go to charity?

Q3 If my spouse or civil partner survives me, do I want to guarantee that my children will inherit when they die by giving my spouse or partner just a life interest in what I own (the benefit of income and the power to trustees to advance capital for their maintenance if they need it)? If so, do I want that life interest to come to an end should they remarry, enter into a civil partnership or cohabit?

Q4 Do I want to gift my interest in a home or other property which I own jointly with my spouse or partner to someone else and, if so, is there anything I need to do apart from making a will in order to achieve this? If you own with your spouse or partner as joint tenants your interest will automatically pass to them on your death, irrespective of what your will may say. You can change this (see chapter 45).

Sign here please

You need to sign your will in the presence of two witnesses so there's a sort of death trio. The pandemic has incited a change to this strict requirement which is intended to be temporary but could become permanent and prove to herald even more changes. The pandemic change came into force on 28 September 2020. However, it is backdated to wills made after 30 January 2020 and continues to cover wills made up to and including 31 January 2022. "Get on with it, Gold. What does it do?" It allows the witnesses to see you signing up on a video conference such as Zoom without being physically present and staring up your nostrils. The two witnesses would then sign up afterwards but they do not need to be in each other's company when they do so. You can watch them signing up – as you must – by video. Please don't take advantage of this change unless you have no reasonable alternative because there could be trouuuuuuuuuuble. The will has got to be conveyed from you to the witnesses and if the witnesses are not together when they sign then from one witness to another. This gives the witnesses a good opportunity to spy out what the will says which you may well have preferred to have enjoyed privacy during your lifetime. Should you unhappily expire or lose your mental capacity before they have both signed up, the will will have no legal effect. And Clive Troublesore who, naturally, has been left out as a beneficiary may argue following your death that the conference screen froze when you signed.

Adult witnesses are preferred although someone under 18 who knows what they are doing will be acceptable if all the big kids are out. No beneficiary – person to be a recipient of a gift in the will – should act as a witness or the gift to them will be lost. Generally, marriage or entering into a civil partnership will automatically revoke a will unless it is clear that the will was made in contemplation of that marriage or civil partnership. A divorce or annulment of a marriage or dissolution or annulment of a civil partnership will automatically cancel out a gift to the spouse or partner or their appointment as executor unless it is clear that the gift or appointment is to be unaffected. Nevertheless, the loser may still have a claim under the Inheritance (Provision for Family and Dependants) Act 1975 (see chapter 44).

Digital property

Your existing will or plans for a new will encompass your digital property like social media accounts, don't they? Of course they don't (or, if they do, you can participate in a draw to win my old smartphone). A Law Society survey reveals that 93% of wills said nothing about digital property. Give your executors a break by addressing the topic in your will. That's what we shall do.

Here goes

I promised it and 'ere it is. The longest will in the world. You can pick and choose the bits you want in and the bits you want out. At the least, the will of Benny Factor (he has been brought in by kind permission of Clive Troublesore who has been too busy drawing up claim forms to find the time to make a will) should promote some ideas. Some of them could lighten the mourners' mood. The bits may also help you to decide what you want your will to say if you intend to see a solicitor about drawing it up for you (and where you want a professional to do the job, make sure it is a solicitor and not a will writing service operating opposite the fruit and veg stall in your local market or online and lawyerless). If you are intending to make a gift to a charity, contact that charity to find out whether they will pay for the solicitor's charges. And each November, the Will Aid scheme (go to willaid.org.uk) has participating solicitors across England and Wales drawing up wills for anyone over 18 without making any charge. Instead they will invite you to make a gift to a charity and what they suggest is £100 for a single will or £180 for two wills where one is the mirror of the other (for example, wills by spouses or partners). That's an invitation only so if you had the nerve, you could decline to pay anything or, if times were that hard, pay something less. But do the decent thing. There's another scheme run each March (go to freewillsmonth.org.uk) spearheaded by well-respected charities who hope that in return for a free will, you'll leave something to one of them. This time you have to be aged 55 or over to qualify.

THIS WILL dated 14 July 2021 is made by me BENNY FACTOR of 31 Deep Water Portsmouth Hants PO5 0P6

1. I revoke all former wills made by me.

2. This will shall not be revoked by my intended marriage to FREDA FACTOR of 31 Deep Water Portsmouth Hants PO5 0BP

3. I wish to be cremated.

or

3. I do not wish to be cremated.

4. I wish that the certainty of my death shall be confirmed by a medical practitioner cutting my wrists and that I shall be buried with a hammer in my coffin into the top of which no fewer than twelve airholes shall have been made.

5. If FREDA FACTOR survives me by thirty days -

a. I appoint her as my sole executrix;

b. I give her the sum of two thousand pounds for her to spend on a party for such of my relatives who have sent me at least one birthday card in the period of five years immediately preceding the date of my death and my friends to be held in the public bar of The Black Death Queen's Street Portsmouth and at which there shall be two minutes' silence in my memory and should the party coincide with the television coverage of a Premier League football match being shown therein during the party then the silence shall be respected in a commercial break of such coverage;

c. I give to the children of my former marriage ESTELLE FACTOR and FRANCIS FACTOR in equal shares or to the survivor of them absolutely such an amount of money which can be given without any liability being incurred for inheritance tax on my death subject to a maximum of three thousand two hundred and fifty pounds PROVIDED that the amount of this gift shall be reduced by the amount of any gifts made during my lifetime or any other gifts made in this will or in any codicil to this will which are liable to be taken into account on a calculation of any inheritance tax payable on my death;

d. I direct FREDA FACTOR as my executrix to encash my premium savings bonds and to give the proceeds of such encashment and any prize money that such bonds may have generated after the date of my death to my friend and neighbour CHARLES BISHOP of 29 Deep Water Portsmouth Hants PO5 0BP in recognition of all the assistance he has rendered to me over the years in the cutting of my hedge and lawns and the emptying of my cesspit; and

e. Subject to clauses 5(b)(c) and (d) of this my will, I give the whole of my estate to FREDA FACTOR.

6.1. I direct that FREDA FACTOR shall do such of the things as are specified in the sub-clauses of this clause of my will or otherwise as shall be necessary or as she shall see fit in relation to my digital property and for the purposes of this clause 'my digital property' shall include my websites and their contents, my social media accounts and passwords and other access codes and information relating thereto my published and unpublished works and other documents or materials in whatever form stored electronically on my computer or otherwise all my copyrights and rights in the same and the hardware on which such property shall be stored.

6.2. Transfer the domain names of websites and close my social media accounts having posted notice on them of my death and any appropriate information relating thereto.

6.3. Destroy files of no material monetary value.

6.4. A list of my websites and social media accounts and all passwords and other access codes and information relating to the same (along with the like information for my financial and any other accounts) is contained in a sealed envelope deposited by me with the Portsmouth branch of Dodgy Bank plc.

7. If FREDA FACTOR does not survive me by thirty days the following provisions of my will shall take effect.

8. I appoint my solicitor MEL PRACTICE of 38 Coke Road Portsmouth PO7 0PR and my friend ROBIN GOODFELLOW of 2 Chorley Grove Cosham Portsmouth PO6 3BT to be the executors and trustees of this my will and I declare that the expression 'my trustees' shall mean the trustees of this my will and of any trusts arising under it.

9. I appoint ROBIN GOODFELLOW and his wife EMELIA GOODFELLOW to be the guardians of any of my children who are under the age of eighteen years.

10. I give to my trustees the sum of two thousand pounds to spend in the same way and subject to the same terms as that sum would have been spent by FREDA FACTOR under clause 5(b) of this my will had she survived me by thirty days.

11. I direct my trustees to encash my premium savings bonds and to give the proceeds of such encashment and any prize money that such bonds may have generated after the date of my death to my friend and neighbour CHARLES BISHOP of 29 Deep Water Portsmouth Hants PO5 0BP in recognition of all the assistance he has rendered to me over the years in the cutting of my hedge and lawns and the emptying of my cesspit.

12. I give to NELLIE CLEANHOUSE of 122 Reinforcement Avenue Portsmouth PO8 0P9 the sum of five hundred pounds provided she is in my employment at my death and not under notice from me for the termination of such employment.*

13. I give to the SOCIETY FOR DISTRESSED FORMER LITIGANTS

IN PERSON of the Royal Courts of Justice Strand London WC2A 2LL the sum of five thousand pounds and declare that the receipt of the person who appears to be a proper officer of the said charity shall be a complete discharge to my trustees.

14. I give the sum of seven hundred and fifty pounds to each of the following persons -

a. ROBIN GOODFELLOW;

b. EMELIA GOODFELLOW;

c. My friend KEVIN DOVAIN of 168 Great Ronan Street Portsmouth PO6 3PQ on condition that he is not at the date of my death a member of the Church of Scientology or any other sect, society or body to which he is under an obligation contractually or morally to give to it any of his property or the income derived or to be derived therefrom and if this condition shall not be satisfied this gift shall fall into residue*;

d. My friend MIRABEL MYERSON of 40 Gregson Arcade Fareham Hants PO16 7AA on condition that at the date of my death she has not married and is not cohabiting with Greaser Gattree and if such condition shall not be satisfied this gift shall fall into residue*; and

e. EMILY MAITLIS of the British Broadcasting Corporation London W1A 1AA in recognition of the many hours of enjoyment she has given to me for the expression of her views on Her Majesty's Government (from time to time) and without seeking to impose any obligation on her I express the wish that she shall use her reasonable endeavours to cause a recording of 'All the Nice Girls Love a Sailor' to be played over the closing credits of one edition of Newsnight on BBC2.

15. I give any motor vehicle in my ownership or possession at my death to my neighbour JOSE PARKER of "Chez Costa" 27 Deep Water Portsmouth Hants PO5 0P6 and if such vehicle is in my possession under the terms of a hire purchase or other credit agreement my trustees shall discharge such agreement out of my residuary estate and take such other steps as may be necessary so that ownership of the same shall be vested in Jose Parker.**

16. I release ARTHURE CON of 11a Prison Villas Guildford Surrey GU1 IRX from his indebtedness to me in respect of the loan of seven pounds I made to him in or about 1984 together with all interest which may be outstanding and which he would otherwise be liable to pay to me.

17. I give to the child of my former marriage SMALL FACTOR whose whereabouts are presently unknown to me my collection of postage stamps.

18. I give to my former wife PENELOPE HARDWARE (formerly FACTOR) of 16 Driftwood Road, Portsmouth PO16 0HB the sum of two thousand pounds.

19. (a) Subject as already set out in this my will I give such of my furniture plate and articles of household domestic or personal use and ornament to my trustees to transfer to each of such of my relatives and personal friends who shall have attended on invitation the party referred to in clauses 5(b) and 10 of this my will and who are not otherwise beneficiaries under this my will such items as each of them shall select to the value in the opinion of my trustees of up to one hundred pounds.

20. My trustees shall hold the remainder of my estate on trust to sell call in and convert into money such parts as do not already consist of the same at such time or times and in such manner as they shall think fit with power to postpone such sale calling in and conversion for so long as they shall in their absolute discretion decide without being liable for loss and

a. to pay my funeral and testamentary expenses and debts;

b. to pay any inheritance tax which shall be payable in respect of property passing under this will;

c. to divide the residue (hereinafter called "my residuary estate") equally among such of my children of my marriage (or expected marriage) to Freda Factor who shall survive me by thirty days and attain twenty one years or marry under that age but if none of such children so survive me or attain a vested interest in my residuary estate my trustees shall divide my residuary estate equally between ROBIN GOODFELLOW and EMILIA GOODFELLOW or the survivor of them absolutely;

d. to pay any money to which a beneficiary who is still a minor is entitled to their parent or guardian for their benefit;

e. to pay or apply capital for advancement of any beneficiary under section 32 of the Trustee Act 1925 as if the said section applied to the whole of the presumptive or vested interest of such beneficiary and not to one half thereof; and

f. and to invest as freely as if they themselves were beneficially entitled.

21. Any of my trustees being a person engaged in any profession shall be entitled to charge and be paid for work done by them or their firm or company including work which an executor could have done personally on the same basis as if they were not one of my trustees but employed to carry out such work on their behalf.

22. The directions contained in clause 6.1 to 6.4 inclusive of this my will shall apply to my trustees in all respects in relation to my digital property as they would have applied to FREDA FACTOR if she had been my executrix and my trustees shall do the same things and have the same powers as set out therein.

23. I wish that my trustees shall read this my will as soon as practi-

cable after my death to a gathering of my beneficiaries and such other relatives and personal friends as my trustees shall in their absolute discretion invite and that immediately before such reading there shall be recited by my trustees in unison the lyrics to "All the Nice Girls Love a Sailor".

24. I wish that my trustees shall consider the appropriateness and advisability of a deed of family arrangement and/or variation and/or disclaimer under section 142 of the Inheritance Tax Act 1984.***

25. This will is made pursuant to an agreement between myself and Freda Factor under which Freda Factor is making a will which where appropriate is in substantially the same terms as this will and such agreement is that neither of us will revoke our respective wills without the written consent of the other.****

26. I have this day made a statement explaining the reasons I have not made provision for certain persons and why I have made only a token gift for my child SMALL FACTOR. *****

SIGNED by the TESTATOR	)
in our joint presence and by	)
us in his presence	)

*It is possible to attach a condition to any gift. But a condition, if challenged in court, may be held to be void and so of no effect where, for example, it is found to be contrary to public policy. "I give to each of my trustees fifteen thousand pounds on condition that they do not disclose to HM Revenue and Customs details of my investments to which relevant documents are to be found in deposit box 15XT24 at Dodgy Bank, 16 Lombard Street...." That would be void. "My trustees shall pay the income from my residuary estate to my son Arthur for life so long as he shall not marry Angela Scrubbit...." That would be valid. And so would this condition. "My trustees shall pay the sum of seven thousand pounds to my son Arthur upon marrying Angela Scrubbit and in default of such marriage taking place...."

In the 1800s, courts held to be valid conditions against marriage to a Scotsman, to a domestic servant and to anyone "beneath" the beneficiary. In more recent years, a gift "provided he shall be a Roman Catholic" was given the blessing of the House of Lords. And so was a direction to trustees to pay income "to the Baronet for the time being if and when and so long as he shall be of the Jewish faith and shall be married to an approved wife". Such a wife was defined as "a wife of Jewish blood by one or both parents and who has been brought up in and never separated from and at the date of her marriage continues to worship according to the Jewish faith as to such facts in case of dispute or doubt the decision of the Chief Rabbi in London of either the Portuguese or Anglo-German community shall be conclusive". Certainly, one way to keep religion alive and a direction which could be adapted to suit other faiths.

Conditions which would effectively require the beneficiary to behave themselves in the future should be quite safe. Take it away with this: "I give to my friend Harry The Lad Scratcher Junior the sum of ten thousand pounds on condition that he has given up low company and is following the path of virtue and the decision of my executor/trustees as to whether such condition has been satisfied shall be conclusive."

**If you make a gift of your "personal chattels" (which are often referred to in those DIY wills you can buy off stationers' shelves) note that they are given a special meaning in wills made after 30 October 2014. That is movable property other than money or securities for money or property which is used solely or mainly for business purposes or you held solely as an investment.

***If you couldn't tell the difference between inheritance tax and margarine and your will was not tax efficient, and so would lead to tax being payable which might have been avoided had gifts been made in a different way, do you have to be recalled from the dead to put things right? No. Section 142 of the Inheritance Tax Act 1984 enables a will to be rewritten – just once – with the agreement of all beneficiaries concerned so that it avoids inheritance tax or reduces the amount of inheritance tax payable. This must be done within two years of death. There are certain procedural steps which need to be taken. The same section 142 can be used where there is no will so that the intestacy laws kick in (see chapter 44 under **Look, no will**) and a rewriting of those laws would avoid or reduce inheritance tax. You'll find a useful HM Revenue & Customs checklist for dealing with a variation at gov.uk/alter-a-will-after-a-death. But I would strongly recommend that independent professional advice is sought on the most tax advantageous way of making changes and on the drafting of the necessary document rather than engage in a DIY job.

****If spouses or partners make mirror wills, saying substantially the same things, and agree between themselves not to change them – a testamentary duet – can the survivor be trusted to keep to the agreement? The general rule is that, while they are both alive, either or both of them could lawfully make changes. However, the position would be different once the first of them died and the other reneged on the agreement. Then, if it could be proved that there had been a no-change commitment by which they intended to be bound then the beneficiaries under the original will ought to be able to secure a court order which effectively ripped up the later will. When the wills are made under a no-change agreement, a suitable no-change clause can be incorporated in them.

*****For more on a statement like this, see chapter 44 under **FOR THE DECEASED'S EYES ONLY**.

All change, please

Blast, you left out the gift of back editions of the *Radio Times* to your friend Jeff Link. A change to the will is needed. But what a criminal waste of time and money to ditch the entirety of the will you made and start afresh. The solution is to add a codicil to your will provided you don't want everyone to see what you originally said and the codicil is not as long as *War and Peace*.

The codicil can be typed or written on the original will or a separate sheet which is secured to the original will. The same witnessing rules which apply to the will also apply to a codicil.

> *THIS CODICIL dated 30 July 2022 is made by me BENNY FACTOR of 31 Deep Water Portsmouth Hants PO5 0P6*
>
> 1.   *If FREDA FACTOR does not survive me by thirty days I additionally give to my friend JEFF LINK of John Snagge House 78 Revolution Road Watford Herts WD6 0BP my back editions of the Radio Times and express the wish that he will cherish them read them cover to cover and keep them in immaculate condition fair wear and tear excepting.*
>
> 2.   *In all other respects I confirm my will.*
>
> SIGNED by the TESTATOR   )
> *in our joint presence and by*   )
> *us in his presence*   )

Where's there's no will there's a claimant

Did you make a will? Where is it? Might it be torn up? For protective measures, see chapter 44.

Chapter 43

Removing Executors

"We want our money!"

A will's executors are meant to get on with the job and wind up the deceased's estate in a diligent and honest way. They may go to sleep: they may have their hands in the till. Infuriating for you beneficiaries who need your legacies for the loft conversions and safaris. The court has the power to kick out an executor and appoint someone else in their place. That someone else could be you. Is it in the best interests of the beneficiaries for a kick out? That's the overriding consideration. There does not need to be proof of friction and hostility between beneficiaries and executor. In fact, their existence will not normally be enough alone to secure the kicking out but if that friction and hostility are present, they may help to persuade the court that a kick out is for the best. The court will be reluctant to go into allegations of wrongdoing or fault on the part of the executor although their existence would be powerful evidence that the executor must go. The fact that the deceased wanted a particular person as their executor will weigh heavily in favour of the executor remaining in post but weighing against it will be the wishes of you and the other beneficiaries. The more of the beneficiaries you can get to back an application for kick out, the stronger your prospects of success. The court can be expected to take into account how much more work is left to be done before the estate is wound up and what would be the likely cost of a kick out and replacement.

The most common and straightforward route to follow to secure a change is to make an application to the court under section 50 of the Administration of Justice Act 1995. That application can be made by a co-executor who is fed up to the teeth with the lack of cooperation of their fellow executor or by any beneficiary and even before probate has been granted. Where there is no will and the laws of intestacy take over (see chapter 44), an application under this Act would have to wait until there had been a grant of representation (letters of administration, that's called) to whoever was entitled to get it (a widow or widower, for example).

It is to the Chancery Division of the High Court that the application is made. The county court cannot deal with these cases. The Chancery Division's judges at London's Royal Courts of Justice have the most experience in hearing them. Otherwise, the application can be made to one of the Chancery Division's outposts in the district registries (attached to the county court) at Birmingham, Bristol, Cardiff, Leeds, Liverpool, Manchester, Newcastle or Preston. The procedure under part 8 of the Civil Procedure Rules 1998 (see chapter 12) should be used.

Chapter 44

No Inheritance Claims

Gone but not forgotten

Where there's a will, we at least know what the deceased intended although, as we shall see, they do not always get their own way. And where there's no will, the laws of intestacy kick in and, as we shall again see, the court may disapply them. The deceased's like or dislike of what would happen on an intestacy may well have determined whether or not they made a will. One senior figure at the Probate Registry, which deals with issuing authorities to executors of wills and relatives of those who died intestate to wind up the deceased's affairs, once told me he had never made a will because the intestacy laws suited his situation and wishes to a tee. He would have said the very same in a will as the intestacy laws said so no point in wasting the ink and a couple of sheets of paper. You may come to think that the intestacy laws are not for you. Do some cardiac walking, consume a low calorie dinner and read on.

Look, no will

The law changed on 1 October 2014. The deceased is survived by a spouse or civil partner and no children? If yes, they scoop the lot. Formerly, the surviving spouse or civil partner only got the first £450,000 and the rest was shared as to one-half to them and as to the other half to the deceased's parents or, if neither surviving, to the deceased's brothers and sisters. A surviving spouse or civil partner plus children (and not just the under 18s but big and ugly children as well)? The first £250,000 to the surviving spouse or civil partner – but that's the first £270,000 if the death was after 5 February 2020 – and then the rest divided as to one half to them and the other half to the children. The principle law change is that whereas the surviving spouse or civil partner formerly got just a life interest (a right to the income generated by invested capital in the estate) in one half of the rest they now get that one-half outright. In these situations, the surviving spouse or civil partner is also inflicted with the deceased's personal chattels and the new law defines what this means. Tangible movable property other than money or securities for money and property which was held solely or mainly for business purposes or was held solely as an investment: pretty wide-ranging.

No surviving spouse or civil partner but children? The children collect 100%. No surviving spouse or civil partner and no children? The parents take the lot and, where neither is still with us, brothers and sisters or their descendants. And so on down to half-uncles and aunts or their descendants and if the only person left is the postman, then the deceased's money goes to the state – and not even a bench commemorated to "a lovely man who spent so many hours sitting in these gardens that he never got round to buying a home made will form."

Left out but litigious

Where you are omitted from the will or do you not qualify for a share of the deceased's estate under the intestacy laws, you may still succeed in a claim for something, thanks to the Inheritance (Provision for Family and Dependants) Act 1975.

Who can apply

- Deceased's spouse or civil partner.
- Same sex partner who had not entered into a civil partnership but had been living with the deceased as a civil partner.
- Former spouse or civil partner so long as they have not remarried or entered into a new civil partnership (unless an order for financial remedies made in matrimonial proceedings excludes the right to apply – and frequently it does so).
- A person who lived in the same household as the deceased as if they were the deceased's spouse or civil partner for at least two years immediately before the death.
- A child of the deceased.
- Any person treated by the deceased as a child of the family in relation to a marriage or civil partnership.
- Any person treated as a child of the family in which the deceased at any time stood in the role of a parent which, for example, would cover a child who was not a child of the deceased but who was brought up by the deceased alone or in the context of cohabitation.
- Any other person who immediately before the death was being wholly or partly maintained by the deceased.

And when

The application for some property or dosh out of the deceased's estate must be made by court proceedings started within six months of probate (in the case of a will) or letters of administration (in the case of an intestacy) having been granted by the probate registry. The court does have the power to extend that time limit but being late is a risky business. Nevertheless, in a 2019 case called *Cowan v Foreman and other parties*, the Court of Appeal ticked off a judge who had refused to extend the time limit where there had been a 13 month delay. The appeal judges said that a robust approach to an extension application was not called for. And in another 2019 case called *Bhusate v Patel and other parties*, a delay of 25 years and nine months was overlooked but the facts of that case were very exceptional (though you might just mention the case when you are asking the court to extend time – "*Judge, Mrs Bhusate got over 25 years, I only want 25 months*").

A change in the law allows proceedings to be started before probate or letters of administration have been granted which is useful in the situation where, say, the prospective applicants for the grant are deliberately dragging their feet or they have little incentive to do anything because the deceased's property bypassed their estate (see below). If time permits, a pre-action protocol letter (see chapter 10) should be sent to whoever has probate or letters of administration, actually or prospectively, and efforts made to negotiate a settlement. These cases often do settle by negotiation.

You can ask the probate registry for what is called a standing search which will tell you over a period of six months if and when probate or letters of administration have been granted and if so, generate a copy. This can be renewed at six-monthly periods and will cost you a bargain £3 a time (reduced from £10 in August 2020). Where you may wish to challenge a will or have some other good reason for preventing the grant or probate or letters of administration, you can achieve this by entering what is called a caveat at the probate registry and for a fee of £3 (reduced from £20 in August 2020). Be careful, though. If, having entered the caveat and then refused the request of whoever wants probate or letters of administration to cancel it, you could be involved in court proceedings. Once probate is granted, you can obtain a copy of the deceased's will from the probate registry, whether or not you have a legitimate interest or are a nosey parker. Everything online.

What are your chances?

In every case the court has to take account of the financial resources and needs of you, anyone else who has lost out and is making a claim and all beneficiaries; any obligations the deceased had towards anyone applying and all beneficiaries; the size and nature of the estate; any physical or mental disability of anyone applying and the beneficiaries; and any other relevant matter which can include the conduct of you and anyone else, a promise to see you alright which has been broken or arrangements before death to make a new will which would have benefited you but were never implemented. The court can also have regard to the reasons given in a written statement signed by the deceased and normally kept with the will and which attempts to justify why some have been omitted and some have been preferred (see below) but the contents of a statement would be far from a cast iron guarantee that they would destroy a claim for provision.

Different rules apply to different classes of applicant. On an application by a spouse or civil partner or former spouse or civil partner, the court must have regard to the age of the applicant and the duration of the marriage or partnership and the contribution made to the welfare of the deceased's family. Where the spouse or partner is applying, the court will look at what would have been awarded if the marriage or partnership had been ended by divorce or dissolution instead of death. A legal change, though, means that the court won't be straitjacketed by this. On an application by a cohabitee, the additional factors to be considered are the age of the applicant, how long the applicant and the deceased lived together and the contributions they made to the family, looking after the home or caring for the family. On an application by a child, the court will additionally look, where appropriate, at how they were being educated or trained. In the case of an old and ugly child, that might involve an investigation into their progress on night school courses in flower arranging and salsa dancing.

In a major case in the Supreme Court in 2017 called *Ilott v The Blue Cross and others*, it was decreed that what the court had to look at was whether the will or the intestacy laws made provision for the claimant which is actually reasonable when the case is heard and, if not, what reasonable provision ought to be ordered. The court should not be considering whether the deceased acted unreasonably. Where there is a will, it might be decided that there were very good reasons for what the deceased gifted or did not gift in it. But the claimant could still end up winning an application because, for example, their circumstances had altered and the deceased did not know what had happened or did not have time to change the will. Conversely, the deceased might have acted out of spite but still made provision for the claimant which is reasonable for them. The state of the relationship between the claimant and the deceased will very much kick in, even though the court will not be considering whether the deceased had acted reasonably

And in claims by other than the deceased's spouse or civil partner, the Supreme Court ruled that all that could be awarded was what was needed for their maintenance, albeit this was not limited to just subsistence level. That maintenance could be reflected in a lump sum being set aside from which both income and capital could be drawn by the claimant over the years and did not have to take the form of regular income payments (like £250 per month). Or the claimant might be awarded a lump sum to buy a car to get to work. There was also no reason why housing could not be provided to the claimant which could be by way of a right to live in a particular property for the rest of their lifetime.

That Supreme Court case involved a daughter's claim arising out of the will of her mother with whom she had fallen out. They had been estranged for 26 years and three attempts at reconciliation had foundered. The daughter was totally excluded from the will. Mother's estate was worth around £460,000. Apart from a modest gift to a benevolent society connected with her late husband's employment, mother had willed the lot to a group of charities in which she had shown little or no interest while she was alive. After court hearings and appeals which had been going on for 11 years (!!), the Supreme Court decided that daughter should be awarded £50,000 out of the estate as against one-half of everything which the daughter had been after. The charities, anxious that a precedent should not be set which might lose them a fortune in bequests in other cases, argued that the daughter should have nothing.

What are the other prizes?

The court has the power to play around with jointly owned property. Take for example a house which the deceased and his widow both owned as *joint tenants*. The deceased's interest in the house would ordinarily bypass their estate and go automatically to his widow, even if his will stated otherwise. However, the court can claw back into the estate what had been the deceased's interest. Obviously the widow would spit brass tacks if that happened on an application by someone other than her and so would be involved in the proceedings and be heard. Most jointly owned properties are held by their proprietors as *joint tenants*. Otherwise, they are held as *tenants in common* which means the proprietors own in specific shares – say 50/50 – and their respective interests can be gifted by them and, will or no will, those interests count as part of their estates when they die. Owners decide whether they want to be *joint tenants* or *tenants in common* (and, if so, what shares each will take) when they acquire a property and their wishes should be clear from the conveyancing documents and land registry entries. Any owner who holds as a *joint tenant* can easily change over to a *tenancy in common* and, unless there is a contrary agreement with the co-owner, this would have the effect of giving them equal shares (see chapter 45).

Which court?

You can bring a claim in the county court and take it or send it to your civil hearing centre. The Part 8 procedure should be used (see chapter 12). You need to put in a claim form and a written statement in support (see chapter 12) and make the personal representatives of the deceased the defendants to the claim. The details of the claim on the claim may go something like this:

> "The claimant claims under section 1 of the Inheritance (Provision for Family and Dependants) Act 1975 as the spouse of Clive Troublesore deceased for financial provision out of his estate and for the costs of the claim to be paid out of the estate."

Leaving it late

The will has nothing for you apart from a few raspberries or maybe you scooped the deceased's false teeth and have nowhere to put them. But didn't the deceased tell you close to death that his signed first edition copy of *Breaking Law* was to be yours, or marginally better still, that they would be leaving you their home (paddock land included)? There is an outside chance that such a gift though not in the will is legally effective. But be warned. The law on so-called death bed gifts – gifts made in contemplation of death or *'donatio mortis causa'* for my Latin readers – is strict. This is because it would be easy to come up with a cock and bull story about what the deceased said and did as the end approached and the deceased cannot readily be called to rebut it. And because of the desirability of preserving a written will as the appropriate means by which we should express our wishes about who gets what when we die.

As it happens, the law has got stricter thanks to a Court of Appeal ruling in 2015 in a case in which four to six months before her death, the claimant's elderly cat and dog loving aunt handed him the title deeds to her home which was not registered at the Land Registry. As she did so she told him; "This will be yours when I go." Her legally effective will gave everything, including the property, to seven animal charities.

Here's a countdown to what you would need to prove to persuade a court to uphold a deathbed (or close to it) gift in your favour.

1. The deceased must have contemplated their impending death. Not simply that they were approaching the end of their natural lifespan but that they had good reason to anticipate their death in the near future from an identified cause. The mere possibility of death weeks or months later will fall short of what is required.

2. The gift must only be intended to take effect if and when death occurs so that the deceased can cancel it at any time. When an early death is inevitable, the court is likely to relax the need for the deceased to have specifically laid down that the property was to be returned to them if they survived.

3. The deceased must have given you physical possession of the gift or some means of accessing it or documentation showing your entitlement to take possession of it.

In one case the deceased, while dying in hospital, slipped into his partner's handbag the key to a strong box containing the title deeds to his unregistered house. As he did so he said to her: "The house is yours, Margaret. You have the keys. They are in your bag. The deeds are in the steel box."

Margaret got the partner's house.

The nephew didn't get auntie's house. He couldn't satisfy all those conditions.

Ownership of most properties and land is now registered at the Land Registry so there would be no title deeds which the deceased could hand over in order to satisfy condition 3 above. That does not rule out that the handing over of something else would do the trick. A conundrum for a court at some time in the future. Stick around.

Are you aware of anyone who might show up close to the end and concoct a deathbed gift story? Of course you are. You could put with your will a statement which could go some way to impugning any deathbed gift claim that might be made. You might integrate it into the statement dealing with anyone who has been omitted from the will (see below).

> "I have this day executed my last will and testament. I have been advised and fully understand that I can change any of its provisions at any time before my death by way of codicil or revocation with a fresh will. I always have ready access to pen and paper and could easily summon prospective witnesses who could be present and actually witness me making a codicil or fresh will. I also have my solicitor's emergency contact number and she has assured me that I can summon her at short notice in the unlikely event that I should wish to make a codicil to my existing will or make a fresh will.
>
> I assess the prospects of me changing my mind about the provisions of my existing will to be non-existent. I have thought about these provisions with great care before executing the will and I regard it as inconceivable that any event (apart from any gift in my existing will being

> destined to fail because the beneficiary has predeceased me) could occur to lead me to change my mind about those provisions."

FOR THE DECEASED'S EYES ONLY

Don't say we didn't tell you. You worked seven days a week for years, saved a few bob, divorced the first wife after you caught her engaging in sexual commerce with the organic fruit and vegetable delivery man and her Botox refiller and you disowned your son for habitual drugs misuse and profligacy. And now you have kicked the bucket, the divorced wife and the son have made Inheritance Act claims. It's too late now for your voice to be heard except through your personal representatives unless you can get a pass back but you could have put a statement with the will as mentioned – naturally, signed by you and dated – which set out in moderate yet firm language why those two parasites would not be getting anything from your estate. The statement would have been in the will envelope and so could have been held back when probate was applied for. The judge would have read it and, though by no means could it have been guaranteed to scupper the parasites' claims, it might still have done the trick.

And tell your mate up there that it's no good screaming on about having hidden his will behind the picture of Blondie on the living room wall. Without knowing it is there, one of his relatives will apply for letters of administration to his estate and the intestacy laws will apply. It's tough that he thinks they stink. We don't have a system of compulsory registration of wills. If a dissatisfied relative rips up a will (a crime so don't try it at home) or the will cannot be found and there is no evidence about what was in it then, again, the laws of intestacy will swoop into action. Your mate could have voluntarily registered the will with the Probate Service or regional probate registry and that would have totally eliminated the risk of his estate being wound up on the basis that he died without a will. The facility is not widely known. I am not saying that they won't tell you all about it if you ask but they haven't yet taken a full page ad in *The Sun* ("Die Laughing. Make a deposit with us. Hurry."). If your mate is interested for next time around, tell him he can obtain details at gov.uk/government/publications/store-a-will-with-the-probate-service/how-to-store-a-will-with-the-probate-service. The one-off registration fee is £20 and there is no charge for withdrawing the will (use form PA7A) if you are still alive and want it back if your executor is after it following your death. Otherwise, you can keep the will with a solicitor, a bank (watch for a charge) or one of the companies that maintains its own registry (watch for a charge). The Probate Service is my hot tip for the best location.

There's an alternative way of seeking to ensure that your will sees the light of day. That is to register it online with the National Will Register run by Certainty (see nationalwillregister.co.uk) which holds records of over 8.4m wills. If your will has been drawn up by a solicitor or a non-solicitor will writer then they can see to registration for you: otherwise, you can handle it personally. What gets registered is the fact that you have made a will and where it is located. But, unlike the Probate Service, they won't hold the will for you. Certainty is especially useful in quickly establishing whether a will exists so could aid your loved ones in deciding whether or not to go to the trouble of organising the wake. The will registration fee is £30. A search of the register to establish whether a will has been made will cost £45.60 and an extensive search for an unregistered will is £114. These figures are VAT inclusive.

Chapter 45

Joint Tenancies

Severing without pain

When you own a freehold or leasehold house or flat (or just a patch of overgrown land on which to graze your pony or best friend) jointly with someone else, it will be as *joint tenants* or *tenants in common*. It should be clear which it is from the deed transferring the property to you or from the Land Register. If you are joint tenants and one of you dies during ownership, their interest will automatically pass to the other. The fact that the deceased's will purported to gift their interest to a third person will not count. But if you are tenants in common, this will not happen. Each of you is free to will your interest or any part of it to the other, to me, to Bradley Walsh, to whomsoever.

Joint tenants can become tenants in common in a relatively painless way and, once that is done, the law will treat each of them as having an equal interest in the property. You need to make a statement to the effect that you are changing the basis of ownership – it is called a *notice of severance* – and ensure that your co-owner receives a copy. Where they are your spouse or partner, the copy can be handed over in the family kitchen after all utensils have been removed to prevent them being launched in your direction. It would be wise to put the notice with the deeds and, if possible, for your co-owner to acknowledge receipt of the copy on the original notice. Just in case your co-owner takes to hiding in a dustbin disguised as garden refuse to evade being handed a copy of the notice, it is good enough to leave it for them at their last known home or business address, even if it never comes to their attention! If the property is registered at the Land Registry – as it will be in the vast majority of cases – apply to the Registry for registration of what is called a *Form A restriction*.

This will usually be the restriction wording: "No disposition by a sole proprietor of the registered estate (except a trust corporation) under which capital money arises is to be registered unless authorised by an order of the court." It will prevent your co-owner dealing with the property without the concurrence of yourself or your executor and tell the world – or, more precisely, anyone who checks at the Registry – that you are no longer joint tenants. There's no Land Registry fee – really – and you can find out how to get that restriction by going to gov.uk/joint-property/change-from-joint-tenants-to-tenants in-common.

In certain situations, a joint tenancy will become a tenancy in common without either owner coming up with a *notice of severance* or their arms leaving their bodies. This will happen on the bankruptcy of one of them and may also happen if a charging order is made against the property or the interest of one of them (see chapter 29) or one of them unlawfully kills the other.

Here's that notice of severance.

To Minnie Mouse, Cheese Cottage, High Street, Titchfield, Hants PO14 4AE

I CHARLES MOUSE hereby give you notice of my desire to sever the joint tenancy in equity of and in Cheese Cottage, High Street, Titchfield, Hants PO14 4AE now held by us as joint tenants at law and in equity.

Dated 14 July 2021

(signed) Charles Mouse

Chapter 46

Squatters' Rights

How to become a landowner without really trying

You can steal a paperclip. You can steal a gold bar. But you can't steal land. That's why you never hear of anyone up before the local beaks charged with theft of a park or a house. However, you do hear of squatters. This chapter is not about the smelly, scary and unkempt squatters who take over land and buildings for a few months until they are evicted. It is about the more sophisticated and sometimes insidious squatters and what the law books call 'adverse possession'.

Look, no rent for 12 years

At the start of my days as the BBC Radio Solent on-air lawyer before I became a judge, I was keen to get hold of a good legal story which is how I came to turn up for the first time on national radio. A lady who worked at Gosport Magistrates' Court recounted to me the tale of her parents and their absent landlord. They had taken a monthly tenancy of a house in the town and 12 years previously had stopped paying the rent. They didn't know to whom to pay it. The landlord had disappeared. Enquiries to trace him came to nothing. "Now why don't you get them to write to the Radio Lawyer for advice?" They did. Presenter Jeff Link interviewed me. I opined that thanks to squatters' rights, in the particular circumstances the couple effectively now owned the property. Early next morning in bed and in a semi-conscious state I heard the voice of Jack de Manio on the *Today* programme and then I heard what I thought was my voice and fathomed out it *was* my voice. Having finished recording the interview with me the evening before, Jeff Link, unbeknown to me, had packaged the item for *Today*. The postscript to the story is that the landlord never did appear and in due course the couple were registered with the Land Registry as the absolute owners of the house which by then was worth over £150,000.

The squatter at work

The more usual route for gaining land through the squatting laws runs quite differently. The squatter begins using land they have not previously been associated with or moves the fence at the bottom of their garden three hundred metres into the adjoining field and extends the fencing to the sides. They may be less adventurous and erect a wall at the side of their house a quarter of a metre into the next door neighbour's land. They go about their business quite openly for this is one of the essentials to getting the squatting laws to work for them. Where appropriate, they will probably cultivate this land. They will never seek approval from the owner of the land for what they do because this would be fatal to their enterprise. Should the owner of the land on which they are squatting ask them to desist they will ignore them unless they fear the owner might punch them about the body or bring civil court proceedings against them (as the owner could) for trespass and even damages and costs to boot. Never ever will they sign a written acknowledgment that the land belongs to the owner for that, squatterlawwise, would waste the time they had occupied it. They will reject any offer from the owner to grant a tenancy or a licence to use the land as such a creature would be a killer of their plans. They will exercise some form of physical control over the land. They will be conscious of the fact that when the time arrives (see below), they will need to show that they intended to possess the land and have been dealing with the land as an occupying owner would have dealt with it and that no one else has done so whilst they have been concerned with it. They will not be guilty about their motives for they know that motives do not matter in the jungle of squatters.

Bye bye

Until the time arrives for them to claim that the land in question is now their land, the squatter who is occupying it cannot sell it. But should they sell their own land, they can certainly transfer to their buyer any "rights" they have to the new land. The time the squatter has been occupying the new land can be added on to the time their buyer occupies, having stepped into their squatter shoes, in order to score the period needed to become the new owner. The prudent buyer will obtain a statutory declaration – a formal written statement signed up in the presence of a lawyer and, indeed, make it a condition of the purchase contract that one is handed over on completion – setting out the squatting history in lurid detail. That's what happened when Christopher Moran bought a house in Dolphin Place, Amersham in 1971. His sellers in the conveyance deed transferred "all such estate right title and interest as the vendors may have in or over ..." a plot of land which had belonged to Buckinghamshire County Council and which it intended to use at some time in the future for a proposed diversion of the A404. From 1967, the sellers whose house adjoined, had cut the grass of the plot, trimmed the hedges and from time to time parked a horsebox on it. A statutory declaration was handed over with the deeds explaining the history and Mr Moran carried on where his sellers had left off. He also padlocked the gate to the plot and kept the key. The county council failed in its attempt to have Mr Moran booted out. Because that time had arrived.

When does the time arrive?

The period required for ownership of the land to effectively pass to the squatter depends on whether or not the land is registered at the Land Registry. Most land is registered. If the land is unregistered, the period was and remains 12 years. If it is registered, the period has been reduced to ten years as from 13 October 2003 by virtue of changes made by the Land Registration Act 2002, unless the squatter had already notched up their 12 years before that date. There is an exception where the squatting is on Crown foreshore. A whacking 60 years of adverse possession is needed there. This embraces "the shore and bed of the sea and of any tidal water, below the line of the medium high tide between the spring and neap tides". Let's hope you aren't too wet to fathom that out. Sorry.

The squatter of *unregistered* land with 12 years under their belt as at midnight on 13 October 2003 can apply to the Land Registry for title to the land to be registered for the first time in their name (unsurprisingly, called an application for first registration of title). The squatter of *registered* land with 12 years under their belt at midnight on 13 October 2003 can apply to the Land Registry to be recorded as the new proprietor but the existing registered proprietor and certain others will be notified and can put forward objections.

And the squatter of registered land (I know you may be finding this tedious) who notches up the lesser period of 10 years but only after midnight on 13 October 2003 can apply to the Land Registry to be recorded as the new proprietor. Again, notice will be given to the registered owner and certain others who can object. No objections? The squatter is recorded as the new owner. Objections? Generally, the registered owner prevails but if they fail to get the squatter evicted or at least to obtain a court order for the squatter to give up possession within the next two years, the squatter can return to the Land Registry and more or less repeat his application. Second time round the squatter will prevail.

One exception to how things go on a first application. Where the squatter and the registered owner own adjoining land – typically in the moving fence or encroaching wall erection situation – the registered owner will not usually be entitled to object to the application after 10 years of squatting if (a) the exact line of the relevant boundary has not been determined under Land Registry rules and (b) during the time of squatting, the squatter reasonably believed that the land they want recorded in their name actually belonged to them. This exception was subject to a controversial decision of the upper tribunal in a 2020 case called *Dowse v City of Bradford Metropolitan District Council*. This is as good as a judgment of the High Court for binding tribunal and county court judges in cases which have to be decided from hereon. It was ruled that, for the exception to apply, the land claimed has to adjoin the whole or substantially the whole of the squatter's land or otherwise the registered owner will prevail.

Dry land

It's all rather complicated, 'aint it?! Should you want more detail, I commend the excellent Land Registry series of guides which you can access on the internet and will guarantee you will never be invited to another dinner party should you mention them at the next one.

The morals

1. Periodically check out land you own.
2. Don't go away for more than ten years less a month or two at a time and as soon as you get back, pop round to *Whiteacres* and check that there's no one there, the grass is longer than you left it, the hedge is reaching for the sky and the next door neighbour does not have a smug look on their face.
3. Avoid any claim of adverse possession by ensuring that when you allow

another person to use your land or buildings they acknowledge in writing that they are doing so with your permission. Adverse possession and consent do not go hand in hand.

Chapter 47

Libel, Slander And Malicious Falsehood

Troublesore v Whitecock – Statement in open court

Solicitor for the claimant: "My Lord, I appear for the claimant who is a highly respected citizen. The defendant is a retailer of pedal cycles and their accessories. He is represented today by my learned friend Mr Francis de Lobowalk.

In August 2020 my client purchased a bell from the defendant which fell to pieces when he attempted to fix it to his cycle. It was defective. When he returned the bell to the defendant's shop he was abused by a staff member and denied any redress. The following day the defendant posted a message on the website vexiandvile.com in which he accused the claimant of having made a false claim against him and demanding £10,000 for not reporting him to trading standards. He went on to allege that the claimant was a serial false complainant and urged any shopkeeper who encountered him to evict him from their premises. The website has in excess of three million followers and a substantial number of whom hail from the claimant's region.

All these allegations by the defendant were untrue, as the defendant now accepts. In particular, the defendant accepts that the bell was defective and that the claimant made no demands of him or his business other than for a full refund of the price paid for the bell and the expenses incurred by him in travelling by bus to and from the defendant's shop. He also accepts that whilst the claimant has in the past made a number of consumer complaints against other businesses, they have always been well founded and that the claimant is not vexatious.

The defendant appears here today by counsel to apologise to the claimant for the damage, distress and embarrassment caused by the online publication. Further, the defendant has agreed to pay to the claimant a substantial sum in compensation and to deliver to him a lifetime's supply of cycle bells of the highest standard and to indemnify the claimant for his legal costs."

Counsel for the defendant: "My Lord, I confirm everything my friend has said. My client extremely regrets that he failed to give satisfaction to the claimant in the matter of the bell, that the claimant's complaint was not dealt with efficiently but most inappropriately by a very junior member of staff who has since been dismissed and that the defendant in a moment of madness after a very stressful day and completely out of character, should have libelled the claimant as he did."

Solicitor for the claimant: "In the circumstances, my Lord, it only remains for me to ask for permission to withdraw the record."

This is the speak of defamation proceedings – libel and slander – which have settled. The claimant makes a statement in court which has been approved in advance by the court and the defendant usually joins in. The hope is that the statement will be reported on by the media and that the public and, in particular, anyone who knew about the defamation will come to hear of the statement in court and will thereupon realise that the claimant is good and pure. The claimant may turn up at court to hear the statement and pose a little on the ways in and out as they insist to their inquisitors that they cannot say how much they are being paid in damages by the erring defendant. Custom has it that actual figures are not mentioned. "Substantial damages" sounds good but they may be only a few hundred pounds. Views differ on whether a statement in court is wise. It effectively repeats the libel or slander and then proceeds to knock it down. Some may think there is no smoke without fire and that the real reason damages are being paid and an apology is being given is that the publisher cannot get the evidence together to justify the truth of what was written or uttered.

Brittan meets Gold

My first experience of an open court statement was when I was despatched off as a naïve trainee solicitor to the Royal Courts of Justice in London's Strand for the making of a statement following the settlement of a libel action brought by the then town clerk of Gosport for whom my principal had been acting. The statement was being read out by a barrister, the late Leon Brittan (pre-MP, Lordship and the rest) who my firm had briefed for the purpose. Back then solicitors from the sticks who had a case in London were required to use a London firm of solicitors for hearings in the capital to act as their agents. So there were Leon Brittan, the London agent and me with the file and one copy of the statement on flimsy paper. Outside court the London agent introduced the naïve trainee to Mr Brittan whereupon he gave him a sneering glance and turned away. An enduring image. The statement having been read out, I was besieged by a multitude of reporters who wanted the flimsy paper which taught me – and my principal – always to go to court armed with ample copies to satiate members of the press whose shorthand is not up to scratch.

Cyril Smith apologises

You may wonder why such an array of talent had to be assembled to read from a piece of paper. Good point. The practice was an irritant to solicitor Alastair Brett who in 1985 was senior legal assistant with Times Newspapers Ltd and, with his employer's consent, was conducting a small private legal practice mainly representing personal friends during the course of which he had been advising the then Liberal MP Cyril Smith. He along with Radio Trent had been sued for defamation by Leo Abse, Tam Dalyell, Bob Cryer, Dennis Skinner and 21 other MPs over a broadcast Smith had made at the time of the Falklands crisis in which he had adversely commented about their conduct in voting as they did. The case was settling. A few days before a statement was due to be read, Brett telephoned his favourite defamation chambers to retain a barrister to read the statement which was to be made. The last time he had used a barrister to show how well they read, his client had paid out a fee of £50. This time he was being quoted £150 for his choice or £75 for a more junior barrister. "The fees have gone up, sir." For some time Brett had harboured the belief that a solicitor should be able to read out a statement which would make the exercise much cheaper. Generally, solicitors were not then entitled to speak in open court unless in hushed tones through the client's right ear. There would have to be a challenge. Brett briefed barrister David Pannick (later Lord Pannick QC) to apply to the High Court for Brett to be given permission to read out the statement. This may not have been an economically viable step in the circumstances but nevertheless, a worthy fight. The High Court judge refused Brett permission. There was only one thing left for it. An appeal to the Court of Appeal. That was proceeded with and failed. But the following year, judges announced that mere solicitors would be permitted to appear in formal and unopposed cases in the High Court when sitting openly which would include reading out a statement where a defamation case had settled: something I later did myself. This was the first step in extending solicitors' rights of audience in the higher courts.

"Pass the magnifying glass, please"

It's useful as part of a settlement to seek to extract a commitment by an offending publication to report the statement and to do so in at least as prominent a position as the offending article. I once represented a television presenter who sued a local newspaper for libel. It made a payment into court which he wanted to unconditionally accept but the paper failed to participate in the making of a statement in open court. It reported on the statement but in the most economical of terms and in a position less prominent than that occupied by the local tide times. I thought that the paper deserved a stricture from the now defunct and formerly feeble Press Complaints Commission. But we wanted anonymity. My client would have been guilty of self-inflicted ridicule if he had been unsuccessful in his complaint, having details of it well publicised with him being fully identified. So I asked the Commission's Mark Bolland (who went on to become deputy private secretary to Prince Charles, with no thanks to me) whether anonymity could be afforded. No. We had to forget the complaint.

Gold gets nervous

It was in 1971 that I had begun my weekly broadcasting on the law for BBC Radio Solent. I forgot to stop and was still at it 25 years later when appointment as a judge compelled me to quit. In the event, a regular round up of legal news was sometimes recorded from a small self-operated studio at Portsmouth Guildhall which linked up with the main studios in Southampton. There, a producer would deal with matters technical – like starting a recording machine. Fairly early on I was commenting on the outcome of a libel action which had concluded that day with Lady Docker, a bizarre socialite, winning her case and being awarded a halfpenny in contemptuous damages (or possibly a penny or a farthing but let's not fall out over quantum) which would suggest that the jury felt obliged to follow the law and find she had been defamed but didn't think much of her or her reputation. I alluded to her in an uncomplimentary way as I started to chat to producer Jeff Link at the other end. Unfortunately, a presenter had failed to switch the broadcast desk at his end on to Radio 2 resulting in my comments being broadcast live over the sports report. A memorandum was issued from on high. It was not to happen again. It didn't. I could have been on the wrong side of a libel writ but maybe Lady Docker didn't listen in to the sports report on local radio.

Gold gets gazebo

In November 1982 I was presenting a current affairs programme for the regional television station TVS when the Chichester and Bognor Regis Promoter libelled me. In a lead story on the front page (they must have been hard up for news that week) under the headline "Local Man Sues TVS Presenter" they reported on the issue of a writ against my law firm by a former client who alleged I had been negligent in litigation I had conducted for him.

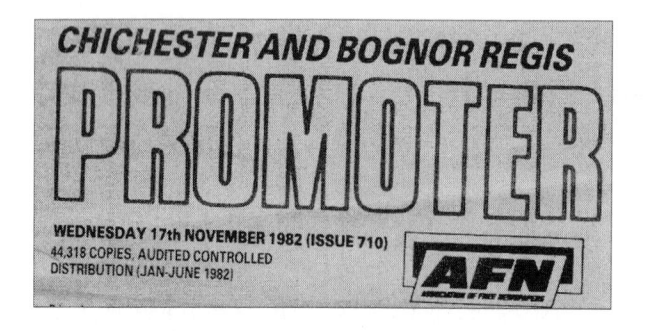

CHICHESTER AND BOGNOR REGIS PROMOTER
WEDNESDAY 17th NOVEMBER 1982 (ISSUE 710)
44,318 COPIES, AUDITED CONTROLLED DISTRIBUTION (JAN-JUNE 1982)
AFN

LOCAL MAN SUES TVS PRESENTER

"Ouch"

The writ was later abandoned and rightly so. With that out of the way, I sued the paper's publishers for libel (see *"I've been libelled"* on page 386). The report had gravely injured me in my character, credit and reputation and brought me into public scandal, odium and contempt. That was how the court papers grandly put it. The paper through its insurers put in a defence, not alleging that I had been negligent but, amongst a couple of things, denying that the article had been defamatory. Five years after the article had appeared and sensing that I was not going away, the publishers paid £1,050 into court to settle the claim (the Part 36 procedure did not then exist – see chapter 10) and I accepted. On top, the publishers had to pay my firm's bill covering the work I had done on their behalf in acting for me in pursuing the claim which was all perfectly legitimate. I had a gazebo built in my garden on the strength of the settlement.

But what about a statement in open court? I decided against it. On balance, I thought I had more to lose than win by having the libel repeated. After all, you know I couldn't possibly have been negligent.

Hacked off

I have to confess to less success with *The Independent*. In 1989 I was contributing to the paper's Law column. A man with a name not dissimilar to my own had allegedly been involved in a bit of computer hacking and a report of the court proceedings appeared in the paper. I was concerned that readers might think that the report referred to me. I asked the then editor Andreas Whittam Smith to publish a statement which distanced the lawyer from the alleged hacker. I asked for not a penny in compensation, not even for a free subscription to the paper. Liability in defamation can arise in such a situation although a publisher would have a defence when the statement complained of was included in a report of court proceedings which was fair, accurate and contemporaneous. Mr Smith was having none of it. He concluded that the risk of confusion was too small to require publication of a disclaimer (see *"Complaint dismissed"* on page 387). I thought it would be a good idea to carry on writing for *The Independent* so took that one on the chin. I have taken no pleasure in seeing its demise in print form. I liked the paper.

Beware

Should you reckon you have been libelled or slandered and want some compensation then a DIY job will be dangerous. The law in this area is complex, the case would have to be brought in the High Court and the costs there can reach astronomical heights. If your case is strong enough then lawyers will take you on a 'no win, no fee' basis (see chapter 7). If it isn't strong enough for that then you probably ought not to be suing. Maybe you are trying to assess your position through the paperback edition of *The One Thousand Things You Didn't Know About The Law by a Struck Off Solicitor* which your aunt bought you for Christmas 1957. Watch it. The defamation law changed for libels and slanders perpetrated after 31 December 2013. There will now be no defamation unless publication (in a newspaper or on radio or television or whatever) caused or was likely to cause serious harm to your reputation. For a claim by a business, including a company, there won't have been serious harm unless serious financial loss has been caused or was likely. This is a high threshold. Juries in defamation cases (one of the rare categories of civil cases in which they figured) have been virtually killed off which means that a judge alone will now try the case. For an internet libel the one-year rule for starting a claim in a defamation case (see chapter 13) is to apply from the date of the first posting and the one year will not rerun from a later publication of the same or substantially the same libel. And a useful power has been introduced which will generally enable the court to order the defendant to publish a summary of its judgment.

Defaming the dead

You can write or say what you like about someone who has died. Or can you? A judgment of the European Court of Human Rights at the end of 2013 suggested that a defamatory statement about a deceased person might, for a relative of the deceased, be a breach of their right to respect for private life under article 8 of the human rights convention. The impact on the relative would have to be pretty monumental for any hope of success on this basis. So if something false has been written or said about late Uncle Jimmy and you've been shunned and avoided by the world since then and have got a couple of hundred thousand to spend on legal costs, have a go, make legal history and get your name into the law reports – so long as the human rights convention is still around for us.

Shut up or else

Perhaps you have been libelled or slandered and have no wish to go near a court of law to do anything about it but want to frighten off the culprit. Never threaten to do that which you are not prepared to do. It will make you look weak and stupid. "Unless within seven days of the date of receipt of this letter you pay me damages of £2,000.00 and provide me with your withdrawal and unqualified apology for your libel, an irrevocable undertaking that you will not repeat or cause, encourage or permit to be repeated the defamatory statement that I am a raving paedophile or publish or cause, encourage or permit to be published any other statement which is defamatory of me, I shall commence proceedings against you in the High Court for damages, aggravated damages, an injunction to restrain you from defaming me in the future and costs without further notice." Forget it unless you mean it. Instead, adopt an ostensibly stern approach without committing yourself to litigation now:

> "At a meeting of Littlecamp Parish Council on 14 July 2021 you stated that I had failed to pay my council tax for seven years, had erected a tablet summarising my marriage vows in the back garden of my property without planning permission and was a serial adulterer. All these allegations are false and amount to the most serious actionable slander of me. You are required to take this letter as formal notice that in the event that these defamatory statements or any of them are repeated by you or any statement which is defamatory of me is made by you in the future or that you cause, encourage or permit any such statement to be repeated or made, I shall, without further notice, institute proceedings against you in the High Court for damages, aggravated damages, an injunction to restrain repetition, interest and costs in respect of the slanders published on 14 July 2021 and any subsequent defamation."

Website libel

If you are libelled on a website and the operator will not remove the statement that causes you concern, you may wish to make a claim against the poster. You know their identity? No problem. You don't know their identity?

You can apply to the court for the operator to identify them or consider taking advantage of the Defamation (Operators of Websites) Regulations 2013 because that could be a passport to a successful claim against the operator for publishing the statement which is otherwise likely to be legally difficult. What you do is to send the site operator a *notice of complaint*. This must:

- give your name;
- set out the statement concerned, where on the website it was posted, why it is defamatory of you, the meaning you attribute to it and the aspects of it which you believe are factually inaccurate or are opinions not supported by fact;
- confirm that you do not have sufficient information about the poster to bring proceedings against them;
- confirm whether you consent to the operator providing the poster with your name and email address; and
- specify the email address at which you can be contacted.

Ensure you get all that in. Generally, the operator must send the poster within 48 hours a copy of the *notice of complaint* (with your name and address concealed if you did not consent to disclosure). The poster then has an opportunity to consent or object to the statement being removed. Should the poster consent or do nothing, the statement should be removed. The operator's failure to follow what the regulations require them to do after they receive a *notice of complaint* will rob the operator of the defamation defence otherwise available to them that they hadn't posted the statement.

> To *vexiandvile.com*
>
> *Below is my notice of complaint. In view of its contents and, without prejudice to your statutory obligations in consequence of the notice, I call on you to forthwith withdraw the statement referred to in the notice which is highly defamatory of me.*
>
> **Notice of complaint pursuant to the Defamation (Operation of Websites) Regulations 2013**
>
> *My name: Clive Troublesore.*
>
> *My address at which I can be contacted: sorebore12@yahooshucks.co.uk.*
>
> *Statement complained of: "Troublesore is a menace and must be stopped. He lies about his purchases being naff and tried to screw my mate out of ten grand for flogging him a bloody bike bell that was a peach saying he was off to trading standards if he didn't pay up."*
>
> *Where statement was posted on your website: Bastard's Corner (on 14 July 2021).*
>
> *Why statement is defamatory: It is untrue and its publication has caused and/or is likely to cause serious harm to my reputation.*

Meaning I attribute to the statement: I am dishonest; a serial frivolous and vexatious complainant and/or litigant; and a blackmailer.

Factually inaccurate aspects of statement: That I am a liar; that I am a menace; that I attempted to extract £10,000 from a bicycle bell seller; that the bell sold to me had been of good or satisfactory quality; and that I threatened to report the bell seller to trading standards if I was not paid £10,000.

Aspects of the statement which are opinions unsupported by fact: That I need to be stopped from pursuing any course of conduct which is objectionable or improper.

Disclosure of my identity: I consent to you providing the poster with my name and my electronic mail address.

Poster's identity: I confirm that I do not have sufficient information about the poster to bring proceedings against that person.

Malicious falsehood

This is one of my favourites. A claim for malicious falsehood can be made when you have been slagged off and caused financial loss as a result.

> *"Clive Troublesore has retired as painter and decorator. I will be delighted to give you a competitive quote for the sort of job he used to do."*
>
> *"If you want a jar of jam, steer clear of anything made by Clive Troublesore. I've heard he mixes up the strawberries and raspberries in his empty paint pots."*

The recipe for a successful malicious falsehood claim is a written or verbal statement which is not only false but has been communicated to someone else, was made maliciously and, generally, has caused actual financial loss as was likely to happen. Malicious falsehood differs from libel and slander in a variety of ways. The most striking difference is that you do not have to prove that the statement has injured your reputation. Nevertheless, if your feelings as well as your pocket have taken a knock, you could claim damages for both, asking for aggravated damages in relation to the injury to feelings. Libel and slander claims are sometimes coupled with an alternative claim for malicious falsehood.

Here is what makes malicious falsehood such a cutie. Whereas a libel or slander claim cannot generally be started in the county court, a malicious falsehood claim can be started there. You might even just be able to get an uncomplicated malicious falsehood claim squeezed onto the small claims track although this would almost certainly mean having to limit the claim to £10,000. As to the ingredient of malice which is needed, that may not be as hard to prove as you might think. The defendant must have acted with some improper motive. Normally, they will be treated as having done so if they knew that the statement was false or made it recklessly, not caring whether it was true or false. If the statement was made in good faith, don't waste the ink on completing a claim form.

Say you have all the ingredients for a successful claim bar being able to prove the statement has caused you actual financial loss? In certain circumstances, it won't matter. That's when the statement was likely to have caused such loss, though it did not, and it was in writing or made during a television or radio broadcast or the performance of a play. You can also succeed without actual financial loss when the statement was likely to have caused actual financial loss in respect of your job or business. Obviously, without financial loss there will be no point in making a claim unless you are after an injunction to prevent a repetition or damages for hurt feelings. The open court statement procedure (see above) is now also available in a malicious falsehood claim that settles.

Particulars of Claim

1. At all material times, the claimant carried on the business of a part-time painter and decorator ("the business") and the defendant was a full-time painter and decorator in competition with the claimant and ordinarily operating in the same localities.

2. Between, on or about 2 to 23 January 2021 the defendant distributed and thereby published in and around Twickenham, Middlesex not less than 200 leaflets ("the leaflets") containing the following words ("the words") relating to the business:

> "Clive Troublesore has retired as painter and decorator. I will be delighted to give you a competitive quote for the sort of job he used to do."

3. The words were false and published maliciously. The claimant had not retired as a painter and decorator and was ready, willing and able to take on new contracts. The defendant knew of their falsity or, in the alternative, published them recklessly, not caring whether they were true or false, in order to induce the recipients of the leaflets to contract with the defendant instead of the claimant.

4. In consequence of the said publications, the claimant has suffered loss and damage in that he has lost profit from contracts into which certain recipients of the leaflets entered with the defendant whereas they would otherwise have contracted with the claimant or, in the alternative, the claimant has lost the chance of entering into contracts with such recipients. Further and alternatively, the words were likely to cause pecuniary damage to the claimant in the business.

And the claimant claims:

a. Damages limited to £10,000;

b. Interest;

c. An injunction to refrain the defendant from publishing, causing *to be published or encouraging any other person to publish the words or any similar words likely to cause damage to the claimant; and*

d.   *Costs.*

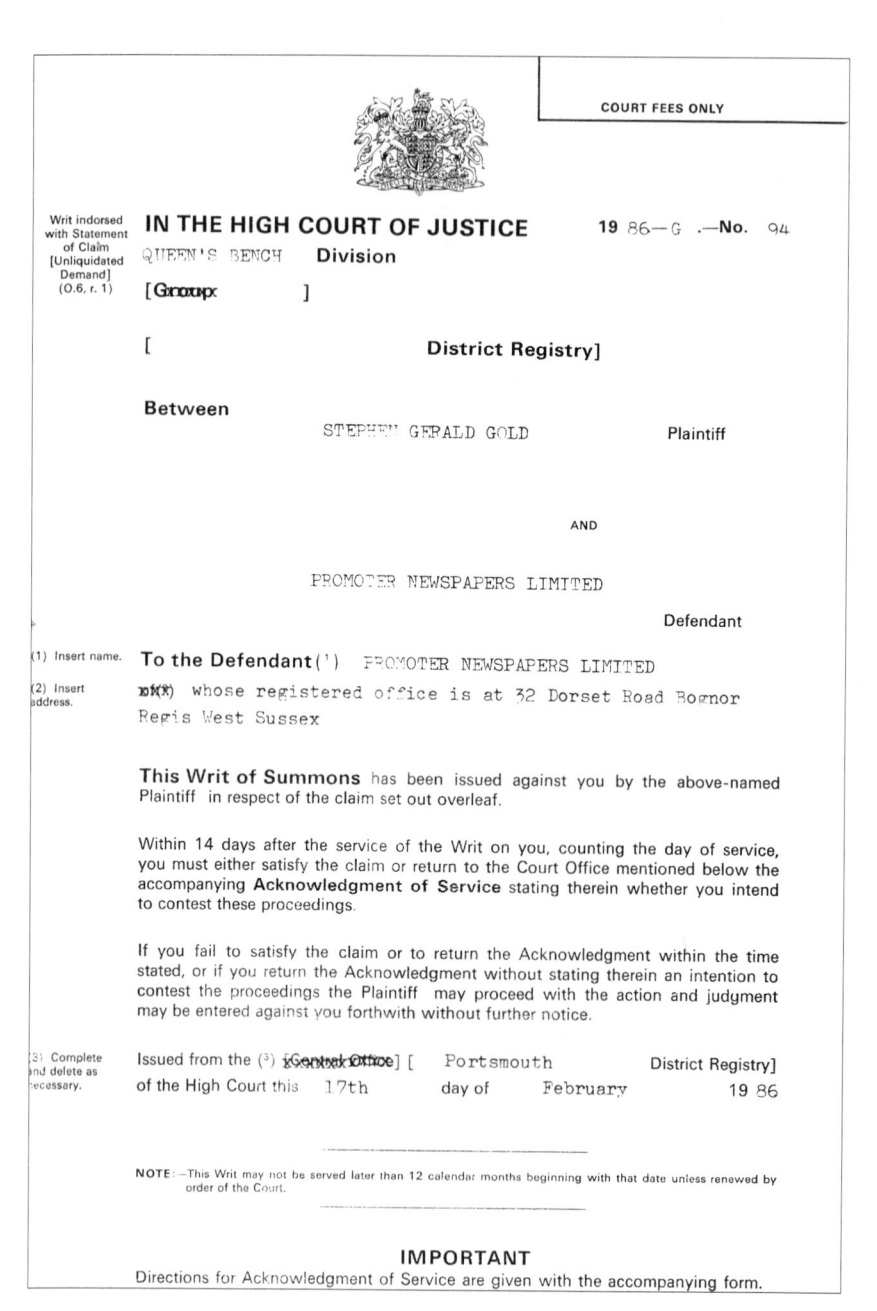

	COURT FEES ONLY

Writ indorsed with Statement of Claim [Unliquidated Demand] (O.6, r. 1)

IN THE HIGH COURT OF JUSTICE   19 86—G .—No. 94

QUEEN'S BENCH **Division**

[Group]

[**District Registry**]

Between

STEPHEN GERALD GOLD   Plaintiff

AND

PROMOTER NEWSPAPERS LIMITED

Defendant

(1) Insert name.
(2) Insert address.

To the Defendant(¹) PROMOTER NEWSPAPERS LIMITED

of(²) whose registered office is at 32 Dorset Road Bognor Regis West Sussex

This Writ of Summons has been issued against you by the above-named Plaintiff in respect of the claim set out overleaf.

Within 14 days after the service of the Writ on you, counting the day of service, you must either satisfy the claim or return to the Court Office mentioned below the accompanying **Acknowledgment of Service** stating therein whether you intend to contest these proceedings.

If you fail to satisfy the claim or to return the Acknowledgment within the time stated, or if you return the Acknowledgment without stating therein an intention to contest the proceedings the Plaintiff may proceed with the action and judgment may be entered against you forthwith without further notice.

(3) Complete and delete as necessary.

Issued from the (³) [Central Office] [Portsmouth   District Registry] of the High Court this   17th   day of   February   19 86

NOTE:—This Writ may not be served later than 12 calendar months beginning with that date unless renewed by order of the Court.

IMPORTANT

Directions for Acknowledgment of Service are given with the accompanying form.

"I've been libelled"

THE INDEPENDENT

NEWSPAPER PUBLISHING PLC
40 City Road, London EC1Y 2DB
Telephone: 01-253 1222 Telex: 9419611
Direct Line: 01-956   Fax: 01-956 1435

16 November 1989

Mr S G Gold
Donnelly & Elliott
Solicitors
38 Stoke Road
GOSPORT
Hampshire
PO12 1JG

Dear Mr Gold,

Thank you for your letter of 29 September. I have discussed your worry about confusion with your namesake, but I have come to the conclusion that the risk is too small to require publication of a disclaimer.

Yours sincerely,

Andreas Whittam Smith
Editor

Newspaper Publishing plc
Directors The Lord Sieff of Brimpton OBE (Chairman), Andreas Whittam Smith (Editor & Chief Executive), Christopher Barton, Stephan Conaway, Ian Hay Davison, George Duncan, Bruce Fireman, Stephen Glover, Adrian O'Neill, Matthew Symonds
Registered in England number 1908967 *Registered Office* 40 City Road, London EC1Y 2DB

"Complaint dismissed"

Chapter 48

Bankruptcy

The ecstasy and the agony

The honourable thing to do is to pay off your debts. Nobody would quarrel with that. Well perhaps they would. Alas, the debts may be so high or your financial position so dire that there is no reasonable prospect of you achieving settlement during the lifetime of your great grandchildren. Or it may be those personal and telephone calls from your more aggressive creditors are getting you down. It's the creditors who have bought the debt from the people you originally owed the money to, sometimes for less than the price of a box of ten *Woodbines*, who can be the most aggressive. Then bankruptcy may be the answer. Let's see what it really involves and, if you find the idea of it to be anathema, are there alternatives?

The nice bits

You can tell your creditors to go to hell. Once you have been made bankrupt, they cannot lawfully chase you for what you owed them. And at the end of one year after you were made bankrupt, generally speaking, the slate is wiped clean. The debts you had are cancelled when you are said to be discharged from bankruptcy and the discharge happens automatically without any application to the court or anyone else. That's a pretty good deal, isn't it? The slate cleaning still comes after 12 months even though you have been made bankrupt before although this period can be extended if you have failed to cooperate with the official receiver who deals with your affairs following bankruptcy. I once had the doubtful distinction of making a bankruptcy order against a man who had been through it twice before. Three bankruptcies over a relatively short period. He deserved some sort of medal for finding so many people to extend credit to him.

Before the Enterprise Act 2002 came into force, discharge generally took three years, though longer for those who had been bankrupted before within the previous 15 years. The radical change in the law was spearheaded by former Prime Minister Gordon Brown when he was Chancellor of the Exchequer, for the ostensible purpose of helping struggling entrepreneurs whom it was felt were encumbered by the stigma and restraints which had traditionally been associated with bankruptcy. So the three years came down to one year for entrepreneurs but also housewives on benefits with a string of credit card debit balances, organ grinders, shysters and old hands (none of them being mutually exclusive). The late Labour MP Michael Meacher was once before me as a claimant complaining about how easy it was for debtors to avoid their responsibilities. I told him who he had to thank when it came to bankruptcy!

There are some exceptions to the rule that bankruptcy wipes out your debts. You continue to be liable for arrears of maintenance to a spouse or former spouse and civil partner or former civil partner and, thanks to a change in the law, for a matrimonial order for payment of a lump sum of money or an order for costs as well. Other exceptions (so you will still be liable) are:

- student loans unless the bankruptcy took place before 1 September 2004 and the loan was received or the entitlement to the loan arose before that date;
- fines;
- outstanding child support;
- debts incurred by means of fraud (which led in February 2021 in a case called *Jones & Pyle Developments Ltd v Rymell* to the High Court allowing enforcement of a liability of around £83,000 notwithstanding that the defendant's bankruptcy discharge had taken place six years ago); and
- money due under most judgments for damages for personal injury.

Creditors who hold security, like a building society to whom you have mortgaged a property or a creditor who has obtained a county court judgment against you and followed it up with a charging order (see chapter 29), can, subject to a suitable court order, dispose of the security and take out of the proceeds whatever they are owed with the remainder being made available for your creditors without any security.

The possibly not so bad bit

Take this scenario. You jointly own your home with your partner. You need money and, with your partner's agreement, you borrow it using the property as security for the loan. You are then made bankrupt. Can your partner tell your trustee in bankruptcy that the property is out of the reach of your creditors because of the loan? Possibly, yes. Your partner would be taking advantage of what is called – altogether now – the equitable doctrine of exoneration. It is a doctrine which was doing the rounds in the 18th and 19th centuries. As a Court of Appeal decision in 2017 demonstrates, it's as good as it ever was.

What happened in the Court of Appeal case was that a husband's law firm had debts. He borrowed more money under an existing mortgage on the family home to pay off them off. The property was in his sole name but it still jointly belonged to him and his wife. In legal eyes, you can be a joint owner without having your name on the deeds or registered at the Land Registry (see chapter 71). Eventually, the law firm closed down and the husband was made bankrupt. The husband's trustee in bankruptcy applied to the court for the property to be sold. The court decided that the doctrine of the equity of exoneration came into play and refused to order the sale. This was because the wife was to be treated as having a charge over the husband's share in the property which exhausted its value.

Exoneration won't work if the loan was raised for the benefit of the person arguing for the doctrine to be applied – where, say, you could both go on holiday or some of the debts were run up by that person. This was the area of main dispute in the Court of Appeal case in which the ruling was that, for the doctrine not to work, the benefit had to be directly or closely connected to the borrowing and be capable of carrying a financial value. There was no such benefit to the wife in that case.

The not so nice bit 1

You lose your assets. Ouch! Ok, so you haven't got any assets. I've always been amazed by the dearth of assets shown in the statements which debtors seeking a bankruptcy order have produced to me. The higher their credit card debts – and it isn't unusual to see someone on benefits having run up liabilities of over £20,000 – the less likely it seems they will have anything to show for it. I do hope, dear debtors, that you haven't been pulling the wool over my bespectacled eyes. Anyway, if there are any assets (and you sure can't hide a house or flat under the bed and if you gave it away in the run up to bankruptcy, it may be retrieved for the benefit of your creditors), you will lose them. That includes your home if you do own it and your interest, with the mortgage debt being deducted from the market value of the property, is worth more than £1,000. Should you jointly own the property with, say, your spouse or partner then it's only your share which will be lost to your creditors. The interest of your spouse or partner will be preserved for them and, when the property is their sole or principal home, the creditors will not usually be after trying to get the property sold until one year from the date you were made bankrupt has elapsed.

The trick in that situation is to buy out the creditors if you can source the money required. You will have to come up with the amount your interest in the home would have raised if it was sold on behalf of your creditors. Perhaps your spouse or partner is in a position to raise the necessary money on a mortgage or you have a relative who can come to your financial rescue. Or perhaps released from all those debts which you owed when you were made bankrupt, your financial position is transformed and you can find a willing mortgage lender to come up with the necessary money. Such lenders do exist but criteria are very strict and you'll find yourself having to pay an interest rate way above that which would have been available to the Archbishop of Canterbury (who has never been bankrupt). Although discharge from bankruptcy comes after one year, the official receiver (or whoever has been appointed outside the Insolvency Service to act on behalf of your creditors – either way they are called the trustee in bankruptcy) has three years from the date on which you were made bankrupt to do something about getting hold of your interest in a home by applying to the court for you to leave or for the property to be sold, or both. The court has power to extend the three years but it is rare for this to happen. Subject to this, at the end of the three years, the property will revert to you.

Like virtually everything else in the law, there are exceptions to the rule that you lose your assets on bankruptcy. Your pension is the Enormously Huge exception for bankruptcies ordered after 29 May 2002. Approved personal pensions are safe although the position is not straightforward for certain final salary schemes. Should you take a lump sum under a pension scheme whilst still bankrupt, that lump sum could be treated as income for the purposes on an income payments order (see below). However, the court cannot compel you to take a lump sum. A High Court decision that this was allowable was rubbished by the Court of Appeal in 2016. But a former bankrupt who had agreed to draw down pension sums of over £48,000 to go to his creditors before the Court of Appeal's ruling, failed in 2020 to get the money back. And also excepted from the 'you lose the lot' rule are tools, books, vehicles (though, if valuable, you may be expected to replace the vehicle with a cheaper alternative) and other equipment which is necessary for you to use in your work or business along with clothing, bedding, furniture, household equipment and provisions which are necessary for the basic domestic needs of yourself and your family.

The not so nice bit 2

For the one year you are an undischarged bankrupt (or longer where you haven't been cooperating and the period is extended), you cannot:

- be a director of a limited company or involved in its promotion, formation or management without the court's permission;
- seek credit for £500 or more without disclosing that you are an undischarged bankrupt with the result that only someone out of their mind would then grant it to you;
- manage a business with a different name without telling people with whom you do business that you are an undischarged bankrupt;
- be a member of a local flood defence committee (oh no) but you can be an MP (so that's alright then);
- pursue certain professional careers such as a solicitor or generally work in financial services; or
- work as an insolvency practitioner!

Your immigration status could be affected and any prospective employer might be put off (discriminating against an individual on the grounds of their bankruptcy or former bankruptcy is no more unlawful than quietly whistling in a public place). If your trustee in bankruptcy reckons that you have been in some way culpable for what has happened then they can seek to have certain of those restrictions continued beyond the end of the bankruptcy and for a period of at least two years and a maximum of 15 years. They would be after what is called a bankruptcy restrictions undertaking or order. So you could find that you are no longer bankrupt and are released from your debts but for some period of time you are subject to the same restrictions to which you were subject during the bankruptcy. You will be asked to sign a bankruptcy restrictions undertaking which will bind you not to seek credit for £500 or more without disclosing you are subject to the undertaking and so on and, if you refuse, an application can be made to the court for a bankruptcy restrictions order.

The not so nice bit 3

If you have got some spare dosh after the basic living requirements of yourself and family have been met then the trustee in bankruptcy may seek to have you make a contribution towards your debts by way of an income payments undertaking or, if you won't sign one, an income payments order from the court. The undertaking or order will be limited in duration to three years from when it was made. As a matter of practice, there won't be an attempt at obtaining an order or undertaking unless you have at the very least a spare £20 per month although it is very rare for an attempt to be made at that rock bottom figure. The court might well decline to make an order on the strength of only £20 per month being available.

The not so nice bit 4

Bankruptcy is a good way to alienate family and lose friends who have lent you money and not been repaid, without really trying. Like the rest of your creditors, they will probably have to wave goodbye to their money or place what they are paid out into a partially used packet of salted peanuts. If you favour them over other creditors in the run up to the bankruptcy then they may well find themselves having to pay the money back at the behest of the trustee in bankruptcy.

The not so nice bit 5

Details of your bankruptcy are likely to stay on your credit reference agency file for six years. They will also have gone on the Individual Insolvency Register where they will remain for up to 15 months (assuming the date of your discharge is not suspended on naughty bankrupt grounds) and will be recorded at the Land Registry against any property you own for five years from bankruptcy but this will not prevent a sale or remortgage of the property where the trustee in bankruptcy confirms they are no longer interested in it.

Easy!

The process of going bankrupt could not be easier. In fact, since 5 April 2016 it's got ridiculously easier. The court is generally no longer involved. You apply for bankruptcy to the Insolvency Service by going online to gov.uk/apply-for-bankruptcy. A paper application is not available. Initiative and a swear box will be required if you haven't got a computer, tablet, mobile phone or a public library you can afford to get to (and get back from) so as to access a computer. The application will be considered by a so-called adjudicator. It isn't necessary for you to don an Oxfam outfit for the occasion as nobody will be watching unless you are in a public library. I once had a man applying to me for his bankruptcy who was wearing a beautiful sheepskin coat which was so new and stiff that the arms were elevated at an angle of 45 degrees to the legs. He had obviously had a last fling on a credit card with a bit of life in it to buy the garment.

Should bankruptcy be refused you can ask for the refusal to be reviewed and if the decision stands you have a right to appeal to the court. The application will be cheaper than the fee which was payable to the court on issuing a bankruptcy petition – £130 instead of £180 – but the deposit which has to be paid on account of the cost of the work which would be carried out by the official receiver if the application is successful did stay at £525 but has been increased to £550. The court was able to remit the petition fee. You won't be able to get either the application fee or the deposit cancelled or reduced but you will have the opportunity of paying them by instalments. In that event, the bankruptcy application will not be processed until you have scored the full amount required. The court will deal with any issues which arise after bankruptcy and will continue to deal with petitions for bankruptcy by creditors against debtors. If having to stump up both the application fee and the deposit presents a problem for you, borrow from father-in-law ("I said she should never have married him!") or Ken next door or try and get the money from a charity. If all that fails and you remain desperate for bankruptcy, wait for one of your creditors to bring bankruptcy proceedings against you instead of doing it yourself. Anyone owed at least £5,000 (the figure was raised from £750 for bankruptcy proceedings started after 30 September 2015) can do so and they will have to pay the court fee and deposit. If you tell one of your creditors you have just come back from a cheapie in the Bahamas they will probably reckon you as good for the debt due to them and bankrupt away.

Cheers!

Once you have obtained your bankruptcy, it's off for a quick pint and then to your bank or building society to notify them of what has happened. You can still run an account with them while bankrupt so long as they want to keep you as a customer. If you owed them money and they don't hold security for the debt, they will lose out and so be pleased to see the back of you. Presentationally, it makes sense for you to take the initiative and reveal what has happened rather than leave it to them to discover from the official receiver that you are bankrupt. It may be you have already opened a basic account with no overdraft facilities in contemplation of the bankruptcy and that you have shared your intentions with the bank or building society. Many do. If an account with a credit balance is frozen the official receiver can be asked to release to you any money you urgently need and also release your partner's share in any joint account you hold with them.

The 'beanless defence' to bankruptcy

It could just be that you don't want to be made bankrupt. The beanless ground of opposition to a creditor's bankruptcy petition is as old as the hills but was revived by a case called *Lock v Aylesbury Vale District Council* in July 2018 in which the debtor was appealing against the bankruptcy order which had previously been made. There the debt was for council tax amounting to £8,067. The debtor was living in social housing and was dependent on financial support from her daughter. There was no proper evidence before the court that the debtor then had any assets or was likely to have any in the future and there was nothing to indicate that an investigation into her affairs would bring any assets to light. The judge ruled that where a bankruptcy petition was based on unpaid council tax, as here, there was a burden on the creditor to show, on the face of it, that bankruptcy would achieve some useful purpose. This the creditor had failed to do. Bankruptcy would achieve no useful purpose at all and the order which had been made was quashed. You could seek to rely on this decision in challenging a petition against you if your circumstances are similar and you can also impress the judge by telling them that the beanless defence was fully investigated and analysed by a High Court judge in another case called *Re Edgeworth Capital and other v Maud* in April 2020. The principle behind the defence could be applied whatever the type of debt but, be warned, the decision may not find favour with a lot of judges but worth a run. The burden will be on you to show that a bankruptcy would be pointless but the court will refuse to accept your uncorroborated evidence that this was so.

The 'I made an offer' defence to bankruptcy

The court may – it has a discretion – dismiss a bankruptcy petition where you have made an offer to secure the debt in question (for example, to grant the creditor a charge on the house or flat you own so that you could not sell it without the debt being paid in full out of the sale price) or you have put forward other proposals to pay up and the creditor has unreasonably refused the offer. Paying up by instalments over a long period of time won't be sufficient. The creditor should reflect on what is being offered. A rigid institutional policy or bureaucratic inflexibility by the creditor will work in your favour. But the creditor is entitled to have regard to their own interests and is not forced to take a chance, or be patient, or generous and can take into account their own financial situation. If you can show that no reasonable creditor would have refused the offer, you should be able to persuade the court to throw out the bankruptcy petition.

The 'creditor cocked up the statutory demand' defence to bankruptcy

Almost invariably, a bankruptcy petition must be preceded by a statutory demand if the petition is to succeed. Where the creditor fails to follow the prescribed rules for service of the statutory demand, the subsequent petition will fail. For more, see chapter 29 under **The special treat**.

The alternatives to bankruptcy

They all involve coming up with some cash but are worth looking at so here goes.

Debt management plan alternative

You hand over regular instalments out of your future earnings or other income which is shared out to each of your creditors in proportion to what they are owed until they are all eventually paid off. Ideally, you need them all to agree. They won't agree unless they are convinced that you have offered the best they are likely to get. There are a number of companies who make a profit from organising and maintaining plans like this. Beware. Some of them are parasites, charging fees which are knocked off each instalment before it is distributed and are disproportionate to the amount of the instalment and the service they provide. It can also be difficult to extricate yourself from the agreement with the company until the agreement with creditors has come to an end. Payplan (payplan.com) is worth looking it. They seem efficient to me and set up and handle the plan free of charge to the debtor. Payplan receives donations from the credit industry.

You can always organise and manage your own plan, seeking an agreement to what you propose from the creditors and then dividing up the agreed weekly or monthly payment among them. When seeking agreement, it is vital that you provide and are seen to provide the fullest information about your financial circumstances and pack this punch. Refusal by the creditors to agree will result in bankruptcy and nothing for them.

> *149 Magnolia Crescent*
>
> *Twickenham*
>
> *KT89 4XZ*
>
> *14 July 2021*
>
> *From Clive Troublesore*
>
> *To my creditors*
>
> *I regret I am presently unable to pay my debts and am in arrears with all payments to you. I am an honourable person and, within reason, I prefer to clear my debts rather than apply for my own bankruptcy which I will be compelled to do if any of you are unwilling to accept my proposals below.*
>
> *I owe a total of £x. I am prepared to make instalments in the total sum of £y per month to commence on 1 October 2021 and thereafter to be made on the first day of each successive month on the basis that each of you receives the proportion of the instalment which the amount of my debt to you bears to the sum of £x. [My offer is conditional on any creditor who is entitled to claim interest on my debt waiving such entitlement as from 1 October 2021 provided I do not default in instalment payments. It is also conditional on all my creditors accepting my proposal]. Should my financial circumstances improve then I will be happy to increase the amount of the instalments and would provide you with full information about my new circumstances at the time.*
>
> *Would you please confirm whether or not you are prepared to accept my offer within 28 days of the date of this letter. If you are, a payment book, standing order details or other directions as to the mode of payment you require should be provided to me. I shall be happy to give you any further information you may require. I hope your response will be favourable.*
>
> *Details of my debts*
>
> *[insert name of creditor and sum owed]*

> *Details of my financial circumstances*
>
> *[insert details of assets, income (after tax and national insurance) including benefits and outgoings including travel to and from work and food when working: add income of spouse or partner and state number and ages of all dependants: if you own your home, state the market value after the amount required to pay off any mortgages has been deducted and where you jointly own it give the value of your share after that deduction. Send copies of some recent pay slips and copies of recent bank statements with a view to demonstrating that you are being as transparent as you possibly can].*

Individual voluntary arrangement alternative

This is a formal arrangement with creditors to pay something towards what you owe them over a period of several years – it will usually be five years – and which will be set up and managed by a supervisor who is an insolvency practitioner. You may be putting income or capital into the pot to be shared by the creditors, sometimes both. Certainly, if you have or are likely to receive some capital during the lifetime of the arrangement, your creditors would expect it or some of it to go into the pot. The proposals you put forward for the arrangement must be sufficiently attractive to the creditors to get 75% of them to agree which is essential for the arrangement to go forward. That's 75% in value which means that where your total debts come to £100,000, creditors owed at least £75,000 must agree and they won't agree unless they are convinced that the voluntary arrangement would be financially better for them than seeing you made bankrupt. You could end up paying off a small fraction of what you owe and avoid bankruptcy. I have approved voluntary arrangements for substantial debts where the creditors were set to collect as little as 5p and 10p in the pound. The bad news is that the insolvency practitioner who organises things will want their money up front for their service and we are here looking at around £3,500 plus. Future fees for maintaining the arrangement will come out of the money you put in. Should you default under the arrangement, the insolvency practitioner will bankrupt you or you can bankrupt yourself.

Debt relief order alternative

This is an amateur debtor's form of bankruptcy and works in a similar way: Insolvency League Division 3 stuff. It's only available where the amount owed is no more than £30,000 (this figure was raised from £20,000 as from 29 June 2021); the value of your total assets is £2,000 or less (up from £1,000 as from the same date) with the value of any single motor car you own that can be disregarded from the total asset figure being £2,000 (up from £1,000 as from the same date); and the level of surplus monthly income you enjoy after tax, national insurance and normal household expenses does not exceed £75 (up from £50 as from the same date). There's a fee to pay of £90 so considerably cheaper than bankruptcy and it's the Insolvency Service to which an application for an order is made – through an approved intermediary such as the Citizens Advice – and not the court.

Administration order alternative

Available from the county court and for National League debtors who owe a maximum of £5,000. You pay off your creditors by regular instalments and usually over a period of no longer than three years. The court may, and often does, reduce the debts to the creditors you have named – they are all given the opportunity to object – so that you only pay them a percentage of the total bill: in that sense, like an individual voluntary arrangement (see above). Once you have paid off what is required by the order, the creditors named in the order can't touch you.

The dodgy bankruptcy

Here we meet the individual attempting to thwart an application against them for property or money in matrimonial proceedings. Once a bankruptcy order is made, as we have seen, the bankrupt, with a few exceptions, effectively loses their assets. With their assets gone, there is nothing for their spouse or civil partner to share. Apart from a claim for maintenance to be paid out of the bankrupt's future income – and this the court can still order and it would be advantageous to the prospective payee to get an application made before the trustee in bankruptcy gets round to applying for an income payments order (see above) – the spouse or civil partner are stymied. Or are they? Supposing the bankrupt hides some of their assets from the official receiver, avoids an investigation and interrogation about their assets in a financial application because that never takes off as a result of the bankruptcy, enjoys automatic discharge from bankruptcy after 12 months and in due course reunites himself with those undisclosed assets? I have seen it happen. Should the spouse or civil partner discover that the bankruptcy was a ruse, they can apply for the order to be annulled (cancelled). Occasionally, an application to annul is linked up to a financial application in matrimonial proceedings and they are heard together.

The bad bankruptcy

In April 2018, most county court hearing centres were robbed of their ability to deal with opposed creditors' bankruptcy petitions – they can deal with unopposed petitions, though – and to deal with certain other insolvency business. This does not apply to the hearing centres at Brighton, Croydon, Medway, Preston and Romford or to the Central London county court which can hear these opposed cases and they can also be heard at the Business and Property Courts in Birmingham, Bristol, Leeds, Liverpool, Manchester, Newcastle and Cardiff. Yes, I know this is very dry stuff but it's about to get moist so stay aboard.

If the petition is started in a county court hearing centre which lacks jurisdiction to hear an opposed petition and the debtor has put in a notice that they oppose the bankruptcy, it must transfer the case to a court that does have jurisdiction to hear it and, in the south-east that must be to the Central London county court. This system is rife for exploitation because by putting in a notice of opposition to the petition, perhaps on spurious grounds, the debtor can earn what to them is highly valuable time (to get together the money needed to settle the debt?) while the process of transferring the case to another venue is actioned. It may not be evident until the first hearing of the bankruptcy petition that it is opposed. The case then has to be transferred and the court to which it is transferred has to relist the petition for hearing there.

But what happens if the hearing centre without jurisdiction to hear the case, nevertheless does hear it and makes a bankruptcy order? The order will be null and void. That's what happened in a 2019 case and then in a 2020 case. In that later case, the debtor had not only put in a notice of opposition but had lodged seven files of documents in support of that opposition.

The debtor's notice of opposition should be with the court along with a copy to the creditor at least five business days before the date fixed for the first hearing of the petition. If it's late then the judge may well take that point and disallow more time if the debtor is trying it on with a farrago, this time, of delusional nonsense.

Gold rush

It sometimes happens that a marriage or civil partnership has broken down and one party is unable pay their debts but has assets which they would prefer to see go to the other party rather than their creditors: maybe they are particularly anxious that the family home should be preserved so that any children should continue to have a roof over their heads. What they do is to collude with the other party in procuring a court order which transfers to the other party their interest in the home, and possibly other property as well, with the intention of outwitting their creditors on the bankruptcy which will inevitably follow a few months later. An order like that is highly likely to be successfully challenged by the transferring party's trustee in bankruptcy and cancelled out once the bankruptcy has taken place.

But should one party get wind of the fact that the other party is heading for bankruptcy, pushing speedily ahead with an application for financial remedies is quite legitimate. Provided there is a court order dealing with financial issues (and the fact that the party heading for bankruptcy has agreed to it matters not) and it is made before the date on which the bankruptcy process has been started, then the likelihood is that the order will stand and the trustee and the creditors will be bound by it. This could mean that the family home and other assets go to the other party and will not be available to be shared out among the creditors towards what they are owed. What is vital to defeat the trustee and creditors, however, is that the final decree ending the marriage or partnership – the decree absolute in the case of divorce – has been made prior to the date on which the bankruptcy application or petition was issued. Generally, a period of six weeks and one day must elapse after the date of the decree nisi before the decree absolute can be applied for. The same situation will apply to the differently named final orders under the new matrimonial law when it comes into force (see chapter 74). Unsurprisingly, a financial order which has been consented to by the bankrupt party should not be mega over-generous to the other party or collusion between the parties may be established which would be fatal to the order.

Chapter 49

Property Buying And Selling

Traps and how to avoid them

Estate agents 00£: Licence to charge

In a poll I conducted in a dream as to who the public would least like to be trapped in a lift with, an estate agent came top. This is a shame because some estate agents are almost human and help old ladies across the road without asking for any commission at all.

In a second poll I conducted in a dream the following night, I asked whether the public would avoid paying an estate agent commission for negotiating the sale of their property if they possibly could, and 123% answered in the affirmative. Which takes me to the Estate Agents Act 1979. What the Act says along with regulations made under it – the Estate Agents (Provision of Information) Regulations 1991 – is that if you go to an agent with a view to possibly instructing them to offer your property for sale, then they must provide you with various prescribed information in writing which includes the amount of their commission and when you would become liable to pay it. The information must be given at the time when you and the estate agent commence communication or as soon as reasonably practicable afterwards. But, in any event, the information must be given before you sign up with the agent and become committed to any liability to them.

If the agent fails to give you the necessary written information at all or gives it late, they cannot recover one new pence of commission from you unless the court gives them permission to do so. The court must dismiss their application for this permission if it considers this is just taking into account the prejudice caused to you by their breach and the degree of culpability for their failure. Even if the court gives the agent permission to sue you, it can reduce the commission or order no commission at all, so as to compensate you for any prejudice you have suffered. If, for example, the agent was acting dishonestly, the delay in giving you the written information was considerable or you reasonably thought the commission rate was less than it turned out to be, the agent might well end up with no commission or a reduction in it.

In a case before the Supreme Court in 2019 – *Wells v Devani* it is called or, if you are an agent, something very rude – the client and estate agent had agreed over the phone that the client's seven flats should be marketed by the agent. Just one week later the agent secured an offer of £2.1m. The sale went ahead. But it was not until the offer had been accepted that the agent sent the client the necessary information which meant it was one week late. The Supreme Court upheld rulings that because of the failure to comply with the law, the agent's commission should be reduced by one-third (to £32,900 inclusive of VAT) having regard to the prejudice suffered by the client. The Supreme Court made it clear that there could be cases where the degree of the agent's culpability was so great that the agent would get nothing even if the client had suffered no prejudice. The importance of the 1979 Act should not be underrated.

The agent must also provide a written explanation, using prescribed wording as set out in the 1991 regulations, of the meaning of 'sole selling rights', 'sole agency' and 'ready, willing and able purchaser' (see below) where they are using them and at the same time as the other required information.

The agreement you did not reach

The agent may well give you the written information in time. But is it accurate? It needs to be scrutinised with care as to whether it misstates what, in fact, was agreed. Any departure from the agreed terms should be challenged with the agent immediately as there is otherwise a risk that you could be taken to have accepted differing terms by saying nothing.

Sole selling rights

Never, never, ever, ever grant an estate agent sole selling rights. If you grant them but succeed in selling the property to your mother-in-law without any involvement of the agent, you would still be liable to pay the agent commission – for doing nothing.

Sole agency

Granting an estate agent a sole agency is fair enough and it should lead to a lower commission rate. Indeed, it may spur the agent on to greater things as their chances of earning on the sale of your property would be higher than with six rival agents battling it out. But it could have the opposite effect and send the agent to sleep and so set a time limit on the sole agency, say six weeks, but be careful not to instruct a second agent during that period because if the second agent finds you a purchaser, you would be at risk of having to pay separate commission to the first and the second agent (see more on this below). An agent who has been granted a sole agency may put the property out with other agents on a joint agency basis so that if one of the other agents comes up trumps, the two agents will share the commission you agree to pay to the original agent. If you don't fancy the idea of a joint agent, ensure the agreement you reach with your agent precludes them from appointing one.

Ready, willing and able

It is not uncommon for a seller to agree to pay commission on the introduction of a buyer who is 'ready, willing and able to purchase', 'ready and able to purchase' or 'prepared to purchase'. There are a number of variations on the same theme. Such forms of words should be avoided. Although virtually every buyer will make an offer which is conditional, like 'subject to contract' or 'subject to survey' or probably both, they might reach the stage when they become, say, 'ready, willing and able' to proceed which could render you, the seller, liable to pay commission to the agent although you end up selling to someone else or not selling at all.

The link

Before an agent can become entitled to commission, there must be a link between the agent and the buyer: the agent must have been an effective cause of the buyer going ahead. And they won't be prevented from being an effective cause because the property had been marketed through a second agent who also played a part in closing the deal or you personally conducted most of the negotiations with the buyer yourself. It is irrelevant that the buyer deceived you into thinking that they just happened to have heard from a friend of a friend that the property was on the market and that they did not come through an agent and that they did not see the 'For Sale' notice erected by the front gate and have an aversion to estate agents' windows and never received particulars of the property through the post and once knew a man who knew a girl who danced with the Prince of Wales.

If you have any doubts about the buyer's story that they did not come through any agent instructed by you, here's some wording you can shove into the sale contract. If it then transpires that the buyer was lying and you have to shell out commission to an agent, you can claim it back from the buyer.

> *The buyer hereby warrants to the seller that;*
>
> *(1) The buyer was not introduced to the property by Grabapound (Homes for the Discerning) (Estate Agency) Ltd ("the agent") or any other agent.*
>
> *(2) The buyer has never observed any 'For sale' or similar sign of the agent in relation to the property, received particulars of the property from the agent, visited the premises of the agent, viewed a photograph, sale particulars or any other document in relation to the property at or displayed at the premises of the agent or in the window of such premises or had any contact or communication of whatsoever nature and by whatever means with the agent in connection with the property.*
>
> *(3) The sole origin of the buyer's knowledge that the property was available for purchase was [insert details].*
>
> *(4) The agent was not an effective cause of the buyer contracting with the seller to purchase the property.*
>
> *(5) The buyer hereby agrees to indemnify the seller against all claims demands actions or other proceedings by the agent for commission, disbursements and other costs in relation to the seller's sale of the property to the buyer.*
>
> *(6) This condition shall not merge with the transfer of the property to the buyer.*

Double the commission

In March 1985 a High Court judge held that a seller was legally compelled to pay commission to two agents, though only one buyer was ever involved. The seller had agreed to pay Lordsgate Properties Ltd if they introduced someone who purchased their property and he had also agreed to pay Brian Lack and Partners Ltd if they were *instrumental* in negotiating a sale. The actual buyer was first introduced by Lordsgate but subsequently made a number of offers through Brian Lack. The last offer was accepted and a sale ensued. There have been many other cases which have been decided by the courts in the same way. I have personally had to similarly decide several cases, with the evidence leaving no alternative. It has also been my pleasure, where evidentially possible, to decide cases the other way.

The risk of a claim by two (or even more!) agents is a real one. The solution is to seek to ensure that under the agreements you reach, there can be no liability to any one agent for any deal negotiated after their instructions have come to an end. At the same time, only agree to pay an agent where they introduce an applicant who not simply agrees to buy but actually competes the purchase.

Judge v Ombudsman

If you find yourself involved in a court case with an estate agent, the likelihood is that you will be the defendant rather than the claimant. That's because the vast majority of estate agency litigation is about estate agents' claims against their clients for unpaid commission. Of course, there are plenty of client complaints along the lines of "You didn't advertise the place properly" or "You sent the office cat to accompany the applicant round the property instead of your chief executive officer." However, under the strict law which will be applied in court, complaints of this nature generally get nowhere if the property ended up being sold through that agent, as no loss will have been suffered except for non-compensatable aggravation.

Enter the Property Ombudsman who, strangely enough, I have not personally fenced with. Must move more. Estate agents now have to be members of an approved redress scheme and the main scheme is run by the Property Ombudsman. As with the Financial Ombudsman Service (and other Ombudsmen) she – yes, it is a she – will decide complaints on the basis of what is fair and reasonable and taking into account the law and the scheme's code of practice. The result is that you may well succeed with a complaint to the Property Ombudsman which would have been treated with derision by a judge in court. Certainly, I reckon you have a better chance of avoiding dual liability for agent's commission through the Ombudsman's decision than through a judge in court having to apply that strict law. And if the Ombudsman is against you? Refuse to accept his decision, as is your right, and let the court decide on a claim, probably by the agent or possibly by you. Both agents in a dual commission case will need to be members of the Ombudsman's redress scheme for the Ombudsman to decide.

This is how a Property Ombudsman's decision went in a 2018 dual commission claim dispute. The seller was elderly, bereaved and lacked experience and knowledge of the sales process. She instructed A on a sole agency basis and then terminated the instruction and instructed B, also on a sole agency basis. Her property was sold through B to buyers who had been introduced by A while the property was still on their books. The seller settled A's commission account but, nearly a year later, B pursued her for commission to be paid to them.

The Ombudsman's code of practice states that an agent, when disinstructed, must explain clearly and in writing to their former client, any continuing liability there might be to pay them commission and how they might become liable to pay dual commission. A did not do so.

The code of practice also states that an agent, when aware that a property has previously been marketed by another agent, should ascertain whether the potential buyer has viewed with that other or any other agent. B did not do so. Had they done so, they should have referred the buyers back to A or sought to negotiate a split fee with A.

The Ombudsman decided that there should be just one lot of commission which was to be split 60% to A and 40% to B. A fair and reasonable result whereas, had a judge been required to decide, the result would almost certainly been that the seller was responsible for commission to each of A and B to the full amount for which they had invoiced.

How to lose £43k

Here's the moral of this story. Never legally commit yourself to buy a property by exchanging contracts unless you can be sure you will be ready, willing and able to complete the purchase on the date which will be specified in the contract.

If you can't complete when the contract says you should, the seller can send you what is called a *notice to complete*. It will set a final deadline for you to produce the cash and that could be as close to five working days from when you get the notice. Still fail to come up with the cash and what will happen? The seller can cancel the contract and probably keep your deposit. Ouch?

In a 2016 High Court case called *Solid Rock Investments UK Ltd v Reddy and another party*, the buyers had paid a deposit of a cool £43,000. One week before completion was required to take place, they told the seller that they might be late because of delay in funds coming through from a Nigerian bank account. They didn't take up offers by the seller to put the completion date back in return for a modest price increase. The completion date arrived and they weren't ready. The seller sent them the dreaded *notice to complete*. The final deadline passed without completion. So the seller cancelled the contract and told them they were keeping the deposit. The next day the buyers were ready with all the cash they needed!

The buyers' attempt at getting the £43,000 returned to them through the court failed despite the fact that the seller later sold the property for an extra £100,000 (albeit with the benefit of planning permission although it had been known that planning permission was on the cards when the original buyers agreed to go ahead).

The key to having a decent chance of securing a deposit return is to come up with some good proposals to compensate for lateness, to keep the seller very closely informed, not to be very late and, with a bit of luck, to be able to rely on some delay on the part of the seller (for example, in answering queries after contracts had been exchanged or in providing relevant details). Any extra money the seller later managed to obtain when selling to someone else will be taken into account but as just one of the considerations.

It's immoral and it makes you sick

Until contracts are exchanged for a house or flat transfer, either side can drop out. If that happens, neither will be responsible to the other to reimburse the expense to which they have been put in legal, survey and mortgage fees and the rest, in expectation that the transaction would be finalised. As a general rule, it leaves open the risk that while you, as prospective buyer, are beavering away settling on the blinds for the living room windows and organising your mortgage and conveyancer, the prospective seller is negotiating a sale to a rival bidder at an extra £5,000 or issuing paperwork to half a dozen other would-be buyers and saying that the first to be in a position to exchange contracts gets the property. Or, as a general rule, it means that you, as prospective seller, could be waiting anxiously for your prospective buyer to be in a position to exchange contracts, only to discover that they have been stringing you along and negotiating to buy another property down the road. You see, all is fair in love, war and conveyancing! Is there a way to protect against the conveyancing liar? I say there is. The lock out agreement.

*THIS AGREEMENT is made on 14 July 2021 BETWEEN ARNOLD TRUSTWORTHY of 20 St Mary's Courtyard Twickenham Middlesex KT42 1LA ("the house") ("the seller") and CLIVE TROUBLESORE of 149 Magnolia Crescent Twickenham Middlesex KT40 1LA ("the buyer")

BACKGROUND

(1)   The seller owns the house.

(2)   The parties have agreed 'subject to contract' that the seller will sell and the buyer will buy the house at the price of £600,000.00 ("the price").

(3)   The buyer has paid a holding deposit as a demonstration of his good faith to Grabapound (Homes for the Discerning) (Estate Agency) Ltd of £250.00 as stakeholder.

(4)   The buyer requires a mortgage advance on the security of the house of £425,000.00 and intends to make application for such an advance, to arrange for the house to be surveyed as part of the application and to instruct a solicitor or licensed conveyancer to act on his behalf in connection with his intended purchase.

IT IS HEREBY AGREED THAT in consideration of the above matters and the parties entering into the obligations provided for by this agreement and specified below:

(1)   If and so long as the buyer complies with his obligations under this agreement the seller and no person or company acting on behalf of the seller will until the expiration of 42 days from the date of this agreement –

(1.1)   seek another buyer for the house;

(1.2)   advertise the house as available for sale;

(1.3)   negotiate or agree with any person other than the buyer for the sale or the terms of the sale of the house whether on a 'subject to contract' or otherwise basis; or

(1.4)   issue a draft contract or other documentation relating to the proposed sale of the house to anyone other than the buyer.

(2)   If and so long as the buyer complies with his obligations under this agreement the seller will –

(2.1)   cause his solicitors to deliver to the solicitor or licensed conveyancer for the buyer a draft contract and other usual documentation for the proposed sale of the house to the buyer within 7 days of the date of this agreement and reply to all reasonable enquiries about the house raised by them with reasonable promptness; and

(2.2)   until the expiration of 42 days from the date of this agreement, provide facilities to the surveyor or valuer for the buyer's prospective lender and for any surveyor or valuer directly instructed by the buyer to inspect the house subject to reasonable notice of their proposed visit.

(3)   The buyer will use his reasonable endeavours to –

(3.1)   procure an offer of a mortgage advance on the security of the house for no more than £425,000.00 as soon as possible;

(3.2)   instruct a solicitor or licensed conveyancer to act for him on the proposed purchase of the house and to approve the draft contract with reasonable promptness; and

(3.3)   be ready, willing and able to exchange contracts with the seller as soon as possible and in any event no later than the expiration of 42 days from the date of this agreement.

(4)   The buyer will answer in an expeditious manner and in any event within two working days of their receipt such questions as shall be put to him by or on behalf of the seller as to his compliance with his obligations under this agreement and, in particular, as to the identity of the solicitor or licensed conveyance instructed by him to act on his proposed purchase of the house and the progress of his application for a mortgage advance.

(5)   If before the expiration of 42 days from the date of this agreement the buyer decides to withdraw from his proposed purchase of the house from the seller, he shall forthwith give written notice of such withdrawal to the seller and shall pay to the seller the seller's reason-

able conveyancing costs and disbursements relating to the proposed sale to the buyer [not to exceed the sum of £x] but shall otherwise be under no further liability to the seller under this agreement or otherwise.

(6)   If at the expiration of 42 days from the date of this agreement the buyer is not ready, willing and able to exchange contracts with the seller, he shall make the same payments to the seller as provided for by paragraph 5 of this agreement but neither party shall be under any further liability to the other party under this agreement.

(7)   If before the expiration of 42 days from the date of this agreement the seller decides to withdraw from his proposed sale of the house to the buyer, he shall forthwith give written notice of such withdrawal to the buyer and shall pay to the buyer the seller's reasonable conveyancing costs and disbursements relating to the proposed sale to the buyer [not to exceed the sum of £x] and the mortgage application survey or valuation fee and any privately instructed survey or valuation fee incurred by the buyer [not to exceed in the aggregate the sum of £y] but shall otherwise be under no further liability to the buyer under this agreement or otherwise.

(8)   If before the expiration of 42 days from the date of this agreement the buyer shall give the seller written notice to the seller that he is ready, willing and able to exchange contracts with him at the price and with completion to take place no later than [insert date] and the seller does not exchange contracts within 28 days of the receipt of such notice, the seller shall make the same payments to the buyer as provided for by paragraph 7 of this agreement but shall otherwise be under no further liability to the buyer under this agreement.

(9)   For the avoidance of any doubt, this agreement does not commit the seller to the sale or the buyer to the purchase and does not form part of any other contract.

SIGNED   Arnold Trustworthy   Clive Troublesore

These paragraphs may be mixed and matched. Whether a holding deposit is paid is optional as is whether there should be provision for either side to have to pay the other side's expenses in certain circumstances if the transaction does not proceed.

Chapter 50

Residential Service Charges

Cutting 'em down

Paying service charges is as satisfying as self-extracting a molar during a pandemic. Paying them when they are excessive is as satisfying as self-extracting a molar and an incisor during a pandemic. With dental treatment, you should feel better afterwards. My aim is to make you feel better over service charges by reading this chapter and seeing how you may well be able to extract their excessiveness.

County court v tribunal

There are two ways of making a challenge to service charges apart from simply telling the landlord or their managing agent they are too high and why, which is likely to be a complete waste of paper and postage stamp or laptop power. You can simply refuse or neglect to pay which will induce your landlord to claim the charges in the county court or you can make a tribunal application in England to – wait for it – the First-Tier Property Chamber (Residential Property) and I am relieved that whoever thought up that title does not compile the words on greeting cards ('*Happiness on Anniversary of Birth (Forceps Delivery)*') or, in Wales, to the Leasehold Valuation Tribunal. Preferable to a failure to pay a single penny would be to pay what you say should be the right figure and leave the difference in dispute or, if you are of a nervous disposition and, as you will read below, you could pay the sum demanded, making it clear that you challenge the amount, and then make the challenge to the tribunal. You would be entitled to repayment of any excess received by your landlord.

Should the landlord claim against you in the county court, it is very, very, very highly likely that the dispute will be transferred to the tribunal. That's because county court judges detest service charge disputes. Tenants – not you, of course – can get emotional about the porter who didn't doff his cap, the paint that started crumbling before the decorator dropped his brush and the common garden that is overgrown with ragwort. Most issues raised in a county court service charge battle can be sent to the tribunal to decide: any issue over the ground rent cannot. You may favour staying in the county court because you reckon it will give you the protection of the costs regime which would normally apply to a service charge case (see chapter 25). Don't let that rank as a consideration. The lease will usually state, in effect, that the landlord can personally charge you up for their costs and expenses in dealing with the dispute. If it doesn't then I am the Lord Chief Justice or a banana (you choose). Generally (but see below), what the lease says will take precedence over the small claims costs regime and so, if you lose in the county court, you won't have its protection and will have to pick up the landlord's bill which could be heavy if they have been represented by a lawyer. Similarly, while the general rule at a tribunal is that losing there will only lead to you paying the landlord's costs if you have acted unreasonably in bringing, defending or conducting a case, what the lease says will take precedence over that. But even if you win at the county court or tribunal, there is a nice big trap awaiting you on costs which we will have a look at shortly.

Tribunal victorious

So where does that take us? If I was at war over a service charge dispute, I would take the initiative and make an application to the tribunal at the outset because that is where the dispute would have probably ended up anyway and the tribunal members are specialists in these sort of cases. They love them. They dream of porters' caps, crumbling paint and weeds. The application fee is £100 and, if there is a hearing, another £200 will be payable. 'Help with fees' is available (see chapter 17).

But does your dispute qualify?

Having got this far, you may be inclined to clock me if you find that my route to challenging service charges is not open to you and I would not blame you which is why I seldom go out. You can take advantage of my route if the dispute regime under the Landlord and Tenant Act 1985 applies to you. The service charges must relate to a residential property so business tenants go back to your premises and take another route. Similarly, council tenants must do the same unless your lease is for more than 21 years. The service charge can directly or indirectly relate to services, repairs, maintenance, improvements, insurance or the landlord's management costs. A service charge for a sum fixed in advance might be challengeable along some other route but such fixed sums are quite rare.

According to the 1985 Act, service charges must be reasonably incurred and the services or works to which they relate must be of a reasonable standard. They must also be reasonable in amount. Your challenge can be under any or all of these limbs. You can additionally argue that some or all of the items that make up the service charge demand are not caught by the lease wording. You may put in evidence cheaper quotes that you have been able to obtain but you should take care to ensure that they are on a like for like basis. I would recommend that you look at the current (third) edition of the Service Charge Residential Management Code issued by the Royal Institution of Chartered Surveyors which you can download free on the internet. It sets out the best practice to be followed by landlords and their managing agents, so a bit like the motorists' highway code. It does not follow as night follows day that breach of the code will automatically mean that you are on to a winner but breach will be taken into account by the court or tribunal and can only help your case. An argument that the landlord's delay in carrying out the works has increased what eventually had to be done and, hence, the amount of the service charges, will not get you anywhere. However, if that failure amounts to a breach by the landlord of their repairing covenant then you can ask the tribunal to reduce the demand by an amount representing the increase and any losses arising. This will not be possible if there has been a change in landlord and it was not the current landlord who was at fault. Any attempt to knock out the entirety of the service charges and to recover compensation from the landlord on top would need to be dealt with by way of a county court claim by you or a defence and counterclaim to the landlord's proceedings in the county court against you.

Can you challenge service charges in a tribunal which have been paid for many years before you acquired the lease? Yes, said the upper tribunal in a 2018 case called *Gateway Holdings v Lynda Mckenzie*. However, if the tribunal agreed that the charges were too high, you would fail in the challenge unless you could show that you, rather than the previous tenants, were entitled to a refund. The trick is to reach an agreement on the subject when you buy. The purchase contract could say that any repayment due following your challenge was to belong to you. After all, it would be you who had shed the blood and sweat (but hopefully not the tears) in making and pursuing the challenge.

The coronavirus factor

I foresee the coronavirus rearing its ugly head in a large number of future service charge disputes. Is it reasonable for the managing agents to charge their usual management fee when they weren't managing as contemplated for the entirety of the service charge year because staff were either off work or working reduced hours? Should not certain services have been stopped or reduced during lockdown? What credit has been given for the no-shows by the window and guttering cleaners? Has the benefit of furloughing been factored into your overheads? Why charge £300 for porter masks when they never wore one? Should major improvements not be put on hold when the vast majority of tenants cannot afford to finance them because of the impact of coronavirus?

The landlord's costs – and that trap

We have already seen how you can be stung, personally and directly, for the landlord's costs if you lose against them on a service charge case. But there is a big trap. Whether they win or lose, the lease will probably allow the landlord to add their outstanding costs and expenses involved in the dispute to a service charge demand. That won't please you and it won't please your co-tenants who could end up having to contribute towards a bill for a dispute with which they not had been concerned and over which they had no control. You may be able to escape falling into this trap on behalf of yourselves and your co-tenants.

Attempt at The Great Escape

This is an application, under section 20C of the Landlord and Tenant Act 1985, for an order which prohibits the landlord from adding their costs and expenses to the service charge. The county court or tribunal will grant such an application if it is satisfied that, in the circumstances, it is 'just and equitable' to do so. It would be madness for you not to apply for such an order. The application should be made on the tribunal form called *Leasehold 7*.

The tribunal's order on an application may let you off the hook entirely, let you off the hook partially or let one or more of your co-tenants off the hook, wholly or partially. You could even apply for an order preventing costs incurred by the landlord in a challenge by a co-tenant being passed on to you. In so far as your own case in a tribunal is concerned, you can ask that an order be made in favour of you and any co-tenant who you name in the form *Leasehold 7*. The form specifically asks for details of other tenants who would wish to avoid being stung for the landlord's costs by being added on to the service charge even though they are not parties to those proceedings. There is no time limit in the tribunal for a section 20C application being made: as indicated, co-tenants who might be effected can make their own application in the same proceedings or subsequently; and co-tenants can apply for a section 20C order even though the tenant making the challenge has been refused a section 20C order.

Whether you can expect to succeed on an application under section 20C of the 1985 Act will depend on such factors as the conduct of each side; the circumstances of each side; who has won (and very much so); and whether or not the landlord does have resources other than service charge income.

In a 2017 appeal case before the upper tribunal called *Bretby Hall Management Company Limited v Christopher Pratt*, the first-tier tribunal had decreed that the landlord could only pass on to the service charge 25% of its costs. That meant that the individual tenant who was challenging service charges would be liable for just 6.16% of the costs which worked out at around £3. The landlord was appealing against that decree but on a number on other points. After some encouragement from the upper tribunal (ridicule, shotgun to the head, astonished faces – that sort of thing) the landlord agreed to abandon that part of the appeal.

But the landlord's costs for the appeal hearing were substantial which was a serious matter for the landlord since its only income was from the service charges it collected from the tenants of the 30 apartments in the development. The tenant pleaded with the upper tribunal to prevent the landlord from adding on its appeal costs to the service charges. The appeal tribunal refused. The landlord had succeeded in the appeal on almost all points and against the tenant's opposition. That the landlord had no resources apart from service charge income was a crucial point. It was just and equitable, said the appeal tribunal, that the tenant should bear his share of the costs by them being added on to the service charges.

The administration charge trick

Some leases seek to overcome a section 20C application by entitling the landlord to treat their litigation costs not as part of the service charge but as so-called administration charges. It so happens that administration charges in the form of litigation costs were not susceptible to a section 20C type regime – until 6 April 2017. Now the county court or tribunal can wipe out or reduce a tenant's liability to have to pay them in connection with a service charge dispute under a section 20C type regime. This time the regime is set by schedule 11 paragraph 5A of the Commonhold and Leasehold Reform Act 2002 (phew!). As with section 20C, in the tribunal you will find that form *Leasehold 3* asks whether you want to ask the tribunal to make a schedule 11 order.

There is no *Leasehold 7* form which can be used in the county court should the landlord have started their claim there. Even if the county court has indicated that it is thinking of transferring the case to the tribunal or you have asked it to do so, it would be prudent for you to do this. Issue in the county court an application notice (form N244) asking for an order under section 20c or schedule 11 (depending on whether the lease says the litigation costs can be recovered by them as part of the service charge or as administration charges) and this will cover the landlord's costs while the case remains in the county court. Then, if and when the case is transferred to the tribunal, complete form *Leasehold 7* asking for a section 20C or schedule 11 order and this will cover the landlord's costs while the case remains with the tribunal.

Service charge arguments at work

Let's have a look at some juicy court and tribunal decisions from recent times which may just give you some ideas. The names of the cases are given after each summary along with citations which should enable you to locate full case reports on the internet, should you want to rely on them in court or at the tribunal.

The 'spending that amount of dosh in the light of the sort of folk who live in our blocks is barmy' argument

In a case which started in a tribunal but was ultimately decided by the Court of Appeal (*London Borough of Hounslow v Waaler* [2017] EWCA Civ 45) the part of the service charge under attack was for the replacement of windows and cladding to 10 blocks of facts at the Ivybridge Estate in Isleworth where the landlord is the London Borough of Hounslow. The Estate comprises council flats and houses and some properties which have been bought under long leases by former council tenants under the right to buy scheme. One lady got a demand for a cool £55,000 as the required charge from her for the new windows and cladding and some other work. The windows had not been in disrepair but suffered from an inherent design fault which was a potential safety issue. The fault related to a hinge failure. Replacement hinges were available at a cost of £140 a pair but the problem would have eventually recurred with new hinges. So after the necessary consultation with lessees, the council decided to replace the windows and deal with the inevitable resulting replacement of cladding as well. The aluminium windows which were used will have a life span of twice that of the UPVC ones which might have been used at a lower cost.

Our aggrieved lady (with other lessees) attacked the council's decision. The Court of Appeal ruled that improvements such as these – and they were to be classified as improvements – had to be approached differently to repairs which the council was obliged to carry out. With improvements, a landlord had to take particular account of the extent of the interests of the lessees who would be charged up, their views on what was proposed and the financial impact of proceeding. It was not simply sufficient to rely on the right to recover the cost of repairs under the lease as a justification in itself for embarking on a scheme of very expensive work.

The landlord was not bound by the views of tenants but where it was exercising a discretionary power at the lessees' expense, it made sense that the tenants' views should be more influential than when repairs were concerned. The landlord need not embark on an investigation into the finances of particular tenants. However, in broad terms, the landlord was likely to know what kind of people were tenants in a particular block or estate. Tenants in a luxury block in Knightsbridge might find it easier to cope with a bill for £50,000 odd than tenants of a former council flat in Isleworth.

The council had not acted as it should have done. The result was that only part of the service charge would be recoverable from our lady and it was left to the tribunal to decide how much.

The 'put your specs on mate and the lease doesn't say you can charge us up for your costs of this dispute' argument

In a case decided by the upper tribunal (*Sinclair Gardens Investments (Kensington) Ltd v Avon Estates (London) Ltd* [2016] UKUT 317 (LC)), the tenant escaped paying the landlord anything towards over £11,000 in legal costs on the ground that the wording in the lease on which the landlord relied did not catch them. It allowed the landlord to employ solicitors for certain things and to charge up the tenant. However, the wording was not specific enough so as to relate to solicitors' and barristers' fees for defending the tribunal cases involved. Any liability had to be clearly spelt out in the lease and the lease in its entirety had to be looked at to decide whether or not the tenant had to pay up as the landlord had claimed.

The 'interim payment asked for is too high because of money coming from Buggins' argument

Your lease probably entitles the landlord to require you to stump up cash in advance of carrying out major works. When assessing what is a reasonable advance sum, does the landlord have to take into account a cash contribution which some third party may be making? If, say, an insurer might be forking out for some of the work, should this be ignored when your contribution is calculated?

The amount of the advance payment can be challenged before a tribunal on the basis that it is unreasonable under the Landlord and Tenant Act 1985. It says at section 19(2) that where a service charge is payable before the relevant costs are incurred, no greater amount than is reasonable can be sought. And after the relevant costs have been incurred any necessary adjustment is to be made by repayment, reduction or subsequent charges or otherwise.

In a Court of Appeal case (*Avon Ground Rents Ltd v Cowley and others* [2019] EWCA Civ 1827), there was the possibility of a payment by NHBC. It was not a certainty. It was, as I say, a possibility. In giving guidance on what significance the landlord should place on this possibility, the Court of Appeal ruled that flexibility in approach was required. Certainty of the third party payment was not necessary for it to be taken into account, it was held. That would constrain the discretion of a tribunal which was deciding on a challenge to the amount of the advance demand when in reality what was required was a test which allowed account to be taken of all relevant matters and to those matters the appropriate weight would be attributed.

So by ignoring a good chance of a third party payment, the landlord may well be in trouble.

The 'interim charge isn't reasonable and you still have a problem with your specs' argument

We've seen that an interim demand must be reasonable in amount. The landlord could fail to follow the lease's regime for requiring an advance payment to the letter. That failure in itself may well not be fatal to the landlord being lawfully able to recover the interim sum you are being told to pay – it will depend on the wording of the lease and how serious has been the lessor's failure – but it might anyway come into the reckoning on whether that sum is reasonable. The other point is that the reasonableness of what is being asked for is to be assessed as at the date on which your liability to pay it arises and not subsequently.

In an upper tribunal case (*Wigmore Homes (UK) Ltd v Superbly Works Residents Association Ltd* [2018] UKUT 252 (LC)), the landlord's interim demands for six years were slashed by one-half. The amount sought for each of those six years had been precisely the same and the tribunal decided that this was a clear indication that the lessor had not carried out a careful assessment each year and that the sum claimed was not based on a genuine estimate of the likely expenditure.

The 'you didn't consult over that fixed period contract, silly, so you can't charge me up for all of that contract' argument

Although the tenant lost, an upper tribunal's decision (*Bracken Hill Court at Ackworth Management Ltd v Dobson and others* [2018] UKUT 333 (LC)) on consultation highlights a very important legal right for tenants. They must be consulted by the landlord under the Landlord and Tenant Act 1985 section 20(1) and section 20ZA(2) – no joke! – about entering into a contract for a fixed period of more than 12 months. Slipping up on this will usually mean that the landlord cannot recover more than £250 from each tenant towards the contract price, unless the landlord is forgiven by the first tier tribunal. What happened in the case is that the landlord engaged a management company to look after a block of flats in Pontefract. The contract was renewed annually and the landlord and the management company always agreed that the new contract would last no longer than 364 days. The upper tribunal ruled that none of these contracts was for longer than one year and so there had been no duty on the landlord to consult with the tenant about renewal. It might well have been that the landlord and the management company had an expectation that in all likelihood the contract would be renewed but an expectation of renewal was not the same as a contract. Either party would have been entitled to decline to renew.

Generally, annual renewals will suit the landlord and save them having to consult. Following this course will keep the landlord out of trouble provided the arrangement is not a sham. If it could be shown that there was really a commitment to keep the management company or other contractor on board for more than 12 months and that the so-called renewal process was not genuine then a tenant should be able to take advantage of the consultation breach.

The 'you shouldn't be forgiven for failing to consult with me' argument

The landlord may well apply to the first tier tribunal to dispense with the consultation requirements (see ***The 'you didn't consult over that fixed period contract, silly, so you can't charge me up for all of that contract' argument***). In order to have a decent hope of defeating the landlord's plea, you need to come up with evidence that the failure to consult has prejudiced you. You may be able to show that, had you and your co-tenants been consulted and been able to make your points, the work would not have been carried out or the particular contract would not have been entered into; would have cost less; or would have been done in a different way and would have been more acceptable or cheaper. If you can prove such prejudice, dispensation will probably be refused. If it is granted, it is likely to be on condition that the landlord pays any legal and surveyor's fees you have incurred and compensates for any prejudice that has been suffered. Spout out to the tribunal the cases of *Daejan Investments Ltd v Benson* [2013] UKSC 14 and *Aster Communities v Chapman and others* [2020] UKUT 177 (LC).

The 'pay and argue' argument

You are precluded from a challenge if you admitted you owed the service charge or if a court (it will almost certainly be the county court) has given a judgment against you for the service charge about which you are arguing. But you will not be treated as having admitted the charge simply because you paid it. There will need to be some evidence other than payment to show you agreed it. An upper tribunal case points to how you can challenge despite having already paid (*Marlborough Park Services Ltd v Leitner* [2018] UKUT 230 (LC)).

You might, for example, be under some pressure from your mortgage lender to pay because forfeiture proceedings are threatened by the landlord if the service charge is not settled. In this sort of situation, either wait until you have issued a tribunal application challenging the charge before settlement or make it abundantly clear to the lessor when settling that you dispute liability for the charge.

> 'This charge is an affront to decency. It is exorbitant, unreasonable and a disgrace. I challenge every new and old pence of it with every fibre of my body and will be taking my challenge to the first-tier tribunal (property chamber). I am paying strictly without prejudice and my action is not and is not to be taken as an agreement to or admission of the charge for the purpose of section 27A (4) of the Landlord and Tenant Act 1985.'

That should do!

If you have a court judgment against you for the service charge and it was obtained by default – you failed to put in an acknowledgment of service or a defence and so there was no hearing about the merits of the claim – then apply to the court for the judgment to be set side (see chapter 14). If the judgment is set aside, the probability is that the issue about the reasonableness of the service charge will be transferred to the tribunal. Then the way will be clear for your challenge as the court judgment will have gone.

The 'building insurance premium is unreasonable and look at the quotes what I got' argument

In an upper tribunal case (*Cos Services Ltd v Nicholson and Willans* [2017] UKUT 382 (LC)), the service charge in issue took the form of buildings insurance premiums for three years in respect of Chiltern Court in Harpenden which is a purpose-built block of 16 flats with separate garages. The tribunal upheld the decision of a first-tier tribunal that the premiums sought (which had to be shared between each flat) for each year in question should be respectively reduced from £12,598 to £2,803, from £12,670 to £2,819 and from £11,150 to £3,017. Wow!

The critical point to be decided was whether the premiums asked for had been reasonably incurred. That meant, said the judge, that consideration had to be given to both the rationality of the landlord's decision making and the reasonableness of the charge. It was not necessary for the landlord to show that the premium charged was the lowest that could be obtained in the market but it still had to be reasonable. A landlord would be required to explain the process by which the policy and premium had been selected, with reference to the steps taken to assess the current market. Tenants might, as happened in this case, place before the tribunal the quotations that they have been able to obtain from elsewhere although they would have to ensure that the policies were comparable.

As also happened in this case, it was open to a landlord with a number of properties to negotiate a block policy covering the entirety. However, the landlord would then need to prove that the block policy had not resulted in a substantially higher premium which had been passed on to tenants of a particular building without any significant compensating advantages to them.

Incidentally, you have a right to a written summary of an insurance policy on your premises from the landlord and to inspect any relevant policy and associated documents and without being charged up for the privilege, although the landlord's expenses in granting inspection facilities can be added to their management costs. This does not apply to a local authority tenancy unless it is for more than 21 years.

Dear Mismanagement (Rachman) Limited

Re Flat 1106B Grandiose Buildings, Balham SW11 6AA

As the long-suffering tenant of the above premises, I hereby request you as agent for the landlord to take this communication as formal notice pursuant to section 30A and schedule 2 of the Landlord and Tenant Act 1985 to supply me within 21 days of receipt of this communication with a summary of the insurance cover which is reflected in the service charge to include the amount insured, the name of the insurer and the risks covered or, alternatively, a copy of the policy. I reserve my right under the 1985 Act to require reasonable facilities to inspect relevant documentation and take copies or to require copies from you.

Yours faithfully

Clive Troublesore

The 'you need to get your clock mended' argument

An 18 month rule applies to service charge demands under the Landlord and Tenant Act 1985. In so far as a service charge demand relates to expenditure incurred more than 18 months previously, you don't have to pay – unless the landlord has told you in writing during those 18 months that the particular expenditure will be incurred and that you will be charged up for it in due course. For some years, it had been thought that the 18 month rule did not apply to interim (or on-account) demands for service charge contributions which are provided for by most leases (see above). But the Court of Appeal has ruled that the relevant law – you will find it in section 20B of the 1985 Act – does in fact apply to interim demands as well as other demands. This means that if, by the time an interim demand is given to you, any of the costs covered by it were incurred more than 18 months earlier, you may not be liable to contribute towards them. Whether or not the landlord can get round this by sending you a supplemental demand will depend on what the lease says. In the Court of Appeal case (*Skelton and others v DBS Homes (Kings Hill) Ltd* [2017] EWCA Civ 1139), the landlord was too late to do this.

Before telling your landlord to get on their bike once they have mended their clock, it would be wise to get some advice from a professional on how you stand, given the wording of your particular lease.

Chapter 51

Eating Out Is Off

Aggro at the bistro

The food was awful and the service was pathetic. Our evening has been ruined.

I do not believe that I should be liable to pay this bill. I will write to you tomorrow with full details of my complaints.

Clive Troublesore
149 Magnolia Crescent
Twickenham
KT89 4XZ
20 8742 9381

Please, please, please ... don't foget to write ...

A large helping of guts is a prerequisite for a customer who wishes to challenge management in a restaurant for they can never be sure who will prevail and, at the best, you could be rewarded by the chef urinating into your dessert or worse. The food and drink must be of a satisfactory quality, reasonably fit to be eaten and as described on the menu or by the waiter when taking your order. The service should be provided with reasonable care and skill. That's the Consumer Rights Act 2015 talking (see chapter 63 for more talk). Obviously, what you get and how you get it – silver service or dropped down onto the table from a great height – will depend on the type of joint you have gone to and how much you are meant to be paying.

Ideally, any food or drink not up to standard should be rejected before much more than a taster has been consumed or you may find it difficult to justify a complaint. But if you are genuinely scared or embarrassed to make too much of a fuss, leave some of the offerings on the plate and draw the waiter's attention to the inadequacies when they are clearing the table and on no account tell the waiter that everything is fine as and when an enquiry to this effect is made at five minute intervals. Stay mute.

Crunch time comes, whether or not you have created a rumpus, when the bill is tendered. Can you scarper without tendering any payment? You have to be very careful here because of the crime of *bilking*. It is an offence under the Theft Act 1968 to *dishonestly* make off without having paid as required and with intent to avoid payment. The magic word there is *dishonestly*. If you genuinely believe that you can leave without payment and have it out with the management subsequently then that would not be *dishonesty* on your part. On the other hand, you don't want to run the risk of an under nourished police constable fresh from being poisoned at the station canteen taking a dim view of your conduct and arresting you. The solution is this. Leave a message on the table and snap in position on your mobile before the scarper.

Message on a plate

It would be a hard task to completely knock out the entire bill where you had consumed quite a bit of the food and drink on it, unless you were proposing marriage to your lover at the restaurant but, because the occasion was so terrible, they irrevocably turned you down. The more likely remedy to which you would be entitled is a reduction in the bill to reflect your complaints – what was the food and drink worth? – and the disappointment of the occasion. In that situation and assuming you do not wish to confront management there and then, deduct from the bill what you feel is reasonable and leave the balance in cash on the plate with a suitably adapted message. No cash? Then you are in trouble and a confrontation will be unavoidable. For the extremely meek, clear your throat a thousand times; tell management you are not a happy bunny; write on the bill *"Paid under protest"*; snap the bill and leave it behind; and pay up in full. Next day send the restaurant a letter of complaint and, if you get nowhere, see if you can take advantage of your credit card 'equal responsibility' or debit card 'chargeback' opportunities (see chapter 41). For the purpose of seeing whether the value of the transaction was over £100, the grand total of the bill can be reckoned.

Bad service charge

Oh yes, the service charge. The menu or bill will often say it is discretionary. In that event, you don't have to pay it. If it is a requirement that you should pay, you don't have to pay if the standard of service did not justify it or the requirement was not brought to your attention before you placed your order. It is an offence for a priced menu to omit reference to a service charge which is to be made and the menu should be displayed outside the restaurant.

No shows

It would be a breach of contract to reserve a table and, for whatever reason short of outbreak of war or destruction of the restaurant, fail to turn up. A cancellation call should be made wherever possible and as soon as possible. Cancellation call or no cancellation call, if you reckon that your restaurant has a likeness for litigation and a dislikeness for people who break their word, it would be wise to check on whether it has been able to book out your table to other customers. This can be done by telephoning and asking for a table – "Sorry, sir but we are fully booked and there is a queue outside but we could fit you in next year on a Monday night at 11.45pm." – or snatching a glance through the window from outside. If the restaurant has served others who would have gone unserved if you had shown up and those others have spent at least as much as you would have done then the restaurant has suffered no loss from your breach and would not have a valid claim against you. Any provable claim would have to be for loss of profit. Restaurants have sued for this loss and won but usually only against persistent no-showers.

Was this chapter to your satisfaction, sir and madam? We hope to see you in our next chapter.

Chapter 52
Change Of Name
From Smith to Brown

Changing your name can be as refreshing and exciting as changing your underpants. A click of the fingers and it's done. Mr Smith becoming Mr Brown is a tad boring, if I may say so, and I do with the greatest respect to all the fascinating and friendly Smiths and Browns I have taken wine with in my lifetime. What I had in mind was Clive Troublesore converting himself to Orlando Mischief. The change can be of any forename, the surname or both. A legal document is not strictly necessary but when your bank and the passport office ask for your fingerprints and life history, you may wish you had made the change in a more formal manner. And that makes sense. Do it with a deed poll and that's not something with which to prod a philanthropist. You will find a template for the deed poll below and for no extra charge. There's also a template for a deed poll to be made on behalf of a child but the position there may not be quite so straightforward.

Changing your name for a fraudulent purpose is likely to get you into criminal trouble, although those cursed with an unspent criminal conviction or diabolical credit rating, break no law in making the change, provided they supply truthful information about the past, if asked. I commend a carefully and honestly crafted new handle to turn heads as you are paged in hotel lobbies and guaranteed the best table by the window at overbooked restaurants. Orlando Mischief might not quite do the trick but it will please him.

It has been suggested that a baptismal name can only be changed by Act of Parliament or bishop on confirmation or adoption. Nevertheless, it is customary to see a deed poll changing a baptismal name as well as a surname and nobody gets worked up about it.

Enrolment

There is procedure for registering – except, just to be difficult, they call it enrolling – a deed poll at no less a place than the Central Office of the Senior Courts of Justice. The procedure, which is an enormous pain in the neck, if not a certain part of the lower rear anatomy, is set out in the Enrolment of Deeds (Change of Names) Regulations 1994 which have been amended a few times. It isn't necessary to take this step in order to make the name change legally effective and, in my view, only a circus clown or a client following the advice of a very expensive firm of West End solicitors which was short of work would go down that path.

Children

A parent can change the name of their child who is a minor so long as everyone with parental responsibility for the child consents and that will usually mean mother and father. The consent of a child aged between 16 and 18 is also highly desirable. If there is a court child arrangements order in force which states with whom the child is to live then the consents should be set out in writing. But where there is a dispute about a child's name change, a court application must be made by one of the parties to settle it. This should be under the Children Act 1989 for a specific issue order. The most frequent applications of this kind arise where the child's mother has the child living with her exclusively or for the majority of the time, has remarried or is cohabiting with someone else whose surname mother has taken and wants the child to be known by the same surname. These disputes are sometimes resolved by the child being known by both surnames: a double-barrelled job and then everyone is happy – hopefully.

In more recent years, judges have shown a desire to be satisfied that a change of forename as against just surname has been in the best interests of the child. In a 2016 case, a local authority which had care of twins went to court with a view to preventing their mother from naming the boy Preacher, which she had chosen, and the girl Cyanide, which the twins' half siblings had chosen. Naming the girl Cyanide, it was ruled, raised the likelihood of her suffering serious emotional harm. Preacher would not do the same for the boy but both names were ruled out. The potential benefit to the boy in having a name chosen by the mother was more than outweighed by the potential detriment to the girl in having a name chosen by the half-siblings.

Deed poll for big and ugly adults

> THIS DEED POLL* made on 14 July 2021 by me ORLANDO MISCHIEF of 149 Magnolia Crescent Twickenham Middlesex KT89 4XZ formerly called CLIVE TROUBLESORE WITNESSES AND IT IS HEREBY DECLARED as follows:-
>
> (1)   I absolutely and entirely renounce relinquish and abandon the use of my former forename of CLIVE and my former surname of TROUBLESORE and assume adopt and determine to take and use from the date of this deed the forename of ORLANDO and the surname of MISCHIEF in substitution for my former forename of CLIVE and my former surname of TROUBLESORE.
>
> (2)   I shall at all times hereafter in all records deeds and other writings and in all actions proceedings dealings and transactions and on all occasions whatsoever use and sign the said forename of ORLANDO as my forename in substitution for my former forename of CLIVE hereby relinquished and the said surname of MISCHIEF as my surname in substitution for my former surname of TROUBLESORE as hereby relinquished to the intent that I may hereafter be called known or distinguished not by the former forename of CLIVE but by the forename of ORLANDO only and not by the former surname of TROUBLESORE but by the surname of MISCHIEF only.
>
> (3)   I authorise and request all persons at all times to designate describe and address me by my adopted forename of ORLANDO and my adopted surname of MISCHIEF.

SIGNED AS A DEED by the above-named) ORLANDO MISCHIEF in the presence of) Witness signature Address Occupation	Orlando Mischief formerly known as Clive Troublesore

*One witness will do. The document does not have to be stamped by HM Customs and Excise. Orlando signs as shown above to the right with his new names and then, underneath, with his old names.

Deed poll of behalf of child

THIS DEED POLL* made on 14 July 2021 by me MAVIS BULWARK of 149 Magnolia Crescent Twickenham Middlsesex KT89 4XZ the mother of PRISCILLA ANNE BULWARK now or lately called PRISCILLA ANNE TROUBLESORE a child born on 12 June 2011 of 149 Magnolia Crescent Twickenham aforesaid on behalf of the said PRISCILLA ANNE TROUBLESORE WITNESSES AND IT IS HEREBY DECLARED as follows:-

(1)   On behalf of the said PRISCILLA ANNE TROUBLESORE I absolutely and entirely renounce relinquish and abandon the use of her former surname of BULWARK and on her behalf assume adopt and determine to take and use from the date of this deed the surname of TROUBLESORE in substitution for her former surname of BULWARK.

(2)   The said PRISCILLA ANNE TROUBLESORE shall at all times hereafter in all records deeds and other writings and in all actions proceedings dealings and transactions and on all occasions whatsoever use and sign the said surname of TROUBLESORE as her surname in substitution for her former surname of BULWARK as hereby relinquished to the intent that she may hereafter be called known or distinguished not by the former surname of BULWARK but by the surname of TROUBLESORE only.

(3)   I on behalf of the said PRISCILLA ANNE TROUBLESORE authorise and request all persons at all times to designate describe and address her not by the former surname of BULWARK but by the adopted surname of TROUBLESORE.

SIGNED AS A DEED by the above-named MAVIS BULWARK in the presence of	))	M Bulwark on behalf of Patricia Anne Troublesore formerly known as Patricia Anne Bulwark

Witness signature

Address

Occupation

*One witness will do. The document does not have to be stamped by HM Customs and Excise. Mavis only signs as shown above to the right with her usual signature. Assuming there is no dispute about the name change between parents or anyone else with parental responsibility which would have to be settled in court proceedings (see above) then it would be desirable, if possible, for the child's other parent to sign an additional paragraph after the other signatures which goes like this: "*I ALBERT BULWARK of Upper Flat 62 Estuary Road Clapham Common London SW4 XET being the father of PATRICIA ANNE TROUBLESORE formerly PATRICIA ANNE BULWARK hereby consent to the change of her surname from BULWARK to TROUBLESORE.*"

Good game, eh?

Chapter 53
Drink Drive
Excess defences

Warning

Drinking and driving is bad for you, your vehicle, your licence, your pocket, your future insurance premium or even your ability to find insurance, your job, your reputation and your sanity. It is also bad for anyone else on the road at the same time. Right that's the preaching out of the way. But what I say is true. It is a criminal offence to drive or attempt to drive or to be in charge of a motor vehicle on a road or other public place (okay on your front lawn) with more alcohol in your breath, blood or urine than the law allows. If you thought it would be a good idea to refuse to provide a 'roadside' preliminary breath test or a police station specimen of breath, blood or urine so that there was no incriminating evidence against you, then you would be wrong. It is an offence to fail, without reasonable excuse, to cooperate with the police over the preliminary testing or to provide a specimen for the later testing.

This is all the Road Traffic Act 1988 this is. An 'excess alcohol' offence they call it. And you just might be charged with this offence when it so happens you are innocent of it or the police failed to follow the proper procedures and you are aggrieved by this. Nobody would quibble with you contesting a charge when you are innocent. Perhaps you weren't the driver or you weren't over the limit and the equipment the police used to attempt to prove their case was up the creek. It's when you take a point about the procedure the police followed or some other so-called technical point that you will be as popular in court as an actuary at an orgy. But the procedures are there to be followed; the consequences of a conviction are severe; we don't do anarchy; and so the taking of a technical point against a prosecution is perfectly legitimate. Despite moaning and groaning from the magistrates and a look of repulsion on their faces, technical defences do quite often succeed. Indeed, the threat of a technical defence may facilitate a compromise with the prosecutor. As a drink-drive solicitor defender in one of my previous lifetimes, I was able on occasions to negotiate an arrangement whereby the prosecutor accepted a guilty plea to failing to provide (now cooperate with) a preliminary test with the more serious charge of driving with excess alcohol being dropped (which gave an opportunity for disqualification being avoided as in this instance it was within the discretion of the court to disqualify and not mandatory). And on other occasions an arrangement involving a charge of driving with excess alcohol being dropped in return for a guilty plea to being in charge of a motor vehicle with excess alcohol (again, giving an opportunity for disqualification being avoided for the same reason). Such occasions are still available and will be of interest to the prosecutor where they reckon there is a risk of not securing a conviction on the more serious and mandatory disqualification charge.

This chapter is devoted to 'excess alcohol' offences and does not touch on separate offences of driving or attempting to drive or being in charge of a motor vehicle when under the influence of drink or drugs or with a concentration of a controlled drug over the specified limit. But those other offences are there.

An 'excess alcohol' charge will be tried by a magistrates' court. There is no right to elect trial by jury. There is a right of appeal against conviction to the Crown Court or, on a point of law only, to the High Court.

Let's look at the defences

The 'they were dressed as Mary Poppins' defence

The preliminary breath test, generally required at the roadside, will usually be your passport to go on your way if you pass it or your passport to be arrested if you fail it. The fact that the action of the police in requiring it was unlawful will be a good defence to a charge of failing, without reasonable excuse, to cooperate over the test (which carries discretionary and not mandatory disqualification, endorsement and a fine) but not, of itself, a good defence to a more serious charge of driving with excess alcohol or failing to provide a specimen for later police station testing etc (although it could play a part in a 'bad faith' defence to such a charge (see below)). Unless it is after an accident, the police can only require a preliminary test if the administering constable is in uniform. Dressed as Mary Poppins, this condition will not be satisfied and you will have a good defence to a failing to cooperate charge if you refused to be tested or deliberately messed up the testing. Likewise, if the constable accompanying the test-requiring constable was in uniform but not the actual test-requirer. The High Court has held in two cases that a constable without his hat was still in uniform for this purpose.

Relevant law – section 6(7) of the Road Traffic Act 1988.

The 'random stop' defence

The police may require a preliminary breath test if they reasonably suspect a relevant offence or, where there has been an accident, they reasonably believe a relevant offence has been committed. Random roadside testing is outlawed but random roadside stopping is permissible. This means that the police can stop you for no apparent reason but then, sniffing alcohol on your breath, require you to cooperate with a roadside test. Random stopping without being followed up with reasonable suspicion of a relevant offence will be a good defence to a charge of failing to cooperate with the preliminary test. It might also be a good defence to a charge of driving over the limit after a positive police station test on the basis that the police station evidence should be excluded because the police had obtained evidence they would not otherwise have had and that prejudiced you.

Relevant law – section 6 of the Road Traffic Act 1988.

Relevant case – *DPP v Godwin* decided by the High Court on 22 April 1991.

The 'out of the way' defence

The preliminary breath test, except after an accident, may only be administered at or near the place where you are required to take it. So if you are stopped and required to give a preliminary blow, that can't take place five miles down the road. Breach of that condition would be a defence to a charge of failing to cooperate with the test. That of itself is unlikely to assist you with any defence to a charge of driving over the limit if you went on and gave a positive test at the police station. In the case of an accident, the preliminary test may be administered at a police station if the police think that is expedient or somewhere else such as a hospital.

Relevant law – section 6A of the Road Traffic Act 1988.

The 'look, no accident' defence

One of the justifications for the police requiring a preliminary test is that the police reasonably suspect that an accident has occurred owing to the presence of a motor vehicle on a road or other public place and believe (not just suspect) that you were driving, attempting to drive or in charge of the vehicle at the time of the accident. If there was no reasonable suspicion of an accident or reasonable belief that you had been involved, then that would be a good defence to a charge of failing to cooperate with a preliminary test. A difficult defence, this one, on no reasonable suspicion of an accident because the courts have given a very wide interpretation to 'accident' for this purpose. It will catch any unintended occurrence which has an adverse physical effect although in one case it was ruled that an 'accident' had taken place where the motorist had deliberately driven through locked gates! Challenging the police on whether there was a reasonable belief that you had been involved in an accident might be a trifle easier provided you weren't sitting in the driver's seat of a smouldering wreck when the police turned up. The outcome of a successful challenge to the prosecution's case on either of these limbs would be the same as for the **random stop defence** as above.

Relevant law – section 6(5) of the Road Traffic Act 1988.

The 'wrong testing result' defence

At the police station, the specimen required for testing will be of your breath. The prosecution will rely on the analysis of the lower of the two specimens which will be required from you. In certain circumstances, the police will instead ask for a specimen of your blood or urine, for example where the breath machine is up the creek. The choice as to which, blood or urine, is down to them. In a decided case, the police swapped from breath to blood because the police station breath machine had failed to produce a written print-out showing the testing results despite the fact that the results had shown up on the machine's visual display unit. Also, the machine's clock had been five minutes out. Both the machine and the blood specimens put the motorist over the legal limit but, at the hearing of the case, the prosecution relied only on the breath testing. The motorist was convicted of driving over the limit but the appeal court quashed the conviction on the basis that the police had treated the breath machine as unreliable and so reliance could only have been placed on the blood test result.

Relevant case – *Badkin v Chief Constable of South Yorkshire*, decided by the High Court on 10 July 1987.

The 'no evidence of breath machine calibration' defence

Police station breath machines self-calibrate before and after the specimens you provide have been analysed. Or they should do. Before you can be convicted of any offence on the strength of the machine's breath analysis, the prosecution must prove that the machine did satisfactorily calibrate. This can be done by the prosecution producing a copy of the machine's print out which will give calibration details or coming up with some verbal evidence from the operating police constable about calibration which will be based on what they saw on the machine's visual display unit. If there is no print-out and no satisfactory verbal calibration evidence, the charge against you should be dismissed. You would be entitled to plead 'not guilty' to the charge and wait and see whether the prosecution could prove its case. If no calibration evidence was adduced then you could ask for the charge to be dismissed on the basis that there was no case to answer. The disadvantage of this course is that if the prosecution comes up with the calibration goods and you then change your plea to guilty, you will have ratcheted up its bill for costs against you and lost the chance of being given credit for an early cough to the charge.

Relevant cases – *Mason v DPP* decided by the High Court on 4 February 1988 and *Owen v Chesters* decided by the High Court on 14 November 1984.

The 'no service of print-out' defence

Although the police can prove the results of the breath testing and the calibration of the breath machine, otherwise than by producing the machine's print-out in evidence (see **The 'no evidence of breath machine calibration' defence**), they will usually rely only on production of the print-out. Not easy for you to allege that a piece of paper is a liar. However, production of the print-out can only be relied on if a copy of the print-out was handed to you when it was produced by the breath machine or served on you no later than seven days before the main hearing of your case. Handed to you? In one decided case, the print-out copies were placed on the police station counter for the motorist to sign but without any indication that one of those copies was for him to take away. The charge of driving with excess alcohol was rightly dismissed because he had not been 'handed' a copy of the print-out and so it could not be relied on at the hearing. There was no other evidence of the machine's readings or calibration. The fact that you keep quiet during the prosecution's evidence about not having been handed or served with a copy of the print-out in time or at all and allow the court to see the print-out will not matter so long as you take the point when you give evidence. It is not fatal to the prosecution that the print-out was not signed by the investigating officer. That was decided in a High Court case where I had represented the motorist in the magistrates' court and taken that technical point against the prosecution. Don't tell anyone that I lost.

Relevant law – section 16 of the Road Traffic Offenders Act 1988.

Relevant cases – *Halser v DPP* decided by the High Court on 17 May 1988 and *Tobi v Nicholas* decided by the High Court on 1 July 1987.

The 'no warning' defence

The police must warn you that failure to provide a police station specimen may render you liable to prosecution (but no such warning needs to be given in relation to the preliminary test). They usually do because this is written down on their aide-memoire but they have been known to forget the warning. If you were not warned, this would be a defence to charge of driving or attempting to drive with excess alcohol or to failing to provide a police station specimen, even where a specimen was provided and showed you to be over the limit. The police officer's notebook would be telling on whether the warning was, in fact, given, though not conclusive.

Relevant law – section 7(7) of the Road Traffic Act 1988.

Relevant cases – *Simpson v Spalding* decided by the High Court on 7 November 1987 and *Murray v DPP* decided by the High Court on 4 February 1993.

The 'me no understand the warning' defence

This is a variation of **The 'no warning' defence**. It works like this. "OK, I accept that a warning was given to me but I did not understand what the constable was on about." A valid reason for not understanding might be your inability to understand English, your anxiety or your mental state. The defence has succeeded on a charge of failing to provide breath specimens at the police station. It ought equally to succeed on a charge of driving or attempting to drive or being in charge of a motor vehicle with excess alcohol. In the decided case, the motorist was of Indian origin. He could understand English to a certain degree but he could not understand long or technical words. What the police sergeant said to him by way of warning under the legislation which has since been amended – but it makes no difference to the principle – was this: "It is alleged you have committed an offence contrary to section 5 or 6 of the Road Traffic Act 1972 as amended by the Transport Act 1981 and I require you to provide two specimens of breath for analysis by means of an approved device. The specimen with the lower proportion of alcohol in your breath may be used as evidence and the other disregarded. I must warn you that failure to provide any of those specimens may render you liable to prosecution. Do you agree to provide two specimens of breath for analysis?" He was somewhat overwhelmed. He said "yes" although he did not understand what he had been told. He then went to provide two specimens but his blowing was insufficient and no analysis could be performed by the breath machine. Where the sergeant slipped up was in not considering the language barrier, not explaining the situation in words the motorist could understand and not thinking it necessary to get in an interpreter. The charge was dismissed and the prosecutor's appeal against the dismissal was thrown out.

Relevant case – *Chief Constable of Avon and Somerset v Singh* decided by the High Court on 12 March 1987.

The 'absent brief' defence

As a general rule, the police can carry on with the excess alcohol procedures at the police station, including putting you on the breath machine, despite you wanting legal advice first and even if you are actually waiting for a solicitor to telephone you or see you at the station. It follows that, generally, a refusal to provide specimens until legal advice has been received would not be justified. But if the police have told you quite clearly that you need not provide specimens until you have consulted with a solicitor and, still solicitorless, the police change tack and require the specimens there and then, you might have a good defence, by way of a reasonable excuse, for failing to supply but this is a difficult defence to run. It would be a question of degree and depend on how long you had been waiting and whether the solicitor was expected pretty quickly or was still waiting for a bus in Outer Mongolia to get them to the police station. Your best chance of success with the defence is to be able to prove that the police knew a solicitor was immediately available and that up to the point of you asking for the solicitor to attend, there had been no significant delay in the procedures. If you say "I promise I will provide specimens but can I see my solicitor first?" the police should not treat that as an outright refusal to provide specimens and proceed to charge you with failing to supply. If they did, you would have a good defence to that charge. Instead, the police should decide whether or not to grant the favour for which you have asked. They could not be faulted for rejecting it.

Relevant cases – *DPP v Billington, Chappell v DPP, DPP v Rumble* and *Corywright v East*, all decided by the High Court on 20 July 1987 and *Causey v DPP* decided by the High Court on 11 November 2004.

The 'dirty play' defence cum 'PACE' defence

The court effectively has a discretion to refuse to take account of certain evidence if, having regard to all the circumstances, it would just be too unfair to do so. It might well say it is too unfair where the evidence was obtained oppressively or by a trick. In one decided case, the motorist, who had been speeding, gave positive preliminary and police station breath machine samples. But he had been stopped on private property to which the motorist had objected. The police officer said the motorist could sue him if he was wrongly arrested. It was ruled that the evidence of the positive testing should be disregarded because of the oppressive behaviour of the police. In another case, the police had followed the motorist onto his driveway and he had told them they were trespassing. The police led or dragged him back to the road where he failed the preliminary breath test and subsequently gave positive breath tests at the station. Again, the evidence of positive testing was excluded because of the police behaviour and the High Court quashed the conviction for driving with excess alcohol. Incidentally, the law now permits police to enter any place after an accident to administer a preliminary test or to arrest in what would formerly have been a trespass situation.

Relevant cases – *Matto v Woverhampton Crown Court* decided by the High Court on 20 May 1987 and *Sharpe v DPP* decided by the High Court on 3 February 1993.

The 'archbishop' defence

You dine with an archbishop before taking to the driving seat. Your liquid intake during the long meal is restricted to two glasses of sparkling mineral water and a bowl of non-alcoholic consommé. You appear quite sober to the archbishop and other diners in your party and to certain others with whom you had contact before going to the restaurant. Oddly, the breath machine at the police station shows you to be over the legal limit.

In the course of your attempt to impugn the breath machine's accuracy, the court may hear evidence of the quantity of alcohol, if any, that you had consumed before patronising the breath machine. The evidence of persons of high moral standing, like the archbishop and any of the others who saw you in the run up to your arrest who look good in a double-breasted suit or cocktail dress, should make the court sit up. But the evidence really needs to be very powerful indeed and, ideally, linked with some evidence suggesting that the breath machine had been off colour lately. The court can hear evidence along these lines and would be entitled to conclude that there was reasonable doubt about the breath machine's accuracy and, hence, about your guilt.

Relevant case – *Cracknell v Willis*, decided by the House of Lords (before it became the Supreme Court) on 5 November 1987.

The 'burden of proof' defence

As in all criminal cases, it is for the prosecution to prove its excess alcohol case against you beyond reasonable doubt (see **The 'archbishop' defence**). The law presumes that the breath machine reading was reliable. This presumption can be rebutted. If you put in some evidence suggesting that the reading was unreliable, it is then the job of the prosecution, if it is to secure a conviction, to prove beyond reasonable doubt that in fact the reading was reliable. It is not your job, if you are to secure a dismissal of the charge, to prove beyond reasonable doubt the reading's unreliability or even that it is more probable than not that the machine was up the creek. The burden of proof on the reliability of the reading is on the prosecution and not you. May sound like semantics but, in practice, which of the prosecution or the defence has that job can be the difference between a conviction and a dismissal.

Relevant case – *Ali v DPP*, decided by the Administrative Court on 27 October 2020.

The 'hip-flask' defence

So there was a delay between you driving or attempting to drive or being in charge of a vehicle and providing positive police station specimens, was there? It is a defence to one of these charges that you consumed alcohol after you ceased to do what is alleged and that, but for that, you would not have been over the limit. It would be down to you to prove both of these factors and to show that it is more probable than not that what you say is truthful and correct. This is a lower burden than the one which rests on the prosecutor's shoulders in a criminal trial to prove their case beyond reasonable doubt. Unless it is as plain as a pike staff that the second factor is established, you won't have a hope in hell in succeeding in the defence without some medical or scientific evidence to back up your assertion.

Relevant law – section 15(3) of the Road Traffic Offenders Act 1988.

The 'I wasn't going nowhere' defence

If you are alleged to have been in charge of a motor vehicle while over the limit, it is a defence to prove that there was no likelihood of you having driven so long as you remained likely to be over the limit. A wheel clamp would help. As with the **'hip-flask' defence** you would have to show it was more probable than not that what you say is truthful and correct in order to succeed and expert evidence from a medical or scientific witness may well be essential where it becomes necessary to show how long it would have taken for the volume of alcohol which was shown to have been in your body to be eliminated.

Relevant law – section 5(2) of the Road Traffic Act 1988.

Chapter 54

On The Road

And off a charge or disqualification?

Speeding

Or, to be precise, not speeding. In *DPP v Marrable** decided by the High Court on 4 February 2020, the motorist was clocked by a police constable using an approved TruCAM device, speeding in a 50 mph limit in his van at 72 mph. The motorist had an unapproved GPS tracking device fitted to the van and a data print out from the device, shown by the motorist to the court, suggested a speed at the relevant time of between 53 and 54 mph which he asserted had been the correct speed. Magistrates found that the constable had carried out all required operational checks on his device before and after use but also that the motorist was a credible witness. They decided there was reasonable doubt about the speed and so dismissed the case. The prosecution was miffed and appealed.

The High Court threw out the appeal. If the motorist had simply given his own opinion of his speed, that would have been one thing. But he had produced the GPS print out to support his account. The TruCAM data was not conclusive. It was true that the magistrates had only needed to be sure that a speed higher than 50 mph had been reached in order to convict. They must have allowed for a small margin of error when considering the GPS data. That was neither perverse nor irrational.

*This decision follows that in the case of *Cracknell v Wills* (see under **The 'archbishop' defence** at chapter 53) where the House of Lords ruled that the readings of a breath machine could be challenged by other evidence, although the strength of evidence produced by type approved devices had to be acknowledged as strong.

The unidentified driver

For a variety of road traffic offences such as speeding, the police can require you as a vehicle's registered keeper to tell them who was driving when the offence was alleged to have been committed. It is an offence in itself not to identify the driver. But it is a defence if you can show that you did not know when asked who the driver was and could not have found out their identity with reasonable diligence. Lord Howard of Lympne (former Conservative leader Michael Howard) was asked by the Met who had been at the wheel when his car had been clocked at 37 mph in a 30 mph limit. It could have been him or it could have been his wife. Neither could remember which of them. Although the magistrates' court judge believed him, she convicted him on the ground that, despite the fact in the first part of the form the police had sent him he had stated "The driver was my wife or myself. We don't know which", he had not gone on in the second part of the form to identify the driver if he was claiming it was not him! He appealed against his conviction to the High Court which meant there were more M'Luds about than usual. His conviction was quashed because the magistrates' court had failed to consider whether that defence – didn't know and couldn't have found out with reasonable diligence – had been made out. The High Court judges criticised the police form for not catering for the registered keeper to explain what steps they had taken in the Howard situation, to try and identify the driver.

The dreaded points

You may be ready, willing and able to cope with the fine for a motoring offence. Points endorsed on your driving licence are something else. Most offences attract points. Some offences such as speeding can be dealt with by the issue of a fixed penalty notice when you are stopped if the police officer is prepared to offer you the option of settling for one. For speeding, the automatic number of points with a fixed penalty is three. The 12th point (add the points which the latest offence attracts to the points already endorsed for offences committed within the three years immediately before the latest offence to reach the 12th point) spells disqualification by which time you will be up before the beaks. The disqualification period will be at least six months. That disqualification will generally wipe the driving licence clean of endorsements. When, as a solicitor, I was pleading to keep my client on the road, I was fond of urging the beaks to refrain from disqualifying so that the points would remain stained on their licence and operate as a Damoclean Sword hanging over their heads and thereby deter them from future transgressions. Alright, it didn't work every time.

There are two possible routes of escape from 12th point disqualification.

Route 1. The special reason for not endorsing any points on your driving licence. This means a reason which is special to the offence and not you, the offender. The ingredients for the special reason are some mitigating or extenuating factor; a factor which does not amount to a defence (for, if you have a defence, you should be pleading 'not guilty'); a factor which is directly connected with the commission of the offence; and a factor which the court ought properly to take into account. Words, words. How does it work? There are a number of conflicting court decisions and what may strike one bench of beaks as a load of codswallop may have another bench eating out of your driving licence.

These are not special reasons. Your previous safe driving. No special reason would lead to up to 12 or more points and that would lead to disqualification which would lead to catastrophe for you and your aged aunt who lives 15 miles away and to whom you deliver breakfast (eggs sunny side up) every weekday morning. You were only 1 mph over the limit.

These have been held to be special reasons. An obstructed 30 mph sign at the start of a restricted stretch of the road. Exceeding the speed limit by 10 mph on a motorway by a driver so worried about his blind and incontinent 80 years old passenger becoming ill that he was anxious to reach the nearest service station and unaware of his speed. A short distance only driven when it was unlikely that the motorist would come into contact with other road users. U-turning on a motorway to avoid a long stationary traffic jam when there had been no oncoming traffic in the opposite direction for some considerable time (although it would have been otherwise if the motorway had been in normal use).

Where you wish to rely on a special reason in court, you will be required to give evidence from the witness box and so exposed to cross-examination by the prosecutor. You cannot succeed with a 'half-way house' in a borderline special reason plea and invite the beaks to reduce the number of penalty points to be endorsed rather than waiving endorsement entirely. It's all penalty points, be the number fixed or subject to the court's discretion within a specified range, or nothing.

Route 2. Mitigating reasons for not disqualifying. A factor which fails to rank as a special reason may nevertheless be taken into account by the court along this route. Here the court can refrain from disqualifying you at all or reduce the period of disqualification from the 12 point minimum of six months. The beaks can do this if satisfied that "having regard to all the circumstances, there are grounds for mitigating the normal consequences of the conviction". A dustbinful or jewelboxful of factors (as the case may be) can be relied on here but do remember that the beaks will probably have heard most of them before so try and be discriminating in what you put forward and, where possible, back up your mitigating reasons with documentary evidence like letters from employers and worthies. I once heard one magistrate ask a clergyman who turned up at court to back up their congregant whether the motorist was a regular churchgoer and the affirmative reply went down very well. That the circumstances of the offence (or any other previously endorsed offence) were not serious is not intended to be a good reason for no or reduced 12 point disqualification although I have never heard an advocate fail to impress the triviality of the circumstances on the sentencing beaks. The most common factor relied on here is the exceptional hardship that disqualification would cause. It has to be exceptional though as, almost always, some hardship will ensue from disqualification.

Motorist shall speak peace unto pedal cyclist – one day

The battle between motorist and cyclist shows no sign of abating. If anything, with the proliferation of cycling lanes (or, at least, those lanes which have not been withdrawn within five minutes of birth), passions run higher than ever. We all know what the highway code says about how motorist and cyclist should react to one another while driving and riding. In a civil claim arising out of an accident between motorist and cyclist, the one of them who has broken the code will usually be presumed to have been wholly or partly to be at fault for the accident.

Cyclists as well as motorists are under a duty to take reasonable care on the roads for their own safety which is pretty trite law. That duty extends to stopping at traffic lights. Quite how those cyclists who fail to do so and give the remainder a bad name can be induced to change their ways is a hard question to answer. Perhaps the police could occasionally prosecute them. Or perhaps pedal cycles, like cars, could become self-operating and automatically stop at red while the riders read up on hip hop. The Law Commission has recommended that motorists in self-driving cars should not be criminally responsible for failing to comply with traffic lights (or speeding and dangerous or careless driving) when the self-drive mode has been activated and that responsibility should fall on the vehicle's manufacturer or developer. The same principle could work with pedal cyclists in self-ride mode. Take no notice. I am being silly again.

This duty to take reasonable care was brought home in 2017 in three civil claims by cyclists who had suffered serious injuries in road accidents. In one case, the cyclist lost the claim entirely: in the other two, the cyclist was held to have substantially contributed to the accident which means that their compensation was reduced by the proportion of their own negligence.

Case 1 (*Elson v Stilgoe*). On the B5414, a single carriageway with one lane in each direction, at 8am on a dull day in January, the claimant was cycling alongside his friend: the claimant was on the outside. Just before reaching a puddle, the claimant veered to his offside onto the other lane as the defendant was driving his car on it in the opposite direction at a speed which was appropriate for the circumstances and road conditions. There was a collision between the claimant's cycle and the defendant's car. The trial judge decided that the claimant had had no good reason for moving to his offside. His friend had avoided the puddle without doing so. The defendant had been confronted at the last moment by the veering claimant. The argument that the defendant should have seen the claimant in time and either stopped or steered to his left was rejected. The claimant's appeal against the dismissal of his claim was dismissed by the Court of Appeal.

Case 2 (*McGeer v McIntosh*). The claimant was riding her cycle and the defendant, ahead of her, was driving his articulated HGV along Whitby Road, Ellesmere Port. They were both going in the same direction. Having driven over a railway bridge, the defendant stopped at traffic lights at the junction of Whitby Road with a road to his left into which he had intended to turn. He was signalling left but straddling two lanes. When the lights moved to green, he started to make that turn. At the same time, the claimant passed along the nearside of his vehicle and across its front. There was a collision. At the civil trial, the claimant was held to have been 30% to blame for the accident and the defendant 70%. The defendant's challenge to that decision was thrown out by the Court of Appeal. In relation to the claimant, she should have realised the defendant was straddling two lanes and she could not have safely assumed he was going to go straight ahead or turn right. She had cycled down the brow of a hill on the railway bridge at some speed and had failed to heed the advice in rule 73 of the Highway Code. ("Pay particular attention to long vehicles which need a lot of room to manoeuvre at corners. Be aware that drivers may not see you ... Do not be tempted to ride in the space between them and the kerb.")

Case 3 (*Rickson v Bhakar*). Just before 7.30am on a Sunday, the claimant was taking part in a cycling time trial on the westbound carriageway of the A27. The defendant in his van was travelling on the eastbound carriageway and went to turn right at a designated gap in the dual carriageway.

He thought he was safe to make the turn. He was wrong. The claimant was coming along and the defendant would be crossing the claimant's path. The claimant collided with the van's rear as it crossed and the collision caused him catastrophic and life-changing spinal injuries. At his speed, it would have taken the defendant approximately four seconds to have moved across the carriageway. The claimant had been cycling at between 20 and 25 mph. He would have been approximately 40 metres away when the van first started to move across the junction which would have given him ample opportunity to apply his brakes and avoid the collision if he had been keeping reasonable observation of the road. The claimant may have swerved within lane 1 but that action was too little, too late. The claimant, for one reason or another, had not been keeping a sufficient lookout. Because of that, a High Court judge ruled that he was 20% to blame.

Chapter 55
Parking On Private Land
The great escapes

Quiz time, folks. What do you hate the most? *Mrs Brown's Boys*, rice pudding with a dollop of marmalade planted in the middle or parking companies? It doesn't get easier than that. Around 6.8 million parking tickets are issued each year by private companies which have been given control over parking on private land, be it a pop up cabbage patch, an area adjacent to a supermarket or a series of postage stamps at the back of a block of flats. One every four seconds, so that's at least two since you started this chapter unless you are a fast reader. The conditions which govern parking on land may cover a multitude of sins: parking without payment or sufficient payment, without displaying a payment receipt or permit in your windscreen, outside the bay's markings, without stuffing an ice cream up your exhaust pipe. Jesting about the ice cream. The biggest nightmare around allegedly unlawful parking used to be the clamp or, worse still, the removal of your car to some compound in the Sahara Desert. This is now prohibited in relation to private land with the exception of airports, ports and some railway car parks. The nightmare these days is the so-called penalty for breaking one of those dreaded conditions which is likely to cost you in the region of £40 or up to £100 if you do not pay up on time and considerably more if you stubbornly refuse to pay anything and end up with a county court claim against you and then a judgment. That presupposes that you are legally liable to pay. But are you?

The scheme for caning you which we are looking at does not apply to local authorities which have separate powers to enforce parking, both on and off the road. And before you get into a fight with the supermarket or hotel manager who unctuously tells you that they are ever so sorry, sir or madam, and have sooooooooo much sympathy for you that they are wanting to weep but that it has nothing to do with their company that you got a ticket and it is those b......s who run the car park who are to blame and you must complain to them etc – they are mainly right! They are also bare faced liars because it was their company that brought in those b......s with the very intention of doing exactly what they are doing.

If, when you are cursed with a parking ticket or chased to pay up, whether as driver or registered keeper, you wish to make a challenge then you should put your representations to the parking company within 28 days. ("I challenge the charge because (set out your reasons). If you do not cancel the charge then I shall appeal and, if the appeal goes against me and you are unwise enough to claim against me in the county court, I shall defend the claim and apply for costs against you if, as I expect would happen, I succeed.") The challenge fails? Appeal to an independent appeals service called 'Parking on Private Land Appeals' (good name?) at popla.co.uk where the ticket has been issued by a member of the trade association British Parking Association, OR the Independent Appeals Service at theias.org where the ticket has been issued by a member of the other trade association, International Parking Community, but the success rate is lower with them. The appeal fails and you are sued in the county court by way of a small claim? Defend the claim but beware. If you lose in the county court, you will add to the bill against you. Only defend where you are satisfied you have a good chance of winning. Sorry to dampen your spirits, though. If the parking company is not a member of the British Parking Association or the International Parking Community, it may not entertain any representations and there almost certainly will not be any appeals procedure available.

Legal Changes Alert!!! The Parking (Code of Practice) Act 2019 was passed to deal with the parking company cowboys. There's been a consultation on a draft code and, if the government is true to its word (don't mock), that code will have been published well before you reached this chapter and the parking operators should have started to follow it by mid-2022, at the very latest. If they all do so, I will be engaging in more eating. Perhaps this time a photo of my favourite traffic warden. And by mid-2022, a free appeals service set up by the government and independent of the trade associations and the parking companies will have gone live. Breach of the code is likely to debar a parking company from obtaining details of registered keepers and that could well put them out of business. The code would also be taken into account in any ticket challenge you may make. The parking companies will additionally have to sign up to an appeals charter which will outline the process they should adopt in representations to them on the grounds of innocent error and mitigating circumstances. And then we come to the level of permissible penalties. These are to be brought in line with what you would be stung by a local authority for a parking transgression. There will be a distinction between London and out of London. In London, the cap will be £80 most of the time but this will rise to £130 for more serious breaches such as abusing a Blue Badge bay, parking on a no stopping zone such as an airport road or parking in a residents' permit-only car park. Outside London, the caps will be £50 and usually £70 respectively. However, within and without London, there will be a 50% discount for payment within 14 days so that, for example, you would get away with no more than a £25 slap on your steering wheel overstaying in a Macclesfield supermarket car park so long as you paid up quickly enough.

But this is for the future and won't help you over an incident yesterday afternoon. Or might it? Add this to your representations to the parking company (see above).

"I suggest that if the code of practice under the Parking (Code of Practice) Act 2019 and the appeals charter were already in force, the parking ticket issued against me would be cancelled. I believe that your company should act within the spirit of the pending code and charter and that the United Kingdom Accreditation Service would take a dim view of a refusal to do so."

The defences summarised below can be utilized for representations, an appeal or a county court claim against you – now and in the future.

The 'there was no contract' defence

The legal basis on which it will be claimed you were obliged to comply with the parking conditions is that you made a contract with the parking company by parking your vehicle where you did, with knowledge of the conditions and you have broken one (or more) of them. It will be asserted that the conditions were displayed on notices here, there and everywhere and, possibly, alongside any ticket machines on the land. The test to determine whether you saw one of more notices will be an objective one. Would a reasonable driver entering the car park and taking the route you would have taken, seen at least one of these notices before parking and making off on foot to their destination? The defence here is that there were no notices (unlikely) **or** that such notices as were up were absent from the route you took, in vehicle, from entrance to bay and, on foot, from bay to exit (possible) **or** that such notices as were up on your routes in and out were obstructed by foliage or in some other way and could not be seen or could not have been taken by their appearance, size and/or inconspicuousness of writing to contain parking conditions (possible). You cannot be taken to have agreed to the conditions and made a contract incorporating them if you didn't know of them and no reasonable person would have known of them. Should the parking company take you to the county court for their money and you defend the case, they may well rely on photographs of the signs. But were the signs up on your visit? Their written evidence may not make this clear and, more likely, their evidence may not establish where the signs were displayed in relation to where you were parked and your routes there. The best evidence you could come up with would be your own photographs backing up your case, taken once you discovered your parking ticket but make sure there is no spittle on the camera lens. Incidentally, if you found out about the conditions only on returning to your car and could not have reasonably known about them earlier, this defence is still intact. You cannot be taken to have made a contract when it was all over!

The 'signs did not catch what I did' defence

You need to check what the parking ticket alleges you did wrong against the parking conditions: what the signage said would be wrong. If, for example, it is alleged that you failed to display a permit and there was nothing in the conditions requiring you to do so then you should not be liable for the charge. Display was not a term of the contract.

The 'signs did not cover the alleged loss' defence

Some parking companies are fond of trying to charge up for the administrative cost of pursuing you where they make a county court claim. The cost of recovery, they call it. However, this is often not allowed for in the signage. If not allowed for, they can't have it. They seek to argue that the trade association to which they belong recommends that they be entitled to a reasonable amount. This alone is not a sound reason for them having it. It should have been covered by the signage. Sometimes, the signage will say that they can add an additional sum if you do not pay, without specifying for what. I suggest that this wording is too uncertain to catch recovery or administration charges and, in any event, they would need to be reasonable and evidence of how the additional sum has been calculated would be needed. Should they win the county court claim, they will usually be entitled to have their court fees paid back by you and, where the claim form has been issued by a solicitor, a fixed amount to cover that work which will usually be £50. These sums are distinct from the recovery charge which they may go for. The fact they are not entitled to the recovery charge would not of itself give you a defence to the charge under the parking ticket.

The 'you were too late' defence

Parking companies have six years to bring a county court claim from the date of the alleged contravention. They will generally be much quicker off the mark. Delay on their part within the six years is not a defence to the charge although, where it was unreasonable and they are asking the judge to award them interest on the charge from the date you should have paid up to the date of judgment, you may be able to persuade the judge to cut them down either on the rate of interest they seek or on the period over they are seeking it, or both. However, an exciting defence may well present itself in another form of delay. Where the company is ignorant of the identity of the driver who it is alleged has done wrong – and unless there was a human attendant on duty who recognised the driver as their maiden aunt, they won't have the foggiest about identity – and of where to find them, they can pursue whoever was registered as the vehicle's keeper for what they seek to have paid to them. And, more often than not, that is precisely what they do.

Time limits differ according to whether a parking ticket has been fixed to the vehicle while it was stationary or handed to the driver OR the transgression has been snapped on a remote camera. Where fixed or handed, the company can apply to the DVLA for registered keeper details (provided the company is a member of the British Parking Association or the International Parking Community) if the ticket has not been paid within 28 days. Then it must write to you as the registered keeper within 56 days of the ticket's issue for either details of the owner or your money. If it is late in doing so, you would have a defence to a county court claim should you not have paid or identified the driver where the driver was not yourself. Where the vehicle has been snapped and so no ticket has been fixed or handed to the driver at the scene of the crime, the company can apply for registered keeper details right away and it has just 14 days to send you a notice to pay up or identify the driver if not you. These 14 days run from the date of the transgression so not long. The notice is often given late. If late, you would have a defence to a county court claim even though you had not complied with the notice. Either notice must be placed in your grubby hands or delivered to you by post within the specified period. It will be presumed that, if posted, you had the notice on the second day after the day of posting, with Saturday, Sunday or any public holiday in England and Wales being ignored but if the postman fell asleep on their round and went home early without servicing your letterbox, you can seek to show that it was actually delivered too late. Should you need chapter and verse – and you may need them at a county court small claims hearing – go to the Protection of Freedoms Act 2012 schedule 4.

The 'there was no means of paying' defence

Every ticket machine was out of order? Or, as in one case I tried, the car park notices gave an option to pay either on your phone through Ringo or by credit card but Ringo was out of order. The driver did not have a credit card on her. She left her car and continued to try Ringo away from the car park. When she ultimately got through, she paid a parking charge based on a period commencing with the time she had actually parked. The parking company issued a ticket and sued her in the county court, arguing that she should have driven off and that for some of the time she had been parked no advance payment had been made. She could not pay retrospectively, they asserted. I decided, as the parking company conceded, that the contract (see **The 'there was no contract' defence** above) had been made when the driver had accepted the displayed conditions by parking her car and that there was nothing in those conditions which precluded parking in the situation that arose. Indeed, the parking company had agreed, through the conditions, to give a driver the option of paying through Ringo. It was the company which was in breach of the contract in that, through no fault of the driver, the option was not available. It was impossible for the driver to exercise the option when she tried and, anyway, a 'penalty' charge was an unfair condition in the circumstances. The driver was entitled to do what she did. The same principles, I suggest, should apply in the no working ticket machine or similar scenario.

The 'you had no authority to control or charge' defence

The parking company will have been brought in to manage what goes on in the car park by the owner of the land or whoever has control over the land. That may be the supermarket, the lessors or management company of the block of flats or whoever. There will be a written contract between the parking company and whoever has brought it in. Often, it will be for a fixed period but that fixed period may have expired. On the hearing of a county court claim, the parking company will usually rely in evidence on a copy of the contract. More than once, I have discovered that when the alleged transgression was committed, the fixed period had expired and I was not satisfied by any evidence that it was more probable than not that the whoever had brought in the company had agreed to it continuing to do its thing. Without authority to charge up, its claim should fail. A contract dealing with the car park at a supermarket or other business such as a leisure centre, should also be scrutinised to see whether it prohibits the parking company from issuing a ticket against or pursuing transgressors in certain situations. This could well include first-time wrongdoers who have parked and gone on to spend money at the business premises. Representations or an appeal should seek a copy of the contract and its production could be compelled on a county court claim, if not voluntarily produced by the parking company.

The 'parking scheme under which you are trying to nab me does not apply to this car park' defence

The scheme does not apply to car parks which are subject to what is described as 'statutory control'. If you are being chased for a parking charge under the scheme we are looking at and the car park concerned was already subject to some form of statutory control, then you should not be liable for the charge. This could well be the case where the car park was at an airport, port or railway station. It matters not that the owner of the land or whoever managed that land signed up to a contract with the parking company which is chasing you. For the contract to be an irrelevance, the statutory control would have to impose a civil or criminal liability in relation to parking generally on that land or parking of a vehicle of the class of yours (car, lorry or minibus). The form of statutory control includes – and is likely to be – a by-law or statutory order or regulation. You would need to do some digging if you suspect that this defence might be available to you and start with the local authority. I have dismissed a claim on the basis of this defence in relation to a car park at Southampton Docks. Go to the Protection of Freedom Act 2012 schedule 4 paragraph 2(1).

The 'charge for my wrongdoing is extortionate or extravagant' defence

If you are being chased for a charge of up to £100 (ignoring any recovery charge – see **The 'signs did not cover the alleged loss' defence** above – and also ignoring court costs), this defence would be a dead loss and was killed off by the Supreme Court (see chapter 65). But it might work if the charge is quite a bit over and the court reckons that it was fixed simply to punish you and your co-wrongdoers and had no legitimate purpose. This line of defence could have particular impetus where your wrongdoing falls within the lower penalty caps the government is committed to bring into force (see above).

The 'I wasn't parked long enough to trigger a charge' defence

This is for when you have been snapped, usually at the entrance and later at the exit. The car park conditions will usually trigger a charge if you have been **parked** for longer than was permitted. Time spent other than parked – getting to the bay and getting out of the park once you have collected your vehicle – should in that event be discounted. If the parking company is a member of the British Parking Association, it will normally allow you a period of at least ten minutes' grace. However, on a busy day that may prove to be insufficient. You can seek to rely on that busyness to reduce your parking period by ignoring your going around in a circle and doing your nut in a queue times.

Chapter 56

Tax Penalties

How to beat the taxman (if you want to)

I will tread carefully here as I no more want to fall out with Her Majesty's Revenue and Customs (HMRC) as my refuse collector, the Lord Chief Justice or the chefs we have met who have inimitable ways of punishing whingeing diners. However, it has to be said. HMRC does make mistakes. Oh to hell with it. HMRC makes far too many mistakes and has to be watched with great care. Those mistakes frequently lead to the imposition of penalties – on the taxpayer and that could be you. This chapter is about getting those penalties cancelled or quashed when they have arisen from an HMRC mistake or they are unjust or unfair and is aimed at assisting you whether or not you have yet made a challenge. They could relate to no or a late tax return or non or late payment of tax, among a series of alleged tax associated misdeeds.

You can appeal against an HMRC penalty to the first-tier tribunal dealing with tax cases. That appeal can be made online and there is no fee (see gov/uk/tax-tribunal/appeal-to-tribunal). You usually have 30 days from the date of the HMRC decision within which to appeal although the tribunal can extend that period for good reason. HMRC advice about your prospects of getting an extension can be misleading. If you or your business have been affected by coronavirus and wish to appeal against a decision made in or since February 2020, HMRC would have given you an extra three months. By now you will be well over the extended appeal deadline but there may still be a good reason for that. The upper tribunal can hear appeals on decisions on a point of law from the lower tribunal and further appeals on the law could go to the Court of Appeal and then the Supreme Court. Unless your case involves a complex tax avoidance scheme based on you investing £10m in a *Big Issue* vendor to make films about cracked paving stones, your case will start and finish in the first tier's basement. Many appeals there are decided on paper without any hearing for each side to attend but you can ask for a hearing if that is what you want. It could now well be by telephone. And you should want it where there is a factual dispute and you are telling the truth.

Where you are appealing against a penalty then you won't have to pay it before the appeal has been decided. If you are appealing against a tax assessment then you will have to stump up before the decision although you can make a hardship application for more time to HMRC and, if that does not lead to a compromise, appeal to the tribunal on that issue.

Most tribunal appeals will revolve around whether you had a reasonable excuse for any default or HMRC has followed the statutory procedures, or possibly both. HMRC has proclaimed that it will consider the coronavirus as a reasonable excuse for missing some tax obligations such as dates for payment and filing returns but there could well be a dispute as to whether there was, in fact, a link between the pandemic and the default. It is sometimes said that HMRC takes a narrower view of what constitutes a reasonable excuse than does the tribunal. The reality is that HMRC misleads on the law on reasonable excuse and has been habitually criticised by the tribunal for doing so. You will shortly see my selection of tribunal decisions on reasonable excuse as well as other appeal grounds so as to give you a flavour of the tribunal's approach on appeals. In all but one of the cases, HMRC lost! That certainly does not mean that it loses in the vast majority of appeals but it does lose very often indeed.

An appeal is not the only challenge route but if you wish to follow the complaint route, ask HMRC to agree in writing to agree to extend your time for appealing to the tribunal until that route has been exhausted or put in an appeal and ask for its progress to be halted pending exhaustion of the complaint route.

Other challenge routes

***Review**. When you appeal, you can ask HMRC to review its decision or it may offer to do so. The review will be carried out by someone at HMRC who was not involved in the original decision. The review will usually take 45 days. Should you wish to carry on with the appeal after the review decision has been notified, you should tell this to the tribunal, usually within 30 days of the decision.

***Alternative dispute resolution (ADR)**. This version of ADR is a little quirky in that it starts with someone from HMRC called a facilitator, albeit that they have not been involved with the case previously, working with you and the HMRC officer who has dealt with the case, investigating whether there can be a resolution of the dispute. In really complex disputes, an outside mediator may be appointed instead of the internal facilitator. ADR would not affect your right to a review or an appeal but HMRC will not generally agree to ADR unless you have already put in an appeal.

***Complain to HMRC and Complain, Complain and Complain**. Kick off under HMRC's own complaints procedure which will initially involve the officer so far dealing with your case looking at the complaint, and if you are dissatisfied with their response, the complaint going to another officer who has not previously been involved. Still dissatisfied? You can complain to The Adjudicator's Office which also covers complaints against the Valuation Office Agency and reviews Home Office decisions on entitlement to compensation under the Windrush Compensation Scheme. You normally have six months from the second HMRC review in which to do this. The Adjudicator will look at whether policy and guidance were applied fairly and consistently; administrative errors including unreasonable delays, mistakes, poor service or misleading advice; how discretions have been exercised; and staff conduct which has led to poor service. Protests about the tax rate are outside its remit. In 2019/20 the Adjudicator substantially or partly upheld 358 out of 817 complaints against HMRC – nearly 44% – and if the myriad of complaints about private debt collectors instructed by HMRC going over the top during Covid-19 are to be believed, that rate can be expected to escalate. Compensation was recommended to be paid by HMRC to the successful complainants for worry and distress totalling £13,896; poor complaints handling totalling £26,365; and for costs totalling £22,593. Demands totalling £64,234 were scrapped.

Ombudsman. Still dissatisfied? You can ask the Parliamentary Ombudsman to deal with the complaint but this has to be done through your MP. The whole process should not take longer than 100 years. The route is probably best used where it's too late to appeal.

Reasonable excuse

A 'reasonable excuse' can get you off having to pay tax penalties not only for failing to get your tax return in on time but for failing to pay the tax you have been assessed to pay on time. It has to be objectively reasonable. That means not that just you thought it reasonable because you could be a biased and arrogant crackpot (although I know you are not as you bought this book or, at least, I hope you did). It means a reasonable person would have thought the excuse to be reasonable. Coming up are some excuses which the tribunal decided were reasonable and one excuse which was not ruled to be reasonable. Even ignorance of the law – not usually a good legal excuse – has been taken into account on consideration of what is reasonable. The upper tribunal of the tax and chancery tribunal has acknowledged that some requirements of the law are simple and straightforward but others are less so. It would be a matter of judgment for tax tribunals in each case, they said, as to whether it was objectively reasonable for a particular taxpayer to have been ignorant of the legal tax requirement in question and for how long. At the same time, it condemned HMRC for its habit of putting forward arguments that a reasonable excuse had to be based on some unforeseeable or inescapable event or on an unexpected or unusual event. That was not the law.

I have given details of case references so that you can look up further details, if you wish.

*In *Pearson v HMRC* [2017] UKFTT 780 (TC) a penalty of just over £91,000 was quashed. It related to late payment of a cool £1,833,000 capital gains tax that the chief executive officer taxpayer had been due to stump up on the sale of company shares. He paid but was around six months late in doing so. The tribunal ruled that what they had to decide was whether the payment was due to an insufficiency of funds and, if so, did that insufficiency arise out of reasons which were outside the taxpayer's control. If the answer was 'yes' to both questions, then the taxpayer had a reasonable excuse for their lateness. It was!

*In *Robert Morris v HMRC* [2017] UKFTT 749 (TC) the taxpayer had been caned for £2,900 in penalties in respect of two separate tax years. But he had completed the returns before the deadline although HMRC denied having received them. When he had dealt with his return online in a previous year, the HMRC website had generated a receipt and a long reference number. However, for these two later years no receipt and no reference number had appeared. Instead, said the taxpayer, he had each time received an on screen message on a very basic web page saying either "Thank you for your submission" or "Submission complete". He treated that as sufficient and thought he had done all that was required of him. HMRC could not say that what the taxpayer was alleging was impossible and put forward no evidence that it was technically impossible or something that was unlikely. The tribunal accepted the truthfulness of the taxpayer's account and decided that they had a reasonable excuse.

*In *Roderick Northam v HMRC* [2017] UKFFT 706 (TC) the taxpayer who was penalised for a late return had not been informed by his accountants that despite the fact he had completed his paper return before the deadline, they were not proposing to submit it to HMRC in time because they needed further information. The tribunal decided that the taxpayer had taken reasonable care to ensure that his return was on time and he had a reasonable excuse.

*In *Hindocha v HMRC* [2017] UKFTT 373 (TC), HMRC accepted that serious mental illness could be a reasonable excuse but went on to argue that where the illness was an ongoing condition, the taxpayer should make arrangements for sending in their tax return on time. The tribunal found that the taxpayer had suffered a serious mental illness which had been ongoing for four years in the form of depression, anxiety and panic attacks. It had affected the taxpayer in such a way that they had been unable to arrange for somebody else to get their returns in for them. They had found it impossible to organise their menial day to day activities, let alone their finances and taxes. Penalties totalling £1,500 for a late return were quashed.

*In *McDonald v HMRC* [2017] UKFTT 265 (TC) penalties totalling £1,300 for a late return were in issue (including some £10 per day jobs). The taxpayer had gone through a prolonged period of difficulty which had been traumatic for them. It had involved them running their own self-employed business, looking after their own home, looking after their ailing parents and their home, attending to their parents' personal needs and, for a time, driving their father to visit their mother in hospitals twice a day. They then suffered the deaths of both parents. After that, they had to deal with the parents' personal affairs, effects and financial affairs. They continued to work beyond retirement age and one reason for that was that they were conscious of the need to sort out their own tax affairs with help from their accountant. HMRC argued that anyone's serious illness could only be taken into account if it meant that the taxpayer was incapacitated from dealing with their own affairs for the whole period from the return deadline until when the return ultimately went in. The tribunal disagreed and decided there had been a reasonable excuse. [A victory for the taxpayer but the decision could easily have gone the other way before a different tribunal.]

*In *Redman v HMRC* appeal number TC/2017/07240 penalties of £97,821 were quashed which had stunned an evangelical Christian who earned his living as a singer/songwriter and musician and for a period of time had been non-resident in the UK. When his accountant came to file his late tax returns for two years subsequent to his return to the UK, the accountant found he was unable to do so because the taxpayer had been removed from his self-employment status. Trouble was that HMRC had failed to notify this fact to either the taxpayer or his accountant. HMRC asserted that the taxpayer had breached the law by deliberately not giving notice of his liability to be charged for tax in relation to those two years. The tribunal decided that the failure to notify had not been deliberate because neither the taxpayer nor the accountant had been told of removal from the self-employment system. It also decided that was reasonable excuse for non-notification. So, no default and no carelessness.

Raggatt v Commissioners for HMRC [2018] UKUT 412 (TCC) was a case which the taxman won but let's have a look at it so as to give a bit of balance to this and to highlight that, in the right case, the defence of 'reasonable excuse' can get you off having to pay tax penalties not only for failing to get your return in on time but for failing to pay on time the tax you have been assessed to pay. Leading barrister Timothy Raggatt QC was stung for late payment penalties relating to two tax years which totalled nearly £13,500. He appealed to the first tier tribunal of the tax chamber (as one does) and he lost. So he appealed again to the upper tribunal (as one does) and he lost again. He was represented by Timothy Raggatt QC (as one would be as it tends to keep legal fees down). Mr Raggatt's argument was that he had a 'reasonable excuse' for late payment. This, he said, was that events out of his control had prevented him from paying on time. He principally relied on the substantial reduction in his income from the cuts in the legal aid budget and his bank's refusal to increase his overdraft facility. Now, to succeed with a defence of 'reasonable excuse' in this sort of situation, you have to show that you exercised reasonable foresight and due diligence and a proper regard to the fact that the tax liabilities concerned would become due on particular dates. The Finance Act 2009 (go to paragraph 16 of the 56th schedule if you must and you can bear it) states that an insufficiency of funds is not a 'reasonable excuse' unless it is attributable to events outside the taxpayer's (or tax non-payer's!) control and that if you rely on any other person to do something, you must have taken reasonable care to avoid their failure to do so. Both tribunals had considerable sympathy for Mr Raggatt's predicament (a fat lot of use that was!) but, as it was put on this second appeal, he could have done more to have avoided that position.

What was made clear by the upper tribunal – and this may be of help to you – is that the principles relating to 'reasonable excuse' are the same in late payment penalty cases as they are in late return penalty cases. There was no legal requirement on the part of a self-employed professional person to reserve for their tax liabilities but a person with such an episodic life as Mr Raggatt would be well advised to take reasonable steps to make some provision for tax liabilities or to ensure that they had appropriate bank facilities to meet their expected tax liabilities if they subsequently wished to plead a 'reasonable excuse'. Taking such reasonable steps might not end up enabling a taxpayer to deal with unforeseen events but if it appeared they had done all that could be reasonably expected of someone in their position then the defence of 'reasonable excuse' might be a winner.

*In *Kevin Brazier v The Commissioners for Her Majesty's Revenue and Customs* [2020] UKFTT 185 (TC) the tribunal was concerned with child benefit. If you or your partner receive child benefit and your annual adjusted net income is over £50,000 then part of that child benefit will be taxable. If you reach £60,000 then the whole of the benefit will be taxable. That's been the score since 7 January 2013 and you have to disclose the benefit to the taxman and register for self-assessment, if not already registered, sending in a tax return. Here, the lorry driver taxpayer's partner had received child benefit for the tax years 2012/13 through to 2015/16. The taxpayer had not disclosed the benefit to the taxman because they claimed they did not know of the obligation to do so. In fact, some of the benefit would have been taxable. The taxpayer did not find out about the obligation until the taxman wrote to them in August 2018 telling them about the high income charge. They then made full disclosure and paid up everything required except for a penalty of £296. The tribunal quashed the penalty on the ground of reasonable excuse. There had been a number of cases where tribunals had decided that ignorance of the law could be a reasonable excuse. It would depend on the nature of the law in question and the characteristics of the taxpayer. HMRC argued that it was not obliged to inform taxpayers of a change in the law but, nevertheless, there had been a national campaign about this scheme. The tribunal concluded that the taxpayer was completely unaware of the new legislation and noted that there had been no targeted campaign to write to all tax payers earning over £50,000 when it had come in.

Returning returns, dodgy notices and no notices

*In *Pidgeon v HMRC* [2017] UKFTT 438 (TC) the taxpayer was appealing against penalties of £1,500 for a late return. They had submitted a return in November or December 2012 but HMRC maintained it was unsatisfactory and sent it back to them. Return of the Return. A second return was submitted in January 2014 which HMRC accepted was satisfactory. The penalties related to the period which elapsed between the two returns. HMRC cannot chuck back a return on a whim. To justify a chuck back for omissions, it must mean that in reality the document does not amount to a return at all. In my book, you could not seriously argue that if you simply signed and dated the return but put in no detail, you had done enough. Whether the document did or did not constitute a valid return was a matter of fact, ruled the tribunal. So what had been wrong with this taxpayer's return when put in the first time? It was for HMRC to say but it had failed to do so. What is more, it had failed to produce a copy to the tribunal. The mere fact that it had been originally rejected was not sufficient for the tribunal to conclude it had not been up to the job. Penalties quashed.

An unjustified chuck back was just one of a series of reasons that HMRC came a cropper in *Tabrez Akhtar trading as Crawley News and Post Office v HMRC* [2017] UKFTT 651 (TC). The taxpayer's partnership return was submitted by their accountant but not logged on by HMRC until ten days later. Then nearly three months later it was sent back. Why? Because HMRC claimed there had been an arithmetical error in the return in that expenses had been overstated by £4. The tax consequence of this alleged error would have been the grand sum of less than £1 per partner. The return was redelivered to HMRC by the accountant who disputed any arithmetical error.

HMRC imposed penalties for a late return of £560. They were quashed. HMRC had been wrong to have sat on the return for ten days; charged daily penalties on the basis that the return was not back in its hands until the accountant redelivered it when it was only out of its hands because it had chosen to send it back to the accountant; overlooked section 12ABB(1) of the Taxes Management Act 1970 which allows it to correct "obvious errors or omissions in the return, whether errors of principle, arithmetical mistakes or otherwise"; and given misleading information to the taxpayer about what it would take to get a penalty quashed on the ground of reasonable excuse.

*In *Anstock v HMRC* [2017] UKFTT 307 (TC) the taxpayer was told by HMRC that it was investigating him. After two meetings, HMRC claimed to have sent him a notice to produce information and documents. When there was no response, a £300 penalty was imposed. The taxpayer never acknowledged the notice or gave any indication that he was aware of it despite subsequently writing to HMRC. The penalty was quashed. HMRC had not proved that the notice had been sent and received. Often, receipt would be presumed where there was evidence of posting. But that could not be done here. Had HMRC proved posting, the penalty would still have been quashed because the notice had been so poorly drafted that, if received by the taxpayer, he would not have known precisely what was being required of him. The notice had also proceeded on the erroneous basis that the taxpayer could be expected to produce documents or information held by third parties including companies of which he was or had been a director. Those documents and that information were the property of the companies and nobody else.

*In *Lennon v HMRC* [2018] UKFTT 220 (TC) the taxpayer had been penalised for a late return. He was subject to PAYE but his employer had under-collected £321 for one tax year and HMRC decided it wanted a tax return from the taxpayer. It imposed a penalty for the late submission of that return. The penalty was quashed. There could not be a valid penalty unless there had previously been a valid notice from HMRC to the taxpayer to submit the return. A notice could be given for the purpose of establishing the tax which the taxpayer had to pay for a given year. In this case, the notice had not been given for that purpose as HMRC was fully aware of how much tax had to be paid. It was just the uncollected £321. Because the purpose of requiring the return was invalid, the notice requiring it was invalid and the penalty based on non-compliance was invalid.

*In *Zainub Takeawav v HMRC* [2017] UKFTT 337 (TC) the tax return had gone in three months late resulting in a £400 penalty. That penalty was quashed because HMRC had failed to establish that the notice of the penalty it had issued had specified the date from which it was payable.

*In *Pantelli v HMRC* [2019] 1 WLUK 42 the taxpayer had been clobbered for penalties for failing to submit tax returns for two years. The taxpayer claimed that he had not been sent the requisite notice for this to be done. The tribunal quashed the penalties. HMRC had to prove it was more probable than not that it had sent him the notice. Adequate evidence about this was a necessity and not a luxury. HMRC had failed to produce any evidence that the notice had been given for either year.

*In *Advantage Business Finance Ltd v HMRC* [2019] UKFTT 30 (TC) daily penalties of £900 were cancelled by the tribunal for a late annual tax on enveloped dwellings return (and you don't get many of those to the kilo). The law required HMRC to notify the taxpayer of the date from which the penalty was payable but it did not do so until after the end of the penalty period. Too late.

Understatement

In *Pandey v HMRC* [2017] UKFFT 0216 (TC) the tribunal judge began his judgment like this: "Well, here we go again." This was not the first time that a tribunal judgment over tax had started with these words. They were used by the judge in a 2015 case about tax credits after there had been a series of such cases marked by a catalogue of errors committed by HMRC. In this latest case, HMRC had messed up again. The tribunal quashed a penalty which had been imposed on a doctor who had omitted from their tax return some of her earnings which had been subject to PAYE deduction. But the omission did not amount to an understatement and that was the end to the matter. The taxpayer had been late in putting in her appeal and had to ask the tribunal for an extension to do so which had been granted. The judge pointed out that the tribunal's power to grant such an extension was wider than HMRC say on the subject in their letters and guidance to taxpayers.

Questions to the taxman

You wouldn't ask your bank manager (if you had one) which was the best bank to which to hand over all your money. So you might wonder why you would ask the tax man for an answer to a tax conundrum. Well, it might be useful to discover how HMRC sees things (it could be favourable to you) and it could save you accountants' fees. HMRC now has an online customer forum where you can post questions on a range of tax topics that are then answered by their experts. Anyone can view the forum. I wouldn't suggest anything like: "I have never disclosed my profit for driving a minicab on the side. Where do you suggest I hide the money?"

But "My ISA provider told me that if I took my interest monthly then I would be taxed on it. Isn't this nonsense?" would be okay. [Actually, I asked that very question and was able to understand the answer. It was to the effect that it was nonsense.]

You too can register to ask questions in the forum. Go to community.hmrc.gov.uk to do so. It's free.

Chapter 57

Knotweed

A knotty problem of the Japanese variety

Japanese knotweed is pernicious. It is more objectionable than a neighbour who insists on talking to you every time you are in their vision. In fact, your very next door neighbour could be responsible for it. The aforesaid knotweed is a bamboo-like perennial plant which grows quickly and strongly and spreads through its underground roots. It can affect drains, patios, paths, drives, boundary walls, retaining walls, outbuildings, conservatories and gardens. It can block drains, disrupt drain runs, grow between slabs of concrete drives, disrupt brick paving, undermine garden walls and overwhelm poorly built buildings and conservatories. Is that enough?

It is estimated that up to one in 20 properties is affected by this bloody – oh, do excuse me – weed. Yours could be that one. It can be treated with chemicals and that could cost around £2,500 or the roots can be dug up but, either way, it has the habit of coming back.

If the roots from an adjoining property have encroached into your land, the likelihood is that you can use the law to do something about it. In theory, the landowner responsible for the weed can be compelled to address the problem by a community protection notice served under section 43 of the Anti-Social Behaviour, Crime and Policing Act 2014 by the local authority or police, and the local authority planning department can serve a notice requiring remedial action under section 215 of the Town and Country Planning Act 1990. But they could well run a very fast mile if you asked them to do so or the knotweed roots could have sprung up in the middle of your living room, blocking your enjoyment of *Strictly*, before they got round to doing anything. It looks like you will have to get directly threatening with the landowner responsible and bring civil proceedings against them if they do not respond positively to your afternoon tea and currant bun plea and pre-action letter follow up.

It's down to you, neighbour

You will have to prove encroachment. If you can prove actual damage having already been caused to your property, then do so. But, to succeed in a claim, this may not be essential where the encroachment is serious enough. The Court of Appeal (the case is *Williams v Network Rail Investments Ltd and another* case in 2018) has recognised that Japanese knotweed is a natural hazard and affects the ability to fully use and enjoy the land. It imposes an increased difficulty in developing the land, if that was wanted. Additionally, you will have to prove that the responsible landowner, knowing of the encroachment and being able to foresee that there was a risk it would cause damage to your land at some stage, failed to act with reasonable prudence to remove the knotweed.

You can claim for the cost to you of eradicating the knotweed and repairing any damage and for compensation to reflect any reduction in the market value of your property because of the possibility of the knotweed's return in the future. As an alternative to getting the eradication work carried out yourself (thanks to your own pocket or an insurer's pocket) you could claim an injunction against the responsible landowner compelling them to fix the problem.

Particulars of Claim

(1) The claimant is and at all material times was the owner and occupier of land and the dwelling erected thereon known as 60 Lighthouse Lane, Langstone, Hants PO8 1RX ("the claimant's property") and the defendant is and at all material times was the owner and occupier of the adjoining land and the dwelling erected thereon known as 62 Lighthouse Lane, Langstone, Hants PO8 1RX ("the defendant's property").

(2) Since at least 2000 there has existed on the defendant's property a large stand of the pernicious weed commonly known as Japanese knotweed ("the knotweed") which has encroached onto the claimant's property along the approximate position indicated on the plan annexed to these particulars marked "A" (which the claimant says will encroach onto the claimant's property unless eradicated).

(3) The defendant has known of the existence of the knotweed on the defendant's property and has known that it has grown onto the claimant's property (or has known or should have known of the risk of it growing onto the claimant's property) since 2016 and at all material times has known of the risk that the knotweed would cause serious damage to the claimant's property unless eradicated. Notwithstanding this knowledge, the defendant has persistently refused or neglected to eradicate the knotweed.

(4) In view of the facts set out above, the knotweed is and at all material times has been a nuisance and has caused the claimant to suffer loss and damage, which continues.

Particulars of loss and damage

a. Loss of amenity and enjoyment of the claimant's property through increased difficulty and cost in developing the claimant's property and/or carrying out repairs and improvements to the claimant's property and/or the risk of future damage to the claimant's property by return of knotweed following action calculated to eradicate it.

b. Cost of eradicating knotweed on the claimant's property – £x

c. Cost of insurance backed guarantee relating to the works at b. – £x

AND the claimant claims:

a. An injunction requiring the defendant to eliminate the knotweed on the defendant's property;

b. Damages limited to £10,000.00;

c. Interest; and

d. Costs.

I believe that the facts stated in these particulars of claim are true. I understand that proceedings for contempt of court may be brought against anyone who makes, or causes to be made, a false statement in a document verified by a statement of truth without an honest belief in its truth.

(signed) Clive Troublesore

Claimant

Dated 14 July 2021

It's down to you, seller

Claiming against your neighbour will, of course, do away with them ever trying to talk to you again. This is a positive. But in the exceptional situation that you like them, you are related to them or you are terrified of their children or they wouldn't have the cash or an insurer to pay you out, you could turn your attention to whether you have a meritorious claim against your seller for fraudulent misrepresentation.

When you bought your property, the seller will have sent you an information pack providing you with all the documents and information that any reasonably interested person would want to know about the place. In the vast majority of cases, that pack will have included a property information form, originated by the Law Society, called the TA6. This form was last updated in February 2020 following criticism of it in relation to Japanese knotweed. The TA6 has a set of standard questions which the seller is meant to answer honestly. This is how the knotweed question now goes:

"Is the property affected by Japanese knotweed? If Yes, please state whether there is a Japanese knotweed management and treatment plan in place and supply a copy with any insurance cover linked to the plan."

A false response to the question could gift you a claim for damages against the seller and the damages might be more extensive than in a nuisance claim against the neighbour. But you would obviously have preferred not to have purchased in the first place. The seller may not be into fraudulent misrepresentation but may be into refraining from answering a question that has not been raised. You might do well to widen the TA6 enquiry along these lines:

"Is the property or any adjoining property affected by Japanese knotweed by the presence of plants or underground stems or in any other way whatsoever? If so, provide full details. If not, has the property or any adjoining property been so affected in the past? If so, provide full details.

Details provided as above should include what treatment or elimination works have been or are intended to be carried out and whether there is a Japanese knotweed management and treatment plan or ever has been and you should supply a copy of any such plan and a copy of any insurance cover linked to that plan."

It's down to you, solicitor or licensed conveyancer

Did your solicitor or licensed conveyancer ask the right questions about Japanese knotweed? Did they check the answers with reasonable care and skill? Did they bring to your attention before you contracted to buy any matters of concern about the knotweed? A NO to any of these questions might well mean that you have a claim against them for damages for professional negligence, as an alternative or addition to a claim against the neighbour and/or seller.

It's down to you, surveyor

Your surveyor should be on guard for evidence of Japanese knotweed. Was it there and would a reasonably competent surveyor have spotted it? If so, did they tell you about it? The higher the standard of survey requisitioned, the stronger your claim for professional negligence against your surveyor, even if they were instructed by your prospective mortgage lender. Certainly, mortgage lenders require surveyors to look out for the knotweed. So a possible claim then against the surveyor, as an alternative or addition to a claim against the neighbour and/or the seller and/or the solicitor or licensed conveyancer.

Chapter 58

Rights To Light

And there was insufficient light. And there was an injunction and damages

If you have a right to light coming through the window of your property, you may well have a passport to power and power can bring dosh. That right could prevent your neighbour adding an extension to the back of their property or raising the height of their boundary wall to stop you peering over the top of it. That right could prevent a developer sticking up a ten floor block of flats on land adjoining your property. On the other hand, you might be prepared to allow what the neighbour or developer want to do in return for an arrangement to compensate you for a reduction in the light to which you are entitled.

The most common way of acquiring a right to light is by having it entering the window for an uninterrupted period of 20 years. Those 20 years can include periods before you became the owner of the property. The right will not exist if it was excluded by the deed which was created when the property was built which often happens with residential property developments so check the deeds or with the Land Registry before booking a one-way ticket to Ambrosia.

An interference with your right to light would have to amount to a legal nuisance before you could call up the law to aid you and so be substantial. The question to be answered in order to establish whether there would be a nuisance is how much natural light would be left in the room if the extension, wall or block of flats went up and whether that would be enough for the comfortable use and enjoyment of the property according to, as judges are fond of putting it, "the ordinary requirements of mankind"? The locality may be relevant to the standard of light to be looked for. The use to which a room can reasonably be expected to be put in the future can be taken into account as well as its present use. If it currently functions as your in-house cinema but it is probable you will be utilising it at some time ahead to compose a brilliant oversized book on the law, then this can come into the reckoning.

There is no rule of law that if you would be left with 45 degrees of unobstructed natural light through a particular window, you have no case. More than 45 degrees of natural light may be sufficient to establish a nuisance. But there is a '50/50' rule which sometimes will impress the court – though it will be far from a slave to it – which is to regard a room as adequately lit if at least one-half of its area receives at least one lumen (a measure of brightness) of light at the level of an imaginary table which is 2 feet 9 inches high. Got it? A surveyor will get it and if a light dispute gets serious, you will need to bring in a surveyor specialising in these cases to give expert evidence for you.

Light interruptus

20 years needed, then, for your passport to power (and we aren't going to Ambrosia quite yet). But it has to be an uninterrupted period of at least 20 years. It is possible to interrupt the 20 years by registration with the local authority for the building of what is called a light obstruction certificate, under the Rights of Light Act 1959. Registration has the same legal effect as if a giant boulder has been planted in front of the window and reduced the light. It counts as a notional interruption but is less inconvenient and cumbersome than the boulder but only just. The Law Commission in 2014 recommended a simplified procedure to the registration but a few things seem to have got in the way of the government implementing the proposals like domestic violence, Brexit, and the pandemic. Not a boulder.

If you aspire to extending at the back, raising your wall or building that tall block of flats and at least 20 years have not yet been clocked up in favour of the nearby light lover, you will want to be thinking about whether those 20 years should be interrupted. Once the certificate has been registered, light lover has to restart counting 20 years from the end of its one year life with the threat that history is to be repeated and 19 years or so later a fresh certificate is registered.

How to procure a light obstruction certificate registration

Application for a certificate is made to the Upper Tribunal (Lands Chamber) in London's Fetter Lane (telephone 020 7612 9710). The fee is £1,320. A temporary certificate can be issued where there is some exceptional urgency and it may not have been possible for anyone – like the light lover – or everyone to have been told about the application. There's an extra £330 fee to pay for the temporary certificate. The Upper Tribunal aims to issue a temporary certificate within three days of getting the application. An application for the full certificate, they say, is "normally given a high priority". So long as the procedure has been followed and the paperwork makes sense, the certificate or certificates will be issued. It's a 'rubber stamping' job. If light lover wished to challenge the temporary or full certificate, they will have to bring proceedings, not in the Upper Tribunal but the High Court or county court. Armed with the certificate, application is then made to the local authority to register the certificate. It is registration, remember, that acts as the interruption and not the issue of the certificate. The Land Registry acts as the registering authority for some local authorities. You can check online whether or not it covers your authority. If it does, the certificate is registered with them and otherwise with the local authority itself and at a fee of £18.

Back to you light lovers

I do apologise. I had to tell the enemy how to outwit you though, in fact, I may have done you a favour. Notification of the application for a light obstruction certificate may have alerted you to what you did not know, namely that development plans were afoot. And, notwithstanding the certificate, you may be able to assert that the 20 years had been clocked up before the certificate was issued, let alone registered. No certificate can rob you of a right of light already acquired. You have one year from registration to challenge it by court proceedings in which you would be asking the court to declare you had a right to light and to order cancellation of the registration.

Remedies for a threatened infringement of your right to light

If you have a right to light and what is proposed would amount to a nuisance, the first word to come into your head should be 'injunction'.

> *Dear Sir or Madam*
>
> *I am the freehold owner of 65 Handover Gardens, Peardrop. It has come to my notice that you are intending to develop land at the rear of my property by the erection of a block of flats. I have enjoyed the entry of natural light into the windows at the rear of my property since its erection and my occupation of it in 1980 and have accordingly acquired a prescriptive right to that light. I regret that I have been expertly advised that your intended development would substantially reduce the quantity of light entering those windows to the degree that constituted a legal nuisance. In those circumstances, I must require you to supply me with your written undertaking within 14 days of the date of this letter that you will not take or cause or permit to be taken any steps to proceed with the intended development as planned or in any other way which would infringe my right to light, without my prior written consent or order of the court.*
>
> *In the event that I do not receive your undertaking as above within the time limited, I shall have no alternative but to institute proceedings against you for an emergency undertaking, declaration and costs.*
>
> *Subject to your compliance with my requirement, I would be happy to meet with you to investigate whether there is scope for the land in question being developed in some way which would not infringe my right to light.*
>
> *Yours faithfully*
>
> *Clive Troublesore*

In 2008 a company redeveloped a five-storey building in Leeds by refurbishing the first to fourth floors, reconstructing and extending the fifth floor and constructing new sixth and seventh floors. The man who owned a listed building opposite with windows facing the development was entitled to a right to light through those windows. From the outset, he had sought to engage the developer in negotiations with him to reduce the scheme but no resolution was reached. The developer, with all the works already completed, commenced High Court proceedings for a declaration that the man had lost his right to any remedy by failing to apply for an injunction to stop the development going ahead. The man sought his own injunction. In July

2010, the judge decided that the accepted interference with the right to light was so significant that damages were not an appropriate remedy and that an injunction should be granted. An injunction for what? To compel the developer to remove one-third of the upper two floors of the developed building! That the top floor had already been rented out as offices to a firm of accountants made no difference. The developer had proceeded in full knowledge of the man's complaint. A decision to be mentioned to any developer who chooses or threatens to push on regardless.

The developer lodged an appeal against the injunction to the Court of Appeal. The appeal was never heard as the parties reached an agreement.

Chapter 59
Ragbag

Here's a selection of some off-beat and intriguing legal rights and some draft particulars of claim (see chapter 12) to go with some of them. The particulars would need to be adapted to the facts of any actual case. And each set of particulars of claim should be ended with a dated and signed statement of truth which says: "I believe that the facts stated in these particulars of claim are true. I understand that proceedings for contempt of court may be brought against anyone who makes, or causes to be made, a false statement in a document verified by a statement of truth without an honest belief in its truth".

Taxi traumas

Some of my best friends are taxi and private hire drivers and I would like to think there will be no impediment to using their services in the future. Yes, some of them do have those wretched highly fragranced packs hanging from the interior rear view mirror to combat passenger armpit aroma and worse and which make me want to vomit but a polite request for them to being taken down has never been refused though the aroma lingers on. And some of them take a liberty.

You fool, Gold. I didn't look at the meter properly before getting out of the taxi in 2017. My excuse is that I was in a hurry and also busy helping to usher out two other passengers from the back of the taxi including a four year old child. But that's no excuse, Gold and there will be serious trouble if this happens again.

So thinking that the meter indicated an amount less than £8 – the return journey was £5.50 but faster – I stupidly said to the driver "How much?" "£10," he replied but there was something about that look on his face that made me think he was taking me for a mug. I gave him a £10 note but no tip because I didn't trust him.

The taxi was ordered through the *mytaxi* (now *Freenow*) app. The fare receipt was emailed to me promptly after the driver had departed. It was for £8. I complained to *mytaxi* which dealt with the matter promptly and efficiently.

> Oct 13, 2017 | 09:33AM UTC
>
> *Rene replied:*
>
> *Hi Stephen,*
>
> *Thanks for getting in touch with mytaxi.*
>
> *I am sorry to hear that you have been overcharged. This is not the usual mytaxi standard and the driver in question has been cautioned.*
>
> *I have now processed a refund and the money should be available in*

> your account in the next 5-7 working days depending on your bank.
>
> I hope that this bad experience did not put you off using mytaxi.
>
> Enjoy the rest of your day,
>
> Kind regards,
>
> Rene

In fact, I was given £5 credit and hope the same driver doesn't turn up next time. Or maybe I'll take a bus.

And there was this guy who didn't know the location I needed on a pre-booked job in north London the other year and kept going round the same one-way system, to my intense frustration and despair. This led to me walking into a judicial training course late and being dreadfully embarrassed. Again, I could not bring myself to tip him.

Anyway, the drivers I've had in the front of my taxis and private hire cars of late assure me that if they or their employer are in breach of contract, it's fine with them for a claim to be made and there's no question of a black listing or any hard feelings so here goes.

Been waiting and waiting

> ### Particulars of Claim
>
> 1. On 13 July 2021 the claimant agreed to engage the defendant to convey him from his home at 149 Magnolia Crescent, Twickenham (the pick up) to Gatwick Airport to fly to Spain and to collect him at 12 noon on 14 July 2021. The claimant informed the defendant that it was essential that he was collected no later than 12 noon or he would miss his flight and suffer loss. It was implied by these circumstances that time was of the essence of the contract. Despite 12 hastening telephone calls by the claimant to the defendant its collection vehicle did not arrive at the pick up until 12.50 pm on 14 July 2021 in consequence of which the claimant did miss his flight.
>
> 2. As a result of the defendant's breach of contract, the claimant suffered the loss of having to pay for an outward ticket with another airline to fly on the same date in the sum of £167 which he claims from the defendant.
>
> AND the claimant claims:
>
> a. £167.00
>
> b. Interest under s 69 of the County Courts Act 1984 at 8% from 14 July 2021 to date of claim of (insert amount) and thereafter at the daily rate of 3p; and
>
> c. Costs.

Eliminating your opposing lawyer

Is this the impossible dream? Not completely impossible but it will only happen extremely rarely and more difficult than getting rid of the judge (see chapter 24). You would have to apply to the court for the solicitor or barrister on the other side to be ordered to cease to act for your opponent in the proceedings. You could do it in any kind of proceedings, be they civil, family or criminal. What would not get them thrown off the case? That you didn't like them, they had sent you threatening correspondence, they had acted for your opponent in previous proceedings against you and won, they had told you that their client would win and they would do all in their power to squeeze every penny you owe or that they are too ferocious in cross-examination and you are frightened of them. What would get them thrown off is if you could show that, because of some situation, a fair-minded and informed observer would have a reasonable apprehension of unfairness if they continued to act in the case: not necessarily actual unfairness but a reasonable apprehension of it. Words, words! I agree but let's look at some examples. Before I do, may I have your permission to make a small point? If you succeed in dislodging them, they will be replaced, perhaps by someone you will regard as more odious or alternatively, I have to accept, perhaps by someone who is an incompetent and whose cross-examination is equivalent to an undernourished sheep maul. Another point: if you apply for a lawyer to be booted out and there has to be a hearing to decide on the application because it is contested, you are more likely than not to have the other side's costs bill for the application hearing to pay should you fail.

Those examples, then, of when the opposing lawyer could be ordered to leave the case. There is a connection between the barrister for one party and a witness on the other side who will have to be cross-examined on factual matters which are in dispute but where the witness is an expert and would be cross-examined only on technical matters, this might not be a concern: it would depend on the nature of the connection. Where the lawyer objected to has previously acted for you, is now acting against you and has relevant confidential information as a result of acting for you which would amount to a breach of confidence if disclosed to your current opponent. But not if they could show there was no risk of this information being disclosed. And in one decided criminal case, a trainee barrister met the accused and discussed his case with him and then subsequently appeared behind the prosecuting barrister at the accused's trial. The Court of Appeal there assumed that no information which the trainee had obtained from the accused was divulged to the prosecution. Nevertheless, it ruled that it was impossible to say in the circumstances that justice had been seen to be done and the accused's conviction was quashed. Incidentally, in another criminal case, the Court of Appeal considered that it was undesirable for a husband or wife or other cohabiting partners to appear as advocates against each other in a contested trial because to do so might give rise to an apprehension that the proper conduct of the case may have in some way been affected by the relationship.

In the most recent case in this area which was decided by the High Court in October 2020, the barrister for the father in proceedings under the Children

Act 1989 was precluded from further acting for her client at the behest of the mother. The mother had previously made a complaint against the barrister to her professional body (it did not pursue any disciplinary proceedings) and had sought to denigrate the barrister to her chambers. This had naturally upset the barrister but her response, rather than being a mere rebuttal, had "become a highly personalised response which would reasonably be regarded as inconsistent with the retention of the requisite objective independence." What would have made the barrister's continued involvement in the case so difficult was in her cross-examination of the mother. Being inextricably bound up in the case, she might have been putting not only her client's case in cross-examination but also her own.

The court will be alert to whether your attempt at booting out the opposing lawyer, whether or not you have made a complaint about their conduct to their professional body, is purely a tactical manoeuvre. And if objection to the lawyer is to be taken, this should be at the start of the main hearing or, if there is an interim hearing, it should be taken there. No interim hearing and the situation you are concerned about is already known to you? Issue a written application (Form N244) and a hearing will be fixed.

"The applicant applies for an order that Archibald Ponsonby-Smythe being counsel (or the solicitor) currently acting for the claimant shall cease to act for the claimant in these proceedings."

Mellor moments

Particulars of Claim

1.   On 14 July 2016 the claimant engaged the defendant to convey him by metered taxi from his home at 149 Magnolia Crescent, Twickenham to Eton Avenue, London NW3. It was an implied condition of the engagement that the defendant would follow a route which would render the duration of the journey as short as reasonably possible taking into account road and traffic conditions of which the defendant was or should have been aware. Further and in the alternative, it was an implied condition of the engagement that the defendant would take whichever route which the claimant reasonably required him to take.

2.   In breach of the above conditions the defendant, having collected the claimant at 2pm, took a route which was not a short as reasonably possible and was circuitous despite the claimant's protests and refused to take the route which the claimant asked of him thereby trebling the duration of the journey from 30 to 90 minutes.

3.   The claimant was charged a fare which was £30 in excess of what he would have been charged had the above breaches not occurred and which he paid to the defendant under protest. The claimant claims its return.

AND the claimant claims:

a. £30.00; and

b. Costs.

No show

You have advertised for a chief executive, nanny, residential rat catcher or secretary, sifted through 789 applications, interviewed six people on the shortlist and finally hired Mrs Troublesore. She was due to start yesterday. She didn't turn up. Mr Troublesore phoned two hours after you were expecting her, to say she had changed her mind and decided she preferred to stay at home and look after him instead. That is a breach of contract and Mrs Troublesore is liable to you in damages for your losses. She might have found it cheaper to start the job and given notice on the first day. The length of notice would be dictated by the employment contract.

Particulars of Claim

1. On 1 June 2020 the claimant agreed with the defendant to employ her as a nanny to commence work on 1 July 2020 at a wage of £450 pw. In breach of the agreement, the defendant failed to so commence and notified the claimant through her husband on 1 July 2020 that she had decided not to work for him.

2. The claimant has suffered these losses as a result:

- cost of re-advertising: £35;
- difference between defendant's agreed wage and agency wage paid for temporary nanny until new employee started: £1,250;
- net loss of income for time spent re-interviewing: £25.

AND the claimant claims:

a. £1,310;

b. Interest under s 69 of the County Courts Act 1984 at 8% from 23 July 2020 to date of claim of £17.22 and thereafter at the daily rate of 28p;

c. Costs.

In a 2019 employment tribunal case, there had been no breach of contract by the solicitor who left the Gravesend law firm which had engaged her, within her first year. She had given notice to her employer which she was entitled to do. Unfortunately for her, though, she had agreed when being taken on that, if she did give notice within her first year, she would refund to her employer the £5,100 fee they had paid to the recruitment agency which had introduced her to them. Her employer withheld £1,578 from her final salary payment towards the £5,100 and she claimed to the tribunal that this had been an unlawful deduction. The tribunal backed the employer. The fee was not so great as to amount to an irrecoverable penalty but the question of a penalty did not arise because penalties were concerned with breaches of contract and here there had been no breach.

Where an employer has been gazumped by an applicant accepting an offer of employment and then securing a better package elsewhere and taken it, this would amount to a contract breach by the applicant. Graduates are adept at the practice. The applicant would be vulnerable to a claim for damages by the disappointed – "what do you think that b.....d has gone and done etc" – employer.

Sue achooer and coronavirus claims

Pre-pandemic, I rhetorically asked in the first edition of this book, why it was that every person we chose to sit next to or pass by always had a stinking cold and why they never carried a handkerchief and, if they did, why they never used it but instead sneezed with the velocity of a tornado directly into our faces and then turned to speak to their companion who had escaped the onslaught as we protested at their disgusting behaviour and why we never failed to be struck down by their harmful virus a day or so later? Until unprotected public sneezing was criminalised, I wanted to see some successful claims for damages which might help to reduce the practice, at the same time as compensating the hapless sneeze (or cough – same principles) victim. But I emphasized the enormous difficulties in the way of the sneezee. They mainly emanated from the necessity for success to be able to prove that the infection was the result of the technical assault on your or negligence of the sneezer. No sneeze claim, successful or unsuccessful, has been reported to me to date so take a black mark, class, for insufficient attention to litigation. Alas, what has overtaken concern about the effects of public sneezing has been the global plague that is coronavirus. When the masks come off, the selfish sneezing could return. However, what can now be expected is an avalanche of coronavirus connected claims and some firms of solicitors and claims management companies are already dropping the idea of such claims into their online advertising.

A successful coronavirus claim against anyone – be they shopper, neighbour, courier, schoolteacher or whoever – would be no easier than a sneezing claim. In fact, probably impossible because of an inability to establish when you were infected, let alone who, among the multitude of people with whom you were in contact over the likely window of infection, was responsible for your misfortune. However, what we are likely to see is claims by residents and employees against certain care homes and employers for failing to take adequate health and safety measures to prevent the spread of the virus within their establishments, fortified by evidence of a failure to adhere to emergency coronavirus legislation and government guidance. Even in these areas, the main battleground will be over the issue of causation: whether it is more probable than not that the acts or omissions of the other party led to the infection. The greater the number of persons infected in the same location at about the same time, the more likely it is that the link can be established. The claims could be brought by the person infected or, where they have sadly died, on behalf of their estate or by dependants of their estate. Insurers are braced.

And what of a claim against the NHS? In a recent High Court case, the judge pointed out that, in the clinical context, a balance had to be struck between the needs of a patient and other competing professional demands placed upon the clinician involved. Sometimes the needs of the patient had to be deprioritised to allow the clinicians to attend to other demands on their time. If courts were not strongly influenced in any coronavirus negligence claim brought against hospitals or clinicians and staff by the inhumane pressures they have been under during the pandemic, I would this time be eating all my hats and my medicine cupboard as well, contents and the wood. Having said that, the pressures cannot have excused blatant recklessness. Some degree of reasonable care reflecting the pressures will have been expected but claims will not be easy.

By all means, start off a coronavirus claim on your own if that is really what you want to do and see what response you receive to your claim letter. However, in view of the fact that you are unlikely to be in small claims territory here, I would strongly urge you to bring in lawyer help if court proceedings are to follow because proving the claim could be hard. Expert evidence from at least an epidemiologist will probably be vital to success. I can think of no good reason for going to a claims management company.

As meritorious as your case may be, it will not get off the ground unless you can identify the sneezer or other infector. Claiming against "the bloke in the green jumper by the cauliflowers in Sainsbury's, Chobham at 1pm on 14 July 2021" is a no-goer. Please don't attempt a private arrest. The chances of persuading a police constable who happens to be standing close by at the red peppers to investigate an assault and battery by sneezing or other infection is remote though you can always try. Your best bet is to ask your prospective defendant for their name and address as you snap them on your mobile before they land you on the ground with blood pouring from your nose at which point the police constable by the red peppers would be more interested. Your even better best bet is to find a staff member who knows them as a regular and can tell you who they are. Out in the street a direct approach is likely to be the only course open to you. Either way, the less confrontational the better. Under no circumstances should you ape the Carlisle man who in October 2015 was given a six month sentence of imprisonment for assaults and public order offences. He had taken exception to five women, mainly elderly, who had sneezed or taken out their handkerchiefs in public.

Drone attack with a touch of Res Ipsa Loquitur

It won't be as big as PPI but litigation over damage to property (or humans) by the operation of drones is an inevitability as the wretched machines proliferate. Operators would be crazy not to see that they are sufficiently covered by insurance for liability to others. Where do you stand as the victim of a drone that has gone out of control and damaged or ruined your property? With luck, your buildings or household insurance policy will see you alright but if you are uninsured, loss or damage by drone is excluded from the insurance risks covered or you just don't want to take advantage of your policy, you can make a civil claim against the drone operator alleging trespass to property. In principle, the same as if I grew a creeper up your wall, dumped rubbish in your front garden or erected a tent in your back garden and planted myself inside it – though more harmful. It would be open to the drone operator to seek to justify the trespass by showing that the loss you claim for was unintentional and without negligence.

You can add on a negligence claim or make one instead of a trespass claim. The probability is that you haven't a clue what went wrong in which event proving the drone operator's negligence could be problematic. There is a special legal approach designed for this situation which shifts the burden from you in having to prove the operator's negligence to the operator in having to prove that they were not negligent. It applies where the facts speak for themselves which lawyers who like to show they know three words of Latin spout off in court and court documents as *Res Ipsa Loquitur* (meaning "the thing speaks for itself"). It's a phrase you can use when in a Roman coffee shop you are asked whether you want to order an espresso or a glass of water. The approach has been successfully applied in court cases where a customs officer was walking in front of a dock warehouse and six bags of sugar which were in the process of being lowered landed on him; where a theatre ceiling fell on the head of a member of the audience; and where a vehicle ploughed into a car which was parked unattended at the roadside. What is needed to pass the buck to the defendant is an unexplained occurrence which in the ordinary course of events would not have happened without the negligence of someone other than them and the circumstances pointing to your defendant rather than anyone else being to blame. Then you can rightly say – altogether now – *Res Ipsa Loquitur* but in Latin and not italics. A very useful rule.

PARTICULARS OF CLAIM

1. At all material times the claimant occupied 149 Magnolia Crescent, Twickenham, Middlesex KT89 4XZ which included a rear garden ("the House") and the defendant was the operator and had control of an unmanned aircraft system ("the drone").

2. On 14 July 2021 at approximately 2.30pm the drone entered the rear garden of the House and struck the claimant's gazebo ("the incident").

3. The incident constituted a trespass to the House and the gazebo. Further and in the alternative, the incident occurred on account of the negligence of the defendant as to which the claimant says Res Ipsa Loquitur.

4. As a result of the incident the claimant suffered loss and damage.

Particulars of loss and damage

a. Cost of repairs to gazebo £x

b. Out of pocket expenses £y

5. The claimant claims interest on damages under section 69 of the

> *County Courts Act 1984 at such rates and for such periods as the court shall determine to be just.*
>
> *AND the claimant claims:*
>
> *a.   Damages not exceeding £5,000;*
>
> *b.   Interest; and*
>
> *c.   Costs.*

Service charges: still waiting

Restaurant misuse of tips, gratuities and service charges collected from customers who wish to reward waiters and staff for what they have received or are embarrassed not to reward them for what they have not received is a national scandal. The government was once ready to introduce a bill to outlaw this conduct. Although it appeared to have been lost without trace, I was assured by a government spokesman in May 2021 that the subject will be addressed in an Employment Bill which will be brought forward "in due course". If there is a third edition of this book, we will see then how things have panned out. Any legislation cannot be expected to be retrospective. As things currently stand, if a staff contract covers who the money is to belong to then the contract will prevail even if it is morally objectionable except that the employer cannot lawfully use tips and so on to top up an employee's minimum wage. But if the employer does not follow the contractual agreement or if there was no contract or no agreement in the contract covering tips then you the employee may be able to claim the money which has been wrongly withheld from you. In that situation you could claim back in the county court for six years. If your employer has covered up what has been going on, you might be able to claim back even longer (see chapter 13). You may have been one of the many to have lost your job in catering. That does not bar you from making a claim so long as your former employer is still in existence. Before starting proceedings, it would be wise to obtain some expert advice on how you stand in the light of the particular contractual documentation in your case.

The Department for Business Innovation & Skills issued a code of best practice on this topic in October 2009 which could be useful in proving industry custom and practice where you are relying on an implied agreement. The code requires that employees should be fully informed on the distribution and breakdown of tips, gratuities and service charges along with cover charges and the level and purpose of any deductions. Businesses should seek to reach agreement with employees on any change of policy.

A claim for wrongly withheld tips could be brought in an employment tribunal under Part II of the Employment Rights Act 1996 but here a much tighter time limit applies.

The particulars of claim in the county court might go like this.

PARTICULARS OF CLAIM

1. Between 1 July 2017 and 14 July 2021 the claimant was employed by the defendant as a waiter at its "Downa Throata Pizzeria" restaurant at 16 Uptown Road, Twickenham, Middlesex ("the restaurant").

2. The terms of the claimant's contract of employment were governed by a written agreement made on 30 June 2012 ("the agreement").

3. It was a condition of the agreement that all tips and gratuities tendered by and service charges added to bills issued to customers served by the claimant would belong to the claimant.

or

3. It was a condition of the agreement that all tips and gratuities tendered by and service charges added to bills issued to customers served during the period of the claimant's employment would be subject to a TRONC to which the claimant would belong whereby such sums would be paid into a fund administered by the manager of the restaurant who was the TRONC master and distributed among the staff of the restaurant who were in the employment of the defendant at the restaurant on the distribution date which would be each quarter (as from the 1st January in each year) in such proportions as the manager deemed fit. It was implied that the manager would make his distribution on reasonable grounds having regard to all relevant circumstances including in particular the seniority of each member of staff, the number of hours worked by each member of staff during the relevant quarter and the extent of the industry displayed by each such member during the relevant quarter.*

or

3. The agreement was silent on the ownership and application of tips and gratuities tendered by and service charges added to bills issued to customers served during the period of the claimant's employment. In the circumstances, it was an implied condition of the agreement that such gratuities which were paid directly to the claimant by the customer in cash would belong to the claimant and that such gratuities and service charges as were added to the bill would belong to and be paid by the defendant to the members of staff who were on duty for the shift in which the added gratuities and service charges were tendered in equal shares or in the alternative in the proportions which each such member's gross pay for the relevant shift bore to the aggregate of the gross pay of the members of staff who were on duty for such shift. Further and in the alternative, the gratuities and service charges collected by the defendant for each shift for which the claimant was on duty were held in trust by the defendant for the benefit of the claimant and the

other members of staff on duty for that shift in equal shares or in the alternative in the proportions which each member's gross pay for the relevant shift bore to the aggregate of the gross pay of the members who were on duty for such shift.

4. In breach of the condition (and/or trust*) specified above, the defendant has refused or neglected to account to the claimant for the tips, gratuities and service charges due to him throughout the period of his employment despite the claimant's habitual requests for it to do so.

or

4. the defendant has refused or neglected to account to the claimant for the full amount of tips, gratuities and service charges due to him throughout the period of his employment despite the claimant's habitual requests for it to do so and the only such payments made by the defendant have been as follows, namely [insert particulars of dates and amounts of the relevant payments].

or

4. no payments have been made to the claimant under the TRONC.**

or

4. the payments to the claimant under the TRONC which have been derisory and unreasonable in amount having been substantially less than the equal share contended for by the claimant as above and bearing no relation to the particular criteria alternatively contended for by the claimant as above. The payments have been substantially less than the sums paid to co-employees of the claimant on duty for the same shifts as the claimant and who have been of the same or less seniority as the claimant and have been no more industrious than the claimant during relevant shifts. The only such payments made by the manager have been as follows, namely [insert particulars of dates and amounts of the relevant payments].**

5. The claimant is unable to provide further and better particulars of the amount of his until disclosure of documents has taken place.**

6. The claimant claims interest on such sums as shall be awarded to him under section 69 of the County Courts Act 1984 at such rates and for such periods as the court shall determine to be just.

AND the claimant claims:

a. An account of all sums due to the claimant as set out above;

b. Judgment for such sums and/or damages limited to the sum of £x;

c. Interest; and

Costs.

*Delete if the existence of a trust and its breach is not alleged.

**The TRONC system is usually an arrangement under which employees decide who is to participate and how distributions are to be made and not the employer. Therefore, in order to succeed in a TRONC claim against the employer it would be necessary to prove that there was a contractual guarantee by the employer when you joined as an employee that you would be a TRONC beneficiary and if there was a guarantee about what share would be paid to you. so much the better: otherwise you would have to rely on an implied condition about how your share would be worked out. Proving an implied condition in a TRONC or non-TRONC case may be difficult where there is vagueness as to what was intended.

Where's my gold bar?

Booking in at hotel reception can be an ordeal. Your arrival will be far too early. "Housekeeping aren't finished yet but we will have your room ready by 4pm and please remember you must vacate by 10 in the morning." You won't be able to remember your car registration number or make up your mind on which newspaper you want the next day or whether you will be eating in or out. You will blush when the receptionist refers to your companion as your wife (or as the case may be). You will be perplexed by this notice on the reception wall:

> **NOTICE**
>
> **LOSS OR DAMAGE TO GUESTS' PROPERTY**
>
> *Under the Hotel Proprietors Act 1956, an hotel proprietor may in certain circumstances be liable to make good any loss or damage to a guest's property even though it was not due to any fault of the proprietor or staff of the hotel.*
>
> *This liability however-*
>
> *(a) Extends only to the property of guests who have engaged sleeping accommodation at the hotel;*
>
> *(b) Is limited to £50 for any one article and a total of £100 in the case of any one guest, except in the case of property which has been deposited, or offered for deposit, for safe custody;*
>
> *(c) Does not cover motor cars or other vehicles of any kind or any property left in them, or horses or other live animals.*
>
> *This notice does not constitute an admission either that the Act applies to this hotel or that liability thereunder attaches to the proprietor of this hotel in any particular case.*

Generally, you see, a hotel will be liable to compensate you for any of your property which is lost or damaged during your stay without you having to show that it was at fault. That's unless it was you who threw the gold bar out of the window to be caught by a thief or took an axe to your baggage. Tough on your Roller, horse or budgie which are excluded from this rule. But provided that a notice like the one above has been conspicuously displayed at or near reception or at or near the main entrance if no reception, the hotel's liability is limited. The limit is to compensate for up to £50 for any one item per guest and up to £100 in total. For Greater London hotels, these limits are higher: £750 instead of £50 and £1,500 instead of £100. Also, the limits to this strict liability do not apply to any item you have deposited with the hotel to hold for you or you asked them to hold but they refused. Should there be no notice displayed, it will probably because you are at a five-star joint and they have insured against the risk of a claim.

Back to that gold bar. It was gigantic and heavy and worth trillions more than £50 in Wigan or £750 in Kensington. The law caters for it. Where you can show that the hotel was to blame in that your property was stolen, lost or damaged through the default, neglect or deliberate act of the hotel or one of its workers, the hotel will have to compensate you in full: no limits. Which takes me to the stay of Victoria Adanda at what was then the Holiday Inn in London's Kings Cross.

Ms Adanda's jewellery and other items were stolen from the safe in her room. While she was at dinner, her room was burgled and the safe was ripped from its fixings in the wardrobe. The hotel asserted that it only had to pay her out £1,500 being the London limit under the 1956 Act. She sued the hotel and claimed in the case which was heard, on appeal, in the High Court in December 2018, that the limit did not apply because the hotel had been to blame. She had complained earlier that her door was not locking properly and been told by the hotel that the door needed to be firmly shut. It had been when she had gone off to dinner. However, an interrogation of the electronic door locking system showed that the lock was working. It transpired that in the previous month, four or five separate rooms at the hotel had been entered and property stolen, without any signs of forced entry and with an interrogation of the door locking system coming up with the same result. The High Court ruled that, having identified that the electronic lock could be breached, it had been incumbent on the hotel to have done something about it. If they had been unable to identify the cause of the breach and resolve the problem, they ought to have changed the locks or taken some other measures to secure their rooms. At the very least, they ought to have warned guests about the known breaches. The hotel was to blame and had to reimburse Ms Adanda in full.

Case no 21P0000678

IN THE COUNTY COURT MONEY CLAIMS CENTRE

BETWEEN

CLIVE TROUBLESORE Claimant

- and -

FELONIA PROMENADE HOTEL LIMITED Defendant

PARTICULARS OF CLAIM

1. At all material times, the defendant was the proprietor of an inn ('the hotel') known as the Felonia Promenade Hotel from which it carried on business at The Promenade, Bognor Regis, West Sussex and the claimant was a traveller for whom sleeping accommodation had been engaged as a guest in room 3B ("the room") at the hotel.

2. On 14 July 2021 upon his arrival at the hotel the claimant had with him a gold bar ("the bar") among his luggage which with other belongings he was permitted to take to the room whereupon the claimant placed the bar in the room safe ("the safe") which he locked.

3. On 15 July 2021 at approximately 3.30pm while the claimant was out of the room, the safe was wrongfully forced open and the bar removed by a person or persons whom the claimant is unable to identify. The bar has not been recovered.

4. The defendant had failed to keep the room and the bar safe and secure.

5. As a result of the facts set out above, the claimant has suffered loss and damage.

PARTICULARS OF LOSS AND DAMAGE

Value of the bar – £25,000.00

6. The claimant claims interest on damages under section 69 of the County Courts Act 1984 at such rates and for such periods as the court shall determine to be just.

AND the claimant claims:

a. Damages not exceeding £25,000.00;

b. Interest as above; and

c. Costs

Give me my ball back

You take your car or boots in for repair and the repairer can hold on to them until their bill has been paid. In fact, they would be mad to let them go. Of course, you knew that and have uttered a few words about it in your time. After all, they may have made a hash of things and once you have paid, your power to argue about the standard of work has diminished. The repairer's right is to retain possession of your repaired property but not to hide it so there is no reason why you should be deprived of an opportunity to inspect and check that everything seems okay. Obviously, the car repairer is not going to fall for your plea to just be allowed to drive round the block to satisfy yourself that the engine has stopped banging. If you are reasonably convinced that the job has been done badly, you should tender to the repairer what, if anything, you reckon they are entitled to and, if nothing, tender nothing. Then you would be entitled to start a county court claim for damages and an injunction to compel the repairer to release your property. You could ask for an urgent interim hearing where justified. If that didn't persuade the repairer to concede release, the court might well order the release of your property on condition that you paid into court the amount in dispute or a proportion of it. That money would be held until the rights and wrongs of the dispute had been determined. All a bit of a fag. Especially for a pair of lace-ups and so the alternative is to pay – and make it clear you are doing so 'under protest' so write those words or have them written on the invoice – and then make a subsequent claim for damages.

It is not uncommon for the shadier repairer to attempt to force your money out of your pocket by invoicing you at some exorbitant rate for the cost of storage of your property, or threatening to do so. That is unlawful unless you agreed to pay for storage when you instructed them, which is probably unlikely. If it transpired that they were in the right, had done the job to a reasonable standard and should have been paid, they could claim compensation against you for storage, without a prior agreement, but that compensation would be limited to their actual financial loss. If they had plenty of space and did not lose a contract to house the Lord Mayor's limousine on their premises where your old banger was sitting at the rate of £1,500.00 per day plus VAT, the loss could be negligible or nought.

Where does the ball come into it? I thought you would never ask. It's all about distress damage feasant. Do what? In 2017 the police visited a 73 year old lady from Bridlington, East Yorkshire on what must have been a slack day. They were investigating her retention of a number of footballs which had been kicked over her fence by local children and damaged her garden plants. She was told she might face a charge of theft. Nonsense. If a ball or some other item turns up uninvited on your land and damages your property, you are legally entitled to hold on to it until whoever was responsible has paid you compensation for the damage, even if you have to accept it by way of a lifetime's supply of lollipops. That is the right called – altogether now – distress damage feasant, which is a bit like a lien. The woman was doing what she was entitled to do. Do remember, though, that to exercise the right there must have been actual damage to your property. The same principle can apply to animals but special rules come into play so if it was a tiger or elephant that paid you a visit and ripped out your daffodils, reserve a copy of this book's third edition and I'll cover your rights then.

Case no 21P0000678

IN THE COUNTY COURT
AT TOYTOWN

CLIVE TROUBLESORE Claimant

- and -

BERTRAM TRYON trading as DODGY BUT FAST REPAIRS
Defendant

PARTICULARS OF CLAIM

1. The claimant is and at all material times was the owner of a Triumph Spitfire motor car registered mark CT1 77 ("the car").

2. The defendant was at all material times a motor vehicle repairer.

3. On 22 July 2021 the claimant delivered the car to the defendant when it was expressly and orally agreed between the parties that the defendant would supply and install a new clutch and exhaust to the car for the price of £1,000.00, and that the work would be completed on 24 July 2021 ("the agreement"). It was implied that the parts fitted would be of satisfactory quality.

4. In breach of the agreement, the defendant installed a used clutch and a used exhaust and neither of which were in any event of a satisfactory quality in that the clutch stuck and the exhaust pipe had a hole in it and for which the claimant says he is under no legal obligation to make any payment to the defendant.

5. The defendant has unlawfully retained the car and refused to release the car to the claimant unless the claimant pays him the sum of £1,000.00 and storage charges of £250.00 per day from and including 24 July 2021 until the date of payment.

6. The claimant has suffered loss and damage.

PARTICULARS

a. Loss of use of the car from 24 July 20201 and continuing.

b. Cost of remedying the defendant's work to include the cost of supply and installation of a new clutch and new exhaust in so far as the cost of such supply and installation may exceed £1,000.00 and further particulars of which the claimant will supply upon inspection of the car by another repairer or other repairers.

AND the claimant claims:

a. An injunction to compel the defendant to deliver up the car to the claimant forthwith;

b. Damages not exceeding £1,500.00;

> c. Interest under section 69 of the County Courts Act 1984 at such rates and for such periods as the court shall determine to be just; and
>
> d. Costs

The particulars of claim are to go with the claim form. In addition and so as to attempt to obtain an urgent injunction to lead to the car being released, a general form of application for an injunction – form N16A it is called – will need to be completed. The terms of the injunction sought should be described in the N16A like this: "To compel the defendant to deliver up to the claimant the Triumph Spitfire motor car registered mark CT1 77." Everything should be completed in triplicate.

Clocked by the police

If a police officer is negligent in the course of preventing and investigating crime and causes you injury or loss as a result, they and their boss in the form of the chief constable may be legally liable to compensate you. But only may. The police could not be successfully sued for failing to protect you from being injured where you created the danger of injury yourself. Or from failing to respond to an emergency call in time to save you from being attacked. Or from failing to arrest a murderer before a potential future victim was killed. Actual court cases have decided this. But these are instances of the police omitting to do something rather than doing something positive and doing it negligently where a legal duty to take care can exist. And so it is that when in 2008 a relatively frail lady aged 76 was walking along a shopping street in the centre of Huddersfield and was knocked over and injured by a group of men who were struggling with one another, there was something she could do about getting compensation. That's because two of the men were sturdily built police officers and the third was a suspected drug dealer they were attempting to arrest. The police officers had been negligent in the way they went about the arrest and the lady had ended up under the group of the struggling three men. But the officer's chief constable argued that they had not owed the lady any legal duty of care. The Supreme Court ruled otherwise. What happened had been reasonably foreseeable and was a result of positive actions and not omissions by the police. The lady was injured because she had been exposed to the very danger from which the officers had been under a duty to protect her.

Subject to contract

We have already met 'without prejudice' (see chapter 10). Here are two equally magical words: 'subject to contract.' They can be used when negotiations are being conducted between parties to a proposed transaction or some dispute which may or may not be the subject of court proceedings. They most commonly crop up in the world of property buying and selling where deals will almost invariably be struck on the basis that either party can drop out without liability to the other up to the point at which contracts can be exchanged (but see chapter 49 for how you can cater for your expenses when the other party does the dirty on you). 'Subject to contract' means there is to be no legally binding contract until a formal written document is prepared, the wording on it is agreed, it is signed up and is intended to take legal effect. The formal document may be prepared in duplicate with each side signing one part, swapping the parts and dating them and, at the point of dating, the deal will have been done. Alternatively, both sides may sign the same document and date it with the intention that it will be legally binding the moment the date is put in.

Whereas the words 'without prejudice' plastered on a letter will generally prevent it being used in evidence in any civil court proceedings that follow, the words 'subject to contract' will make it clear that what is stated in the letter cannot commit the sender. And it cannot amount to an offer that the recipient can accept so as to create a binding contract: more would be needed for that in a formal document. In a case in the Court of Appeal in November 2020 called *Joanne Properties Ltd v Moneything Capital Ltd and another party*, solicitors on behalf of the parties exchanged a series of emails or letters while trying to settle the residue of outstanding issues in court proceedings which were already in existence. The crucial communications from both sides which demonstrated they were agreed on the outstanding matters were headed 'without prejudice and subject to contract'. Yes, both sets of magic words so a belt and braces approach and one I would commend to you when you are after Protection Plus. Anyway, despite that agreement, it was clear that the parties contemplated that a formal document setting out the agreement would be entered into and, as there were court proceedings, this would be an order of the court made with their consent: a consent order, we call it, which makes sense. But one side did not like the draft consent order drawn up by the other and so it was never completed. And because it was never completed there was no legally binding agreement and only the 'subject to contract' stuff which meant nothing. That was the decision of the Court of Appeal who ruled that in the context of negotiations to settle proceedings which were made 'subject to contract', the consent order was the equivalent of the formal contract. The mere fact that the parties are of one mind is not enough. There must be a formal contract or it must be clear that the parties intended to expunge the 'subject to contract' qualification. It was not so in this case.

Chapter 60
Privacy, Dignity And Confidentiality
Keep your nose out
Secret affairs

Before you take to stringing me up in a market square and bombarding me with rotten apples, let me make it plain where I stand. If you are married, in a civil partnership or in some other established relationship, I am not advocating or encouraging you to embark on a relationship with anyone else. Glad I've got that out of the way. But if you are or have been in a relationship with someone else or played away from home one afternoon or even later in the day, there could be a plethora of reasons why you would not want this to get out: to your spouse or partner, to your children, to a tabloid newspaper, to the other members of your parish council. You may well be able to prevent anyone who is threatening to spill the beans from doing so: similarly, if you have credible evidence that their plan is to do this. You can seek an injunction to stop them, which would typically be from the High Court. That would be on the ground that disclosure of what had happened would be an infringement of your right to privacy, with possibly an allegation of breach of confidence thrown in for good measure in the appropriate case.

Once upon a time, the law did not recognise a right to privacy. That was starkly exposed in the case brought by the late actor Gordon Kaye, way back in 1991. He was hospitalized, having suffered a severe brain injury and was not in a fit state to be interviewed by any journalist, let alone to give his valid agreement to be interviewed. But a journalist did barge into his hospital room, ignoring notices at the entrance to his ward and on his door asking visitors to see a member of staff before going in. And the journalist did interview him and took photographs of him. Many can probably still remember those images. Gordon Kaye was denied an injunction to stop publication of the interview and photographs because the law did not allow it.

And then came the much maligned Human Rights Act 1988 with the European Convention on Human Rights (they haven't disappeared under Brexit though they may be played around with in due course) which introduced a legal right to privacy – everyone has the right to respect for their private and family life, their home and their correspondence – but to be balanced against the publisher's right of freedom of expression. The balance battle has been fought out in a succession of court cases ever since. In a 2002 case a celebrity (I know, I know!) failed in his injunction attempt to prevent disclosure of the fact that he had visited a brothel and photographs of the visit. Not only had the rights to privacy and freedom of expression to be taken into account but also the rights of the prostitute who plainly took a different view from the celebrity (I know, I know!) as to whether, what she did and with whom she did it, was a private or confidential matter as far as she was concerned.

In a 2011 Court of Appeal case, disclosure of an affair in a newspaper was forbidden on the basis that weight had to be given not only to the right to privacy of the adulterous claimant, who worked in the entertainment industry (I know, I know!), but, again, of the other party concerned and – stand by for very big factor coming up which could well swing it in favour of a claimant in an otherwise borderline case – the claimant's wife and children. The wife had opposed publication, as had the other party, so that a reconciliation with the claimant might be facilitated.

The court pendulum swung even further towards the adulterer in 2016 in a case against a newspaper which went up to the Supreme Court and in which one Justice proclaimed that there was no general public interest in other people's sex lives (oh, no?!). Lord Mance stated:

> *"Every case must be considered on its particular facts. But the starting point is that (i) there is not, without more, any public interest in a legal sense in the disclosure or publication of purely sexual encounters, even though they involve adultery or more than one person at the same time, (ii) any such disclosure or publication will on the face of it constitute the...invasion of privacy..."*

And in November 2011 a Premier League footballer was granted a temporary injunction preventing his ex-girlfriend from publishing further information from their relationship. This came after she had posted screenshots on their private messages on *Instagram*.

For an injunction to do the trick, the person seeking it should not apply too much after-shave or perfume (as the case may be) before leaving home for their lawyers or court, or else their partner could become suspicious, and ensure that the court hearing is in private and that the case title is anonymised. The judge will usually oblige on these points but won't have any control over the after-shave or perfume.

"Lights, camera, breach of privacy, action!"

Most of us have gawked at television footage of criminal suspects being brought to their front windows at 3am by the noise of five squad cars outside, by erring motorists being pulled up in the hard shoulder (if there still is one) by a police patrol car and bailiffs going about their work. All by courtesy of the television cameras who were there to film for our edification. Sometimes, where obvious misfortune lies behind those to be subjected to televisual scrutiny, and its consequential public opprobrium or ridicule, sympathy might go out to certain subjects. High profile publicity of this kind may be more damaging than any court judgment. Of course, in the case of a crime suspected and later found to have been committed which was highly repellent, the publicity attracted may be regarded as an inevitable and expected outcome.

But broadcasters can go too far as did Channel 5 in an episode of its *Can't Pay? We'll Take It Away* series broadcast in 2015 and featuring the work of High Court enforcement agents (see chapters 29 and 30). One of their primary functions is to deal with evictions of tenants and mortgage borrowers who have been ordered out after a court hearing. An agent and a trainee turned up at the home of a husband and wife with an authority to evict them. They were accompanied by a camera crew for the programme which was made by an independent production company. The couple had been through county court possession proceedings but had remained in their home after the local housing authority had warned them that if they left before eviction, they would be treated as having made themselves intentionally homeless and so be deprived of the allocation of council accommodation. They had fallen behind with their rent: the husband had lost his job and injured his leg earlier that year. The eviction process had been transferred from the county court to the High Court and in those days an enforcement agent could turn up without prior notice to those facing eviction. The broadcast film showed the couple being evicted without prior warning; in a state of shock and stress; and being taunted by the son of the landlord who assisted with his father's affairs. It would have been seen by over 9 million viewers and 230,000 viewers online. The couple sued for damages for what they said was an intrusion into their private lives. The trial judge accepted that the programme had contributed to a debate of general interest but the inclusion of the couple's private information had gone beyond what had been justified for that purpose. The focus had not been on matters of public interest but upon the drama of the conflict between the landlord's son and the couple which had been encouraged by the enforcement agent to make what he had regarded as 'good television'. The invasion of privacy had not been justified by the public interest or by Channel 5's right of free expression. The Court of Appeal upheld this decision but rejected the couple's appeal against the award of £10,000 damages each which they had argued was too low.

Next time you encounter a film crew on the trail of an enforcement agent after you, or anyone else who has come to enforce a court order, on no account consent to a recorded performance – an argument raised by the broadcaster in the Channel 5 case that the couple had consented to a waiver of their privacy rights got nowhere. In fact, make it plain that you object to the filming, if that be so, and that you will claim damages if anything of the process of eviction, seizure of your goods or whatever is persisted with.

Sir Cliff Richard had no opportunity to do anything about the police search of his Sunningdale, Berkshire home in 2014 in connection with a vigorously denied allegation of a historical sex offence. The BBC had been tipped off that the search was to be conducted and gave it prominent and extensive coverage as it was happening while Sir Cliff was in Portugal and afterwards. He had been taken by surprise by the search for which the police had obtained a warrant. The police investigation was subsequently abandoned. Sir Richard sued the BBC for invasion of his privacy rights and in 2018 the High Court ruled that those rights had not been outweighed by the broadcaster's right to freedom of expression. The usual balancing exercise in these cases. Sir Richard was awarded general and aggravated damages totalling £210,000. Sir Cliff had also sued South Yorkshire Police on the same basis and they had agreed a £400,000 plus costs settlement with him. The High Court decided that the aggregate damages bill of the BBC and the police were to be shared as to 65% by the BBC and 35% by the police. Sir Cliff was totally vindicated in relation to both the criminal allegation and civil matters. One of the rare occasions on which the BBC had gone over the top.

Under police investigation but uncharged

Since Sir Cliff Richard's experiences, the Court of Appeal has controversially upheld the High Court's ruling that, in general, a person has a reasonable expectation of privacy in relation to a criminal investigation against them. The case involved an article on Bloomberg News's website. That expectation ran up to the point of any charge being made. If the person sued the broadcaster or article publisher for damages or an injunction or both on the ground of breach of their privacy right, the court would have to ask itself what a reasonable person of ordinary sensibilities would feel if placed in the same position as them and faced with the same publicity. And it would have to carry out the usual balancing test between the right of privacy and the right of freedom of expression. The anonymised claimant had been awarded £25,000 in damages and an injunction. In January 2021 the Supreme Court granted Bloomberg permission to appeal against the Court of Appeal's decision. There won't be a media outlet in the land which prays for the appeal to fail. We shall wait and we shall see.

Dignity in death

The right to privacy – to respect for private and family life – figured in an unusual way in a tragic case which reached the county court at Leeds in January 2021. A 25 year old wife and mother of two children met her untimely death from a brain injury. Her body was initially taken to the mortuary at Leeds General Infirmary where it was refrigerated. Just over six weeks later it was transferred to Bradford public mortuary where it remained, also in refrigeration, for just short of one year. Refrigeration of a body slows down the progress of decomposition but does not arrest it. What arrests it is freezing and that did not happen until the coroner directed it. By the time of freezing and for a period significantly earlier, the body had decomposed to the extent that it would have been very distressing indeed for the deceased's family to have seen the person in death. Six members of the deceased's immediate or extended family sued Bradford Metropolitan District Council and Leeds Teaching Hospitals NHS Trust claiming that, in failing to freeze, the defendants had failed to treat the body of their loved one with dignity and respect which had been incompatible with their own convention rights to a private and family life under the Convention we have already met. There had been cases in Europe in which it had been held that the ways in which the body of a deceased relative was treated as well as issues regarding the ability of them to attend the funeral and pay respects at the grave, came within the scope of the private and family life Convention right but the argument in the Leeds case was pretty novel for the UK. Bradford settled the case agreeing to pay the relatives £13,250 and costs but Leeds disputed it and argued that any breach of the right was justified. The judge ruled in favour of the relatives, declared that Leeds had acted unlawfully and awarded them a further £7,500 damages in the aggregate plus some expenses reimbursement.

Confidentially...keep your mouth sewn up

If you receive confidential information from someone else, then you may well be under an obligation to keep it confidential and could be prevented by the court from breaching the confidence. That's often the case between employer and employee. It was the case as between a local authority and one of its residents in a May 2020 case. The authority's social services department had written to the resident in connection with her family but had inadvertently included other information in the envelope relating to another family. The resident returned the documents but first made copies which she gave to her solicitors. It was common ground that the inadvertently disclosed information was highly confidential. The court granted the authority a temporary injunction forbidding the resident from publishing the information.

And it could equally be the case between spouses and civil partners who will be regarded as owing a duty of trust and confidence to each other. We will see at chapter 75 how, when one spouse or partner spies on the confidential information of the other when financial proceedings between them are looming or pending, the court may intervene. One party to a broken relationship might well be able to secure an injunction against the other of them from the court, forbidding them to publish details of their 'marital' secrets. This would be on the basis of a threatened breach of confidence which could well be linked to a claim based on a right to privacy (see **Secret affairs** above).

But it wasn't the case between the late 'Beatle' John Lennon and his former wife Cynthia when she was planning to publish marital secrets and he objected and went after an injunction against her. The Court of Appeal would have none of it. The parties' relationship, it was ruled, had ceased to be their own private affair. They themselves had put the relationship in the public domain. There had been no breach of confidence.

Part 8

GONE SHOPPING: SEE YOU IN COURT?

Chapter 61

Supermarket Struggles

Lousy plastic bags, parking machine clocks, suspected shoplifting and expired vouchers

I spend more time in supermarkets than reading statutes. Well. I did before Covid-19. I know that serving me as your 123rd customer of the day is no joy but the slightest hint of a smile would be ever so nice. Anyway, the contract for the sale and purchase of supermarket goods does not carry an implied term that the cashier will be pleasant so don't even think of claiming for a bad day because the cashier put on a hatchet face. My views have been softened by cashiers' valiant efforts throughout the pandemic. Carrier bags are another matter. I plead guilty to stoking a successful campaign in my first book *Gold's Law* for supermarkets to supply free bags to take the goods sold. I followed it up on a variety of radio and television programmes with the idea that, having reached the cashier, you should refuse to proceed with the purchase if the bags were not thrown in and leave it to staff to replace the goods onto the display shelves. I'm not sure that this makes me responsible for global warming though things have turned full circle. You get the plastic bags alright if you have the nerve to ask for them but you pays.

Having in 2016 packed a bottle of wine into a *Waitrose* plastic bag alongside a small packet of the lightest feathers, I left the store and as I went to bypass a *Big Issue* vendor, the bag exploded and the bottle rolled onto the pavement. And who brought the bottle's roll to a summary end? The *Big Issue* vendor. This got me thinking about buying a copy of *Big Issue* every time I saw one move – and a bag for life. It also reminded me that I have never succeeded in carrying home a cucumber which has not split through a supermarket plastic bag. The splitting process can be very embarrassing and lead to much pointing and ribaldry by passing students. As with flowers, there should be a conically shaped and strengthened plastic bag which is exclusively devoted to the cucumber.

And a supermarket ticket machine clock got me thinking about innocents being induced to pay parking charges and occasionally penalties which were not actually due though, in fairness, in my case I got customer services to stamp the ticket and the lady smiled – and knew the clock was wrong as other customers had already complained (so why hadn't they fixed the clock or gone over to free parking?).

Been shopping

> ### Particulars of Claim*
>
> 1. On 14 July 2021 the claimant purchased goods from the defendant's Twickenham store and was provided with (or sold) through the cashier a plastic bag into which to pack and carry the goods. The bag should have been reasonably fit for its purpose and of a satisfactory

standard but it was neither in that although the goods weighed no more than (state weight) the bag split within about two minutes of commencement of carriage whilst the claimant was on the highway outside the store and most of the goods fell onto the ground and either containers were smashed or the goods were otherwise ruined.

2. The claimant lost the value of the ruined goods and the plastic bag being a total of £50.00.

OR

1. On 14 July 2021 the claimant purchased goods from the defendant's Peardrop store and was provided with (or sold) through the cashier a plastic bag into which the cashier packed the goods. It was implied that the cashier would not pack goods of a weight which was greater than that which the bag could bear with reasonable safety and that the bag should have been reasonably fit for its purpose and of a satisfactory quality. The goods were too heavy for the bag and/or the bag was neither reasonably fit for its purpose nor of a satisfactory quality. Before the claimant reached the store's exit doors with the goods, the bag burst open and the goods fell to the ground and were ruined.

2. The claimant lost the value of the ruined goods and the plastic bag being a total of £50.00.

*When you claim online and can squeeze in your particulars of claim, a statement of truth will be generated for you to confirm along with an invitation to add interest. Otherwise, you should finish off your particulars of claim showing the relief you are seeking (for example, a sum of money, interest and costs) and with a statement of truth as shown in previous templates.

Been charged 10p for a plastic bag

Whether or not in England you should be charged 10p for a plastic bag (5p before 21 May 2021) may be less certain than the checkout assistant suggests. If you agree to pay then you may be stuck with the charge. "Bag for 10p?" "Yes, please." But if you paid under the mistake that you were liable when you were not and you would otherwise have been supplied with a free bag then you ought to get your 10p returned. I would not recommend for one moment that you commence county court proceedings for its recovery with interest and costs unless perhaps you are a shopaholic and have shelled out a fortune for 10p jobs. However, you could ask the store to do the right thing and return the money mistakenly paid over or next time make a polite challenge to the cashier who may have to send for the supervisor who may have to send for the assistant manager who may have to send for the manager who may have to telephone head office which isn't open that day but I beg of you not to do it when I am next in the queue or, as tiny and timid as I am, I may try and punch you on the nose.

So when don't you have to pay? Generally and ignoring the pandemic relaxations which are now over:

- when, before 21 May 2021, the business within all its branches employed a total of fewer than 250 full-time employees (now all businesses should charge and that includes airport retailers who were previously exempted);
- when the bag is non-plastic or plastic but more than 70 microns thick;
- when the bag is used;
- when the bag is not supplied for the purpose of enabling your purchases to be taken away, so if the store accepts that you simply want to take the bag home empty or you want to pack purchases from other shops into it and to carry away their goods bagless then they don't have to charge you but, on the other hand, they don't have to give you a free bag either;
- when the bag is to be used only for unwrapped or partly unwrapped food for human or animal consumption – ensure no other item is added to the bag – so there's an incentive to select at least one food item which is not wholly wrapped (but removing part of the wrapping of a wholly wrapped item pre-checkout may earn you a permanent barring from the store and a charge of criminal damage as goods selected in a shop do not become your property until the shop agrees to sell them to you which will usually be when the cashier rings up the price for them on the till);
- when the bag is intended to be used only for uncooked fish or fish products, meat or meat products or poultry or poultry products but, again, ensure that no other non-exempt item is added;
- when the bag is intended to be used only to carry medicine sold under a doctor's or dentist's prescription, live fish in water or only unwrapped axes, knives, knife blades or razor blades (and, frankly, if your store sells unwrapped axes or razor blades, I suggest you take your custom elsewhere or shop wearing iron gloves);
- when the bag has no handles (some of those titchy ones are handleless) or is of woven plastic;
- when the bag is intended to be used to carry goods on board a ship, train, plane, coach or bus (which could just about be anything and especially a vomit bag but probably not a copy of *"Why I never travel by public transport"*);
- when the bag is sealed after alcohol or tobacco purchased in a designated airport security area has been placed in it.

Been parking

> ### *Particulars of Claim*
>
> 1. On 14 July 2021 at 1.10pm the claimant was automatically issued with a ticket to the defendant's Peardrop store car park at the point of entry and parked his car. Unbeknown to him at the time, the

ticket wrongly showed the time of issue as 1.00pm. At 3.05pm on the same date the claimant was compelled to pay £25.00 into the defendant's exit ticket machine so at to procure a receipt validation in order to leave the park with his car whereas, under the ticket's conditions of issue, the claimant was entitled to free parking because his car had been parked for less than three hours and he had spent in excess of £20.00 in the store. The defendant has refused to make any refund to the claimant.

2. The claimant claims return of the sum of £25.00.

OR

1. On 14 July 2021 at 1.10pm the claimant parked his car in the car park at the defendant's Peardrop store with the intention of buying goods at the store. It was an implied condition of the parties' contract for parking that the defendant would attend to the claimant at one of its checkouts with reasonable dispatch so as to enable the claimant to depart from the car park when he intended to do so and not incur car park charges in excess of what he had intended. At 2.45pm on the same date the claimant sought to pay for the goods he had selected with the intention of departing from the car park by 3.10pm. At 3.11pm the car park charge was due to increase from £3.60 to £30.00 on account of a 'penalty' for parking in excess of two hours. Two of the cashier checkout points were unserviced and there were long queues at the other points with three of them being serviced by part-time trainees who were slow. There were no facilities for self-payment (or The Claimant did not have a prior arrangement to use the self-payment facilities OR The claimant did not have the confidence or expertise to use the self-payment facilities for which he has an abhorrence OR the self-payment checkouts were log jammed with customers OR the self-payment machines only accepted credit or debit cards and the claimant wished to pay in cash*). In the event, the claimant was not served until 3.20pm thereby compelling the claimant to pay £26.40 more than he had intended or wished so as to be able to remove his vehicle from the car park.

2. The defendant, in breach of the above condition, failed to attend to the claimant with reasonable dispatch and should have contemplated that the claimant as a result would be obliged to pay the charge which in fact he did pay.

The claimant's loss as a result of the defendant's breach was £26.40 which he claims.

*Warning: if there were self-payment facilities of which you could have taken advantage and, had you done so, they would have seen you on your way in time for the football results then the claim might be looking dodgy.

Not been thieving

If you are wrongfully arrested by a store detective and detained, you may have a claim against them or, more interestingly, their employer for damages for false imprisonment. For a valid claim, it is not essential for you to be carted off to one of Her Majesty's playgrounds: you can be falsely imprisoned in the manager's office. A store detective does not have the same power to arrest as a police constable: in fact, no greater power then a private citizen like Madonna or Harry Bloggs next door. The net result is that, should it transpire that you had not, in fact, stolen anything plus the store detective compelled you to go with them plus your free movement was prevented, you ought to be on to a winner. It matters not that the store detective genuinely thought you had already committed a crime. But if they had reasonable grounds for suspecting you to be in the course of committing an indictable crime (that's a crime for which you can be tried at the Crown Court and would include theft) they would be justified in making an arrest even though it turned out that you were innocent. Where their suspicion was that the crime was complete (say you had by then left the shop) that would usually be too late to justify the arrest. In short, no actual crime and no suspicion that you were being caught in the act means no private arrest permitted. The store detective who has recently been on a training course and remembered everything they were taught will simply invite you to accompany them to the manager's office whilst the arrival of a police constable is awaited. If you agree and go voluntarily then that would end a false imprisonment claim before it had started. But sometimes they jump too early and make it clear by words or action or both that you have no choice but to go with them. Accompanying them when it is obvious you have no real choice would not be counted as a voluntary action. Often the store detective will be in the employ of a security firm which has been engaged by the store and is left to get on with prowling and nabbing without any direction from the store. The law calls the security company an independent contractor and, in this situation, the store would probably deny any responsibility to you and lay the blame on the security firm. So you might have to claim against the security firm and not the store. Should it appear that the store was more involved than it suggests, you may be wise to claim against both and leave it to them to scratch each other's eyes out.

The trend seems to be for shops to refrain from providing a paper receipt for a more modest purchase – usually up to £10 – if they can avoid it. This can only serve to compromise you if you are challenged. The likelihood of a challenge is enhanced by the understandable public response to the 10p plastic bag law in slinging purchases into the trolley without prior committal to any form of bag, to merge with purchases made elsewhere and possibly goods they have just selected but overlooked in the trolley.

I recently took to the internet to ask Marks and Spence about the paperless transactions.

> "I am a long-standing and regular customer of yours. I am concerned and perplexed by your new practice of discouraging customers from taking a receipt on purchases. Why are you doing this? Is it to save money? What would happen if I had no receipt and was challenged

> about whether I had paid? Have you stopped this sort of challenge and, if so, are you not encouraging shoplifting? I would be glad to hear from you.
>
> Stephen Gold"

Here's the reply – and talk about not answering the question?

> "Hi Stephen
>
> Thanks for letting us know about your recent visit to one of our stores. I'm sorry to hear you're unhappy the assistant asked if you would like your till receipt.
>
> Our assistants like to give customers the option if they would like the receipt if the total is under £10. I'm sorry this has disappointed you.
>
> I have passed your comments on to our Policy Team as I know they are consistently reviewing customer feedback and will take this into consideration for future planning.
>
> Thanks again for getting in touch.
>
> Kind regards
>
> Lauren C
> Retail Customer Services
> Your M&S Customer Service"

Incidentally, I have never met my new friend Lauren.

No, I have not been falsely imprisoned by a supermarket (although I have to confess to fantasizing about such an experience) but I did help out two ladies who were stopped by a store detective at the late House of Fraser in London's Kensington. The ladies had made purchases which the assistant had packed into a store bag and, at the same time and unbeknown to them, chosen to pack a garment from stock to which a security tag was still affixed. The tag activated the alarm system as they left. A claim for damages for false imprisonment was made and judgment entered in default of a defence being submitted in time. The store, through its insurers, then applied for the judgment to be set aside. The ladies made much of the fact that the store would have to demonstrate to the court that it had a real prospect of successfully defending the claim if the judgment went. A settlement was negotiated whereby the insurers paid out £2,000, the judgment was set aside and the claim was dismissed.

> **Particulars of Claim**
>
> 1.   On 14 July 2021 at about 12 noon the claimant who had been a visitor to the defendant's Peardrop store was in High Street, Peardrop (the store) when a store detective employed by or under the direction and control of the defendant apprehended the claimant by seizing him

by the right arm and said to him in the presence and hearing of not less than six members of the public: "I was watching you in Tuppencehalfpennyplus, sonny. You've got a packet of razor blades and some sliced smoked salmon in your jacket pocket for which you have not paid and I am arresting you for theft. You will accompany me back to the store and to the manager's office and the police will be called."

2.   Against his will, the claimant was taken to the manager's office in the store in which he was forced to wait until the manager appeared 15 minutes later. He was told to empty out his jacket and trouser pockets which he duly did. They contained neither of the goods allegedly stolen. The store detective said: "He must have dropped them on the way up. The manager said: "We'll let you go this time, Troublesore."

3.   The claimant was distressed and humiliated by his ordeal and his feelings were injured.

4.   The claimant claims compensatory damages and aggravated damages for false imprisonment. In support of his claim for the latter, the claimant relies on the conduct as set out above of the store detective and store manager and their adherence to the allegation of dishonesty despite no stolen goods being found on his person.

AND the claimant claims:

a.   Damages;

b.   Aggravated damages;

c.   Such interest as shall be deemed just;

d.   Costs.

Voucher oucher

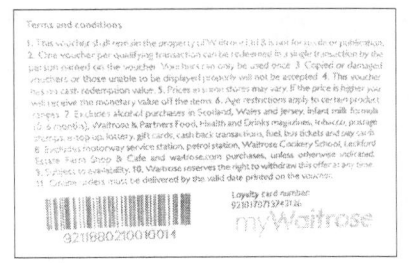

Discount vouchers are all the rage. They will encourage you to buy that which you do not want and exceed the minimum spend needed because you panicked that you had not already scored enough. I love them. That is why I was so excited when I received a few of them from my good friends at *Waitrose*. I placed an online grocery order with them on 4 October 2020. Using this medium obviates the risk that if I enter one of its stores, a staff member may recognise me as a troublemaker and poke their tongue out, though an extremely remote chance as Partners aren't normally like that. I intended to redeem one of the vouchers for £16 on a minimum spend of £100 which I healthily topped. The voucher was stated to be valid until 11 October 2020 which was one week later. I sought a delivery date before 12 October 2020 but none was available. The earliest date available was 14 October 2020. I booked it. The voucher was disallowed.

I complained to a member of customer care with whom I had a lively exchange of emails – not rude but forceful from each side and she was quite a toughie – until she guillotined me. On 8 October 2020 she wrote:

> "I have spoken with our Head Office via a phone call, regarding this. As I have presented you with all of the information we have to offer on this basis, there is nothing else for me to communicate with you at this point. I apologise if I could not satisfy this query, however I have done so to the best of our capability. The terms listed in this email thread and on the vouchers offered as a privilege to our customer base are clearly stated, and I cannot deviate from them.
>
> Please be aware that I will not be discussing this further. I would like to wish you well."

Good wishes are always to be welcomed. I returned the same day with this:

> "Thank you. If it will not unduly strain you to do so, please provide me with an email address for the office of the CEO. It is more expedient for me to email than write by post."

No reply. I duly wrote to the CEO. The main issue was whether *Waitrose* could rely on the small print condition on the back of the voucher that delivery had to take place by 11 October 2020. My argument was that the voucher implied *Waitrose* would be in a position to effect delivery within a reasonable period of an order being placed. Notwithstanding the pressures of Covid-19, ten days from order was not within a reasonable period. If, because of the pressures, delivery could not be effected within a reasonable period then this should have been provided for in the voucher conditions. Additionally, the delivery deadline was in conflict with the text on the face of the voucher which implied that the voucher would be actioned if the order was placed and money spent on it by 11 October 2020. That conflict should have been resolved in my favour as the customer. Also, the deadline was unreasonable and so unenforceable (see chapter 65). The text on the face of the voucher was in the upper case and bold and prominent as compared with the small print on the back.

I heard nothing from the CEO for over a month and so I made contact with the John Lewis press office to the effect that I was writing up my experience. This was on 13 November 2020 at 3.31pm. At 6.00pm the same day I heard from the case manager in *Waitrose*'s executive office, no less. Not quite the

CEO but good enough and later in the evening came this:

> "Further to my email earlier this evening, I would like to apologise to you for the way in which your concerns have been handled. Our customer care team is here to help resolve our customers' queries and I am sorry that this has not been done to a satisfactory level. I will be speaking to all those involved as I can see that we do have an opportunity here to improve on the service we are offering and for it is so important that we do right by our customers at all times.
>
> ......To put this right for you, I would like to offer you a £50 gift card to replace the £16 voucher that we sent to you and the additional is for a gesture of goodwill from us to you to welcome you back to Waitrose & Partners.
>
> I wish you and your family safe and well."

I graciously accepted the £50 gift card, asked some pertinent questions and told the manager:

> "I look forward to hearing from you and, in the meantime, I can tell you that I have just received a delivery of groceries etc from _____ Waitrose!"

The delivery arrived including one vegetable curry and one chicken curry instead of the two vegetable curries ordered. The price for the wrong curry – we are vegetarians – was refunded. I digress.

Back came the manager.

> "The way in which our online loyalty vouchers can be redeemed, which has been the same process since we introduced them, is that your delivery date must take place by the expiration date, the last date displayed on the vouchers showed being included. The reason for this is that we don't charge our customers until the day of delivery as all orders are picked, packed, and charged for on the day of your delivery. Should any of our customers miss out on the opportunity to redeem their vouchers we always ask that our Partners use their discretion to refund the amount once the order has been charged for or to send a gift card as a replacement option. Once again, I'm sorry that this hadn't previously been offered until my involvement and please be assured that this has been fed back to our customer care team. I have also shared your feedback around the way in which we word these vouchers with our marketing team for future consideration."

If you find yourself initially rebuffed in a **Voucher oucher** situation, let's hope this material will be of help to you. Leave the press office alone, though – unless you're on the *News at Ten*.

Chapter 62

Receipts And Sale Goods And Cheques

And planes and boats and trains

This is my true story as related in my letter to Jaeger's chief executive. I know he probably never saw it but there's always the chance of somebody other than a customer services rep picking up your opening missive.

16 November 2014

Chief Executive
Jaeger
57 Broadwick Street
London W7F 9QS

Dear Sir

Myself and Jaeger

I was in a relatively good mood when I entered your Portsmouth outlet yesterday. My intention was to both make some purchases and return a blue shirt which I had purchased in July 2014 for £25 (less, I think, a percentage discount). Indeed, in July 2014 in the course of three visits to the outlet whilst visiting the area I had spent around £250 – no doubt you will be able to identify the purchases from my account record as I hold a loyalty card with you – and the shirt in question had to be rejected because, whereas the affixed ticket represented that it was sized 16 which is my size, a subsequent sighting of the small label on the shirt itself just before I was about to unwrap and wear it, showed it was sized 15. In view of the fact it was patently obvious that the shirt had come from you and that my case for an appropriate payment was not capable of resistance by any reasonable business or staff member, I had not taken steps to take the receipt with me. In the event, the assistant present remembered me from my previous transactions and could confirm in the presence of the supervisor referred to below that the shirt had been sold to me. I should add here that this was the first time I had been back in Portsmouth and been able to return the shirt to the outlet.

I was confronted by a young lady who, on enquiry, informed me she was a supervisor and adopted the charm of a tyrant. She was economical with words and, judging by her facial expressions, perceived me to be objectionable for complaining about the mistake you had made. No apology. No offer to accept the shirt back. Nothing bar a proclamation that no action could be taken without a receipt. I was amazed and quite upset and forced in due course to leave with the shirt which I now hasten to enclose. Perhaps against my better judgment, I proceeded to buy further garments at the price of £315.20. Fortunately, the supervisor played no part in the further transaction and was absent for most

> *of my additional time in the outlet.*
>
> *I require you to please pay to me the gross value of the shirt which is £65 plus the cost of the postage which this parcel bears. The gross value is the measure of my loss.*
>
> *I have since been able to locate one of my July 2014 receipts and enclose a photocopy. It may or may not cover the shirt in question. You will see that I purchased a series of shirts on the date to which the photocopy relates.*
>
> *Yours faithfully*
>
> *Stephen Gold*

I have not included the shirt or photocopy receipt with this book. So what happened? Jaeger wins the *Breaking Law'Posthumous Inside Leg Award*. They promptly telephoned and agreed to pay me £65 together with £25 travelling expenses (for which I had not asked) and to gift me a £25 voucher. This is customer relations at its zenith.

The experience is instructive on a couple of counts over and above appraising you of my collar size. Was the Jaeger supervisor correct to insist on seeing a receipt before she would consider any refund? No. When you have a claim against a seller which is legally valid, the absence of a receipt should not prevent you from pursuing it. You would have to prove in court that you made the purchase so it is fair enough that you should prove the same thing to the shop when you complain but there is nothing wrong with your word for proof (although a bank or credit card statement could always be produced as a substitute for the receipt even if it could spoil a good argument). There is obviously scope for deception by a customer so one can empathise with a trader's wish to ensure that they are not being taken for a ride. How empathetic you are may well depend on the attitude of the trader. Mr or Ms Jobsworth may well deserve The Treatment.

> "Do you accept I am a truthful person?"
>
> "Yes."
>
> "Well, I as a truthful person am telling you that I purchased this item (a) from you; (b) when I say I did; and (c) for the price marked on it."
>
> "Sorry, sir but our policy is that we must have a receipt."
>
> "Which means I have to sue you and claim the price, interest, court fee and my travelling and car park expenses for today and you will have no defence. What a complete waste of time."
>
> "I'll just get the manager."

The girth of my neck had got me into difficulties before. As I look through my archives of trivia, I see that in 1979 I bought what I thought was a shirt with a 15" collar but mistakenly selected one sized 15.5". From whom? Jaeger. They kindly exchanged it. And then subsequently, I opened a new shirt

I had selected on one of my 2014 visits to them and thought it a little tight. The collar was 15.5" instead of the 16" to which it had grown and, this time, the label had given the correct measurement. My fault entirely. Would you be prepared to take it back for me? Actually, that may not be necessary as I had the courage to return to Jaeger and the Portsmouth branch to boot. This was on 26 February 2016 (with that false moustache and beard – joking) when I bought a discounted suit and was overcharged £10 for posting on the trousers to me which required shortening by two feet. They quickly made a refund when I raised the overcharge two days later.

The assistant manager of Robert Dyas in Petersfield told me in 2014 when I returned a water filter cartridge which turned out to have been smashed in its box when purchased that I could not have a refund but only an exchange. This was because I could not produce the receipt which I had discarded. I was going to leave it at that but eventually concluded that this would be unfair to you so here are my letters.

2 January 2015

The Manager
Customer Services
Robert Dyas Ltd
Cleeve Court
Cleeve Road
Leatherhead
Surrey
KT72 7SO

Dear Sir or Madam

I have suffered three shattering blows in recent times. In July 2014 I purchased a Brita Classic Single Pack Cartridge (100214) from your Havant branch for £4.29 and when in due course I opened it, I found it had literally shattered. I had not subjected it to any trauma between purchase and opening by way of dropping it onto the ground or throwing it at a wall and so it is as evident as night follows day that the product was in this unhappy state when I had the misfortune to remove it from your shelf as an act preparatory to purchase. This then was the first shattering blow.

The second shattering blow came when I went to return the product to your Havant branch. I found the branch was no more. It had metamorphosed into an outlet vending products at the price of £1 each.

The third shattering blow was when I subsequently took the trouble of calling at your Petersfield store with the product and encountered the assistant manager Damian. I cannot provide you with his surname because he declined to provide it to me although I had no intention of stalking him or holding him up to public ridicule. No doubt you know him. You should be proud of him because he steadfastly held rigidly to what I believe must be company policy, without insulting me or at-

tempting to throttle me. The blow was that although he accepted back the substandard product and offered to allow me to exchange it for a like product without charge, he would not refund the price. I was unable to provide a receipt for the purchase which appeared to be the stumbling block. It is hardly no more likely that I would have retained a receipt for a single Brita cartridge than that I would have done so for using a cubicle at the gentlemen's toilets at Waterloo Station. He said that I could have bought the product at Asda which is perfectly true but the deficiency in his argument was that he expressly accepted I was acting in good faith. My good faith was also implicit in the exchange opportunity and the acceptance back of the product. I pointed out to Damian that it would be appropriate for him to exercise his discretion on this occasion as I would otherwise feel obligated to bring proceedings for the recovery of the price, the court fee payable on this institution of such proceedings and out of pocket expenses. I left him with my contact details when there was no hint of the exercise of discretion so that he could contact you and you would see sense. But I have not heard from you.

The law is against you. I bought the product from you and it was not of satisfactorily quality or reasonably fit for its purpose as it should have been. As a matter of principle, I want my money back. Therefore, I call on you to repay me £4.29 within 14 days of the date of this letter and in the event of you failing to do so I will institute proceedings and seek in them the relief I mentioned to Damian.

It has been several months since my visit to your Petersfield branch. I have been too heavily occupied in writing a legal work on the rights of consumers and apologise for not communicating with you earlier. Fortunately my claim does not become statute barred for another circa five years and six months.

Yours faithfully

Stephen Gold

(see "Water cartridge disappointment" on page 503)

25 January 2015
Lauren P
Customer Services Manager
Robert Dyas Ltd
Cleeve Court
Cleeve Road
Leatherhead
Surrey
KT72 7SO

Dear Lauren P

Thank you for your undated letter received on 23 January 2015. I note all you say and, I will, of course, accept the £10 offered. Please send me a cheque in my favour for this amount to the above address.

I would not wish Damian to miss out on the next Robert Dyas Christmas party or to be in any way disadvantaged by what has happened because, as I indicated in my previous letter, he did very well and was at all times respectful. It is just that I fancy he may not have been blessed with sufficient discretion in the particular circumstances. If I were in your shoes, I would want a bucketful of Damians (provided the buckets were supplied by Robert Dyas).

Incidentally, the cartridge was in a damaged state on purchase which was unbeknown to me at the time.

Yours sincerely

Stephen Gold

Robert Dyas

Mr S Gold

Dear Mr Gold,

Thank you for your letter dated 2 January 2015 and please accept my apologies for the delay in responding. As I am responsible for Customer Service here at Robert Dyas, this matter has been brought to my attention.

Firstly, I would like to offer my sincere apologies the pack of cartridges became damaged so soon from purchase. As you rightly point out, this does not reflect the standard of products we aim to provide. Whilst I believe this to be a one off I understand it has left you disappointed.

Furthermore, I was sorry to learn our colleagues failed to provide a more suitable resolution. Like most retailers, we encourage colleagues to act in line with our Policy which is designed to protect both customer and the business. However, with this said, we also encourage colleagues to treat each customer as an individual and use discretion where required. Clearly, this experience has left you with a rather poor impression and I would like to give you my personal assurance feedback will be provided to the colleagues involved to improve the service going forward.

In order to bring this matter to a more satisfactory conclusion, I will be happy to provide a refund to the value of £10.00. In order to arrange this, I would be most grateful if you could contact me on 0191 600 0601 at your earliest convenience. I trust this more tangible token of my regret will go some way to restore your faith as I am confident the service you receive from Robert Dyas in future will more closely match your expectations.

Yours sincerely,

"Water cartridge disappointment"

I was paid the £10, just a little late but with a suitable apology.

There is an important caveat to this no receipt business. If the goods are perfectly satisfactory but you are after a refund or exchange because:

- you changed your mind;
- you bought the wrong size and that was down to you;
- your boss fired you when you got back from shopping;
- your partner says that green stripes against a pink background with black stars do not suit your complexion; or
- you decided on reflection that Tuesday was an unlucky day to make a purchase,

then you will have to go along with the trader's terms and conditions for making a return. They will probably say.......you must produce a receipt.

Sorry to dance about but I must get back to Jaeger and that shirt and the next nugget to be extracted from the experience. Jaeger asked me to phone them to give them my credit card details.

"[in trilly voice] Hello, Jane. Customer Services."

"It's Stephen Gold. You left a message for me yesterday."

"Oh yes. I have been asked by the customer service manager to deal with this. If you could please let me have your credit card details..."

"I'd like a cheque, please."

"I'm afraid we don't issue cheques."

"So how do you pay your bills? Surely you can send me a cheque."

"Could you hold on, please and I'll speak to my manager........................
...................I've spoken to my manager. On this occasion. We can send you a cheque but it will take a little longer."

"That's fine."

And the cheque duly arrived which means that the *Breaking Law Posthumous Inside Leg Award* to Jaeger has not been forfeited. Could they have insisted that I accept a credit card payment? As the law then stood, no. In so far as I was being compensated for my actual loss, I was entitled to be paid in cash or cheque. Transferring into a credit card account is not always convenient. You don't get the benefit of the credit until your next statement and, for a substantial credit, it may take a while to be able to exhaust it. So Jaeger, thank you. But when a trader is refunding to a consumer on a transaction made on or after 1 October 2015 under the Consumer Rights Act 2015 (see chapter 63) they may be entitled to insist on the same means of refund as the consumer used to make the original payment. The law is not completely clear but, anyway, this would not apply to damages over and above the price refund to which the consumer is entitled or to other transactions outside the 2015 Act.

I should not leave the subject of the receiptless complainant without three little stories. The first concerns some rotting nectarines and Marks and Spencer. Over to extracts from my email exchange with them.

> **From Stephen Gold On 28/03/2016**
>
> *Message:* The box of nectarines I purchased from your Kingston upon Thames store on Thursday last was returned by me to your Richmond upon Thames George Street store today. Each and every one of the four nectarines inside was bad when the box was opened on the evening of purchase which must be something of a record. I obtained a refund of £3 but nothing for my trouble although I did not ask for it but expected some small gesture for a breach of the Consumer Rights Act 2015. What concerned me more however is that I was told I would not have been given a refund if I had been unable to produce a receipt – this information was passed on by the manager to the staff member who attended me – and that I should have returned the product to the branch of purchase. I would like your comments on these matters. As to the receipt which I was able to produce, what was explained to me as your company's policy is surely unlawful. Obviously proof of purchase is reasonable and necessary but there is no limitation on the method of proof which is used, the customer's word may be enough. Certainly production of the product – even if it is festering – with the original labelling still affixed as in my case would be pretty good proof of purchase? Does your store manager think I might have robbed a pedestrian of four rotting nectarines so that I could then pass myself off as the buyer and extract £3 from you? As to returning to the branch of purchase, this of course is legal nonsense. Why instruct your staff to utter it?

> **From: M&S Service Team** <retailcustomer.services@customer-support.marksandspencer.com>
> Date: 29 March 2016 at 11:45:47 BST
> Subject: M&S Ref: 334657
>
> Hi Stephen
>
> Thanks for your email. Sorry to hear about your nectarines. I'm concerned to hear that they were rotten and it's really good of you to return them back to store. Please be assured that the store staff will follow this up with the supplier of the nectarines so they will be monitored for any future quality issues.
>
> I was very surprised to hear you were told by the staff at Richmond you should have returned them to the store where they were purchased. There are hundreds of M&S stores in London and surrounding areas. Realistically, we understand that you're not necessarily going to be shopping in the same store all the time. Therefore, as long as you go back to a store which sells food, which you did, this is fine.

The nectarines were clearly not up to standard, so you're entitled to a full refund in accordance with your legal rights. You were right, the fact that you were able to produce the product with its original packaging was more than enough for us and I'm sorry you were told differently.

I've followed this up with our management team at Richmond. Clearly, they need to make sure they're all up to date with the refund policy so that this doesn't happen again.

I'd also like you to have an e gift card for £10 as an apology for what happened. This will be sent to your email address and you should receive this in a few days time. Please also check your junk and spam folders, as it may get directed there. I hope my reply has helped to clear this up, but if you still have any other queries, feel free to email again and we'd be happy to help.

If you'd like to give any feedback about the reply I've sent you today, please feel free to fill in the short survey we've sent on the email separate to this one. I'd really appreciate your comments.

Take care and have a good week.

Anne G
Retail Customer Services
Your M&S Customer Service

For the second little story, please meet Scribbler, the greetings cards people

To Scribbler

3 May 2016

I made a purchase this morning from one of your stores. The receipt with which I was issued stated: "Returned goods will NOT be accepted without a valid receipt." This statement surely falls foul of the law. If, for example, goods are not of satisfactory quality then your customer would be entitled under the Consumer Rights Act 2015 to a refund if they were returned within 30 days. Obviously you would want to satisfy yourself that you had sold the goods and when but there is no legal obligation on the customer to produce a receipt for this purpose. The customer's word might be sufficient, particularly if it was a chief constable, the Pope or Dame J Dench or a credit card statement proving the transaction. Can you assure me that you will immediately alter this misleading statement on your receipts.

Yours sincerely

Stephen Gold

From Gemma R

5 May 2016

Dear Stephen,

Many thanks for your email to customerservice@scribbler.com. I attach a pdf of our returns policy which is on the backs of our receipts. Can you confirm whether or not your receipt stated this. If it doesn't apologies for the confusion.

Kind Regards,

Gemma

Scribbler

---

scribbler
in store | online | mobile
Visit us at scribbler.com

- Personalise cards with a name or photo
- Send cards anywhere in the world
- Free delivery when buying 2 or more cards

Use code **SCRRWEB20** for **20% off** your next online order!

Keep up to date with the latest news, discounts and fun stuff by signing up to our newsletter.

f y 🅖 ⓟ

We love our products and hope you do too, but on the off chance you change your mind...we promise to refund your purchase in full via the original payment method upon production of this receipt within 30 days. Without a receipt we'll give you an exchange. This does not affect your statutory rights.

Registered Office:
9 Harmsworth Street
London SE17 3TJ
VAT. 672405736 Co. No 1863486

From Stephen Gold

5 May 2016

Dear Gemma

Thank you. I have examined the back of the receipt and can confirm that it does set out your returns policy and makes it clear that the policy does not affect the customer's statutory rights. This is all well and good but the words of which I complained were the words on the front and, hence, the more prominently displayed words which are also in bolder type than the words of the policy on the back. There is no indication on the front of the receipt that the requirement for production of the receipt relates to goods returned after a change of mind. "Returned goods" impliedly includes goods returned because they do not satisfy the standards set by consumer legislation. So will you revise those words?

Yours sincerely

Stephen Gold

From Gemma R

10 May 2016

Stephen,

Many thanks for your email. I can confirm the text has been changed.

Kind Regards,
Gemma R
Scribbler

From Stephen Gold

10 May 2016

Dear Gemma

That is excellent news and I commend your company for responding – and so swiftly – to a customer concern and accepting it was in the wrong. I would be very interested to see the new text – before having to buy another card! Perhaps I may?

Yours sincerely

Stephen Gold

From Stephen Gold

13 May 2016

Dear Gemma

You have not come back to me but I could not resist so made a purchase from you on 11 May 2016. The wording on the receipt is exactly the same! That's a blow. Do you suggest I buy myself a condolence card?

Yours sincerely

Stephen Gold

From Gemma R

Stephen,

13 May 2016

Thank you for your email and apologies I haven't been able to respond before now. We're currently going through a companywide upgrade and rollout of our EPOS system which has been requiring the majority of my attention. The text has been changed on sites with the upgraded EPOS. It's unfortunate you have been to a site that has yet to be upgraded. Once all of our sites have come on board to the new system all receipts will reflect these changes. If you can tell me which site it is you visit I can inform you when this shop will be upgraded.

Thank you for your understanding with this matter.

Regards,

Gemma R

Scribbler

Well I gave Gemma the store location and she then came back with the new receipt wording. "If you want to bring something back please save your receipt. This does not affect your statutory rights." This passes the Gold test. If I had been Scribbler, I might have been tempted to tell me to mind my own business so, all in all, I reckons that Scribbler does deserve my continued patronage. Pity they don't sell noodle pots.

And the third story is about how HP almost wore me out. I had bought from John Lewis an HP printer which was defective. The seller took it back and I replaced it with an upgraded model. In the meantime, I had ordered a supply of cartridges from HP which were compatible with the returned printer but not the replacement printer. I wanted my money back for the cartridges for which I had no use. Strictly, that was a claim against the seller but I foolishly thought it would be more expedient to direct it to HP. They wanted proof of purchase of the cartridges (from the company which had since become an associate company due to some restructuring) but I had not been supplied with an invoice. HP was becoming difficult on this issue though at the same time signing off emails with "warm regards". So, this was my next email to them.

From: STEPHEN GOLD

Subject: Re: HP [ref:_ooDGoh8qk._50027maJgb: ref]

Date: 8 September 2016 12:53:29 BST

To: HP Support

I have now blown a fuse and I fear that a gasket blow is imminent.

You are asking for proof of purchase. I have sent you a copy of the dispatch note issued by your associate company. That I have been able to send you the copy would suggest, would it not, that I hold the original and, if I hold the original, would that not suggest that the original came with the goods and, if the original came with the goods, would that not suggest that the goods were supplied to me and, if the goods were supplied to me, would that not suggest that I paid for them or do you suppose that your associate company decided to give away cartridges for free because they liked me although they had never met me or communicated with me before?

For the third time, would you give me an answer – preferably, a straight one – to the straight question you have so far ignored twice, namely what are your proposals for redress for the inconvenience I have suffered and time I have wasted on this matter. Claim getting even bigger.

Regards (not too warm at the moment)

Stephen Gold

The recipient referred the dispute to six other persons in her organisation calling me difficult (me??!!) and unwisely copied me in on the email.

HP Support

> **To: STEPHEN GOLD** celeste.court@hp.com oliver.dyson@hp.com Cc: jmill117@ec.sitel.com RE: MD Complaint 3030144616 [ref: _00DGoh8qk._50027maJgb: ref]
>
> Hello All,
>
> Sorry there was no initial routing email for this MD complaint:3030144616
>
> Update:
>
> - Robert Request we provide refund for this customers Cartridge
>
> – Customer has been difficult from the start not wanting to provide POP
>
> - Sourced the invoice from HP store
>
> - Customer is persisting for further compensation.
>
> - I have explained 3 times we will not give him any further compensation
>
> - Asked him if he wants the refund, however keeps going on about further compensation
>
> - Will ask BO to process refund to customer as promised initially and will close case.
>
> Warm Regards
>
> Charlotte

You see, you never know what may turn up. I fancy that this carelessness helped with further negotiations.

> **From Stephen Gold**
>
> 21 September 2016
>
> To: HP Support
>
> Re: Refund [ref: _00DGoh8qk._50027maJgb: ref]
>
> Dear Charlotte

> ....*You have libelled me in your circulated separate message of the same date to no less than six persons in that you have falsely alleged I was difficult over providing proof of purchase and in that you have implied I have persisted in pursuing an unjustified claim for further compensation and conducted myself vexatiously in relation to the claim. You have failed to mention to the recipients of the message that I DID provide proof of purchase and in the only appropriate form I had available given that I had not been supplied with an invoice (as I clearly explained to you and note that it was proof that I had made the purchase and not proof of what I had paid for the purchase for which you were asking) .....*

It was then conceded I could have a refund in full and, for my trouble, two cartridges (one was offered and I counter-offered two).

> **To: STEPHEN GOLD Cc: CCRT_BackOffice**
>
> 03 October 2016
>
> RE: HP Reference: 3031954967
>
> Dear Mr Gold,
>
> Herewith I confirm that HP Inc. will refund you at the price of £55.97.
>
> As soon as you have provided us the refund form attached (you should fill in your bank account details and send back to this email address a scanned copy of the form), we will proceed with the re-imbursement process.
>
> Kind regards,
>
> Elena
>
> EMEA PPS CSS Customer Relations Back Office

Claims for compensation for inconvenience where a contract has been broken may not be easy according to the strict letter of the law (see chapter 33) – especially if directed to a business other than the one you contracted with! – but, if you don't ask, you don't get.

Chapter 63

The Newish Consumer Laws

Buyers' kit to be carried at all times when away from home

You obtained goods before 1 October 2015? Go away! Well, not quite. There are plenty of good laws to protect you but the newish stuff which is in the Consumer Rights Act 2015 only applies to purchases and goods hired or acquired on HP or under conditional sale agreements on or after 1 October 2015. And the newish stuff only applies when your supplier is a trader (a person acting for purposes relating to their trade, business, craft or profession) and you are a consumer (an INDIVIDUAL acting for purposes which are wholly or mainly outside their trade, business, craft or profession). It follows that the newish stuff does not apply when a trader acquires from another trader or a consumer acquires from another consumer: nor does it apply if when you acquired you were not a crying, talking, sleeping, walking, litigating human being but a limited company because a limited company is not an individual. Again, there are plenty of other laws which would protect you if you have been taken for a ride (even a short one) in one of these other situations but not the newish stuff. Incidentally, an individual who acquires goods in the course of their business may still be able to take advantage of the newish stuff if the acquisition was made for combined business and personal uses so long as the personal element was the prevalent one. Take the purchase of a computer which is intended for 80% personal use and 20% private use. You would be ranked as a consumer despite the business element and the newish stuff would be at your disposal.

The newish law – and this is a first for consumer protection legislation – extends to digital content including that supplied free with items purchased and supplied on a DVD. There are some exclusions: for example, the newish law does not operate in respect of goods bought at an auction open to individuals who can attend in person or in respect of coins and notes which are to be used for currency which means it would still apply where they were sold as a collector's item.

What you can expect

The old favourites are regurgitated but with knobs on. Goods must be:

- Of satisfactory quality which means they must meet the standard that a reasonable person (not Clive Troublesore) would reckon to be satisfactory. Taken into account will be how they were described, what you paid (though even sale goods with a last day 70% off must still work and for longer than it takes to get them home but a lower standard will usually be expected for second hand goods) and all other relevant circumstances including any public statement which the trader or manufacturer or their representatives have made about specific characteristics of the goods. Particularly relevant will be anything said in advertising (for example, on television, radio, in the papers and on the tube) or on labelling. In looking at the quality, regard will especially be had to whether the goods are up to the job for which they are usually supplied, their appearance and finish, whether they are free from minor defects, and their safety and their durability. But you cannot moan about a defect which was drawn to your attention: "*Seconds – some scratch marks*" or "*I must tell you, Mr Troublesore, the colour of the jumper has slightly faded from the garment being in our window display for a couple of months.*" Where you have examined the goods before you agreed to acquire, you cannot complain about a defect which the examination should have revealed. The moral? If you are going to examine, put your specs on and take the item into the natural light but don't walk down the road with it or you might be arrested on suspicion of theft. When you test drive a used car, the bodywork will look immaculate but the defects may be hidden and an inspection of a dozen scones is unlikely to reveal that they are oozing bacteria so missing latent defects should not present a problem for you. From a legal viewpoint, probably better not to examine goods and then it can't be said that you should have spotted the defect. As a matter of common sense, if the supplier insists on an inspection you may smell a rat and take your litigation elsewhere.

- Reasonably fit for a particular purpose (and there may here be a cross over with the requirement that they are of satisfactory quality). That purpose must have been made known to the trader before the supply was agreed but, more often than not, this will be by implication. If you ask for a bottle of pickled onions it will be implied that you want it to eat the onions inside. If in fact you want the onions for firing out of your son's toy gun, this would be a particular purpose which you would have needed to make known to the supplier. You won't be able to complain about unfitness for purpose where it would be unreasonable for you to rely on the supplier's skill or judgement. "*I really can't say, Mr Troublesore, whether this lagging is suitable for that sort of job. I've never heard of anyone doing that with it.*" "*Don't worry, my surveyor told me to get it.*" Troublesore 0 Trader 1.

- A match with what was described to you by the trader when you agreed to acquire and that extends to any information given to you about the main characteristics of the goods. Generally, this information has to be given by the trader when an agreement is made on or off trade premises or is a distance transaction such as a phone or online sale in compliance with – all together now – the Consumer Contracts (Information, Cancellation and Additional Charges) Regulations 2013. If it could be important in your case, check with the regulations or an advice centre that none of the exceptions to the trader's obligation to give this information applies. One of the main exceptions is day to day sales at the trader's premises where the consumer will be very familiar with what they are getting. "*A rice pudding, the Sun, a bag of spuds and a packet of crisps for the old sod at home today, Cyril, please.*"

- A match with the sample you have been shown where you have agreed to acquire on the strength of that sample – except to the extent that any differences have previously been brought to your attention before you agreed to acquire. *"The edges will be slightly rounder, Mr Troublesore and the colour shade will be much darker."*

And what you can do about it when you are let down

Some excited talk about the newish laws has clouded the fact that they do not afford you any remedy unless the trader has broken the contract. It may be that you want to be shot of the purchase because Mrs Troublesore doesn't like it or you have changed your mind or you have been made redundant or you have seen an identical item round the corner at half the price. If the trader operates a returns policy and you can comply with it then you gets your money back or an exchange or a credit note but the newish laws have nothing to do with this.

The usual rule in the civil law about proof applies so that if you are alleging that the goods or their installation are not up to legal scratch or some specific requirement in the contract has been breached and the case goes to court, it will be your responsibility to show that what you allege is correct. Of course, there are exceptions here which you will like. Where (see below) you are after repair, replacement, price reduction or exercising the right to long-term rejection (but not short-term rejection) on the strength of things being wrong within six months of you getting the goods, it will generally be presumed that things were wrong when you got them. It will be down to the trader to try and show that all was well on delivery and that the goods have met with some misfortune since then. Sounds a bit technical, I know, but important as it puts the trader on the back foot.

> *"Dear Trader*
>
> *The idea that the goods were in tip top condition when I took them away from your shop and that:*
>
> - *I dropped them on the way home;*
> - *My baby must have thrown them out of the cot;*
> - *I have wrongly used them;*
> - *I have not followed the manufacturer's instructions;*
> - *I have submerged them in water;*
>
> *is arrant nonsense. I drew your attention to the defects within six months of the goods coming into my hands and section 19(14) of the Consumer Rights Act 2015 treats the goods as not having conformed with my contract with you on (and from) the date I got them.*
>
> *Yours faithfully*
>
> *Clive Troublesore"*

Now where one of these old favourites has been breached by the seller, you get a right to reject the goods or have them repaired or replaced or have a price reduction – but not the lot! Don't forget that you may well be entitled to compensation as well.

Short term right to reject

Your primary aim could be to get rid of the bloody thing. *"I told you, Clive. I told you it was tat. I told you he was a crook. You wouldn't listen. I told you. Didn't I tell you?"* [pause while Clive turns off the record].

There's a long term right to reject which we will come to later but this one is the early right so they call it the short term right (but you cannot use it for digital content). This is how it works. You are entitled to get rid of the bloody thing (do excuse me) and to a full refund when you exercise the right (generally) within 30 days of getting the goods but for perishable goods substitute any shorter period before which perishing would occur. If you agree to or request a repair or replacement and the goods are still not up to legal scratch, you won't be prejudiced. You will be able to short term reject up to seven days after the goods are back with you purportedly repaired or replaced or, if later, up to the original 30 days with the period you waiting for the repair or replacement added on.

The short term right to reject is really valuable. It entitles you to a full refund (plus compensation for any losses) and without a reduction for any use you have had out of the goods before rejection. But 30 days isn't a long time especially bearing in mind that it could take that time, if not more, for the defects to show themselves. Here's the trick. Get the supplier to agree to extending the 30 days. You acquire on condition that they agree and then you will have a right to short term reject throughout that longer period. You will insist on the agreement being recorded on the invoice. The supplier can agree to an extension after acquisition though you are in a stronger bargaining position for that extra time before you have agreed to buy.

> *We Whitewash Ltd agree that Clive Troublesore's short term right to reject these goods under section 22 of the Consumer Rights Act 2015 is extended from 30 days to X days.*

No vacillation. You cannot exercise the short term right to reject once you have required or agreed to the trader repairing the goods, without giving the trader a reasonable time to carry out the repair. *"I'm back. Where is it?" "You only brought it in this morning, Troublesore. Give us a break."* There is an exception. You can change your mind about the repair if giving the trader that reasonable time would cause you significant convenience.

Short term rejection: how to do it

You must sock it to the trader – but not with your fists. You need to make it clear that rejecting is what you are doing and that can be by something you say or do. *"A plague on your shop and you can stick this up your till"* would leave little room for doubt as Mr Troublesore thrusts the goods into the unwelcoming hands of the trader. You can't rule out the possibility of a dispute in the future about whether you did or did not reject so, particularly with expensive items, put it in writing. When you come to reject, you will need to deal with actual return of the goods. If you take them with you and hand them over when you reject, no problem. Otherwise you can reach an agreement with the trader about how they get the goods back and, if no agreement, you must make the goods available for the trader to collect. And as to the price you paid, the trader must refund it to you – in the same form as you paid the price unless you agree otherwise so if you paid in cash you should be paid back in cash and if you paid by credit card then your card must be credited – and do so without undue delay. The trader must get on and put hands in pockets rather than pleading a bellyache or a need to send the goods to head office to scrutinise under a telescope. You should also have any return costs. If the trader actually agrees you are entitled to a refund then it must be made no later than 14 days from when they do agree. With a HP agreement, you are entitled to a return of all payments made to date. So let's have a look at what that letter of rejection on a purchase, if you choose to send one, may look like and you can adapt appropriately where rejecting having hired or taken out a HP or conditional purchase agreement.

> *14 July 2021*
>
> *Dear Trader*
>
> *I enclose a copy of my invoice for the goods purchased from you on 7 July 2021. I regret that the goods are:*
>
> *not of satisfactory quality as required by section 9 of the Consumer Rights Act 2015; and/or*
>
> *not reasonably fit for purpose as required by section 10 of the Consumer Rights Act 2015: and/or*
>
> *not as described as required by section 11 of the Consumer Rights Act 2015; and/or*
>
> *not in accordance with the sample I was shown before purchase as required by section 13 of the Consumer Rights Act 2015; and/or*
>
> *not in accordance with the model I was shown before purchase as required by section 14 of the Consumer Rights Act 2015.*
>
> *Details of your breaches of contract as above are that [and here set out concisely what you say is wrong avoiding the use of vulgar abuse and **not** marking the letter 'without prejudice'* and remembering one sweet day you might have to listen to the letter being read out in court].*
>
> *In view of the breaches of contract, I hereby exercise my right under section 22 of the Consumer Rights Act 2015 to short term reject the goods and treat my contract with you at an end and require you to:*
>
> *a.   refund to me without undue delay the purchase price paid; and*
>
> *b.   at the same time, pay to me damages in the sum of £a. Par-*

ticulars of the damages are £b for travelling expenses and car park charges I estimate I shall incur in sourcing and acquiring substitute goods; £c for loss of enjoyment of the goods purchased which have not been used and have not been usable for the period of an estimated two weeks from purchase of the goods until when I estimate I will be able to take delivery of substitute goods**; and £d which is the difference between the price I paid you and the price I am satisfied from enquiries I have made that I will be required to pay elsewhere for closely comparable goods***.

Or

b.   note that I reserve my right to claim damages for breach of contract against you and that it is my intention to provide you with particulars of such claim as soon as I am in a position to formulate it.

I acknowledge that I am under a duty to make the goods available for collection by you. Please let me know when you would like to collect from my address, giving me reasonable notice****. If I do not hear from you in satisfactory terms within seven days of you receiving this letter, I shall be obliged to bring proceedings against you without further notice for the refund and damages to which I am entitled along with the court commencement fee and interest.

Yours faithfully

Clive Troublesore

*But you could write a separate letter marked "without prejudice" (see chapter 10) which indicates a willingness to accept a lesser sum for damages provided the trader settles without undue delay.

**These are called damages for loss of enjoyment or loss of amenity which you may be entitled to where an important object of the supply was to give you "pleasure, relaxation or peace of mind" so they could arguably be claimed where, for example, the goods comprised a TV set or luxury food which you had purchased shortly before a carefully organised dinner party (see chapter 33).

***You may be able to buy a substitute at the same price which you should certainly take reasonable steps to attempt to do so that there will be no price difference claimable. But you could have a good case for a difference in price where, for example, the goods were originally bought at a discount and the trader could not replace with identical goods which were up to legal scratch and you had to pay more elsewhere for the same goods or goods which were as identical as you could find.

****If you prefer to return the goods to where you obtained them then say that is what you will be doing, state the expenses (reasonable) which this will involve if you want to claim them back and add them on to the refund total.

I once tweeted (to be precise, it was George who tweeted – see chapter 6) that I had jars of honey for sale containing live bees. Just a joke, you understand. No offers to purchase were received but I gained a health shop as a follower which quickly decamped upon more careful consideration.

Alas, nothing funny about one of the two jars of natural raw buckwheat blossom honey I ordered through Amazon. One of them had the corpse of a bee inside (or alternatively a wasp but I could not be sure until I had had an autopsy performed although a quickly convened jury reckoned, on balance, that it was a bee). I decided to reject both jars. I notified rejection through Amazon – on line, of course – and asked for the supplier to arrange collection. In response, I was given a list of option returns. Waiting for the supplier to call was not among them. Not being a litigious type, I decided to be merciful and to indicate I could return via a locker at a local store. However, when I was informed that the locker reservation would only be available for what was a very short period, I changed my mind. This was my web question and chat with Amazon from its own transcript.

> *Initial Question: I cannot return during the limited locker time allowed and revert to my original request that the seller arrange for collection. It is not my legal obligation to be put to the inconvenience and expense of repackaging and redelivering.*
>
> *Surendar (Amazon): Thank you for contacting Amazon. My name is Surendar. Am I chatting with S Gold?*
>
> *S Gold: Yes.*
>
> *Surendar: Hello, Gold. I can understand your concern regarding this. Let me check and help you in this.*
>
> *Surendar: Just to confirm. Is this the item you are referring for: Natural, raw buckwheat blossom honey (1 kg)?*
>
> *S Gold: Yes, two jars.*
>
> *Surendar: Thanks for confirming. Please bear with me 2 minutes while I check this for you.*
>
> *Surendar: I have checked and see that the return label is created today, you can return within 3 working days. You no need to worry for the package, please return the item with any box you may have.*
>
> *S Gold: Please reread what I have already said. I am NOT prepared to be put to this trouble. There has been a most serious breach of contract – a dead insect in one jar. My legal right is for a return of the price paid for the two jars and reimbursement of consequential losses. The seller must collect.*
>
> *Surendar: Just to confirm, is the insect found on both the jars you have received?*
>
> *S Gold: No, one but the contract is not severable. If the product cannot be trusted – one is unfit for human consumption – then I am entitled to reject both jars as I do.*

> *Surendar: Okay Gold, I'll forward this issue to the internal team and they will reach you via email in 24 hours.*
>
> *S Gold: Noted. My name is Stephen Gold.*
>
> *Surendar: I'm sorry, I will forward this issue to the internal team and they will reach you via email in 24 hours.*
>
> *S Gold: OK.*

And then, within 24 hours, Amazon – not the actual seller – returned to say they were refunding the full purchase price which they duly did and nobody wanted the products back. The honey and the bee made it to the household dustbin.

So pressure there on Amazon resulting in a waiver of its normal complaints scheme and a claim directly against the seller being obviated.

Repair or replace

Quite why you would want to put up with a repair, I am not sure. Perhaps you are soft, silly or sentimental – or all three. I suppose you might have fallen in love with the kettle having taken it to bed for three consecutive nights or maybe there's just nothing else like it on the market and only the supplier has the necessary parts. Accepting a replacement is understandable if you are convinced that what was supplied to you was an isolated rogue and there isn't something intrinsically wrong with the design or manufacture. Anyway, the general rule is that you can require the supplier to repair or replace and if that's what will turn you on, it makes sense to do so before your time for making a short term rejection is up (see above under **Short term rejection: how to do it**). Having made that requirement, the trader must comply within a reasonable time and without significant inconvenience to you. Whether or not the trader has done so will depend on the nature of the goods (that kettle or sophisticated technological equipment) and the purpose for which you were acquiring them (a toilet or a tin of treacle). The trader must bear any necessary costs involved including, in particular, the cost of labour, materials or postage. If you have gone for repair, you must give the trader a reasonable time to comply before opting for replacement or short-term rejection unless that would cause you significant inconvenience. Again, if you have gone for replacement, you must give the trader a reasonable time to comply before opting for either repair or short term rejection unless that would cause you significant inconvenience.

But you cannot go for repair or replacement where that would be impossible or disproportionate compared to the other remedies available to you. They will be considered disproportionate if either imposes costs on the trader which are unreasonable compared with the other remedies, taking into account the value of the goods if they had been up to legal scratch, the extent to which they were below scratch and whether you would be caused significant inconvenience. So, for example, if it would cost more to repair than replace, you would probably not be entitled to repair and vice versa.

14 July 2021

Dear Trader

I enclose a copy of my invoice for the goods purchased from you on 7 July 2021. I regret that the goods are:

not of satisfactory quality as required by section 9 of the Consumer Rights Act 2015; and/or

not reasonably fit for purpose as required by section 10 of the Consumer Rights Act 2015; and/or

not as described as required by section 11 of the Consumer Rights Act 2015; and/or

not in accordance with the sample I was shown before purchase as required by section 13 of the Consumer Rights Act 2015; and/or

not in accordance with the model I was shown before purchase as required by section 14 of the Consumer Rights Act 2015.

Details of your breaches of contract as above are that [and, as before, here set out concisely what you say is wrong avoiding the use of vulgar abuse and **not** marking the letter 'without prejudice' and again remembering one sweet day you might have to listen to the letter being read out in court].

In view of the breaches of contract, I hereby exercise my right under section 23 of the Consumer Rights Act 2015 to require you to:

repair the goods

or

replace the goods

You should comply with your statutory obligation as above within a reasonable time. I regard this to be within 28 days of the date of your receipt of this letter. You must also bear the necessary costs incurred in you complying with my requirement.

I also require you to pay to me damages in the sum of £a. Particulars of the damages are £b for loss of enjoyment of the goods purchased which have not been used, for the period of five weeks from acquisition to estimated compliance with my section 23 requirement and £c for my out of pocket expenses comprising postages, telephone calls and travel.

I am returning the goods to you with this letter. You should please let me know as soon as possible the latest date by which you expect to comply and as soon as you have complied.

If you do not comply with my section 23 requirement within the time specified above, it is my intention to end the contract and exercise my right to short term rejection and the return of the price paid and to damages for breach of contract.

Yours faithfully

Clive Troublesore

Price reduction or final right to reject

You have a choice: price reduction or final rejection (as distinct from short term rejection). But when? Only after one repair or one replacement have not worked OR repair or replacement are not available because of impossibility or disproportionality (see above under **Repair or replace**) OR the trader has failed to repair or replace as required within a reasonable time and without significant inconvenience to you. It follows that you can't demand a price reduction at the very start. When it comes, the reduction should be for an "appropriate amount" which obviously means the amount by which the value of the goods has lowered because of the contract breach and you will be entitled to a refund of any money you have paid the supplier over and above the reduced value. The reduction could conceivably be 99% of what you paid (I shouldn't spend too long arguing that it should be 100% though you might be right) where the goods are valueless.

Here's the rub with final rejection. Once six months have been clocked up since delivery or installation (where your supplier had to install), what you get back through final rejection may be reduced to take account of your use of the goods and, again, that could conceivably be 99% of what you paid (or the trader might argue for 100% so you don't get back a penny). That's fair enough. Otherwise you could do all manner of things on the duff settee for a couple of years and then demand you had all your money back without a discount. Even Troublesore wouldn't try that one on. Or maybe he would. There won't be any reduction if you finally rejected within six months of delivery or installation. Obviously, there's an exception to the six month rule. You will suffer a discount for use during the first six months where the goods are a motor vehicle other than a mobility scooter or the like.

14 July 2021

Dear Trader

I enclose a copy of my invoice for the goods purchased from you on 13 December 2020. We have reached the end of the road. The goods were:

not of satisfactory quality as required by section 9 of the Consumer Rights Act 2015; and/or

not reasonably fit for purpose as required by section 10 of the Consumer Rights Act 2015; and/or

not as described as required by section 11 of the Consumer Rights Act 2015; and/or

not in accordance with the sample I was shown before purchase as required by section 13 of the Consumer Rights Act 2015; and/or

not in accordance with the model I was shown before purchase as re-

quired by section 14 of the Consumer Rights Act 2015;

and you have

attempted to repair the goods but without success in that they still do not conform to legal requirements because [set out outstanding deficiencies]; or

you have replaced the goods but the replacement goods, like the original goods, do not conform to legal requirements because [set out deficiencies]; or

you have refused to repair or replace because this would be impossible; or

you have failed to accede to my requirement that you repair in that you have not done so within a reasonable time and without significant inconvenience to me [give details]; or

you have failed to accede to my requirement that you replace in that you have not done so within a reasonable time and without significant inconvenience to me [give details].

In view of the above and under section 24 of the Consumer Rights Act 2015, I now require you to allow me a price reduction in an appropriate amount which I claim to be £a [give details of how you have reached the reduction figure] and in addition pay me damages in the sum of £b, particulars of which are [set out details and have a look at the short term rejection template letter above to see the sort of things you might be claiming for]; or

take this letter as formal notice that I finally reject the goods and treat our contract as at an end and repay to me the purchase price of £a* and in addition damages in the sum of £b, particulars of which are [set out details and have a look at the short term rejection template letter above to see the sort of things you might be claiming for].

Unless the amounts claimed** are paid to me within seven days of the date of receipt of this letter, I shall be compelled to bring proceedings against you for the sums specified along with the court fee and interest.

Yours faithfully

Clive Troublesore

*If you have allowed more than six months to elapse before final rejection, the trader may well ask for credit to be given to them for the use you have had out of the goods (see above) but you could leave it to the trader to take the point: alternatively you may feel it is fair to take it yourself and say what you are knocking off the claim to reflect use.

**You could write a separate latter marked "without prejudice" (see chapter 10) which indicates a willingness to accept lesser sums provided the trader settles with you without undue delay.

Installation

If it is part of your agreement that the trader will install the goods and they are incorrectly installed whether by the trader or on the trader's instructions, that will amount to a contract breach. The trader is under a strict obligation there. They must do more than use reasonable care and skill: they must install correctly! The result of incorrect installation? All the remedies we have been looking at will apply except the right to short term reject.

Other contract breaches and other remedies

We have been focusing on specific terms that the law says will be treated as included in the contract. There may be other terms which do not have to be treated as such and which amount to specific requirements which the trader agreed to honour. Where one of these has been breached and it is appropriate, you can go for repair, replacement, price reduction or long term rejection (but not short term rejection) under the scheme of the Act as you can with the terms that are treated as included. Tell the trader you are relying on section 19(4) of the Act. You can also go in either case for what the general law has on offer for a contract breach including damages and an order for specific performance ("You shall get on and do that which you agreed you would do or the law says you should have done").

Where is it?

"We'll let you know when it's in, Mr Troublesore and may I say that it's a pleasure to do business and my best wishes to Mrs Troublesore." The answer is to try and pin down the trader about the time for delivery before you commit and have what is agreed written down by the trader on all copies of the invoice or on some scrap of paper or the plaster cast on one of your limbs. Then you can treat the contract at an end and have any deposit you have paid returned to you if the trader fails to keep to the delivery date so long as the importance of the date being kept to was made absolutely clear.

> *"Delivery agreed for 14 July 2021 and this date is absolutely essential; or*
>
> *Delivery agreed within 14 days of today and this period is absolutely essential".*

So you haven't agreed a particular date or period for delivery? In that case, the trader must deliver without undue delay and, anyway, no longer than 30 days after you have reached your agreement. The trader may say they still have every intention of delivering the very second the goods come in and they had spoken to the manufacturer only that morning who are very sorry about the delay but the goods have been so popular that they have got behind with orders and how is Mrs Troublesore. You don't have to wait for ever. Once the 30 days are up, you can specify a period for delivery that is appropriate in the circumstances and require the trader to deliver by the end of that period. Where still no show, you can treat the contract at an end: refund and go order elsewhere. Clearly you won't want to make it too far ahead for your own sake. Equally, you have to be careful not to make it unreasonably soon or you could really come a cropper with the trader being able to effectively force you to accept delivery or pay the price or compensation for loss of profit as you didn't give them long enough. Remember, you have to specify a period which is appropriate in the circumstances and that period is not and cannot be cast in legislative or any other kind of stone. You are unlikely to come a cropper if you have given the trader another 28 days.

> "I regret that you have failed to deliver the goods ordered in accordance with your obligation under section 28 of the Consumer Rights Act 2015. I need the goods without further delay. Therefore, I require you to take this communication as formal notice that unless the goods are delivered by (insert date), I shall treat the contract as at an end and call on you to reimburse me without undue delay for all payments I have made to you and claim damages for my losses* arising from your breach of contract. These damages will reflect the fact that I will have been deprived of the use of the goods for an appreciable period of time"

*You can claim for the same sort of losses you could have suffered where you cancelled the contract because the goods were not up to legal scratch – see above.

Your bicycle will be delivered next Tuesday between 5am and midnight

If, when you made your agreement, you failed to cater for delivery to your home at a time which did not coincide with the local foxes' investigation of your dustbin, you may be stuck with a wide and unsociable delivery window. But how do you stand when a delivery time or window is fixed, you are twiddling your thumbs awaiting their arrival and the goods don't appear? Unless the trader has allowed for a 'no delivery guarantee' opt out in their terms and conditions, you should be entitled to claim compensation from the trader for any loss you suffer. The most likely loss is a day's or half-day's net earnings. The object of compensation is to put you in the same position as you would have found yourself had the goods been delivered as agreed. Strictly speaking, no loss as you were actually intending to take the time off work. Same position: just no goods. The real loss would be in relation to the rearranged delivery date if your salary was docked and it was not reasonably possible or convenient to rearrange delivery for when you or someone on your behalf could have taken the goods in without time away from work. Where you are after compensation for the rearranged delivery, it would be prudent to have your salary docked rather than have the time off in lieu of holiday as some judges take the view that time of in lieu cannot lead to compensation. The small claims rule that a winner can recover lost holiday time on going to court for the hearing of their case (see chapter 25) is a special situation and does not apply here.

"I never have to deliver to you. Go away"

The trader sometimes argues that there wasn't a firm deal to supply: just an agreement to make an agreement and so no contract which was capable of being broken by either side. And that is precisely what the trader said in a case which was decided by the Court of Appeal in January 2016. Kevin Hughes ran two garages and was heavily into Porsches. In 2011 he got to hear that Porsche would be manufacturing a limited edition of the 911 GT3 RS4 model which was the last four litre 911 it was to produce. He wanted one and went for it to Pendragon Sabre Ltd which was a Porsche dealer in Bolton. He rushed to place an order and paid a deposit of a cool £10,000 on the basis that if one of the new model was allocated to Pendragon then Mr Hughes would get it. He didn't. Because they thought Mr Hughes would re-sell it at a profit, they decided it should go to another customer. Mr Hughes sued for damages for non-delivery.

Pendragon contended there was no enforceable contract. When the arrangement was made there was no car, no price agreed and no delivery date agreed, they argued. It didn't matter ruled the Court of Appeal. The Sale of Goods Act 1979 section 5 (which catches contracts made on or after 1 January 1894 so ought to just about be of potential benefit to you if not your great great grandfather) is unaffected by the Consumer Rights Act 2015 to the extent that it says there can be a binding contract for the supply of future goods: goods albeit not yet made or acquired by your supplier. Equally, there can be a binding contract for goods to be sold to you although their acquisition may be subject to some contingency which may or may not happen – like the manufacturer allocating goods in demand to your supplier instead of a competitor. And, as to the price, this can be dealt with under section 8 of the 1979 Act (which is also still intact). It says that where the contract does not give it then it may be determined in some manner fixed by the contract or by the course of dealings between the parties and otherwise the buyer has to pay a reasonable price. The law would have required delivery within a reasonable time. On this last point, the Consumer Rights Act 2015 has changed things but it is unlikely that the Court of Appeal's decision would have been any different if reached under the newish law. And how much did Mr Hughes get awarded to him? £35,000.

Excloooooooooooooooooooooosion

"Sale goods – no warranty" "We cannot deal with any complaint about the goods unless it is notified to us in red pencil enclosed within a sealed jam jar to be received by us no later than 93 seconds after you have taken delivery" "No short term rejection on our goods as they are so cheap – thank you for buying".

You know the sort of thing. Exclusion clauses is what the law calls them. You might call them small print although it can often be brazenly large print. Not legally worth the cardboard they are scrawled on? When it comes to the contract conditions we have been looking at – and this includes what I have said about when goods should be delivered – these exclusion clauses are totally ineffective and count for nothing although they often mislead consumers into abandoning their rights. Equally ineffective in legal eyes are words that appear to make any rights you have subject to some restrictive or onerous condition that is not in the Consumer Rights Act or allow a trader to put you at some disadvantage as a result of pursuing a remedy.

> *"Dear Trader*
>
> *I am advised that the condition you seek to rely on is not binding on me by virtue of section 31 of the Consumer Rights Act 2015 and that you seek to rely on it when you know or should know of its ineffectiveness is a matter I view with considerable seriousness. Hence, I am referring the contract and our correspondence to trading standards."*

Here is another no-no. A term in a contract is blacklisted in law where it suggests that a trader who has been negligent, as a result of which the consumer has died or been caused personal injury, is not liable for what happened. It has no legal effect and the position is the same if the trader, though not trying to completely escape liability in the contract in this situation, does still have a go at limiting it. *"The trader will not be liable to the consumer or their estate in the event of death or personal injury for damages exceeding £100,000."*

At your service

If it is a service that you are getting (whether or not some goods are thrown in as with a decorator who provides paint, wallpaper and glue or a vehicle repairer who throws in a new engine or some plugs in which event those goods have to be up to legal scratch in the same way as if you had bought them yourself from a trader) there are mirror type requirements. They are set out in the Consumer Rights Act 2015 as well which will apply, as in the case of goods, where you are a consumer and the supplier of the service is a trader in respect of an agreement made on or after 1 October 2015 and this is in place of the Supply of Goods and Services Act 1982. The service is to be provided with reasonable care and skill. If you haven't agreed when the service is to be performed then it must be within a reasonable time. What's reasonable? Good question, reader. Depends on the facts of each individual case, says the Act. Crikey.

> *"Dear Trader*
>
> *You said you would start as soon as you could. I am advised that you were obligated to perform our agreement within a reasonable time by virtue of section 52 of the Consumer Rights Act 2015 and you have failed to do so. I require you to take this letter as formal notice that unless you commence work within 14 days* of the date of receipt of this letter I shall treat the agreement at an end and claim from you the deposit I have paid you and damages reflecting losses I have and will have suffered as a result of your breach of contract to include any sum I have to pay to another contractor to do the work you had agreed to carry out over and above our contract price. Of course, you will also be required to complete the contract if and when you commence it as promptly as possible and in any event within a reasonable time which*

> *I consider to be 28 days of the date of receipt of this letter.**

*These deadlines may be too long or too short. As we have seen, what is reasonable depends on the facts of each individual case. If in doubt, err on the side of caution and allow a bit longer.

If you agreed a time for the work to start and the words of the agreement or circumstances made it abundantly clear that it was vital for this date to be adhered to and the trader has defaulted, you can tell the trader you are treating the agreement as at an end. Your remedy would again be recovery of whatever money you had paid over plus damages along the lines set out in the threatener above.

How much are you obliged to pay for the service? Generally, whatever you agreed to pay and if you made a bad bargain, I'm afraid that's tough on you. Sometimes the price or at least the means by which it is to be calculated – £50 call out charge plus £40 for each 30 minutes of service or part thereof (to include talking about the weather and looking out of the window) plus £10 in lieu of a tea break – will not have been agreed in advance. In that case, you have to pay a reasonable price and no more. What is reasonable again depends on the facts of each individual transaction. If you are being swizzed, pay what you say is the reasonable price and explain how you got there. You will not usually be legally justified in paying nothing on the ground that an excessive amount has been demanded.

> "Dear Trader
>
> You have invoiced me for £1,568.75 for unblocking my drain. We did not agree the price in advance. The job took 45 minutes. The amount of the invoice is exorbitant. My legal obligation under section 51 of the Consumer Rights Act 2015 is to pay you no more than a reasonable price for the service. I have made enquiries of several other drains specialists in the area and none of their estimates for the work exceed £250 inc VAT. I am satisfied that £250 inc VAT is more than a reasonable figure. I enclose my cheque for £250 in satisfaction of your entitlement and await your VAT credit note. If you are misguided enough to bring proceedings against me for the balance then I can assure you here and now that such proceedings will be defended. I am reporting you to your trade association whatever your response to this letter as I am convinced that your conduct justifies such action. In future, I shall be taking my drains elsewhere.
>
> Yours faithfully
>
> Clive Troublesore"

Where the trader told you something about the service, verbally or in writing, and you took it into account when deciding to give them the job, that something is now treated as a term of the agreement and must be complied with. These somethings include information provided under regulations 9,

10 or 13 of the Consumer Credit Regulations which we met above in respect of goods.

Duff service remedies

The 2015 Act establishes a regime for dealing with a trader who has not used reasonable care and skill. The general law which applies to contract breaches may well entitle you to other remedies: in particular, to throw the trader off the job but you should be confident that the law is on your side before taking such a drastic step or you could be in trouble with a trader's claim against you for damages, including the profit they have lost from not being able to see the contract through. Perhaps not too much to worry about if it's the gardener you are dispatching who had a penchant for mistaking your delphiniums for weeds. It's when we come to big money building contracts, for example, that the order of the boot could be a bit risky.

So what's the Act's remedy regime for services then? You have an entitlement – if you want to exercise it and it's not an impossibility – for a repeat performance and that doesn't mean messing up again. The trader would be obliged to make right what they have done wrong and to do so within a reasonable time and without significant inconvenience to you. Any costs in doing so, including labour and materials, would have to be borne by the trader. Should a repeat performance be impossible or the trader have failed to repeat within a reasonable time and without significant inconvenience to you then you have a right to a price reduction which could be up to 100%. A price reduction is also available where the job has not been done within a reasonable time.

> *"Dear Trader*
>
> *You have failed to carry out our contract using reasonable care and skill so that you are in breach of section 49 of the Consumer Rights Act 2015. I attach a separate list of 169 deficiencies in your work. I hereby require you to remedy these deficiencies by way of repeat performance under sections 54 and 55 of the 2015 Act. It will be your obligation to bear all costs involved in the repeat performance and I consider that the remedial work should reasonably be completed within 7 days of your receipt of this communication.* If you fail to repeat within this time frame, I intend to instruct another builder to do the work and to claim their bill against you together with damages for breach of contract which will reflect the stress and disruption we are suffering and will continue to suffer until things are put right.*
>
> *Yours faithfully*
>
> *Clive Troublesore"*

*The time allowed should be reasonable. Longer than seven days may well be appropriate. It depends on the particular circumstances. Err on the side of allowing more rather than less time than may be needed.

Where you are supplied with goods along with a service – say bricks by a bricklayer – then, as already noted, the goods must be up to the same legal scratch as a computer bought from a shop and the service must be performed with reasonable care and skill. This means, for example, that you could exercise the short term right to reject the goods along with the right to a repeat performance of the service.

> "Dear Trader
>
> Certain of the materials supplied by you under our contract were not of satisfactory quality as required by section 9 of the Consumer Rights Act 2015 (the Act) and/or reasonably fit for purpose as required by section 10 of the Act. I enclose a separate list of the relevant defects. Further, you have failed to carry out our contract using reasonable care and skill so that you are in breach of section 49 of the Act. I attach another list of 169 deficiencies in your work. I hereby require you to replace the defective goods under section 23 of the Act. In addition, I require you to remedy the defects specified in my second list by way of repeat performance under sections 54 and 55 of the Act. It will be your obligation to bear all costs involved in the repeat performance and I consider that the materials should be replaced and the remedial work should reasonably be completed within 7 days of your receipt of this communication. If you fail to replace and repeat within this time frame, I intend to treat our contract as at an end, reject the materials under section 24 of the Act and instruct another builder to make the replacements and redo the work and to claim their bill against you together with damages for breach of contract which will reflect the stress and disruption we are suffering and will continue to suffer until things are put right.
>
> Yours faithfully
>
> Clive Troublesore"

Excloooooooooooooooooooooooosion

In the same way as a trader's attempts at excluding or restricting your rights under the Act in relation to goods will be in vain, so it is in relation to the provision of a service. You have similar safeguards under section 57 of the Act.

Present prescience

Supposing that instead of popping up to the attic and dusting off the cherry stoner or smart phone overcoat to gift to Auntie Vera for her birthday, you actually dip into your pocket and buy her a present. And, worse still, supposing the present falls to pieces in Auntie's hands. We have an awkward contractual situation. When Auntie identifies the trader who supplied the present from the tiny sticky label on the box and takes a trip to their premises, she could legitimately be sent packing. *"Push off, Auntie. Our contract was with your nephew. You have no status to make a complaint, let alone* a claim. Goodbye – unless you want to pay for something yourself rather than moaning about somebody else's purchase."

There are two ways round the problem which avoid Auntie Vera suffering the embarrassment of telling you that you gave her rubbish and please could you take it back for her or pretending that the cherry stoner was a better invention than underpants or that her smart phone looks ever so cute in its overcoat but she can't find it at the moment.

First way round is using the Contracts (Rights of Third Parties) Act 1999. Tell the trader that the goods you want to buy are a gift for Auntie Vera. You are sure she will be delighted with them but, in case they turn out to be defective, you want her to be able to enforce the same rights against the trader as you would have been able to do as the purchasing consumer. If the trader agrees then they should write some magic words on the invoice or till receipt and you can go ahead and buy. This would satisfy the requirement of the 1999 Act that the contract expressly states that a named third party can enforce it. Put the invoice or till receipt in with the birthday card which will have the bonus of Auntie seeing how much you have spent and being extremely impressed.

Magic words: *These goods are being bought for Vera Troublesore and we agree that she shall be entitled to enforce all terms of the contract for their sale as the third party.*

The second way round is to assign – transfer – your rights to enforce the contract to Auntie Vera when you hand over the gift or subsequently. This would not involve any concurrence or action on the part of the trader.

> **Assignment** *To Auntie Vera Troublesore: I Clive Troublesore hereby assign to you the benefit of all rights and remedies including those treated as applying by the Consumer Rights Act 2015 to which I am entitled under my contract for the purchase of this gift, namely a cherry stoner which I made on 14 July 2021 from The Ridiculous Kitchen Utensil Store, Macclesfield under invoice/till receipt number 679WQZ16. Many Happy Returns. Love Clive.*

If Auntie Vera decides to follow through a complaint or claim she will need to give the trader a copy of the assignment.

Incidentally, despite the general rule that a person who is not a party to a contract cannot enforce it, there are exceptions in relation to holiday contracts. In the case of a package holiday (within the Package Travel, Package Holidays and Package Tours Regulations 2018 as recently amended – see chapter 24), a claim can be pursued by members of a party on whose behalf a single individual has made the booking. And in the case of a non-package holiday, a claim can be pursued by the person who made the booking on behalf of themselves and the other members of the party.

Distance sales cancellation

We have already met in another context the Consumer Contracts (Information, Cancellation and Additional Charges) Regulations 2013 which now incorporate the law on cancellation of goods, services and digital content such as music and software downloads and streamed films contracted for DISTANTLY on or after 13 June 2014 by a consumer from a trader. Cancellation (because you changed your mind or for whatever reason which may have nothing to do with the fault of the trader) will apply to the vast majority of deals which do not involve you going into a shop (including a pop up shop) or other business premises of the trader and making your agreement to buy or have some work done there and then. Or, to use what you may find to be the indigestible words of the regulations, cancellation will apply to distance contracts and off-premises contracts. This means that the most usual deals to be caught are those fixed up on the internet, by phone, by mail order or at your home. Distance selling requires some organised scheme for transacting with you so if you ring a bookshop and ask them as a one-off to send you six copies of *Breaking Law* (you fool) you will be stuck with them once they arrive even if the picture of the author turns your stomach. Not an organised scheme.

The right to cancel, wherever the deal was done, is excluded for:

- medical products and services (which would fall within what the regulations describe as 'sealed goods which are not suitable for return due to health protection or hygiene reasons, if they become unsealed after delivery' and sleepers should please note, when awake, that the European Court of Justice ruled in March 2019, in relation to the directive on which the regulations were founded, that a German consumer could cancel the online purchase of a mattress notwithstanding that they had removed its protective film when delivered);
- passenger transport services such as bus, rail or flight tickets;
- personalised goods;
- perishable goods ("liable to deteriorate or expire rapidly");
- urgent repairs or maintenance where you have specifically called out the trader;
- the supply of accommodation, vehicle hire and leisure activities for specific dates;
- goods bought at auction but eBay and other online auctions are caught where a trader is involved; and
- some others so check regulations 27 and 28 to ensure you are not ruled out before getting too stroppy when the trader has not told you that there is a right to cancel.

For deals which were done off the trader's business premises – so generally we are not here looking at internet and other distance situations – there is no right to cancel unless you had to pay more than £42.

There's no doubt that reaching a deal with a right to cancel often gives you an advantage over going into a shop which does not offer a returns policy because then you have no such right. Against that, you will be denied the opportunity of being coughed or sneezed at in the face by other shoppers (see chapter 59) and to fully examine goods and even try them on or try them out.

How long do you have in which to cancel? Generally, 14 days starting the day after you made the contract. But with goods it's generally 14 days after the day on which they came into your possession or the possession of someone else to whom you asked them to be delivered. There are special rules for multiple or regular deliveries. The time for cancelling is extended if the trader has not supplied you in the prescribed way with prescribed information about your right to cancel (see part 2 and schedules 1 and 2 to the regulations). The extension is to 14 days from the date on which you get the necessary information from the trader. However, once 12 months from the date on which the trader should have come up with the information are up, the right to cancel disappears.

How do you cancel? You can use a template cancellation form which you will find in schedule 3 to the regulations. You don't have to. Instead, you can use an online form provided to you by the trader – but again you don't have to – or you can just communicate with the trader using you own words (or mine!) and you don't have to give any reasons for cancellation.

> *"I require you to take this communication as formal notice that in accordance with regulation 29 of the Consumer Contracts (Information, Cancellation and Additional Charges) Regulations 2013 I hereby cancel my contract with you numbered 000001XB4 made on 14 July 2021."*

So long as you have sent off the cancellation communication before the end of the cancellation period you will be treated as having cancelled in time even if the trader does not receive it until outside that period.

What next? You get back any money you have paid to the trader including any original delivery costs. If you had asked for an expedited or otherwise enhanced form of delivery which was more expensive than the trader's basic form on offer then only the cost of the basic form is refundable. You cannot lawfully be charged a cancellation fee. If you have damaged the goods – diminished them by any amount "as a result of handling...by the consumer beyond what is necessary to establish the nature, characteristics and functioning of the goods" – the amount may be deducted from your refund. In the case of services, the trader can deduct the cost of any of them supplied at your request during the cancellation period.

You must return goods to the trader within 14 days of notifying cancellation at any address they have specified unless the trader has offered to collect them. If no address has been specified, you can use a trader's contact address and, if none, any address at which they carry on their business. The cost of return is to be borne by you unless the trader has agreed to pay it. But when giving you details of your cancellation rights, you should have been told that the responsibility for bearing the return cost would be down to you if the trader was not intending to meet it. Where the goods could not normally be returned by post (because, for example, they were too large), you should have been told what the return cost would be. If the trader failed to give you this information, they must pick up the bill for return.

The refund due to you is to be paid without undue delay and within 14 days of cancellation unless you have to return goods. Then, you should be refunded within 14 days of the goods arriving back or, if earlier, within 14 days of the trader receiving proof that you have sent the goods back. Unless you have agreed otherwise with the trader, the refund is to be made with the same payment method as you originally used.

Brexit Alert!!! This is potentially very boring indeed. Some contracts say that the law of a foreign country outside the EEA shall apply to it. A foreign jurisdictional clause they call it. So long as the contract has a 'close connection' with the UK, such a clause has been unenforceable when attempting to rob the consumer of rights which they would otherwise enjoy under the Consumer Rights Act 2015. That remains the position with pre-1 January 2021 contracts. For contracts made since 31 December 2020, the Consumer Protection (Amendment etc) (EU Exit) Regulations 2018 meddles with the lingo in the Consumer Rights Act 2015. UK law will generally apply to UK consumer contracts and no contract can rob the consumer of rights under parts 1 and 2 of the 2015 Act by applying the law of an EEA state.

Chapter 64

Unfair Trading

The price (and possibly any one of a dozen other things) is not right

You cannot compel a trader to sell to you. In legal eyes, when the trader displays goods they are inviting you to make an offer to buy them. You make that offer once you present the goods to the cashier or to the assistant manager or to the big shot down from head office who is checking out the cashier and the assistant manager or to whoever happens to be standing or sitting at the purchase point and they decide whether they will accept the offer. It matters not that you have been queuing all night to bag the rug or tin of silver plated baked beans marked down to 50p and nobody else wants them. Because you have no right to insist on a sale to you, it follows that you have no right to insist on a sale to you at a particular price.

But say the goods were mistakenly marked at £10 when they should have been marked at £100 and the shop won't sell to you at the lower price despite you having travelled 26.3 miles to get them? It makes no difference. The same principle applies although the conversation at the purchase point – by which time you have been joined by the store manager and six other shoppers who are pretending to be inspecting the nearby itching powder or staring at the fascinating white ceiling – could go something like this:

> "I accept I can't make you sell them to me but you do know you have broken the law, don't you?"

> "We never break the law. We pride ourselves in discharging our legal obligations to the letter."

> "You are conversant with the Consumer Protection from Unfair Trading Regulations 2008, I am sure. They make it an offence for a trader to mislead customers about the price of a product and lots of other things like the existence of a specific price advantage if that misleading would lead them or would be likely to lead them to purchase the product or simply go into the shop. It's in regulation 5."

> "Would you like to sit yourself down and partake of some refreshment?"

Now it would be quite improper for you to use a trader's commission of an offence as a device to harass or intimidate them into bending to your demands. However, where it is brought home to the trader that what they have done amounts to an unfair commercial practice and constitutes an offence, they may well be only too pleased to relax their attitude towards you. After all, you are giving them the opportunity to avoid a visit by trading standards and possible prosecution. The trader has a defence if they can show that they made a mistake, the offence was due to an accident or another cause beyond their control but also that they took all reasonable precautions and exercised all due diligence to avoid an offence – and this is where they may come unstuck.

Where do you stand when you have actually been charged for goods at a higher price than the displayed price? In a strong position. As chance would have it, I had a bit of bother along these lines myself. I was after 96p, an apology and greater care.

> *From: STEPHEN GOLD*
> *Sent: 30/12/2015 18:26*
> *To: customersupport@waitrose.co.uk*
> *Subject: Overcharging*
>
> *Did you know it can be an offence to display goods at a price less than that which you intend to charge? On 22 December 2015 I purchased from your Richmond, Surrey store goods for which I was charged £146.24 (till 003 seq no 126436). These included four Kabuto ramen noodle pots which were on display at £3.50 for two. I was charged and paid £1.99 per pot which was 96p in excess of what I should have been charged. I did not notice the overcharge until I had arrived home. If this had been the one and only occasion this had happened to me at Waitrose, it would have been one thing. But it has happened before and it is presumably resulting in a host of customers who need to count their pennies being deceived where they are less diligent than I was (belatedly) on this occasion. I am fed up with this happening and equally fed up with having to waste the time and take the trouble to return to the store and queue up to complain. Would you please take greater care and would you reimburse me the overcharge?*
>
> *Whilst writing, may I point out that your displayed bananas are habitually soft and/or black and/or blacken within a couple of days of purchase. This is no doubt due to them being frozen or over refrigerated before display. I am advised that consumption of overripe bananas is not conducive to good health because the sugary content is increased.*
>
> *Yours faithfully*
>
> *Stephen Gold*

> **On 2 Jan 2016, at 16:26, Waitrose Customer Service** <customerserviceteam@waitrose.co.uk> wrote:
>
> Thank you for your email Mr Gold.
>
> I'm sorry to hear of your disappointment on your recent visit to our Richmond store.
>
> I have double checked our product database and I'm afraid the Kabuto Noodle range has not been on offer since January 2015. The selling price is £1.99.
>
> Mistakes at our tills are thankfully rare, but I can understand that your confidence in us has been dented. Following your feedback, I've made

the Richmond branch management team aware. They will discuss this with their cashiers and we're confident this won't happen again.

As a gesture of our goodwill for the disappointment caused, I'd like to send you a gift voucher. Please can I ask you to provide us with your full postal address and I will be happy to arrange this for you.

Thanks again for telling us about this and I hope we can look forward to seeing you again soon.

Kind regards

Katie S

Waitrose Customer Service

Case Reference: 01361887

From: STEPHEN GOLD
Sent: 02/01/2016 17:28
To: customerserviceteam@waitrose.co.uk
Subject: Re: Overcharging [ ]

Thank you for your message.

I am very concerned – indeed irritated – by your third paragraph. I care not what your database discloses. The display of the product in question was accompanied by a prominent and unequivocal notice to the effect that two were available for the price of £3.50. I had this independently verified the following day. That is why I purchased four. If you made the mistake of allowing the notice to be in position when you intended otherwise then please say but do not insinuate as you are doing that I have given you a false account or that I was suffering from some hallucination. I expect an apology and an acceptance that you were in error. I will address your offer of a gift voucher when I have heard from you in more satisfactory terms. You may also wish to say something about my banana comments which you have ignored.

Yours faithfully

Stephen Gold

On 4 Jan 2016, at 08:18, Waitrose Customer Service <customerserviceteam@waitrose.co.uk> wrote:

Thank you for your email Mr Gold.

I am sorry you are dissatisfied with my previous response and I am sorry for any upset caused.

I'm afraid I cannot comment as to the location of the sign at the time of your visit as this may have been moved since. I have spoken to the branch and I have asked that they double check all of the offers to ensure that the shelf edge tickets are clear and accurate so we do not mislead any of our customers.

I'm also sorry to hear of your disappointment with the bananas purchased from our store. I'd really like to look into this for you. So I can do this, please can you reply with as much of the following information as possible:

- your full name, address and phone number;
- product barcode/product name;
- cost of the product;
- use by/best before date;
- packer's/batch code (this is usually printed near the use by/best before date).

Once we have this, we'll pass this matter on to our merchandise complaints department for full investigation and then we will write to you.

Thanks again for letting us know and I look forward to hearing from you.

Kind regards

Katie S
Waitrose Customer Service
Case Reference: 01361887

From: STEPHEN GOLD
Sent: 04/01/2016 18:19
To: customerserviceteam@waitrose.co.uk
Subject: Re: Waitrose Customer Feedback [ ]

Thank you for your further message from which it seems you accept you were in error. Is this so?

The mischief is in failing to update your tills with offer data and, incidentally, in failing to display reduction notices in a way that does not confuse customers into thinking they relate to goods immediately by them or to all goods immediately by them when they do not. I cannot see how cashiers can be blamed as you previously suggested. You should be apologising to them for having to suffer protests about wrong pricing.

In the matter of the bananas, my complaint was of habitual problems. I fear I would have to go to the refuse tip to answer most of your questions.

I give my contact details below.

Yours faithfully

Stephen Gold

The exchange continued with my new best friend Katie who responded to each of my messages with commendable speed and never lost her cool. I accepted a voucher for a fiver and let matters rest after an acknowledgment that she was not suggesting that my complaint was false or indeed that I had suffered a hallucination BUT *"however as previously mentioned, without any evidence of the ticket in branch, I cannot confirm or deny what was on display at the time of your visit."* I regard the acknowledgment as tantamount to an admission that *Waitrose* had been at fault, albeit I accept this had been due to a human error. Why not have the grace to say so in the first place? There are drawbacks for the trader in going overboard with open contrition.

The fiver was more than adequate compensation for me. What I didn't know at the time was that, within a matter of weeks, I should have a spot of similar trouble at *Tesco* over the matter of an overcharged cucumber. I will let the emails tell the story.

To: "Customer Service
Subject: Tesco Customer Service Enquiry Call Form

Sent: 23/01/2016 20:16
Title: Mr
First Name: Stephen
Surname: Gold

I today made purchases from Tesco Metro, George Street, Richmond (till receipt no 309700710344043) including two cucumbers: one organic at £1 and one non-organic at circa 45p. I now notice from the receipt that I have been charged for two organic cucumbers. I have the cucumber labels which are available for inspection by appointment. I do not have the time at the moment to return to the store. Would you please make me an appropriate refund to the address at the bottom and be more careful in the future because overcharging albeit by mistake is an offence when lack of care is involved. It might also be a good idea for you to advise your customers to check their receipts for instances of overcharging because I fancy that not all shoppers are as vigilant as me.

Yours faithfully

Stephen Gold

From: customer.service@tesco.co.uk
Date: 24 January 2016 at 11:02:54 GMT
Subject: Re: Tesco Customer Service Enquiry Call Form

Dear Mr Gold

Thank you for your email.

I was very sorry to learn that you had paid more than you expected for one of your cucumbers at your local Tesco Metro in Richmond and I can appreciate how disappointed you must be.

It is very disappointing that the product was incorrectly scanned and as a result of this you were overcharged. Our overcharge policy is to refund double the difference.

Whilst there is little more that can I say to alleviate the disappointment this situation has caused you, I'd like to thank you for taking the time to bring this matter to our attention. I do hope that despite this incident, you will give us the chance to restore your confidence in our operation.

As you are unable to return, for me to issue a Tesco Moneycard please could you provide a copy or a photo of the receipt and the labels you have available?

Finally, thank you for bringing this to my attention: I eagerly await your response so I can resolve this issue for you.

Kind regards,

Ryan K

Tesco Customer Service

To Customer Service

Sent 24 January 2016

From Stephen Gold

Dear Mr K

Thank you for your message. I congratulate you on its promptness. I regret what has happened although I would not say I was as disappointed as you suppose.

I have sent to you by separate message copies of the till receipt and labels. I have no problem with your request. Whilst I would not expect my request to materially affect your company's share price, I can understand that you must protect yourself against what could in theory be an attempt at obtaining money by deception. Should you wish to send the branch manager along to authenticate the copies against the original documents then I would be happy to see him by appointment and perhaps he would care to partake of some organic cucumber sandwiches whilst he is here although I can see that his bus fare may exceed the sum of money in issue.

In passing, I am particularly impressed by the freshness of your bananas.

Yours sincerely

Stephen Gold

> **From: customer.service@tesco.co.uk**
> **Date: 25 January 2016 at 06:56:36 GMT**
> **Subject: Re: Overcharge**
>
> Dear Mr Gold
>
> Thank you for your email and for the photo provided.
>
> I think maybe my colleague in store presumed they were both organic based on the other items purchased but we can't be caught making assumptions as in this instance it's caused you to be overcharged.
>
> As requested, I've issued a Tesco Moneycard for £5.00 so that you can make some extra sandwiches. This will be with you in 7 to 10 working days.
>
> Finally, thank you for taking the time to bring this to my attention. We value your custom very highly and we always do our best to put things right. I hope you give us another chance to deliver and provide the service you expect and deserve. If you have any further questions please don't hesitate to contact us again.
>
> Kind regards,
>
> Ryan K
>
> Tesco Customer Service

Poor Ryan K. Does he never go to bed? That matter was settled in less than one and a half days and, for the first time in my experience, someone from a customer services department displayed a sense of humour. I can overlook that my suggestion was not addressed. Well done *Tesco*. Well done Ryan K who wins the 'Breaking Law Life Award for Services to Sliced Cucumber Sandwiches with a Pinch of Salt'. Incidentally, legal pedants would be quite correct to point out that I could have insisted on a cash refund of the overcharge which would not have committed me to return to *Tesco*. But I love them – and their bananas.

And legal pedants really on the ball would also point out that, in this situation, the changes to the 2008 regulations now kick in. They are a gem. Previously, the erring trader could face a prosecution but not a county court claim simply on the basis that they had breached the regulations. The changes can give you the consumer the right to redress in a noodle pot situation – as indeed with a multitude of misleading actions and also aggressive practices – which has occurred since 30 September 2014. You will need to show that you entered into a contract with the trader or you made a payment to the trader PLUS that an average customer would have been likely to have done so (an objective test and, therefore, we are not concerned with what a very weird customer would have done) PLUS the action you are complaining about was a significant factor in your decision to enter into that contract (which is a subjective test).

So prove those things where the trader has done something misleading under regulation 5 of the 2008 Regulations, and you can get out of the deal within 90 days from when you received the goods or service (yes, services and even digital content are also covered) so long as you haven't fully consumed the goods or fully received the service. It's called a right to unwind. You must return the goods and you are entitled to your money back.

Alternatively, and, possibly of more interest, you can keep the goods and enjoy a discount where you have paid the price or some of it. How much? For a minor transgression, 25% of the price; if it is significant, 50%; if it is serious, 75%; and if it is very serious, 100%! The degree of seriousness will be judged according to the trader's behaviour, the impact on you and the time that has elapsed since the transgression. There is an inevitable exception where the purchase price is over £5,000, the market value of the goods was less than you agreed to pay and there is clear evidence of the difference between the two figures. Then, you are entitled to the same percentage of the price as market value bears to what you agreed to pay. In certain circumstances, you may also be entitled to damages.

In addition to an unwinding or a discount or instead of them, you can claim damages for any financial loss you have incurred which, but for the trader's misleading you, would not have been suffered as well as for any alarm, distress or physical inconvenience or discomfort you have been caused. These rights do not affect any other rights you may have under the general law for breach of contract or misrepresentation but you cannot collect duplicate compensation. Unlike the position with a prosecution, it is no defence to a civil claim under the regulations to unwind or for a discount for the trader to say that what happened was due to a mistake, accident or somebody else or was beyond their control and that they took all reasonable precautions and exercised all due diligence. But that defence can be put forward for a claim for damages.

The new rights do not apply to house and flat sales; property lets apart from assured shorthold tenancies and holiday accommodation; pensions, mortgages, insurance, banking and other financial services though there is plenty of other protection there; or generally to credit agreements (but again, plenty of protection elsewhere).

A claim can be brought in the county court. I have yet to come across one despite this being a valuable right.

PARTICULARS OF CLAIM

1. The claimant brings the claim under regulation 5 ("regulation 5") of the Consumer Protection from Unfair Trading Regulations 2008 as amended ("the Regulations").

2. At all material times the claimant was a consumer and the defendant was a trader within the Regulations.

3. On 14 July 2021 the claimant entered into a contract with the defendant ("the contract") for the purchase of a 'Brain Scramble' laptop computer ("the computer") for the price of £1,250.00 ("the price"),

paying the price and taking delivery of the computer on the same date.

4. The defendant engaged in a prohibited practice ("the prohibited practice") in relation to the computer within regulations 5 and 27A(4)(a) of the Regulations (or the manufacturer of the computer engaged in the prohibited practice within regulations 5 and 27(4)(b) of the Regulations of which the defendant was aware or could reasonably be expected to be aware as at the date of the contract).

Particulars of prohibited practice

[Set out the false information relied on which must relate to any one or more of the matters referred to in regulation 5 – for example, the amount of the price or how the price has been calculated; the existence of a price advantage (for example, "50% off"); the extent of the trader's commitments (for example, saying the trader gives a full guarantee when it turns out to be only for parts and not labour); indicating by a statement or symbol that the goods or the trader are sponsored or approved (for example, "By Appointment to Dame Judi Dench" or "Approved Platinum Member of He'salrightmate"); the need for a service, part, replacement or repair (for example, "All parts last for life"); the attributes of the trader (which includes their qualifications, status, approval, affiliations and connections and awards and distinctions); and information on the main characteristics of the goods which includes among a long list their benefits, risks, composition, after-sale customer assistance, method and date of manufacture, results to be expected, fitness for purpose, usage and specification – **you will detect some crossover with the Consumer Rights Act 2015 and we touch on this below: alternatively, you may be able to rely on a misleading omission – omitting or hiding material information or providing it unclearly, unintelligibly or ambiguously etc under regulation 6**].

5. Pursuant to regulation 27E of the Regulations, on 20 July 2021 the claimant exercised the right to unwind the contract on account of the prohibited practice by indicating to the defendant that he rejected the computer and informing the defendant that the computer was available for collection from his home subject to 24 hours' prior notice to the claimant of the defendant's intention to call in order to collect.

6. The defendant has neither refunded the price to the claimant nor collected the computer from the claimant.

7. The claimant claims the return of the price.

Or

5. The defendant has not exercised the right to unwind in respect of the contract.

6. Pursuant to regulation 27I of the Regulations, the claimant claims a discount in respect of the contract.

7. The relevant percentage discount within regulation 21I of the

Regulations which the claimant says is just and appropriate is:

25% on the basis that the prohibited practice was minor;

Or

50% on the basis that the prohibited practice was significant;

Or

75% on the basis that the prohibited practice was serious;

Or

100% on the basis that the prohibited practice was very serious.

Pursuant to regulation 27J of the Regulations, the claimant further claims damages for financial loss incurred by him and for distress and physical inconvenience or discomfort suffered by him which he would not have respectively incurred and suffered if the prohibited practice had not taken place.

Particulars of financial loss

[insert particulars]

Particulars of distress and physical inconvenience or discomfort

[insert particulars]

And the claimant claims:

a. return of the price of £1,250;

or

a. a discount limited to £x;

b. damages limited to £y;

c. interest at such rate and for such period as the court shall deem just; and

d. costs.

I believe that the facts stated in these particulars of claim are true. I understand that proceedings for contempt of court may be brought against anyone who makes, or causes to be made, a false statement in a document verified by a statement of truth without an honest belief in its truth.

(signed) Clive Troublesore

Claimant

Dated 16 September 2021

Crossover with Consumer Rights Act 2015

The newish laws in the 2015 Act do the consumer proud (see chapter 63). Sometimes you will have a remedy under both the 2015 Act and the 2008 regulations. If goods are not reasonably fit for purpose and the trader has convinced you that they are reasonably fit, for example, that could amount to a breach of both pieces of legislation. You may be too late for a short term rejection under the Act but in time for an unwinding under the regulations. Or you may get a better result by going for a discount (especially in the case of a very serious case of misleading) under the regulations than a price reduction under the Act. Provided that your case falls within both pieces of legislation, there is no shame in making claims as alternatives which rest on both and relying on the general law to boot if that is justified although do not over complicate the claim if you can avoid it. You would need to appropriately adapt the particulars of claim in this chapter and template communications in chapter 63.

Oh, I almost forgot

Having tested out customer relations on price at *Waitrose* and then at *Tesco* it would have been ungallant to have neglected *Marks & Spencer*. My sentiments are genuine.

"Price not so happy"

Sent from my iPad

Begin forwarded message: On 20/02/2016 22:34,

Message: I bought a packet of five "Happy Easter" cards from you today. The product reference is T21/7790/3428E. The price label appeared to be £2. When I got to the checkout the cashier pointed out that the price was in fact £2.50 and on the closest inspection I see that this is so. But the 50p is a small fraction of the size of the £2 and is in less bold print. Since 50p is more than I ordinarily spend on my afternoon tea, I consider that giving it so little prominence is very misleading and that many of your customers, particularly the elderly with poor eyesight, will be deceived. I would welcome your observations. I can send you a copy of the packaging. Alternatively you may be able to source a packet of the cards at your end but I should put on a pair of strong specs first.

On 22 Feb 2016, at 19:52, M&S Service Team <no_reply@customersupport.marksandspencer.com> wrote:

Hi Stephen

Thanks for contacting us about the Happy Easter cards you bought from us today. It sounds like I'd need my super strong glasses on to see how small the pricing was on the packaging of these cards. This is quite unusual as normally the font size of the numbers on the price is the same.

I've passed your feedback onto out Stationery/Card team, they'll be keen to look into this further and to see if this is just a one off on this particular pack of cards. They'll also take your comments into consideration when discussing this with our supplier as we want to make sure all of our customers are happy with our labelling.

Thanks again for getting in touch, we look forward to seeing you in store again soon.

Kind regards

Karen B
Retail Customer Services
Your M&S Customer Service

From: STEPHEN GOLD
Date: 22 February 2016 at 21:56:21 GMT
To: M&S Service Team <no_reply@customersupport.marksandspencer.com>
Subject: Re: M&S

Dear Ms B

Thank you for your prompt response. However, I see from a revisit to the store that this misleading practice is being adopted with a number of other cards — including cards on display for what appear to be £1 but which an inspection with one's nose almost touching the packaging reveals are priced at £1.50. Can I have your assurance that all these cards will be immediately removed from display and relabelled. This may have sounded a trivial complaint from a lunatic but it really is a serious matter. I await your early response.

Yours sincerely

Stephen Gold
Sent from my iPad

From: M&S Service Team
To: Stephen Gold
Date: 25 February 2016
Subject: M&S

Dear Mr Gold,

Ref: 310957

Thank you for getting back in touch.

I hope you don't mind me replying on behalf of my colleagues Karen and Paul. I can appreciate your frustration as I've also noticed the labelling has changed when purchasing a Mother's Day this weekend and I found it very hard to read the notably smaller decimal and 50p.

My colleagues have passed your comments and feedback onto our Stationary Team along with our Marketing Team who will evaluate your comments along with any further feedback we receive on our label pricing.

I'm afraid I'm unable to say whether the cards with the current labelling will be removed from sale as this is something our teams will review and they will do this by using the feedback we've received. Your comments are incredibly important and will play a part in this review.

Thank you again for getting in touch and for your valued feedback.

Kind regards
Lucy M
Retail Customer Services
Your M&S Customer Service

Waitrose revisited

You'll never guess what happened. Or perhaps you might.

From: STEPHEN GOLD
To: Waitrose
Sent: 02/04/2015
Subject: False representation as to price

Dear Team

I have had to complain to you in the recent past on the above subject. I regret I have to return to you on the very same subject.

Today at your Richmond branch I selected two bags of creme eggs which were displayed as having been marked down from 37p to 19p each. At your till, however, I was asked to pay the original price. This is another instance of reduction data not having been input into the till. Fortunately, I was alert to the possibility of an overcharge attempt being made on this occasion and was able to draw your assistant's attention to the error before the transaction was closed. You really must be more diligent or I fear that sooner or later you will face prosecution for this practice (although you may have a defence) independently of any claim for compensation that may be made as a result of breach of statutory duty. Can I have an assurance that you are going to be more careful for I shall otherwise find shopping with you too much of a nervous experience.

Yours faithfully

Stephen Gold

On 5 Apr 2016, at 09:11, Waitrose Customer Service <customerserviceteam@waitrose.co.uk> wrote:

Thanks for getting in touch with us Stephen, though I'm sorry to hear what happened when you were shopping in our Richmond branch recently.

From looking at our records, the reduced price of 37p came into effect on the 31st of March. Could I ask if the 19p price was on a reduction sticker on the product? I'm unable to see this further reduction.

Once I've heard back from yourself I'll then investigate this for you and then once I've gathered all the information I need, I'll then respond to you in full.

Thanks again for getting in touch, I look forward to hearing from you.

Kind regards

Kieran D
Waitrose Customer Service
Case Reference: 01784361

From: STEPHEN GOLD
Sent: 05/04/2016 11:48
To: customerserviceteam@waitrose.co.uk
Subject: Re: Waitrose Customer Feedback (Case No. 01784361)

Thank you. The reduction to 19p was clearly notified on the shelf by the product display although not on the selected products. You do not usually mark products with their price, do you?

Stephen Gold

From: Waitrose
To: Stephen Gold
Date: 5 April 2016
Subject: Re: Waitrose Customer Feedback (Case No. 01784361)

Thanks for your reply Stephen and for confirming those details for me.

We may on occasion have a reduced sticker on a product to indicate a further reduction.

As I can't see this on our system, I'll speak with the buyer and highlight to them about this. It may have been a change that was not communicated to the relevant team to put the price into action on our checkouts, if so they'll review the way they communicate such changes for the future to avoid such issues.

I'm sorry that we've let ourselves down in regards to the service provided, but I hope that knowing this will be reviewed by the right Partners shows you how we're dedicated to getting things right and improving our customers experience when shopping with this.

Thanks for giving me the opportunity to look into this for you Stephen, I hope this doesn't deter you from shopping with us and that we'll see you in our Richmond branch again soon.

I hope my response has been helpful today and if you'd like to provide feedback we have a link to a short survey. It'll only take a few minutes and as a thank you for your time you'll be entered into our prize draw where you could win £500 in gift cards.

www.waitrose-cs.com/?certcode=011

Kind regards

Kieran D
Waitrose Customer Service
Case Reference: 01784361

We'd love to hear your thoughts on your contact with us. If you'd like to take a couple of minutes to fill in our survey you could win £500 of vouchers – www.waitrose-cs.com/?certcode=011

From: STEPHEN GOLD

Date: 9 April 2016

To: customerserviceteam@waitrose.co.uk

Subject: Case number 01784361

Thank you for your last communication. I note what you say but the misleading continues at the same branch. Please see photo of display at the store today. Does the money off notice not imply that it relates to the product immediately above it (which I selected and for which I was charged the higher price). This is the third complaint I have had to make as to misleading pricing in rapid succession. Once is careless. Twice is reckless. Three times is a scandal.

Sent from my iPad

Stop the press!

I promise that I do not go out with mischief on my shopping list. But they did it again.

From: STEPHEN GOLD

Sent: 11/04/2016

To: customerserviceteam@waitrose.co.uk

Subject: 01784361

Please see extract below from the relevant receipt. I was charged £1.99 for the displayed Unoco coconut water. You will appreciate that the shelf label indicated that the reduction applied to this product by virtue of its proximity to the Unoco display. This was misleading. Would it be wise for you to warn customers to carefully check their till receipts as there is a good chance they will be overcharged? I would welcome your particular comments on this suggestion.

Yours sincerely

Stephen Gold

"Shelf snap"   *"£1.99? How dare you!"*

From: Waitrose Customer Service [customerserviceteam@waitrose.co.uk]

Sent: 14/04/2016

To: Stephen Gold

Subject: Waitrose Customer Feedback (Case No. 01784361)

Thanks for the photo of your receipt Stephen.

I'll contact the branch management team to investigate why this keeps happening. Once I've looked into each of your concerns I'll then be back in touch to respond to you in full.

Kind regards
Kieran D
Waitrose Customer Service

**From: Waitrose
To: Stephen Gold**

On 14 Apr 2016, at 15:37, Waitrose Customer Service <customerserviceteam@waitrose.co.uk> wrote:

Thanks again for getting in contact with us Stephen.

Further to my last email as discussed, I've contacted the branch management team at our Richmond branch.

I've spoken with Liam, branch manager, who would like for me to pass on his apologies.

Having discussed this we agreed that it was quite clear that we've clearly let ourselves down on delivering excellent customer service. Liam can't provide any reasons for this shortfall in standards, however it is a Partner error and should not have happened. Going forwards Liam and his management team will be speaking with Partners and offering refresher training to those who they feel may not be completing any tasks given to them correctly.

If you'd like to speak with Liam regarding this, he's more than happy for him or his assistant managers, Kate or Vicki, to sit down and discuss what the branch are doing to resolve these issues and what they'd like to do for you as our customer. Please do ask for Liam, Kate or Vicki upon your next visit to the branch if you wish to do so.

Thanks again for bringing this to my attention, I hope that the above goes some way to showing you how we want to get it right and deliver brilliant customer service.

Kind regards

Kieran D

Waitrose Customer Service

From: STEPHEN GOLD

Date: 14 April 2016 at 21:07:16 BST

To: Waitrose Customer Service <customerserviceteam@waitrose.co.uk>

Subject: Re: Waitrose Customer Feedback (Case No. 01784361)

Dear Keiran (if I may)

Thank you for your message. As delightful as a meeting with Liam, Kate or Vicki (in whatever combination) might be, I feel I must plead the hair washing defence. However, I would be prepared to police the pricing practice at the branch for a limited period on your behalf if that might help – I do not think that I am known as the troublemaker so would not be rumbled – and could report back to you. What do you think? Also, I would appreciate your view on the suggestion I have already put forward about warnings to customers. It could be watered down a bit if you thought that appropriate by reference instead to the slight possibility of an overcharge.

Yours sincerely

Stephen Gold

From: Waitrose
To: Stephen Gold

Date: 15 April 2016

To: Stephen Gold

Subject: Re: Waitrose Customer Feedback (Case No. 01784361)

Thanks for your reply Stephen.

We'd recommend the best course of action is to speak with the branch management team. As they're at the branch and focused on delivering the best service possible, it's always good to feedback directly to the branch. As previously mentioned, Liam is more than happy to meet with you and discuss whatever you might find in the branch, if he's not available then Kate or Vicki would be able to assist.

In regards to your suggestion, we wouldn't use this at the checkout, we empower our Partners and put our faith in them to ensure that they carry out their duties to the best of their ability. Again, if you do find something that isn't right, please highlight this to a branch management team Partner who'll be more than happy to help.

Once again I'm sorry for the service you've received but hope we can welcome you into branch again soon and show you that the branch is turning things around.

Kind regards

> Kieran D
> Waitrose Customer Service
> Case Reference: 01784361

And again.

> **From: STEPHEN GOLD**
> **To: WAITROSE**
>
> Sent: 04/12/2016
>
> Subject: Grapes (not sour)
>
> As your records may disclose, I have felt it necessary in the recent past to make several complaints to you regarding pricing issues at your Richmond-upon-Thames store. I regret it is a case of 'here we go again'.
>
> Below you will see a snap of yesterday's grape display at the store. On the upper shelf, three kinds of grapes are displayed – sable, sapphire and cotton candy. There are price notices for the sable and cotton candy but not for the sapphire. The absence of a sapphire notice creates a
>
> *"Grape gripe"*
>
> misleading situation as customers would be forgiven when they select what are sapphire grapes for believing they are sable or cotton candy. This would probably result not only in them getting the wrong kind of grape but paying more than they intended as I gather that you intend charging £3.29 per carton for the sapphires as against the cheaper £2.99 or £2.50 (as the case may be).
>
> The display depicted by the snap has been the state of the grape display at the store for about three weeks!

Would it help if I made a sapphire price notice for you and came and affixed it at what would be the correct position?

Yours sincerely

Stephen Gold

And then this exchange

From: Waitrose
To: Stephen Gold
Date: 9 December 2016

Thank you for your patience while I looked into this Stephen.

I have had a response from the branch regarding the ticketing on our grapes in our Richmond branch. The duty manager has assured me he has spot checked the fixture and can confirm there is a ticket for each product. He has advised that the sweet sapphire ticket that was missing has a date for 5/12/16 on, so was printed the following day.

The duty manager would like to apologise for any confusion and disappointment caused and is more than happy to discuss this with you when you are next in branch.

I hope my response has been helpful today and if you'd like to provide feedback, please click on the link below.

Kind regards
Kelsey
Waitrose Customer Care

From: STEPHEN GOLD
To: Waitrose
Date: 9 December 2016

Thank you for your message. I think that what you are saying is that, after a period of about three weeks with no price ticket for the sapphire grapes, one was printed out the day after and as a result of my communication to you. Is that correct and do you accept that this latest lapse is very serious? Further, are you prepared to bring the lapse to the attention of your customers in an appropriate way and inform them that, if they have been misled into paying more than they intended for the sapphire grapes, you will make reimbursement to them? Surely this is the very minimum action you should take?

I will not trouble the duty manager when next in the store in case he feels constrained to propel a large grapefruit in my direction!

Kind regards

Stephen Gold

FROM: WAITROSE

Date: 9 December 2016

Thanks for getting back in touch Stephen.

Unfortunately I'm unable to comment about the last few weeks, however I can confirm that the branch periodically check our products to ensure the correct ticket is being displayed. Sometimes mistakes do happen which appears to have been the case on this occasion.

The branch do always welcome any comments or feedback from our customers, if you have any problems in the future please do speak to a Partner at the time and they'll be pleased to resolve this for you.

I hope my response has been helpful today and if you'd like to provide feedback, please click on the link below.

Kind regards
Kelsey
Waitrose Customer Care

From: STEPHEN GOLD

To: WAITROSE

Sent: 09/12/2016

Dear Kelsey

Thank you but, if I may dare to suggest it, you are avoiding giving me any specific answers to the specific questions I posed. Given that I appear to have been responsible for bringing an end to a misleading state of affairs, I think you should at least favour me with those answers.

Kind regards

Stephen Gold

From: Waitrose

To: Stephen Gold

On 13 Dec 2016

Dear Stephen

Thanks for your return email, although I'm sorry you remain unhappy with Kelsey's response.

We do everything we can to make sure all our prices are clear on shelf edge tickets and have rigorous procedures for checking that our prices are correct. We certainly don't intend to mislead our customers in any way. In this instance it would seem to be a case of human error on this occasion for which we apologise.

I'm sorry you had a disappointing experience at Waitrose. To say sorry, I'd like to send you a gift card. Please could you reply to confirm your full postal address and I'll arrange this for you.

I hope we can look forward to seeing you again soon.

Kind regards

Mel

Waitrose Customer Care Team

From: Stephen Gold

To: Waitrose

Sent: 14/12/2016

Dear Mel

Thank you for your message. Let me make it clear. I am not saying I was deceived and, save to the extent that I have suffered the frustration of not getting you to give straightforward (or any) answers to straightforward questions, I have not suffered on this occasion anything that could be categorized as a loss. However, if you remain insistent on sending me a gift card, I will not look a gift horse (or card) in the mouth and provide my address below but you may wish to reconsider.

My concern is for those who have been deceived. What are you going to do about it? I have already made a suggestion. Come on, answer that please and no more evasion.

Kind regards

Stephen Gold

From: Waitrose
To: Stephen Gold
Date: 14 December 2016

Dear Mr Gold

I'm sorry you feel that I have evaded your query that was certainly not my intention.

If any of our customers come forward and make a complaint of a similar kind then we would of course compensate them for that. I have arranged for the gift card to be sent to you. You should receive this within the next couple of days. I hope my response has been helpful today and if you'd like to provide feedback, please click on the link below.

Kind regards

Waitrose Customer Care

The value of the gift card was a fiver. I donated that amount to charity. On one of my other complaints to *Waitrose*, though, the gift card had a chocolaty flavour about it. Bite into this.

> **From: Stephen Gold**
>
> To: Waitrose
>
> Sent: 26/10/2019
>
> Subject: Car Park at Richmond-upon-Thames Store
>
> Hello
>
> *I would like to both congratulate and apologise to you. As to congratulations, this is on the occasion of the first anniversary of the perverted automated announcement in your centre lift from ground floor to car park that the lift is descending rather than ascending and thereby sending its passengers into a state of intense confusion. As to the apology, this is on account of the lateness in conveying my congratulations which has been due to pressure of shopping.*
>
> *I have previously drawn your attention to the lift problem which you had stated was being fixed. I am wondering whether the engineer has been caught in dreadful traffic?*
>
> *May I offer a solution? I would be prepared to take up an honorary position in the lift in question and personally announce its direction of travel at appropriate intervals. All I would ask is that you made available to me a slice of your exquisite chocolate cake from the new Waitrose 1 range during tea breaks, assuming, of course, that I would be entitled to such breaks. I could arrange for my cat to take over duties during them.*
>
> *I look forward to hearing from you.*
>
> *Yours sincerely*
>
> *Stephen Gold*
>
> *[Sitting down and not up]*

> **From: Waitrose Customer Service**
>
> Sent: 28/10/19 19:27
>
> To: STEPHEN GOLD
>
> *Thank you for the offer of manning the lifts, however I am going to have to decline your help as I have now spoken to Jasmine, one of the duty managers in store this evening. She has advised that she will bring this to the attention of the maintenance team to get this fixed as quickly as possible, as we do not want to continue to confuse our customers anymore.*

Apologies that this had not been rectified when you first queried this. I hope you will accept a small gift card so you can purchase that lovely chocolate cake you so desire. Please reply with your full home address and I will get this arranged for you. If you'd like to comment on the service I've given you, click the link below to take part in our quick survey – as a thank you, we'll also enter you into our monthly prize draw where you could win Waitrose & Partners gift vouchers.

[link provided]

Kind regards

Kristina

Waitrose & Partners Customer Care

And that labelling problem again

FROM: STEPHEN GOLD

Sent: 29 JULY 2018 19:05

TO: customersupport@waitrose.co.uk

I plead guilty to being a frequent complainant but I merely seek to encourage you to comply with the law in relation to the price labelling of goods which you offer for sale. Given the spirit in which I draw attention to my experiences at your Richmond-upon-Thames branch, it is my earnest hope that I shall not be barred from it or any of your other branches and that you will take your responsibilities more seriously.

Twice last week I had cause to complain at Richmond (disregarding the episode of the water melon which due to an aberration attributable to the intense heat I had selected for purchase notwithstanding that it was gashed and soft to the touch on one section and for which I received a refund and a free replacement in accordance with your policy).

The first cause for complaint was over a sign which represented that upon purchase of an Alpro Almond 'milk' an Alpro Go On would be provided free of charge. Do take a look at the sign.

In characters the size of fleas you may be able to discern (provided you are wearing strong spectacles) '150g'. Those characters are not repeated on the prominent red section of the sign. It would have made sense if you were intending to ensure that no customers were misled to have displayed the free product next to the priced product. But no. The free product was apparently to be found in a refrigerator on the opposite side of the aisle. My shopping companion who was in charge of the proposed selection enquired of a senior member of staff as he was flying along the aisle as to the location of the free product whereupon he pointed to the opposite refrigerator and continued his journey. My companion selected the product he had pointed to and in due course

I presented the checkout assistant with both products. Having paid and checked my till receipt I found I had been charged for the Go On. Customer Service informed me that the selected Go On was a larger size than 150g. We had been misled. The assistant there mentioned that there had been a number of enquiries that day by customers about the size of the product being provided free. Of course, there had. A number of other customers taken in like us. 'Go On' you might say. You had the good sense to refund the price charged for the ostensibly free product.

The second cause for complaint was the charge for two tubs of 'Happy Pear' hummus which according to the price label were on promotion at two for the price of one, yet once again this was not picked up at the till and I was charged for two tubs instead of one. This I discovered on checking my receipt and I obtained a refund. Here is the till receipt.

Two instances of price misrepresentation experienced in one week in the same store by one customer. How much in a year is Waitrose wrongly inducing its customers nationwide to hand over? Not only is this unlawful but it is reckless and grossly unfair on your customers, the majority of whom I fancy do not check their receipts.

On the way out of the store (before entering the lift which is STILL auto announcing it is going down when in fact it is going up) I encountered an acquaintance who was having trouble with her car park ticket for the fourth time. I suspect she thinks I have been hard on you in the past but by the look of fury on her face she probably reckons I have let you off lightly.

Yours sincerely

Stephen Gold

FROM: Waitrose Customer Service

Date: 3 AUGUST 2018 13.36

TO: Stephen Gold

Thanks for letting us know we charged you incorrectly at our Richmond branch recently. I'm sorry about this and can imagine how frustrating this must have been for you.

Mistakes at our tills are thankfully rare, but thank you for letting us know about the double scanned item that happened recently. Thank you also for bringing the poor quality melon to our attention. I'm pleased the branch were able to refund you for these issues, and we've discussed with the branch to try and prevent similar issues in future.

I'm sorry you also felt our recent promotion for Alpro milk was misleading. We do take great pains to make sure all our prices are clear on promotional shelves, and have rigorous procedures for checking that our prices are correct. I can assure you we don't intend to mislead our customers in any way and we will certainly consider your comments at our future reviews.

Kind regards

Paul

Waitrose Customer Care

Case Reference: 05118145

And *M&S* revisited.

On 01/05/2016 21:16, STEPHEN GOLD *wrote:*

I regret that I am back but to report a different transgression. In your George Street, Richmond branch today you were displaying bottles of Oudinot medium-dry rose champagne at a price of £21. However, the price programmed into the till just a few feet away was £23. Your assistant sought to charge the higher price – "The till is always right," she said – but when I pointed out the representation of the lower price she dealt with the matter properly and courteously, taking the lower price. I have lost nothing but how many customers had been charged the higher price believing they were purchasing for the lower price? I have had to tackle your good friends at Waitrose about this practice. I hope it is not going to catch on with you and that you will be more careful. Do you realise it could get you into deep trouble?

Yours sincerely

Stephen Gold

Good afternoon Stephen

Our ref: 355048

I am sorry that you were charged the incorrect amount for our Oudinot medium-dry rose champagne in our store.

It is never our intention to let our customers down but clearly an error occurred within our system on this occasion. It is a new offer at the moment with £2 off selected wine products and this had not been programmed into the till.

I have forwarded your experience to the Store Management team who will review how this offer could have been missed. The store will ensure this does not happen again.

I do apologise and thank you for highlighting this error and ensuring we rectify it.

I hope this won't deter you from shopping with us and that you'll enjoy your next visit. Thanks again for getting in touch.

Kind regards
Julie R
Retail Customer Services
Your M&S Customer Service

Coffee break

A bit of light relief from unfairness, albeit that it covers a dilemma. Which size coffee cup to order when patronising an *M&S* cafeteria? You might have thought that the quantity of coffee injected into a cup would always increase pro rata with the size of the cup. Not so, it appears. Medium and large get two shots: large gets more milk. So if you thought you would be able to keep awake for a couple of days by downing a large as against a medium, you would be mistaken. I thought you should know.

My short exchange with *M&S* Customer Service reveals all. By the way, they came back to me within five hours of my enquiry. Really on the ball. Must be drinking medium or small with two shots.

On 24/06/2018 11:09, STEPHEN GOLD wrote:

Subject :Contact Us-In-store service and feedback

Product Description: coffees

Store Name: Havant

Date of visit: 23/06/2018

Your coffees (and other beverages) come in three sizes. In relation to coffees, I have noticed that the larger the size, the weaker the drink. This leads me to the conclusion that the same quantity of coffee goes into the cup, whatever the size ordered and that the larger the size, the more the milk (and froth). Am I correct? If so, I shall restrict myself to the smallest size in future. If I am incorrect, what is the explanation for the weakness I have identified, please?

On 24/06/2018 15.53 M&S SERVICE Team replied:

Hi Stephen

Thanks for getting in touch with us about our coffee. I'm sorry to hear you've found the coffee is weaker the larger the cup size.

I've just spoken to Gemma, who works in the cafe at Havant, and she's let me know that one shot of coffee is used for a small cup and two shots of coffee are used for the medium and large cups. The large cup will be slightly weaker as this will have more milk in than the medium. She also let me know that they do offer extra shots but these are for a small charge.

I hope this has helped Stephen. Thanks again for getting in touch and we look forward to seeing you in store again soon.

Best wishes

Sian

Retail Customer Services

Your M&S Customer Service

Use by and best before dates

Back to more serious business. Yes, I know that coffee is serious. Generally, all foods up for sale must be marked with a date of minimum durability. Use by dates are concerned with safety and reserved for food that goes off quickly. Best before dates are concerned with quality. Food may be safe to eat after this date but may not be at its best. *M&S* took to displaying fruit and vegetable one day after the use by date had expired. I observed this while on duty at its Richmond-upon-Thames store. For example, on 6 October 2017 it was proclaiming that fruit and veg were best before 6 October 2017. I took that to mean that it was best if consumed on 5 October 2017 at the latest.

M&S just didn't get it. Take a look.

FROM: Stephen Gold

TO: Marks & Spencer

Date *On 06/10/2017 17:02*

Today you had on display white peaches, blackberries and tomatoes all marked 'best before 06 Oct 2017'. Today is the 06 Oct 2017! There was no apparent price reduction because of the age of this produce. This is not the first time I have observed this sort of thing happening at the store. It is not good enough, is it? I have photographed the 'offending' produce. I would like your comments. Would you recommend that no fruit is purchased from the store or that customers take a magnifying glass with them to the store and scrutinise every perishable product with it before selecting for purchase?

FROM: Marks & Spencer

TO: Stephen Gold

On 8 Oct 2017, at 10:09,

Hello Stephen

The quality of our food is extremely important to us. We want you to enjoy our food at its very best and we carry out extensive tests to establish the natural life of each of our products. We also want you to enjoy food that is as natural as possible and free from any unnecessary additives or preservatives. As a result, some of our foods may have a shorter life than our competitors' products. We believe the benefits of our approach outweigh the negatives of a shorter shelf life, and help us achieve the higher quality our customers have come to expect.

We label all our food with dates, so you can see how long it should last and encourage customers to check this information before they decide to buy.

We do reduce some of our products at the end of the day, these are clearly labelled with a yellow sticker. It's important to note that this doesn't apply to all products.

I hope this helps and thanks for getting in touch.

Have a great day.

Kind regards

Richard Retail Customer Services

Your M&S Customer Service

FROM: Stephen Gold

TO: M&S

On 08/10/2017 12:48

Dear Richard

Thank you for your message but you appear to have responded to me using an inappropriate template. I respectfully suggest that you re-read my original message and refer the matter to your manager. You are not seriously suggesting that you deliberately display fruit for sale when it is beyond its best date for consumption and at a non-discounted price to boot, are you? This would represent an outrageous practice for a leading supermarket and suggest you are trading in old perishable stock.

Regards

Stephen Gold

FROM: M&S

TO: Stephen Gold Service Team

Date: 9 October 2017 14:06:17 BST

Dear Stephen

I'm sorry you're unhappy with the response from my colleague and I can understand you're disappointed about your recent visit to one of our stores.

Just to clarify, we can sell items with a 'best before' date on the same day, as they are not off. What items get reduced at the end of the day is down to the Store Manager's discretion. We encourage our customers to check the dates on the products, so they can make the informed decision to buy them.

I've recorded all your comments on our central system, could you

> please let me know the store you've visited, so I can let the Store Manager know about this.
>
> Thanks for getting in touch. I look forward to hearing from you.
>
> Kind regards
>
> Marcel
>
> Retail Customer Services
>
> Your M&S Customer Service

Tesco had a spot of bother in 2020 over use by dates. Local authority environmental health officers had conducted visits to three of its stores and found food items on display after their use by dates. The company was charged with offences under the Food Safety and Hygiene (England) Regulations 2013. *Tesco* sought to argue that, no matter the date of display, the items were actually quite safe for consumption and wanted to call expert evidence to back this up. The High Court ruled that it couldn't. The law deemed the items to have been unsafe and evidence to the contrary could not be relied on. Stores were under an obligation to label highly perishable foods with a use by date and they could not be placed on display after that date. However – and watch out for this – food could be relabelled when that date had passed provided it was reassessed for risk.

Chapter 65

Small Print

And bigger print

We have seen how a trader's attempts at wriggling out of legal responsibility for breaching their specific obligations to a consumer which are treated as part of the contract under the Consumer Rights Act 2015 can be thwarted (see chapter 63). That same Act may well thwart attempts at doing you down in a multitude of other ways where you are a consumer and your contract was made with a trader on or after 1 October 2015. There are similar rules for contracts made before then which you will find in the Unfair Contract Terms Act 1977 and the Unfair Terms in Consumer Contracts Regulations 1999 but the new laws are an improvement for the consumer.

Having a laugh

A contract term that the law now says is unfair will not bind you. Yes, you can laugh in its face unless for some reason it suits you to rely on it. If it looks unfair and smells unfair, the probability is that it will be unfair under the law. It must not cause a significant imbalance in the rights and obligations of each side which is to your detriment. If the term is ambiguous so that it could have different meanings then the meaning which is the most favourable to you as the consumer will prevail.

Train tickets and car park notices

The fairness law applies not just to written contracts but to verbal contracts too and not just to standard form contracts which are offered to one and all on a 'take it or leave it' basis but to contracts which have been individually negotiated. And it applies to what are called *notices* which catch a written or verbal announcement or other communication which creates a contract. This would typically include a car park sign proclaiming that by leaving your car there you will be agreeing to pay 50p per 15 minutes or part thereof, mortgage your home if you stay longer than two hours and kill yourself if you lose your ticket. However, the law does not catch an employment or apprenticeship contract (although there may well be other laws which can come to the rescue of a downtrodden employee or apprentice).

Core law

You have a problem when it comes to *core terms* of the contract because the general rule is that you cannot challenge them as being unfair. A *core term* is one that goes to the core of the contract. I know, I know! It will specify the main subject matter of the contract. What it is you are buying or hiring or what service you are getting. What you are paying. This means that if you decide you don't like the goods or services involved or you have paid more than they are worth, you cannot use the unfairness law to effectively escape from or reopen the deal.

But you could still challenge a term that allowed the trader, without your consent, to change the goods or services you were due to be getting. Also, there are certain price terms which would be susceptible to challenge. A term which provided when and how the trader might increase the price you agreed to pay would be one: or a term which said you had to pay an administration charge but no service was being performed by the trader in exchange for it, because the challenge would not be based on value. Similarly, a term in an agreement made by a landlord with their property letting agency that if the landlord came to sell that property, they would have to pay commission to the agency even though they offered nothing and did nothing to achieve the sale. And if the object or effect of a core term is to allow the trader to get away with something that the law says is probably unfair (see below), it can be challenged.

Okay then. Whether or not the term is a *core* job might involve a head scratch. If it is *core*, hold on to your weep. There may still be hope. A *core term* will not be binding on you unless it is transparent and prominent. It has to be in plain and intelligible language and, if in writing, it has to be legible but remember that verbal contracts must also be fair. And it must be prominent so that an average consumer who is reasonably well-informed, observant and circumspect would have been aware of it. Nevertheless, the reality is that we do not read every single word which appears in a contract and most judges would not expect you to do so. In deciding whether a term is transparent and prominent, the court will look at such things as technical mumbo jumbo, long sentences, killer text the size of a pinprick and whether, though it is burdensome on the consumer, it appears at the bottom left of the 126th page of the contract. Hidden extras could well be successfully challenged. The more onerous on you the consumer, the clearer the meaning and the greater the prominence that the law would expect to be given to the term. Beware, however, of the trader trick of surrounding a detestable term which appears in giant flashing light text with other terms equally prominent with the intended result that you ignore the lot of them.

Grey talk

In the Consumer Rights Act 2015 you will find a list of terms which may be considered by the court to be unfair. It's called the *grey list* and you will find it in schedule 2 to the Act. I suppose we could reproduce schedule 2 here and now but that could add another £1.50 to the price of this book which you might be buying on the internet for 1p plus postage so I'll tell you what. Let's have a look at the juiciest terms in the list which is the Act's way of giving guidance on how it works and at a series of examples of terms that would fall foul of the guidance. Some of them have actually appeared in contracts and traders have been forced to delete or change them. If one or more of the terms with which you reckon you have been stitched up is described in the list or is similar to the description, then you may well be onto a winner. These are potentially unfair terms which the court could say were not binding on you. Some may be blacklisted and automatically unenforceable against you although deft word play by the trader may disguise the fact that they fall into this category.

Some are patently and blatantly unenforceable: some are unenforceable because the trader has gone too far with terms that are too wide and exclude or restrict liability for every conceivable eventuality whereas exclusion or limitation in certain eventualities might have been fair.

Grey (nasty) list

(and note that some of the terms could fall into more than one category).

A term that has the object or effect of limiting the trader's liability if you die or are injured because of some act or omission on their part

Like:

"If we kill you due to our cock-up we won't have to pay your estate more than £10,000."

A term which has the object or effect of inappropriately excluding or limiting the legal rights of the consumer in relation to the trader in the event of total or partial performance or inadequate performance by the trader of any of the contractual obligations including the option of offsetting a debt owed to the trader against any claim which the consumer may have against the trader

Like:

"Sold as seen."

"This car wash is used entirely at the customer's own risk and we will not under any circumstances be liable if it damages your property while on these premises."

"The company does not accept responsibility for any fire protection equipment it has supplied in the event of fire." [really!!!]

"We will not be responsible for any injuries to pregnant passengers."

"No guarantee is given as to the use or mileage of the vehicle and any information provided on these matters is without prejudice."

"The hirer shall not make any claim for loss or damage to any property left in the vehicle."

"No complaints can be accepted after the carpet has been cut."

"It is the customer's responsibility to make sure that goods have been tried before delivery and that they are fit for the purpose for which they were intended."

"Your signature constitutes acceptance that you are 100% satisfied with the goods."

"The company will not be responsible for consequential losses due to damage caused by the installation."

"The company will not be responsible for damage or theft of clothing or other possessions brought into the gymnasium."

"We will not be liable for any monetary loss."

"Payment is due on completion. The buyer shall not be entitled to withhold payment by reason of any minor defect."

"You must pay the balance due under this contract without any deduction."

A term which has the object or effect of permitting the trader to retain sums paid by the consumer where the consumer decides not to conclude or perform the contract, without providing for the consumer to receive compensation of an equivalent amount from the trader where the trader is the party cancelling the contract

Like:

"If the customer falls into arrears for not less than two monthly instalments, this agreement shall stand automatically cancelled and the deposit held by the trader shall be forfeited. If the company cancels this agreement for reasons beyond its control, it may retain the deposit it holds."

A term which has the object or effect of requiring that, where the consumer decided not to conclude or perform the contract, the consumer must pay the trader a disproportionately high sum in compensation or for services which have not been supplied

which we will look at in conjunction with:

A term which has the object or effect of requiring a consumer who fails to fulfil his obligations under the contract to pay a proportionately high sum in compensation

A host of dodgy terms are covered here like requirements to:

- pay excessive interest on arrears such as a rate well over and above what the trader is paying its bank on a loan or overdraft;
- pay the whole contract price if you cancel without grounds to do so but the trader could find another customer to fill your shoes;
- when a contract runs indefinitely (say, from month to month instead of for a fixed period), to pay an excessive amount of money to the trader for not having given them the amount of notice they were looking for; or
- pay on ending a contract an excessive disconnection fee (which is a disguised penalty).

Terms such as this are loosely called penalties and until recently courts would disapply them both under general contract law and under the consumer fairness law which applied before the Consumer Rights Act 2015 came into force. If the defaulting consumer was being told to pay the trader an amount which was over and above the trader's genuine advance estimate of the financial loss they would suffer because of the default then the courts would say this amounted to a penalty and was unenforceable.

There has been a shift in the law in this area with the decisions of the Supreme Court in November 2015 in two cases including that of Barry Beavis who overstayed his welcome in a parking bay. Courts will in future be asking themselves whether a term which costs money to the consumer who defaults is simply to punish them or whether it has a legitimate purpose, and, if so, what the purpose is. If the consequences of the term are extortionate or extravagant in relation to that purpose, the term will be struck down and the consumer will be off the hook. The fact that the trader has come up with a term which gives them more money than they will lose as a result of the consumer's default, whilst relevant, will not of itself make the term a penalty and so unenforceable and unfair.

We can see this test at work in the car parking case. Let's go to the Riverside Retail Park in Chelmsford where visitors could park for free for up to two hours but if they stayed put for longer they would be charged £85. Mr Beavis left his car for a total of 2 hours 56 minutes. He subsequently received a demand for the £85 although he was told this would be discounted to £50 if he paid up within 14 days. Reckoning that £85 for a 56 minute overstay was ridiculously steep, Mr Beavis decided he would pay neither the £85 nor the £50 and when he was sued in the county court he defended the case. He lost there and lost again when he appealed to the Court of Appeal. It was a case of general public importance and thousands of other claims involving the same legal issues were dependent on its outcome. That is how the case ended up in the Supreme Court.

The Supreme Court ruled that the £85 was not a penalty and was fair under the law which was in operation when Mr Beavis was 56 minutes late. The result would be the same now as that part of the law has been replanted in the Consumer Rights Act 2015 which we are now enjoying (aren't we?). The £85 had two objects: to deter drivers from staying for too long and so depriving other shoppers from being able to park, and to provide an income stream to the company which ran the park so that it could operate the scheme and make a profit. This did not give the company a licence to charge what it liked but there was no reason to suppose that £85 was out of all proportion.

A term which has the object or effect of enabling the trader to alter the terms of the contract unilaterally without a valid reason which is specified in the contract*

Like:

"If for any reason the company is unable to supply a particular item it will notify the customer. It will normally replace it with goods of equivalent or superior standard."

"The company may at any time vary or add to these terms as it deems necessary."

*The trader can legitimately vary in this way if the contract is not for a fixed period and requires the trader to give you reasonable notice of their intention to do so and leaves you free to escape from the contract if you are unhappy.

A term which has the object or effect of limiting the trader's obligation to respect commitments undertaken by the trader's agents or making the trader's commitments subject to compliance with a particular formality

Like:

"The company reserves the right to sub-contract any of its obligations under this agreement without the consent of the customer and the company shall not in the event of doing so be liable for the acts or omissions of any agent so sub-contracted whether or not the company would be liable to the customer if the acts or omissions were those of the company and whether or not loss may be incurred by the customer."

"Proceedings for breach of this agreement must be brought within 12 months of delivery of the goods."

"You must give written notice of any claim within three days of receipt of the goods."

A term which has the object or effect of excluding or hindering the consumer's right to take legal action or exercise any other legal remedy, in particular by:

a. **requiring the consumer to take disputes exclusively to arbitration not covered by legal provisions;**

b. **unduly restricting the evidence available to the consumer; or**

c. **imposing on the consumer a burden of proof which, according to the applicable law, should lie with another party to the contract.**

Like:

"Although this contract was entered into in England and Wales, the customer is resident in England and Wales and the goods and services supplied hereunder were so supplied in England and Wales, any claim by the customer for the alleged breach of any provision of this contract on the part of the company must be brought in France and the law governing such claim and this agreement shall be the law of France."

"Any dispute between the parties under this agreement must be referred to arbitration* by an arbitrator selected by the company before whom the customer shall not be entitled to legal representation and the decision of the arbitrator shall be binding on the company and the customer and shall be final."

*The drive is relentless to persuade warring parties to take their disputes to an arbitrator (or for some other form of alternative dispute resolution such as mediation or adjudication) (see chapter 10). But it may not be on to force arbitration down a consumer's throat and deny them the right to take their case to court instead. Any attempt to do so may be branded as unfair and so unenforceable. In fact, section 91 of the Arbitration Act 1996 automatically outlaws anything in a contract which says that arbitration is compulsory where it relates to a claim for £5,000 or under. It is blacklisted and so it does not have to be shown that it is unfair.

"The company shall not be under any obligation to provide any records, data or documentation relating to any dispute between the parties which was created more than 12 months before the customer gave notice of the dispute to the company."

"The meter reading shall be conclusive proof of its accuracy and of the volume of gas/electricity/water consumed under this agreement."

"The company shall not be under any obligation to entertain any claim against it by the customer unless the customer proves beyond any doubt that the company is in breach of any of its obligations under this agreement."

And some miscellaneous other terms which have been regarded as unfair

"The company shall not be responsible for any assistance given with measuring."

"If a staff member assists you without our written authority we will not be responsible."

"We will accept liability for defective goods only to the extent that we can make a corresponding claim under the manufacturer's warranty in our favour."

"The customer agrees it is fair and reasonable to exclude liability for negligence."

"Your installation is guaranteed for five years provided the invoice is paid in full upon completion of the work."

"The management reserves the right to refuse access to the member without giving any reason for doing so."

In court

The outcome of a court claim against you may well depend on whether certain wording of the contract passes the fairness test or is automatically blacklisted. The judge is now obliged to consider fairness whether or not you, as the consumer, have raised it as an issue in your defence to the claim. But this obligation will not apply unless the judge has before them sufficient legal and factual material to enable them to consider fairness. There is a very real danger that the judge will not have sufficient factual material to come to a sensible conclusion on what can be a difficult matter. Then the judge could adjourn the case to another day and direct each side to put in evidence on the subject. Otherwise, the judge could decide that, because sufficient material is absent and you haven't take any point on fairness, the question of fairness will have to go out of the window. So don't take a chance. Raise fairness in your defence. And unless it is plain that the term is not automatically blacklisted, it may be prudent to start off by alleging blacklisting. That way, if the court is with you on blacklisting that would make the term automatically unenforceable and it would not need to trouble with deciding on fairness.

Case no 21P0000678

IN THE COUNTY COURT MONEY CLAIMS CENTRE

BETWEEN

WHITEWASH LIMITED Claimant

- and -

CLIVE TROUBLESORE Defendant

DEFENCE

1. In so far as the claimant relies on clause 16(3) (clause 16(3)) of the contract between the parties referred to in paragraph 2 of the particulars of claim (the contract), the defendant says that clause 16(3) is not binding on him because it excludes or restricts the claimant's liability as covered by section 31 of the Consumer Rights Act 2015 (the Act) and, further and in the alternative, it is unfair within the meaning of section 62 the Act.*

2. If (which is denied) clause 16(3) is a core term of the contract within section 64(1) of the Act, the defendant says that it is still assessable for fairness under section 62 of the Act because it is not transparent within section 64(3) or prominent within section 64(4) of the Act.

3. Further and in the alternative, the defendant says that clause 16(3) is ambiguous in that it could mean either that notice by the defendant that he did not wish to renew the contract had to be given so as to expire within the initial fixed period of the contract or it could mean that such notice could expire outside such fixed period so long as the defendant made a pro rata payment for the period of the notice which so fell outside the fixed period. Therefore, and in accordance with section 69 of the Act, the defendant says that the latter meaning should prevail.

4. For the purposes of the matters alleged at paragraphs 1 and 2 of the defence, the defendant relies on the subject matter of the contract and all the circumstances existing when clause 16(3) was agreed and to all the other terms of the contract and in particular (but not exhaustively) on the following factors:

    a. the claimant neglected to explain clause 16(3) to the defendant before the contract was concluded notwithstanding that, as the claimant well knew or should have known, the defendant had no experience of contracts of this nature or of the operation of contract renewal terms and conditions.

> b. the language of clause 16(3) is highly technical and complicated.
>
> c. the font size of clause 16(3) is small.
>
> d. clause 16(3) is not in a prominent place and appears among other terms and conditions which are of less and/or little importance.
>
> e. the defendant was given no indication by the claimant in the contract document or otherwise of the importance or significance of clause 16(3).
>
> f. the claimant neglected to afford the defendant sufficient opportunity to read and/or to attempt to understand clause 16(3) or the other terms and conditions of the contract in that the claimant's representative tendered a biro to the defendant so that he could sign the contract at the same time as he presented the contract to him and told the defendant that he was in a hurry and he had 20 other customers to see that day who wanted to "sign up with us for this great deal before it is withdrawn."
>
> g. the period of notice of non-renewal required of the defendant was too long.
>
> h. the deadline fixed by the contract on the claimant's interpretation of the meaning of clause 16(3) for the giving of notice of non-renewal was too early.
>
> I believe that the facts stated in this defence are true. I understand that proceedings for contempt of court may be brought against anyone who makes, or causes to be made, a false statement in a document verified by a statement of truth without an honest belief in its truth
>
> (signed) Clive Troublesore
>
> Defendant
>
> Dated 14 July 2021

*Adapt if you are not alleging that the term is blacklisted under section 47 of the Act.

The next defence could be suitable in a Barry Beavis type car parking claim or any other claim involving the consumer being required to make a payment to the consumer for terminating a contract early.

Case no 21P0000678

IN THE COUNTY COURT MONEY CLAIMS CENTRE

BETWEEN

WHITEWASH LIMITED Claimant

- and -

CLIVE TROUBLESORE Defendant

DEFENCE

1. In so far as the claimant relies on clause 16(3) (clause 16(3)) of the contract between the parties referred to in paragraph 2 of the particulars of claim (the contract), the defendant says that clause 16(3) is not binding on him because it is void at common law as a penalty in that-

    a. its sole purpose was to punish the defendant if he defaulted under clause 16(3); and

    b. there was no legitimate purpose for the imposition of the payments the defendant would be liable to make under clause 16(3) if he defaulted under it or, if (which is denied) there was such a legitimate purpose, the consequences so imposed were extortionate and/or extravagant in relation to such purpose.

2. The defendant says that the following factors in particular are relevant to the matters alleged at sub-paragraphs 1 (a) and (b) above-

    a. the payments the defendant would be liable to make under clause 16(3) if he defaulted under it were in excess of the loss the claimant was likely to suffer as a result of such default;

    b. the payments the defendant would be liable to make under clause 16(3) if he defaulted under it were in excess of any estimate, genuine or otherwise, which the claimant made or might have made if he had conducted an estimate of the loss the claimant was likely to suffer as a result of such default;

    c. upon entering into the contract the subject of the claim, the defendant had no bargaining power in that the provisions of clause 16(3) were not open for negotiation and the defendant was obliged to 'take it or leave it' if he wished to take advantage of the service or facility available to the defendant under the contract; and

    d. the matters set out at paragraph 5 of this defence.

3. Further and in the alternative, the defendant says that clause 16(3) is unfair within the meaning of section 62 the Act.

4. If (which is denied) clause 16(3)is a core term of the contract within section 64(1) of the Act, the defendant says that it is still assessable for fairness under section 62 of the Act because it is not transparent within section 64(3) or prominent within section 64(4) of the Act.

5. For the purposes of the matters set out at paragraphs 3 and 4 of the defence [continue as at paragraph 4 of the draft defence above, adapting appropriately].

I believe that the facts stated in this defence are true. I understand that proceedings for contempt of court may be brought against anyone who makes, or causes to be made, a false statement in a document verified by a statement of truth without an honest belief in its truth.

(signed) Clive Troublesore

Defendant

Dated 14 July 2021

Who claims?

So far, we have assumed that the trader has claimed against you on the basis that you have not paid up under a blacklisted or unfair contract term. As it happens, you don't have to wait to be sued before you take the point that the term is not binding on you. You can always ask the local authority's trading standards department, the Competition and Markets Authority or the Consumers' Association to help you – they are among a group of regulators which can take enforcement action against a trader who flouts the Consumer Rights Act 2015 – but it could be that circumstances demand some swift and definitive action in your particular case which might not be achieved through a regulator so that you know where you stand. For example, when you are anxious to escape from a contract, do you risk ignoring a term which calls for you to give what seems to be an interminably long period of notice to end the contract in the hope that it is unenforceable or do you honour it? So long as you reckon your case is a good one, you can bring your own county court claim against the trader and ask the court to make a declaration to the effect that the term does not bind you. But beware: if you do this and lose, you could have to pay the trader's legal bill. Your ability to take the initiative could give you a useful bargaining tool with the trader, especially if they twitch at the prospect of a court declaring the term to be unenforceable, possibly in a blaze of publicity, and so run the real risk that thousands of other customers, displeased like you, will get to know that the term is useless.

> *"Dear Trader*
>
> *It is my misfortune to have entered into contract numbered XBF1239555666/yx with your company dated 14 July 2021. I wish to bring the contract to an end but I am unwilling to make the payments specified under clause 16(3) which suggests that they would be due upon me doing so. I now have the benefit of expert advice on clause 16(3) which is that no payments as specified could be lawfully demanded of me because the clause is not binding on me. The reasons for this are that the payments amount to penalties at common law and that the clause is unfair within section 62 of the Consumer Rights Act 2015.*

The advice given to me takes account of the judgments of the Supreme Court in Parking Eye Limited v Beavis and another appeal on 4 November 2015.

In the above circumstances, I require you to confirm to me within seven days of your receipt of this letter, that your company will release me from the contract as from the date of your confirmation and that your company will not make any claim against me for any moneys allegedly due or allegedly to fall due under the contract at any time. In the event of receiving that confirmation within the period mentioned, I agree not to publish to any third person that this confirmation has been given save and except as I might be compelled by law to do so. If I do not hear from you as required and within the period specified, I shall institute proceedings against your company in the county court for a declaration that clause 16(3) is not binding on me and for an order that your company should pay the costs of the proceedings."

"But I'm not a ruddy consumer, Gold"

Calm down. If, as a non-consumer, you have signed up to the other party's standard terms of business – maybe you are a professional property owner and apparently saddled with an estate agent's standard contract – then any term which excuses the other party for a contract breach has to be reasonable before it can be used against you. That's the Unfair Contract Terms Act 1977 at work. It's down to the other party to prove that the condition under attack is reasonable. The court will look at such factors as the strength of each party's bargaining position; whether you had the opportunity of transacting with another business without being bound by the same sort of condition; and whether you knew or ought to have known of the existence and extent of the condition. On that last point, previous dealings with the people you contracted with will be taken into account.

One of my all times favourites

Be you a consumer or a trader there is always one of my favourite cases you might be able to fall back on where, for whatever reason, the legislation we have been looking at doesn't cover your situation. Alternatively, perhaps you simply want to demonstrate how senior judges were prepared to do justice and how your judge might try and follow in their footsteps. Over to *Interfoto Picture Library Ltd v Stiletto Visual Programmes Ltd* decided by the Court of Appeal in 1987. Interfoto ran a photographic transparency library. Stiletto were in advertising. Stiletto telephoned Interfoto and asked whether they had any 1950's transparencies which were wanted for a presentation. The same day, Interfoto sent them round 47 transparencies which were packed in a bag. Also in the bag was a delivery note. It specified the return date and included nine prominently printed conditions set out in four columns. Condition 2 required the return of the transparencies within 14 days and imposed a fee of £5 plus VAT per day per transparency for every day of lateness. Stiletto went over the return date and so received an invoice for …. £3,783.50! You guessed it. They refused to pay and were sued. The Court of

Appeal knocked the invoice down to £350. It was felt that Stiletto could not have known of the "very high and exorbitant charge" as their attention had not been drawn to Condition 2. That should have been done. This ruling reflected the words of Lord Denning in a previous case. The more unreasonable was a condition, the greater the notice of it that had to be given to the customer. "Some clauses which I have seen," he said "would need to be printed in red ink on the face of the document with a red hand pointing to it before the notice of it could be held to be sufficient."

The impossible dream

A condition in a contract which is impossible to comply with may well be unreasonable under the Consumer Rights Act and so not binding on you. It may also not bind you simply because it is impossible to comply with it and that's a handy argument for when you are a trader who is the customer and the Act does not benefit you. Have a look at chapter 41 and the case involving PayPal where it had to PayOut.

Part 9

HOME UNDER ATTACK

Chapter 66

Behind With The Mortgage

Keeping out the lender

I made my first repossession order against a borrower who owed more than a million in 2011. Now that level of mortgage indebtedness comes without shock. Many fail to treat mortgage repayments with the priority they command: many just don't have the cash to pay. Either way, the lender's repossession of your home can more often than not be avoided if you keep your head above the sand. And more often than not there's hope right up to the nanosecond before you and your family are evicted. What needs to be appreciated by every borrower is that the lender requires an order of the court to evict through the bailiff or a High Court enforcement agent and it is the judge who decides whether you must go and not the lender.

Talking to the animals

Well, actually, not all lenders graze in the zoo and even some of the aggressive ones have been obliged by regulatory control and media publicity to temper their attitude with a modicum of reasonableness. Indeed, most mortgage lenders have honoured what the Financial Conduct Authority has expected of them during Covid-19 providing you with support tailored to your individual circumstances including allowing mortgage payment holidays which were due to come to an end by 31 July 2021. Alas, these holidays have not excused payment of missed instalments for ever and borrowers are now having to address with their lender how they will clear the arrears which have clocked up due to the virus. What will continue to help keep lenders in line is a pre-action protocol in residential mortgage cases and which was revamped in April 2015. It contains rules which lenders are expected to follow before they ask the court to evict. If your lender has failed to comply, you can legitimately ask the judge at the hearing of any possession claim that is brought to put off the case for a period. "Please adjourn the hearing so that the lender can do what it should have done and has failed to do – follow the protocol. It has jumped the gun." This will not give you a defence which could lead to the case being thrown out but it could earn you valuable time.

Under the protocol (which does not apply to buy-to-let mortgages) and before any court proceedings are started, the lender must provide you with information about where you can get help, the amount of the current monthly instalments and what you have paid over the last two years and the amount of the arrears (including an estimate of any interest or charges that may be added). A reasonable request by you to change the day of the month you make your payment or how you pay must be considered and, if refused, you are to be given written reasons for the refusal within a reasonable period. The lender must respond promptly to any payment proposal you make. If it is rejecting a proposal then you should have its written reasons within ten business days of making the proposal (that excludes weekends, bank holidays, Good Friday and Christmas Day). Where the lender makes a payment proposal to you there should be sufficient details to enable you to understand its implications and you are to have a reasonable time to consider it. You have made an agreement to pay off the arrears and then broken it? Before starting a possession claim, the lender is to give you written warning at least 15 business days beforehand.

And there's more. The lender must consider not taking you to court when you can demonstrate to it that you have submitted a claim to the Department for Work and Pensions for mortgage interest help or universal credit, a mortgage protection policy insurer or a local authority mortgage rescue or other homelessness prevention support scheme and have provided all the evidence needed to process that claim. But there must be a reasonable expectation that you will be eligible for the assistance you have sought and that you can cope with what has to be paid which will not come from the DWP or elsewhere. The lender should also consider waiting where you have a specific personal or financial difficulty and need time for debt advice or you have a reasonable expectation of an improvement in your financial circumstances and, where possible, can provide evidence of this. Again, the lender should consider holding on for a realistic period if you can show you have or will put the property up for sale at an appropriate price based on reasonable estate agents' or other professional advice. You are then expected to take reasonable steps to actively market the property. If, despite it all, the lender decides to press on to court it must give you written reasons for its decision at least five business days before starting proceedings.

You have made a complaint about the potential possession claim to the Financial Ombudsman's Service? If it is a genuine complaint, the lender must consider postponing starting proceedings until the Ombudsman has decided on it. Where the lender is not prepared to wait, it must tell you that it intends to start proceedings and its reasons for not waiting.

More of the protocol later.

You are taken to court

You will receive a claim form telling you where and when the case is to be heard. Along with the claim form will be a defence form. Complete it and return it to the court. It will ask whether you want the court to consider allowing you to pay the mortgage arrears by instalments and how much you can afford to pay in addition to the monthly instalments.

More talk – and pay

Before the hearing, keep up or start up a dialogue with the lender. There's nothing to stop you trying to reach an agreement with them even at that stage and even though you may believe them to be the biggest parasites in the financial services market. Not only talk, pay as well even though the payment may fall substantially short of the monthly instalment due and not even address the arrears. To say to the judge that you didn't pay a penny because you could not afford the amount required or because you were coming to court never goes down well. You can also source free legal advice about your situation before court (see chapter 7).

Thou shalt participate

Your lender must follow the same procedural route when bringing possession proceedings to have you evicted as a landlord must follow in a quest to have their tenant evicted. Covid-19 resulted in possession proceedings by both lender and landlord being halted for many months during which new possession cases could not be progressed and possession orders already made could not be enforced by county court bailiffs or High Court enforcement agents. An enormous backlog of possession cases has built up which the county court is slowly clearing. A modified procedure has been organised for the listing of cases which is live as we go to press. For how long it will last is anybody's guess. What is it? Possession cases which were halted – those started before 3 August 2020 – and those started afterwards are given a preliminary 'review' hearing date, though the subsequent final hearing date may be fixed at the same time. The object of the 'review' is to investigate whether the claim can be settled with the free assistance to the borrower of a duty scheme lawyer or other professional adviser. Where settlement cannot be achieved there and then, consideration will be given to mediation between lender and borrower through a pilot scheme funded by the government. It is very much in your best interests to participate in the review, if not personally at court, then remotely. The lender will have its representative at court or remotely participating. You probably won't see a judge on the day.

Should the case not settle at the review, a hearing before a judge will take place but no earlier than four weeks from the review. If there still remains any dispute between you and the lender come the day of the hearing, you stay away from that hearing at your peril. Again, a duty scheme lawyer or professional adviser should be on hand to help you at no charge. Where necessary, they should be prepared to speak on your behalf to the judge. You can take advantage of this independent help even though you may not have participated in the review or done anything else in response to the case up until then. The judge will listen to your proposals notwithstanding that you failed to return a defence but could be disgruntled because of that failure.

Getting technical

There are various rules to be complied with and steps to be taken by the court and the lender before this hearing. If they have not done as required and you would welcome the extra time that an adjournment of the hearing would afford you – perhaps to get a job or borrow from friends or family or progress your own marketing of the property for sale – that's when you can go for it and ask the judge to adjourn so that things can be put right. You ought to get a four week breather out of it at the least. Here is when you can go for it:

- when the lender has not followed the protocol (see above);
- when the lender's representative does not have with them at court a completed form – it's called form N123 – which shows what they have done to comply with the protocol;

- when the hearing date is less than four weeks after the lender issued their claim but that's unlikely to happen unless you are reading this in 2031 or later;
- when you have not been sent the court paperwork (the claim form and particulars of claim) at least three weeks before the hearing;
- when the particulars of claim omit some compulsory information such as:
  ◊ the amount needed to pay off the mortgage at a stated date no more than a fortnight after the claim started and showing how much in solicitors' costs and administration charges has been included;
  ◊ the rate of interest payable when the mortgage started, immediately before arrears arose and when the proceedings were started; and
  ◊ whether anyone who is claiming a right to occupy the property (we are effectively looking here at a spouse or civil partner with whom you have fallen out) has registered that claim at the land registry or land charges registry;
- when the lender has left compulsory information out of the court papers originally sent to you and it is intending to rely at the hearing on written evidence to plug the gap and to update what has been happening and that further evidence has not been sent to the court and you at least two days before the hearing;
- when the proceedings were started after 2 August 2020 and before 29 March 2021 and the lender failed to include with the documents sent to the court at the start, a statement setting out what knowledge it had as to the effect of the coronavirus pandemic on you and your dependants (and if it complied, the court would have passed on a copy of the statement to you);
- when within five days of receiving notice from the court of the date fixed for the hearing, the lender has not sent details of the proceedings including the hearing date, to the mortgaged property addressed *"to the tenant or occupier"* (the property may be a buy-to-let or you may have unlawfully let in a tenant without the lender's consent and, in either event, you are living elsewhere); the local authority's housing department; and any other lender (there may be a prior lender, this being a second mortgage or a subsequent third etc mortgage); or
- when before or at the hearing, the lender does not produce a land registry or land charges registry certificate – positive or negative – about any registration of a right to occupy the property (see above); official land registry documents showing what information about the property is on the land register (these are called *office copy documents*); a copy of the mortgage deed; and copies of the notices to *"the tenant or occupier"* etc (see above) and evidence that they have been sent.

The judge does have the power to shorten the time limits I have mentioned. It is more likely that you can persuade the judge not to shorten and to adjourn the hearing because of the lender's non-production of essential information or documentation if you can show that you will be prejudiced in some way by the rules not being kept to. If you can throw in some detail about oppressive behaviour towards you by the lender then more strength to your elbow. Don't be frightened to ask at the hearing to see any document or be given any information which you think is missing and should have been provided.

What the judge can do

The judge will usually have the option to take a course which would save you from eviction if that would be justified in the circumstances whether you have a repayment or interest only mortgage or a mixture of the two or are in arrears with a first, second or 11th mortgage. Judges have heard of Covid-19. They know only too well of the financial disaster it has been for such a large part of the population and they will be quick to assess whether the arrears accumulated in your case were partly or wholly attributable to the effects of the virus. And so you can expect them to be particularly sympathetic to virus inflicted situations. The stance of the lender will vary from one institution to another. Nevertheless, the interests of both sides have to be taken into account and the judge's discretion on what to do must be exercised within the confines of the law. It would be a mistake to go to the full hearing of the case believing that because the arrears were virus related, your security in the property is guaranteed. Also, the judge will not be able to save you where the mortgage required you to repay the lender *on demand* (for example, a mortgage securing a bank overdraft) or a mortgage has come to an end (where, for example, you had an endowment mortgage for 25 years and, at the end of the 25 years, the policy has matured and what has been paid out by the life company falls short of the amount you need to pay back to the lender). Here, your position will be weak though if you need just that little bit of extra time to vacate the property under a possession order or to repay the lender pretty quickly, the judge might just be prepared to grant it.

The lender may have accepted your proposals but want them incorporated in a court order and that is why it has started or continued the proceedings. This will happen where the lender is after a suspended order for possession which would involve the court ordering you to leave by a specified date but then to go on to paralyse the order: suspend it so long as you keep to the agreement which, no doubt, would be to pay the monthly instalment plus something each month off the arrears. In this situation, the suspended order could have been agreed on at any review which had taken place and in which you had participated. Of course, it may be that you would prefer the proceedings to be adjourned indefinitely to a suspended order and that is an option you could ask the judge to consider. Any such adjournment would be on the basis that you paid the agreed money but that the lender could return to court in the same proceedings if you defaulted.

Should you have made no proposals or any proposals made been rejected, then the lender will almost certainly ask you to be ordered to leave at the end of 28 days from the hearing, allowing it to sell the property, take for itself the amount required to pay off the mortgage and hand over any surplus to you. Any shortfall would be your liability and where it is one you cannot reasonably tackle then bankruptcy might be a sensible escape route (see chapter 48).

The case for the lender will be put by someone with legal qualifications or training whose mouth has been hired for the outing and, more often than not, a specialist in mortgage possession claims. Before the hearing, they may want to chat to you or any adviser you have helping you out: no harm in going along with that as it may be possible to negotiate a settlement even at the court doors. Some of these representatives have a heart and will not oppose (or only do so in a token way) any fair proposals you put to the judge whereas others follow to the letter the written instructions they have been given to secure an order ousting you after 28 days so that they can report back to the lender that they have won and they would like to do loads more cases for them, thank you very much. Occasionally, they only get paid for the outing if the court makes the very order they were instructed to obtain. Do not be intimidated by what they say to the judge. Again, it is the judge who decides on the court order, not the lender or their court representative.

Faced then with a demand for that 28 day order for possession, you put forward your proposals to the judge. The last thing the judge wants to see is somebody booted out of their home. But they do have to apply the law and take account of the interests of both sides.

"Please let me stay put with a suspended order"

To achieve a suspended order, you must be able to demonstrate not only that you can pay the monthly instalments but that you can clear the arrears by regular payments as soon as reasonably possible and certainly before the mortgage is due to come to an end. Say you have a mortgage which was granted for 25 years, there are five years left and the arrears are £8,000. In that event, the very least the judge would find acceptable would be a commitment to pay the monthly instalments plus £8,000 divided by five years (60 months) = £133.33 per month. With a second or subsequent mortgage there may be greater flexibility.

"But I can't afford monthly payments and £133.33"

Then you must set out to persuade the judge that what you cannot afford today, you may be able to afford tomorrow – or at some time in the foreseeable future. Perhaps your wife will be taking a part-time job, your son is going to get off his backside and obtain a job and make a meaningful contribution to the household finances or you are expecting promotion. The judge might make a suspended order for possession and fix a hearing at which the position will be reviewed when the change in your circumstances is likely to have materialised.

When you have no or only a meagre income and any help towards the mortgage from the Department for Work and Pensions or elsewhere will fall short of what is required to address the monthly payments let alone the arrears, the judge may still be prepared to adjourn the hearing for a short period if satisfied that there is a good chance of you obtaining a job offer (but not a bequest under the will of your aged uncle who you are intending to murder). The lender's representative will hit the roof at the idea of current monthly instalments not being met for any period at all. "Judge, you cannot interfere with my client's contractual right to receive the monthly instalments as and when they fall due. If the borrower cannot afford to pay these – and he accepts he cannot – then you have no alternative but to make a possession order today." Should the judge look like wavering, pitch in fast with this:

> *"With respect, I am advised that under section 36 of the Administration of Justice Act 1970 you can allow the monthly instalments to go unpaid for a period **if it appears likely that the borrower will be able within a reasonable period to pay those sums**. I also submit that you can adjourn today's hearing under your Civil Procedure Rules case management powers. I am told that these cases are regularly adjourned or suspended possession orders made under which monthly payments are allowed to be missed for a little time so long as the court is satisfied the borrower will be able to make them up within a reasonable period. There is nothing in the 1970 Act or anywhere else to say you cannot do this. On the contrary, the Act says you can. Only the lender says you cannot. What is the lender's authority for this?"*

Or you may have reluctantly decided you cannot afford the mortgage and the property must be sold. A private sale by you will almost invariably generate a higher price than a forced sale, often at auction, by a lender who has obtained possession through the court. Pin back your lugholes. Unless and until you have lost possession to the lender, it is your legal right to market the property for sale yourself. The lender's representative at the possession hearing might well sneeringly say to the judge: "There's no buyer. There's no offer. It could be months before a buyer is found and even then the sale could fall through. My client's cuddly general manager will cry if you give the borrower more time. The borrower isn't paying a penny at the moment. You MUST order a sale." Now there's a challenge!

Judges are increasingly more ready to consider allowing the borrower time to sell themselves so long as they are satisfied that the borrower is genuine about wanting to get rid of the property, would accept a realistic price and there is a good chance of a sale within a few months. More time for finding a buyer can be achieved by the judge making an order for possession on a date later than the conventional four weeks: eight weeks is popular. Should a buyer surface within that period and at the very least, be close to commitment by an exchange of contracts, there would be an excellent chance of procuring an extension either with the lender's consent or by referring the case back to the court yourself via an application for the time for giving possession to be extended. Your preference should be for an adjournment to allow marketing and sale rather than an extended date for giving possession. The judge could find that idea to be attractive if it is on the basis that you pay current monthly instalments or an appreciable proportion of them during the adjournment period and with the lender being allowed the option of an accelerated return to court if you default.

What to take to court

- *Accompaniment number 1* – the joint owner be it your spouse, civil partner or mother-in-law because this demonstrates the seriousness with which the household is treating the predicament. It also establishes that the co-owner is in the loop and so should ensure that any proposals you put forward will be kept to. It is commonplace for an owner to hide the co-owner's court papers which would normally have been sent in the post and to stay mum about what is going on. Perhaps they have drunk or gambled the mortgage money? In one sad case I dealt with, the husband was an honourable man who had suffered a series of misfortunes leading to financial difficulties, had kept from his wife that the mortgage was not being paid and destroyed her court papers. He turned up at court alone and without the wife's knowledge. I was obliged to make an order for possession. He left the court and it transpires he then tried to take his own life. All then came out and, whilst he was in recovery in hospital, the wife put together an emergency plan and made an application for the possession order to be set aside. I was eventually able to approve her proposals and the order for outright possession was changed to a suspended order.

- *Accompaniment number 2* – a valuation of your property which can be an estate agent's assessment (not simply of the suggested asking price but what the property would actually go for) which you should be able to obtain free of charge where you are contemplating putting the property on the market with them. The object would be to show, hopefully, that there is a comfortable equity in the property – its market value less the aggregate of what it would take to pay off the mortgage and selling fees and expenses. That could make the difference between being ousted and being allowed to stay put, as a comfortable equity removes or diminishes any possible prejudice to the lender. Of course, if the valuation would establish an equity of a tenner or less, you would be better off leaving the valuation on the bus. Where you are resisting an order for possession in favour of a lender under a first mortgage and you have a second mortgage as well, the amount required to pay off the second mortgage can be ignored for the purpose of calculating the equity. The reason is that the first lender would pay itself out on a sale if it repossessed, before handing over any balance to the second lender. If no balance or a balance insufficient to pay off the second lender, that's tough on the second lender. The sale would still go ahead. But the judge may want to know if you are behind with a second mortgage and, if so, what the second lender is doing about it. A second lender can itself go for repossession if you have defaulted though the first lender has not brought proceedings and is bound to be more aggressive or proactive about doing so because, being second in the queue, it would be more exposed should the equity be small. On a sale by a second lender which has repossessed, it would have to pay back the first lender before taking any money for itself.

- *Accompaniment number 3* – where the property is already on the market, a letter from marketing estate agents to confirm that they are marketing the property, the asking price, the likely actual price which will be achieved and the prospects of an acceptable offer and within what time frame. Please, please, please put the property on the market sooner rather than later if you cannot afford the mortgage. Doing so five minutes before the hearing will raise the suspicion that you are not in earnest. And it may sometimes be prudent not to put all your proposal eggs in one basket. If you have proposals for a suspended order which are shaky, put the property on the market as an alternative. Then you can say to the judge: "I would like to stay and this is my plan for dealing with the monthly instalments and arrears but just in case you are going to be against me, this is what I have done about selling. Please adjourn to enable me to find a buyer."

- *Accompaniment number 4* – up to date details of your household income and expenses backed by wage slips or business accounts (even if you have completed a defence and given figures there).

- *Accompaniment number 5* – if you are relying on a loan or other financial help from a friend or family member, that friend or family member should be at court so that they are available to be questioned by the judge. If their attendance is impossible without frogmarching them to court with a gun in their back, obtain a letter from them explaining their connection with you, what help they are willing to give and on what terms and setting out some information which will satisfy the judge that their own financial circumstances allow them to help and when the money will be available.

Second, third etc mortgages: the time order

The court usually has broader powers to assist you where the lender has granted you a second or subsequent mortgage provided it was not taken out with a bank or building society to buy your home. It is by way of a magical *'time order'* under section 129 of the Consumer Credit Act 1974. We are looking at secure loans for such things as home improvements and the facilitation of spousal or partner extravagance. The powers may not exist if the mortgage was taken out before 6 April 2008. For loans before 1 May 1998 the amount borrowed must be less than £15,000 and for loans between the 1 May 1998 and 5 April 2008 the amount must be less than £25,000. There is no limit for loans taken out on or after 6 April 1998. The court can assist to cater for temporary difficulties. It can reduce the monthly payments and refrain from obligating you to make a contribution to the arrears for the time being. It can even allow payments to be made after the mortgage term has come to an end. Regard will be had not only to your interests but to those of the lender. You won't get anywhere unless you can satisfy the court of the likelihood that you will be able to resume payments at some stage at the rate you originally agreed.

- You don't have to wait for your lender to take you to court for a possession order before going for a time order. You can make your own application to the court but only after your lender has sent you an arrears notice, a default notice or a termination notice. One of these titles will be on the document so you should realise you have had it! Use court form N440. The application will strongly indicate to the judge how seriously you regard the situation and puts you into a tactically advantageous position. Back up the application with a written statement.

> Case no 21P00000678
>
> IN THE COUNTY COURT
>
> AT PEARDROP
>
> BETWEEN
>
> CLIVE TROUBLESORE Applicant
>
> - and -
>
> DODGY BANK PLC Respondent
>
> I CLIVE TROUBLESORE state as follows:
>
> 1. I live at 149c Magnolia Buildings, Twickenham, Middlesex KT89 4XZ.
>
> 2. I ordinarily work as a double glazing salesman and painter and decorator but am presently unemployed due to injuries sustained in an assault.
>
> 3. The facts referred to in this statement are of my own knowledge and it has been composed by me and is in my own words.
>
> 4. On 14 July 2014 I entered into a mortgage agreement with the defendant for a principal loan of £30,000 with interest payable at the rate of 12% per annum which was repayable over a term of 20 years by monthly instalments of £429.83. The loan was raised to pay for my engagement party, a car, a home cinema and a ten-day cruise with David Essex and other 1960's bands.
>
> 5. On 3 January 2021 I was wrongfully arrested by a store detective at the High Street, Peardrop branch of Farthing Universe who alleged I had stolen three toothbrushes. I tried to free myself from the store detective's hold and, in an attempt to restrain me, he kicked me in the groin and I fell to the ground and exacerbated a long standing back condition which has since incapacitated me from work. My present financial circumstances are particularised in my form N440.
>
> 6. Up to the date of the assault I had paid all instalments due to the respondent regularly and punctually. However, since the assault I have been unable to comply with my obligations in full. I have made

what payments I could afford but have fallen into arrears in the sum of £y which represents three monthly instalments.

7. I have kept the respondent closely informed of my situation. However, I have found it hostile and totally lacking in empathy. On 1 July 2021 the respondent served me with an arrears notice.

8. I am advised by my GP that I should be fit to return to my-pre-assault work by the end of this year. In the meantime I am having regular physiotherapy.

9. I have instructed Piranha Hector & Co on a claim for damages against the store detective and his employers on a conditional fee basis and am advised that I have a good prospect of recovering damages of not less than £8,000 including loss of earnings.

10. In the circumstances, I ask that the court should make an order under section 129 of the Consumer Credit Act 1974 which reduces the monthly mortgage repayments to £z, and suspend the payments of interest on the basis that I pay all arrears in full within 12 months from the date of this statement and against my undertaking to make such payments earlier should I recover damages arising out of my assault claim at an earlier date. I would keep the respondent fully updated on the progress of my damages claim. I accept it is appropriate that these terms should be incorporated in a suspended order for possession of the property.

11. I submit that the conduct of the respondent has been totally unreasonable and that the court should debar it from adding its costs of this application to the security* and order it to pay me my costs of the application to be summarily assessed on the litigant in person basis. I will provide the court and the respondent with a statement of those costs before the hearing**.

I believe that the facts stated in this witness statement are true. I understand that proceedings for contempt of court may be brought against anyone who makes, or causes to be made, a false statement in a document verified by a statement of truth without an honest belief in its truth.

(signed) Clive Troublesore

14 July 2021

---

*Mortgage agreements invariably entitle the lender to recover its legal costs and expenses in taking any action or doing any work arising out of the borrower's default by adding those costs and expenses to the secured mortgage debt. In exceptional cases, the court has the power to veto this.

**See chapter 35.

You can make a similar application to the court if your lender has brought repossession proceedings against you and the application and the lender's proceedings would then be heard together. Even without a specific application, you can ask the court when it comes to hear the lender's case to make a *time order* but this could lead to an adjournment because longer than has been allocated would be needed for the court to consider the application. Make the application in advance if you possibly can. Otherwise, in the most unlikely event of the judge going red in the face with fury and gnashing their teeth when you put forward your proposals, you might gently say: *"May I respectfully draw attention to the fact that it is a second mortgage I entered into and humbly ask you to consider exercising the special powers you possess to make a time order to cater for my temporary difficulties?"*

Time orders are not restricted to mortgage agreements. They can be made in respect of any agreement which is regulated by the Consumer Credit Act 1974 such as a hire-purchase agreement.

"But it was an unfair relationship"

If you have been taken for a ride by your lender, you may be able to persuade the court to reopen the agreement's terms and do you some justice. This is an option for second or subsequent mortgages where your lender has started proceedings against you because you have defaulted or you can start your own proceedings against it. Your legal peg is sections 140A and 140B of the Consumer Credit Act 1974 relating to existing agreements made since 5 April 2007 or made before 6 April 2017 but which have come to an end since 5 April 2008. There are not dissimilar but narrower laws for agreements which ended before 6 April 2008. Incidentally, these laws can also be used for a host of other credit agreements (see, for example, chapter 40). You would be alleging that there was an unfair relationship between you and your lender. Steady on. This is nothing about the lender's rep taking you out for a *Babycham* and making indecent suggestions. It is about things such as ridiculously high interest and secret commissions. The fact that the lender had the upper hand in negotiations will not itself be sufficient. That's usually the position and will not of itself give rise to a relationship that is rendered unfair. What you are complaining about really needs to offend against the ordinary principles of fair dealing. The lender has the task of justifying the fairness of the point under attack. The court can do all sorts of things to remedy the unfairness: most notably, change the interest rate and order the lender to refund you money. That would certainly get the arrears down and so, where you have good grounds, the unfair relationship argument is well worth a try.

Where you intend to allege an unfair relationship in the course of the lender's proceedings against you, then you should let the court and the lender know about this within 14 days of getting the claim form.

Case No 21P00000678

IN THE COUNTY COURT
AT PEARDROP
BETWEEN

DODGY BANK PLC Claimant

-and -

CLIVE TROUBLESORE Defendant

NOTICE OF INTENTION TO SEEK REOPENING OF CONSUMER CREDIT AGREEMENT

TAKE NOTICE pursuant to Civil Procedure Rules 1998 Practice Direction 7B that I CLIVE TROUBLESORE, the above-named defendant, intend to seek an order in these proceedings under sections 140A and B of the Consumer Credit Act 1974 relating to an unfair relationship between myself and the claimant in respect of the mortgage agreement the subject of the claimant's claim and will rely on the following matters:

a. the contractual rate of interest which I contend is exorbitant or alternatively grossly excessive;

b. the excessive and otherwise unjustifiable amount of administration charges debited to my mortgage account when I have defaulted with repayments or sought modest extensions of time for complying with the terms of the agreement when due to circumstances beyond my control I have been short of money; and

c. the Claimant's failure to disclose to me the fact that it received or would receive substantial commission as to the amount of which I shall seek disclosure upon my taking out a payment protection policy incidental to the mortgage agreement which policy was mis-sold to me by the claimant (but for which such mis-selling I have been compensated).

Dated 14 July 2021

(signed) Clive Troublesore

To the Court

And to the claimant

The chances are that the hearing of the claimant's claim which will have been listed for up to just ten minutes will be adjourned on the day and the court will give directions for that claim and your attempt to get the court to reopen the mortgage agreement to be heard together at a later date.

Taking a shtum powder

Because you can legally sell your property at any time before you are evicted, you can market it and carry on marketing it even after an order for possession has been made by the court. Not a good idea to mention the order for possession to any viewers or prospective buyers for they may just get it into their heads that they could do well by capitalising on your situation and offering a stupid price or reducing the price they have agreed. Bearing in mind that all is fair in war and home transactions, they might – and I have seen it happen – delay exchanging contracts and withdraw at the last moment with the result that you are evicted and they subsequently purchase from your lender at a substantially reduced price. Keeping quiet about the possession proceedings is perfectly legitimate. I wouldn't mention it to the marketing agents either. They have the habit of leaking confidential information to applicants like a gigantically holed sieve.

"How long do I have?"

You are expected to vacate the property – family, furniture, back editions of the *Radio Times* and cats included – by the date for possession specified in the court's order. You won't be committing a criminal offence by staying on. Once your lender realises that you remain in residence, it will apply to have you evicted by a bailiff if the case is with the county court or by an enforcement agent if the case has been transferred for enforcement to the High Court. The bailiff or enforcement agent will fix an appointment to come and evict you and must now give you at least 14 days' prior notice of when this will be in a special form N54 which was introduced in August 2000. The likelihood is that this process will allow you around a further four weeks in the property from the date by which you should have vacated before you are evicted. Dependent on how quick off the mark is your lender in applying for your eviction, this could be longer. The process can be expected to be slower with a bailiff than with an enforcement agent through the High Court. The court does have the power to extend the 14-day period and an application could be made for it to do so but I would not expect it to be prepared to do so where there were no grounds for suspending the warrant or writ of possession instead.

The N54 gives a flavour of what will happen on eviction. "A representative of the claimant will attend with the Authorised Person (the bailiff or enforcement agent.) That representative will change any locks, or take any other steps necessary to prevent re-entry. If you have not removed all of your belongings when the eviction takes place, you will only be allowed time to do so if the claimant's representative agrees."

How will the N54 reach you? It is to be inserted through your letter box in a sealed transparent envelope. If that is not practicable (because you have sealed up the letter box or placed a ferocious dog in the hallway which is known to be a proficient hand biter) then the notice may be attached to the main door or some other part of the property so that it is clearly visible. And if even that is not practicable, stakes may be placed on the land where they are clearly visible with a copy of the notice, contained in a sealed transparent envelope, being attached to each stake. If the notice fails to come to your attention because these requirements have not been followed or you have been given short notice, you could apply to the court to direct that the eviction appointment be cancelled and that a fresh and sufficient notice be given to you before the eviction proceeds. Should you already have been evicted, it would be arguable that the eviction was unlawful and you could apply to the court to reinstate you in the property. If you succeeded, the eviction notice procedure would then have to be restarted.

You can issue a court application to extend the time you were given to go before you get form N54 or wait until then to issue the application which should be for suspension of the warrant of possession in the county court or suspension of the writ of possession in the High Court. Either way, an urgent hearing of the application will be fixed by the court and your lender will have an opportunity of attending the application. Many borrowers wait for the very last moment and apply for the warrant or writ to be suspended the day before the bailiff or enforcement agent is due to evict: sometimes on the very day of the eviction. The judge may construe this as playing the system and take an adverse view of the borrower's conduct. Two key points: firstly, try and ensure that when you make your application, your case for earning time is at its strongest and, hopefully, that there have been developments in your favour since the case was last before the court; and, secondly, make the application before the bailiff or enforcement agent has evicted.

More time refused

You can seek to appeal against a judge's refusal to grant you more time (or the original possession order itself). You will have to proceed at hare type speed should the refusal come on the day of eviction or very close to it. You will want to get before the appeal judge prior to being evicted although if you happen to be evicted and then go on to win the appeal, you would be let back in but just think of the upheaval and you may miss *Coronation Street*. The appeal would be to a circuit judge (see chapter 28). You need permission to appeal either from the judge who refused the application or from a circuit judge. So, if you want to appeal:

- Tell this to the judge who refuses the application immediately they have done so and ask them for permission to appeal and, whether or not permission is granted, ask the judge to "stay the warrant (or writ) of possession pending the appeal" which means halting the eviction so that you can get the appeal under way. If the judge seems reluctant, invite them to do as requested on condition that you issue your notice of appeal that day.

- Issue your notice of appeal which will include an application for permission to make the appeal if it was refused by the first judge. Because you will be under intense time pressure, you might have got hold of the form of notice of appeal from the hearing centre's office before your application was refused and, even more cheekily but practically, you might have already completed it or most of it. If you are going to need to apply for remission of the court fee on the application (see chapter 17), get the application for that too and complete it in readiness to lodge with the notice of appeal.

If permission to appeal has been refused by the judge who refused the application for more time, you must get before the circuit judge and ask them to "stay the warrant (or writ) of possession pending the appeal". The court staff should put you in front of a circuit judge as soon as humanly possible and hopefully on the same day so that you can do this. A particular problem arises where, as is often the case, there is no circuit judge sitting at the hearing centre where your hearing took place. You will be told at what centre a circuit judge can be found who can urgently hear you. You might even be told that you have to take the appeal papers to that other hearing centre. What is essential is that the bailiff or enforcement agent, who may be waiting outside the property ready to carry out the eviction process, is aware of the steps you are taking because they may be prepared to hang fire to allow you to take them. A lack of liaison between staff at the hearing centre and the bailiff or enforcement agent outside the property has been known to lead to the eviction being carried out whilst the borrower is waiting to see the circuit judge.

FOR LENDERS' EYES ONLY

As to the eviction notice in form N54, the court does have power to shorten or extend the service time or even dispense entirely with the need for it. It could well shorten, dispense or even direct alternative service where there is evidence that the defendant is or is likely to attempt to frustrate the eviction process.

FOR ALL EYES

You will find more on the eviction process, which is the same for mortgage borrowers and tenants, at chapter 67.

Chapter 67

At War With Your Home Landlord

Armaments store

REFORM ALERT. The government is committed to major reform of the housing law in England: in particular, to the abolition of assured shorthold tenancies and strengthening the existing grounds for eviction. Its public consultation on the subject closed in October 2019. Almost 20,000 responses were received. Some thought that its appetite for upsetting landlords whose ability to have erring tenants evicted during the coronavirus may have been muted. Nevertheless, its line to me in February 2021 was that the pandemic had rightly meant that resources across Whitehall had been prioritised to tackle the virus and economic recovery and that a Renters' Reform Bill would be produced once the responses had been carefully considered. On my rough estimate, it would take over three years at half an hour a response working on an eight-hour day to get through that lot. And then, just to wind me up (obviously), the Housing Minister announced in May 2021 that a white paper would be published in the autumn of 2021 which would include proposals to abolish assured shorthold 'evictions'. One day, you will need to tear up much of this chapter but by the time any major changes come into force, you should have got your money's worth out of it. In Wales, the Renting Homes (Amendment) (Wales) Act 2021 will effect major changes from the spring of 2022. A minimum letting for 12 months and notice periods up. A minimum letting for 12 months and notice periods up from two to six months where the tenant is not alleged to be at fault.

There are many advantages to residential renting. No risk of escalating mortgage interest which you are unable to pay. Many essential repairs down to the landlord. The chance for the kids to draw Bugs Bunny on the hallway stairs (in red), the dog to foul the living room carpet and you never to clean the cooker and then to argue when the deposit comes up for return time that the drawing (red) was fair wear and tear to be contemplated from any reasonably normal brat, the dog has been permanently constipated since the letting began and the oven was like that at the start of the tenancy – and that your mother-in-law came in on the last day of the tenancy with four of her friends and they spent 47 hours between them scrubbing and vacuuming and shining and scraping and hosing and the place looked like a museum when they had finished.

Watch for the landlord mortgage trap

The one gigantic disadvantage is that you may have to leave the house or flat which is your home earlier than you would have wished. Generally, your landlord can't evict you without a court order. To be precise, they can do so but if they do, you'll be in the money as the eviction will be unlawful and entitle you to damages. If the landlord takes you to what will be the county court to get you out, you will have the opportunity to put forward a defence or ask for more time to go than the landlord would like. Much of our guidance given to mortgage borrowers who are taken to court by their lender (see chapter 66) applies to tenants who are taken to court by their landlords. If you would prefer to stay put, participate in the court proceedings in the same way as a mortgage borrower should do. You can obtain free advice about your legal rights even before any court hearing has been fixed (see chapter 7). Free advice will also be available to you at court from a lawyer or other professional, though you have not sought it earlier.

Before you sign a tenancy agreement, check whether the landlord has a mortgage and, if they do, that their lender has consented to the tenancy. Where a mortgage exists, it is virtually certain that it will preclude the landlord from granting a tenancy without the lender's prior approval. Should the landlord let on regardless, the tenancy will be regarded as unlawful and the lender will not be bound by it (unless it subsequently finds out about it and acquiesces in the way it acts towards you). The knock on effect of the lender not being bound is that, should the landlord default with payment of the mortgage instalments and a possession order be made against the landlord, you will be stuffed and evicted. True that the Mortgage Repossessions (Protection of Tenants etc) Act 2010 would give you some protection – a breather of up to two months to go if you follow the procedure it sets up – but that's it. That you had a two year tenancy which is still running and you paid six months' rent in advance and you paid a dilapidations deposit and you spent a grand on improving the place count for nothing as between you and the lender. Of course, it's another matter as between you and the landlord but if the landlord has effectively lost the property the prospect of you squeezing any compensation out of them would be as good as getting the mother-in-law to the moon by next week.

So how do you check? Ask the landlord or the letting agents to see the lender's written confirmation that they are okay with the tenancy and if the landlord says there is no mortgage, check this out at the Land Registry: you could make an online search. I have seen countless evictions where the tenancy has been unlawful and the lender has legitimately swooped. I have also seen a number of cases where the tenancy has been granted between the start of mortgage repossession proceedings and the hearing of those proceedings, with the landlord mercilessly pocketing the up-front rent and deposit, well knowing that a couple of months later, the tenant would be thrown out.

AND ANOTHER THING

Like a glass of beetroot juice, the Tenant Fees Act 2019 which came into force on 1 June 2019 could do you a lot of good. It is aimed at rogue landlords and their agents, even if they occasionally give money to charity, and dictates what you can and cannot be charged up for when taking on and during a tenancy. It now impacts on all residential assured shorthold tenancies in England as well as most residential licences and student lettings although the suffering for landlord breach is more severe where the tenancy was granted after 31 May 2019. For a tenancy granted before 1 June 2019, the landlord could charge for sums which would now be prohibited, but only up to 31 May 2019.

If a payment required by the landlord ain't permitted by the Act, it will be treated as prohibited. Among the banned charges against you the tenant are those for viewing the premises, setting up the tenancy and preparing inventories when you go in and when you come out. However, do not lose sight of the fact that the Act will not let you off liability for breaking a condition of the tenancy agreement which is not prohibited and so, for example, if the kids do draw Bugs Bunny on the hallway stairs (in red or possibly green), this would still cost you.

Let's see what is prohibited.

- A deposit for more than five weeks' rent (or more than six weeks' rent where the annual rent is a cool £50,000 or more). But landlords and their agents have taken to circumvent this prohibition by asking for a greater amount for up front rent. Instead of requiring say a fortnight's rent by way of a deposit which they hold on to until the end of the tenancy or dip into if you default, they seek three months' rent in advance which they can pocket when they receive it.

- A reservation deposit of more than one week's rent. But listen to this. The deposit, whatever you paid, must be refunded to you if you subsequently enter into a tenancy agreement; the landlord decides not to rent out; an agreement with the landlord is not reached before a deadline of 15 days, or longer if agreed in writing; or the landlord imposes some prohibited requirement or acts in such a way as to make it unreasonable to expect you to enter into a tenancy agreement with them (for example, by putting forward unfair conditions for the letting). But the deposit may be kept by the landlord provided they give their written reasons for doing so if you have provided false or misleading information which reasonably affects their decision about whether to let to you (for example, you are a parish priest who has just won the lottery whereas, in fact, you have been taken on by a television reality show and are an escaped convict); you have failed a 'right to rent' check; withdrawn from what was intended; or, unlike the landlord, failed to take all reasonable steps to enter into an agreement. Geddit it?

- A default fee for rent which is not at least 14 days overdue; isn't permitted by the agreement; or attracts an interest charge of more than 3% over the base rate (currently 0.1%) – it's just the excess that is prohibited.

- A default payment for loss of a key or security device to obtain access to the premises unless that payment was reasonably incurred by the landlord and there is written evidence to support it, such as an invoice.

- More than £50 or a reasonable amount for dealing with a variation to the tenancy agreement or a tenant's request to transfer the tenancy to someone else – it's just the excess again that is prohibited.

- Frontloading the rent at the start of the tenancy to cover prohibited fees (for example, by charging rent of £1,000 in the first month and £750 in the second month in which event the £250 difference will be a prohibited payment).

- A payment to the landlord for letting you out of the tenancy or letting you out of giving the required notice to terminate the tenancy, at your request, where the payment exceeds the landlord's actual loss as a result of the termination – it's just the excess again that is prohibited.

- A payment to the letting agent for arranging for you to be let out of the tenancy or letting you out of giving the required notice to terminate the tenancy, at your request, where the payment exceeds the reasonable costs of the agent – it's just the excess again that is prohibited.

And now let's see what happens if the landlord collects a prohibited payment. They must refund it to you. Until it has been refunded, they cannot go through the assured shorthold tenancy possession procedure under section 21 of the Housing Act 1988 (see below under **Private tenancies**) where the tenancy was granted after 31 May 2019. But this ban will not apply where, with your consent, the prohibited payment has been applied towards a permitted deposit or rent which you owed. Enforcement is usually by the local authority's trading standards department (or what is left of it) or by the district council where there is no such department. They will have the option of bringing proceedings against the landlord in the magistrates' court for committing a civil offence or itself imposing a fine on the landlord of up to £30,000 which it may retain and so the fine route has quite an appeal for them. They will also be able to require the landlord to make you a refund, along with interest from when you paid over the money at the rate of 8%. A landlord under an old tenancy granted before 1 June 2019 who accepts a payment that is prohibited will escape a prosecution or local authority fine provided they refunded the prohibited payment within 28 days of accepting it. You, or someone else who has guaranteed the rent, can personally apply for a refund of the prohibited payment to the first-tier tribunal (property chamber) unless the local authority has brought criminal as opposed to civil proceedings against the landlord for a second breach. Use tribunal form number TFA1. If the application goes in your favour but the landlord still refuses to dip into their pockets, you can make a claim in the county court to get your money. You should be able to get help from trading standards if you bring the proceedings yourself on a tribunal application or enforcement in the county court.

In relation to a tenancy granted before 1 June 2019, the landlord is not prevented from serving you with a two-month notice (longer thanks to temporary coronavirus legislation – see below) under section 21 of the Housing Act 1988 until the prohibited payment has been refunded.

We've talked about the landlord's liability as if cuddly letting agents didn't exist. But they do and are just about capable of doing dirty work for the landlord. Requirements by and payments to letting agents which are prohibited will attract the same sanctions and have the same effect as if they had been made or received by the landlords for whom they act.

A claim against the landlord or letting agent, or both, may be made even after the tenancy has come to an end and you have ceased to live in the premises.

> Dear Landlord*
>
> 61 Trionoble Close, Peardrop
>
> On 31 July 2015 I took a tenancy from you of the above premises and as from 1 June 2020 the Tenant Fees Act 2019 applies to that tenancy.*
>
> or
>
> On 31 July 2020 I took a tenancy from you of the above premises and the Tenant Fees Act 2019 applies to that tenancy.
>
> and
>
> Prior to taking the tenancy and in contravention of the 2019 Act, you required me to pay you a reservation fee of two weeks' rent amounting to £500.00 whereas the Act prohibits a requirement to pay a reservation fee of more than one week's rent and, in any event, provides for a refund of the fee if an agreement is entered into. Accordingly, the full £500.00 which I duly paid is repayable to me.
>
> and/or
>
> Prior to taking the tenancy and in contravention of the 2019 Act, you required me to pay you a security deposit of six weeks' rent amounting to £1,500.00 whereas the Act prohibits a requirement to pay a security deposit of more than five weeks' rent. Accordingly, £250.00 of the £1,5000.00 which I duly paid is repayable to me.
>
> and/or
>
> The tenancy agreement provided for me to pay rent for the first six months of the tenancy at the rate of £250.00 per week payable four-weekly and thereafter at the rate of £200.00 per week payable four-weekly, whereas the Act prohibits a rental during the first year of a tenancy at an amount which subsequently decreases during that year. I duly made the higher payments for a period of v weeks amounting to £w. If I had paid at the lower rate subsequently provided for during the first year, the total paid would have been £x. Accordingly, the difference between £w and £x, namely £z is repayable to me.
>
> and/or
>
> The tenancy agreement provided that in the event of me falling into arrears with the payment of rent for a period of seven days, I would be liable to pay interest on the amount in arrears at the rate of 10% per annum, whereas the Act prohibits any default charge which is not at least 14 days overdue and in any event at a rate higher than 3% over the base rate from time to time prevailing. I have fallen into arrears

under the tenancy agreement. In some instances, I have cleared the arrears in less than 14 days but have paid the interest charge demanded of me and, in other instances, I have cleared the arrears outside 14 days but paid interest at the contractual rate. Accordingly, the full interest paid where I have been in arrears for less than 14 days is repayable to me and the interest paid in excess of 3% over base rate where I have been in arrears for more than 14 days is repayable to me. The total wrongfully required of and paid by me is £x and the breakdown of this figure is contained in the attached schedule [set out breakdown showing how you have reached the £x on a separate sheet].

and/or

When I lost the front door key and you had to replace the lock and obtain duplicate keys, you charged me £350.00 inclusive of your administration charge whereas, in such circumstances, the Act prohibits a requirement to pay more than a reasonable sum and prohibits an administration charge. Further, the Act requires the provision of written evidence to support the charge, whereas you provided no such evidence to me. My enquiries establish that a reasonable charge for replacement of the lock and supply of replacement keys would have been £150.00 inclusive of VAT. I paid you £200.00 in excess of a reasonable amount for which I would be entitled to a refund but, as no written evidence whatsoever in support of any amount and, in particular in support of £350.00, was provided to me, the full amount of £350.00 is repayable to me.

and/or

You agreed to release me from my tenancy before the expiration of the fixed term of two years in consideration of the payment to you of £2,000.00 which I paid and you duly accepted, whereas the acceptance of a sum in excess of your actual loss resulting from the release was prohibited by the Act. I have now established that prior to the agreement and acceptance, you had arranged to relet the property to another tenant for a fixed term of two years commencing on the day after my vacation of the property at a rent in excess of that which I had been obligated to pay. It follows that you suffered no loss as a result of my release. Accordingly, the full amount of £2,000.00 is repayable to me.

and (where tenancy granted before 1 June 2019)**

I now require you to repay to me the total sum of £x which you have accepted from me since the Act applied to the tenancy. If less than 28 days have elapsed since acceptance then you will be released from further liability if you repay me the full amount before the expiration of those 28 days. If you fail to make such repayment within 28 days of the date of this letter, then I shall bring proceedings against you before the first-tier tribunal (property chamber) for the recovery of this amount, subject to such action as the local authority may take against you by way of prosecution for an offence or the imposition of a fine under the

> Act. *[Add where landlord is a company – Local authority enforcement may be against not only your company but any director who has approved or connived at contravention of the Act]*.
>
> or
>
> (where tenancy granted after 31 May 2019)
>
> I now require you to repay to me the total sum of £z within 14 days of the date of this letter. If you fail to do so then I shall bring proceedings against you before the first-tier tribunal (property chamber) for the recovery of this amount, subject to such action as the local authority may take against you by way of prosecution for an offence or the imposition of a fine under the Act. I should draw your attention to the fact that, so long as the entire sum of £z has been repaid to me, no notice served by you under section 21 of the Housing Act 1988 will be of any effect. *[Add where landlord is a company – Local authority enforcement may be against not only your company but any director who has approved or connived at contravention of the Act]*.
>
> Yours faithfully
>
> Clive Troublesore

*If the payment has been required by the landlord's letting agent, then this letter should be appropriately adapted and sent to the agent. Where both letting agent and landlord are involved in requiring a prohibited payment, they may both be liable to you and this letter can be adapted so that it is addressed and sent to each of them although you cannot recover repayment twice! It may be that each of them has required different prohibited payments which would require different letters to each of them. Should you have to go to the first-tier tribunal then you can apply against both landlord and agent.

**For tenancies granted before 1 June 2019, remember that the prohibited payment is only refundable if the landlord or agent have accepted it after 31 May 2020 although it could have been requested beforehand.

GETTING YOU OUT

FOR TENANTS' EYES ONLY BUT LANDLORDS MAY TAKE A PEEK

A landlord who is out to recover the property they have let must first serve a notice on their tenant requiring them to leave. I discuss below for how long the notice must be. The periods mentioned were temporarily lengthened for residential premises which had been let in England by the Coronavirus Act 2020 from the original periods of between 14 days and two months (depending on why the landlord was requiring possession) in generally every instance. In respect of a notice given on or after 26 March 2020 and up to and including 28 August 2020, a standard three months' notice had to be given. In respect of a notice given on or after 29 August 2020 and up to and including 31 May 2021, the period was doubled to a standard, stonking, six months except (a) for notices in relation to anti-social behaviour, rioting and making a false statement to obtain the tenancy where the notice periods were restored to those which applied before coronavirus and except (b) for rent arrears cases where the period was four weeks where at least six months' rent was owed and six months where the arrears were lower. As for notices given on or after 1 June 2021, the six months have been reduced to four months and there have been further changes where the landlord is relying on rent arrears. If at least four months' arrears are due, four weeks' notice are required: less than four months' arrears, then four months' notice. And for notices given on or after 1 August 2021 and up to 30 September 2021 there will be a tapering down with the landlord having to give two months' notice if less than four months' rent is due. The notice period for the ground for possession where the tenant is unlawfully present in the UK in breach of immigration rules or in the event of the tenant's death will reduce to two months when given on or after 1 June 2021. In Wales, the temporary notice period was three months from 26 March to 23 July 2020 and this has been extended to six months until at least 30 June 2021. There has been an exception for anti-social behaviour cases which were set to remain at three months until 28 September 2021 and then return to pre-coronavirus periods. You should check on my blog whether or not, after 30 September 2021 in England and 30 June 2021 in Wales, the pre-coronavirus notice periods have been restored.

There is a real likelihood that your landlord has given you insufficient notice during coronavirus (or even out of it). If you as tenant are still involved in a possession case where the notice was served in any of those temporary periods and it was for less than what the law called for, you have a defence to a claim for possession based on the short notice and the landlord is in trouble. In that situation the landlord would need to serve a fresh notice for the appropriate period then prevailing and bring fresh possession proceedings against you if you are still in occupation at the end of that notice period. Fresh proceedings could not be validly brought before the second notice period had expired.

FOR TENANTS' EYES ONLY

Private tenancies

We are looking here at non local authority and housing association tenancies. Things to watch out for if you want to stay put – for a while or longer than a while.

- Is the landlord trying to get you out too early? The landlord cannot take any steps to get you out for the first four months of an assured shorthold tenancy **provided you have behaved**. Check what the tenancy agreement says about how long the tenancy is to last. If the tenancy was granted for 12 months and only six months are up and, again, **provided you have behaved**, the landlord cannot generally call for you to go until the entire 12 months have expired, unless, that is, the agreement contains what is called a *break clause*. Many agreements are for 12 months but go on to say that the landlord can bring the tenancy to an end following the first six months by giving the tenant two months' notice that their time is up. This is lawful. Before ever signing a tenancy agreement you should scrutinise it for any mention of what amounts to a *break clause*. It could be buried among several pages of smallish print. Why have to go before your two eggs are hard boiled?

- The landlord will generally only be able to attempt to get you out if your time is up under a tenancy agreement for a fixed term (like 12 months), you are on a periodic tenancy (usually weekly or monthly and often following the expiry of the original fixed term) or you have broken the tenancy plus they have presented you with a written notice to go. Most private tenancies these days are *assured shorthold* tenancies so I'll restrict myself to these. If you have an *assured shorthold tenancy*, the agreement will probably say so but not necessarily so. Whatever the agreement does say, it will not be an *assured shorthold* if granted to a company or at a rent of £100,000 per annum or more where granted after 30 September 2010 (and, if that's what *you* are paying, go and hire a QC for advice instead of sponging on this book). There are a couple of other exceptions.

- Assuming the *assured shorthold* landlord is not after closing the front door permanently behind you before the end of the fixed term of your assured shorthold tenancy or later on the ground of a tenancy breach, you must have at least two months' notice (judges, lawyers, professional landlords and letting agents who have a language of their own – no, not Polari – call it a section 21 notice) unless the longer coronavirus notice period applies as explained above. In England, the notice has to be in a prescribed form where the tenancy began after 30 September 2015. It has a very sexy title – form 6A – and if you want to see what it looks like – and I suggest you do check that the correct form has been used – feast yourself for a couple of minutes on the Assured Shorthold Tenancy Notices and Prescribed Requirements (England) Regulations 2015 and you'll find it at the back. It was last revised to cater for temporary coronavirus changes when given on or after 1 June 2021. The landlord hasn't used the correct form or a form which substantially follows it? Notice invalid. In Wales, the landlord must explain in writing that they are serving an eviction notice under section 21 of the Housing Act 1988. Giving the notice can be down to the whim of the landlord. Perhaps you have won the Ms Wonderful Tenant of the Year Award for each successive 12 months of the tenancy. Perhaps the landlord has broken a tenancy condition by failing to repair the premises. It generally matters not. The landlord's whim provides you with no defence to a claim for possession though, in the event of the landlord's breach of a tenancy condition (for example, by failing to repair), you may still have a valid claim for damages against them. But if the landlord is after your exit before the fixed period is up on the ground of a tenancy breach, the notice period is usually shorter at a fortnight (unless a longer coronavirus period applies as explained above). The use of a different prescribed form of notice is essential. For England it is form 3 which was revised in April 2015 and April 2016; as from 26 March 2020 and 29 August 2020 to take account of the coronavirus changes explained above; as from 4 May 2021 to take account of the breathing space and mental health crisis moratoria; and. finally, as from 1 June 2021 to take account of the latest coronavirus changes. Judges and the rest call this a section 8 notice. The shorter notice may also be relied on by your landlord if the fixed period is up and the tenancy is continuing as a monthly tenancy but the landlord says you have broken its terms and prefers not to have to give you a full two months' (or extended coronavirus) notice. A notice which is too short is not worth the paper on which it is written.

- The grounds on which the landlord can rely are limited where they seek possession during or after your fixed period and they want to give you less than the non-coronavirus two months' notice. The most common ground is that the rent is in arrears: two months' worth (or eight weeks' worth where payable weekly or fortnightly) both when the notice is given and at the date of the court hearing. So long as all the necessary procedural requirements have been met by the landlord, possession would then be mandatory. The trick then is to reduce the arrears to less than the threshold required before the hearing although the court might even then have a discretion to boot you out because of persistent delay in paying the rent but you would be unlucky for that to happen if it looks to the judge that the arrears still left will soon be cleared and you are good for future rent. No, I can't lend you the money. And, no, the judge should not adjourn the hearing simply to enable you to come up with the arrears or a sufficient part of them to bring the figure down to less than the required threshold – though you can always try it! – unless there are exceptional circumstances such as you having left the cash on the bus on the way to court. Where rent arrears are relied on by the landlord as a ground for possession and the landlord has broken their repair obligations, you may be able to escape a possession order by defending and, at the same time, making a counterclaim for damages for breach of repair which could be set off against the arrears and bring them down to less than the magic threshold amount required.

- Check that the notice makes sense. If it is confusing about when the landlord would like to see the back of you or on other information, it might well be legally ineffective. The court would have to decide what a reasonable person who had received the notice would have made of it. Steady on, I didn't say you were unreasonable just because you think the mouth of a pillar box is the place through which you can insert your used cheese sandwiches. But you might be. The court may be prepared to forgive the landlord for an ineffective section 8 notice by dispensing with the need for a notice to have been given but it would have to be satisfied that it would be 'just and equitable to do so'. More often than not, it will refuse to do so. However, the court does not have power to dispense where the landlord is relying on possession on the ground that the arrears amount to at least the threshold for a mandatory order (two months' or eight weeks' worth of rent behind).

- Check the date you were given a section 21 notice against the date that court proceedings against were issued, which you will find on the claim form. The reason for this is that the period between the two dates must not exceed six months or, under temporary coronavirus legislation, ten months where the notice was served on or after 29 August 2020 or eight months where served on or after 1 June 2021. In other words, the proceedings must have been started within the six, ten or eight months of the notice being served. Where more than the appropriate period is up, you would have a cast iron defence to the possession claim and the landlord would have to serve a fresh notice and bring fresh proceedings when it expired if you had not vacated. Check my blog as to any future change to the life of the section 21 notice after 30 September 2021.

- Where your landlord is relying on a section 21 notice there is an evens chance that they will mess things up. That's because the law has come up with an almost unintelligible set of rules for them to follow. If they have gone wrong, be it innocently or deliberately, then the section 21 notice will probably be invalid. This would result in them having to restart court proceedings once they had taken corrective action by giving you a fresh notice and any court proceedings based on the invalid section 21 notice would be thrown out or abandoned.

- The most likely area in which your landlord will have come a cropper is over any deposit paid when the tenancy was taken out. The deposit protection legislation was well meaning. However, unfortunate statutory wording and various technical amendments have turned it into a sick joke for landlords and a sweet respite and moneyspinner for many tenants. The deposit must have been protected with one of the three government approved schemes which are Deposit Protection Service, MyDeposits and The Dispute Service – Capita Tenancy Deposit Service provided a scheme for a short period only and any deposits paid to them have been transferred over to MyDeposits – and with you being notified of protection information. All of this unless your landlord is a *resident landlord* in that they live in the premises, the rental is over £100,000 a year (cool), the tenancy has been taken by a company or you have rented student accommodation from a university or college. That protection information is formally called *prescribed information* and is set out in the Housing (Tenancy Deposits) (Prescribed Information) Order 2007. You would be doing yourself a great favour by checking whether you have had each and every item of information. Failure to protect or to give you the protection information where required will mean that the section 21 notice is ineffective and the windfall for you of a penalty entitlement from the landlord which might sweeten the ultimate eviction (see below).

You may feel that it would be unfair to cane a good landlord with a penalty where they have innocently failed to protect on time and remedied their default as soon as they realised what they should have done. The only escape route for your landlord who has not protected the deposit and provided protection information in time is to do both late – this should have been done within 14 days of deposit receipt or within 30 days for deposits received from 6 April 2012 – but prior to giving you the section 21 notice or to return the deposit to you before giving you the section 21 notice. While enabling the landlord to proceed to get you out, this belated action will leave them exposed to a successful penalty claim by you. The deposit protection regime originally caught only tenancy agreements granted after 6 April 2007. However, it now even impacts on deposits paid before then. If you have moved on to a monthly tenancy prior to 6 April 2007 (say you went in with an agreement for 12 months which expired on 1 February 2007 and you have stayed put as a monthly tenant since then) the landlord must return your deposit or protect it now before they can give you a section 21 notice but you will not be entitled to make a penalty claim. If your original tenancy started before 6 April 2007 and you did not move on to a monthly tenancy until after then, your landlord cannot give you a section 21 notice until they have returned the deposit to you and you will have an entitlement to a penalty claim – UNLESS the landlord protected the deposit and provided protection details to you late but by 23 June 2015. See what I mean!

- The deposit will probably be the money you paid over which your landlord could use at the end of the tenancy for redecorating and repairing the premises after you had wrecked them. But it could be something else. The definition of a deposit for the purposes of this protection law is "money intended to be held (by the landlord…) as security for (a) the performance of any obligations of the tenant, or (b) the discharge of any liability of his, arising under or in connection with the tenancy." This would extend to a sum paid at the start of the tenancy as security for rent: not advance rent for say the first month or two of the tenancy but a sum to be set aside into which your landlord could dip if you missed a rental payment which fell due (sometimes called a *deposit security* fund or *agreement*).

- If you haven't heard from the landlord about deposit protection the chances are that they have broken the law. You should check out with the three schemes whether any of them is holding the money. All the schemes allow you to make the check online, if you wish.

- You can still claim a penalty if the tenancy has come to an end but you must do so within six years of the landlord having defaulted.

- If it wasn't you but Mummy or Daddy or Uncle Russell who to the landlord's knowledge shelled out the deposit then they instead of or in addition to you may be able to claim a penalty.

- Okay then. Your landlord has scored full marks for their performance over the deposit? All is not lost. If the premises are in multiple occupation, the local authority probably required them to be licensed for it. If unlicensed, a section 21 notice will be invalid. Where appropriate, check with the council whether they should have been licensed and, if so, whether they were licensed. The licensing requirements in England were toughened up as from 1 October 2018. A licence is needed for a building with fewer than three storeys – formerly, three storeys or more – if, as before, they are occupied by five or more people in two or more households. And flats above shops on traditional high street locations where the building comprises three or more storeys are now more likely to be caught by the licensing requirement than before. See **Multiple nice little earner** below on how to get a rent refund if your landlord has broken the law on multiple occupation licensing.

- Also for a tenancy granted after 30 September 2015 you must have been provided with an energy performance certificate and gas safety certificate before being given a section 21 notice. That gas safety certificate should have been given to you before you occupied (sometimes it can be alternatively displayed in the premises in a prominent position). Additionally, you should have been given or been able to see and obtain records of later gas inspections carried out during the tenancy. Those inspections are required every 12 months. If the landlord is late in giving you this gas stuff then the law forgives them – the Court of Appeal ruled on this point in a 2020 case – so long as you had it before the section 21 notice. And there's more. You must also have been given the then current version of the eight-page checklist published by the Department for Communities and Local Government called *How to rent: the checklist for renting in England*. It's available free (and there's a money making opportunity lost) on gov.uk/government/publications/how-to-rent. It was revamped for tenancies granted on or after 1 February 2016. The landlord is to provide it – so it's not good enough for the landlord to rely on the copy you picked up in the street – and to do so in hard copy or by email where you have given an email address for receiving documents. This obligation in relation to the checklist does not extend to social landlords such as local authorities and housing associations. Once provided, any revised version published during the same tenancy need not also be provided. The landlord (or someone on their behalf such as the letting agent) hasn't come up with all these documents before giving you the section 21 notice? The notice will be invalid.

- Hell hath no fury like a landlord scorned. Just in case you have been complaining about the state of the premises and the landlord has decided you would be better off on the street than in the hovel they have rented out to you, the law now comes to your rescue so long as you didn't cause the damage yourself. Any section 21 notice may be invalidated where you have complained to the landlord about the condition of the premises, then complained to the local housing authority after the landlord has failed to respond to you adequately or at all or served a section 21 notice and the authority has sent the landlord an improvement or emergency action notice. And your landlord is in any event prevented from giving you a section 21 notice within six months of them receiving from the local authority an improvement notice or a notice to take emergency remedial action concerning the state of the property, whether or not this has arisen from your complaint. Unhappily, they don't seem to have thought about invalidating a section 21 notice if it was triggered by the tenant claiming a deposit protection penalty from the landlord during the currency of the tenancy. That would have been of much wider benefit.

- The nightmare scenario for you is that your landlord has done everything according to the book and you have no defence to the possession claim. You will usually be ordered to give possession within 14 days of the hearing. Often there is no hearing because the landlord is relying on having given you two months' notice (or extended notice for the coronavirus period) and is asking for the case to be accelerated and dealt with by the judge on the papers and in the absence of the parties. Where this has happened the 14 days will run from when the judge has looked at the papers and decided that you must go and you should receive a copy of the judge's order through the post a couple of days later. The maximum period the judge can allow for you to go is 42 days but they will only allow more than 14 days where you can show you would otherwise suffer exceptional hardship. You can ask that you be allowed more than 14 days and up to 42 days to leave in your defence – you will receive the defence form with the claim form and you should complete it and send it back to the court – and state why you want more time. What will then happen is that you will get an order to give possession within 14 days of the date of the order and, at the same time, details of a court hearing at which the judge will decide whether to extend the 14 days to anything up to 42 days (as from the date on which the order for possession was made). Occasionally, the landlord would have stated on the claim form that they would be content for the judge to decide whether to grant more than 14 days if asked for, without fixing a hearing on that one matter. Then the judge could allow anything up to 42 days in the original order they make.

- What happens once the 14 or 42 days (or something in between) are up? Do you get locked out whilst up at the chippie? No. The landlord requests that the court orders your eviction through the county court bailiff or, if the case has been transferred to the High Court for enforcement, an enforcement agent and you are – and generally must be – served with a notice of eviction at least 14 days before the planned eviction appointment. The bailiff or enforcement agent are to use a special form N54 for this and, failure to do so or give you adequate warning could provide you with grounds to apply to the court for a later eviction appointment: alternatively, if you have already been evicted, to apply to be reinstated and then the eviction procedure would have to be restarted. You will find more on the eviction procedure and the N54 at chapter 66 dealing with mortgage repossessions. The same principles apply to tenant evictions. All in all, you are likely to have around 18 days plus from the expiry of the date by which you should have given possession before being actually forced out by the bailiff.

- If ordered to give possession within anything less than 42 days, you could apply to the court for the time to be extended for up to 42 days from the date of the possession order should circumstances amounting to exceptional hardship have arisen since the order. Remember, the longer the period you are allowed within which to give possession, the longer the landlord has to wait before they can ask for the bailiff to get to work.

Multiple nice little earner

Anyone having control of or managing a property in multiple occupation which should have been licensed but was not, commits an offence under the Housing Act 2004. Where that has happened, you can apply to the first-tier tribunal for your offending landlord to repay you the rent you paid out while the property was wrongly unlicensed with a limit of 12 months' worth. It's called a rent repayment order. Any part of that rent included in your universal credit would go to the local housing authority. The tribunal will take into account the conduct of both your as well as the landlord's financial circumstances. An upper tribunal case in June 2020 decided that the landlord was not entitled to have any fine he had been liable to pay for committing the offence deducted from the tenant's award. Likewise, money they had spent out during the unlicensed period in repairing or enhancing the property. Money paid for utilities, however, could be knocked off.

A rent repayment order can be made against not only your landlord but your landlord's own landlord (who may or may not also own the freehold of the property) where, having control of or managing the property, they have themselves offended. They might have let out the whole or part of the building to your landlord who then let out a few rooms to you and 246 other tenants.

A bit more on one of those penalty claims – or how an estimated 284,000 landlords are holding an unprotected £500,000,000*

(*The estimates were made by the Centre for Economics and Business Research in a report published in January 2016).

Alright then. I can't resist it. If you have a claim you should notify it to the landlord before rushing into court proceedings. Once upon a time, the defaulting landlord could be ordered by the court to repay the unprotected deposit to the tenant or pay it into a scheme and to stump up for the tenant a penalty equal to three times the amount of the deposit. The law has now gone softer on the landlord. They can still be ordered to repay the deposit or, where the tenant is still renting, pay it into a scheme but the penalty may be mitigated. It will be a minimum of an amount equal to the deposit and a maximum of three times the amount of the deposit. It could be the deposit x 1.5! Judges are alive to the harshness of the deposit protection law and only in the most diabolical case – say your landlord was fully aware of the law but steadfastly refused to do anything about complying with it, ripping up your letters pleading with them to protect and returning the tiny pieces in an unstamped envelope dipped into horse manure and treated the previous tenant in exactly the same way – it is likely that the maximum penalty would be imposed. Otherwise, you would be lucky to achieve a triple penalty. Your letter to the landlord might go something like this:

> Dear Landlord
>
> Re 61 Trionoble Close, Peardrop
>
> You are in breach of your obligations under the Housing Act 2004 (as amended by section 213) in relation to the deposit of £500.00 which I paid you on entering into my tenancy agreement with you of the above premises dated 14 July 2018 in that:
>
> as I have established on enquiry of the three approved schemes for deposit protection, you have failed to protect my deposit.
>
> or
>
> you have failed to provide me with the prescribed information as to deposit protection.
>
> I hereby claim against you the return of the deposit and a statutory penalty of £1,500.00 representing three times the deposit sum. If you do not pay me the total sum claimed of £2,000.00 within 14 days of receipt of this letter, I shall be obliged to commence proceedings against you in the county court in which I shall claim that total sum together with interest and the costs of the proceedings.
>
> **Without prejudice***
>
> With a view to obviating court proceedings I am prepared to accept the sum of £1,250.00 from you inclusive of the deposit return in full and final settlement of my claim against you provided I receive payment from you within 14 days of the date of this letter. Otherwise, I will institute proceedings against you without further notice in which I shall seek the full £2,000.00 plus interest and costs as set out above.
>
> Yours faithfully
>
> Clive Troublesore

*See chapter 10.

You may be under pressure from your landlord to get out. A different tactic is then required. You could advance a penalty claim in response to receiving a section 21 notice from your landlord or later if your landlord starts county court possession proceedings against you. Those proceedings could be based on the fact that you have stayed put when the section 21 notice expired or have been inspired by your non-payment of rent.

Why would you want to respond then and how would you do it? If you have had a section 21 notice and been a good tenant – or you haven't been too bad – and you want to stay on in the premises, the landlord may be dissuaded from following up the section 21 notice with possession proceedings by the legitimate threat of deposit protection proceedings. The same tactic could be applied on being given a section 8 notice (see above).

> Dear Landlord
>
> Without Prejudice*
>
> 61 Trionoble Close, Peardrop
>
> You have served me with a notice under section 21 of the Housing Act 1988. If I am obliged to vacate then, of course, I shall vacate but would do so with regret. I would prefer to continue in possession. I have been a good tenant. Unfortunately, you have not complied with the Housing Act 2004 in relation to my deposit. Even though it was protected and I had been given the prescribed information when the notice was served:
>
> > the deposit was protected late;
> >
> > or
> >
> > the prescribed information was sent to me late.
>
> I am advised that I am entitled to claim or counterclaim for the return of the deposit and a penalty equal to three times the amount of the deposit and interest. However, if you are prepared to withdraw the section 21 notice and to grant me a new tenancy for 12 months on the same terms as my last fixed term tenancy, I am prepared to forgo any claim for relief on the ground of your breach. This offer shall be treated as withdrawn if I do not receive written confirmation that you accept it within 14 days of the date of this letter.
>
> Yours faithfully
>
> Clive Troublesore

*See chapter 10.

Should your landlord not accept your kind offer but bring proceedings because you are still in occupation, you could counterclaim for the deposit return, penalty and interest, when you answer the proceedings. This would enable you to request the court to set off any costs awarded to your landlord on their claim, against the money awarded to you and to collect the balance awarded on your counterclaim. You may have one technical difficulty with the counterclaim. The landlord will probably have used the accelerated procedure for gaining possession and the defence form for your completion sent out with the court papers does not cater for a counterclaim. The solution is to draw up your own form of counterclaim, staple it to the defence and send both documents in to the court. You may wish to wait and see if you are asked to pay a counterclaim fee. Otherwise, you can refrain from counterclaiming and bring your own claim (see below on procedure) which the court will probably deal with separately to the possession claim but may link up with the possession claim.

If your landlord is relying on rent arrears and a section 8 notice (see above) to get you out, it is possible that a combination of the return of the deposit and a penalty would wipe out those arrears or would, at least, reduce them to below the level at which the court would be obliged to oust you.

> **Defence**
>
> *I set-off against the arrears in the sum of £z which I admit, the amount of the deposit of £y and a penalty for three times the amount of the deposit (or such sum as the court shall think fit) and interest thereon at the rate of 8% from the date of the claimant's breach until judgment on the grounds that the claimant has:*
>
> *failed to protect my deposit;*
>
> *or*
>
> *failed to give me the prescribed information;*
>
> *or*
>
> *has protected my deposit late in that it was only protected on 2 January 2016;*
>
> *or*
>
> *has given me the prescribed information late in that it was only given on 2 March 2016.*
>
> *Insofar as the amount of the claim is less than the aggregate of the deposit, penalty and interest, I counterclaim the difference.*

And another bit more on one of those penalty claims

If you decide to take your landlord to court for some deposit penalty cash independently of any claim by them, you cannot do it, or, at least, you should not do it by claiming online. There is considerable confusion about the procedure to be followed and some of it is fuelled by internet advice websites. You should start proceedings in the county court at the civil hearing centre for the district covering the premises in question. If you don't, they will be sent on there. You start them by using claim form N208 which is for what is known (to judges, lawyers, court staff and anyone who has already had a go) as a Part 8 claim (see chapter 12). This form is different from the one used for claims for money to be paid to you and the procedure is different from that which applies to money claims. You pay a flat fee in the county court of £308 when you kick off unless you qualify for fee remission (see chapter 17) and you don't quantify the precise amount you are after on the front of the form. Also, although some particulars of the claim must be given, they may not be as comprehensive as the particulars of claim in say a money claim and, at the same time as you issue the claim form, you must put in a written statement of your evidence. These documents should be presented to the court in triplicate.

Should court staff query whether you are in need of mental treatment because you have used form N208 and are attempting to start the proceedings at their hearing centre, tell them to have a gander at the Civil Procedure Rules 1998 rule 56.1(1) and Practice Direction 56 paragraph 2.1 – and don't be cocky.

Where your landlord contests the claim and it looks as though the case could be protracted in view of the lengthy, complex and boring points they take, write to the court and ask that the judge reallocate the case to the small claims track (see chapter 25). You have a very good chance of that happening. The different procedure means that you cannot obtain a default judgment against your landlord should they do nothing about contesting: there must be a hearing.

Let's just see how the details of your claim on the claim form might go.

> 1. At all material times, the claimant was the tenant of 61 Trionoble Close, Peardrop ("the premises) and the defendant was his landlord. The premises were let to the claimant by the landlord under a written assured shorthold tenancy agreement dated 14 July 2015 ("the agreement") for a term of 12 months.
>
> 2. On 14 July 2020 the claimant paid the defendant the sum of £1,000.00 ("the deposit") which was a tenancy deposit within the definition contained in section 212(8) of the Housing Act 2004 ("the Act").
>
> 3. The defendant has failed to pay the deposit into an authorised scheme in compliance with section 213(3) of the Act.
>
> or
>
> 3. The defendant paid the deposit into an authorised scheme on 2 November 2020 which was outside the period of 30 days beginning with the date of its receipt and, accordingly, the defendant failed to comply with section 213(3) of the Act.
>
> or
>
> 3. The defendant paid the deposit into an authorised scheme in compliance with section 213(3) of the Act but failed to give the claimant prescribed information in compliance with section 213(5) and (6) of the Act and the Housing (Tenancy Deposits) (Prescribed Information) Order 2007.
>
> or
>
> 3. The defendant paid the deposit into an authorised scheme in

compliance with section 213(3) of the Act but did not give the defendant prescribed information until 2 November 2020 which was outside the period of 30 days beginning with the date of receipt of the deposit and, accordingly, the defendant failed to comply with section 213(5) and (6) of the Act and the Housing (Tenancy Deposits) (Prescribed Information) Order 2007.

or

3. The defendant paid the deposit into an authorised scheme in compliance with section 213(3) of the Act and gave the claimant what was purportedly prescribed information but such information was insufficient so as to comply with section 213(5) and (6) of the Act and the Housing (Tenancy Deposits) (Prescribed Information) Order 2013.

or

3. The claimant has been notified by the defendant that the x [insert scheme name] authorised scheme applies to the deposit but has been unable to obtain confirmation from its administrator that the deposit is being held in accordance with such scheme.

4. In the above circumstances the claimant claims:

a. an order that the defendant repay the deposit to the claimant.

or

a. an order that the defendant pay the deposit into the designated account held by the scheme administrator under an authorised custodial scheme.

and

b. an order that the defendant pay to the claimant a sum equal to three times the amount of the deposit.

and

c. interest under section 69 of the County Courts Act 1984 at the rate of £8 per centum per annum on such sum and for such period as the Court shall deem just.

and

d. costs.

And the statement that has to go in? If there are relevant aggravating facts of which you are aware then they should go in as they could make the difference between a penalty of the deposit x1 and the deposit x3. Evidence, for example, that your landlord knew of what the law required of them; that they had "form" with regard to breaking this particular law; that you repeatedly reminded them that they must comply; and that you were prejudiced in some way by their default. Something along these lines but depending, of course, on which of the alternative grounds you are resting on.

IN THE COUNTY COURT
AT PEARDROP
BETWEEN

Case no 20P00068

Claimant C Troublesore

1st

CT1-CT"

1 December 2020

CLIVE TROUBLESORE Claimant

– and –

WHITEWASH LIMITED Defendant

I CLIVE TROUBLESORE state as follows:

1. I live at 61 Trionoble Close, Peardrop ("the premises").

2. I am a local authority pest control officer.

3. The facts referred to in this statement are of my own knowledge.

4. The premises were let to me by the defendant under a written assured shorthold tenancy agreement dated 14 July 2020 ("the agreement") for a term of 12 months. Immediately before the agreement was completed I paid the Defendant's lettings administrator Mr Archibald Daredevil the sum of £1,000 in cash of which receipt was acknowledged in the agreement. This sum was intended as a deposit to secure my performance of the obligations to maintain the premises in a state of good repair as set out in the agreement. I produce a true copy of the agreement marked "CS 1". Mr Daredevil told me when I handed over the deposit to him that although he and the directors of the defendant regarded the law of tenancy deposit protection to be "bloody mad", he would personally see that the deposit was protected and that I would receive details of this as soon as he could get them to me. He said that the defendant has already had its fingers burnt with a previous tenant of the premises and it would not happen again.

5. I took up possession of the premises on 14 July 2020.

6. By 28 July 2020 I had heard nothing from the defendant about deposit protection and so on that date I telephoned Mr Daredevil on six occasions. On each occasion he told me he could not speak because he was tied up on urgent company business but that he would write to me.

7. I waited about one week and heard nothing from Mr Daredevil or anyone else on behalf of the defendant and I then began telephoning the defendant's office. Over a period of three weeks I made about 79 telephone calls to the office. I was never able to speak to Mr Daredevil. I was given a variety of excuses for the non-availability of Mr Daredevil by the series of staff members I spoke to ranging from him being crippled with stomach ache and unable to converse to him being in conference with the defendant's managing director and not to be

disturbed. Each time I gave my name and address and asked that Mr Daredevil contact me urgently about the protection of my deposit.

8. On 1 August 2020 I wrote to the defendant about the deposit demanding a reply within seven days and warning that I would bring proceedings against the defendant if I did not have a satisfactory response within seven days. I produce a true copy of my letter marked "CT 2". I heard nothing back.

9. The amount of the deposit is substantial to me and I can ill-afford to lose it. Not only have I had been considerably inconvenienced by the time wasted in chasing the defendant but I have been worried that my deposit may have been dealt with improperly or may in some other way be in jeopardy.

10. This statement has been composed by me and in my own words. I believe that the facts stated in this witness statement are true. I understand that proceedings for contempt of court may be brought against anyone who makes, or causes to be made, a false statement in a document verified by a statement of truth without an honest belief in its truth.

Signed

C Troublesore

Dated 1 December 2020

Tenancies from social landlords

Here we are looking at tenancies granted by councils and certain other social housing sector landlords. As with private tenancies, there are specific grounds which the landlord must establish to obtain a court possession order but, generally, the landlord must go on and prove that it is reasonable to order possession (though not with an *assured shorthold* tenancy but see below). Because of this, the court has considerable scope to allow the tenant who has broken a tenancy condition to stay put by:

- dismissing the claim (rare but possible where say you got into arrears only because the housing benefit people lost your documents and wrongly ceased payments);
- ordering possession but suspending the order (effectively, paralysing it) so long as certain conditions are observed by you (for example, paying off the arrears in addition to paying future rent as and when it falls due or no longer using the back garden to cultivate cannabis);
- adjourning the possession claim for as long as you keep to agreed terms (for example, where there are rent arrears but they are modest); or
- postponing possession.

A few words on postponement. This is an alternative to a suspended order and involves the court making a possession order but not fixing a date for you to go. Instead, the court leaves it to the landlord to apply for an order fixing the date should you break any of the terms of the order which will usually relate to payment of the arrears by instalments and payment of current rent. A postponed order would be better for you than a suspended order. The reason is that the landlord needs an additional court order before requesting the bailiff to evict when you breach a postponed order but, with breach of a suspended order, the landlord can go straight to the bailiff. Social landlords hate postponed orders: many judges love them.

The tenant is sometimes stumped because they lack the security given to the so-called conventional secure tenant who rents from a council. Or do they? A homeless person who has been granted temporary accommodation by a local authority under a licence instead of a tenancy can be evicted without a court order. But take a homeless person who has been put into temporary accommodation by the council as a tenant or a council or housing association tenant who has an assured shorthold tenancy. They won't have the same security as the conventional council tenant: in short, it's easier for the landlord to get them out through a court order. Still, for such a non-secure tenant there might just, just, just be a modicum of hope in defeating the landlord who has overstepped the mark with a (drums roll, trumpets fanfare, George Clooney and his wife enter stage left)....**public law defence or human rights (or both) defence**.

The public law defence involves arguing that the landlord's actions are irrational or disproportionate. The human rights defence is along the lines that the landlord has breached article 8 of the human rights convention. That says everyone has the right to respect for their private and family life, their home and their correspondence and that there is to be no interference with this right by a public authority (such as a council landlord) except where it is in accordance with the law and is necessary in a democratic society in the interests of national security etc etc. Often, both defences are run. If the landlord has called a meeting at the request of the tenant to review its decision to bring possession proceedings and sat with cotton wool in their ears and laughter on their faces as the tenant addressed them or the tenant owes only £25 in rent and they have mental health problems then the landlord may well be denied possession. The defences are usually raised – and stand the best chance of succeeding – where the tenant is vulnerable as a result of mental illness, physical or learning disability, poor health or frailty. Incidentally, that public law defence will never be available to the tenant of a private landlord so there is no scope for the private tenant to argue, for example, that their landlord's decision to have them ousted was disproportionate. The idea that this defence could be successfully run was put to bed by the Supreme Court in June 2016.

The social landlord (now including housing trust) is obliged to follow a pre-action protocol which was last revamped in January 2020. If they fail to do so, the court may order them to pay any costs you have incurred whether or not you have been represented by a lawyer. It may also be persuaded not to order you to pay the landlord's costs in making the claim which you would otherwise almost certainly be stuck with and it can take the landlord's naughtiness into account in deciding what order to make when it has a discretion about what to do. And where the landlord is solely relying on one of those grounds we have been looking at where you are normally stumped because you lack the security of a conventional tenant, the court can adjourn the hearing to give the landlord the opportunity to take the protocol steps it should already have taken – or even throw out the claim!

When you have run up rent arrears, the social landlord must:

- contact you as soon as reasonably possible to discuss the case, your financial circumstances and any entitlement you may have to benefits or other help;
- try and agree a plan for you to pay off the arrears;
- send you quarterly statements showing the rent due and the sums received for the past 13 weeks;
- arrange for the arrears to be paid by the Department for Work and Pensions out of your benefit, if you meet the appropriate criteria;
- offer to assist you in claiming housing benefit, discretionary housing benefit (where you have been hit by the bedroom tax) or the housing benefit element of universal credit; and
- withhold taking you to court if you can demonstrate a reasonable expectation of eligibility for housing benefit or that element of universal credit and you have provided all the evidence required to process an application for it so long as you have paid all sums not covered by the benefit.
- inform you of the date and time of any court hearing and advise you that, because your home is at risk, you should attend.

The procedure for getting you evicted once the time for you to give possession has expired is generally the same for a tenancy from a social landlord as it is for a tenancy from a private landlord (see above in connection with form N54 etc). However, it is unlikely that a social landlord will use a High Court enforcement agent to evict you: it will almost certainly be the county court bailiff.

Water and sewerage bonanza

In 2019, the High Court ruled that Kingston-upon-Thames Council had been overcharging its tenants for unmetered water charges and sewerage charges for over 14 years up to August 2017. It pains me to have to tell you this because I have fond memories of walking past the council's headquarters on my way to grabbing a lunchtime egg and watercress sandwich at M&S. Anyway, for the period concerned, an agreement between the council and Thames Water allowed the council to enjoy a commission and an allowance to reflect the fact that certain properties would be unoccupied from time to time when no services by Thames Water would have to be provided. However, the council did not pass on these reductions to their tenants. The judge ruled that as the council was bound by the Water Resale Orders 2001 and 2006, it had charged more than the permitted sums for these services and the tenants had a right to recover what they had been overcharged. The Court of Appeal upheld this ruling in October 2020.

As a result of the ruling, hundreds of thousands of council and housing association tenants in similar situations are likely to be in for refunds, either at the instigation of their landlords or former landlords – the fact that they may have moved on to other accommodation does not take away this entitlement – or through making county court claims for what they were overcharged plus interest. It is likely to be near impossible for a tenant to work out the refund due and so it may be necessary when suing to claim 'an account for the amount due' and judgment for that amount rather than a specific sum which has been arrived at with the assistance of a pin while blindfolded. This would allow the court to carry out an enquiry into the figures on the strength of documents from the council or housing association.

Lodgers

Most lodgers can be required to leave without a court order so long as they have been given reasonable notice to go and the notice period has expired. This applies provided that the landlord lived on the premises as their only or principal home when you moved in and they are there on this basis when your time is up. You must also be sharing some living space with the landlord: bathroom, kitchen or whatever. Notice period? 28 days is the norm but more could be needed where you have lived in the accommodation for a very long time and less could be sufficient where you have been there for five minutes. Should you have beaten up your landlord then very short notice might suffice. In one case I tried, I decided that a lodger who had kicked and bruised his elderly landlady in the course of a dispute could be required to go the next day.

FOR PRIVATE LANDLORDS' EYES ONLY

"I smell trouble"

Your *assured shorthold* tenant misses one month's rent. Unless the premises are unfit for human habitation so that you will never find another mug to move in or you are having a passionate affair with the tenant, consider very carefully whether to serve notice requiring possession (provided, of course, the law gives you the grounds to do so at that stage), even though you do not follow it up with a court claim for possession. More often than not, one month missed means further trouble down the line.

A notice will concentrate the tenant's mind on their obligation to pay and if further arrears accrue and you have already served a notice then you may be able to start a claim immediately or very soon. If it's say a monthly tenancy (either because it always was a monthly tenancy or the fixed term has come to an end with the result that the law treats the tenant as staying on as a monthly tenant) you can serve a two months' notice under section 21 of the Housing Act 1988. Longer notice would have been required under the temporary coronavirus legislation (see above). If a fixed term is still running then there may be a break clause in the tenancy which you can invoke and the section 21 notice may well be sufficient to trigger the break – or it may not. Study the tenancy wording. That's one good reason to have a break clause in a fixed term tenancy: ideally, one that entitles the landlord to end the tenancy by giving two months' notice. The prohibition against the landlord ending an *assured shorthold* tenancy during the first six months of its life does not apply to lettings after 27 February 1997. But for a tenancy granted on or after 1 October 2015 there has been a prohibition on an end within the first four months of the tenancy. The section 21 route will entitle you to utilise the accelerated possession claim regime and you can seek the arrears in a separate online claim.

You can explain your point of view to the tenant without prejudicing your legal position.

> *"Dear Mr Troublesore*
>
> *I very much regret that you have failed to pay your rent due on 14 July 2021. I am hopeful that this is due to some unexpected difficulty and that you will shortly clear the arrears and not default again as I would prefer to keep you as my tenant and not be compelled to take steps to recover possession of the premises from you. However, I am sure you will understand that I must protect myself as I am heavily reliant on receiving the contracted rent from you regularly and promptly. Accordingly, I enclose a formal notice under section 21 of the Housing Act 1988 and ask you to please acknowledge receipt. If I am able to withdraw the notice, I will let you know but, subject to this, its terms must stand.*
>
> *Yours faithfully,*
>
> *P Rachman"*

Section 8 v Section 21

Where two months'/eight weeks' arrears are already outstanding you can serve a 14 days' notice (it was longer under the emergency coronavirus legislation) under section 8 of the Housing Act 1988 during a fixed term or monthly tenancy. But in that situation you will not be entitled to use the accelerated possession procedure and there will have to be a court hearing leading to a slower process. Against this, you will be able to make a claim for the arrears in the same proceedings. Should the arrears be cleared or brought down to less than the equivalent of two months/eight weeks before the hearing then your right to a mandatory possession order will have been lost. You can always serve a section 21 notice when the law permits it at the same time as the section 8 notice (telling the tenant that each notice is without prejudice to the other). Once the time for giving possession under the section 21 notice has expired, you can restart proceedings on the strength of it should you still be on a quest for possession and the section 8 notice not have led to it.

Dodgy notices

The notice required to be given to the tenant under section 8 of the Housing Act 1988 that you are seeking possession may be defective. The earliest date on which you will start court proceedings has to go in. The date you give may be incorrect – it frequently is – or you may insert other information that is wrong or leave out information which should have gone in. A mistake is not necessarily fatal. The court will have to decide what a reasonable tenant would have made of it when reading it in the context of the prevailing circumstances. If a reasonable tenant would have realised there was an error and appreciated what the notice was intended to convey then it will be interpreted that way to see whether it does everything required by law. Take the case before the Court of Appeal in 2020 called *Pease v Carter and Carter*. There the notice gave the earliest date for starting proceedings as after '26 November 2017', which had passed, instead of '26 November 2018'. The Court of Appeal decided (despite what some had regarded as previously conflicting Court of Appeal decisions) that the 'reasonable tenant' test did apply and that any reasonable tenant would have realised there had been a mistake and what it was. The notice was valid. It was also made clear that in deciding what a reasonable tenant would have made of the notice, a court could take into account any covering letter sent with the notice which contained a correct date in respect of when proceedings could be started.

If a notice is invalid then, except where you are asking for mandatory ground 8 possession because of at least two months' rent arrears when the notice was given and at the hearing, the court has the power, which we have already met, to dispense with the requirement to have given a valid notice on the ground that it would be just and equitable to do so. Don't bank on the court doing so. It is more likely than not to refuse you. Rather than waiting to find out, you may prefer to abandon obtaining possession on the strength of the dodgy notice and serve a fresh and compliant notice. Alternatively, you could battle on with court proceedings on the strength of the dodgy notice and, pending the hearing, serve a second notice while making it clear when doing so that the second notice is 'without prejudice to my contention that the notice served on x is fully valid and compliant with the law.'

Accelerated possession no-show

The normal order in an accelerated possession claim is that the tenant must leave the premises within 14 days of the court order which will be made without a hearing provided the judge is satisfied with what they have seen on the papers. But the tenant may have asked for more time: up to 42 days instead of 14 days. The claim form will have invited you to say whether you consent to a request for more time being decided on paper. It may be a bad idea to give that consent. At a hearing on whether there should be more time, there may be matters you can bring to the judge's attention which will have a bearing on whether the tenant would suffer exceptional hardship in having to leave within 14 days. Where there is a hearing devoted to whether more time should be given the initial order on the papers will still have been for possession within 14 days.

Friends for breakfast

When the eviction is through the county court, the bailiff will do the deed and the same procedure will apply as for the eviction of a mortgage borrower. There is a trend for some persons facing eviction to invite 50 or so friends for breakfast to coincide with the eviction appointment and for the friends to gather in the front garden before the baked beans are heated, possibly with a drum or two and some trumpets and maybe an accordion and some flags and notices unflattering to the bailiff and the claimant and some menace. When this happens, the bailiff who has respect for his physical health and pension takes fright, although the accompanying claimant or their representative on hand to board up the property once possession has been achieved, is occasionally up for some muscle action. The process is frustrated. With a view to outwitting the defendant and their friends – and, more often than not, the friends are part of an organised group who are heavily into this nonsense – a special scheme has been devised for the county court.

Where the bailiff has been frustrated first time around, the claimant will be given the opportunity of agreeing to a second eviction to be set on a date and at a time which will not be notified to the defendant. A notice with the new appointment will be served on the defendant by a minimum of two bailiffs, no less, with appropriate protective equipment, at least seven days before the date of the intended eviction. It informs the defendant that bailiffs will reattend at any time without further notice after a stated date to conduct the eviction. With gritted teeth, it gives the unfriendly defendant user friendly guidance. It will be accompanied by a scary warning to the occupier that their home is at risk if they ignore the notice and provide details of the usual agencies who can help. Before the secret eviction attempt, bailiffs who have been specially trained will conduct a risk assessment and formulate an action plan to mitigate any noted risks. The police will not become involved in the eviction but may attend to deal with any breach of the peace. If there is reason to believe that the defendant has got wind of the second eviction date, that will be aborted and a new date set although no further notice will be served on the defendant.

Here's the rub. Bailiffs are advised that they must withdraw from enforcement if there are risks of threats of harm or violence. They must assess the risk throughout the eviction. This procedure is a commendable attempt at avoiding an organised protest but it is no panacea. There are alternatives for the obstinate defendant. One is to seek to have them evicted through the High Court by an enforcement agent who is likely to be readier for some bother and almost certainly will be able to give an earlier eviction date than a county court bailiff. To achieve this you have to get the case transferred to the High Court. It is by no means a forgone conclusion that the county court judge considering the matter will agree to transfer. Some judges feel that the trusted county court bailiff should be left to get on with enforcing a county court judgment. You can apply orally to the county court judge from whom you obtained the possession order for the case to be transferred to the High Court for enforcement by a writ of possession or you can apply subsequently on paper using an application notice in form N244 and accompanying it with a request for a certificate of judgment in form N293A. Attempts by enforcement agents acting for landlords to bypass the county court because it was taking too long to process the form N244, by applying directly to the High Court without notice to the tenant for possession to be dealt with there have now been thwarted: any such application must in future be made on notice to the tenant. On the N244 to the county court you should apply for an order that *"the claim to be transferred to the Central Office of the Queen's Bench Division of the High Court for enforcement of the order for possession dated [insert date]"*. You will need to support the application with a written statement giving viable reasons for transfer.

> *The defendant is making no payments to me for his occupation of the property and is currently £4,560.72 in arrears of rent. I have a mortgage on the property and am reliant on rental income from it. I have been unable to service my mortgage since the defendant's default began and I am in grave danger of possession proceedings being brought against me imminently if I cannot re-let to a new tenant.*

> *I am informed by the bailiff's clerk at this hearing centre that a bailiff cannot offer an appointment for eviction for at least five weeks. I have been in touch with an enforcement agent who assure me that he could act immediately on a High Court writ of possession subject to giving appropriate notice to the defendant of an eviction appointment.*

> *The defendant has informed me that if I seek to enforce the possession order he will do everything in his power to prevent the bailiff from getting near the property. He says that bailiffs are the scum of the earth and he would rather punch them into a pulp than lose his home.*

A copy of any N244 should be attached to the N293. The county court may impose a condition to transfer that the enhanced costs of enforcement through the High Court instead of the county court be met by you.

And the other alternative? Apply to the county court for the defendant to be committed to prison for their contempt of court in not obeying the court order for possession. A prison sentence for contempt will get them out of the property but they may well be evicted while the contempt hearing is taking place . High Court enforcement is probably the fastest route if you can persuade the county court to transfer the case.

Beware letting agents

Many letting agents offer their landlord clients an all-in service which includes serving a section 21 or section 8 notice and dealing with a subsequent court claim for possession. They do not have the legal status to conduct proceedings on the landlord's behalf and very often they blunder over the timing and form of notice used and completion of the claim form. The consequences of a blunder for the landlord could be monumental. I beg of you, take legal advice if only to check over the documentation which the agent has prepared and ensure that any claim form prepared by the agent is signed by you and not the agent and has your contact details down and not those of the agent. That is what the court rules require if a lawyer is not involved and that way you know what is going on. I have seen many instances of agents' cock-ups which have been hidden from the landlord for ages because court documents have been sent out to the agents and not to them.

Deposited!

That's what you will be if the tenant's deposit has not been protected when it should have been or you have protected but failed to give the tenant the necessary protection information in time and you serve a section 21 notice. It will be legally ineffective and any possession claim you make on the strength of that section 21 notice will fail. You will have to protect late and serve a fresh section 21 notice and then start a new possession claim. Excellent for blood boiling and internal combustion. Fast fix? Refund the deposit to the tenant before you serve the section 21 notice though it won't work as a barrier to a tenant's claim to a penalty for non-protection (see above). Calm down. We know there are rent arrears and the tenant has taken a hammer and saw to the double wardrobes and telly and the deposit was your only realistic hope of gaining some recompense. But the alternative is a delay of around at least three months before you can secure a possession order.

FOR THE EYES, EARS AND JOY OR ALARM OF LANDLORDS AND TENANTS

Unlawful eviction. Stupid for you, the landlord, because it is a crime and you will probably find it very expensive. Dreadful for the dispossessed tenant because you may find yourself out on the street but what could keep you going is the thought of the compensation to come.

Any landlord who physically throws out someone occupying premises as their home – this will usually be a tenant but see **Lodgers** above – or does anything else to get the tenant to leave such as threatening them, changing the locks or turning off the gas or electricity supplies, can be sued under the Housing Act 1988. How does the tenant play it? They may or may not want to go back. If they do, they can apply to the county court for an emergency injunction to compel the landlord to allow them back and not interfere with their right to remain there. They would almost certainly be awarded their costs if an injunction is granted but they would not get compensation as well: that would be the end of it.

They may well prefer to be away from the landlord and their henchpersons forever and collect some cash. How much? If the claim is made under the Housing Act 1988, the compensation will be the difference between the market value of the premises with the tenant in and the market value with the tenant out. That difference could be modest or it could be considerable where, say, the tenant has been there for donkeys' years and has Rent Act protection, they are an assured shorthold tenant with a long tenancy at a lowish rent or the premises or building have development potential.

In assessing the Housing Act compensation, the court may give the landlord a discount, if that is reasonable, on account of the tenant's conduct or that of someone else in the premises before the tenant's exit. And if, before the tenant started proceedings, the landlord offered to let them back in, then the compensation may be reduced where the tenant unreasonably refused the offer. If by then the tenant had already obtained alternative accommodation, there might be a reduction where it would have been unreasonable to refuse had the tenant not obtained it. The landlord could defend and escape a compensation award if they can prove they believed or had reasonable cause to believe either (a) that the tenant had left for good before they swooped or (b) that they had reasonable grounds for their behaviour.

But as an alternative to relying on the Housing Act, the tenant may bring a claim for what are called common law damages alleging breach of the tenancy agreement and, where they have been assaulted, trespass to the person. In that event, the reductions talked out above will not arise. And then how much? In an appeal case which went to the High Court in November 2019 called *Regency (UK) Ltd v Alb-Swalin and Heartland Property Ltd* the locks were changed which kept the tenant out and earned him an award of £19,900 against the owner and head-landlord – £150 per day for 60 days being the two months' notice period the tenant should have been given, £5,000 for the loss of his possessions, exemplary damages for 'a disgraceful case' (they are aimed at punishing the payer) and £1,000 in aggravated damages (they are aimed at compensating the claimant for distress and injury to feelings caused by the defendant's conduct). The award was confirmed on appeal.

In an August 2020 High Court case a church organisation had been unlawfully evicted from its premises and sued the landlord. It had what the law categorised as a business rather than a residential tenancy. It had been kept out of the premises for 40 hours. It was awarded £1,500 to reflect loss of use and inconvenience and exemplary damages equal to three months' rent. Aggravated damages could not be awarded because the tenant was a company and not an individual.

Chapter 68

Unfit Premises

Damp dumps

This is about a war with your landlord over the state of the home they let to you. Generally, that home must be fit for human habitation. The law in this respect has changed through the Homes (Fitness for Human Habitation) Act 2018 and now applies in England to all periodic tenancies (weekly, monthly and yearly) whether your tenancy was granted before or after the Act came into force on 20 March 2019. Tenancies for fixed periods of less than seven years which were granted before 20 March 2019 are caught where you stay on, probably on a monthly tenancy basis, at the end of the fixed period. If the landlord has granted a tenancy for a fixed period of seven years or longer but included a break clause, giving them the right to bring the tenancy to an end before time, the tenancy will be treated as for less than seven years and so you will have the protection of the 2018 Act.

And it's not just private tenancies that have protection. Social housing tenants benefit from it too so that council and housing association tenants can have a go under the 2018 Act as well. Similar laws apply to tenancies of homes in Wales under the Renting Homes (Wales) Act 2016.

What the landlord must do is to ensure that your home is fit for human habitation, both when your tenancy starts and throughout its run. In deciding whether or not the premises are unfit, the court must look at their condition in respect of freedom from damp along with repair, stability, internal arrangement, natural lighting, ventilation, water supply, drainage and sanitary conveniences and facilities for preparation and cooking of food and for the disposal of waste water. Any one or more will do. If it's a flat that has been let to you, then the landlord's obligation will extend to the common parts like landings and staircases (not common because they spit at anyone who walks on them but as they are shared with other tenants in the building and their visitors) because the condition of these parts could impact on the condition of your bathroom or kitchen. Any attempt by your landlord to avoid having to comply by putting into the tenancy agreement words to the effect that they do not warrant the premises will be fit for human habitation, will be null and void so you can ignore them.

The landlord will be off the hook for unfitness which is wholly or mainly attributable to some failure on your part. This could well crop up where you are alleging dampness and the landlord can show – or they think they can show – that the dampness is down to you never opening a window and keeping warm through habitual running on the spot rather than conventional heating. But if, for example, the true reason for dampness is the landlord's disrepair of the property's structure, the law will be on your side. You ought not to have to go to the trouble of showing that it's the disrepair what did it. Judges will leave the discomfort of their courtrooms and visit the claim scene where that is practicable and reasonably necessary. *"Judge, please di-*

rect that you will visit my dump in the course of hearing this case. Wear a trench coat over your robes and, though these days you only don a wig for important occasions like Brian Ferry concerts, I suggest you stick two wigs on your head for this visit. When you are there, the damp will eat into your judicial bones. The intensity of it will be sufficient to prove my case that this dump is not fit for human habitation. Incidentally, I am a human."

The landlord's breach of their fit for habitation obligation could be very costly for them. Where, say, there has been dampness and no hot water or both, over a lengthy period of time, and that has led to some medical condition, the award of compensation (which could include diminution in the rental value of the premises so that a refund of a proportion of each month's rent was justified), the claim's total value could well exceed the small claim limit of £10,000 (see chapter 25). In that situation, a solicitor – pick one who specialises in housing cases – may well be prepared to act for you under a no win-no fee basis (see chapter 7). Otherwise, where you are claiming an order for 'specific performance' which requires the landlord to carry out works to make the premises fit for habitation, that part of the claim could qualify you for legal aid if you can show that the condition of your home raises a serious risk to health or safety. Even if legal aid is not obtained, on a small claim which includes a claim for specific performance, the winner can be awarded up to a modest £260 towards their expense of obtaining legal assistance in the case.

Before starting court proceedings, you should comply with the pre-action protocol for housing conditions (see chapter 10) which takes account of the new fitness for human habitation law and which you will find with the Civil Procedure Rules 1998. This applies to premises in England and it has some useful information about alternatives to court proceedings for tenants of councils, housing associations and other social landlords. There is an older protocol called the pre-action protocol for housing disrepair cases for premises in Wales which is on the same lines.

PARTICULARS OF CLAIM*

1. On 5 January 2020 the dwelling known as and at 61 Trionble Close, Peardrop ("the premises") were let to the claimant by the defendant on a monthly tenancy ("the tenancy") as from and including 6 January 2020 at a rental of £1,250.00 per month. The claimant was born on 1 July 1950.

2. The following were implied terms of the tenancy by virtue of section 9A of the Landlord and Tenant Act 1985, namely that (a) the premises would be fit for human habitation on 6 January 2020 and (b) the premises would remain fit for human habitation throughout the duration of the tenancy.

3. In breach of the implied terms specified at paragraph 2 above, the premises were not fit for human habitation on 6 January 2020 and have remained so unfit throughout the tenancy.

Particulars of unfitness

(a) All rooms in the premises suffered from extreme dampness and as from in or about 14 December 2020 mould began forming on walls in the main bedroom and the living room.

(b) The roof was not watertight and leaked.

(c) The toilet flush only functioned intermittently.

(d) The bath was cracked and could not be used.

(e) The radiators in the main bedroom and living room did not function.

4. Further and in the alternative, it was an implied term of the tenancy by virtue of section 11 of the Landlord and Tenant Act 1985 that the defendant should keep in repair the structure and exterior of the premise and should keep in repair and proper working order the installations in the premises for sanitation and for space heating and heating water.

5. The Defendant breached the implied term specified at paragraph 4 above.

Particulars of breaches

The claimant relies on the particulars specified at paragraph 3 above.

6. Further and in the alternative, the claimant has at all material times owed to the claimant a duty by virtue of section 4 of the Defective Premises Act 1972 to take such care as was reasonable in all the circumstances to see that the claimant was reasonably safe from personal injury or from damage to his property caused by what for the purposes of the said Act of 1972 was a relevant defect.

Particulars of breach of duty

The claimant relies on the particulars specified at paragraph 3 above.

7. By numerous written and oral communications from the claimant to the defendant personally and through its managing agents Nice, Earner & Co, the claimant notified the defendant of the condition of the premises and the matters specified at paragraph 3 above. Despite various promises to attend at the premises and rectify any defects which were apparent, nothing was done by or on behalf of the defendant and no attendances were made except for a cursory visit on the 19 June 2020 by a plasterer sent by Nice, Earner & Co who left for a tea break after ten minutes and has not been heard of since.

8. As a result of the matters specified above, the claimant has suffered injury, loss and damage.

Particulars

(a) Personal Injury. The dampness has caused the claimant to suffer from respiratory problems, sickness and sinusitis from which he has received medical treatment and which has led to him taking time off from his employment as a local authority pest control officer. The claimant's symptoms are continuing. A medical report from Dr Adrian Crochet dated 30 June 2021 on which the claimant relies is attached to these Particulars of Claim.

(b)   Loss of Earnings – £5,268.70 net.

(c)   Diminution in the value of the claimant's enjoyment of the premises.

AND the claimant claims:

(a)   An order for specific performance requiring the defendant to repair the roof of the premises and otherwise carry out such works as shall be required so as to eradicate all dampness and mould at the premises and to repair or replace (as shall be necessary) the defective toilet and bath at the premises;

(b)   Damages;

(c)   Such interest as shall be deemed just; and

(d)   Costs.

I believe that the facts stated in these particulars of claim are true. I understand that proceedings for contempt of court may be brought against anyone who makes, or causes to be made, a false statement in a document verified by a statement of truth without an honest belief in its truth.

(signed) Clive Troublesore

Claimant

Dated 14 July 2021

*The unfitness for human habitation allegation may of itself be sufficient to earn you success in a claim. The other allegations have been included on a belt and braces basis. You can never be certain how the evidence may evolve at a trial and, if there are alternative legal arguments you can put forward in support of your case, then, within reason, throw them all in.

Chapter 69

At War With Your Business Landlord

Tenants rule, OK

Outwitting the enforcement agent

The landlord of business premises can send in an enforcement agent (see chapter 29) to seize goods on the premises which, when sold, will pay off rent arrears. This is without a prior court judgment for the arrears. It's done under what is called the commercial rent arrears recovery scheme which the enforcement agents, discussing their hauls in the salon bar at the end of a perfect day of seizures, call the CRAR. The Taking Control of Goods Regulations 2013 must be followed by the landlord and the enforcement agent. In normal times the scheme can only be used if the arrears amount to at least one week's worth of rent. That threshold has been temporarily and incrementally raised in England and Wales during the pandemic. On 25 April 2020 it went up to 90 days' rent; on 24 June 2020 to 189 days; on 29 September 2020 to 276 days; on 25 December 2020 to a celebratory 366 days; on 25 March 2021 to 457 days; and from 24 June 2021 to 554 days. Worth checking on this book's blog of the threshold if and when you receive an enforcement notice from the enforcement agent. If the threshold has not been reached in relation to any enforcement which has already taken place, you may have a claim against your landlord, the enforcement agent or both. Any interest which the lease states is attracted on arrears and VAT on the rent, if chargeable, can be added in together with enforcement fees but charges for services, repairs, maintenance and insurance are excluded from the scheme.

A landlord can usually forfeit a business lease if rent arrears accrue and that would bring an end to the lease and the landlord's right to rent from when forfeiture takes place (the tenant can apply to the court for relief from forfeiture – see below). But say the landlord has sent in an enforcement agent under the CRAR scheme and then wants to forfeit the lease? Can the landlord do this? NO. The point was decided by the Court of Appeal in 2019 in a case called *Brar and another party v Thirunavukkrasu* where the enforcement agent had taken control of goods on the tenant's premises to cover £10,533 which the tenant then stumped up three days later. Six days later, the landlord purported to forfeit the lease. The tenant went to court claiming a declaration that the forfeiture had been unlawful and for damages. The Court of Appeal ruled that the landlord had waived their right to forfeit. This was because, in principle, using the CRAR scheme amounted to an acknowledgment that the lease continued. If the landlord had wanted the tenant out they should have just gone for forfeiture and then attempted to recover what the tenant owed them by suing for the money.

Other waivers

If the landlord has taken other steps to forfeit your lease – for example, by starting a court claim for forfeiture on the ground of rent arrears or serving you with a notice under section 146 of the Law of Property Act 1925 because you have unlawfully sub-let the premises – and then gone on to demand or accept rent, they may be in trouble. If they knew of what you had done when they demanded or accepted, they will have waived their right to forfeit. In a Court of Appeal case in January 2021, it was ruled that there could even be an effective waiver in this situation. You breach the lease. Rent later falls due. Landlord then unaware of the breach. Landlord subsequently demands or accepts payment of that rent but by then they are aware that the breach has been committed. That, said the Court of Appeal, could amount to a waiver.

Relief from forfeiture

This has nothing to do with self-medicating with paracetamol. It has to do with beating the landlord's attempts to get you out on the basis of rent arrears. Even in these straitened times, the landlord may prefer to see the back of you. Perhaps they have designs on converting the premises into two flats or a massage parlour. In that situation, the landlord is likely to tell you that your lease is forfeited – brought to an end along with any liability to pay future rent – and then take court proceedings for a possession order and judgment for the rent arrears and costs. If you want to stay put and can come up with the money that is due or a credible plan to restart rent and pay off the debt, then the court can be expected to bend over backwards to help you. This involves you applying for – that drum roll again, please – relief from forfeiture.

If you have already been booted out, you can issue your own claim for relief (form N5A) accompanied by particulars of claim. This can be done in the High Court or county court but the former should only be used in exceptional cases. How long do you have? The Common Law Procedure Act 1852 fixes six months from boot out but this is treated as a guideline only. In a 2020 High Court case called *Keshwala and another party v Bhalsod*, the judge stated that over six months could be allowed "so long as the elasticity of reasonable promptitude had not snapped". The landlord may have to put that in their pipe and smoke it. It cannot be argued by the landlord that you have delayed, so long as you keep to those six months.

More commonly, you will be putting in a counterclaim where the landlord has brought proceedings against you. The counterclaim should be sent to the court as early as possible before the hearing and no later than 14 days after you have been served with the landlord's court papers. But if you are late, the judge may well not question the lateness and, even if they do, the probability is you will be forgiven in this kind of case. Although it is not strictly necessary, it is good practice to send the landlord or their solicitor (if they have one) courtesy copies of your documentation at the same time as you send the documentation to the court, rather than have them wait to receive these from the court.

In a counterclaim*, state:

> 1. The defendant admits the facts stated in the particulars of claim.**
>
> 2. The defendant counterclaims for relief from forfeiture on the terms set out at paragraph 3 of this counterclaim or on such other terms as shall be just.
>
> 3. In determining the counterclaim, the defendant asks that the court do take into account that the reasons for the arrears having accrued are that (during the Covid-19 statutory restrictions the premises at which he conducted his business were closed and the defendant's income was limited to etc) and his proposals are that he should recommence the payment of contractual rent on X and settle the arrears of rent and the claimant's costs by monthly instalments of not less than £Y commencing on Z.

*Ideally, the counterclaim should be backed up by a witness statement adding flesh to the bare bones of paragraph 3 of the above counterclaim and containing copies of all relevant documentation.

**You may dispute your landlord's claim to be entitled to forfeit the lease and obtain possession. Perhaps the landlord has sent in an enforcement agent under the CRAR scheme (see above). Perhaps they have waived their right to forfeit (see above). Perhaps you paid all rent due to the landlord in cash and they are on the fiddle. Then you will need to put in a defence (concisely explaining why you dispute the claim) as well as the counterclaim in the same document. The template counterclaim above will need to be adapted along these lines:

> 1. If, which is denied, the claimant is entitled to a money judgment, forfeiture and possession as alleged, the defendant counterclaims for relief from forfeiture on the terms set out at paragraph 2 of this counterclaim or on such other terms as shall be just.
>
> 2. [continue as set out at paragraph 3 above].

You have neither issued your own claim or put in a counterclaim and the landlord's claim is due to be heard tomorrow and you've got the wobbles. Turn up at court, apologise to the judge for not doing what you should have done but ask them to still grant you relief from forfeiture. The judge, having slapped the palm of your hand with a plastic ruler and given you an earful, can still grant that relief on the day. Alternatively, they may adjourn the hearing to another day if your request for relief is contested by the landlord and you could be ordered to pay the landlord's costs for that day's hearing, whatever the final outcome of the case.

Where you are a sub-tenant, you will have the same rights as the tenant in relation to relief from forfeiture.

If the judge is against you at the hearing and makes an order for possession, it will nevertheless be suspended for 28 days to enable you to pay up what is due during that time. Even if you fail to make payment, it would be open to you to issue an application for more time. Indeed, even though you had previously failed to ask for relief from forfeiture, you could apply for such relief at any time within six months of the landlord recovering possession through the court. Where the landlord has relet to somebody else, it would take a miracle for you to succeed.

In a 2019 Court of Appeal case called *Golding v Martin*, the order in a forfeiture case stated that the lease was forfeited and that the landlord should have possession of the premises. The order was defective for two reasons: firstly, it should have stated the date by which the tenant was to give possession and, secondly, it should have allowed the tenant to pay up what was due within 28 days. It did neither and that effectively meant an end of the order. And that was a pity for the landlord because just short of two months after obtaining the defective possession order, they had gifted the premises to their daughter and she had sold the property on to someone else. A good idea to check the wording of any forfeiture order against you.

Part 10

RELATIONSHIPS: BEFORE AND AFTER

Chapter 70

Domestic Abuse Damages Claims

Bill for battery

A spouse, civil partner or cohabitee who assaulted you can be sued for damages as well as forbidden to repeat the exercise. This is quite independent of any criminal proceedings that may be taken against them and in which the criminal court might order them, if convicted, to pay you some compensation, though probably only a token amount.

You also have an option of making an application for compensation (not through any court) under the Criminal Injuries Compensation Scheme which you can be sure will be paid should it be awarded 'cos it's state money. You will need to be patient and have a reasonable expectation of a few years' life since the process would embarrass a snail. An application has to be made as soon as reasonably practicable and, anyway, within two years of the incident but this time limit may be extended in exceptional circumstances. Compensation may be refused where you have not reported the incident to the police as soon as reasonably practicable. Nevertheless, consideration will be given to whether the effect of the incident on you would explain any delay. There is a knock out condition which could scupper you before you have posted the application form. You will be ineligible for compensation if, when injured, you and your assailant were both at least 18 and were living together as part of the same family. However, you will be okay should you and your assailant be apart when you make the application provided you are unlikely to live together again. You will also be ruled out if your assailant may benefit from the award. That okay bit did not apply to pre-1 October 1979 injuries. The victim then was denied compensation simply because they and their assailant were living together as part of the same family at the time of the incident, whatever happened later. But the law was very recently reversed for them and they had until 13 June 2021 to make an application, or a second application if they were turned down first time, and they were then set to qualify for compensation provided they separated after the incident and were unlikely to live with them again. I could have written this return book sooner. I know, I know.

A court claim for damages can be made under the Protection from Harassment Act 1997 and, if required, be linked to an application for an injunction or (and this would be more appropriate for a claim based on a single incident) you can simply make a common law court claim alleging an assault and battery which comes under the umbrella of what is called the tort of *trespass to the person* ("If you trespass my person again, I shall punch you up the bracket.") This claim can also be linked to an application for an injunction or be made separately. The further alternative to seeking an injunction under the 1997 Act is to do so under the Family Law Act 1996 (when it is called a *non-molestation order*) which is more commonly relied on by someone associated with the assailant such as a cohabitee or former cohabitee. A damages claim cannot be made in 1996 Act proceedings but can be made separately, relying on allegations of assault and battery.

Small bills and big bills

What might a claim for damages be worth to you? This depends on the nature of the injury, the extent of the pain and suffering you endured and whether you have a continuing disability and, if so, how long it will last. These are some of the considerations. Guidelines followed by judges (last updated at the end of 2019) suggest that a transient eye injury from which complete recovery is made within a few weeks is worth between £2,070 to £3,710; a very minor wrist injury requiring a plaster or bandage for a matter of weeks with a full or virtual recovery within a year is worth between £3,310 and £4,450; a moderate hand injury is valued at between £5,260 and £12,460; moderate post-traumatic stress disorder following a serious incident from which you have recovered or largely recovered could earn an award of between £7,680 and £21,730; and trivial scarring could bring in £1,600 to £3,310. At the other end of the scale, if you had the extreme misfortune to lose an eye, the court would most likely say that the compensation had a value of between £46,240 and £51,460. On top you would be entitled to be compensated for specific losses flowing from the incident – they are called special damages – such as medical expenses and loss of earnings and any future losses which you expect and can establish.

Another route to compensation

It may be possible to get the court to convert your assailant's violent behaviour into money for you when it comes to deal with a financial application in matrimonial proceedings (such as divorce). It should be prepared to do so when it would be inequitable to disregard it (see chapter 75). But what the hell does that mean? These days it means that the conduct in question must have been pretty diabolical to affect the outcome of the capital share out. Judges are keen to discourage what can become an acrimonious and very time consuming and so potentially costly investigation into the reasons for the relationship breakdown with a view to increasing the innocent party's pay out, not only because of the expense of it all but because both parties may well have contributed to the breakdown. Nevertheless, such investigations are sometimes permitted and sometimes they work. In one case, the husband's share of the capital was reduced to 25% where he had attacked the wife with a bread knife in front of the children and been sentenced to 12 years' imprisonment for the attack. In another case the husband's share in capital was reduced from 50% to 33.33% where he had struck the wife in the chest with a kitchen knife and then attempted suicide. The wife had suffered deep psychological damage along with a superficial wound.

Should the seriousness of your assailant's conduct fall short of what is required to cut down their share of the assets in matrimonial proceedings then you might be well advised to bring a civil claim for damages against them and, if that claim is contested, it can be linked with the matrimonial application and heard at the same time. That way, whilst the violence may not be serious enough to enable the court to reflect it in the matrimonial application award, it can deal with the damages claim in the same way as if you had been assaulted by a complete stranger. Then, the damages you are awarded in the civil claim might be ignored in the matrimonial application with you being treated as not about to receive the damages and your assailant being treated as not having a liability to pay them. Get it?!

How does your assailant's bankruptcy affect any unpaid lump sum or damages? With both, you can now chase any assets they may have along with their other creditors by putting forward a claim to their trustee in bankruptcy. If some of the lump sum still remains outstanding then your assailant will not be released from the obligation to pay when the bankruptcy order comes to an end and they are discharged: they remain liable to you until you have received payment in full. With a damages award, however, anything unpaid may well be lost with the general rule that liability for damages for personal injury survive the end of the bankruptcy arguably not applying where for assault and battery.

It is possible that your assailant is a maniac. If making a claim for damages might promote more trouble from them in the future from which you do not feel a court injunction can adequately protect you, this is a factor which you will obviously consider when deciding what to do.

A claim under the Protection from Harassment Act 1997 must be brought under part 8 of the Civil Procedure Rules (see chapter 12). You should drop off or post the papers to a county court civil hearing centre instead of the County Court Money Claims Centre but it must be the hearing centre which serves the address at which either you or your assailant reside or carry on business: otherwise there will be delay whilst it is sent on to the right place. With the claim form must go statements of your written evidence and the evidence of any other witnesses you intend relying on (see chapter 19). Your own statement will put flesh on the allegations in the claim form and your witnesses will corroborate where necessary. This is what the claim form may look like.

Case no 21P0000678

IN THE COUNTY COURT

SITTING AT PEARDROP

BETWEEN

MAVIS MAGNOLIA Claimant

- and -

CLIVE TROUBLESORE Defendant

Details of claim

1. The claimant claims for relief under section 3 of the Protection from Harassment Act 1997.

2. At all material times the parties cohabited together.

3. Between, on or about 31 December 2017 and 14 July 2021 ("the

period") the defendant pursued a course of conduct which amounted to harassment of the claimant and which he knew or ought to have known amounted to such harassment.

Particulars of harassment

4. Throughout the period the defendant bombarded the claimant with texts, emails and telephone calls which were abusive and/or insulting in content and refused to heed the claimant's request that he desist. The claimant would hear from the defendant by one or more of these media on most days and not less than 20 times a day: sometimes as many as 120 times a day or thereabouts. He would frequently telephone her in the early hours of the morning thereby disturbing her sleep.

5. On 1 January 2021 the defendant posted a message on his Facebook page calling the claimant a "whore" and a "fat cow".

6. On 4 January 2021 at 149 Crescent, Twickenham the defendant assaulted the claimant by slapping her across the face with force using his open hand five times causing her to fall to the ground whereupon he kicked her on both legs not less than six times using both feet whilst wearing heavy boots. He then placed his hands around her throat whilst she remained on the ground and squeezed tightly for about 25 seconds so that she thought she might die and only withdrew them and departed when the next door neighbour rang the front doorbell.

7. By reason of the defendant's conduct as set out in paragraphs 4 to 6 above, the claimant has suffered personal injury, distress and anxiety and loss and damage.

Particulars of personal injury etc and loss

8. The claimant relies on the medical report of Dr A G Ramakin dated 2 June 2021, a copy of which is annexed hereto.

9. The claimant incurred prescription charges of £13.00 and loss of earnings from her employment of £614.91 net.

10. The claimant claims interest on damages under section 69 of the County Courts Act 1984 at such rates and for such periods as the court shall determine to be just.

AND the claimant claims:

a. An injunction* restraining the defendant from pursuing any conduct which amounts to harassment in relation to her until further order;

b. Damages in excess of £5,000 but not in excess of £15,000;

c. Interest; and

d. Costs.

I believe that the facts stated in these particulars of claim are true. I understand that proceedings for contempt of court may be brought against anyone who makes, or causes to be made, a false statement in a document verified by a statement of truth without an honest belief in its truth.

(signed) Mavis Magnolia

Claimant

Dated 16 September 2021

*If you are wishing to obtain an interim injunction pending the full hearing of the case, you should issue an application in form N16A indicating where asked, towards the top, that you are applying in pending proceedings. Where you feel that you need some protection when your assailant receives the court paperwork, you can ask the court to grant you a temporary injunction before they come to know anything about the proceedings. This is known as an ex parte (pronounced party) injunction or an injunction without notice. Your written statement would need to set out why you say this is necessary. The reasons would need to be pretty compelling.

The one-off

You won't get anywhere with a Protection from Harassment Act claim, be it for an injunction or damages or both, unless your assailant has been responsible for at least two incidents. You can still go for an injunction (and one which is temporary and, in a serious case, one obtained ex parte) and damages in an assault and battery claim on the strength of just one incident. This time your claim should be brought under part 7 of the Civil Procedure Rules (see chapter 12) and so you would need to prepare a claim form and a separate document called *particulars of claim*. They might go something like this.

Case no 21P0000678

IN THE COUNTY COURT

SITTING AT PEARDROP

BETWEEN

MAVIS MAGNOLIA Claimant

- and -

CLIVE TROUBLESORE Defendant

PARTICULARS OF CLAIM

1. On 14 July 2021 at 149 Magnolia Crescent, Twickenham whilst the parties were cohabiting together at that address, the claimant was assaulted and beaten by the defendant. The defendant slapped the claimant across the face with force with his open hand five times causing her to fall to the ground whereupon he kicked her on both legs

not less than six times using both feet whilst wearing heavy boots. He then placed his hands around her throat whilst she remained on the ground and squeezed tightly for about 25 seconds so that she thought she might die and only withdrew them and departed when the next door neighbour rang the front doorbell.

2.   By reason of the assault and battery, the claimant suffered personal injury and loss.

Particulars of personal injury

3.   The claimant relies on the medical report of Dr A G Ramakin dated 2 June 2021, a copy of which is annexed hereto.

Particulars of loss

4.   The claimant incurred prescription charges of £13 and loss of earnings from her employment of £614.91 net.

5.   The claimant claims interest on damages under section 69 of the County Courts Act 1984 at such rates and for such periods as the court shall determine to be just.

AND the claimant claims:

a.   An injunction restraining the defendant from pursuing any conduct which amounts to harassment in relation to her until further order;

b.   Damages in excess of £1,000 but not in excess of £15,000;

c.   Interest; and

d.   Costs.

I believe that the facts stated in these particulars of claim are true. I understand that proceedings for contempt of court may be brought against anyone who makes, or causes to be made, a false statement in a document verified by a statement of truth without an honest belief in its truth.

(signed) Mavis Magnolia

Claimant

Dated 16 September 2021

The clock

There are usually time limits for bringing civil proceedings (see chapter 13). A claim under the Protection from Harassment Act must relate to conduct within the previous six years and a claim for damages for personal injury arising out of an assault and battery to an incident within the previous three years (so it may be that you will be too late to claim damages for the latter but in time to do so for the former). Raising your assailant's conduct in the course of a financial application in matrimonial proceedings is possible, however long ago it occurred, although its likely impact on the result will be minimal, if non-existent, where it is very stale.

Chapter 71

Cohabitation

Kit for claims against swines

Don't be fooled. The rights of cohabitees on the breakdown of their relationships are rubbish. The Law Commission would have it otherwise as would many politicians and marchers: the talk about reforming the law to strengthen rights has been incessant for some years. But the law 'aint going to be reformed yet. As the talk goes on, many are obliged to walk away from the relationship with…nothing. The law treats cohabitees in an entirely different way – a substantially inferior way – to the parties to a marriage or civil partnership when the end comes about. Cohabitees have no entitlement to maintenance in respect of themselves although the party who has the main care of a child of the relationship is likely to score child support, if not more, for the child's benefit. And the courts lack the ability to do what is fair between the parties by dividing up their assets. As a general rule, what they own is what they can keep. The message is clear. Marry or enter into a civil partnership and take advantage of the matrimonial laws if the relationship fails. Bully them (though not duress, dear and please no violence), trap them, humiliate them in front of their parents or propose on network radio or television so that they dare not embarrass you with a refusal. All is fair in love, war and getting hitched.

And the message is the same to a person of the Islamic faith who has gone through a religious Nikah ceremony which has not been followed through with a civil ceremony. Get that civil ceremony organised post haste. The reason is that, on a breakdown of the couple's relationship, the Nikah alone will not suffice to obtain a nullity, divorce or judicial separation from a court in England and Wales. Without that, an application for the financial remedies that a party to a marriage ceremony our courts would recognise would not be available. A High Court judge had held to the contrary in a bold decision in 2018. The decision was overturned by the Court of Appeal in February 2020. A Nikah-only bride or bridegroom, though, could take advantage of the same laws available here to a cohabitee who has never gone through any ceremony of marriage with their partner, religious or civil.

If, despite it all, cohabitation is your fate, let's see what we can do for you as, in this book, there's always hope.

The home – on the deeds

If both parties are registered as owners – this would be at the Land Registry where registration takes the place of those lovely old parchment title deeds written out with a blotchy quill pen and making perfect lamp shades – then both can expect the law to deal with the property more or less in the same way as with any other joint owners. It will be evident from the Land Registry documentation whether each party owns one-half of the property or they own it in different shares. One of them may have stumped up a large deposit against nothing from the other when the property was bought and so, by agreement, taken a larger stake in ownership.

If the home was acquired as, or later became, the home of the couple and their relationship is over then the likelihood is that the court will order it to be sold at the instigation of one of them when the other is resisting a sale or just dragging their feet. Again, the likelihood is that the court will go on to direct how the property should be marketed, by which agents and at what price; which of the parties is to organise the sale (frequently, this will be both of them); and that the sale price after deductions for what is required to pay off the mortgage, any estate agent's commission and the legal costs on the sale be divided in accordance with the parties' respective shares in ownership.

Now you might think that what the title deeds say about the shares in which the property is owned is conclusive. Most certainly this is the most powerful evidence that could be available and will usually carry the day. However, it is still open to one of the parties to say that the other has practised some fraud on them (for example, got them to sign the deed which shows the shares pretending it was a request for tickets to attend the recordings of six back to back editions of the *The Chase*) or that they (or the lawyer who drew up the deed) simply made a dreadful mistake.

The law does recognise that a couple's intentions about those shares may change over the course of time. Pin back your lugholes for this case which was decided by the Supreme Court in 2011. Ms J and Mr K were cohabiting and bought an Essex property in their joint names in 1985 for £30,000. In 1993 Mr K moved out. Ms J stayed put with the couple's two children and took full responsibility for the mortgage and other outgoings. In 1995 the couple cashed in a joint life policy and split the proceeds between them. Mr K used his money as the deposit on a new home for himself. By 2008 the value of the Essex property had increased to £245,000. The Supreme Court decided that by then the couple's intention about how they shared had changed from a presumed 50/50 to 90/10 in favour of Ms J! As you might say, you never can tell.

The home – off the deeds

Constructive trust

It may well be possible to establish an interest in property despite the fact that only one person is registered as the owner – that swine of a former co-habitee. If you are out to establish that interest then you will have to prove that you both intended you should have the interest – there was an agreement, arrangement or understanding between you to this effect, usually before the property was bought but sometimes later on – and that you acted to your detriment in the reasonable belief you were acquiring it. This is known to the law as a *constructive trust* claim.

Let's look at what is needed to prove the intention you should have the interest. The fact that the swine used to call the property "our house" won't get you far unless, say, it was to lawyers or accountants and evidence of discussions between the two of you may be crucial. *"You're going through a divorce right now. I won't put your name on the deeds as this could mess up the financial case between you and your hubby." "As you're 21 you'll have to stay off the deeds at the moment."* This sort of comment by the swine would be very useful and they will be taken to have been telling the truth even though they now say they were palming you off with a pack of lies. Nice one, eh?

A financial contribution by you towards the purchase price would be particularly strong evidence of an intention that you were getting an interest. And so might some other financial payment such as conveyancing or survey fees or mortgage instalments (under a repayment mortgage with interest payments only usually being insufficient) or bearing the cost of substantial improvements to the property.

Where a financial contribution has been made, the payment should additionally serve to prove that you have acted to your detriment.

Proprietary estoppel

This, I agree, sounds painful. To Ms B six years ago it was anything but painful. She couldn't prove a constructive trust, though she tried. Nevertheless, she could prove she had an interest in the home in which she had cohabited with Mr T, through the doctrine of proprietary estoppel. This is how it works. You score by proving that the property owner has made a promise to you relating to the home – usually, it's that you can live there until whenever- and that you relied on it to your detriment (which has to be not insubstantial) plus that the owner has acted unconscionably.

In Ms B's case, she had come out of a failed marriage with about £25,000 of which she spent some £15,000 fitting out and furnishing a housing association property she had secured for herself and two daughters in Manchester. Then she met Mr T who was a single man working as a claims manager. The trial judge found him to be "by nature, shrewd, cautious and guarded." But he was to come a cropper. He was against the idea of marriage but wanted to live with Ms B and her daughters. They found a house in Droitwich which was purchased in his sole name. He used £140,000 from the house he had previously owned and otherwise financed the purchase with a mortgage. He reassured Ms B – here comes his downfall – that she would always have a home and be secure in this one. On the strength of that assurance she gave up her Manchester tenancy and moved into the Droitwich home with the girls. She spent £4,000 to £5,000 towards setting up the new home although Mr T paid the mortgage and never suggested that he regarded or intended Ms B to be a joint owner. Around nine years later after a breakdown in the relationship, Ms B and her daughters found themselves homeless. That promise was broken.

The Court of Appeal upheld the trial judge's ruling that the doctrine of proprietary estoppel applied and in relation to the argument that Mr T's behaviour had not been unconscionable, it regarded the repudiation of his promise as unconscionable. That was enough. Ms B was to be compensated for the prejudice to her by Mr T's failure to honour his promise. She had been awarded what the £25,000 she had shelled out on Manchester and Droitwich would be worth when the case was heard: £28,500. The award would stand.

And in March 2016 the Court of Appeal upheld a trial judge's decision that a cohabitee in a 15 year relationship with the man who owned the home in which they lived had acquired an interest in the property thanks to proprietary estoppel. She had contributed £200 per month towards the mortgage instalments. They were said at the time to be "towards the house" and all the evidence showed that meant "towards ownership of the house".

Equitable accounting

You could conceivably be laughed out of court on all your main arguments along the above lines but still leave with some money in your hands. If, say, you have shelled out money towards substantial improvements or repairs or paid or contributed to the mortgage instalments without, in law, earning a proprietary interest in the property, the court might say it was only fair and equitable that the swine should pay you back. It's called *equitable accounting*.

It's litigation time

The party after sale or compensation should send a pre-action letter to the other party (see chapter 10) and, if that results in no shift or a brick though the letterbox, it's off to court. A claim should be made under the Trusts of Land and Appointment of Trustees Act 1996 which lawyers call a *TOLATA* claim so that, as usual, nobody else will know what they are talking about. In such a claim, sections 14 and 15 of the 1996 Act say that the court is to take account of all relevant matters (when shouldn't it?!) effectively including the intentions of the person you will be claiming against, what the property is being used for and the welfare of anyone under 18 who is occupying it or might reasonably be expected to occupy it.

Any moment you will see *TOLATA* particulars of claim with some mix and match paragraphs which can guide you on the sort of argument you could advance in your case. The particulars would be used in conjunction with a Part 7 claim form (see chapter 12) to start the case in court. If you are not expecting what the law calls a "substantial issue of fact" (and I call "a punch-up") to have to be decided in the case then you can use the Part 8 procedure (see chapter 12) but in that event you would need to put in a witness statement (see chapter 19 for how to set it out) instead of particulars of claim. The statement can follow the drift of what would have been in particulars of claim but give more factual detail and, of course, be in the first person ("I left the defendant..." etc).

IN THE COUNTY COURT   Case no 21P0000678

AT PEARDROP

In the Matter of the Trusts of Land and Appointment of Trustees Act 1996

BETWEEN

MAVIS BULWARK Claimant

- and -

CLIVE TROUBLESORE Defendant

PARTICULARS OF CLAIM

1. Between [insert date] and 1 November 2020 the parties cohabited together.

EITHER

2. On 14 July 2007 the parties purchased the freehold property 149 Magnolia Crescent,, Twickenham, Middlesex KT89 4XZ ("the property") registered at HM Land Registry with title absolute and which on that date was transferred to them as joint tenants. On the same date the parties entered into a charge of the property to Parasite (No 3) Building Society ("the Building Society") for the principal sum of £240,000 ("the mortgage") and the claimant contributed one-half of the mortgage instalments and buildings insurance premiums in respect of the property as from acquisition of the property until on or about 1 November 2020.

3. The property was purchased by the claimant and the defendant with the intention that it should be their home for the subsistence of their relationship. On 1 November 2020 the defendant left the property with the intention of bringing cohabitation with the claimant to a permanent end.

OR

2. On 14 July 2007 the defendant purchased the freehold property 149 Magnolia Buildings, Twickenham, Middlesex KT89 4XZ ("the property") registered at HM Land Registry with title absolute and which on that date was transferred to him in his sole name. On the same date the defendant entered into a charge of the property to Parasite (No 3) Building Society ("the Building Society") for the principal sum of £240,000 under a repayment mortgage ("the mortgage).

3. The property was acquired by the defendant with the intention that it should be the parties' home and at all material times such intention has subsisted. Further, between 14 July 2007 and 1 November 2020 the parties occupied the property as their home. The defendant holds the property on a constructive trust for the benefit of the parties in equal shares. Further and in the alternative, the claimant has an interest in the property by virtue of the operation of a proprietary estoppel.

Facts relied on by the Claimant in support of her claim for a constructive trust

a. Immediately before the purchase the defendant said to the claimant: "You won't be on the title deeds. The only reason is that the solicitor told me it would delay the conveyancing if you had to sign up too."

b. At the request of the defendant, the claimant organised removal to the property of the contents of the defendant's previous home.

c. At the request of the defendant, the claimant paid one-half of the fee for the survey on the property requisitioned by the Building Society and one-half of the conveyancing costs and disbursements on the purchase.

d. Shortly after the purchase, the defendant suggested to the claimant that the property be called 'Chez Magnolia-Troublesore'.

e. Between 14 July 2007 and 1 November 2020 the claimant almost invariably made payments out of her earnings as a mobile hairdresser and pedicurist towards the mortgage and the premiums for the buildings and contents insurance cover on the property and, more often than not, such payments were for one-half of the sums due. Further, during the same period the claimant purchased numerous household items for the property and thereby freeing the defendant from any obligation to purchase them and facilitating his payments or contributions towards the mortgage and insurance premiums.

f. The claimant assisted the defendant in internally decorating the property shortly after its purchase and again in 2018.

g. In 2015 the claimant asked the defendant to construct a patio area at the rear of the property whereupon the defendant said to her; "If you want a bloody patio, stick it down yourself." The claimant did thereafter construct the patio with her own labour and using materials for which she paid in excess of £1,000.00.

h. At all material times the claimant acted to her detriment in believing that the defendant was to hold and/or held the property on trust for herself and the defendant.

Facts relied on by the Claimant in support of her claim for a proprietary estoppel

a. The claimant relies on the facts set out in support of her claim for a constructive trust in addition to the facts set out at sub-paragraphs (b) to (d) below.

b. The claimant met the defendant in or about April 2004. By then, she had acquired the tenancy of 689 St John's Wort Parade, Southend, Essex which had been granted by the local authority and following the breakdown in a long-standing relationship with a man who had subjected her to domestic violence. She had spent £10,000.00 on furniture and household equipment for the accommodation and had done so with the intention and expectation that her occupation of it would be permanent, She had also established a network of clients for her business as a mobile hairdresser and pedicurist.

c. In May 2006 the defendant told the claimant that he loved her and wanted to live with her for the rest of his life. He further stated that he wanted the claimant to move into a property with him to be purchased in Twickenham, Middlesex and that, if she did so, she would be secure in it, would never have to leave and could give up her tenancy without having any qualms about her future. The claimant relied on these statements and, in consequence of them, she surrendered her tenancy and ceased carrying on her business in the Southend area, losing her clients, and moved in to the property with the defendant on 14 July 2007.

d. On 1 November 2020 the defendant locked the claimant out of the property and thereafter barred her entrance so that she was rendered homeless and has had to return to the Southend area where she is living with relatives and is currently unemployed.

PLUS

4. The relationship between the parties has irretrievably broken down and the object of the trust claimed by the claimant has failed. The defendant has remained in the property and currently has exclusive possession of it.

AND the claimant claims:

a. A declaration that the defendant holds the property on trust for the claimant and the defendant in equal shares or in such other shares as the Court shall determine.

b. An order for the sale of the property.

c. Such other relief as shall be just.

d. Costs.

I believe that the facts stated in these particulars of claim are true. I understand that proceedings for contempt of court may be brought against anyone who makes, or causes to be made, a false statement in a document verified by a statement of truth without an honest belief in its truth.

(signed) Mavis Bulwark

Claimant

Dated 14 July 2021

And when there are children

We have seen that one of the considerations for the court on a *TOLATA* claim is the welfare of an under 18 year old occupying the property. If the claim is against a parent of the child then it may be prudent for the claimant who is the child's main carer and who either wants to stay put or to get back into the property or, alternatively, is after buying another property, to make a separate claim under schedule 1 to the Children Act 1989. This is a family law claim and is procedurally governed by the Family Procedure Rules 2010. The *TOLATA* claim and the Children Act claim would almost certainly be linked together by the court and heard at the same time (it being necessary to ensure that the judge is qualified to deal with both civil and family cases). A mother, for example, might fail to persuade the court that the father holds the home on trust for her or that there is any merit in her proprietary estoppel argument but succeed in getting the court to allow her to live in the property or in another property which he must provide until the child has completed tertiary education up to and including first degree.

For swines only

The time: approaching midnight.

The place: a romantic French bistro (though part of a large chain) in Clapham Junction.

Clive Troublesore has wined and dined Mavis Bulwark. Unbeknown to her, whilst Mavis pops to the ladies, he proposes to pay the bill with a selection of vouchers and a 'two for the price of one after 10pm weekdays only' coupon torn out of the *Poodle Clippers Weekly*. It is possible that the bistro may end up owing him money.

The verbal intercourse:

> "Mavis."
>
> "Yes, Clive."
>
> "We get on well don't we?"
>
> "Yes, Clive."
>
> "I've got my rambling place number 149 with all that space and you are cooped up in that matchbox next to the station. Come and stay at my place. You can help towards the Xs and we will make music together. You can sign a piece of paper so that you can't take me to the cleaners. As if you would (laughs nervously)."
>
> "Ooooh, yes, Clive."
>
> "That's settled then."

Let's leave the bistro and go over to the agreement I have devised for you. I've kept it short and uncomplicated. It gives the prospective cohabitee a licence to occupy the property into which they are to move and should eliminate or reduce the risk, if and when the music stops and the relationship ends, of any allegation being made that you made promises which would enable them to advance a case of proprietary estoppel (see above).

> THIS AGREEMENT is made on 14 July 2021 BETWEEN CLIVE TROUBLESORE of 149 Magnolia Crescent Twickenham Middlesex KT89 4XZ ("the House") ("Mr Troublesore") and MAVIS BULWARK of Upper Flat

62 Estuary Lane Clapham Common London SW4 XET ("Ms Bulwark") (together called "the Couple")

BACKGROUND

1. Mr Troublesore owns the House.

2. The Couple are in a relationship.

3. Mr Troublesore is desirous of Ms Bulwark living with him at the House and she is desirous of doing so.

4. Ms Bulwark acknowledges that her present living accommodation is unsatisfactory and that in relation to her employment base and the locations of her family and friends it would be as convenient if not more convenient for her to live in the House instead of remaining in her present accommodation.

5. Mr Troublesore does not intend that Ms Bulwark should acquire any legal or beneficial interest in the House beyond the terminable right to occupy it as hereinafter granted or to become entitled to a tenancy or the right to exclusive possession of the House or any part of it and Ms Bulwark acknowledges and accepts that this is the position and further that this is fair and reasonable.

6. Ms Bulwark acknowledges that she has read this agreement and fully understands it and has either obtained independent legal advice on it or that she is aware of her right to do so and of the preparedness of Mr Troublesore to pay the cost of her obtaining such advice.

7. Ms Bulwark acknowledges and accepts that should during the currency of this agreement she make any payments in respect of the House and/or for the entire or partial benefit of Mr Troublesore which she is not obligated to make by the terms of this agreement then she shall nevertheless not be acquiring a beneficial interest in the House or any rights relating to the House to which she would not otherwise be entitled by the terms of this agreement by making such payments.

8. The couple intend and acknowledge that this agreement shall be legally binding on each of them.

IT IS HEREBY AGREED THAT in consideration of the above matters and the mutual acknowledgements and concessions made by them:

1. Mr Troublesore grants to Ms Bulwark the personal licence to live with him in the House and to use the fixtures fittings furniture and equipment in the House with Mr Troublesore and in common with any other person whom Mr Troublesore may from time to time permit to live in or otherwise occupy the House.

2. Ms Bulwark agrees with Mr Troublesore that during the currency of this licence she will:

a. pay to Mr Troublesore the sum of £100 per week payable weekly with the first payment to be made seven days after the date of this agreement or such other weekly sum as the parties may from time to time agree in writing towards the living and other expenses arising out of her occupation of the House.

b.   not cause or permit any other person to occupy the House without the prior consent of Mr Troublesore.

3.   This licence shall come to an end:

a.   forthwith upon Mr Troublesore giving Ms Bulwark written notice that he revokes the licence and why so in the event that Ms Bulwark fails to comply with paragraph 2(a) and/or (b) of this agreement; or

b.   forthwith upon Ms Bulwark permanently vacating the House with the intention of never returning; or

c.   at the expiration of not less than one month's written notice by Mr Troublesore or in the event of his death by his personal representatives.

IN WITNESS whereof the parties have executed this instrument as a deed on the day and year first before written

SIGNED AS A DEED BY   )
CLIVE TROUBLESORE in   )
the presence of:-   )

SIGNED AS A DEED BY   )
MAVIS BULWARK in   )
the presence of:-   )

Pet time

If you have or may have a pet while living together then you can deal in this agreement with what is to happen to them on separation. You will find some suitable wording in our pre-nuptial agreement at chapter 72. It will need some tweaking to suit the different type of relationship.

Dead or alive?

Should one cohabitee expire with either the survivor inheriting nothing under the will or, there being no will, inheriting nothing under the intestacy laws, then the survivor could still be smiling, of course after a suitable period of mourning (see chapter 44).

An alternative cohabitation agreement

You will find another template for a cohabitation agreement – trendily called a *living together* agreement – along with a checklist, both of which you can download, on advicenow.org.uk. It covers every conceivable situation which could arise during a relationship but you can pick and choose the bits you want and disregard the rest. For couples in for the long haul, I commend it. The difficulty is that if one of you produces it to the other before a relationship is given a cohabitation try out it could frighten the other off unless one of you is a forensic accountant and the other is an actuary. Some of my best friends are forensic accountants or actuaries so please do not take umbrage if that happens to be your calling.

Chapter 72

Pre-Nuptial Agreements With What Should Happen To Fifi Thrown In

"I loves you but…"

And it's a big but. It's the but about being terrified your hard grafted dosh and that fat inheritance Aunt Dora left you could go down the drain if and when you marry or enter into a civil partnership and the relationship later fails. Not quite down the drain but to your partner, though the drain would be the destination of your perception. Personally, I don't know how you could do it: how you could be so smitten as to want to spend the rest of your life with this man or woman and at the same time contemplate the destruction of the relationship and that they would then want to take you to the matrimonial bleed-dry cleaners? How could you seek their signature to a pre-nuptial/partnership agreement – the agreement that dare not speak its name? There must also be a modicum of risk that your partner will tell you to get on your bike. There are special, exceptional situations of course. The couple in the late summer or autumn of their lives who have children may be desperate to preserve a good chunk of their assets for them when it's mortal coils time. He or she who has been married before and after bitter proceedings has saved the matrimonial home at great personal expense and is apoplectic at the idea of losing it should the new relationship come to a summary end. For them I can have some sympathy.

Still, it has nothing to do with me. If you want a pre-nuptial agreement, have one. As a solicitor-advocate, I represented plenty of defendants who pleaded 'not guilty, my Lord' when I was convinced in my heart that they were guilty. It wasn't for me to decide on guilt or innocence. It was for the court. And so it is not for me to pass judgment on you (well not now, anyway). It is for you to decide whether to go pre-nuptial and I'll do my best to give you a reasonably digestible agreement which you can use.

There's something you need to understand about a pre-nuptial agreement. It won't be watertight. It could go wrong but, on the other hand, it could go right so it has the potential to save you a fortune. It could go wrong when your partner decides to challenge it in court in financial proceedings which are allied to the nullity, divorce, partnership dissolution or separation case. The court may uphold it or reject it.

Here are the ground rules:

- The agreement must be freely entered into by both sides with a full appreciation of its implications. Duress (gun to the head or as good as) or fraud or misrepresentation by one party to the other aggrieved party will secure the consignment of the agreement to the matrimonial court waste paper bin. Undue pressure ("I know it's all happening tomorrow and you've got two hundred members of your family coming and Neil Diamond is doing the cabaret and we are honeymooning in the Bahamas but if you don't put your signature where I am pointing, you can count me out") will tarnish the agreement and may well render it worthless. The court may take into account a party's emotional state, what pressures they were under to agree, their age and maturity and whether they have been married or in a partnership or a long-term relationship before. To ensure that appreciation of the agreement's implications exist, each side should obtain independent advice from a lawyer. Sorry, but you can't jeopardise the whole enterprise by going lawyer-shy.

- The agreement must be fair to both sides. It is likely to be unfair if it leaves one side in a predicament of real need, while the other enjoys sufficiency or more. If, for example, one side has been incapacitated during the marriage or partnership and thereby incapable of earning a living, this might justify not holding them to the full rigours of the agreement as it would be unfair to do so. It is also likely to be unfair where the devotion of one side to looking after the family and the home has left the other free to accumulate wealth which the agreement says they can keep for themselves.

- There must have been full disclosure of financial information by each party to the other.

- The agreement cannot be allowed to prejudice the reasonable requirements of any children of the family (that is to say children of the union or other children who have been treated as such).

- Respect should be accorded to the decision of a couple as to the manner in which their financial affairs should be regulated, particularly where the agreement addresses existing circumstances (especially where it seeks to protect property acquired before the start of the marriage or partnership) and not merely the contingencies of an uncertain future (for example, a term of the agreement which effectively says: *"The Husband's business may or may not win very substantial contracts at some point in the future, which if won could earn him an additional annual income of in excess of £69,000,000 and which could even reach a figure which is double or triple that but, in that event, the Wife shall not been entitled to enjoy any part of such income by way of periodical maintenance, a capitalised sum or otherwise."*)

So here's the sort of agreement that can be entered into which would need to be adapted according to the circumstances of each individual case. It can also be the model for an agreement between a couple who are contemplating entering into a civil partnership in which event revisions to the agreement should record that it is intended that the agreement should still hold good and be effective if the civil partnership is followed by a marriage and it is the marriage which fails. And as a special treat, the agreement deals with what is to happen to the family pet on breakdown. Judges will be eternally grateful to parties who can reach an agreement on such a subject as pet disputes are about as judicially popular as cases involving a determination on who keeps the sugar tongs. Even the Law Society recommends that parties address pet care in the event of a breakdown. For pet haters, please tweak the agreement suitably and perhaps take in a human but check their teeth first.

> THIS DEED is made on *14 July 2021* BETWEEN CLIVE TROUBLESORE ("Mr Troublesore") and MAVIS BULWARK ("Ms Bulwark") (together called "the couple") both of 149 Magnolia Crescents Twickenham Middlesex KT89 4XZ
>
> BACKGROUND
>
> 1. The couple intend to marry one another no later than 30 September 2021.
>
> 2. The couple have the earnest hope and expectation that their marriage will last for the entirety of their joint lives but have decided after the most careful consideration and with the benefit of the legal advice referred to below to enter into this agreement with the wish that its provisions shall govern their financial affairs in the unfortunate event that the marriage breaks down and it is annulled, dissolved or the subject of a judicial separation upon a decree in favour of either or both of them or in the event that there is an equivalent order under the Divorce, Dissolution and Separation Act 2020.
>
> 3. It would be anathema to the couple to face the potentially heavy cost and, in particular, the unpleasantness of contested financial proceedings following a breakdown of their marriage. It is a matter of comfort to the couple to know in advance albeit without absolute certainty how they would financially stand following a breakdown of their marriage and they perceive this to be one of the many advantages of this agreement. Whilst they recognise that this agreement cannot prevent a court from examining this agreement and that the court's discretion to depart from its terms, wholly or in part, cannot be excluded, it is the couple's strong wish that the court should uphold it in its entirety.
>
> 4. The couple are in no doubt that it is and would continue to be fair to them both and to any children of the family for this agreement to govern their financial affairs should the marriage break down. This conclusion is based on all the relevant circumstances including the disclosure of the present financial circumstances of them both as referred to below and the legal advice they have obtained which is also referred to below.
>
> 5. The couple accept that the other of them has acted honourably in wanting this agreement and in their discussions and conduct preceding the agreement and are satisfied that its terms not only satisfy the legal test of fairness but are morally fair and right.
>
> 6. The couple acknowledge that neither of them has been put under any pressure by the other or by anyone else to enter into this agreement and that, for example, neither of them has threatened or indicat-

ed by themselves or anyone on their behalf that they would not proceed with the marriage if this agreement were not made.

7. The couple have each received legal advice on the draft of this agreement (which was in exactly the same terms as the agreement itself). The advice was in plain English which each of them fully understood. The advice was given to each of them independently of the other and was given to Mr Troublesore by Mr Freeman Hardy-Willis of Speakeasy, Solicitors of Twickenham and to Ms Bulwark by Ms Amelia Doughty-Fighter of Sodscrews Law, solicitors of Richmond-upon-Thames.

8. Mr Troublesore declares that (a) he owns or has some interest which he specifies in the capital assets which are set out in Part 1 of the schedule to this agreement; (b) he has done what has been reasonably possible to provide an approximate figure as to the open market value of those capital assets where their actual value cannot be readily quantified; (c) he is satisfied that all values are reasonably accurate; and (d) he is entitled to the income particularised in Part 2 of the schedule to this agreement.

9. Ms Bulwark declares that (a) she owns or has some interest which she specifies in the capital assets which are set out in Part 3 of the schedule to this agreement; (b) she has done what has been reasonably possible to provide an approximate figure as to the open market value of those capital assets where their actual value cannot be readily quantified; (c) she is satisfied that all values are reasonably accurate; and (d) she is entitled to the income particularised in Part 4 of the schedule to this agreement.

10. The couple accept and agree that the terms of this deed cannot and shall not affect the rights of any child of the couple or treated as a child of the couple as at the date of the marriage or who shall hereafter be born to Ms Bulwark by Mr Troublesore or become a child of the family and that the jurisdiction of the courts to order provision for any such child is preserved and shall not be ousted or in any way affected by the terms of this deed and the couple further accept and agree that the birth of any such child or the fact that a child shall come to be treated as a child of the family is not intended to be a circumstance which would justify Ms Bulwark becoming entitled to any financial or other provision from Mr Troublesore over and above that set out in the hereinafter mentioned Part 5.

NOW THIS DEED WITNESSES as follows:

1. This agreement is conditional on Mr Troublesore and Ms Bulwark being lawfully married to one another no later than 30 September 2021 and shall come into full force and effect forthwith on the celebration of such marriage.

2. In the event of the marriage being annulled, dissolved or the subject of a judicial separation upon a decree in favour of either of Mr

Troublesore or Ms Bulwark or in the event that there is an equivalent order under the Divorce, Dissolution and Separation Act 2020 (a) the financial and any other provision that Mr Troublesore shall make for Ms Bulwark shall be as set out in Part 5 of the schedule to this agreement ("Part 5") and subject to clause 4 of this deed; (b) in respect of the couples' pet dog Fifi ("Fifi") or any other dog which the couple may own in succession to Fifi as at the date of such annulment, dissolution or judicial separation or equivalent order as stated ("the pet") the provisions set out in Part 6 of the schedule to this agreement ("Part 6") shall apply; and (c) the couple shall take all steps that are reasonably possible if called upon by the other of them to do so to cause an order of the court to be made incorporating the provision set out in Part 5 and the provisions of Part 6 and subject thereto dismissing all claims for capital property and maintenance by each of them against the other (the dismissal of Ms Bulwark's maintenance claims to take effect upon her entitlement to maintenance under this deed coming to an end) and debarring each of them upon the death of the other from applying for provision under the Inheritance (Provision for Family and Dependants) Act 1975 as amended and in the event that the court is precluded from dismissing any such claim in proceedings for a judicial separation or separation order the couple shall take all such steps that are reasonably possible if called upon by the other of them to do so to cause an order of the court to be made in subsequent proceedings for annulment or dissolution or equivalent proceedings as stated dismissing all such claims that have not already been dismissed in like manner as hereinbefore specified.

3.   In consideration of the financial and any other provision as set out in Part 5 Ms Bulwark agrees that she will make no financial claim of whatsoever nature against Mr Troublesore or any company and/or business in which he shall have an interest arising out of the couple's relationship or the marriage save and except for the purpose of complying with her obligations under clause 2 of this deed.

4.   The couple acknowledge and agree that (a) in the event that, contrary to their understanding and intention, any part of this deed shall be void or otherwise invalid and/or unenforceable then the remainder of the deed shall remain fully valid and enforceable; (b) the provisions of this deed shall remain in full force and effect notwithstanding the annulment or dissolution of the marriage or the grant of a judicial separation or equivalent event or order as stated to either or both of Mr Troublesore and Ms Bulwark; and (c) in the event that the marriage is annulled or dissolved or a decree of judicial separation (or the equivalent thereof as stated or otherwise) is granted to either or both of Mr Troublesore and Ms Bulwark by a court outside the jurisdiction of England and Wales then the provisions of this deed shall nevertheless have full force and effect and if unable to take the steps set out at clause 2 of this deed for lack of jurisdiction within England and Wales they shall take equivalent steps in the appropriate court outside England and Wales.

5. The couple agree that neither of them shall on the death of the other make any claim for provision against the estate of the other under the Inheritance (Provision for Family and Dependants) Act 1975 (as amended).

THE SCHEDULE referred to above

Part 1

149 Magnolia Crescent Twickenham Middlesex KT89 4XZ – open market value with vacant possession £950,000 less outstanding mortgage of £60,000.00.

Land adjoining 149 Magnolia Crescent as above (including allowance for development potential for 12 detached dwellinghouses) – £3,750,000.

Back editions of Radio Times – £3,000.00.

Copy of Gold's Law published in March 1989 – £1,500.00.

Copy of Gold's Law published in March 1989 signed by the author – £1.50.

Collection of antiques – £150,000.00.

Building Society investments – £1,750,000.00.

Stocks and shares – £3,000,000.00.

Part 2

£750,000.00 per annum.

Part 3

Wet Wet Wet CD – 5p.

Jewellery (Primark) – £2.50.

Part 4

Nil.

Part 5

A: Upon nullity, dissolution or judicial separation decree or equivalent order as stated within two years of the date of the marriage

Mr Troublesore shall pay Ms Bulwark a lump sum of £750,000 within 28 days of decree absolute or decree of judicial separation or equivalent order as stated.

Mr Troublesore shall pay Ms Bulwark maintenance for herself at the rate of £5,000 per annum during their joint lives for a term of three years as from the date of decree absolute or decree of judicial separation or equivalent order as stated.

In the event that there is a child or there are children of the family the lump sum shall increase from £750,000 to £850,000.

B: Upon nullity, dissolution or judicial separation decree or equivalent order as stated within two to six years of the date of the marriage

Mr Troublesore shall pay Ms Bulwark a lump sum of £1,500,000 within 28 days of decree absolute or decree of judicial separation or equivalent order as stated.

Mr Troublesore shall pay Ms Bulwark maintenance for herself at the rate of £7,500.00 per annum during their joint lives for a term of six years as from the date of decree absolute or decree of judicial separation or equivalent order as stated.

In the event that there is a child or there are children of the family the lump sum shall increase from £1,500,000.00 to £2,000,000.00.

Mr Troublesore shall transfer to Ms Bulwark his interest in his signed copy of Gold's Law.

C: Upon nullity, dissolution or judicial separation decree or equivalent order as stated after six years of the date of the marriage

Mr Troublesore shall pay Ms Bulwark a lump sum of £3,000,000 within 28 days of decree absolute or decree of judicial separation or equivalent order as stated.

Mr Troublesore shall pay Ms Bulwark maintenance for herself at the rate of £10,000.00 per annum during their joint lives for a term which shall end upon Ms Bulwark attaining the age of 65, as from the date of decree absolute or decree of judicial separation or equivalent order as stated.

In the event that there is a child or there are children of the family the lump sum shall increase from £3,000,000.00 to £3,500,000.00.

Mr Troublesore shall transfer to Ms Bulwark his interest in his signed copy of The Return of Breaking Law.

Part 6

Fifi is owned by the couple in equal shares.

Any pet acquired by the couple or either of them in succession to Fifi shall be owned by each of them in equal shares notwithstanding how as between the couple the cost of and incidental to acquisition and the cost of maintenance and care have been borne.

Subject to any contrary agreement which the couple may make from time to time:

- the pet shall live with each of Mr Troublesore and Ms Bulwark for alternate weeks save and except that when for any period ("the period") it is not reasonably possible or convenient for the pet to be in their care Mr Troublesore and Ms Bulwark shall give the other of them the first option to care for the pet during the period and in the event of such option not being taken up Mr Troublesore or Ms Bulwark (as the case may be) shall ensure the pet is cared for at the expense of the one of them who should have been caring for the pet by a responsible adult in their stead during the period and shall notify the other of them of the name and address of the carer and the other of them shall be entitled to contact with the pet during the period.

- The parties shall during the lifetime of the pet take out annually a pet insurance policy in standard terms to include cover for veterinary fees and expenses and neither of them shall do or omit to do any act or thing which may invalidate the insurance.

- During each and every period that the pet is living with Mr Troublesore and Ms Bulwark each of them shall (a) use their best endeavours to ensure the safety and welfare of the pet including complying with the requirements of the Animal Welfare Act 2006 ("the Act") and all regulations and codes of practice made thereunder and any other legislation from time to time in force relating to the safety and welfare of animals and shall not commit any offence under the Act or any other such legislation or any such regulations; and (b) pay for the cost of feeding and otherwise maintaining the pet save and except that all fees and expenses of veterinary surgeons and the premiums on such polices of insurance as the couple shall from time to time take out in respect to the pet shall be borne equally by them.

IN WITNESS whereof the parties have executed this instrument as a deed on the day and year first before written

SIGNED AS A DEED BY)
CLIVE TROUBLESORE in)
the presence of:-)

SIGNED AS A DEED BY)
MAVIS BULWARK in)
the presence of:-)

Chapter 73

The No Sex Agreement

A customised marriage or civil partnership

This is positively not a joke. There *are* couples who wish to marry or enter into a civil partnership without the sex. More than you may think. This can be for a variety of reasons, the most likely to be age, incapacity, repugnance or simple disinterest in sexual activity. For them, companionship may be quite sufficient.

The courts have recognised that some degree of sex is the norm in a marriage between parties of the opposite sex and there is no reason to suppose they would take a different view with a same sex marriage or civil partnership.

In a 1964 case on the ground of cruelty – the precursor, and less onerous ground, of the modern yet soon to be departing unreasonable behaviour – the parties married when the wife was 18 and the husband 33. They had a child soon afterwards but sexual intercourse ceased about one year later. After 15 years of the husband refusing intercourse, the wife left home. She alleged her health had suffered. She was refused a divorce and her appeal was thrown out. "I'm not satisfied," said the appeal judge, "that the husband was guilty of inexcusable conduct. In view of his natural disinclination for sexual intercourse, to find him guilty of cruelty is rather like beating a dog because it will not eat its food."

And in a 1977 case, the wife was refused a divorce because of her husband's alleged unreasonable behaviour which was based on an unsatisfactory sex life. She said he had been cold and indifferent to intercourse. This had taken place about once a month and, when it did, the husband quickly withdrew. There were upsets and the wife also left home. Even though her word was accepted, the judge hearing the case decided that unreasonable behaviour had not been proved and an appeal court came to the same conclusion.

In 1980 the Court of Appeal ruled that sexual intercourse once a week over a three month period did not amount to unreasonable behaviour when the 30 year old husband used this as the foundation for his divorce petition against his 31 year old wife. The couple had two children during a ten-year marriage. The couple had had sexual difficulties over the years and the husband had undergone a vasectomy. The wife's rationing had followed that procedure. Lord Justice Ormrod said: "I find it wholly unreasonable to say that she (the wife) was behaving unreasonably."

If these first two cases were to be rerun now, I would be surprised if the results would be the same. So it is that the party for whom sex is off the matrimonial agenda is vulnerable to their spouse using this as justification for seeking a marriage annulment or, exceptionally, having it taken into account when finances come to be looked at in matrimonial proceedings or those arising out of a breakdown of a civil partnership (see chapter 75). It all depends on the circumstances of each individual case but vulnerability does exist. The introduction of the no-blame Divorce, Dissolution and Separation Act 2020 (see chapter 74) does mean that sexual complaints will no longer play any role in getting a divorce, civil partnership dissolution or a separation although, as indicated, they may be raised in connection with financial issues.

My no-sex agreement can be adapted to a civil partnership and to cater for limitations in sexual activity between parties. Apart from being of possible use in financial proceedings, it could scupper an attempt at an annulment of an opposite sex marriage in which incapacity to consummate and wilful refusal to consummate are and will continue to be grounds which can be relied on. However, there is a risk that the court would say that the agreement had to be ignored on the ground that it was contrary to public policy and unreasonable. Be that as it may, in the right circumstances, worth a try and, at the least, the agreement could well deter both parties from bringing the bedroom into their matrimonial dispute. That cannot be a bad thing: bedrooms are better left as places of privacy.

THIS AGREEMENT is made on 14 July 2021 BETWEEN CLIVE TROUBLESORE of 149 Magnolia Buildings Twickenham Middlesex KT89 4XZ and MAVIS BULWARK of Upper Flat 62 Estuary Lane Clapham Common London SW4 XET (together called "the parties")

BACKGROUND:

1.	The parties are engaged to be married to each other and this agreement is made in contemplation of such marriage taking place by 31 December 2021.

2.	The parties intend to display their love and affection for each other during the marriage but have agreed that this shall not extend to engaging in sexual intercourse (or any form of sexual commerce) with each other (or any other person).

3.	The parties are desirous that their agreement as described in sub-paragraph (2) above and on incidental matters shall be formally recorded as set out in this document.

4.	The parties have each obtained independent legal advice on this agreement and fully understand its terms and its legal implications.

NOW IT IS HEREBY AGREED as follows:

1.	This agreement shall come into full force and effect forthwith upon the celebration of the marriage of the parties.

2.	During the subsistence of the marriage, neither party shall require or expect the other party to engage in sexual intercourse (or any form of sexual commerce) with them.

3.	In any proceedings during the subsistence of the marriage or after its dissolution between the parties or their personal representatives in which the conduct of the parties or either of them may be relevant:

a. neither party to the proceedings shall rely or seek to rely on the abstinence of either party to the marriage from sexual intercourse (or any form of sexual commerce) with the other or the refusal to engage in sexual intercourse (or any form of sexual commerce) with them; and

b. the parties to the proceedings shall invite the court concerned to refrain from taking such abstinence and/or refusal into account in determining any question or issue which shall be relevant to the determination of the proceedings between the parties to the proceedings.

4. Neither party to the marriage nor their personal representatives shall bring any proceedings against the other or the estate of the other of any nature whatsoever during the subsistence of the marriage or after its dissolution which rely wholly or partly on either party to the marriage having abstained from sexual intercourse (or any from of sexual commerce) with the other.

5. Each party shall affirm this agreement in writing if required by the other to do so at any time after the celebration of the marriage.

IN WITNESS whereof the parties have executed this instrument as a deed on the day and year first before written

SIGNED AS A DEED BY   )
CLIVE TROUBLESORE in   )
the presence of:-   )

SIGNED AS A DEED BY   )
MAVIS MAGNOLIA in   )
the presence of:-   )

Chapter 74

Divorce, Judicial Separation, Nullity And Dissolution

That's 'yer lot!

I do solemnly declare that I know of no lawful impediment why I Clive Troublesore may not be joined in marriage to...

Hold on a mo, Mr Registrar. If this goes badly tonight, can I cancel and have my money back?

This is most unorthodox, Mr Troublesore. No cancellation.

What about with six months' notice?

The law does not provide for any notice period.

For a fixed term of 12 months with an option to renew the marriage exercisable no later than half an hour before the first wedding anniversary?

No option.

So how long would I have to wait for a divorce?

12 months, Mr Troublesore, before you start the divorce proceedings and then a few months before you are legally free. That's so long as you have grounds, of course, and your wife doesn't defend the case.

I thought divorce was fault-free now and you didn't need grounds?

You'd have to come back later in the year for that. The Divorce, Dissolution and Separation Act 2020 revolutionises the law on ending marriages and civil partnerships and it's on the statute book. Parliament liked it and her Majesty liked it but it has not been brought into force yet.

So what are they waiting for, Christmas?

Actually, it could be near to Christmas 2021 before it is in force. The target date for it to be up and running is the Autumn of 2021. There are lots of complicated rules being put together about the procedures that will have to be followed under the new laws, forms to be drawn up, the online system for bringing matrimonial proceedings to be revamped and piloted, practice directions to be compiled and rewritten...

Give us a break, Mr Registrar. I don't want all that nonsense. Wouldn't irreconcilable differences be good enough?

This isn't California.

I need time.

The bride doesn't. She walked out three questions ago with the engagement ring still on her finger. She can almost certainly keep it. The law presumes it was a gift but Clive can always have a go at showing the contrary was intended. I don't rate his chances. There's no hope of damages on a claim for breach of promise of marriage. That quaint route to some appeasing lolly was abolished years ago. As for engagement and wedding presents, the law presumes them to belong to the person whose relatives or friends gifted them but the court might be persuaded in a particular case that the couple intended an equal sharing. That's another story. This story is about getting unlocked from a marriage or civil partnership that has broken down – or keeping the lock on!

Current law

The registrar was right. Until the Divorce, Dissolution and Separation Act 2020 is in force, there can be no divorce unless the party who brings proceedings has grounds and so it is with same-sex marriages as well. Two of the grounds require proof of the other party's misconduct and the other grounds depend on a period of separation. Dissolution is a civil partnership's version of divorce and this works in a similar way.

Adultery

The other party's adultery is the first ground so long as the party asking for divorce finds it intolerable to live with them. The intolerability does not have to arise out of the adultery. You could have the situation in which the adultery does not trouble you – because, say, you had had 149.5 affairs yourself – but you could not tolerate living with your spouse by reason of their incessant snoring. That's good enough. Once upon a time, those after a divorce had to personally attend court to give evidence. There I was having a pre-hearing discussion with a petitioner at court on the day – the case had been prepared by an executive in my firm and I was dealing with the advocacy – and I was running through the evidence they would be required to give.

> *So, madam, do you find it intolerable to live with your husband?*
>
> *No.*
>
> *I beg your pardon.*
>
> *I could tolerate living with him.*
>
> *But he has committed adultery, is living with another woman by whom he has had a child and you have chosen to bring divorce proceedings against him.*
>
> *Yes, I know but I could still tolerate living with him again.*
>
> *Is there any chance of a reconciliation? Would he ever come back to you?*
>
> *No, but I could still tolerate living with him again.*

This candour was admirable albeit coming rather belatedly. It could have been overcome by the lady changing her grounds to unreasonable behaviour on the basis of an improper relationship on the husband's part. She would in effect have been saying that she could not reasonably be expected to live with him in view of the behaviour although she herself would have been prepared to do so if he was prepared to come back which he wasn't! – though this would have involved an adjournment. In the event, after, I must confess, a few table thumps and some eyebrow raising (on my part, not hers) plus a reminder of how much the lady had spent on the case so far, she decided she could not tolerate living with her husband again. I gave four internal cheers when she said so in the witness box.

Should you have committed adultery yourself and have brought divorce or judicial separation proceedings, you can lawfully keep quiet about what you have been up to. Under old law, it was otherwise. The eyebrows of the judge at Portsmouth County Court (as it then was) before whom I was appearing shot up to the rafters as his mouth simultaneously dropped open in disbelief. He has just read my client's discretion statement. Eh? The law used to be that if you were relying on your spouse's adultery to get a divorce or judicial separation and you yourself had committed adultery then you had to confess that in a statement to the court which would then have a discretion to refuse you what you were asking for. The confession had to be in writing and lodged with the court in a sealed envelope when the case was started. At the court hearing, the envelope would be opened with a flourish by the court clerk and be shown to the judge. On this occasion, my client had confessed to committing adultery during the marriage with 24 different women over a period of three years. He was mighty proud of his conquests. It would have been a paradigm case for the judge to have refused a divorce but he was obviously impressed at the client's prowess – and honesty – and a divorce was duly granted.

Some other points on adultery:

- You are not obliged to name the person with whom adultery is alleged. If you do, they must be made a co-respondent – man or woman – and served with the court papers. It is rare for the person to be named: instead the petitioner usually alleges adultery with "an unnamed person" or "an unknown person". Why would you want to name them? Because you want them to pay the costs of the case. You could apply for costs against your spouse or the co-respondent or both. Your quest for costs against the co-respondent would probably fail if you could not prove they knew your spouse was married when adultery occurred or the court decided that the marriage was dead and buried well before the co-respondent came onto the scene. Or you might want to name them so as to cause them maximum discomfort. Any prospective co-respondent would be well advised to carry a mock-up of a summons for jury service or a county court claim form in their back pocket so that they can do a quick swap should a divorce petition land on the breakfast table over toast and coffee with their spouse.

- Adultery is not a ground for divorce in a same-sex marriage or for civil partnership dissolution (which is the civil partnership version of divorce) and when you come to think of it, that makes pretty good

sense.
- There's no adultery without sexual intercourse.
- If actual intercourse cannot be established by direct or circumstantial evidence but it is possible to prove a romantic relationship then a divorce could be sought on the ground of unreasonable behaviour (see below), relying on an "improper relationship".
- Not so many years ago, when there was an actual hearing of even an uncontested divorce case, the practice was to prove the adultery with evidence from a private enquiry agent who had taken written statements from the other party and the co-respondent in which they confessed to adultery. The statements were often obtained in a seedy hotel room and the agent would have observed items of male and female attire in close proximity. I sometimes wondered whether the very same items of attire were featuring in all the cases and if they were ever washed. As a solicitor, I once instructed a firm of private enquiry agents run by ex-police officers to attempt to gather adultery evidence against a wife who was denying to her husband a relationship with another man. This wasn't hotel room stuff but overnight bungalow close encounters stuff and called for discreet observations. Having spotted the other man's car parked close by at around 3am, two agents commenced observations and waited for the man to emerge. Some eight hours and about £200 later they got a bit peckish and decided – both of them! – to make a quick visit to the local chippie. By the time they had got back, the man had gone. I never instructed them again. Nowadays, the norm is for the other party to confirm in the form of receipt for the divorce papers – the *acknowledgment of service* it is called – that they admit the adultery alleged and for the petitioner to say why adultery is alleged and that will be quite sufficient proof.
- And what pain can be inflicted on the co-respondent? There's that order for costs. Sometimes there's a punch on the nose though that could lead to a criminal charge so do not go there. There used to be a right for the petitioner to claim damages for adultery against a male co-respondent. Such claims were only occasionally made. I once negotiated settlement of a claim where the wealthy co-respondent had lured the wife away from her hapless husband with gifts of jewellery and crispy bank notes. The co-respondent paid up what in today's money would amount to around £20,000. Damages for adultery are no more.

Unreasonable behaviour

We are talking here about the respondent having behaved in such a way that you cannot reasonably be expected to live with them. Sometimes the most ludicrous behaviour is relied on and if the respondent does not defend, the divorce goes through but you can never be sure how relaxed the court is going to be about allowing a weak petition to succeed. The trick is to particularise sufficient unreasonable behaviour in the petition but not go over the top because that could provoke the respondent into defending. After all, he wouldn't want his mum or new girlfriend to see that he is in to black eyes and blue moods more than once a month, would he? Some general allegations and then some examples of specific incidents including the most recent one are recommended.

Respondents are often hesitant about allowing an unreasonable behaviour petition to go through undefended because they fear this could prejudice them in the financial aspects of the case. They should fear not. It is only in the most extreme and rare cases that the respondent's conduct which has founded the petition will increase the money or property the petitioner will be awarded when the court comes to decide on the finances (see chapter 75).

The separation grounds

The remaining grounds depend on the parties having lived apart for a minimum set period. The most straightforward of these is that there has been a separation lasting at least two years and that the respondent consents to divorce or dissolution of a civil partnership. Potential problems are that the court will not usually be prepared to order the respondent to pay the petitioner's costs on a two-year separation petition unless the respondent agrees to do so and, for a variety of reasons, the respondent may not wish to actively consent to the divorce or partnership dissolution. Here's a suggested way round these problems.

> *Dear Clive*
>
> *Sued anyone lately?! There is no hope for our marriage and you know I have decided to divorce you. It is regrettable that you have so far been hostile to the idea but, be in no doubt, I will not be deterred. I can divorce you on the ground of unreasonable behaviour on which I have a very strong case. However, I am prepared to refrain from having to make allegations in the divorce papers about the disgusting way you have treated me throughout the marriage and instead to divorce you on the ground that we have been separated for over two years and you consent to the divorce. My conditions are that you confirm to me within the next week that you will consent and also that you will agree to the court ordering you to repay my divorce costs which will be the court fee amounting to £550.*
>
> *Yours*
>
> *Mavis*

If the other party has deserted the petitioner for at least two years then consented to divorce or partnership dissolution is not needed. Desertion occurs when one of the parties walks out on the other against their will.

Say the other party will not consent to a divorce or partnership dissolution on the ground of two years' separation and there's no desertion because the party after divorce or dissolution was the one who walked out, threw out the other party or was overjoyed to see the back of them? In the absence of the respondent's adultery or unreasonable behaviour, the party after divorce or dissolution is in a bit of a jam. The tactic sometimes adopted is for them to start their own proceedings in which they make puerile allegations of unreasonable behaviour against the other, not with the intention that they will be the party obtaining the divorce or dissolution but so as to provoke the other into action and seeking the divorce or dissolution themselves.

> *"Look at this Maude. That b......d Clive has started a divorce against me! He says I distressed him by refusing to support him in meritorious civil proceedings he instituted during the marriage, failed to fan him in hot weather and forbade him from having sexual relations more than twice a week. I'm not having it. He's not having a divorce against me. I'll defend and divorce him. You mark my words!"*

And that has been known to work. If it doesn't, the party after divorce or partnership dissolution will have to wait until the separation has lasted for at least five years. Divorce or dissolution then is almost certainly assured no matter how diabolical their own conduct may have been. *Almost* certainly assured? That's because the party hostile to divorce or dissolution can scupper it if they can satisfy the court that divorce or partnership dissolution would result in grave financial or other hardship to them and that it would be wrong to end the marriage or partnership. It's a notoriously difficult defence to succeed with. Where the financial implications of divorce or dissolution are relied on by the respondent – for example, a wife may be saying that she would lose out on a substantial amount of money under the husband's pension scheme in the event of him dying before her as she would no longer be his widow, if divorced – the petitioner may have to come up with some proposals for compensation so as to combat the defence. Otherwise, the respondent may be saying that divorce or dissolution is contrary to their religious beliefs or would make them a social outcast.

I once represented a man whose wife steadfastly refused to cooperate in bringing an obviously moribund marriage to a respectable end all because she could not accept that it was over. To reinforce the point, with weekly regularity she washed and rewashed the husband's shirts he had left behind and dried them on the garden clothesline. When five years of separation were finally clocked up, the husband issued his divorce petition relying on that lengthy separation as his solitary ground. After some initial resistance, the wife caved in and the case went through as undefended. Hopefully, the wife's washing powder bill dramatically fell.

Separation trap

A spouse or civil partner against whom a divorce or dissolution petition has been presented on the grounds of either two years' separation with their consent or five years' separation can hold up the decree absolute. They do so by relying on section 10(2) of the Matrimonial Causes Act 1973 or section 48(2) of the Civil Partnership Act 2004 which requires a specific application. It is for the court to consider what will be their financial position after divorce or dissolution. Then the decree absolute or final dissolution order will be postponed until the court has either decided that financial provision for them should not be required or that the financial provision made is reasonable and fair or the best that can be made in the circumstances. There is one route out of the decree absolute or final order blockage. The party after the divorce or dissolution can give an undertaking to make financial provision for the other party – concrete and specific proposals must be put forward – and if the court reckons they are not too far wide of the mark and it is desirable that the decree absolute or dissolution should be made without delay, it has a discretion to allow the decree absolute or final order to be issued. The application for the court to consider the post-divorce or dissolution financial position is more often than not coupled with the more usual financial remedies application for maintenance, property transfer etc though it is a useful device to get the best deal out of the petitioning party whose tongue is hanging out for liberation and remarriage or repartnership. The section 10(2) or section 48(2) device is not available where one or more of the other divorce grounds are relied on.

Two households: one roof

It is legally possible for parties to live apart under the same roof so long as they are running separate households in the property. For the purposes of the two and five years' separation grounds, there could be divorce or civil partnership dissolution though the parties have been at the same property for the entirety of the separation period. Likewise, carrying on living at the same address for over six months after adultery was discovered by the petitioner or after the final incident of unreasonable behaviour will not prejudice the petitioner if separate households under the same roof can be established. And why the hell not? The fact that the marriage or partnership has irretrievably broken should not have to mean that the parties sell up or that one of them moves out. I have come across cases where the divorced parties are living at the same property many years after marriage breakdown as it suited them to do so for financial reasons or because they thought this was better for their children. Nevertheless, the court tends to be a little suspicious in these same address situations so deal with the point when you make your statement in support of the petition: otherwise, the court will probably raise queries which would lead to delay. Whatever happens, do not answer the question posed in the statement form about whether you have lived with the respondent since you became aware of their adultery etc in the affirmative. The correct answer will be 'No'. And you might be saying something like this:

> "I have continued to live at 149 Magnolia Crescent, Twickenham since 14th July 2014 to the date of this statement. Throughout this period, the respondent has also lived at the same address. However, we have not lived together but in separate households under the same roof. The reason for this is that neither of us was in a position to obtain what would have been a necessary mortgage advance to buy alternative accommodation for single occupancy. At all times, we have slept in separate bedrooms and no sexual relations have taken place. We have

prepared our own meals and eaten them separately. We have been responsible for our own washing and ironing and the cleaning of the parts of the accommodation we have separately occupied. We have maintained separate bank accounts and contributed equally to the mortgage repayments and other outgoings on the property. We have not socialised together or taken holidays together. We have not entertained our respective friends at the property on any joint function. We have behaved civilly towards each other but in all respects have led our own lives for the whole time and in contemplation that one of us would bring divorce proceedings against the other when the law permitted."

But there's no irretrievable breakdown

A respondent implacably opposed to their marriage or partnership coming to an end could say to the court; "Yes, I have committed adultery. Yes, I have behaved unreasonably. Yes, I deserted the petitioner, Yes, we have lived separately for over five years. But I love her, I want her and I know it can work." I doubt that William Hill would take any bets on that defence succeeding but it is theoretically possible for a respondent to admit to what is alleged against them but still contend that there is still hope for the marriage or partnership.

Reconciliation attempts

The law encourages parties to try and mend their relationships but a party after divorce or partnership dissolution is under no legal obligation to enter into mediation or counselling with a view to doing so. Either party can begin divorce or dissolution proceedings without going within a square mile of a mediator or counsellor or mentioning what they think about reconciliation prospects to the court (although there are different rules when it comes to financial applications within matrimonial proceedings and cases involving children under the Children Act 1989). Curiously, the procedure changes when a lawyer is acting for a petitioner for divorce or civil partnership dissolution for they must notify the court when starting the case whether they have discussed the possibility of reconciliation with their client and given them the names and addresses of people qualified to help over a reconciliation. However, they don't have to discuss and give this information but simply say whether they have done so and the court will not bat an eyelid even if they say they have not done it!

Where the law is active about reconciliation is in permitting parties to live together for certain periods without destroying the grounds for divorce or partnership dissolution. So it is that if parties have lived together for up to six months (in one go or in the aggregate) any adultery of which the respondent was aware beforehand can still be relied on. As we have seen, after six months, it cannot. But if the adultery is wiped out because they are together for more than six months, any fresh adultery, even with the same person, which occurred after the reconciliation attempt began may afford a fresh ground. Similarly, in an unreasonable behaviour case, the parties can live together for up to six months after the final incident being relied on without the ground being destroyed but if the respondent returns to kicking and beating or whatever after the six months, the old behaviour will be revived and the petitioner will be able to rely on the old and the new stuff. And in calculating whether there has been desertion for two years or a separation which has lasted for two or five years, living together for up to six months after the separation started will not destroy the grounds but neither can it be reckoned towards the two years or five years.

Divorce/partnership dissolution v nullity

A thumping enormous away win when it comes to this match. If the marriage or civil partnership is ended by nullity instead of divorce or dissolution then the parties are treated as though they had never been in the marriage or civil partnership. You could have twenty marriages annulled and advertise yourself as new goods. Among the nullity grounds for opposite sex marriages are non-consummation due to the incapacity of either party (so that the petitioner can rely on their own incapacity) or the respondent's wilful refusal to consummate. For all marriages, a nullity could be secured on the grounds that at the time of the marriage the respondent was suffering from venereal disease in a communicable form or that the respondent was pregnant by someone else but in both these situations the case must be started within three years of the marriage. And with all the nullity grounds mentioned it is a defence that the petitioner led the respondent to believe that they would not bring nullity proceedings when they knew it was open to them to do so and that it would be unjust to the respondent to grant an annulment.

Is anybody there?

Usually no, when it comes to undefended matrimonial cases. Nowadays, the petitioner's evidence will be given in a written statement and, generally, the only hearing will be when the judge pronounces a decree in court. Then the parties can attend if so inclined but the entertainment factor is minus 1,000,000. A generic "I hereby pronounce the decrees in these cases to which the relevant parties are entitled in accordance with the certificates which have been given" (or words to this effect) will be declared in relation to thirty or so cases at a time. If anyone turns up it will probably be a respondent to argue about whether they should have to pay the petitioner's costs or one of the parties after the decree absolute being expedited (see below). The application for the decree absolute when made by the petitioner is again a paper exercise.

I have fond memories of attending matrimonial hearings as a trainee solicitor when the petitioner had to turn up to give evidence in support of their petition for divorce or whatever. Judges could find the endless repetition of substantially the same stories a tedious business and many a yawn was stifled. At Southampton one afternoon the judge who was a crusty and mature part-timer playing the part of a High Court member of the judiciary enquired, with a jolt, of the petitioner's barrister: "Mr Field-Fisher, where am I?" to which Mr Field-Fisher calmly responded "Your Lordship is sitting in Southampton." Come to think of it, there was not much else he could have said.

The race is on

Pre-pandemic, an undefended divorce, partnership dissolution or nullity case was taking anything from around three to six months from start to finish depending on pressure of work at the administrative centre at which the case was being handled and the level of efficiency there. Procedural changes which came about in 2015 have resulted in a faster process and the ability in relation to divorce only to apply and progress online (75% of divorces are now being digitally pursued) has accelerated the procedure. A period of six weeks and one day must elapse from the date of the first decree – the decree nisi or, in the case of partnership dissolution, the conditional order – until the petitioner can apply for the second decree which is called the decree absolute or, in the case of partnership dissolution, the final order. Not until the second decree or final order will the parties be legally liberated and free to try it again. Should the petitioner fail to promptly apply for the decree absolute then the application can be made by the respondent once three months have elapsed from the earliest date on which the petitioner could have applied: effectively after six weeks and one day plus three months.

But is there a way of accelerating progress to the first decree? Yes. For a start, ask the court to send you the papers which have to be delivered to the respondent instead of the court posting them. Arrange for the respondent to have them – you are not allowed to personally serve them yourself but you can get a responsible adult, preferably a process server, to do the job for you – and to complete and return to the court the form of acknowledgment of service of the petition which will be included with the papers. Should the respondent fail to cooperate over the completion and return of the acknowledgement of service then you can rely on a certificate of service from whoever handed the papers to the respondent. While waiting for that to be done, you can be drafting out the statement of your evidence in support of the petition – you can get the form of statement from the court or online at gov.uk/government/collections/court-and-tribunal-forms – so you are ready to pounce as soon as you can prove the respondent has had the papers and assuming they are not defending the case. That will be through either the acknowledgment they have sent to the court and a copy of which the court has copied to you or certificate of service. You won't be able to finalise the statement of evidence until you have the evidence that the respondent has had the papers. In suitable circumstances, you could apply to the court when lodging your statement to expedite the pronouncement. You would need to explain fully in the statement why you are asking for expedition and you should try and extract a letter from the respondent consenting to it which you can include with the statement. Then you could turn up at court when the decree is due to be pronounced – the time, date and venue will have been notified to you – and ask the judge to expedite (cut down on the six weeks and one day) the making of the second decree. Again, a letter from the respondent consenting to expedition would be essential if you were to succeed with the application on that occasion. An application for expedition can also be made after decree nisi but this would involve a fee and a special hearing for the application. You wish to ensure that the child you or your partner is expecting can be born legitimate or to remarry a terminally ill person? This may be sufficient reason but expedition is the exception and not the rule so anything less than such a reason is likely to fail.

The divorce centre has gone quiet

The pandemic, understaffing or a host of other factors may be behind the divorce centre's failure to promptly deal with an application you have made in your case: perhaps it was for the decree absolute to be expedited. They won't be deliriously happy about it, but you could ask your local family court to take over the application. It does have jurisdiction to do so and, if it suggests it does not, ask for its authority for saying so. It would be essential for you to make available to the local court copies of the log-jammed application and all the relevant paperwork in the case so that it effectively had the whole court file.

And now for something a little different

Judicial separation is available on the same grounds as divorce and partnership dissolution (though it is simply called separation in the case of a partnership). *Irretrievable* breakdown of the relationship is not alleged. The legal effect of a decree of judicial separation is that it is no longer obligatory for the petitioner to cohabit with the respondent. Big deal! The attraction of judicial separation in practice is that it can be sought, unlike divorce and partnership dissolution, within one year of cutting the cake – within five minutes if you like – and a decree empowers the court to grant the same financial remedies like maintenance, lump sums and sales and transfers of property (but not dismissal of claims for financial remedies or pension sharing) as on divorce and partnership dissolution. There is nothing to prevent either party going for divorce or partnership dissolution at a later date. The petitioner who has obtained a judicial separation can rely on the same grounds for the subsequent divorce or partnership dissolution.

For the party who, for whatever reason, does not wish to give the other freedom from the marriage or partnership and prefers to see them sweat out five years' separation before they can start their own proceedings as they have no other grounds, judicial separation tends to do nicely.

Defending

So you don't fancy the idea of the petitioner obtaining the decree they are after? You can defend by putting in an *answer* which is a defence to the petition. Relatively few cases are defended. The reason is that the grant of a decree to one party no longer has any impact on what the other party is going to be paying or receiving when finances are decided (see chapter 75). But if your wife has falsely alleged that you are a sex-crazed arsonist who murdered his mother, I can understand you might not be prepared to let that go uncontested. Frequently, a respondent to an unreasonable behaviour petition will negotiate with the petitioner for particular allegations in the petition which they find obnoxious or highly embarrassing to be deleted in return for not defending the case.

In addition to defending, the respondent who has grounds could issue their own petition in the same proceedings seeking a divorce, partnership dissolution or separation. And there's an alternative course that could be taken. The respondent is able to issue their own petition in the same proceedings without defending the petition against them. Then, for example, you might have the wife asking for a divorce on the ground of the husband's unreasonable behaviour and the husband asking for a divorce on the ground of the wife's adultery. In fact, it is common for both parties to ask for a divorce on the ground of the other's unreasonable behaviour! The court will generally go along with an arrangement which involves the grant of a divorce to each party. An order from the court will be needed converting what is technically a defended case because of the two petitions into an undefended case with double decrees. Then both parties can justifiably brag that they got the divorce.

Wallets out

To start off the matrimonial cases we have been looking at (and there will be a separate fee for any financial application made in the course of the proceedings), you will have to shell out £550 to the court (I predict this will soon rise to £592) or £365 if you are after a judicial separation. Though it's consoling to weigh against that what you will be saving in anniversary and birthday presents, it is less consoling to ponder on how much you spent on the wedding celebrations. Presenting your own petition in response to the petition against you will set you back the same amount. Putting in an answer (defence) to a petition against you will cost a court fee of £245. Should you both defend with an answer and put in your own petition, you will be looking at a court fees bill of £795 (with a little less when you go for judicial separation). For getting any of these fees remitted, see chapter 17.

New law

Kind warning and disclaimer to hopefully prevent you from saying unkind things about me

My summary of the new law is based on the Divorce, Dissolution and Separation Act 2020 which is on the statute book but not yet in force. It will remain intact for the next 100 years. It is also based on procedural rules and practice directions approved by the rules committee which loves this stuff. My bet is that there may be some tweaking of the rules and will be some more practice directions.

If you are reading this after the Divorce, Dissolution and Separation Act 2020 has come into force (it was to have been in the Autumn of 2021 but has now been put back to 6 April 2022, though that's not guaranteed), should you rip out the preceding pages of this chapter and use the margins for shopping lists? Don't as this could damage the integrity of the book's binding; the law on nullity (as above) is unaffected; and cases started before the 2020 Act comes into force can be expected to continue under the old law. However, if a pre-2020 Act case has become defended and looks set for a couple of days' worth of allegations and counter-allegations, consideration should be given to the abandonment of the case and the start of fresh proceedings under the new law. How the costs of the abandoned proceedings are dealt with would have to be matter for negotiation or decision of the court. What you can be sure the court would not do is to try the allegations and counter-allegations simply to decide who should bear the costs. For the procedural route to follow on an abandonment and restart, do go to my blog.

The plan is that the current system for starting cases and pursuing them online will have been adapted so as to be ready for patronage by both lawyers and litigants in person as soon as the new law is in force. It should be available for divorces, civil partnership dissolutions and civil partnership separations although I have a sneaking feeling that civil partnership cases could lag behind. I would be prepared to wager a bag of hummus chips which are very close to my heart – but I won't – that the adapted system will not be available for nullity and judicial separation cases for some time to come. It is questionable whether it will be possible for joint applications by both parties to a marriage or civil partnership (see below) to be conducted online. If it becomes possible, it may still be that just one party will kick off and the other party will then join in. Where online is unavailable, the good old fashioned way of bringing and pursuing your case offline will be open. You'll just need some postage stamps.

I will update on developments on my blog at breakinglaw.co.uk. Here goes.

No more dirt

Irretrievable breakdown of the relationship is still the basis of divorce for a marriage and dissolution for a civil partnership. The revolution comes with the scrapping of all the grounds which were available to prove the irretrievable breakdown – adultery, unreasonable behaviour, desertion, two years' separation with consent or five years' separation without consent. Not one of those grounds now has to be established. Instead, once the marriage or civil partnership has lasted for at least one year, either party – or, if they are still communicating, both parties – may start divorce or dissolution proceedings by issuing an application with the court accompanied by a statement in a prescribed form that the marriage or civil partnership has irretrievably broken down. Why would both parties want to apply? To prevent the other bragging to their pals that it was they the court favoured with the divorce or dissolution and so implying that they had been preferred. A joint application will not be materially more difficult than an application by one of the parties only. Despite the fact that both parties have played by jointly applying for the divorce or dissolution, one of them alone can go on to take the subsequent steps to secure freedom and without the concurrence of the other (but see below about giving notice to the other party of a sole request for the final order where the conditional order was made in favour of them both on a joint application). Before committing to a joint application, take a butchers at **Delay in seeking final order** below. Name changes mean that the document that starts the proceedings will be known as the application instead of the petition and the party who kicks off will be known as the applicant instead of the petitioner or, where both parties kick off, they will be known as the applicants.

New law proceedings for divorce or dissolution (or, indeed, for separation as well but more of that later) for which legal aid is not available, can be brought by you without a solicitor or other legal professional. Unless you run into trouble in dealing with service of the court papers on an awkward respondent, you should find the procedure simpler than under the current law. Proceedings for financial remedies which are linked to the divorce or dissolution are another matter.

Service and the 20 weeks' count

Once the application has been issued with the court, start counting. When you reach 20 weeks, you can pounce and apply to the court for the first order – the conditional order, they call it – immediately afterwards. If both parties kicked off then both parties or either of them can ask for the conditional order, as already indicated. Name change alert. The conditional order will be the equivalent of the current decree nisi in divorce so a welcome jargon switch. In civil partnership dissolution, we already have the conditional order. It doesn't have to be 20 weeks later, on the dot, that you apply for the conditional order but it is to be presumed that you won't want to hang about. One good reason for getting on with it sooner than later is that the court will lack jurisdiction to make financial remedy orders in divorce or dissolution until the conditional order has been procured although a financial remedy application can be started beforehand. Do not attempt to send the court the application for the conditional order until the 20 weeks are up and do not date the application or accompanying statement before the expiration of the 20 weeks.

The 20 weeks' count really does start the moment proceedings are commenced by the application being issued with the court? Yes. I know it sounds crackers but the law makers were concerned that, if the count instead started on a single party application from when the respondent (the other party) was served with the court papers, they might seek to frustrate the progress of the case by evading service. The craziness of the situation is that, although the court will need to be satisfied before granting the conditional order that the respondent has been served, it is conceivable that service has not been effected until well into the 20 weeks and that they will be shocked about the prospective proximity of the final end to their marriage or civil partnership when they receive them. The court can shorten the 20 weeks but has no power to extend. It would require a mighty powerful argument to persuade it to shorten: perhaps that the applicant or respondent are pregnant and the child would be born out of wedlock without a shortening or that either of them is terminally ill and wishes to remarry.

What happens during the 20 weeks? You the applicant eat healthy breakfasts and, in the majority of cases, do something about applying for financial remedies or, at the least, start up financial negotiations with the respondent. And there is the not insignificant step of having the respondent served with the court papers. Unless you are jointly bringing the proceedings, the court will ensure that the respondent is aware of what you are up to and that the person served is the respondent and not someone else masquerading as the respondent. Service should take place within 28 days after the date of the issue of proceedings. When starting the case, you will be required to give the court both the respondent's email address (which should be in active use by them and service to a business email address of the respondent is to be avoided where possible) and postal address, if you know them. Usually, the court will serve a respondent in England and Wales and by email unless you ask otherwise in which event service will be by first-class post or through any other organisation which provides for next business day delivery. If that doesn't work in that the respondent fails to return to the court a receipt for the papers (an acknowledgment of service) or the papers are whizzed back as 'not delivered' or 'left here 79 years ago', the court will notify non-service to you and you can come up with a different email or postal address. With a second failure, the court will give up and leave it to you to find out where the respondent can be located.

You personally must not serve the respondent. You can ask the court bailiff, a process server (who probably doubles as an enquiry agent) or some other responsible adult to do the job and they will need to complete a certificate of service when they succeed. Where asking for the bailiff's help, you will have to satisfy the court that email, where appropriate, and post have been tried and failed but, if you have a lawyer acting for you, the court is unlikely to allow the bailiff to do the deed and will expect you to instead use a process server. Notwithstanding the lawyer's involvement, you may be hard up and that could swing use of the bailiff in your favour. The simplest course where the respondent has a solicitor acting for them is to ask that they give you written confirmation that they will accept service of the papers on behalf of the respondent and request the court to email or post to their address. Alternatively, service on the solicitor by document exchange will be permitted, if they are willing to accept it, provided the DX box number is printed on their notepaper. This will be particularly useful where the respondent is outside England and Wales and the solicitor is inside. Otherwise, the respondent can provide an email or postal address in England and Wales at which they are prepared to be served and this can be used. It need not be their usual email address or home or work address. Whether email service is by the court or by you, it must be followed up with written notification, confirming email service, being sent – the procedural rules impliedly require it to be done on the same day – to the respondent's postal address by first-class post or other next-day delivery method.

The court can extend the 28-day time limit for service where service attempts have failed. You should apply for an extension within the 28 days. The court will then make an order setting a further time limit. If service remains unsuccessful, you should apply for a further extension before the deadline under the court's order. A late extension application will only be allowed where there is good reason for the delay in making it. Any extension application must be backed with written evidence (see chapter 19) but may be made without prior notice to the respondent and, on the application, the court will consider all the circumstances including whether non-service was the court's fault; whether you have taken reasonable steps to have service take place; and whether you have acted promptly. There is no automatic sanction for having sat on your backside and done nothing constructive about service or made your extension application late. But in an extreme case where your inertia was quite diabolical, I suggest the court would have the power to kill off your case by striking it out. That would have the effect of obliging you to start all over again – including paying a fresh court fee unless you were exempt from doing so (see chapter 17).

If you believe when you start proceedings that the respondent will refuse to cooperate over the proceedings, the prudent course is to arrange personal service on the respondent, albeit not by you personally. The court would probably refuse to sanction bailiff service if email or postal service had not been attempted or you were in a financial position to bring in a process server.

Where all appropriate service attempts have been made but proved unsuccessful, you must apply to the court to order service by some alternative method or at some alternative place. Your written statement supporting the application should explain why you are asking for an order, what alternative method or place you are proposing and why you believe service by that method or at that place is likely to reach the respondent. Who knows, a national or local newspaper advertisement might be regarded as sufficient to bring the proceedings to the respondent's attention. The *Grasshopper Collectors' Daily* is unlikely to be entertained by the court as suitable. Where the respondent has disappeared into oblivion and service is just not practicable, you can apply to the court to dispense with it. The application must be supported by written evidence. On such an application, the court might well take steps to extract the respondent's address from HM Works and Pensions (you can take a stab at getting the address yourself before making an application) or HM Revenue & Customs. Also, the court might wish to ensure that the other party has not already obtained a divorce or dissolution without your knowledge. After all, they might have procured an order dispensing with service of proceedings on you! The same marriage and the same civil partnership can only be killed off once. The court can be satisfied about this by you producing evidence of the result of a search of the Central Index of Decrees Absolute which is kept and controlled by London's Central Family Court (see gov.uk/government/publications/form-d440-request-for-search-for-divorce-decree-absolutedecree-absolute).Notwithstanding its limited title, the search will throw up all divorce decrees absolute granted by courts in England and Wales since 1858 and of all civil partnership final orders of dissolution made since they came into existence. Final divorce orders will be covered too once they get going. The search will cost you £65 for every ten-year period that is searched. The courts service guidance leaflet contradictingly says the fee is £45 and £65. It is £65, honest! Help with fees (see chapter 17) is not available for the search. If you were only married 18 months ago, don't bother to search back to 1858. Use form D440. You can pre-empt a court request that you produce a search certificate and so cause delay by attending to the search before you make the application to dispense with service. Before applying, you should also make efforts to establish the other party's whereabouts from any known relatives and friends of theirs, any last known employer and landlord, bank or building society with which they held an account and the Child Maintenance Service if there is or was a child support assessment against them.

The diligent respondent should send to the court so that it arrives within 14 days of getting the court papers the form of acknowledgment of service we have already met. They or their lawyer will need to sign and give an address where future documentation for them in the case can be sent. The form must indicate whether or not they intend to dispute the proceedings. The scope for disputing is as narrow as you pray your waist-line will become. More of that later. It won't be the end of the proceedings or the world if the respondent who has been served with the papers has failed to put in the acknowledgment so long as you can show that they have had the papers. A certificate of service can do this where they have been personally served (see above). Otherwise, you can apply to the court for an order deeming them to have been served but you might first just try this.

> *"Dear Former Darling. You haven't sent back a completed form of acknowledgment of service to the court even though I can prove you have had the papers. If I have to apply to the court, as I can, for an order that you be deemed to have had them, this will cost money and I would have to ask the court to order you to pay my costs involved in getting the order. You can save yourself being compelled to pay me those costs, by sending the completed form back. If the court tells me by the end of seven days from now that you have not done as asked, then I will make the application."*

A typical situation in which a deeming order is likely to be made is where in a written statement with your application you can talk of conversations with the respondent following service of the papers and can produce an email or note from them along the lines of "Dear Maude, I've got the divorce papers from the court, you cow. You'll have a divorce over my dead body. I've flushed the papers down the loo. You know I love yer." Relying on the papers having been sent to the respondent's postal address for a deeming order will rarely be enough of itself although it is one factor the court can take into account. But was it the correct address? Where you have reason to believe they are no longer at their usual or last known address, you will be expected to have taken reasonable steps to ascertain their current postal and email addresses.

With a joint application for divorce or dissolution, the court will have sent out the papers to both parties and each must send in a completed acknowledgment of service.

Special rules govern having to serve the respondent in Scotland and Northern Ireland and outside the UK and service on members of the regular forces and US air force.

20 weeks on

Assuming the respondent does not take the required steps to dispute the proceedings, you will be able to apply for the conditional order once 20 weeks have been counted out. As with current procedure, the application will be dealt with on paper, without any personal attendance at a court hearing. The application form and accompanying statement will be provided by the court or accessible online. In the statement, you will be required to confirm that there have been no changes in the information given in the application that kicked off the case and to identify the respondent's signature that hopefully appears on an acknowledgment of service. Nothing about the history of the marriage and any hatred you harbour for the respondent. If all is procedurally okay, the application will be listed at the next available date for the making of the first order. A similar procedure to the current one under which a case is listed before a judge for the formal pronouncement of a decree nisi. You won't need to turn up to the making of a first order ceremony (unless applying for expedition of the next order – see below). If you do, you will be extremely disappointed. The case is likely to be listed with one hundred others and challenge for glamour the opening of a brown envelope containing a tax demand.

Almost there

With the conditional order in the bag, you can celebrate with a shandy (half bottle). Now, another wait but this time much shorter. It is six weeks and one day. The final order – name check: equivalent to the divorce decree absolute under current law and the same as the civil partnership final order under current law – cannot be made until the end of six weeks from the making of the conditional order so that's why one day has to be tacked on to the six weeks. The final order will be made administratively by a court clerk without any further hearing. You will need to give the court notice that you wish the final order to be made. Do not do that until the 43rd day after the date of the conditional order at the earliest and do not put an earlier date on the notice form. In the same way as the court has the power to shorten the 20 week wait (see above), it has the power to shorten the six week wait. Similar grounds would be needed and they would have to be exceptional. There is probably a stronger chance of the time it will take for the application for a conditional order after 20 weeks to be considered or the six weeks between conditional order and final order to be shortened rather than the 20 weeks being shrunk. You could twin applications by seeking an order that "The applicant's time for applying for the conditional order be shortened to x days/weeks or in the alternative, the time for the making of a conditional order be expedited and, subject to a conditional order being made, the applicant's time for giving notice to the court that the applicant wishes the conditional order to be made final be shortened to forthwith upon the conditional order being made/x days/weeks." If, before the conditional order is made, you have not applied for a shortening of the six weeks, you can apply to the judge at the hearing when the conditional order is made to allow a reduction in the six weeks. Getting the other party to consent to a shortening or expedition application and arming yourself with a statement to this effect will only strengthen the prospects of the application meeting with success.

Procedural alert. If the conditional order was made in favour of both you and the other party, you must give the other party notice of your intention to go for the final order at least 14 days before you communicate your notice to the court and that communication must be accompanied by a certificate that you have done so. Where the conditional order was made solely in your favour, notice to the other party is unnecessary.

You have the final order? You can celebrate with a shandy (full bottle) or champagne (full bottle).

Delay in seeking final order

There may be good reason for holding on before going for the final order. The most common is that an application for financial remedies is pending or is to be made and whoever is applying wants the application to be settled or decided by the court because their pension rights could be lost or prejudiced by the other party passing away after the marriage or civil partnership had been brought to a final end. If you fail to go for the final order within 12 months of the conditional order, you will have to explain the delay to the court in writing. Save time by doing it when you give notice to the court that you want the final order rather than waiting to be asked and add and sign a statement of truth to the explanation at the end ("I believe that the facts stated in this witness statement are true") and date it.

But the delay may be forced by the other party. Under the current law, the respondent to a divorce or civil partnership case on the grounds of two years' separation with the respondent's consent or five years' separation can hold up the decree absolute or final civil partnership dissolution order by applying to the court to consider what will be their financial position after divorce or dissolution (see **Separation trap** above). It's section 10(2) of the Matrimonial Causes Act 1973 and section 48(2) of the Civil Partnership Act 2004 that allow them to do so. The procedure remains under the new law but with a vengeance. This section 10(2) or section 48(2) application can now be made in any divorce or dissolution case with a resultant block on freedom. As they have scrapped the two years' separation with consent and the five years' separation grounds, they have had to scrap the current limitation of the block to cases involving only those two grounds! Inevitably, the application, if made, will be made by the respondent. If the conditional divorce order or civil partnership dissolution order have been made in favour of both parties then the party who wishes to go down the section 10(2) or section 48(2) route, will have to withdraw from the divorce or dissolution application. Provided the respondent has done what is necessary, the court must not make the final divorce order or the final civil partnership dissolution order unless and until the court is satisfied that no financial provision should be made for the respondent or that the provision made is reasonable and fair or the best that can be made in the circumstances.

There will be a massive hike in these applications being made. They provide a bargaining weapon for the respondent against the other party who is desperate for freedom. It may be appropriate for the application to be linked with a separate application for conventional financial remedies. But can the respondent be outwitted? Possibly. The court is given a discretion to give its blessing to the final divorce or civil partnership order being made if there are circumstances making this desirable and the other party has provided a satisfactory undertaking to the court that they will make whatever financial provision for the respondent as the court approves. An application that looks weak on the papers will help to obtain that blessing.

An application under section 10(2) or section 48(2) can be obviated by an undertaking by the party who has the conditional divorce or dissolution order in their favour to the respondent that they will not request the final order until an application for financial remedies has been made by the court or without the written consent of the respondent. It might be unwise to accept such an undertaking unless the undertaking party is legally represented.

Time check

Assuming that time limits are not shortened (see above), how long will it take for you to secure your freedom from the marriage or partnership? Much will depend on how quick off the mark are you and the judges and court staff who have to take the steps I have bored you with as the case progresses. Much will also depend on how efficient the modified online procedure turns out to be. Online is faster than the post. Be that as it may, my best prediction at this stage is that an undefended snagless online divorce case with you, judges and court staff acting as quickly as reasonably possible, will go something like this:

Day 1	Start case
Day 143	Court receives your application for a conditional order
Day 157	Court certifies that you are entitled to a conditional order
Day 164	Judge makes a conditional order
Day 207	You request final order
Day 209	Final order made

So wrap it up in 209 days which they tell me is just short of 30 weeks. Beat that and I'll buy you a packet of cheese and onion crisps

"Hold on. I don't want this relationship to end"

Then you may have a problem. The reason is that when the court comes to decide whether to grant the conditional divorce or conditional civil partnership dissolution order, they must treat as conclusive the statement made by the applicant when first kicking off the proceedings that the marriage or partnership had broken down irretrievably. The court cannot go behind that statement. If you are the other party – the respondent – you cannot be heard to say that you have never laid a finger on the other party in anger or that although they may believe there has been an irretrievable breakdown, you have high hopes for the future and have booked a suite at The

Grand, Eastbourne for a fortnight as a second honeymoon. And you cannot be heard to say that you and the other party are still living under the same roof. All irrelevant, I'm afraid. That doesn't mean that you are struck down speechless if something isn't right and you are bursting to dispute the case. You could do that if: when proceedings were started, the marriage or civil partnership had lasted for less than one year; you deny that the marriage or civil partnership took place; you deny that the marriage or civil partnership ceremony was valid and complied with the law; you deny that the overseas marriage or civil partnership should otherwise be recognised by the law of England and Wales; you deny that because of where you and the other party are domiciled or reside, the court has jurisdiction to deal with the case; you deny you were served with the court papers when you should have been or at all; or you assert that the applicant has acted fraudulently in relation to the case. What amounts to fraud for this purpose is likely to be the subject of judicial debate. Say that, notwithstanding the other party's assertion that the marriage or civil partnership had irretrievably broken down, it was as plain as a pikestaff that it had not? You continued to share the same bed, to eat together, to socialise together, to holiday together. Only the day before they started the case, the other party wrote to you to say that you were the best thing since sliced bread (medium cut and wholemeal but have you tried charcoal bread which is delicious?), they loved you very much and looked forward to spending the rest of their life with you? In my book, that shows that the statement of irretrievable breakdown is untrue (unless there had been some overnight drama for which no reasonable partner could forgive you) and I suggest it would be a violence to the law and common sense to preclude you from disputing the case. Relying on the apparent falseness of the statement of truth, the appropriate course for you might well be to apply to the court for the application to be struck out as an abuse of the process of the court. The court's obligation to treat the statement of irretrievable breakdown as conclusive does not arise, I suggest, until later on when it is considering whether to sanction a conditional order and not on an earlier application to strike out. What you cannot do is to put in an answer (the document needed for a disputed case) to challenge that the marriage has irretrievably broken down. Expect an appeal court decision sooner or later on this controversial area of the new law.

And now for something completely different under the new law

We've had a look at judicial separation under the current law (see above. The civil partnership equivalent is separation, without the 'judicial'. The big deal comes with the evidence needed to procure a separation. Under the current and new law, separation does not require evidence that the marriage or civil partnership has irretrievably broken down. Not even that they have broken down but simply that whoever is going for the separation order wants it. Currently, you have to prove a ground which is akin to the divorce or civil partnership grounds except that adultery does not figure in same-sex divorces or civil partnership dissolutions. Under the new law, you don't. The case under the new law will be started and followed through in a similar way as a divorce or dissolution case with just one party or both parties applying for it. But in the statement accompanying the separation application it will be said that either or both seek separation – nothing about breakdown, irretrievable or retrievable – and, on the strength of that, the court must make a separation order when it is asked to do so after the court papers have been served. There is no 20 week wait.

Unlike divorce and civil partnership dissolution, a separation may be sought within the first year of the ceremony – above, I suggested, for the current law, within five minutes but you could always try for a reconciliation and make it the next day, if you like – and there's only one order you get which is the separation order (no longer called a decree of judicial separation as is currently the case with a marriage) without a final order being necessary.

The reasons for preferring separation over divorce have changed with the new law. It will no longer be possible to use it as a bargaining tool for a better financial deal against a party who has no grounds available to seek a divorce or civil partnership dissolution as the new law will facilitate either of them with such ease. But it can be employed as a means of securing financial remedies (albeit not dismissal of claims for such remedies or pension sharing orders) at the same time as keeping the marriage or civil partnership alive for a party who believes that the relationship is not totally dead or finds divorce anathema for religious or social reasons. Divorce or civil partnership dissolution proceedings may be brought by either party subsequent to a separation order.

Take this scenario under the new law. You want a divorce or civil partnership dissolution and apply for one but the other party only wants a separation order or, conversely, you want a separation order and they want a divorce or civil partnership dissolution. Or say you want a divorce or civil partnership order and the other party wants a nullity order (see below). The other party must apply for what they want in the same proceedings – putting in an answer (see below) is not necessary unless they seek to dispute your application on one of the limited bases referred to above – and do so within 35 days of being served with your application. The court can grant permission for the 35 days to be extended. If it's the party only wanting a separation who is after more time, I would reckon they could struggle to be granted it.

Once the other party's application has gone in, the court will fix a case management hearing at which procedural directions will be given. The hearing is to be within six weeks of the application being lodged with the court. I fancy that in one of the scenarios we are examining, the judge at the hearing would indulge in some banging together of heads – nothing traumatic and more like a gentle meeting of ears. If the party seeking only the separation order will not concede, I would expect that their application would be stayed (halted) so as to allow the other party to proceed on an undisputed basis with their divorce or civil partnership dissolution application. The separation order application could be resurrected if the divorce or dissolution application was not pursued within a reasonable time frame. But if one wants a divorce or end to a civil partnership and the other a nullity, that might well have to be fought out in the absence of some compromise because nullity, if established, would prevail over the other remedies.

Both parties want the same – or sometimes different – things

Another scenario. Both you and the other party desire divorce, civil partnership order or separation. Can you both bring proceedings for the same thing? No. Once one of you has kicked off with their application, the other has lost the race and can't brag in the saloon bar that it was they what won it! Exception alert. The court can grant permission for a second application to go in. The most likely situation in which it would do so is when the first applicant has gone to sleep: started off quickly enough but then failed to do anything further about progressing the case within a reasonable period of time. Whereas under the present law, it is not uncommon for the court to allow each party to have the same relief – for example, a divorce to both on the ground of the other's unreasonable behaviour which is known in the business as 'cross-decrees' – I cannot see equivalence happening under the new regime for there is objectively no point. Of course, it is always open to the beaten party to apply for the application to be amended to join them as a joint applicant but without the consent of the race winner, I would doubt that the court would permit this although it would be theoretically empowered to do so.

Permission for a second application is not required where the first application was made for a separation order within one year of the marriage or civil partnership and the applicant then wants a divorce or dissolution instead. And permission is again not required where the applicant has gone for separation and, after 12 months from the date of the marriage or civil partnership, the respondent is after divorce or dissolution.

Nullity

The nullity law is left intact although there will be some procedural treats, including a conditional and final order of nullity of marriage or civil partnership in place of current terminology. For what nullity is all about, see **Divorce/partnership dissolution v nullity** in relation to the current law.

Disputed cases

As soon as an answer is put in, which will turn the application into a disputed case, the court will fix a case management conference within the following six weeks at which procedural directions for it to be tried on a later date will be given although it is conceivable that the judge will suggest some compromise which could enable the case to proceed as undisputed. Under current procedural rules, a conference is fixed at a later stage although, in practice, the court, more often than not, will fix it as early as it will be fixed under the new law.

Costs

The question of what is to happen about who bears the costs of undisputed cases has so far been left in the air by rule makers. However, I now fancy that a practice direction on the topic will be issued before 6 April 2022. I have little doubt that applications for costs will be generally discouraged and it may well be that the documentation required to initiate a case will not even invite the applicant to ask for an order for costs to be considered. That would not debar costs being pursued but would necessitate a specific and separate costs application. My prediction is that judges would usually decline to make a costs order unless there was consent to such an order or there was some exceptional factor relied on which would make it unjust to expect the party who has brought the proceedings to have to pick up the bill for the lot. That factor might well be an obstructive stance in the proceedings by failing to deal with paperwork and causing grief and expense to the applicant in proving that the papers had been served. The would-be applicant might well wish to negotiate an arrangement with the other party to consent to a costs order being made against them in due course before kicking off proceedings or even collect their costs contribution from them before kick off. It will depend on how badly freedom is wanted. It should be borne in mind that a costs order might well be more readily made under the current law than under the new law: for example, where adultery, unreasonable behaviour or desertion could be relied on now.

Changing court documents

An application for a divorce etc can be amended if alterations or amendments are needed. In nullity cases only, a supplemental application can be made, for example, to add particulars of allegations or acts which have occurred since the original application. The document will then be treated as an amendment of the original application.

BREXIT ALERT!!!

You or your partner may be living abroad or only been here for five minutes. When can the courts of England and Wales deal with your divorce or other matrimonial case? For cases started before 11pm on 31 December 2020, the law is unaffected. From then onwards, the EU regulations that governed jurisdiction are no more. The Domicile and Matrimonial Proceedings Act 1973 and the Civil Partnership Act 2004 as amended by the Jurisdiction and Judgments (Family) (Amendment etc) (EU Exit) Regulations 2019 (SI 2019/519) take over. I thought you had better have that detail as it might be helpful for your next pub quiz. For divorce, civil partnership and judicial separation, you can bring proceedings here – that's in England and Wales – where you are both habitually resident here; you were both habitually resident here and one of you continues to reside here; the other party is habitually resident here; you are habitually resident here and have resided here for at least one year immediately before you start proceedings; you are both domiciled and habitually resident here and have resided here for at least six months immediately before you start proceedings; or one or both of you are domiciled here. That should give you a sporting chance of enjoying our justice, eh?! For marriage nullity proceedings, the law is the same except there is an addition to deal with jurisdiction where one of the parties has died and nullity is available.

Pre-Brexit, where each party had brought matrimonial proceedings but in different EU member states, the first case to be started prevailed and the second case would be halted. That has now changed with Brexit so that the court here will have a discretion to deal with the case brought here even if it was started after the other case brought abroad. The court will decide which is the fairest country to have the case.

Chapter 75

After The Breakdown

The anti-stitch up guide

The marriage or civil partnership has broken down. That phase of your life is over. How the next phase progresses is likely to be deeply affected by how you financially come out of the relationship. The law strives to achieve fairness for both parties. However, there are no scientific formulae to be applied to how income and capital are to be shared for the future. The range of fairness can be very wide indeed: ten different judges may give you ten different ideas of what on a specific set of facts is fair to them. "Please may I not be stitched up." This should be your prayer.

This is a massive topic. My aim is to give you a taster of what orders the court can make and how they will approach these financial remedy cases with some tips on dealing with the slippery customer who is worth chasing for that fair deal. The Divorce, Dissolution and Separation Act 2020 (see chapter 74) which is expected to come into force in the Autumn of 2021 but may be delayed, does not affect financial remedy applications except in so far as final order blocking is concerned (see below). In any event, cases already started when the Act does come into force will continue under the current law.

The menu

The court can make orders against your opponent which cover both income and capital. So far as income is concerned, it can order maintenance for you by way of *periodical payments* which will normally involve equal monthly amounts and, where the payments are temporary and ordered in an emergency type situation (see below) they are called *maintenance pending suit* or *interim periodical payments*, depending on whether or not the final decree has yet been made. It will not usually make an order for maintenance in respect of a child except if you and your opponent agree that there should be an order and how much is to be paid. Child maintenance is otherwise dealt with through the Child Maintenance Service (see chapter 76).

If your opponent is patently untrustworthy and they have some capital to their name, the court might be persuaded to secure the maintenance (for example, by charging a property owned by your opponent) so that, come default in maintenance payments, you can get what you are owed out of the security.

Maintenance for you will last for a period which the court will set: for so many months or years or until you cohabit or remarry but never beyond the grave so that an order will automatically lapse on the death of you or your opponent. If you want maintenance to continue to be payable after your opponent's death out of their estate, they will have to agree and you would need a commitment on this through a deed which would bind their estate. Where the maintenance has lapsed on your opponent's death and they have not made acceptable provision in a will to take the place of the maintenance then you may be able to successfully claim against their estate under the Inheritance (Provision for Family and Dependants) Act 1975 (see chapter 44) unless the right to do so has been excluded by the court when it made a final order in the financial remedies proceedings. A maintenance order can be varied by the court or cancelled where circumstances change.

The court does not like to see a party who has the responsibility or the main responsibility of caring for the children giving up a claim for maintenance before the children have say reached 18 (and sometimes until they have completed tertiary education beyond then) unless they are faring particularly well on capital to compensate for this. Remember that the court will not make an order unless it is satisfied that it is reasonable to do so. The court is no rubber-stamper.

So far as capital is concerned, the court can order your opponent to pay you a lump sum; transfer to you property, like the family home; alter the basis on which property is owned (perhaps that the property be transferred from your opponent's sole name into your joint names so that you become equal owners); postpone the sale of property (perhaps that the family home should not be sold until your death, cohabitation, remarriage or the youngest child attains a certain age or finishes full-time education). And the court can give you a share of your opponent's pension (a pension sharing order) or direct that maintenance should be paid to you out of the pension (a pension attachment order). How pensions are dealt with can be a complicated area. I commend a report from the Pension Advisory Group on how the courts will deal with pensions. You can access it at nuffieldfoundation.org/sites/default/files/files/Guide_To_The_Treatment_of_Pensions_on_Divorce-Digital(1).pdf but take a cold bath before you do so.

When it makes its order, the court can be asked to dismiss certain claims of either party or both parties. For example, if one party is scoring over the odds with the capital share they are to walk away with, it might be appropriate for their claims for maintenance to be dismissed. This is known as the *clean break*. Where one party has a good chance of obtaining a sizeable maintenance order but still has a bit of life and hormone jangling about them, it may be prudent for them to take a larger slice of the capital and forgo maintenance because any maintenance order could have a short life on account of good cohabitation or remarriage prospects. The capital would not be repayable on remarriage or cohabitation. Conversely in that situation, the other party would be well advised to suffer the maintenance order and keep the capital at a more modest level.

Match rules

In deciding what is fair, the court must have as its first consideration the welfare of any child of the family who is under 18 but look at all the circumstances of the case so that, for example, if it is especially important to one party to have adult children of the family still living with them, the court may be prepared to factor this wish into its decision. Of particular importance to the court will be:

- The income, earning capacity, property and financial resources of the parties – now and in the foreseeable future.
- Their financial needs, obligations and responsibilities – now and in the foreseeable future.
- The standard of living enjoyed by them before the breakdown.
- Their ages and the length of the marriage or partnership.
- Any physical or mental disabilities they may have.
- Their contributions already made or likely to be made to the family's welfare including looking after the home or caring for the family.
- Any benefit they may lose on account of a divorce, dissolution or nullity.
- Any conduct of the parties which the court reckons it would be "inequitable to disregard".

The court will always look to see how equal the parties will be in terms of capital if it makes the order it has in mind. In fact, in a large proportion of cases the court will use equality as a starting point when it comes to the division of the property and the judge will say to themselves: "Let's calculate what a 50/50 split would give the parties and how that can be achieved and then see if there is any reason to depart from that equal split." The parties' lawyers will be fully alive to this sort of approach and set out to persuade the court that there are sound reasons for it to depart from equality. The most common arguments used are that the other party should not have the benefit of:

- property which one party has brought into the marriage or partnership and to which the other party has not contributed;
- property which one party has inherited during the marriage or partnership; and
- property acquired after the breakdown.

However, the longer the marriage or partnership has subsisted (and the shortness of a marriage or partnership may of itself justify a departure from equality but, for the purpose of the arguments, usually add the cohabitation period to the marriage or partnership period and stop when the parties separated), the more likely that all property (except for post-break up wealth) will be reckoned and particularly when the needs of one of the parties so dictate. In what judges and lawyers call a *needs case*, the court can and often will depart from equality so that it can ensure that one of the parties – especially the party who has the responsibility or the greater responsibility for caring for the children – has enough to satisfy their needs.

Your own cohabitation should not deny you the fair share of the assets you would have enjoyed had you not been cohabiting. You have earned it. However, where the cohabitation has materially improved your financial position and your opponent might suffer hardship if you got that full share then you might just suffer a reduction in the share, especially if there are children under 18 or continuing their education who are living with your opponent. And your own cohabitation will not bar you from seeking and being awarded maintenance, particularly if you have children still being educated living with you the whole time or for a material part of it. Much will depend on the finances of your cohabitee and the extent to which those finances benefit you. When your cohabitee has just snapped up their seventh terrace of empty shops for redevelopment, you would probably be strained to establish that you still had a need for maintenance from your opponent.

"Darling, let's give the court a miss."

Now there are some decent people around, or so they tell me, who want to do the honourable thing on breakdown. If the expense, acrimony and stress of contested proceedings can be avoided, then go for negotiation. You may be able to settle heads of agreement between yourselves or through other means that do not involve the court doing very much apart from approving what has been agreed or decided out-of-court. After all, if the case goes to court and through to a fully contested hearing, the legal costs of both sides effectively come out of the matrimonial pot. It is rare for the 'winner' (in so far as anyone ever wins these cases) to have to pay the costs of the loser (in so far as anyone ever loses) and so each side will generally have to bear their own legal costs. This makes anathema the prospect of running up heavy legal bills and is the main reason that both parties should be sensible in their demands and responses and be prepared to give and take. Does it matter that much if the dog spends half its time with your husband or your partner keeps the David Hockney?

There's another powerful reason to take the non-court route. The court route can be a very slow one. We now have Financial Remedies Courts which are part of the Family Court and they cover everything you would expect which touches finances and the family including enforcement of orders which have not been complied with (but not claims under the Inheritance (Provision for Family and Dependants) Act 1975 – see chapter 44 – or the Trusts of Land and Appointment of Trustees Act 1996 – see chapter 71). They run out of 18 geographical zones and their cases will be dealt with by judges who specialise in the business coming their way. You won't get a judge who has spent their professional life determining whether tabloid papers have libelled celebrities, telling you what percentage share of your partner's pension should be awarded to you. I am a judge of the Financial Remedies Courts. So there.

That's the landscape. The unhappy reality is that the pandemic took a heavy toll on court timetables and listings and the Financial Remedies Courts, like their siblings, are still far away from catching up. So, what else is on offer? We'll have a look but do not lose sight of the fact that, whatever the negatives, the judge in court is cheap. Lawyers' fees there may be, but for court proceedings, all you have to shell out is £255 to start the case (although I predict an increase soon to £275). Unless you have to make some procedural application after that (for example, to compel the other side to obey a direction that has been given by the judge) which will attract a court fee of £155

(I predict an increase soon to £167), there are no other court fees required where the case is to run to a final contested hearing. It's better value than a cheese sandwich at Fortnum and Mason.

Negotiating with the enemy

A good precursor to negotiations is for each side to complete the comprehensive statement of financial information which they would be compelled to do if the finances went to court. It's called a Form E (or there's a shorter form called the E2 for variation applications – see below) and you can access it at justice.gov.uk. Parties are encouraged to comply with what is called a pre-action protocol for the exchange of information before financial proceedings are ever started. The protocol can be found as an annex to practice direction 9A with the Family Procedure Rules 2010 (see the same website). If your opponent has a lawyer and you do not, the chances are that the lawyer will do the running in respect of the protocol. There is no immediate sanction for non-compliance with the protocol and the court will not refuse to accept a financial application because the parties or one of them have failed to follow it. The worst that can happen is that non-compliance will be taken into account by the judge when the costs of the proceedings come to be decided should there be no settlement but a contested hearing and the non-complying party has generally behaved unreasonably over the proceedings. But the worst could be expensive. You can expect financial remedies court judges to now toughen up on costs where a party has failed to negotiate "openly and reasonably". The senior judges have urged them to do so. In a 2021 High Court case the judge was concerned with the wife's quest for maintenance pending suit. On an interim application like this, the general 'no order for costs' rule I mentioned above does not apply and the loser could easily have to pay the winner's costs of the application. Here, the wife won in that an order for maintenance pending suit was made but at a lower figure than she had sought. More damaging for her was that the judge ruled she had failed to negotiate maintenance with her husband in that "open and reasonable" way looked for. For these reasons, she was ordered to pay one-half of her costs of the application.

With both sides lawyerless, the chat may go something like this:

> "I'm more than happy to keep the bloody lawyers out. Just complete this form which I downloaded. I'll do the same. Then we'll both know everything we need to know about the numbers and when we reach an agreement, neither of us will be in jeopardy of the other trying to wriggle out of the agreement in a year's time because we were hoodwinked on the numbers."

> "For goodness sake, I'll have to give up work if you expect me to fill this lot out. Statements for every bank account for the last twelve months and the cash equivalent value of every one of my pension policies and do I expect to be cohabiting. I want a settlement, not a Spanish Inquisition."

> "Well don't worry about all the documents right now. Just fill out the

form so I can see what you are worth."

"No wonder this marriage never worked. No trust. Well, if you think I'm a trillionaire, instead of trying to scratch a living running a back street used car business, go ahead and prove it. See you in court."

Arbitration

There is the option of using a financial arbitration scheme run by the Institute of Family Law Arbitrators instead of having the court decide. It has its own website at ifla.org.uk and a small group of its pool of arbitrators – a particularly impressive group – has established an even more informative site at Familyarbitration.com. There is a pool of around 220 lawyers (but do remember my dodgy maths) including a couple of retired judges trying to supplement their income – the things these old boys and girls will do! – and from which you and the other party can select an arbitrator to decide your dispute in much the same way as it would be decided by a family court judge. You could call it a private court. As things currently stand, arbitration is going to be much, much faster than court proceedings. There's also the added advantage that no member of the media will be admitted to the arbitration hearing so you won't be appearing in the papers walking a poodle away from the hearing having poured a jug of water over counsel for the other side. If you can cope with the cost, it could be of especial use when there are only a couple of issues and time is of the essence. On top of any lawyers' fees, the arbitrator has to be paid by the two of you and a sum well in excess of the court fees that would have to be shelled out if the case took a conventional course.

A number of the arbitrators on the panel have been prepared to tell me their charging rates. Barristers were generally higher than solicitors. The barristers first. *One QC expects £5,000 for Day 1 and £1,000 per half-day thereafter but on a five-day arbitration he would be looking for £32,500. He regards his fees at the higher end "but perhaps Europa League rather than Champions' League." *Rhys Taylor wants £3,000 to £3,500 for a two-day arbitration including writing up his decision (which in arbitration speak is called an award but we will call it a decision just to be awkward). *David Walden-Smith is after £2,500 for Day 1 and £2,000 per day for each successive day. *One of the top family barristers (we would call them a senior junior with knobs on) who is shy about telling the world what they charge goes for £4,000 a day plus £1,500 a day if the case continues into a second or successive day. *Arbitrating barristers at Southampton's College Chambers, which are strong on family law, would want £1,750 for a one-day hearing and an additional £525 for writing up the decision. *The Breaking Law Transparency Award of the Decade goes to London chambers Queen Elizabeth Building which, to the chagrin of some of their eye scratch inflicting learned competitors, advertise their arbitrators' price list on their website. For a one-day arbitration to include writing up the decision, Stewart Leech QC would pocket £6,000 plus £500 for an additional file and £4,000 a day for a second and successive day. The three other QCs in the chambers want the same except that their fixed fee is £5,000. The junior barristers (non-

QCs) ask for £4,000, £3,500 or £3,000 for the fixed fee, £500 or £350 for an additional file and £2,250, £2,750 or £3,000 a day for a second and successive day of the hearing.

A couple of barristers provided me with specimen fees that were lower than those quoted to me by their clerks which tends to indicate that it may well be possible to negotiate down, especially in the current hard times.

Now the solicitors. Malcolm Martin asks for £1,500 for Day 1 and £750 for each half day thereafter plus £500 for writing up his decision. The arbitrators at national firm Mills & Reeve charge £1,750 for a one-day arbitration or £1,000 for a half-day arbitration plus something for writing the decision as to which a quote will be given when the nature of the case is known. For more complex cases, preparation time and preliminary hearings will be charged at £300 to £385 per hour. Tim Melville-Walker might be able to deal with a straightforward case for £500 and would not expect a 'medium asset' case to cost more than £2,000. David Hodson is after £400 per hour but will consider a fixed fee wherever possible. Norman Hartnell (no, not a reincarnation of Her Majesty's former dressmaker) asks for £300 per hour with a free initial exploratory meeting with the parties and any representing lawyers. Peter Jones for what he classifies as an 'average' arbitration seeks £1,500 a day, £500 for reading the papers and £500 for writing up his decision. If a hearing goes short by more than half a day then he will make a proportionate reduction in his fee.

VAT has to be added to charges and there may be extra charges for directions hearings where they are necessary. I fancy that in most instances the arbitrator will throw in the facilities of their chambers or office at which the arbitration can take place but otherwise the venue would have to be organised and paid for by the parties.

If you would find ringing around a pain in the neck, you might like to make use of the innovative 'booking agency' type service run by Fomas (Family Online Mediation and Arbitration Service) which you will find at fomas.co.uk. For £100 plus VAT per party, they will source you an accredited barrister, solicitor or part-time or former permanent judge to take your arbitration. This service is available to solicitors as well as litigants in person. On the strength of the online case information you have provided, they will give you a selection of prospective arbitrators who they regard as best suited to take your case and if you and your opponent can agree on one of them, you will make the necessary arrangements with the chosen arbitrator or their clerk. The lowest fees for one of their stars would be £1,500 for a one-day financial dispute resolution appointment and £2,500 for a one-day final financial remedies hearing: VAT on top. They can also source your MIAM mediator for you (see below).

An order from the court in the matrimonial proceedings incorporating the arbitrator's decision will need to be obtained to ensure everything is legally watertight but only in the most exceptional of cases where the parties are content, will the court interfere with the decision and there is a special fast track procedure for securing the order from the court. But if one side is unhappy with the arbitrator's decision, can it be challenged? It had been generally believed that such a challenge could only be made when the arbitrator had made a mistake on the law, the arbitrator had not had the jurisdiction to do what they had done or there had been some serious irregularity with the proceedings (something like one side had not been allowed to give evidence or the arbitrator had fallen asleep during the hearing). Pretty narrow grounds. But the belief was murdered by the Court of Appeal in a 2020 case. It held that the grounds for setting aside an arbitrator's award in a financial remedies case were wider and that there could be a challenge to the fairness of what they had decided, as in an appeal against the decision of a judge in court. The challenge should be made when an order based on the award is put before the court to approve. The challenging party should explain in writing why they challenge and, if the judge decides they have a real prospect of getting the award overturned, a review hearing by a circuit judge in the financial remedies court or by the High Court will be directed at which the challenge will be fully considered.

Mediation

This isn't about getting someone else – judge or arbitrator – to decide who gets what. It's about getting someone else – a mediator who will often be a lawyer – to help you thrash out an agreement instead of troubling the court to do so. We have already met mediators in civil as opposed to family cases at chapter 9. The law takes a tame step towards nodding you towards mediation. It does so by requiring whoever starts a financial application to have attended a short meeting with a trained mediator – they call it a Mediation Information and Assessment Meeting or MIAM for short – who will provide them with information about possible settlement through mediation and assess suitability for mediation. Nevertheless, you cannot be compelled to mediate even though the other party is keen or willing to do so. You will have to accompany any financial application you make with a form stating whether or not you have attended this meeting and, if not, why not. For help finding a mediator, go to familymediationcouncil.org.uk. There are a large number of exemptions from attending the MIAM. If you were to wrongly claim to be exempt, it is possible, but more unlikely than likely, that this will be picked up by the judge at an early stage of proceedings and that they will adjourn the application so that what should have happened does happen.

Cost? The MIAM is likely to set you back £99 and £49 for a certificate for court purposes that you have been subjected to it, though some mediators will view the MIAM as a sprat to catch a mackerel and waive these charges if you and the other party follow up with actual mediation through them. Different mediators charge different fees for post-MIAM mediation. The norm is around £150 per person for each 90 minute session. But how many sessions might it take?!

If you are on a low income, you may qualify for legal aid for both the MIAM and, if mediation is to take place afterwards, the first session of it. If only one of you is eligible for legal aid, then the MIAM and the first session will come free to the other party as well notwithstanding that they have quids coming out of their ears. Good deal, eh?

Mediation can be conducted even after a court application has been made. The proceedings may be taking an eternity or you may decide that you would prefer a mediated settlement which can only occur if you both agree as against a judge's decision being forced down your throat or you may be very close to an agreement but require some outside intervention to crack the outstanding issues. Just ask the court, with the consent of the other party, to put the brakes on the application for a specified period so that mediation can take place. The court will be delighted to oblige.

A MIAM can also be arranged through Fomas (fomas.co.uk) (see above under **Arbitration**) at no extra cost. That's in connection with financial and children cases and they will fix whether you are a firm of solicitors or are a litigant in person. They promise an enhanced session.

Collaborative law

This is a process whereby each party appoints a lawyer to try and thrash out an agreement. It will involve four-way meetings and probably meetings between the representatives only beforehand. If the process fails then each lawyer will drop out and you would have to find a new lawyer to continue the battle for you. Spot the difference between the collaborative law process and mediation? With the latter, no lawyers for either side actively participating and advising. I have never been an enormous fan because it can be costly and if no agreement is ever reached that's money down the drain. In one case I tried, the parties had expended over £18,000 on the process by which time they had agreed...nothing. The court had to decide after all. Nevertheless, I have come across a number of cases where it has worked. You want to be satisfied that the other side is genuine about trying to reach a settlement and is being completely open about what they have got. In the same way as an arbitrator's decision has to be okayed by the court so does an agreement reached through the collaborative law process.

Financial dispute resolution appointment

No arbitration. No mediation. No collaborative law. Do not despair. There may be a settlement even after proceedings have been started. The court will encourage one. It will happen at the financial dispute resolution stage (see more below).

Court: no option

But if you are faced with an oily spouse or partner who you cannot trust further than you can throw them, going to court is probably the only feasible course you can follow, carrying with it the mechanism for forcing out the truth about their financial circumstances. And if advice comes too late and you have already come to an agreement when the relationship was on the rocks or finally broke down, can you be held to it? Depends! The agreement may well be effectively torn up by the court if you press ahead with a financial application despite its existence *where you had no legal advice (and possibly where you had legal advice but it stank); *where the other side has subjected you to undue pressure to sign up; *where there has been an important change in circumstances which was either unforeseen or just overlooked when the agreement was made; or *in a David v Goliath situation with an inequality of bargaining power (say, the other side has been in a dominant position which they have abused). Then the court may divide capital and income in a way which bore no relation to what you had agreed.

Getting ready for court and being ready to pounce

For many, the idea of getting ready has an unconventional twist. It's getting ready to grab the realisable assets and plead poverty. It involves your spouse or partner emptying the joint bank account and paying off the loan their brother supposedly made to them in the previous century and the repayment of which has taken on an extreme urgency which could irredeemably damage the sibling relationship if it went unheeded. It involves transferring a couple of buy-to-let properties to a distant cousin on the pretext that they had paid for them and were always regarded as the true owners. It involves a sudden cessation of overtime, a rising debit balance on the current account, a threat of redundancy, and the rewriting of the in-laws' wills to disinherit their son or daughter "because on no account is that bitch/bastard (please delete, as appropriate) going to get their hands on my hard earned money when I kick the bucket."

If you get wind of planned monkey business on the part of your spouse or partner, it may be wise for you to pounce before the deed is done. The court has the power to prevent them from disposing of assets where their intention is to reduce what you might be awarded on a financial application, if not totally frustrate your application, or frustrate or impede any enforcement action you might be taking in respect of a financial remedies order you have already obtained. Should you be too late to prevent the disposal, the court can be asked to set it aside. These powers are contained in section 37 of the Matrimonial Causes Act 1973 where the parties are or have been married, schedules 5 and 7 to the Civil Partnership Act 2004 where they are or have been partners and section 24 of the Matrimonial and Family Proceedings Act 2004 which relates to financial proceedings here following an overseas divorce. The court application form to be used is the cutely entitled D50G (see justice.gov.uk) and this would need to be supported by your witness statement.

In very urgent cases the court may be prepared to make an order preventing disposal of any property – it could be money in the bank, an antique, a house – even before you have had an opportunity of making a financial application to the court. The asset at risk of dissipation might also be a pension entitlement where the pension holder may seek to draw a lump sum which is available under the pension conditions or to take advantage of the right to trade in an annuity for cash. If the judge was with you, a temporary order would be made which would last until a further hearing soon afterwards at which time your spouse or partner would be heard and have the right to ask for it to be revoked. A temporary order might also be wise where there is a real danger that the disposal would otherwise be made at some stage between the court papers for a preventative application being served and the hearing of that application taking place.

Obtaining a preventative order is not a doddle. The evidence must be there. The court will not make an order in your favour unless satisfied it is more probable than not that your spouse or partner intends to dispose of assets to do you down in your financial application. If in fact the disposal would have the effect of frustrating or diminishing what you are claiming, the law presumes that this is what is intended with the result that the task shifts to the spouse or partner to show otherwise.

Where the evidence justifies it and usually only in really big money cases, the court can prevent a spouse or partner from removing assets from England and Wales and dealing with them wherever they may be by way of a so-called 'freezing order'. There is also power in exceptional cases for the court to order that the applicant's legal team may go into the other party's premises to search for and seize documents and to remove computer records – without any prior warning. Wow! This is called a search order. They used to call it an *'Anton Piller'* order. If you are divorcing the head of a global organisation who eats his fish and chips out of twenty pound notes, mention 'Anton' as he is eavesdropping on you speaking on the phone to your girlfriend and watch the blood drain from his ruddy face. Or perhaps don't. The stuff of dreams.

"What have you done with my gold studded toothpick?"

Here's a gem that is property specific and should ensure that the property comes to no harm before the court decides on its ownership. Pray silence and welcome your uncomplicated saviour. Ladies and Gentlemen. I give you section 4 of the Torts (Interference with Goods) Act 1977. This effectively provides that the family court has the power to order any goods which are or may become the subject of litigation to be handed over pending a final court decision about them. We could be looking at chattels of monetary or sentimental value to you, jewellery, motor vehicles: any goods. The court might order that the goods be held by your lawyer or some independent third party and you could possibly take the sting out of strong opposition to an order by offering to pay into court a sum of money approximating to the value of the goods where it would remain until the dispute was resolved. The procedure is governed by Part 20 of the Family Procedure Rules 2010.

Fings 'aint what they used t'be

What did a spouse do in the old days when they sensed that, sooner or later, there would be matrimonial proceedings and the court would be dealing with the finances? They did the obvious thing. Rifled through the other spouse's personal papers, photocopied those which related to foreign bank accounts and the land in South Africa bought in a false name and kept them up their sleeve until the other spouse hanged themselves with a pack of lies about what they possessed. When the spouse was tech-savvy enough to use a computer, even a file or two might be invaded. So long as what was downloaded and copied did not include correspondence passing between the other spouse and their solicitor and the possession of the copy documents was disclosed to the other spouse at a specified time in the proceedings, nobody except the other spouse would be troubled. The documents could be used in evidence and, faced with that prospect, the less-than-honest spouse would frequently bow to the inevitable and do a deal which well suited the vigilant spouse.

This all changed in 2010 with the Court of Appeal ruling out that sort of conduct as usually breaching the civil and criminal law. Gird your loins for new tactics. The least contentious course to follow is, immediately after the honeymoon – actually you could start this on the honeymoon itself – take as deep an interest in the financial affairs of your other half as they will permit. Become their personal assistant, if they will wear it. That way, surreptitious raids will be unnecessary. You will have all the information you need at your fingertips in the unhappy event that the relationship breaks down.

Catering for shrewdies

If the other half has accumulated substantial wealth, they will be too shrewd to fall for that one. The action plan to cater for shrewdies demands the greatest care. The crux of the legal objection to what used to be commonplace rifling and hacking is that they amount to breaching confidence. Now, the other party can recover copies or the originals of unlawfully obtained documents under court order which could also forbid use of the documents without their consent and the court might even compel the party who has copied or removed them and then shown them to their lawyer to disinstruct that lawyer and go elsewhere for legal representation.

If the other party has got wind of what you are up to, they might just make an emergency application to the court in which financial proceedings are progressing so as to protect their position. Or even a beefier application to the Queen's Bench Division of the High Court which specialises in breach of confidence cases. And that's precisely what happened in a February 2021 case called *Santi v Santi*. Proceedings were already on foot in the High Court's Family Division. The husband suspected that his wife had accessed and misused his private information. He applied to the Queen's Bench Division for an order preventing her from disclosing any information she had obtained; requiring her to hand over copies of documents she had obtained and to make a statement setting out what information she had obtained and how; and requiring her computer and any other devices to be immediately subjected to forensic imaging because he alleged his wife had had electronic access to his bank account. The wife gave undertakings in the terms of the injunction sought except in relation to the forensic imaging which the judge felt would have been an unjustified and intrusive step. And the wife was ordered to pay 60% of the husband's legal costs. She also had to bear her own. An expensive exercise for her as the husband had solicitors and a QC on his side and the wife a QC and junior barrister under the direct access scheme.

But do not be too downhearted. What you have obtained in breach of confidence might just turn out to be of some use. If you can establish that the documents reveal that the other party has committed some unlawful conduct or intends to do so which could include holding back from the court information about their finances then the court might say that you can rely on them after all. And the court could reach the same decision in relation to very important documents if, taking into account a host of matters, it reckons it is fair to do so. The alternative course which the court might follow before deciding whether to order the other side to produce confidential documents which you have seen, is to allow you to give evidence about the nature of the documents and their contents. So if you happen to innocently come across tasty documents, remember what you have read but leave the documents in place and perhaps recite the details before you retire at night so that they are well implanted in your memory.

> *"Darling, why do you keep saying account number AXD45669209888 sort code 14-78-04?"*

But it's not confidential!

That's another matter. If the documents are not confidential then they can be copied, if not 'borrowed', and used in evidence. Confidentiality, though, is not dependent on a lock and key. And, as the Court of Appeal has put it, if a husband leaves his bank statement lying around open in the kitchen, living room or the parties' bedroom (they actually called it the marital bedroom – *"I'm tired, darling. Let's repair to the marital bedroom." "Oh. Let's and no conjugal rights tonight"* – the statement may not be confidential so far as the wife is concerned. If the statement was kept by the husband in his study, it is more likely to be regarded as confidential and even more likely if in a drawer in his desk and even more likely still if kept locked in his desk.

"No rush, darling" or "Let's talk about it ..... for the next 30 years"

There's a trap here. If you remarry or enter into a civil partnership after a divorce, annulment or dissolution without having applied for financial remedies against your former spouse or partner, then it will be too late to do so, except for a pension share. An application in the petition or answer (for old law matrimonial cases) or an application in the equivalent to the petition (for new law matrimonial cases) would do or a later application in the prescribed form. Just the right words in the document are looked for and not any court hearing. If you made the application in time, your new status may well have some impact on what you will be entitled to but you can nevertheless pursue the application which could, for example, be for an order for transfer of property or its sale and split of the sale proceeds. Maintenance for you would no longer be payable.

Provided you have not remarried or entered into a civil partnership, there is no time limit for making a financial application against your former spouse or partner. The court might be unsympathetic if you left it for ages and then suddenly pounced when your former spouse had thought they were out of the woods.

A Supreme Court case where the wife had delayed making a financial application for 19 years after divorce hit the headlines in March 2015. The publicity was manic and innocently deceptive. When they separated the parties were leading a nomadic lifestyle and there was nothing about the husband's circumstances to excite court proceedings. But how things changed with time. When the wife ultimately made her application the husband was alleged to be worth £107m. The appeal judges gave the wife the green light to pursue her belated application though the husband had fought to have it chucked out on the ground that after all this time there were no reasonable grounds for making it. But that green light was switched on because the Supreme Court ruled that there was no legal ground in this situation to summarily kill off a financial application before a ball had been kicked. The wife was entitled to have her case heard. This was an exceptional case. A substantially belated application will be afforded a decent hearing, unless there are really compelling reasons against it. But it will then be afforded a decent burial and the applicant could end up paying the other party's costs if the court reckoned the applicant had behaved unreasonably in making and persisting with the application.

The very peculiar payer

You can't afford to pay but desperately yearn for legal representation, especially when the opposition is blessed with high powered and higher charging lawyers. Please discount the idea of abducting a barrister from their chambers. That leaves the courses we have looked at previously (see chapter 7). And something else I have saved up for you. The court can order your spouse or partner in war to pay for YOUR lawyer as the case progresses under a *legal services order*. I know it is hard to believe but it really can be done and the prospect of having to shell out not only for their lawyer but your own could well induce 3-D nightmares for your opponent and enhance the chances of a decent deal for you. (Who said this was licensed blackmail?). You won't find securing such an order a walkover but they are regularly being made in the family court for financial remedies cases so it's worth looking into. Obviously, the court will have to be satisfied that your spouse or partner can afford to pay and payment won't want to stifle their ability to get a lawyer for themselves.

To succeed, it is essential for you to prove that you cannot reasonably obtain representation without the opposition dipping into their pockets to help you. Don't you have assets you could sell to pay for a lawyer yourself? The court is unlikely to expect you to sell or mortgage your home or deplete a modest fund of savings. Can't you raise a litigation loan from a bank or some other lender (see chapter 7)? The court may look for evidence of two rejected loan applications. If you can only borrow at a very high rate of interest, you probably won't be expected to have taken up the loan unless your opponent were to offer to pay the interest or, at least, cover the 'excess' element of it.

Won't solicitors be prepared to act for you in return for a mortgage in their favour over any assets you recover in the case? This is known as a *'Sears Tooth' charge*? Not that many solicitors will be happy with such an arrangement. Can't you tap up family or friends?

Your spouse or partner may have the benefit of financial support from a family member of friend. When they contend that the support has been withdrawn but the position is ambiguous or unclear, the court may well treat the support as likely to continue for the time being.

The *legal services order* will more likely than not provide for monthly payments to be made rather than a lump and can reflect your legal costs up to and including the financial dispute resolution appointment (see below) after which a further order could be made. Any intransigence by you in negotiations with the opposition or other unreasonable behaviour in the proceedings will go down badly on an application for an order. Whether or not your opponent has legal representation will be a relevant factor. An order can be made to cover not only costs already incurred under solicitors' unpaid bills but future costs. Your solicitors may be saying: *"We love you and feel for you, little clientipoo, but you owe us £15,000 and we just can't afford to continue to act for you unless you settle what you already owe us and something more for future work. We have rent to pay, mouths to feed and law books to buy".*

If you are after legal representation for arbitration or mediation in the course of proceedings that have already been started (see above), the court can still oblige you with a *legal services order* and will approach your application in the same way as for an order to cover a court hearing.

Getting to the truth – and may be a court promoted settlement

There are three possible stages to a financial application, which have been sharpened up by the new financial remedies courts. You may be able to reach a settlement at or before any of them. They are the first appointment, the financial dispute resolution appointment and the contested final hearing. The sooner the truth emerges, the earlier a settlement becomes a possibility. Exception alert. There may be just one stage to the most straightforward cases. This is under a 'fast-track' procedure which you can indicate you want to be utilised when you make your application. The procedure mainly applies where you are asking just for an order for maintenance ('periodical payments' in law speak) or for an existing maintenance order to be varied (unless at the same time you are asking for some other order to take its place such as an order for a lump sum which might be appropriate where it is proposed that regular payments are stopped in return for a once and for all cash payment). Under the fast-track procedure, the court will fix a hearing at which it is hoped the application can be dealt with there and then without any other procedural paraphernalia having to be engaged in.

Back to the more usual application which will go ahead under the so-called 'standard procedure'. The first lap of the journey to the truth runs from when you make your application up to and including the first appointment. A lapse of 12 to 16 weeks. Both sides will be expected to attend at court on the first appointment in person or remotely – with lawyers, if they have them – but where all procedural directions and documentation have been agreed by both sides, an attempt can be made to get the court's approval to by-pass the first appointment with copies of everything being emailed to the court at least 14 days before the hearing date fixed. Then an order will be issued by the court setting out what each side has to do and by when they have to do it in readiness for the next stage and this will be done without a court or remote attendance. It would save on costs. Casually ask any lawyer acting for you: "I suppose you have organised the accelerated procedure?" Otherwise, the first appointment is likely to last around 30 to 40 minutes. If the case looks complex, a further 15 minutes will probably be added on. Where it is so complex that even around one hour may not be sufficient, ask the court to allow longer and say why. You can do this when completing a questionnaire – allocation questionnaire – that the court should ask you do so with the application or soon afterwards and, if you are not given the opportunity, just write in, as soon as you can. The name of the judge set to conduct the first appointment will be notified to you and so you will know whether to organise a sickie! At least five weeks before the first appointment, you will each have completed a comprehensive statement of your financial circumstances (even if you have voluntarily shared information prior to the application). This is the famous Form E. E doesn't stand for Edith or Edgar or anything in particular but they thought it was a good idea because it slotted nicely between Forms D and G.

The completed Form E must be sent to the court and the other side at least five weeks before the first appointment. You and the other party should actually swap your completed forms – that is what is meant by exchanging them – so that neither of you has seen the other's statement before you have parted with your own or you might just be tempted to modify what you disclose in the light of what you read from them or rant on about what they have said and raise the temperature. Guidance is available on completing Form E (or, in the case of an application for variation of an earlier order, Form E2) at gov.uk/government/publications/form-e-financial-statement-for-a-financial-order-matrimonial-causes-act-1973-civil-partnership-act-2004-for-financial-relief-after-an-overseas. Your spouse or partner may be late with their Form E or go into complete paralysis mode. Where this happens, send your own completed Form E into the court and tell the court and the opposition that you will withhold sending the opposition a copy of your Form E until they are ready to exchange with you.

The questionnaire

Let's assume that you have both done as required and that your opponent's Form E is overflowing with fiction instead of fact. The tool for digging out the truth (and exposing the fiction for what it is) is *The Sizzling Juicy Questionnaire*. It needs to be compiled and sent to the court and the opposition at least a fortnight before the first appointment so that you may have just three weeks to do what has to be done. In practice, you may have much less time because of frequent delay in Forms E being exchanged. Your opponent may be deliberately late so as to shrink the time available to you to compose those searching questions. If you feel that you have insufficient time – particularly if you want to obtain legal help and advice with your questionnaire – you can legitimately seek more time, even if this would result in the first appointment having to be postponed. Ask your opponent to agree. If they refuse or won't answer, write to the court and ask for more time and, if necessary, for a postponement of the first appointment. Where the court refuses or fails to respond, participate at the first appointment hearing but again request a postponement. You can also ask the judge to order your opponent to reimburse you any expenses you have incurred on the abortive hearing. The court ought to be with you.

This crucial questionnaire should set out all the further information and documents you want from your opponent. One of the other documents to be produced by each side and to accompany their questionnaire is a concise statement of what they are arguing about – the issues between them. That's why it is called a statement of issues (sometimes, a position statement) and, unless there are good reasons, it should not be longer than five pages (at least 12 point font with 1.5 or double spacing). Issues? For example, should the family home be sold and, if so, how should the sale proceeds be divided up; should your opponent pay you maintenance and, if so, for how long (for a fixed number of years, until the youngest child has ceased full time education or indefinitely so long as you are both alive and you have not remarried or entered into another civil partnership); and whether you claim that your opponent has assets or income or both which they have failed to disclose in their Form E. The further information and documents you go after must be linked to the issues: something often forgotten. The judge who scrutinises the questionnaire at the first appointment should be on alert for questionnaire requests which are irrelevant or disproportionate. Your questionnaire should positively not be used merely to draw out admissions from your opponent which you think might be helpful to your case (for example, "Does the respondent accept that the applicant worked her guts out for the entirety of the marriage and in 1989 during the course of a streaming cold she single-handedly laid the foundations for a rear extension at the matrimonial home?"). The financial remedies court does not like questionnaires that go on for longer than four A4 pages (again, at least 12 point font and 1.5 or double spacing). You will have to justify exceeding this limit. Here's what your questionnaire might look like.

Case no 2016F2016

IN THE FINANCIAL REMEDIES COURT

SITTING AT PEARDROP

BETWEEN

MAVIS TROUBLESORE Applicant

- and -

CLIVE TROUBLESORE Respondent

APPLICANT'S QUESTIONNAIRE UNDER FAMILY PROCEDURE RULES 2010 RULE 9.14(5) (c)

QUESTION 1 *The respondent has failed to answer 1.8 of his Form E ("Are you living with a new partner?") and 1.9 ("Do you intend to live* with a new partner within the next six months") and, if appropriate, 4.6 (as to the financial circumstances of a cohabitee or intended cohabitee). These questions are repeated.

QUESTION 2 *If the respondent does not intend to live with a new partner within the next six months but does intend to live with a new partner outside that period, when does the respondent intend this should happen?*

QUESTION 3 *The respondent has failed to attach to his Form E at 2.3 statements for the last 12 months with Dodgy Bank. He should produce these statements.*

QUESTION 4 *In respect of the respondent's current account with Barclays plc numbered X49701B7 disclosed at 2.3, he should provide details (including payer or payee where not evident) of every credit and debit entry for a sum of £500.00 or more for the period of three months prior to separation (on 14 July 2021) and since separation.*

Or

QUESTION 4 *The respondent should produce statements of his accounts disclosed at 2.3 where not already attached to his Form E for a period of 12 months prior to separation (on 14 July 2021) to date. He should further provide details (including payer or payee where not evident) for every credit and debit entry on all statements for this period for a sum of £500.00 or more.*

QUESTION 5 *The respondent has failed to disclose at 2.3 or elsewhere, his accounts with Dodgy Bank numbered 2866421/3/4. He should state the reason for non-disclosure and produce statements for the accounts for the last two years.*

QUESTION 6 *The respondent should produce a full and complete copy of his passport and state the purpose of each trip abroad in respect of which an entry has been endorsed since separation on 14 July 2021.*

QUESTION 7 *The respondent should produce copies of his tax returns, forms PIID (as to benefits and expenses not put through the payroll) and all notices of assessment to tax issued by HM Revenue & Customs in relation to him for the last three complete tax years.*

QUESTION 8 *The P60 produced by the respondent for the last tax year does not indicate the receipt of any bonus from his employer and the respondent is silent on bonus entitlement at 2.15. The respondent should (a) produce copies of his contract of employment and any variations of the contract and other documents issued to him by his employer relating to bonus entitlement; (b) explain the non-receipt of a bonus for the last tax year; (c) state when he expects any bonus referable to the last tax year to be paid to him and how much he expects to receive; and (d) state what future bonuses he expects to receive.*

QUESTION 9 *The respondent should state his current mortgage ca-*

> pacity, support the figure with a letter from a financial adviser; and produce a copy of his letter of instruction to the adviser.
>
> **QUESTION 10** The respondent should produce a copy of his application to the Halifax for the further advance on the family home which he raised in 2012.
>
> **QUESTION 11** The respondent should produce particulars of properties which he asserts would be suitable for occupation by the applicant and the respondent respectively in the event of a sale of the family home, limited to six properties in each category.
>
> **QUESTION 12** The respondent should particularise all private cash transactions into which he has entered in the course of his part-time business as a property development adviser during the last 12 months.
>
> **QUESTION 13** The respondent should state what he believes his employment promotion prospects to be and the likely impact of his salary and benefits and should produce copies of all correspondence passing between himself and his employer in the past 12 months relating to these matters.
>
> (signed) M Troublesore
>
> Dated 26 November 2021

Bank, credit and store card statements may reveal sources of income which the respondent has failed to disclose in their Form E and a level of expenditure and style of living inconsistent with the penury being suggested. However, the judge at the first appointment may be reluctant to allow you to embark on a fishing exercise which could involve the respondent in time consuming and potentially costly enquiries to answer your questions. Be prepared, therefore, to substantiate your line of enquiry by reference to the contents of the statements of issues and to highlight to the judge some choice examples of the respondent's apparent high living or suspicious transactions close to and since the separation. "Madam, he has been on three holidays abroad this year alone, his Dodgy Bank statements show he withdrew £12,000 in the three months before he left me and when he came to collect his son last week, he pretended to be on foot but he had parked a brand new Ferrari with a personalised number plate round the corner."

The threshold for explaining debit and credit entries on statements is usually a matter of contention. Better to pitch for a higher threshold – like £500 as in our specimen questionnaire – than one which is too low and might lead the judge to conclude you are being unreasonable and so disallow the request entirely or restrict the number of entries for which an explanation is ordered and raise the threshold, to boot.

Costs and the first appointment

A new regime for watching the cash register in financial remedies cases came into force on 6 July 2020. Each party must now ensure that a costs estimate (in form H) is with the court and the other party at least one day before the first appointment. This is to give details of that party's legal costs incurred up until then and an estimate of the further costs to be incurred up to the next stage which is the financial dispute resolution appointment. A copy of the form is to be taken to court on the day. My advice is to take three copies so that you can dish them out to the judge and the other side at court and have one for yourself because if the copy you sent in has reached the court file, I would eat yet another hat, which by then could give me indigestion. For a remote hearing, email as necessary and be ready to email again during the hearing. If you have a lawyer, they must verify in the form that they have discussed it with you. That should ensure that you have not been left in the dark about the bill you have run up and are likely to run up to reach the financial dispute resolution appointment.

Armed for the first appointment

There could be a settlement at court on the day of the first appointment. Pressure on you to settle may come from the lawyer for your opponent. The majority of lawyers will treat an unrepresented litigant on the other side fairly and courteously but there are others who are bullies and ready to intimidate so as to achieve the best result for their client. Even the judge who is conducting the first appointment may urge you to seize the opportunity of attempting to come to an agreement that day. It is not uncommon for the judge to allow more time for negotiations between the parties and any lawyers who represent them to take place throughout the rest of the court day in the court building or remotely with technology allowing you to confer with the other side and also with any lawyer you may have, out of the vision and the ear shot of the judge. In fact, the judge may decide – whether or not you and your opponent agree – to convert the first appointment into a financial dispute resolution appointment which is the next stage of the application and which, with no settlement, would otherwise follow several months later. Watch it. You cannot be forced into a settlement against your will and the judge will not allow this to happen but, with the combination of pressure from the other side and judicial urging along with the attraction of an end to what has probably been a long period of contention, you might just find yourself highly tempted to settle on terms that you come to regret. Negotiate in haste and repent at leisure.

If a settlement is agreed without qualification on the day of the first appointment, you will find it hard if not impossible to extricate yourself from it later. Obviously, where the settlement is too good to be true – whether this be due to keenness on your opponent's part to avoid an investigation of their finances by paying over the odds to get off the hook or for some other reason – you would be wise to accept it. Otherwise, refuse the offer *or* say you would be happy to continue with the negotiation process after the conclusion of the first appointment *or* say that you want to take legal advice on the offer and ask for the first appointment to be adjourned to a later date so that you can do so. When there is a settlement between the first appointment and the financial dispute resolution appointment, the court can be asked to make an order encompassing what has been agreed without a further hearing and for the financial dispute resolution appointment to be cancelled. So:

- if you are without a lawyer at the first appointment and you are unsure whether or not to accept an offer there and then, don't accept; and
- if possible, hire a lawyer for the first appointment (so at least you are on a level playing field with your represented opponent when it comes to any negotiations which may take place) and even though you may have been acting for yourself up to that stage and intend to act for yourself in the future (see chapter 7).

The financial dispute resolution appointment

You may have thought that the first appointment scored high points on negotiation talk. Well, you 'aint seen nothing yet. There should have been attempts or further attempts at negotiating a settlement after the first appointment but as you are at the second stage of the proceedings, they have not come to anything – yet. The directions given by the court at the first appointment should have been complied with: in particular, some common ground ought to exist on the value of the assets (okay, only the values of the bedside lamps and the coal scuttle are agreed) and each side should have answered the questionnaires.

In an effort to beat you down, your opponent's lawyer will have prepared another position statement (which this time might be called a *skeleton argument* and which has nothing to do with what might be found under a Leicester car park). It should usually be restricted to ten A4 pages and you can put one in too. Indeed, you could have been ordered to do so at the first appointment and lodgement with the court of copies of all offers and counter-offers exchanged since the first appointment would probably have been ordered as well but this should be done anyway, at least seven days before the resolution appointment. The statement will summarise the factual background and comment on what remains in dispute and why your opponent maintains that you are a despicable liar, in surreptitious cohabitation, deliberately under employed and with family members who will be bank rolling you in perpetuity. Or the position statement may be moderate in its language and balanced. When you read it (and this may not be until the day of the appointment and at court or by email with a remote hearing) you might visualise your case collapsing before you. When you read it again, you will probably visualise your case suddenly rejuvenated and realise the document is a balloon of hot air. My advice about taking in a lawyer for the first appointment is even more apposite for this second stage. If you are represented, your lawyer will have produced a position statement on your behalf, perhaps even more aggressive and inflammatory than that from your opponent.

The costs changes effective on 6 July 2020 impact on the financial dispute resolution appointment as well. A similar procedure is to be followed as for the first appointment and this time the estimated costs are to run up to the final hearing, assuming the case is not going to settle.

The judge (not necessarily the same judge who conducted the first appointment) will go into crack mode, discovering what offers, counter offers, counter-counter offers and counter-counter-counter offers have been made and what now separates the parties. Having listened to both sides and any lawyers, the judge will do their best to indicate what they consider to be a fair settlement. That won't be easy where there are fundamental factual issues between the parties. You will be allowed time to negotiate at court or remotely on the day, as with the first appointment (see above).

The judge will dip into and out of the negotiations by asking you back to find out how you are getting on and becoming irritable if they are told that neither side has budged an inch. And then as darkness draws in, the public outside make their way home or your children are screaming for their tea and you and your opponent and any lawyers check your wrist watches (or fobs) and yawn with exhaustion, the judge will want to know whether you have settled.

As before, nobody can force you to settle. Should the best offer from your opponent fall short of the realms of reasonableness, refuse to settle. The judge will then give directions for a contested hearing to take place at a later date. It is unlikely to be for at least three months: it could be considerably later. But negotiations could continue after the appointment and lead to a settlement with both sides having chewed over the arguments which were ventilated at the appointment and the judge's suggestions for how the case should be settled. Many cases which failed to settle at this stage do go on to settle soon afterwards. Bear this in mind, though. The judge at the financial dispute resolution appointment will have directed various things to be done by the parties before the final hearing: statements from the parties and any relevant witnesses of the evidence to be relied on in relation to particular issues, experts' reports (maybe from a pensions expert or a business valuer), property valuations – that sort of thing. These will cost money and that money will be coming out of the parties' assets so you don't want to run up this expense or too much of it if the case is to settle – and you know it.

Incidentally, if the case does proceed to a contested hearing and you thought the judge's settlement proposals at the financial dispute resolution appointment were off the mark, don't worry. You won't be seeing that judge again for the financial proceedings unless you join them in the same ice-cream queue at teatime. They are disqualified from playing any further part in the financial dispute, except to deal with procedural matters.

Private financial dispute resolution appointments

Can't get a hearing date for a court financial dispute resolution appointment for months? Hate all the judges at the court in which the case is proceeding? Then a private resolution appointment is just the ticket so long as you, with your opponent, can afford to pay the charges of whoever is going to conduct it and are willing to do so. Choose from the pool of lawyers who conduct arbitrations in financial cases (see above). Their fee is likely to be at the same level as for an arbitration and the appointment can probably take place at the chambers (for a barrister) or office (for a solicitor) of the lawyer concerned. There's another prominent lawyer who has recently become available to conduct private resolution appointments. That's retired circuit judge and barrister Philip Waller CBE who can be engaged through clerks@corachambers. He is a consultant editor of the leading textbook *Rayden and Jackson on Relationship Breakdown, Finances and Children*.

Basically, with one of these private jobs, everything is the same as in a court except no judge. Whoever conducts will be giving an indication on how they assess the case should settle and encouraging a settlement along those lines. If a settlement is reached, a judge in court will be asked to approve its terms – most unlikely to be a troublesome step – and, if no settlement, the case will go back to court for the fixing of a contested hearing. The family court chief is on record as encouraging the use of these private appointments. Help to clear the backlog of court cases!

The final hearing

As indicated, the majority of cases settle before the final hearing commences even though there has been a financial dispute resolution appointment which has not generated a settlement. Some settle five minutes before everyone is at the starting line. It's a game of brinkmanship. Another big change which has been in operation since 6 July 2020 is that after a failed resolution appointment, each party must send to the court and the other side details of the terms of settlement they are proposing. And not details marked 'without prejudice' or hidden way in a sealed envelope. No, 'open' proposals which the judge can read before the case starts and which can be taken into account when the court comes to decide at the end of the case whether one side has behaved so unreasonably by refusing a patently fair offer, that they should pick up the other party's legal bill or part of it. The proposals must be sent out within 21 days of the failed resolution appointment or, where, for whatever reason, there has been no resolution appointment, no later than six weeks before the final hearing. The 21 days will often be unworkable because things need to be done before both parties can formulate sensible proposals – property and pension valuations to be carried out and up-to-date statements to be put in by the parties and any other witnesses, for example. The court can grant longer than 21 days. Where appropriate, ask the judge to do so. Either side can modify proposals made although, if still no settlement, the judge will be unimpressed by a subsequent set of less favourable proposals, unless there has been a change in circumstances to justify the changes.

No settlement, even five minutes before starter's orders? Good luck!

Interim relief: interim pain

Should you be in financial difficulty (perhaps you have been relying on regular voluntary maintenance or housekeeping from your opponent which has dried up or been reduced), you can apply to the court for temporary maintenance: that's *maintenance pending suit* up to decree absolute or final civil partnership dissolution order (or the equivalent under the new legislation) and *interim periodical payments* from then onwards. This is particularly useful where you are in the family home and the mortgage repayments are not being made. The object of temporary maintenance is to deal with immediate needs: we'll see what that really means in a moment. It will almost invariably be pitched at a figure which is lower than the maintenance you could expect from the court after a final hearing. You can indicate an intention to apply for temporary maintenance on your initial application form: sling it in, just in case and it will not matter if you never follow it up. On the hearing of a temporary maintenance application, each side will be required to produce statements of their financial circumstances where the Forms E are not yet ready. It would be rare for any oral evidence to be allowed on the hearing of the application which is usually decided on consideration of the papers and after representations from both sides. Where you are applying for a legal services order (see above), it will be convenient for that matter and temporary maintenance to be dealt with together.

In an urgent situation, the court may be prepared to make a *'Segal Order'* (named after the judge who invented it) for global maintenance for the applicant and the children in the applicant's care although in due course the Child Maintenance Service (see chapter 76) may need to be involved.

Maintenance pending suit applications were given a boost by the Court of Appeal in a January 2021 case. There it was ruled that:

- while it had always been understood that maintenance pending suit was intended to deal with immediate needs, this meant no more than that it was intended to deal with maintenance pending the final hearing. The fact that some items of expenditure were not incurred every month did not mean that they would be excluded for the purpose of determining what amount of maintenance pending suit was reasonable.

- it was unnecessary for a party applying for maintenance pending suit who was relying on basic expenditure and had already put in a Form E (see above) to produce a separate list of income needs for the purpose of that application.

- school fees could be included in the maintenance pending suit order.

Don't get bogged down by making a temporary maintenance application unless you are really in trouble because its life will be relatively short and the cost of an application if you are legally represented may make it a disproportionate exercise. On the other hand, it can sometimes give you a tactical advantage, demonstrating to your opponent that even the lower maintenance level is somewhat higher than they may have believed and, if they comply with the temporary order as the application progresses, that's pretty good evidence that they have the financial ability to pay what was ordered. "Blimey, if that's the interim, I'm going to be stung by the final order." Could help in negotiations.

"The Delivery Manager
The Family Court
Family Hearing Centre
Toytown
BE4 9JG

URGENT

Dear Sir or Madam

Troublesore v Troublesore

Case no 216F2016

I am the applicant/petitioner. In my application for financial remedies, I have asked for an order for maintenance pending suit. I request you to please list the application for maintenance pending suit (I respectfully suggest a time estimate of one hour) as soon as possible and prior to the first appointment (or at the same time as the first appointment if the time estimate for the first appointment can be appropriately increased) (delete as necessary). I am desperately short of money because the respondent is not maintaining me and the matter is extremely urgent.

Yours faithfully

Mavis Troublesore"

Register this

It would be a pity if, before your financial application could be heard, your opponent sold or re-mortgaged some (or all) assets over which they had control and walked off with the money. There are ways in which you can effectively prevent this without procuring an injunction (see above for the injunction). Take a property which is or was intended to be the family home and it is in the sole name of your opponent. By registering a *notice of home rights* you will frustrate any efforts to sell or mortgage the property without your concurrence. The notice will last until the final decree or order but the court can extend its life. Unless it is Hampton Court Palace the property will almost certainly be registered at the Land Registry. Use form HR1 (see landregistry.gov.uk) and there is no charge. If the property is unregistered – one of those parchment title deeds jobs – there is a different procedure you can follow with the Land Charges Registry. For properties other than the family home which are owned by your opponent but not jointly with you, it is possible to achieve the same frustrating result by registering at the Land Registry a *notice* (but different from a *notice of home rights*) or a restriction (which will probably be more appropriate). There is a mirror entry which can be registered at the Land Charges Registry for parchment title deeds jobs. Be warned. Registering a notice or restriction without reasonable cause could subject you to a claim for damages if your action causes loss to your opponent. So no messing about.

'Aint got it: can't get it

You have asked your opponent to produce certain documents and they say they do not have them and cannot obtain them. Perhaps, they are simply silent. Or in relation to the financial circumstances of a cohabitee or intended cohabitee, your opponent says: "We discuss our love for one another and the storylines of *Emmerdale* but about our finances, we never speak. I don't know where she works. Maybe she doesn't work." The most effective way of dealing with this situation is to apply to the court to order whoever has the relevant documentation to attend with it at court on an appointed occasion so that you can inspect it. Such an order (or just the threat of an application for one) may well lead to your opponent coming up with what is required after all. In the case of the cohabitee, their means may be relevant to what they are or should be contributing towards expenditure which your opponent is incurring and to what with their income being taken into account, your opponent could jointly with them raise on mortgage where your opponent's ability to rehouse is material. Of course, they are under no obligation to maintain *you* or help out your opponent to come up with a financial package for *your* benefit but if the court finds that your opponent and their partner do intend to purchase together, that is going to be highly relevant. The cohabitee can be required to produce pay slips and other specified documents which are calculated to establish their financial circumstances. The procedure to be followed is in rule 21.2 of the Family Procedure Rules 2010.

Stay – just a little bit longer

You may need to keep your opponent on a lead or not too far away from a telescope so that an order preventing disposal of assets pending the resolution of your application (see above) will not be frustrated. Or it may be imperative to achieve a just decision on your application that your opponent should attend the final hearing in person to be cross-examined. But he is about to scarper. The court does have the power on a special application by you to forbid them from leaving England and Wales and, as a backup, to order them to surrender their passport. Such an application will be pretty exceptional and will not be lightly granted because an order of this kind restricts liberty. The court will definitely have to be satisfied that, without the beast being present in court, with or without a battery of lawyers, your case will be materially prejudiced.

Any order made is likely to be for a very limited period. However, in the case of the late tycoon Scot Young who was involved in protracted and acrimonious financial proceedings with his wife, his passport had been impounded for nearly three years when the court extended the period by a further nine months. Mr Young died in tragic circumstances in 2014.

Wot a business!

If your opponent's business is a one-man/woman band and simply a vehicle for them to earn a living, its value (if any) as opposed to what they are earning from it, is unlikely to be of relevance. Of course, if the business has substantial assets, some of which could be realised or used as security for a loan, that is another matter. And it is even more of another matter where say your opponent's business is a sizeable one with goodwill which will one day be sold for a packet or is again sizeable and run through a company in which your opponent has more than a peanut shareholding. In such a situation, you may wish to ask the court to order a business/share valuation. Such a valuation can be expensive and so the court will wish to be satisfied that it would be proportionate to order one. The smaller the business, the more disproportionate the court would reckon the expense of a valuation to be. Any valuation ordered is likely to be by a single valuer who is instructed jointly by both sides and, in all probability, with each party initially paying one-half of the valuer's fee. Asking for a single valuer and not one valuer for each side will make the idea of a valuation more acceptable to the judge.

Conned

The court has made a final order for financial remedies – perhaps with your actual consent – and you have now discovered that your opponent acted fraudulently, misrepresented some matter, failed to disclose some information that should have been disclosed, or accomplished all three! Or maybe you made a dreadful mistake about their financial circumstances or perhaps some event has occurred which you say invalidates the basis on which the order was made. If what you know now but did not know or realise then would have made a material difference, you may be able to upset the order. What is essential is that once the truth or whatever has come out, you act expeditiously to challenge the order. The way of doing so, whether or not you consented to the order, is by an application to the court to cancel the order (set aside). The procedure here, where you are not suggesting that the court went wrong (in which event you should be following the different route of appealing), is dictated by rule 9.9A of the Family Procedure Rules 2010 and came into force in October 2016 (just after the first edition of *Breaking Law* dropped into the bookshelves and I was proudly proclaiming that it was bang up to date) and Practice Direction 9A. The application should generally be made to the court which made the order and be heard by the very same judge who dealt with the case, provided they have not expired or been sectioned. The judge will order a rehearing of the application where the original order is set aside or, if they have sufficient information available, make a substitute order there and then.

Sometimes the less than frank party will procure the inclusion in the original court order of words to the effect that the other party does not accept that the less than frank party has been....frank. They may do so in the belief that this will preclude the other party from challenging the order when ultimately the truth emerges. "You said you thought I lied so how can you complain about it now? You consented to that order with your eyes wide open." This argument won't wash. Words like these in the order will not achieve what was intended by the less than frank party.

The other situation I have touched on where you may be able to procure the ripping up of an order you feel is no longer fair is where some supervening event has occurred since the order was made. The supervening event must have occurred soon after the order was made – probably no more than a few months afterwards with 12 months afterwards almost always being too long – and you must act quickly to challenge. In the leading case on the subject, the husband agreed to transfer the former family home to the wife in consideration of him being relieved of any obligation to pay her maintenance and five weeks later, she killed the two children and committed suicide. The wife's mother resisted the husband's attempt at getting the court order overturned but the husband succeeded.

A remarriage by the other party soon after the order was made which did make a difference and which had not been contemplated by the aggrieved party, might be enough to secure a set aside. And so might the other party having intended to remarry but kept quiet about it: a case of misrepresentation or failure to disclose material information to you and the court.

Mistake and cladding

Making a mistake, as I have indicated, could be the basis for an order being set aside. However, you will fail if you are unable to show that you could not have discovered the true state of affairs by exercising due diligence. Take the case of the wife who in February 2021 was trying to get a judge to cancel an order to which she had agreed requiring her to pay her husband £300,000 for his interest in the family home. This was a flat in an East London block which the parties had agreed was worth £1,100,000. It had cladding outer walls. After the wife had committed herself to the deal which the court had approved pending a formal order being drawn up, she was informed that there was no fire safety certificate for the building and, because of government guidelines after the Grenfell Tower tragedy, the surveyor for her building society from whom she needed to borrow money, had been obliged to give the flat a nil value. She genuinely believed that, while a problem existed, it was of a technical nature which was capable of being overcome with the production of suitable paperwork and that there was no problem with the cladding itself. Had the wife chosen not to go along with the formal order being made, she would most likely have been off the hook. But she chose to allow the formal order to be made. She took a gamble that the problem would sort itself out in time and that she would not be affected by it.

You guessed right. After the formal order had been made, the dreaded news arrived. The whole cladding required replacement and, although, the cost of this was unclear, it could be in the region of £40,000 for each flat.

The judge ruled the case fell into the 'know unknown' category where something is known and assumed but later eventuates to an extent that was not expected. A set aside of an order in such a situation would not be granted unless what turned out to be the state affairs could not have been foreseen. That the cladding might be dodgy was obviously something the wife could have foreseen as much as she must have prayed that all would be well. She should never have taken that gamble. It cost her the refusal of her set aside application.

A coronavirus set aside

I predict a mass of challenges – they have already started – to financial orders made before the virus which one party asserts would never have been made had the onset and impact of the virus on them and their affairs (which may not yet be fully ascertainable) been known or contemplated at the time. These challenges will come under the rule 9.9A procedure we have just looked at. But will they or any of them succeed if the other party does not agree with them?

In a 1994 case called *Cornick v Cornick* there had been a dramatic upward hike in the husband's company shareholding after an order was made and the wife was seeking to have the order set aside. The judge (Mrs Justice Hale, as it happens, who went on to do greater things in the Supreme Court) ruled that a change to an asset's value within a relatively short period of time owing to the natural process of price fluctuation, was not sufficient to secure a setting aside. What could be sufficient, she held, was the happening of something unforeseen and unforeseeable which has altered the value of assets so dramatically as to cause a substantial change in the balance of the assets as brought about by the order. But she stated that the circumstances in which this could happen were very few and far between and that previously decided cases did not suggest that the natural value fluctuation, whether in houses, shares or any other property, and however dramatic, would fall within this principle. The wife's case effectively amounted to her saying it was all terribly unfair. This was not good enough.

And then came the financial crash case in 2010 of *Myerson v Myerson* where the Court of Appeal adopted the analysis of the law applied in the *Cornick* case. This time, the challenging husband who was a fund manager, had been ordered to pay his wife a lump sum of £9.5m. Because of the sinkage in the value of his company's shares, he was no longer left with the £14.5m of the joint assets which was intended by the original order but with no assets and, on the contrary, liabilities of £529,000. The husband's challenge went the same way as the wife's in the *Cornick* case and for the same reasons and with several more thrown in for good measure. They included that the husband, with all his knowledge and experience, had agreed the order (that was hard on him!) and he still had opportunities. "Unusual opportunities are created for the most astute in a bear market'" it was said. The judges indicated that the husband might pursue an application to just vary the outstanding £2.5m instalments of the lump sum. By the way, there is an advantage to a lump sum payer being ordered to pay the sum by instalments instead of in just one go as that gives the court the power to later vary which it lacks when there is no provision for instalments.

One coronavirus challenge has already met with defeat. In a case called *HW v WW* (to give the parties anonymity) and decided in March 2021 a circuit judge, "not without hesitation" threw out the husband's attempt at having an order set aside which, among other things, required him to pay the wife a series of lump sums totalling £1m. He was the managing director of a company carrying on the business of wholesale distribution of commercial photocopiers and printers and associated software. When he consented to the financial remedies order providing for the £1m (and the order expressly stated that the lump sums could not be varied which was on the basis that they were a series of sums amounting to £1m and not one sum divided into instalments!) he would have been expecting to raise the money within the company by using cash reserves or borrowing or both. However, because of the economic impact of the coronavirus on the company, he now had trouble stumping it up. The wife accepted he had this trouble. But was it foreseeable? The judge had to ask himself whether the husband could reasonably have foreseen that the coronavirus might have a significant impact on the company's trading position. If the answer was 'yes' then, even if its full extent and impact could not have been reasonably foreseen, the order would stand. The difficulty for the husband was that the order had been made with his consent on 12 March 2020 which was a mere 11 days before the UK entered its first lockdown. The intervening event of the virus was, as the judge put it, "continuing to develop before the ink was dry on the order". And in an expert's report on the value of the company compiled in July 2019, the author had drawn attention to the risks to the company of Brexit, loss of exclusive distribution and paperless offices. The husband had accepted those risks. He could not be put in a better position, ruled the judge, in respect of coronavirus than these other risks.

The outcome was that the order was not set aside but there is the prospect that obligations under the order other than for the payment of the lump sum will be mitigated. The wife, said the judge, was not immune from having to share in some of the pain.

But the judge did accept that, in principle though not in this case, the coronavirus could open the door to a successful set aside application. The decision on *Myerson* could be distinguished from the coronavirus situation, he thought.

Judges may be keen to avoid deciding a case in a way which will open the floodgates to similar cases coming before the courts. But it seems to me that, sooner or later, a set aside application involving catastrophic coronavirus consequences is going to succeed. Where there is a failure to secure a set aside, a reduction in lump sum instalments and/or maintenance obligations could well fare better. Alternative applications for a set aside or variation may well be the most prudent way ahead for economic victims of coronavirus.

Maintenance postscript

I cannot allow you to turn to the next page or chuck this book into the dustbin (whichever your preference) without touching on the court's current approach to applications for one party to pay maintenance to the other party for the benefit of the other party rather than for the benefit of any children. Whenever it makes a financial remedies order, the court must consider bringing to an end as soon as it is 'just and reasonable' the financial obligations of the parties towards one another. That involves considering whether there should be an immediate 'clean break' which would kill off the idea of either of them making a future maintenance application against the other. If the court won't go there and it decides that there should be ongoing maintenance, it will need to look at the period for which this should last – for life until the payee remarries or enters into a civil partnership or the payer expires, known as a 'joint lives' order, or, more commonly, for a shorter period which, in the jargon of the law, means a 'term order'. A frequent order is for maintenance for the wife who is the sole or main carer of the children (although it could be for the husband or civil partner) until they have attained 18 or finished secondary or tertiary education, if later. The approach is by no means uniform and will vary from judge to judge but the trend is increasingly towards getting the party after maintenance out to work and self-supporting sooner instead of later. In a 2014 case Mr Justice Mostyn, probably advocating the most extreme anti-maintenance approach, explained the relevant principles in play on a maintenance application. He said it was proper for there to be a maintenance order where choices made during the marriage had generated hard future needs on the part of the party wanting maintenance. Here the duration of the marriage and the presence of children were pivotal factors. Apart from the most exceptional cases, the order should only reflect what were the needs of the party wanting maintenance. In every case, the court had to consider a termination of maintenance with transition to independence as soon as it was just and reasonable. Limiting the duration of a maintenance order (for, example, to a specific number of years or to a specific event like the youngest child finishing tertiary education as against an order which ran so long as both parties were alive and the payee had not remarried) should be considered unless the party receiving maintenance would be unable to adjust to no maintenance without undue hardship. A degree of hardship in making the transition to independence was acceptable so long as it was not undue hardship.

In 2018 Mr Justice Mostyn was back with the same idea in another case. A term order, rather than a joint lives order, he said, should be imposed unless the court was satisfied that the party after maintenance would not be able to adjust to a cut-off without undue hardship. Normally, that decision would be easily reached because the payee would have a capital base to fall back on in later years.

And in February 2015 Lord Justice Pitchford in the Court of Appeal had refused to give the 51 year old wife permission to appeal against an order which was to scale down over six years the maintenance order originally made in her favour for £33,200 per year. At the time of the original order the judge had made it clear that they had expected the wife to begin working within the following two years but she had made no attempt to find work. The 59 year old husband had complained that he had planned to retire at 60 but as he had been unable to afford to make sufficient pension contributions, he had had to postpone retirement until 65. By virtue of the reduction in the maintenance, the husband will now be completely off the maintenance hook when he comes to retire.

One thing to watch. Maintenance orders are variable by the court and one of the variations available with a term order is for its duration to be extended beyond the date specified for it to end. Exception alert. When making a term order, the court can debar the payee from being able to seek an extension in the future. The payee may resist this happening in case her plans go awry: the payer will push for it so that they have certainty from what they will perceive as relief from penury. It will be a matter for negotiation but back to Mr Justice Mostyn in that 2018 case. Generally, where a term order is made, he said, it should not be extendable unless good reasons otherwise could be shown. Ultimately, the court's goal should be wherever possible, to achieve, if not immediately, then at a defined date in the future, a complete economic separation between the parties.

Whether maintenance is to be ordered for a fixed term or joint lives, it can be by way of the 'step down' variety. Such an order would provide in advance for the amount of maintenance to be reduced on the occurrence of a certain or certain events: say, from £500 per month to £100 per month (or, otherwise, to 5 pence per annum just to keep it going and capable of being increased on an application to the court) from a specified date by when the payee can be expected to be in employment, then down further when the younger of two children attains 18 and then down even further when the younger child hits 18. The payee may find such an order to be more palatable than a term order at a constant figure although it would still carry the risk for the payer of a variation application by the payee.

Kids

Children can cause a bit of a headache. Not in the sense of bad table manners or disobedience to your lawful commands but by sometimes making it difficult to reach a deal with your opponent under which you would agree not to pursue them for child maintenance. You might be more interested in a higher capital payment in return for no maintenance for yourself and the children. Dropping maintenance for yourself should not be a hindrance. Your opponent's concern over the children is that you may say you are dropping claims for them as well but then go running off to the Child Maintenance Service and secure a fat assessment from them. Do go to chapter 76 where you will find some ideas about how this headache might be fixed without the ingestion of a box of paracetamol.

Consent orders

As you will have gathered, a large number of financial remedies applications settle at some stage on the way towards a final hearing. If there is a settlement, no final hearing is needed but just an order of the court encompassing what has been agreed and that order can be obtained 'on paper': no hearing and so no court attendances or remote participation. "Why waste time with a ruddy court order? If it's agreed, it's agreed and the court can mind its own business." Steady on. It is perfectly true that if you are both happy with what has been agreed, there's nothing to stop you going on to implement it without involving the court further. That would be highly dangerous for a host of reasons: the chances are that the agreement reached does not cover everything that it would be advisable to cover and obvious lacunas would be picked up by a judge; one party may later decide that they had done a bad deal and want to come back to court and restart their application – and the court could decide they were not bound by the agreement; and, without an order, the agreement might be unenforceable if one party failed to keep to it. That will do.

If an agreement can be reached without a financial remedies application having been issued – and that happens all the time – an order encompassing the agreement can be sought in the course of the matrimonial or civil partnership proceedings between you and your opponent (see chapter 74). Those proceedings will almost certainly be needed to give the court the power to order what you would be asking of it. There is then an online system for obtaining a consent order in divorce cases only, although it is expected to be extended to nullity, separation and civil partnership cases in the future. It is used in around 75% of divorce cases. It is much faster than seeking the consent order through the post. Here's the catch. It is not available unless the party taking the lead in applying for the order is represented by a lawyer. If your opponent has a lawyer and you do not, let them be the applicant. The system cannot be used unless a decree nisi of divorce has already been pronounced (that will be known as a conditional divorce order when the new law is in – see chapter 74) and it is not available for applications for variation of a previous order or maintenance pending suit, which must be dealt with by post.

Whether the consent order is to be sought online, when that is possible, or through the post, the necessary documentation will have to include a statement setting out the finances of you both – it can be done in separate forms but judges prefer a consolidated form to which you both contribute – and a draft of the order. Yes, you heard me right. The responsibility for drafting the order is down to you and not the court. My strong advice is to get a lawyer to do the drafting. Sorry. To keep the expense down, one of you can go to the lawyer (you might share their bill) and the other of you go lawyerless but, ideally, you should each have independent legal advice. If you can find a solicitor who will act for and advise you both, I will eat the Lord Chief Justice's wig washed down with a pint of methylated spirits and lime. Their code of professional conduct permits them to act for clients jointly where those clients have a substantially common interest in the matter concerned or where the clients are competing for the same objective. Arguably, that could be the case with the drafting of a consent order if, for example, the financial affairs of husband and wife are modest and straightforward and the consent order is going to be simple but I fancy that, even then, no solicitor in their right mind is going to run the risk of taking on the couple together as joint clients.

You may have heard of various non-lawyer businesses which offer help to both parties in drafting a consent order and the documents to go with it. One business has been charging £300 to do this and the High Court has ruled that in doing what they did in the uncomplicated case involved, they had not broken the law which forbids a non-lawyer from charging for services which are the preserve of lawyers. Other similar businesses operate on a similar model. Where there is little or nothing to be shared out and each party has complete and utter trust in the other (why has the relationship broken down then???) and are fully aware of their legal rights and the implications of the order being drafted for them, perhaps these businesses have something to offer to parties who do not want to perform a DIY job.

"A DIY job did you say?" I sure did. There's nothing to stop you drawing up the paperwork to lead to a consent order yourselves and so avoid shelling out fees to a lawyer or a £300 a time type business. You can access template orders by going to judiciary.uk/publications/practice-guidance-standard-financial-and-enforcement-orders and clicking on the zip file link there. If you then take a butchers at template 2.1, you will find wording to cover about every conceivable topic that could arise on breakdown (though I'm not sure there's anything about pets, ownership of collections of the back editions of the *Radio Times* or reading the meters before banging the front door closed for good but never mind). You would even find it useful to take a butchers when negotiating with the opposition because I guarantee you will find stuff there you never imagined might arise and be relevant.

Just because the draft order is all agreed – that's why it's called a consent order – the judge who considers it is not bound to approve it. The job of the judge is to ensure that it clearly expresses what the parties intended, they understand what it means and it is fair to them both. If the judge is not satisfied on all these points, they will probably raise queries and suggest some drafting changes or, where troubled on fairness, indicate how the order could be made fair. Where still not convinced or as an alternative, they will set a directions hearing at which you will both need to participate and at which these points will be addressed further. It will not be an adequate answer to the judge's points to insist that the order is what has been agreed and so the judge will just have to lump it. The order will not be made and I have already dealt with the risks of implementing an agreement without an order.

More often than not, a draft DIY order will be chucked back by the judge at the first attempt at gaining approval to it. You can attempt to avoid a chuck back by addressing in the original draft order or the statement of financial information which would go with it (whichever is appropriate) these factors which would otherwise lead to tears: *where the paperwork is being submitted before the final divorce, nullity or civil partnership dissolution order, ensure that the order is expressed as being made subject to the final order (for example, with a divorce: IT IS ORDERED SUBJECT TO DECREE ABSOLUTE (or, under the new law, IT IS ORDERED SUBJECT TO FINAL DIVORCE ORDER); *whether you have both obtained independent legal advice and, if not, why not; *how the needs of any children of the family are to be met; *why the proposed division of assets is fair; *that the assets of each of you as shown are the current assets and, where the order is to change the asset position, what you will each end up with if and when the proposed order is implemented; *if there is provision for child maintenance which is for more than one child, how the total amount to be paid is to be apportioned between them (as otherwise what would be payable once one of the children had ceased to be dependent?): *where you show that you have no capital but are proposing to pay the other party a lump sum where that money is coming from; and *where the family home is being transferred, whether the mortgage lender has been notified and objected and whether the transferring party is to be released from the mortgage and, if so, when and, if not, why not.

Consent orders: nil loot passing

Here's an idea for which someone will want to have me locked up. Neither of you makes a claim against the other. No squabbling. You each go your own way. You each keep what you have got. Neither of you relies on the other for any form of financial support now or in the future. I'll give you a few spaces to get back up off the ground and recover. Okay?

A judge would refuse to make such an order unless it was fair to do so. If, for example, neither had any capital or next to nothing and similar pension scheme values and both had incomes which were not miles part, that would almost certainly be fair. Exception alert. It might be considered unfair if there was a dependent child: most judges would take some persuasion that it was fair for the parent with the entire or main care to abandon their own maintenance claims, lest they should become unemployed before dependence ceased.

Here's a template for a nil loot order in a divorce or nullity case.

IN THE FINANCIAL REMEDIES COURT   Case no: TT21D789

AT TOYTOWN

BETWEEN

CLIVE TROUBLESORE Applicant

- and -

MAVIS TROUBLESORE Respondent

UPON each of the parties having obtained independent legal advice

or

UPON each of the parties being aware of their right to obtain independent legal advice and being fully cognizant of the provisions of section 25 of the Matrimonial Causes Act 1973 in relation to financial remedies

AND UPON each of the parties being satisfied that the other has made to them a full, accurate and truthful disclosure of their financial circumstances

AND UPON each of the parties being satisfied that it is fair and in accordance with their deeply held wishes that no financial provision should be made for them by the other now or in the future and that they should be financially and permanently independent of the other

IT IS ORDERED BY CONSENT AND SUBJECT TO DECREE ABSO-

LUTE (or FINAL DIVORCE ORDER) that-

1. The applicant's claims for periodical payments orders, lump sum orders, property adjustment orders, pension sharing orders and pension attachment orders shall be dismissed and they shall not be entitled to make any further application in relation to the marriage for an order under the Matrimonial Causes Act 1973 section 23(1)(a) or (b) and they shall not be entitled on the respondent's death to apply for an order under the Inheritance (Provision for Family and Dependants) Act 1975, section 2].

2. The respondent's claims for periodical payments orders, lump sum orders, property adjustment orders, pension sharing orders and pension attachment orders shall be dismissed and they shall not be entitled to make any further application in relation to the marriage for an order under the Matrimonial Causes Act 1973 section 23(1)(a) or (b) and they shall not be entitled on the applicant's death to apply for an order under the Inheritance (Provision for Family and Dependants) Act 1975, section 2].

We hereby consent to an order in the above terms

(signed) C Troublesore

Applicant

(signed) M Troublesore

Respondent

Dated 14 July 2021

Chapter 76

Money For The Kids

Paying for the smart phone

Your relationship has broken down and you have the entire or some care of the child. You will be keen on the other parent paying towards the child's maintenance unless you are daft, very rich or care is fairly evenly shared and your financial circumstances are about equal. Assuming that child maintenance does not flow freely from the other parent's pocket into your purse or won't continue to do so, there are three ways you can go after securing it – from the court, from the Child Maintenance Service (CMS) which now deals with all new maintenance cases in place of the Child Support Agency or, with a bit of nudging, threatening or wrestling, from a formal agreement with the other parent.

Maintenance from the court

Generally, disputes about child maintenance have to be dealt with through the CMS. There are some exceptions which we will look at later where the CMS has to keep out and the court gets a look in. And whether or not the CMS can touch, the court does have jurisdiction to make a child maintenance order if there is an agreement between the parties. Almost always, that agreement and order will specify that maintenance will be paid, how much, on which dates and for how long. This is how a typical order will read:

> B shall make periodical payments to A during their joint lives for the benefit of C born on 14 July 2014 ("the child") at the rate of £1,000 per calendar month payable calendar monthly as from and including 14 July 2016 until the child attains the age of 17 years or ceases full-time tertiary education to first degree level (whichever is the later) or further order.

In practice, 18 years is often substituted for 17. The life of such an order can be extended if when it is due to end the child will be continuing in education or training for their career or special circumstances exist, such as the child's disability, which would justify an extension of its duration. So far as an extension for more brain feeding is concerned, it is common for maintenance to be ordered to continue for secondary and tertiary education but rarely, if ever, will it go on beyond first degree. It is doubtful that any court has ever ordered an extension to cover a post-graduate professional qualification such as a lawyer or doctor but never say never. In a 2020 High Court case, the issue was whether the married and living together parents of a vulnerable 41 year old solicitor who had depended on his wealthy parents to financially support him for years, could be ordered to pay him maintenance in the future. The relationship between the man and his parents had deteriorated of late. The High Court ruled that it had no jurisdiction to order such maintenance.

If the parties have been married or in a civil partnership then the court has the power in matrimonial proceedings such as divorce or partnership dissolution proceedings to make an agreed order for the maintenance of a child against a party to the proceedings who is a non-parent but has treated the child as their own. In proceedings in the High Court but usually the family court under schedule 1 to the Children Act 1989 the court can only make a maintenance order against a parent of a child, whether or not the parents have been married or in a civil partnership, if it is not a case which has to be dealt with by the CMS. But even where the CMS has to be involved, the court can order a lump sum payment for a child's benefit though this would usually only occur in a 'big money' case. In the same situation, the court can also order the parent to provide accommodation for the child by, say, buying a property for the child to live in with the other parent, usually up to their 18th birthday, or make available a property they already own to be occupied in this way. In a February 2021 case called *CA v DR*, a High Court judge emphasised that there was no power on a schedule 1 application to make financial provision for the child's carer beyond that element attributable to the child's actual care. In that case, the court refused the mother carer's attempt at obtaining £40,000 a year to put into a pension on the ground that by concentrating on the child's care, she would be unable to build up a pension pot of her own. The child's father was worth £190m with a gross annual income of £3.8m and had confirmed that he could meet any order the court might make although he resisted the pension attempt.

The court cannot make a schedule 1 order after the child has reached 18 but a child who is continuing education or training may be able to make their own application after 18.

How much to go for under court order

There is no set figure. However, maintenance is usually agreed at or around what would be payable under the CMS regime for the obvious reason that in the absence of agreement that is all you could achieve. But in those cases where the court has the power to decide, it will use its discretion on the amount to be paid with the CMS figure probably being the starting point. The court will particularly take into account the child's financial needs; any income or earning capacity of the child and their other financial circumstances; any physical or mental disability of the child; the manner in which the child was being educated or trained and what the parents were expecting about that; and the other considerations which apply where you are applying for maintenance for yourself (see chapter 74). If you are after child maintenance against a spouse or former spouse and it is not their biological child, the court will additionally look at the extent to which and basis upon which they had assumed responsibility for the child and whether they knew the child was not theirs when they did so. The liability of any other person such as the child's natural father to maintain them will come into the reckoning. The court should be asked to reflect the fact that maintenance has to cover not only the food that goes into the child's mouth and the clothes that go onto the child's back but the outgoings on the child's home which will be greater because of the child's presence there. For example, if in order to accommodate your child you have a two-bedroomed flat instead of a one-bedroomed flat, your mortgage instalments, for a start, are going to be higher.

A multi-millionaire has moved into your place and you hope the two of you will live together happily hereafter? The multi-millionaire is not legally responsible for maintaining your child and your relationship does not of itself relieve the other parent of their financial responsibility in relation to the child's maintenance or reduce what they would otherwise have to pay. But if your new partner is ploughing money into your household with the result that you are released from other financial burdens you would have to discharge then the court can reflect that fact in its award.

Keeping out the CMS

Where a court order for child maintenance was made before 3 March 2003 neither parent can go to the CMS. It won't touch. The parent after an increase or decrease in maintenance may go back to court for the order to be varied. But where the court order was made on or after 3 March 2003 the CMS can only be kept out for 12 months: after that either party can go to the CMS. This state of affairs carries its risks for the paying parent who may wish to enter into an arrangement with you which is generous in capital provision but in return for reduced child maintenance or perhaps even no child maintenance at all. Risky as you might make your way to the CMS once the 12 months are up and seek a juicy maintenance assessment from them as any agreement by you which purports to restrict your right to apply to the CMS is legally void!

There are ways around this but they are very tricky for the other parent, yet they are occasionally used though, so far, have not been the subject of an authoritative court decision as to their effectiveness. You can agree and undertake to the court that you will not go to the CMS and the other parent can pray that you will keep to your word and the court will restrain you from breaking it if you attempt or threaten to do so. You can also agree and undertake to repay to the other parent any maintenance they are compelled to pay over as a result of you getting the CMS involved – and you can back that up with a charge on your property (provided you own it or are going to do so) for a sum equivalent to any CMS maintenance the other parent ends up paying out which they had not expected to pay. This would put the other parent in the position of a mortgage lender from whom you had borrowed that amount of money. Lawyers call it a 'chargeback'. Or the other party can seek the adjournment of certain financial relief capital claims, such as for a lump sum, until a while after the youngest child can no longer figure in a CMS assessment and with a view to restoring those claims if you break your word. However, where there is still a spousal maintenance order in force for you, the other parent might well apply to the court for that maintenance order to be reduced to reflect their liability under the CMS assessment – and succeed! – in a word break situation.

Here are two templates for wording to go in to either a chargeback which has been agreed as part of a financial remedies order or an order for adjournment of claims in the course of a financial remedies application. They are based on wording that has been approved by some judges although, as indicated, untested by a binding court decision.

Chargeback

The property known as [name of property] shall be charged with payment to the respondent of an amount equal to the total of the following sums paid by the respondent:

a.   any sums paid under any CMS calculation to the applicant in respect of the children of the family inasmuch as such sums exceed the monthly equivalent of £[amount] for each child

b.   any sums paid under sections 106 and 108 of the Social Security Administration Act 1992.*

together with simple interest on these sums at the rate applicable for the time being to a High Court judgment debt from [date], [the payment to be due and the charge to be enforceable] on the first to occur of:

i.   the death of the applicant;

ii.   the applicant's remarriage;

iii.   all the surviving children of the family attaining the age of 18 years or ceasing their full-time tertiary] education to first degree level, whichever is the later, save and except that if prior to this all the surviving children of the family have ceased to live permanently with the applicant respondent, the determining event shall arise upon such cessation;

iv.   the sale of the property hereby charged; or

v.   a further order of the court, for which both parties shall be at liberty to apply to the court

provided that the amount as to which the property shall be charged shall not exceed one half of the gross proceeds of sale of the property, or if it shall not have been sold, one half of the gross value, any dispute as to such value to be settled by a surveyor agreed between the parties or in default of agreement appointed by the President for the time being of the Royal Institution of Chartered Surveyors.

*These sections of the 1992 Act deal with benefits having been paid to the parent with care (the applicant here) and some of that money being recouped from the other party (the respondent here).

Order for adjournment of claims

A In circumstances where the parties have agreed that (i) the provision made by this order fulfils the respondent's responsibilities to the children of the family; (ii) the applicant does not intend to seek any

> [further] financial provision for the maintenance of the children of the family [including school fees and/or any other extras for the children] whether through the court, the CMS or otherwise; and (iii) in the event that the respondent becomes liable to make any [further] financial provision for the children of the family, the applicant will indemnify the respondent against any liability, and in default of the applicant performing their agreement to indemnify the respondent, the respondent shall be entitled to make claims for a lump sum order and/or property adjustment order for the purpose of recompensing the respondent, the respondent's claims for a lump sum order and/or property adjustment order in respect of [name property] shall be adjourned generally with liberty to the respondent to restore
>
> B In the event of the respondent not having restored their claims by [date] then such claims shall stand automatically dismissed without further order of the court.
>
> C The applicant shall indemnify the respondent against the liability of the respondent to make any [further] financial provision for the children of the family.

When can't the CMS poke its nose in?

The CMS has no jurisdiction when:

- the court made an order for child maintenance before 3 March 2003 in which event either of you would have to go back to the court for any sort of variation;
- the court made an order for child maintenance on or after 3 March 2003 and it has not yet been in force for 12 months;
- the child is a step-child of the other parent (but it does have jurisdiction in respect of an adopted child);
- the child is resident abroad; or
- the other parent is resident abroad unless abroad because they are serving in the civil service, the armed services, certain local authorities or with a United Kingdom based company paying wages in the United Kingdom.

In these situations, the court will be able to decide maintenance except where a step-child is involved unless the step-child is a child of the family where you and the other party have been married or in a civil partnership.

"My Jimmy is 32 but prefers not to work as this would clash with Judge Rinder"

The CMS can only deal with maintenance for a child who is:

- under 16; or
- under 20 where child benefit would be payable (even if it is not

claimed for, say, tax reasons) and they are receiving full-time education up to A level – provided they weren't fast workers and have been married or in a civil partnership.

How much under the CMS regime?

The present regime has been preceded by two previous schemes with different rules. Cases under the old schemes are being progressively closed down and the parent entitled to maintenance (where the money due from the other parent is not being taken out of their bank or building society account following default) will be required to make their own arrangements or apply under the new regime. Nearly 92% of applications are against men. Let's have a look at how the maintenance will be calculated.

There are nil, flat and reduced rates which will not generate anything or only sufficient for a haircut and a bag of chips. The nil rate is scored by, among others, someone with an income of less than £7 per week and prisoners. Full time students no longer automatically qualify for the nil rate. The flat rate is for those out of the range of the nil rate but with a gross weekly income of £100 or less or on certain benefits. It's £7 per week. The reduced rate applies where the weekly gross income is more than £100 and less than £200 generating, for example, a liability of 17% of that income for one child. Where the CMS cannot find out the amount of the other parent's income, it may apply a default weekly liability of £38 for one child, £51 for two children or £61 for three or more children.

With a bit of luck, the basic and basic plus rates will be effective in most cases. Assuming the other parent is not responsible for other children by another relationship who come into the reckoning, the basic rate maintenance for gross weekly income between £200 and £800 is:

- 12% for one child;
- 16% for two children; and
- 19% for three or more children.

Where the gross weekly income is over £800 – this is the *plus* bit of basic plus – then add on a percentage of the income in excess of £800 BUT UP TO A MAXIMUM OF £3,000 depending on the number of children like this:

- 9% for one child;
- 12% for two children; and
- 15% for three or more children.

Should the other party be caring for other children in a new family their gross weekly income for the purposes of calculating child maintenance to go to you will be reduced by 11% for one child in the new family, 14% for two and 16% for three or more. Your own income will not be taken into account.

Gross income for child support purposes means the income of the payer which is charged to tax. As a result of legislation which came into force in July 2019, expenses incurred by the payer which are allowed by HMRC are discounted from the gross figure.

A notional income is attributed to the paying parent in respect of certain assets held by them. Assets worth no more than £31,250 will be disregarded but where they exceed this figure the entire value of them will generally be treated as earning the parent an income of 8% of its value. Assets subject to a trust of which the parent is a beneficiary will be taken into account to the extent of the parent's interest. But among the disregards are assets used in the course of the parent's business, the main residence of the parent of the child and assets which would need to be sold to meet the maintenance payments where a sale would cause hardship to a child of the parent or would be unreasonable in the circumstances.

And maybe a bit more

Provided you have applied to the CMS and it has calculated what the other parent is to pay and their gross income is more than £3,000 a week, you could apply to the court for a *top up* as you hop, skip and jump down the road. You would have to show this was "appropriate". You can also go to the court whether or not the CMS has been involved, for an order for the other parent to pay or contribute towards school fees (including extras and uniform), training for a career or for expenses attributable to your blind or disabled child's condition.

Ignoring the chips

Gambling winnings are not generally reckonable for child support calculation purposes and the position is the same when it comes to assessing the gambler's liability for income tax or entitlement to welfare benefits. If the winnings were taxable as self-employed earnings then gambling losses could be set off against other profits or gains, possibly to the point at which the gambler might be entitled to claim benefits. Should the winnings be an adjunct to a trade or profession – say someone making their winnings as a dealer at a gambling club they own – the position would be different.

Shared care

The maintenance payable will be reduced if the other parent has one or more of the children stay overnight with them for at least 52 nights a year although even then the maintenance payable can never fall below £7 per week. The maintenance bill goes down by one-seventh for 52 to 103 nights, two-sevenths for 104 to 155 nights, three-sevenths for 156 to 174 nights and one-half plus £7 per child for 175 or more nights. The stay over must be with the other parent and not say with grandparents while the other parent is elsewhere.

There may be a dispute between parents about how time is actually split. What is relevant is the number of nights the paying parent is expected to have overnight stays during the 12 month period ahead of when maintenance is being calculated. Consideration should be given to the terms of any contact agreement or court order or, if there is neither, whether a pattern of shared care has already been established over the previous 12 months.

There has to be a good reason for any conclusion that an arrangement between parents that has been up and running is not going to reoccur in the future 12 months.

It would be cynical for me to say that a parent who is well-informed will sometimes factor these reductions into the proposals for child contact which they formulate, especially when an extra one or couple of nights would raise them into a higher reduction band. But I will be cynical. 51 nights a year won't earn them a reduction of one new pence: one more night and their liability is cut by one-seventh. Court contact orders sometimes provide for such reasonable contact as the parents shall agree. This does of course have the merit of encouraging a harmonious relationship between the parties and maximum flexibility but if any argument over child maintenance shared care reduction is anticipated, it might be better to have a more specific order.

> A shall make C available for contact with B and do all things reasonably necessary to facilitate such contact taking place as from the date of this order on alternate weekends from 4pm on Friday until school on Monday commencing on 9 July 2021 with B being present with C overnight and for one-half of school holidays (including half-terms) and such other reasonable contact as the parties shall from time to time agree.

Going to the CMS

Before you can apply to the CMS you have to make contact with Child Maintenance Options (0800 988 0988 childmaintenanceservice.direct.gov.uk) which runs a live chat service. You will be encouraged to reach a family-based arrangement which is a romantic invention involving parents actually agreeing on a figure and payments being made. If no arrangement is made or if it is made but not adhered to, then you can get on with the application. There is a £20 fee unless you are under 18 or in the eyes of the CMS a victim of domestic violence or abuse.

> Week 1: "I don't think I can do better than £20 a week but let me have a look at my bank statements and I'll check how much longer I have to run on the plasma credit agreement."
>
> Week 2: "Daddy is not available to answer your call. Please leave a message."
>
> Week 3: "So sorry I didn't get back to you. I can't find my bank statements anywhere. I'll get a print out this afternoon."
>
> Week 4: "Daddy is at present away on a short break to the USA and offline. He will reply to your email as soon as he returns. Best wishes."

You don't want to hang about for too long in trying to get an agreement because the liability to pay maintenance once the CMS gets to work will not arise until two days after the other parent has been sent notification of the application and they clearly cannot be notified until you have made it! The CMS will calculate the amount of maintenance to be paid and then there's an option – Direct Pay or Collect and Pay. With Direct Pay, payments are made – direct to you! With Collect and Pay (where the other party consents or the CMS reckons they won't otherwise pay), the CMS collects, stings and takes immediate enforcement action where necessary. Stings? Yes. You pay 4% of the maintenance which is deducted from what you receive and the other parent pays 20% which is added to what they have to shell out. If that doesn't make the collections service pretty unattractive, what does?!

> "Dear Father
>
> *I may have said a lot of uncomplimentary things about you but never that you lacked intelligence. That is why I cannot understand the reason for you not agreeing to put a standing order in force immediately to pay the maintenance which the Child Maintenance Service has calculated you must pay for Jimmy. Do you realise that if you won't change your mind about this my only option is to use the Collect and Pay system which between us will cost 24% of the maintenance, 20% of it coming from you on top of the maintenance. That's not in your interest. It's not in my interest. It's certainly not in Jimmy's interest. Please confirm now that you will do as reasonably asked.*
>
> Best
>
> Mother"

Varying an assessment

An application can be made to vary a CMS assessment on the ground that some specified factor will not have been taken into account in the assessment calculations. One of the factors is that the payer has assets worth more than £31,250 (see above). Also that the payer has certain unearned income (not reckoned in the gross income used to calculate the assessment), such as building society interest and rental for letting a property, amounting to £2,500 a year or more or has played the 'diverted income trick' by directing it to someone else. And certain special expenses being met by the payer may be treated as a good reason for reducing the assessment. Included are the cost of exercising contact with any child to whom the assessment relates, necessary expenses for the long-term illness or disability of such a child, prior debts incurred before the parents separated, boarding school fees for a child to whom the assessment relates and mortgage payment on a property occupied by such a child and the other parent.

An application for variation will be considered by the CMS who may chuck it out or allow it. If either parent is dissatisfied with the way it is dealt with, they can appeal to the first-tier tribunal (social entitlement chamber). The tribunal has variation applications coming out if its ears and is never taken by surprise to find that the CMS has cocked up. I wouldn't say that the CMS is short of calculators: just that I wouldn't leave it to them to add up my

Ocado order.

Reaching an agreement

Your contact with Child Maintenance Options could lead to an agreement over maintenance and you and the other parent signing a form (cmoptions.org/en/pdfs/Private%20Form.pdf). It contains the parents' promise "to keep to the arrangements, for the sake of the children" and warns that the document is not legal though it is a clear statement of their commitment to the children. Some lawyers suggest that this wording is inaccurate and misleading as the agreement would entitle the court to make an order for maintenance in its terms which in turn would have the effect of keeping out the CMS for 12 months. I am not so sure. It could be strongly argued that the agreement is not binding as the wording shows that the parents did not intend it to be so.

So what do you do if there is arrangement but you want the comfort of being sure you can enforce it should the other party default? It may be safer to steer away from the Child Maintenance Options form and use another agreement form which can be enforced in the same way as any contract. If payments were not made you could sue in the county court for what you were owed under the agreement as a straightforward debt and the usual means of enforcing a civil judgment would be available to you (see chapter 29). True that these means would not be as extensive and robust as available to the CMS when it is collecting and there is default (for example, disqualification from driving, imprisonment and, since December 2018, disqualification from holding a UK passport). But against this, an agreement does give you the opportunity to obtain an amount of maintenance which is over and above the amount which would have been required under a CMS calculation (though the other parent could at some stage apply to the court to alter the agreement by reducing the amount or go to the CMS themselves). And you could even seek an agreement against a former partner who is not the parent of the child but treated the child as their own to maintain them in the future and, provided by deed, the agreement would be legally enforceable. It may be that the very safest course if the CSA calculation is to be used and the other party is a parent, is to apply to the CMS and, if appropriate, opt for the direct payment scheme without collection charges. Should the CMS not have jurisdiction (for example, because the other parent is living abroad) then an agreement is a useful alternative to a court order.

That agreement of your own

The agreement – call it a deed, please – may go something like this.

> THIS DEED is made on 14 July 2021 BETWEEN MAVIS BULWARK of 149 Magnolia Crescent Twickenham Middlesex KT89 4XZ ("Ms Bulwark") and CLIVE TROUBLESORE of 2b Magnolia Crescent Twickenham Middlesex KT89 4XN ("Mr Troublesore")
>
> BACKGROUND
>
> 1. Ms Bulwark and Mr Troublesore formerly cohabited together.

2. Jimmy Troublesore-Bulwark ("the child") was born to Ms Bulwark on 14 July 2015.

3. Mr Troublesore is the biological father of the child.

4. Ms Bulwark and Mr Troublesore ceased cohabiting together on 1 March 2020.

5. Mr Troublesore acknowledges his legal and moral commitment to contribute towards the maintenance of the child and to play a full part in the child's life.

6. Ms Bulwark and Mr Troublesore agree that the child should live with Ms Bulwark and that it is in his best interests to do so.

7. Ms Bulwark acknowledges that it is in the best interests of the child that the child should have extensive contact with Mr Troublesore.

NOW THIS DEED WITNESSES as follows:

1. Mr Troublesore covenants to pay or cause to be paid to Ms Bulwark maintenance for the benefit of the child at the rate of £1,500.00 per month payable calendar monthly by way of standing order to the credit of the current account of Ms Bulwark with Dodgy Bank plc numbered 45799003 at its Twickenham branch sort code 32-19-01 or to the credit of such other account as Ms Bulwark may from time to time direct. The first payment shall be made on 7 August 2021 and subsequent payments on the 7th day of each successive month.

2. Subject to sub-paragraphs 3 and 4 below, the payments shall be made until the child attains the age of 18 years or if later until he ceases full-time tertiary education up to first degree level.

3. The payments shall cease upon a maintenance calculation being made by the Child Maintenance Service or such other statutory authority as may perform its or similar functions.

4. The payments shall cease upon the death of Ms Bulwark.

5. The payments shall not cease by virtue of the death of Mr Troublesore and in the event of his death whilst payments continue to be due they shall be made by the personal representatives of his estate.

6. Ms Bulwark shall apply the maintenance hereby covenanted to be paid for the benefit of the child and for no other purpose.

7. Ms Bulwark shall make the child available for contact with Mr Troublesore and take all reasonable steps necessary to facilitate such contact each Tuesday and Thursday for two hours at times to be agreed between them commencing on 3 August 2021 and as from 13 August 2021 for one weekend each fortnight from 2pm on Friday until 2pm on Sunday and for such other reasonable contact as Ms Bulwark and Mr Troublesore shall from time to time agree.

IN WITNESS whereof the parties have executed this instrument as a deed on the day and year first before written

SIGNED AS A DEED BY)
CLIVE TROUBLESORE in)
the presence of:-)

SIGNED AS A DEED BY)
MAVIS BULWARK in)
the presence of:-)

Chapter 77

Missing Persons

Gone fishing?

If your marriage, civil partnership or other relationship is a bit rocky, beware of being talked into taking an extended holiday abroad. The Guardianship (Missing Persons) Act 2017 fills a legal hole. It allows for the appointment of a guardian (who may not turn out to be an angel) to administer the property and financial affairs (or some of them) of a missing person. That person must have been domiciled in England and Wales or habitually resident here for at least one year before performing a disappearing act. Administering financial affairs could be as straightforward as making monthly mortgage instalments or renewing the subscription to *Private Eye*. With the court's permission, a relative other than a spouse or partner, or even a friend, can apply for the appointment. The procedure covers the situation where it is not possible to presume that the missing person is dead under the Presumption of Death Act 2013, because they are not thought to have died or have not been heard of for at least seven years.

Missing? They must have been absent from their usual residence and day-to-day activities with their whereabouts unknown or not known with sufficient precision to enable them to be contacted to make the decisions they should be making. For how long? At least 90 days although a shorter period might be sufficient in an emergency. Absence in prison could be enough so that could be of use if your spouse is locked up abroad for urinating in a public place and they are not able to communicate relevant decisions about their affairs.

The government has published a code of practice with guidance which will be taken into account by the court. It states that in most cases it will be helpful if a police report on the disappearance can be provided to the court and that is certainly what the court will be looking for in most cases to ensure that whoever is applying for the appointment of a guardian is not on a fraudulent mission. The Public Guardian will supervise an appointed guardian for which they will charge a setup fee of £200 and an annual supervision fee of £320.

The application for an appointment is to be made to the High Court only, through its family or chancery divisions. The procedure is laid down in part 57 and practice direction 57C of the Civil Procedure Rules 1998. Part 8 of the 1998 Rules is to be used.

Remember to serve documents on the missing person. April Fool. Only joking.

Index

A

Accelerated possession 625
Acknowledgment of service 155, 676
Addressing the judge 205
Administration of Justice Act 1970 327
Administration of Justice Act 1995 361
Administration order 398
Adultery 674, 675, 680, 684
Adverse possession 375
Advice now 100
Advocate 95, 96
Affiniti Finance 85
After-the-event policy 82
Age Co 99
Age UK 99
Anti-Social Behaviour, Crime and Policing Act 2014 455
Anton Piller order 709
Appeals 249
    fees 254
    grounds 250, 254
    judge's note 253
    notice of 252
    permission 251
    route 249
    transcript of judgment 252
Arbitration 116, 704
    charging rates 704
    consumer arbitration schemes 116
    ombudsman schemes 116
Arrears notice 592
Article 8 ECHR 621
Assets on bankruptcy 391
Assigning rights 531
Assignment of debt 131
Assured shorthold tenancies 542, 599, 607, 617, 621, 623, 624
Attachment of earnings 261
    application 261
Augusta Ventures 86

B

BAILII 215
Bankruptcy 271, 389
    administration order alternative 398
    appealing against bankruptcy order 394
    bankruptcy restrictions undertaking 392
    charging order 264
    conduct of bankrupt 392
    contribution towards debts 393
    costs 272
    creditor's petition 394
    credit rating 393
    debt management plan alternative 395
    debtor's notice of opposition 399
    debtor's petition 393
    debt relief order alternative 397
    defences to 395
    discharge of 389
    disposition of assets 391
    employment prospects 392
    exoneration 390
    favouring creditors over others 393
    immigration status 392
    individual voluntary arrangement alternative 397
    jointly owned home 390
    jurisdiction to hear an opposed petition 398
    null and void order 399
    limitations on undischarged bankrupt 392
    loss of assets 391
    matrimonial/civil partnership order before bankruptcy 398, 399
    notifying bank/building society 394
    Payplan 396
    pension 391
    process 393
    refusal of 393
    remaining liabilities 389
    short hearings 212
    statutory demand 271
    transfer of case to different court 399
    trustee in bankruptcy 223, 391, 393
Barristers 88
    advertisements 91
    direct access 90
    fixed fee arrangement 91
    instructing without a solicitor 90
    instruction of 89
    selection of 87
    treatment of litigants in person 127
Behaviour in court 211
Best before dates 562
Bias 209
Breach of confidence 709
Breach of contract 153, 222, 247, 343, 467, 542
    interest on award for 297
    legal aid 79
    right to bring a claim 148
    time limits 130, 147, 153
Break clause 607
Breathing Space Moratorium 139

Brexit   121, 234, 289, 301, 306, 481, 534, 696, 697, 728
Bundles
   See Court bundles
Business and Property Courts   186
   Practice Direction 57AC   186
Business/share valuation   725

C

Case management conference   212
Certificate of judgment   627
Certificate of satisfaction   245
Challenging judge's decision
   See Appeals
Change of name   423
   children   423
     consent   423
     dispute   424
   deed poll template   423
     adults   424
     child   425
   enrolment   423
   for a fraudulent purpose   423
Change of position, defence of   318
Chargeback scheme   346
   exceptions   344
   payment by credit card   343
   payment by debit card   346
Charging order   264
Chartered legal executives   93
Child maintenance   735, 740
   Child Maintenance Service   735
     application   742
     assessment amount   740
   Children Act 1989 Sch 1 application   736
     agreement template   737
     gambling winnings   741
     jurisdiction   739
     keeping out   737
     adjournment of claims   738
     chargeback   737
     payment options   743
     regime   740
     shared care   741
     top up   741
     varying an assessment   743
   court order   735
     amount   736
Child Maintenance Options   744
Children Act 1989   424
Children Act 1989, Schedule 1   656, 736
Choice of lawyer   88
Chronology   181
Citizens Advice   94
Civil claims online   144
Civil hearing centres   143
Civil legal advice   96
Civil Mediation Council   120
Civil Partnership Act 2004   696, 708
Civil partnership dissolution
   See Divorce
Civil Procedure Rules 1998   105, 120, 134, 148, 617, 632
   See also Part 36 offer
   part 7   645
   part 8   361, 643, 747
   part 23   146
   part 31   159
   part 36   133
   part 57   747
   part 69   268
   part 81   270
   practice direction 7B   340
   practice direction 22   184
   practice direction 32   183, 184
   practice direction 56   617
   practice direction 57AC   186
   practice direction 57C   747
   practice direction 70B   139
   rule 3.3   105, 176
   rule 12.3   156
   rule 23.9   105
   rule 27.9   229
   rule 31.16   160
   rule 31.17   162
   rule 32.9   180
   rule 32.14   180
   rule 39.9   253
   rule 40.9A   258
   rule 40.11   258
   rule 45.39(5)   310
   rule 52.14   252
   rule 56.1(1)   617
   rule 65.28   329
Civil restraint order   193, 197
   extended   197
   family cases   198
   general   198
   limited   197
Clean break   700
Clerksroom   90
Codicils   358
   See also Wills
Cohabitation
   constructive trust   650
   equitable accounting   652
   joint ownership of property   649
   living together agreement   658
   maintenance of   649
   proprietary estoppel   651
   rights of   649
   title deeds   649
Collaborative law   707

Index

Commercial rent arrears recovery scheme 635
Commonhold and Leasehold Reform Act 2002 412
Communication and Internet Services Adjudication Scheme 122
Company directors 321
   disqualification of 324
      Conduct Assessment Service 324
      length of 324
   fraudulent and wrongful trading 323
   misconduct 321
      coronavirus suspension 323
      director's disqualification/under-taking 321
      phoenix company 321
Company Directors Disqualification Act 1986 324
Compensation 299
   due to court error 313
   interest on late receipt of money 314
   referral to the Parliamentary and Health Service Ombudsman 314
   due to director misconduct 324
   for assault 641
   for hassle and mental distress 300
   for inconvenience 299
   for injury to feelings 329
   for libel or slander 381
   for loss of time of witness 180
   for out of pocket expenses 299
   for personal injury 147, 150
   funder's cut 82, 85, 87
   interest on 293, 297
   reduction of 134
   under Consumer Protection Act 1987 149
   under Housing Act 1988 for unlawful eviction 628
Competition and Markets Authority 287, 577
Conditional divorce order 731
   See also Divorce
Conditional fee agreements
   See No win, no fee agreements
Conduct
   during proceedings 127
   in matrimonial proceedings 642
Conduct Assessment Service 324
Conference 88
Confidentiality 711
Consent orders 725, 730
Consequential loss 343
Constructive trust 650

Consumer Contracts (Information, Cancellation and Additional Charges) Regulations 2013 514, 532
Consumer Credit Act 1974 138, 149, 337, 343, 345, 591, 594
Consumer Protection Act 1987 149
Consumer Protection from Unfair Trading Regulations 2008 300, 542
Consumer rights 513–579
   cancellation 532
   delivery delay 525
   exclusion clauses 526
   final rejection 522
   matching description 514
   matching sample 515
   reasonably fit for purpose 514
   satisfactory quality 513
   services 527
   short-term rejection 516
   small print 526
Consumer Rights Act 2015 287, 513, 527, 545
Consumers' Association 577
Contracts (Rights of Third Parties) Act 1999 223, 531
Controlled goods agreement 279
Copyright claims 232
Costs 79, 82, 87, 92, 120, 127, 130, 134, 135, 156, 161, 195, 219, 221, 259, 272, 296, 309, 409, 465, 593, 621, 628, 675, 676, 685, 695, 703
   financial dispute resolution appointment 719
   first appointment 717
   'fixed recoverable costs' regime 312
   insurance policy 84
   litigant in person 309
   management order 311
   of landlord 411
   statement of 310
   third party litigation funders 84
Counterclaim 194
County court bailiffs 275
County Court Money Claims Centre 146
County Courts (Interest on Judgment Debts) Order 1991 259
Court bundles 189
   electronic 191
   in family cases 191
   in non-small claim cases 190
   Integrated Dispute Resolution 191
   procedure 189
   who prepares 190

751

Court fees	167, 170
bands of	170
claiming from loser	309
defended civil cases	169, 170
failure to pay	171
fee saving tips	167
financial test for fee remission	167
help with	167
matrimonial cases	684
payment deadline	170
remission	167
retrospective application	168
remission in exceptional circumstances	168
with or without a hearing	170
Court hearings	212
addressing the judge	205
adjournment	210
behaviour	211
cross-examination	214, 215
crying	218
doing a runner	200
dress code	201
evidence	213, 216
evidence in chief	213
judgment	219
jury	205
nature of	212
preparation	231
public or private	204
remote	205
ushers	201
witness familiarisation	217
Court location	143
Covid-19	75, 287
cancellations and refunds under consumer contracts	287
claims against NHS	468
force majeure	287
frustration of contract	288, 289
issue of foreseeability	288
obtaining redress	290
variation clause	288
Credit cards - equal responsibility	343
See also Consumer Credit Act 1974	
Credit/debit card scheme	343
chargeback	346
exceptions	344
Creditors	
debt collectors	333
demanding payment of the debt	327
duty of care	333
harassment by	327
protection from	327
Credit reference agencies	243
Credit reference agency file	393
Credit repair services	245

Criminal Injuries Compensation Scheme	641
Cross-examination	181, 214, 215
Cyclists	437
duty to take reasonable care	437

D

Damages	
special damages	
See also Compensation	
Damages based agreements	84
Death bed gifts	367
Debt	
advice and assistance	131, 139
assignment of debt	131
debt counsellor	141
defence against claim	132
execution	275
goods exempt from seizure	275
moratorium (debt relief)	139
permission to take enforcement action	141
qualifying debts	139, 140
register of	140
appeal against refusal to withhold address from	141
request for address to be withheld	141
review of	141
rules	139, 140
notice required from enforcement agent	277, 278
pre-action protocol for claims	132
Debt collectors	333
Debt management plan	395
Debt protocol	131
obligations on the debtor	132
Debt relief order	397
Debt Respite Scheme	139
Decree absolute	678
Defamation	
See Libel, slander and malicious falsehood	
Defamation (Operators of Websites) Regulations 2013	383
Default notices	138, 592
new form	138
Defended cases	193, 683
Delivery of goods	524
Departure from equality	701
Deposit Protection Services	609
Deposits	610
Deposit security fund	610
Determination	259
Direct access	90
Directions	212
Directions questionnaire	193, 228

Directors
    conduct leading to disqualification
        324
        disqualifaction of   324
        fraudulent and wrongful trading   323
        personal liability   321
        undertakings   324
Direct recovery of debt (DRD)   273
Disbursements   309
Disclosure   159, 715
Dispensing with a hearing   228
Display price for goods   536
Disputed debt   164
Dissipation of assets   708
Dissolution
    See Divorce
Distance sales cancellation   532
Distance selling   532
Distress damage feasant   477
Divorce   673
    current law   674
    defended cases   683
    grounds for   674
        adultery   674
        separation   677
        living in same house   679
        unreasonable behaviour   676
    new law (no-fault)   684, 685
        acknowledgment of service   689
        amending application   696
        conditional divorce order   731
        conditional order   686
        costs   695
        defended cases   692
        disputed cases   695
        final order   690
        delay in seeking   691
        jurisdiction   696
        nullity   695
        separation order   693
        service   686
        timing   692
    reconciliation   680
    timeline   682
Divorce, Dissolution and Separation Act 2020   684–696
Domestic violence damages claims   641
Domicile and Matrimonial Proceedings Act 1973   696
Donatio mortis causa   367
Dress code for court   201
Drink driving   427
    avoiding disqualification   427
    defences
        absent brief   432
        administering constable not in uniform   428
        behaviour of police   432
        burden of proof   433
        consuming alcohol after alleged offence   433
        evidence of others   433
        no accident   429
        no evidence of breath machine calibration   430
        no likelihood of having driven   434
        no service of print-out   430
        no understanding of prosecution warning   431
        no warning of prosecution   431
        place where administered   429
        random stop   428
        wrong testing result   429
    'excess alcohol' offence   427
    offence of failing to cooperate with preliminary test   427
    Road Traffic Offenders Act 1988   431
    technical defence   427
Duration of the marriage   729
Duress   649, 661
Duty of care   333

E

Early neutral evaluation   137
Eating out   419
    dishonestly leaving without paying   420
    no shows   420
    reasonable deduction from bill   420
    service charge   420
    when to complain   419
Employment Rights Act 1996   471
Enforcement   257
    appointing a receiver   268
    attachment of earnings   261
    charging order   264
    imprisonment   260
    obtaining information about debtor   269
    statutory demand   271
    third party debt order   262
    time limit   260
    timing of   258
    warrant or writ of control   262
Enforcement agents   275
    acting illegally   280
    controlled goods agreement   279
    costs of   279
    during Covid-19   283
    goods exempt from seizure   275
    national standards   283
    notice before seized items are sold   278
    notice of intention to re-enter   278
    notice required   277

time and place of seizure	277	Executors	361
vulnerable debtor	279	removal	361
Enforcement of maintenance orders	270	Experts	229
Enrolment of Deeds (Change of Names) Regulations 1994	423	fees	226
		reports	230
Enterprise Act 2002	389	Extension of time	252
Environmental Protection Act 1990	83		
Equitable accounting	652	**F**	
Estate Agents Act 1979	401		
Estate Agents (Provision of Information) Regulations 1991	401	Family court bailiffs	275
		Family hearing centres	143
Estoppel by representation	317	Family Procedure Rules 2010	195, 252, 656, 703, 709, 724
European Convention on Human Rights	481		
		Fees	
European Online Dispute Resolution Platform	121	*See Court fees*	
		Final right to reject	522
European Order for Payment Procedure	234	Finance Act 2009	451
		Finance (No 2) Act 2015	273
European Small Claims Procedure	234	Financial Conduct Authority	121
Eviction		Financial dispute resolution appointment	707, 719
See also Possession proceedings			
breach of the tenancy agreement	629	Financial Ombudsman's Service	117, 584
by landlord	599	Financial remedies	699
Housing Act compensation	629	allocation questionnaire	714
through the county court	626	arbitration	704
assessing risk	626	business/share valuation	725
trespass to the person	629	capital payments	700
unlawful	628	children	730
Evidence	231	clean break	700
See also Cross-examination; Without prejudice; Witness statement; Witness summary		collaborative law	707
		consent orders	730
		approval by court	732
expert	229	costs	703
giving of	216	costs estimate	717
hearsay	182	exchanging Form E	714
in chief	213, 214	fairness	700
longer hearings	213	fast-track procedure	713
new	214, 215, 250	final hearing	713, 721
oral	212	financial dispute resolution appointment	707, 713
questioning witnesses on	214		
similar fact	7	first appointment	713
truth of	216	Form E	703
Exceptional funding	81	fraudulent behaviour	725
See also Legal aid		going to court	707
Excess alcohol		interim periodical payments	699
See Drink driving		maintenance	699, 728
Exchange of documents/statements	179, 231	maintenance pending suit	699, 721
		mediation	706
Exclusion clauses	526	Mediation Information and Assessment Meeting (MIAM)	706
Execution	275		
costs of enforcement agent	279	mistakes	726
during Covid-19	283	non-court route	702
illegal action of enforcement agent	280	obtaining private information by stealth	709
items exempt from seizure	275	pensions	700
national standards	283	periodical payments	699
notice from enforcement agent	277	private financial dispute resolution appointments	720

Index

settlement 718
skeleton argument 719
standard procedure 713
unforeseen and unforeseeable events 727
First appointment 718
Fixed fee 90
'Fixed recoverable costs' regime 312
Food Safety and Hygiene (England) Regulations 2013 565
Force majeure 287
Forfeiture relief 636
Forms
   D11 195
   D50G 708
   D50K 270
   D440 688
   E 703, 714
   E2 714
   EX105 252
   EX160 168
   EX160A 168
   EX343 313
   EX343QA 313
   Leasehold 7 411
   N1 146
   N5A 636
   N16A 329, 479
   N54 596
   N123 585
   N208 146, 617
   N215 145
   N242A 134
   N244 141, 156, 159, 160, 276, 280, 333, 413
   N245 259
   N260 310
   N260A 310
   N260B 310
   N293 627
   N293A 262, 627
   N316 269
   N316A 269
   N336 261
   N440 592
   PA7A 369
   Precedent H 311
Fraud 150, 323, 650, 661
Fraudulent and wrongful trading 323
Free legal help 94
   Advocate 95
   Citizens Advice 94
   Free Representation Unit 97
   in possession cases 100
   IP Pro Bono 99
   Law Centres Network 95
   LawWorks 97
   Pro Bono Connect 94
   RCJ Advice Bureau 94
   Shelter 98
   Tax Aid 98
   Tax Help for Older People 98
Free Representation Unit 97
Freezing order 709
Frustration of contract 288, 289
   issue of foreseeability 288

G

Guardianship (Missing Persons) Act 2017 747

H

Harassment 327, 328
   discriminatory 329
   particulars of claim 644
   right to claim damages 328
   time limits 646
Hearsay 182
High Court 143
HMRC penalties 447
   alternative dispute resolution 448
   appeal against 447
   complaints procedure 448
   coronavirus 447
   ombudsman 449
   online customer forum 454
   reasonable excuse 449
   reasonable excuse for default 447
   review 448
   tax returns 452
Holidays 301
   arbitration/mediation through ABTA 303
   contract broken by package holiday organisation 301
      further obligations 301
   flight cancellation and delay 306
      time limit 307
   gastric illness claims 302
   Package Travel etc Regulations 2018 301
Homes (Fitness for Human Habitation) Act 2018 631
Hotels
   liability for lost/damaged property 474
Housing Act 1988 623
   section 8 624
   section 21 609, 624
Housing Act compensation 629
Housing (Tenancy Deposits) (Prescribed Information) Order 2007 609
Human Rights Act 1988 481
Human rights defence 621

I

Imprisonment	260
Individual Insolvency Register	393
Individual voluntary arrangement	397
Inheritance (Provision for Family and Dependants) Act 1975	364, 700
Inheritance rights and claims	363
against deceased's estate	364
time limits	364
no surviving spouse/civil partner but children	363
no surviving spouse or civil partner and no children	363
surviving spouse/civil partner and no children	363
surviving spouse or civil partner plus children	363
Inheritance tax	349
allowance	349
gift to charity	349
home gift	349
lifetime gifts	350
Residence Nil-Rate Band	349
tapering of	350
re-writing will with agreement of all beneficiaries	358
spouse or civil partner exempt	349
Inheritance Tax Act 1984	358
Inherited wealth	701
Injunction	645
Insolvency Act 1986	321
Insolvency Service	393
Insolvent liquidation	321
Institute of Family Law Arbitrators	704
charging rates	704
Integrated Dispute Resolution	191
Intellectual Property Enterprise Court	232
Interest	259
business to business	296
court's discretion	297
defence against	295
interim payments	297
on unpaid debts	293
rate of	293
Interim periodical payments	699, 721
Interim third party debt order	262
Intestacy	
See Inheritance rights and claims	
IP Pro Bono	99

J

Japanese knotweed	455
claim against seller for fraudulent misrepresentation	457
claiming cost of removal from neighbour	455
obligations of solicitor/licensed conveyancer/surveyor	458
property information form	457
Joint tenants	366, 371
death of one owner	371
how to become tenants in common	371
automatic change	371
Form A restriction	371
notice of severance	371
Judgment	219
default judgment	156
enforcement abroad	156
extension of time for defence	156
late defence	156
request for judgment	155
summary judgment	156
without a hearing	155
Judgment enforcement	257
appointing a receiver	268
attachment of earnings	261
charging order	264
more than one creditor	266
imprisonment	260
third party debt order	262
time limit	260
timing of	258
warrant or writ of control	262
Judicial Conduct Investigations Office	247
Judicial review	119
Judicial separation	673, 683
Jurisdiction and Judgments (Family) (Amendment etc) (EU Exit) Regulations 2019 (SI 2019/519)	696
Jury trial	205

L

Landlord and tenant
   See Assured shorthold tenancies; Eviction; Forfeiture relief; Homes (Fitness for Human Habitation) Act 2018; Housing Act 1988; Housing (Tenancy Deposit) (Prescribed Information) Order 2017; Landlord and Tenant Act 1985; Penalty claims against defaulting landlords; Possession proceedings; Rent arrears (social landlord obligations); Renters' Reform Bill; Renting Homes (Wales) Act 2016; Renting property (business); Renting property (home); Rent repayment orders; Repossessions

and repossession orders;
Residential service charges;
Tenant Fees Act 2019; Unlawful
tenancy
Landlord and Tenant Act 1985   410
Late Payment of Commercial Debts
    (Interest) Act 1998   296
Law Centres Network   95
Law for Life   79, 100
Law Reform (Frustrated Contracts) Act
    1943   289
LawWorks   97
Legal aid   79
    denied on financial grounds   79
    exceptional funding   81
    inquests   80
    payments disregarded   80
    qualifying for   79
Legal executive   88
Legal expenses insurance   98
Legal help   94
Legal precedents   215
Legal services order   712
Letter before action   223
Libel and slander   377
    avoiding court   382
    compensation   381
    difference from malicious falsehood   384
    of the dead   382
    one year rule   381
    statement in court   378
    website   382
Limitation Act 1980   147, 153
    See also Time limits
Litigant in person   105
    communication with   127
    costs   160, 309
    McKenzie Friend   101
    non-compliance with court direction   105
    online help   79
    treatment from the courts   105
Litigation finance   84
Litigation friend   150
    See also McKenzie Friend
Living together agreement   658
Lodgers   623
Long term right to reject   524
Losses exceeding interest   296
Loss of earnings   226

M

Maintenance and maintenance orders   143, 683, 699, 700, 728
    duration of   729
    enforcement of   257, 270, 271
    global   722
    needs   729
    pensions   700
    temporary   722
    variation of   700
Maintenance pending suit   699, 721
Malicious claims   327
Malicious Communications Act 1988   327
Malicious falsehood   377, 384
    See also Libel, slander and
    malicious falsehood
Malicious prosecution in civil cases   175
Matrimonial and Family Proceedings Act
    2004   708
Matrimonial Causes Act 1973   678, 708
McKenzie Friends   101
    negligence of   103
    permission to use   103
    pros and cons   103
    risk of using   103
Media   203
Mediation   120, 706
Mediation Information and Assessment
    Meeting (MIAM)   121, 706
Mental Health Crisis Moratorium   140
    making the application   140
MIAM
    See Mediation Information and
    Assessment Meeting (MIAM)
Misrepresentation   247, 343, 542, 661
Missing persons   747
    appointment of guardian   747
    criteria   747
    Public Guardian   747
Mistake of law   151
Money Claim Online procedure (MCOL)   144
Money wrongly received   317
    defence of estoppel by representation   317
Mortgage Repossessions (Protection of
    Tenants etc) Act 2010   600
Multi-track claims   310
    costs management order   311
    Precedent H   311

N

Name
    See Change of name
National standards for enforcement
    agents   283
National Will Register   369
Needs in matrimonial finance   701
Negligence   470
No-fault divorce/dissolution   685
    acknowledgment of service   689
    amending the application   696

conditional divorce order	686, 731	Parliamentary and Health Service	
consent orders		Ombudsman	116, 314
approval by court	732	Part 36 offer	133
costs	695	alternative approach	135
defended cases	692	before or after start of court	
disputed cases	695	proceedings	133
final order	690	consequences if not accepted	133
delay in seeking	691	limited to issue of liability	134
jurisdiction	696	pitching at the right level	134
nullity	695	withdrawal of	134
separation order	693	Passing off	199, 232
service	686	Payment protection insurance (PPI)	337
timing	692	commission	337
Non-standard restriction	265	time limits for bringing a claim	337
No sex agreement	669	extension of	338
Notice		unfair relationship	337
of appeal	252	Payplan	396
of complaint	383	Penalty claims against defaulting	
of hearing	200	landlords	613
of home rights	723	Pension attachment order	700
registering	723	Pension sharing order	700
Notices	567	Periodical payments	699
Novitas	85	Perjury	217
No win, no fee agreements	82	Permission to appeal	251
success fee	83	Personal injury	232
Nullity	673, 681	Police negligence	479
		Possession proceedings	
O		extending time	597
		modified procedure (Covid-19)	585
Oaths Act 1878	216	notice of eviction	596
Objections	181	order for possession	592
Official Injury Claim	233	postponement (Covid-19)	585
Ombudsman Association	116	rules to be complied with	585
Omission from will	364	unfair relationship with lender	594
application for money from deceased's		vacating the property	596
estate	364	Post break up wealth	701
time limits	364	Postponing possession	620
Online Civil Money Claims procedure		Pre-action	
(OCMC)	145	disclosure order	159
Open court statement	378	letter	652
Order of evidence	213	protocol	621, 703
See also Evidence		protocol for debt claims	132
Out of court negotiations	137	protocol letter	159, 365
		Pre-marital assets	701
P		Pre-nuptial agreement	661
		Preparing for the hearing	231
Package Travel, Package Holidays and		Prescribed information	609
Package Tours Regulations 1992		Preventative orders	709
	531	Price reduction	522
Parking		Price terms	568
challenging parking ticket	441	Privacy	
fines	491	European Convention on Human	
on private land	441	Rights	481
defences to	443	Human Rights Act 1988	481
time limit to bring claim	444	right to	481
Parking on Private Land Appeals	441	Private hearings	204
Parking (Code of Practice) Act 2019	442	Probate	
		standing search	365

Index

Probate Service 369
Pro Bono Connect 94
Property buying and selling 401
  estate agents
    commission 401
    disinstructed 405
    link between agent and buyer 403
    prescribed information 401
    Property Ombudsman 404
    ready, willing and able buyer 402
    sole agency 402
    sole selling rights 402
  Estate Agents Act 1979 401
  Estate Agents (Provision of Information) Regulations 1991 401
  exchange of contracts 405
  lock out agreement 406
  notice to complete 405
Proprietary estoppel 651
Protection from creditors 327
  civil claim for Protection from Harassment Act damages 329
  communications between creditor and debt collectors 333
  creditor's conduct 327
  debtor given credit 333
  injunction 329
Protection from Harassment Act 1997 147, 327
Protection of Freedoms Act 2012 444
Public hearings 204
Public law defence 621
Public Law Project 81

Q

Questionnaire (financial remedy applications) 714

R

RCJ Advice Bureau 94
Reasonable care and skill 529, 530
Reasonable price 528
Reasonably fit for purpose 514
Receiver
  appointing 268
Recording hearings 203
Recusal of judge 209
  request for 209
Redetermination of judgment rate 259
Refund without receipt 500
Register of Judgments, Orders and Fines 137, 157, 223, 235, 243
  cancellation of registration 244
  certificate of satisfaction 245
  change of name 245

judgments which should not be registered 243
length of registration 244
satisfaction of judgment 245
Registration
  of a notice 265
  of a restriction 265
Relief from sanctions 212
Remote hearings 75, 205, 206
  negative aspects 75
  positive aspects 75
Rent arrears (social landlord obligations) 622
Renters' Reform Bill 599
Renting Homes (Wales) Act 2016 631
Renting property (business) 635
  commercial rent arrears recovery scheme 635
  forfeiture of lease 635
    relief from 636
    rights of sub-tenant 637
  right to send in enforcement agent 635
  threshold of arrears 635
Renting property (home) 599
  deposits 613, 628
  enforcement agents 612
  eviction 599
  landlord mortgage trap 599
  notice to leave from landlord 605
  pre-action protocol for housing conditions 632
  prohibited tenancy fees 600
  properties in multiple occupation 613
  unfit premises 631
Rent repayment orders 613
Repairers
  paying under protest 477
  right to retain possession of property 476
Repair or replace 520
Repaying lender on demand 587
Repeat performance 529
Repossessions and repossession orders 583, 584
  extra time 587
  paying mortgage arrears by instalments 584
Residence Nil-Rate Band 349
  tapering of 350
Residential service charges 409
  18 month rule 418
  challenging 409
    administration charge v service charge 412
    arguments 413
    coronavirus 411
    County Court v Tribunal 409

landlord's costs 411
Leasehold 7 411
qualifying disputes 410
schedule 11 application 412
section 20C application 411
when charges have been paid previously 411
fixed period contract 415
interim payments 414
Landlord and Tenant Act 1985 414
right to a written summary of
insurance policy 417
Service Charge Residential
Management Code 410
unreasonable building insurance
premium 417
Resident landlord 609
Res Ipsa Loquitur 469
Rights of Light Act 1959 460
Rights to light 459
20 year uninterrupted period 459
acquiring 459
interference with 459
injunction 461
light obstruction certificate 460
application for 460
registration of 460
Road Traffic Act 1988 427
Road Traffic Offenders Act 1988 431

S

Sale of goods
See Consumer rights
Satisfactory quality 513
Search order 709
Sears Tooth charge 712
Section 8 notice 624
defective 625
Section 21 notice 615, 624
Segal Order 722
Seizure of goods
See Execution
Self-driving cars 438
Service
acknowledgment of 155
date of 155
Service charges 409–418, 471
Setting aside judgment or order 155, 156
application 156
promptness 156
real prospect of success 157
relief from sanction 157
Settlement 163, 718
full and final 163
Shared care 741
Shelter 98

Shopping 489
cheques 499
contract for the sale and purchase of
goods 489
discount vouchers 495
parking 491
plastic bags 490
receipts 499
refund without receipt 500
sale goods 499
wrongful arrest 492
Short term right to reject 516
Similar fact evidence 7
Single county court 143
Single family court 143
Single joint expert 230
Skeleton argument 719
Slander 377
compensation 381
Small Business, Enterprise and
Employment Act 2015 324
Small claims 221
absence of claimant 228
costs 225
dispensing with oral hearing 228
experts 229
expert's fees and expenses 230
limiting a claim 227
mediation scheme 232
personal injury 232, 233
pre-action protocol 233
preparing for the hearing 231
whiplash 233
level of compensation under new
regime 234
new regime 233
Society of Mediators 101
Solicitors 88
fixed fee 90
free advice session 99
guidelines 127
instructing 89
rights of audience 379
selection of 87
to find a barrister 89
unbundling services 93
Solicitors Regulatory Authority rules 89
Specific performance 524
Speeding 435
disqualification 436
fixed penalty notice 436
points endorsed on driving licence
436
routes to escape disqualification 436
mitigating reasons 437
special reasons 436
TruCAM device 435
unidentified driver 435

Index

Squatters	373
adverse possession	375
of registered land	375
of unregistered land	374
rights when landlord absent	373
statutory declaration when selling property	374
time limit for ownership	374
Standard restriction	265
Standing search	365
Statement in court	377
Statement of costs	310
Statement of truth	183
Statements of the evidence	231
Statute barred claims	147
Statutory declaration	374
Stautory demand	
See Bankruptcy; Enforcement	
Stay enforcement action	259
Striking out	200
Subject to contract	479
Summary judgment	193, 195
application	193
Summing up	215
Supply of Goods and Services Act 1982	527
Support Through Court	104
Suspended order	588

T

Taking Control of Goods Regulations 2013	275, 635
Taking of Goods (Fees) Regulations 2014	279
Tax	
See also HMRC penalties	
penalties on the taxpayer	447
procuring settlement of unpaid tax bill	273
Tax Aid/Tax Help for Older People	98
Tenancies from social landlords	620
Tenancy agreement	600
Tenant Fees Act 2019	600
Tenants in common	367, 371
death of one owner	371
Termination notice	592
Testamentary duet	358
Theft Act 1968	420
Therium	85
Third party debt order	262
Third party litigation funders	84
Affiniti Finance	85
Augusta Ventures	86
Novitas	85
Therium	85

Time limits	147
acknowledgment and part payment	151
acknowledgment or part payment of debt	151
breach of contract	147
breach of contract including debt	153
breach of contract made by deed including debt	153
calculatation of date time starts running	148
civil cases arising out of sexual abuse	150
claim for provision out of deceased's estate	153
claims for provision out of a deceased person's estate	148
claims relating to defective products	149
compensation for a personal injury	147
credit card debts	149
defamation (libel or slander) or malicious falsehood	147
defence against late claim	152
for bringing civil proceedings	646
fraud, concealment or mistake	151
judicial review application	153
libel, slander or malicious falsehood	153
mistake of law	151
money claim under Protection from Harassment Act 1977	153
negligence	147, 149
negligence not including personal injury	153
nuisance	147, 153
on taking any enforcement action	260
personal injuries or anxiety compensation	147
personal injury	153
running out	152
table of	153
unfair relationship claim	153
unpaid rent	147
Time order	591, 594
Time to Pay arrangement	274
Title deeds	649
TOLATA claims	652
when there are children	655
Tomlin order	235, 245
breaking	238
defaulting debtors	238
Torts (Interference with Goods) Act 1977	709
Town and Country Planning Act 1990	455
Tracking down a claim	172
Trade mark claims	232

761

Transcript 252
Travelling expenses 180, 225
Trial bundles
    See Court bundles
Tribunals, Courts and Enforcement Act
    2007 257, 280
TRONC system 474
Trustee in bankruptcy 643
Trusts of Land and Appointment of
    Trustees Act 1996 652

U

Unbundling 93, 227
Undisputed debt
    lump sum payment 165
    payment by third party 165
Unfair Contract Terms Act 1977 288, 567, 578
Unfair relationship 334, 337
    time limits for bringing claim 337
    extension of 338
Unfair terms 568
Unfair Terms in Consumer Contracts
    Regulations 1999 567
Unfair trading 535
    best before dates 562
    labelling 558
    use by dates 562
Unlawful tenancy 600
Unreasonable behaviour 227, 676
Unreasonable loser 226
Use by dates 562
Ushers 201

V

Verbal contracts 567
Vexatious litigant 193, 197

W

Warrant of control 262, 275
Water Resale Orders 2001 and 2006 623
Website libel 382
Welfare of the child 700
Whiplash claims 233
    new regime 233
Whiplash Injury Regulations 2021 234

Wills 349
    beneficiary as witness 352
    challenging 365
        court considerations 365
    codicil 358
    condition to a gift 357
    digital property 352
    divorce/dissolution or annulment 352
    executors 361
        application for change of executor 361
        power of court to kick out 361
    gift of personal chattels 358
    mirror wills 358
    National Will Register 369
    Probate Service 369
    revocation of 352
    re-writing with agreement of all beneficiaries 358
    signing of 351
    template will 353
    testamentary duet 358
    Will Aid scheme 352
    witnesses to 351
        during pandemic 351
'Without prejudice' 128, 165, 182
Witnesses 179
    See also Cross-examination; Witness statements
    approaching 180
    familiarisation 217
    summary 180
    summons 180
    uncooperative 180
Witness statement 179
    compliant 184
    disclosure of process by which it was prepared 184
    exchange of 179
    formalities 182
    further evidence 182
    irrelevant or disproportionate material 181
    letting witnesses use their own words 181
    statement of truth 183
Writ of control 275
Wrongful arrest 492